DO NOT SPECIAL LOAN

Human
Artificial Insemination
and
Semen Preservation

Human Artificial Insemination and Semen Preservation

Edited by
Georges David
and
Wendel S. Price

Centre d'Etude et de Conservation
du Sperme Humain (CECOS)
Bicêtre, France

PLENUM PRESS · NEW YORK AND LONDON

Library of Congress Cataloging in Publication Data

International Symposium on Artificial Insemination and Semen Preservation, Paris,
  1979.
  Human artificial insemination and semen preservation.

  Includes index.
  1. Artificial insemination, Human—Congresses. 2. Semen, Frozen—Congresses. 3.
Sperm banks— Congresses. I. David, Georges, professeur. II. Price, Wendel S. III.
Title.
RG134.I57 1979   613.9'4   80-19402
ISBN 0-306-40547-4

Proceedings of the International Symposium on Artificial Insemination
and Semen Preservation, held in Paris, France, April 9—11, 1979.

© 1980 Plenum Press, New York
A Division of Plenum Publishing Corporation
227 West 17th Street, New York, N.Y. 10011

PREFACE

Even though artificial insemination is a simple technique that
has been practiced for over a century, it has long been carried out
under poor conditions due to an inadequate understanding of reproductive physiology and antagonistic socio-ethical attitudes. Accordingly, until fairly recently it was a medical act with a limited
scientific basis which was practised more or less clandestinely.

The development of semen preservation has totally changed the
conditions of artificial insemination, especially in regard to
flexibility and safeguards in its application. Although the use
of fresh semen continues, it is now clear that the future of artificial insemination is closely linked to semen preservation.

During the past two decades, semen banks have been developed
in many countries. This has most often been the result of the
initiative of individual physicians in either the private or public
sectors. In France, a national system of semen banks(CECOS) was
begun in 1973. Although there has been cooperation within this
system in the areas of both research and management, a need to communicate and compare experiences with those from other countries
was perceived. Thus, the first International Symposium on Artificial Insemination and Semen Preservation was planned and held in
Paris, France in April 1979. Thirty-seven countries were represented
by individuals from many concerned disciplines.

This volume contains nearly all the communications given at the
Symposium and constitutes an attempt to provide an up-to-date assessment of accomplishments and the body of scientific knowledge in
artificial insemination as well as to identify challenges which this
field faces. This task is complex since artificial insemination is
confronted by a diversity of clinical, biological, psychological,
legal, social and ethical problems.

The works presented in this volume underscore the important
place that artificial insemination and semen preservation has taken

in the treatment, and even prevention, of male sterility. They
also reveal that these techniques present a unique opportunity for
the study of human reproduction. Furthermore, they reflect the
dynamism of investigators in this field and lead us to anticipate
important advances in the coming years.

This first Symposium has provided an opportunity to increase
exchanges on an international level which we hope will continue and
multiply.

As chairman of the Symposium and on behalf of CECOS, I would
like to thank all who attended and participated in the Symposium
for having made it such a success.

                                        Georges David, MD

ACKNOWLEDGEMENTS

We would like to express our gratitiude to the French Ministry of Health for its support of the Symposium and of this book's publication. Special thanks are due Dr. Françoise Czyglik who with the able assistance of Clementine Giocondese and members of the French Centers for the Study and Preservation of Semen organized the Symposium. Finally, we are indebted to Hélène Arbésman for her patient and skillful typing of the manuscript as well as to Danielle Blanquart and Francine Quinton for their secretarial contributions.

CONTENTS

IV. ARTIFICIAL INSEMINATION WITH DONOR SEMEN
(AID): CLINICAL RESULTS

IX.   ARTIFICIAL INSEMINATION WITH HUSBAND SEMEN (AIH)
CLINICAL RESULTS, SEMEN IMPROVEMENT AND
AUTOPRESERVATION

PRESENT STATUS OF AID AND SPERM BANKS

IN THE UNITED STATES

John H. Olson

Cryogenic Laboratories, Inc.
1935 West County Road
Roseville, Minnesota, U.S.A.

INTRODUCTION

The current status of cryobanking utilizing frozen-thawed human semen in the United States is an ever changing clinical and research application in human reproduction. Since Spallanzani, over 200 years ago, first reported data concerning his observations on the effects of low temperatures on human spermatozoa, the concept of cryobanking as utilized in the United States was essentially non existent until the middle nineteen fifties when Sherman and Bunge first presented a method of cryopreservation along with demonstrating that frozen-thawed human spermatozoa was capable of *in vivo* fertilization with resulting normal embryonic development.[1,2]

The use of cryobanking was relegated to university based banks in terms of both research and clinical applications until 1970. At that time, several private cryobanks were originated applying the research data developed and obtained from earlier investigators. It is the purpose of this presentation to summarize current data regarding the applications, functions and clinical results of cryobanking human semen in the United States.

APPLICATIONS

The primary application for the cryopreservation of human spermatozoa is clearly for the treatment of infertility. With the changing moral, legal, religious and political attitudes towards abortion and marriage resulting in the unavailability of adoptive children, the demand for frozen-thawed semen for AID has increased signifi-cantly in the U.S. All participating U.S. cryobanks have reported

1

a 400% increase over the past five years.[3] Not only have social, legal and moral attitudes influenced the need for AID but also the realization that male infertility is not a disease but rather a physical impairment which can be minimized. More clinicians are beginning to practice AID which appears to be directly related to the increased notoriety artificial insemination has been receiving in the United States. Television documentaries, talk-show interviews, along with nationwide magazine and newspaper publicity has awakened the general public to the dilemma many infertile couples are facing. Sherman in 1964 suggested that the modification of the moral, religious and legal attitudes were moving towards toleration if not support of AID.[4] Fifteen years later one could say with certainty that the support for AID and AIH is substantial not only in academia but also within the general population.

An integral function of most United States cryobanks is the cryopreservation of human semen for future AIH. Many pre-vasectomy, pre-radiation, pre-chemotherapy, and pre-surgery patients have opted to store semen prior to their impending sterility. Although most United States cryobanks, past and present, originated as essentially a storage facility for patients such as those described above, the past nine years have demonstrated that most individuals facing sterility have chosen not to cryo-preserve semen. Some oligospermic specimens are being collected, stored, thawed, pooled, and then concentrated for use in AIH. Generally the success of these procedures have limited their application.

Finally, there has been an increased awareness of carcinogenic materials with which men come in contact which could result in sterility in time.[5] Attention is focusing on the possibility of serious chromosome mutations, blood abnormalities, and cancer brought on by exposure to electromagnetic radiation.[6] These realizations have prompted many individuals to cryopreserve their semen for future progeny and subsequent utilization through AIH. The medical profession has become increasingly aware of the limitless possibilities which cryobanks offer the clinician and his patient, however the geographical locations of the United States cryobanks often dictates an individual's opportunity to utilize their services.

FUNCTIONS

Currently in the United States, eleven cryobanks are recognized as active centers for human semen cryopreservation.[7] The geographical distribution is found in Figure 1. This number of established cryobanks does not include smaller private banks which are maintained by infertility clinicians for their patients only. It is estimated there are fifteen of these facilities in the United States. Not all cryobanks perform the same functions relative to the cryopreservation of human semen. One bank utilizes heterologous donor semen for private patient applications within the clinic itself. One bank provides donor semen only to clinicians in their surrounding medical community while nine cryobanks not only maintain and supply donor semen specimens for physicians but also facilitate long term storage for future homologous insemination of physician referred patients. Four of the cryobanks are university based while the remaining seven are privately owned or commercial facilities.

LEGAL STATUS OF AID IN THE UNITED STATES

The use of AID in the United States has been the pivotal point around which significant social policy issues have been discussed. For the most part, the United States legal system has focused its attention on the legal identity of offspring, the marital relationship, and the adoption of AID as a recognized and accepted medical procedure. Much publicity has arisen in the past year stemming from the work of Steptoe and Edwards. This has brought AID to the attention of the U.S. populace resulting in a deluge of communications suggesting uncontrolled asexual reproduction and genetic manipulation and engineering. It is to the credit of the United States legal system that these issues, which certainly influence the family concept in our society, have not been an area of concentration in the courts.

In general, the majority of the United States medical profession have declined to practice AID due to the potential liability which is similar to liability in other areas of legal medicine and family law. As of 1976, there had been no reported liability cases based upon either medical malpractice or the theory of "wrongful life".[8] It is not the intent of this document to review specific litigation with respect to AID. It is apparent however, that due to the lack of specific legislation in most states the courts have been inconsistent in determining AID cases.[9] Court cases, state legislatures and proposed uniform legislation have been used to determine the issues of AID. Certain courts have considered the legitimacy of offspring[10] while others concentrated their efforts in dealing with the obligations of the husband of the mother of the child.[11]

As of 1976, seven of the fifty states had definite statutes dealing with AID.[12-18] The legislation concerned the legality of practice, written consent, and legitimacy of progeny. Although each of responding cryobanks reported no difficulties with legal issues, it is still apparent that comprehensive legislation is needed to alleviate the stigma of potential liability. Religious obstacles inherent in AID procedures have not been detrimental even though Pope Pius XII in 1949 declared AID to be contrary to Christian principles and morals.[19]

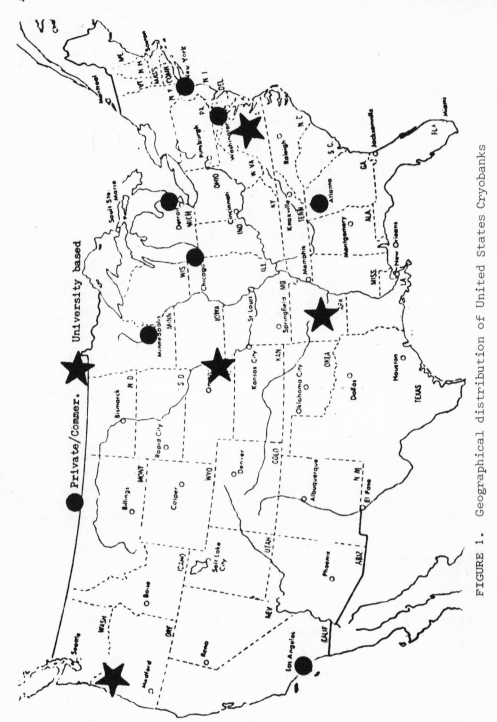

FIGURE 1. Geographical distribution of United States Cryobanks

CLINICAL RESULTS

The last reported data concerning births resulting from cryopreserved human semen in the United States were submitted by Sherman
in 1977.[7,20] Further investigations since that report have demonstrated a significant 61% increase in the number of births resulting
from frozen-thawed semen. A comparison of the data obtained prior
to 1977 with findings from 1977 to 1979 is presented in Table 1.
The nine cryobanks which provided data and to which the author is
indebted, are listed in this text. As previously noted, ten of the
eleven active U.S. cryobanks provide frozen-thawed semen specimens
to clinicians outside of the bank's immediate area. The problems
associated with obtaining pertinent data relative to clinical results
stems from the difficulties which some cryobanks experience in maintaining systematic analyses of insemination results. This is due,
in part, to the required anonymity which must be observed by both the
cryobank and the physician. This obstacle results in physicians
neglecting to respond to surveys, incomplete responses and inaccu-
rate data prompted by incorrect interpretations to submitted questions. Furthermore, data was not available from cryobanks that are
not active members of the AATB or from those that declined to submit
clinical results. It is imperative to point out that the recent data
supports previous findings of lower percentages of spontaneous abortions and abnormalities than that which is found in the normal reproductive population. One participating cryobank reported a third
trimester pregnancy resulting from AIH using frozen-thawed semen
which had been cryopreserved for six years, two months.

CURRENT METHODS

Within the proposed standards set forth by participating members
of the Reproductive Council of the American Association of Tissue
Banks are certain guidelines with respect to accepted laboratory
procedures.[7] It is not the intent of this presentation to dissemi-
nate these proposed standards but rather to present an overview of
data obtained regarding basic methods and charges for services rendered by the nine reporting cryobanks (Table 2). Within the framework of the proposed standards of the AATB, each cryobank has adopted
its own methods of laboratory operation, which is evidenced by the
variations depicted in Table 2. The apparent discrepancy in charges
for cryobank services is due to many factors such as geographical
considerations, private or university banks, and whether or not the
cryobank maintains its own infertility clinic.

TABLE 1. *Clinical results using frozen-thawed human spermatozoa*

	Prior to 1977	1977-1979	Total
No. of AIH Patients	*	2906	2906
No. of AID Patients	*	1778	1778
No. of physicians served	*	2333	2333
No. of current pregnancies	71	339	–
No. of pregnancies (other than current)	*	2333	2333
No. of normal children born	1464	2393	3857
No. of abnormal children born	0.7%	1.3%	1.0%
No. of spontaneous abortions	12.0%	5.0%	8.5%
Male/Female ratio	*	51% male	–

* Data not available.

    The applications of cryobanking of human spermatozoa in the
United States has again been demonstrated to be a significant and
integral part of the medical community. The data presented here
represents a definite trend toward the increased use of frozen-thawed
semen in AID. In view of a few somewhat negative reports from certain researchers concerning the longevity of cryopreserved semen
specimens and the possible higher incidence of abnormalities and
spontaneous abortions, it is truly rewarding to present the current
data obtained from United States cryobanks which directly refutes
previous data. Certainly much should and will be initiated with

TABLE 2. *Laboratory methods and charges of nine United States cryobanks*

		No of banks
Method of storage	Liquid nitrogen	9
Method of shipping	Liquid nitrogen	8
	Other media	1
Shipping carrier	Air	7
	Bus	6
	Other	3
Semen storage container	Glass vials	4
	Straws	4
	Other	1
Cryopreservative used	Glycerol	4
	Buffered Glycerol	1
	Buffered Glycerol/Egg Yolk	4
No. of available donors	1-15	5
	16-30	3
	31+	1
Increased demand for heterologous donor semen		9
Increased demand for preservation for AIH		6
No legal difficulties associated with AID		9
Charges : Heterologous donon semen		$38-$175 per specimen
Homologous donor semen		$25-$ 55 per specimen

respect to the future involvement of cryobanking in the United States. In addition to the roles which cryobanks now assume in the medical field, they have the potential for having a broader and more social-ly oriented role in the future. Through the efforts of the Repro-ductive Council of the AATB and its members, the next decade will be one of significant achievement in the field of cryobanking of human spermatozoa.

ACKNOWLEDGEMENTS

Data obtained for this presentation were contributed by the following members of the Reproductive Council of the AATB : Frozen Human Semen Bank, University of Arkansas for Medical Sciences; Genetic Semen Bank, University of Nebraska Medical Center; Cryogenic Laboratories, Inc., Roseville, Minnesota; Idant Laboratories, New York, N.Y.; Cryo Lab. Facility, Chicago, Illinois; Frozen Semen Bank, University of Oregon Medical School; Reproductive Genetic Center, Vienna, Virginia; Michigan Infertility Center, P.C., Birmingham, Michigan; Xytex Corporation, Atlanta, Georgia.

REFERENCES

1. Bunge, R.G. and Sherman, J.K. Fertilizing capacity of frozen human spermatozoa. Nature, 172:767, 1953.

2. Bunge, R.G., Keettel, W.C. and Sherman, J.K. Clinical use of frozen semen. Fertil. & Steril., 5:520, 1954.

3. Jacobson, E. Up 400% : Artificial insemination. Sexual Medicine today, dec. 6, 1976.

4. Sherman, J.K. Research on frozen human semen. Fertil. Steril. 15:487, 1975.

5. Whorton, D., Krauss, R.M., Marshall, S. and Milby, T.H. Infertility in male pesticide workers. Fertil. Steril., 29:710, 1978.

6. Reid, W.W. EMI causing increasing concern in U.S. Environment Midwest, United States E.P.A., February, 1979.

7. Sherman, J.K. Clinical results and proposed standards in cryobanking of human semen. In : K.W. Sell, Vernon P. Perry, Monroe M. Vincent eds., Proceedings of the 1977 Annual Meeting, American Association of Tissue Banks, AATB, pp. 139-40, 1977.

8. Healy, J.M. Jr. Legal aspects of artificial insemination and paternity testing, in: Milunsky, H. and Annas, G.J. eds. Genetics and the Law. New York, Plenum Press, p. 206, 1976.

9. Sherwood, H.J. Some legal implications of frozen semen banks. Journal of Reprod. Medicine. 8:190, 1972.

10. Doornbos v. Doornbos. 23 U.S. Law Week 2308, 1954

    Anonymous v. Anonymous. 246 NYS 2n835, 1964.

Gursky v. Gursky. 242 NYS 2n 406. 1963.

11. Strnad y. Strnad. 78 NYS 2d 590, 1948

    People v. Sorensen. 68 Cal 2d 280, 1969

    In the Matter of the Adoption of Anonymous. 345 NYS 2d 130, 1973.

12. Georgia Code 74-101.1.

13. Oklahoma Statutes, Title 10. 551 to 553.

14. Kansas Statutes. Sections 23-128 ; 23-129 : 23-130.

15. California Civil Code Section 216, California Penal Code Section 270.

16. Arkansas Statutes 61-141.

17. North Carolina General Statutes. Section 49A-1.

18. Maryland Code, Article 43. Section 55.

19. Barwin, B.N. and Beck, W.W. Jr. Artificial insemination and semen preservation. In : E.S.E. Hafez ed., Techniques of Human Andology. Elsevier/North-Holland Biomedical Press. Amsterdam, p. 429, 1977.

20. Sherman, J.K. Cryopreservation of human semen. In : E.S.E. Hafez ed., Techniques of Human Andology, Elsevier/North Holland Biomedical Press, Amsterdam. Chapt. 24. 1977.

AID AND SPERM BANKS IN GREAT BRITAIN

David. W. Richardson

MRC Unit of Reproductive Biology
Edinburgh, Scotland

INTRODUCTION

In Great Britain, it has been estimated that approximately 1,000 to 1,200 marriages out of the 400,000 marriages each year will be possible candidates for artificial insemination with donor semen (AID).[1,2] If each couple were to have 2 children by donor insemination, then about 2 000 children would be born for each year's marriages. This figure would represent 0.15-0.3% of the total 650 000 annual births in Britain.

The Report of the British Medical Association Panel on AID in 1973 recommended that centres for AID should be established in Great Britain. However, this recommendation has only been partially implemented. At present, there is no national coordinated system of AID centres, though there are at least 24 centres which provide some type of AID service. The governmental Department of Health and Social Security is responsible for the organisation and administration of the National Health Service and recommending the general policy to be pursued by the Aera Health Authorities who operate the health service throughout Great Britain. However, though the Department of Health and Social Security is unlikely to actively endorse the establishment of a national system of AID centres, each Health Authority has latitude in its own policies, and any such Health Authority could establish AID centres within its area.

One Area Health Board has inaugurated an AID service in its region, and its operation and performance will be followed with considerable interest.

Much of the succeeding information was derived from answers given to a questionnaire on AID sent from the Royal College of Obstetricians and Gynaecologists, London, in 1977, to 38 university departments, clinics and private doctors who were thought to be providing an AID service, or were interested in such a service. Twenty-seven centres replied and of these 22 were already providing an AID service. Since 1977, at least two more centres have been set up. Of these 24 establishments, 19 have semen banks, and 4 centres use frozen semen exclusively ; however, the majority use both fresh and frozen semen. Two semen banks are run by commercial organisations and provide services in 4 towns.

The location of the AID centres in the United Kingdom is shown in Figure 1. The geographical distribution of these facilities is uneven. Seven centres are located in the London area, four are in Scotland and three in the north of England. However, there appears to be no AID service at all in Wales, East Anglia, north eastern England, Cumbria and the sparsely populated north west of Scotland. Patients from these areas have to travel long distances for treatment.

The geographical distribution of the AID centres needs to be rationalised and new facilities inaugurated.

THE DEMAND OF AID

There is a growing demand for AID in the United Kingdom. In 1976 there were 1,585 referrals of patients who were possible candidates for AID (Table 1), whereas in 1977 the number had increased by 34% to 2,396, with 1,200 couples actually receiving treatment. If this increase is maintained and extrapolated, in excess of 3,000 referrals would be anticipated for 1978.

731 pregnancies were achieved with donor semen in 1976 and of these, between 70 and 90 were with frozen semen. Between 1977 and 1979, of the order of 210 to 230 pregnancies resulted from frozen semen insemination.

Only 12 centres pursued any form of follow-up of families into which AID children were born and only 1 centre followed the progress of the children for more than one year.

The replies to the questionnaire showed that there was no standard procedure for the selection and examination of donors, nor was there a standardised protocol for investigating couples referred for AID. Most centres charged a fee for the service, although often it was nominal. In 14 centers, medical or dental students were used as their principle source of donors and only one group recruited by advertising. Donors were paid by 19 of 24 centers.

TABLE 1. *Referrals for AID treatment in the United Kingdom*

Year	Couples referred
1976	1,585
1977	2,396

FIGURE 1.   AID centres in the United Kingdom

TABLE 2. *Storage of frozen semen*

Type of Storage unit	Number of centres using each system
Glass ampoules	2
Plastic ampoules	8
French straws	9
Pellet	0

Every centre utilised liquid nitrogen for semen storage, with storage in French straws and glass or plastic ampoules being most widely employed (Table 2).

The predicted increase in demand for AID within the normal in-fertility service should move us to anticipate this demand and establish a semen exchange system which would include specimens from all ethnic groups.

In Great Britain, there is a clear requirement to provide a nationwide network and to rationalise the location of AID centres. A centre to collate and analyse the nationwide results of AID should be established. If methods can be refined to precisely predict ovulation, and significant progress is achieved in improving semen cryopreservation, we may anticipate a marked increase in the successful use of frozen semen during the next five years.

ADDENDUM

The opinions expressed in this paper are solely those of the author, and do not represent the policy or views of the Medical Research Council.

REFERENCES

1. Levie, L.H. Donor insemination in Holland. Wld. Med. J., 19: 90, 1972.

2. Richardson, D.W. Artificial insemination in the human. In : Modern trends in Human Genetics, 2, p. 404-448, Butterworths, London, 1975.

THE ORGANIZATION OF THE CENTERS FOR THE STUDY

AND PRESERVATION OF SEMEN IN FRANCE

Georges David and Jacques Lansac

Centre d'Etude et de Conservation du Sperme(CECOS),
    Paris-Bicêtre. Kremlin-Bicêtre, France
Centre d'Etude et de Conservation du Sperme(CECOS),
    Tours. Tours, France

Because of religous and moral opposition, Artificial Insemination with Donor Semen(AID) in France long remained what was essentially a clandestine practice carried out by a limited number of
private gynecologists who used fresh donor semen.[1] It was not until
the creation in 1973 of the first two sperm banks in Paris at Necker
and Bicêtre hospitals that AID was accepted as a service of the
Public Hospitals. This has greatly assisted the development of AID
by facilitating its practice and enabling government authorities to
recognize it officially. Therefore, its development has been directly linked to that of sperm banks and semen preservation. Artificial
insemination with fresh semen practiced only by gynecologists in
private practice in France is steadily regressing due to the instal-
lation of a network of sperm banks serving the entire country.

Presently, there are 15 sperm banks in France: 14 which make
up the Centers for the Study and Preservation of Semen(CECOS in
French) and 1 which is independent, the Center of Human Functional
Exploration(CEFER) in Marseille.

Structure and Functions of CECOS

The CECOS Centers are located in University-Hospital centers
(Figure 1, Table 1) and are usually the principal activity of the
Reproduction Biology service. They are not directly under hospital
jurisdiction but rather are managed by an Administrative Board which
includes representatives of the Ministry of Health, the hospital
administration, Social Security(the national health service division)

15

TABLE 1. *Sperm banks in France*

Region	City	Address	Director
Paris	Bicêtre	Centre Hospitalo-Universitaire 78, av. du Général Leclerc 94270 Kremlin-Bicêtre	Pr G. David
Franche-Comté Bourgogne	Besançon	Centre Hospitalo-Universitaire Place Saint-Jacques 25000 Besançon	Pr C. Bugnon
Aquitaine	Bordeaux	Hôpital Xavier Arnozan 33604 Pessac	Pr J. Meunier
Nord	Lille	Service de Gynécologie Obstétrique 10, rue Malpart 59000 Lille	Pr M. Delecour
Rhône	Lyon	Centre Hospitalo-Universitaire 8, av. Rockefeller 69373 Lyon Cedex 2	Pr J.C. Czyba
Sud-Est	Marseille	Centre Saint-Pierre 165, rue Saint-Pierre 13006 Marseille	Dr A. Matté
Lorraine	Nancy	Université régionale rue du Dr Heydenreich 54000 Nancy	Pr G. Grignon
Bretagne	Rennes	Hôpital Pontchaillou 33043 Rennes Cedex	Pr Y. Chambon
Alsace	Strasbourg	Faculté de Médecine Institut d'Embryologie 11, rue Humann 67085 Strasbourg Cedex	Dr A. Clavert
Midi-Pyrénées	Toulouse	Hôpital C. La Grave 31000 Toulouse	Pr F. Pontonnier
Centre	Tours	Hôpital Bretonneau Boulevard Tonnellé 37033 Tours	Pr J. Lansac
Normandie	Caen	Centre Hospitalo-Universitaire Côte de Nacre 14033 Caen	Pr J. Izard
Alpes	Grenoble	Hôpital des Sablons 38700 La Tronche	Pr A. Jalbert

TABLE 2. *Evolution of AID requests by year in CECOS according to center. The center at Caen is not reported since it opened in 1979. Data from Paris-Necker is included only since its entry into the CECOS system*

	1973	1974	1975	1976	1977	1978	Total
Paris-Bicêtre	278	348	512	481	498	711	2828
Paris-Necker	–					281	281
Besançon	–	37	55	44	54	49	239
Bordeaux	–	6	67	97	102	102	374
Grenoble						73	73
Lille	–	53	75	115	110	125	478
Lyon	–	109	131	198	120	200	758
Marseille	–	124	167	191	151	181	814
Nancy	–	42	67	72	83	110	374
Rennes	–				191	219	410
Strasbourg	–					55	55
Toulouse	–			34	70	70	174
Tours	–			112	86	109	307
Total	278	719	1074	1344	1465	2285	7165

FIGURE 1.   CECOS Centers in France and their dates of opening

TABLE 3.   *Assessment of activity on March 12, 1978*

AID requests accepted	7,160	
Women treated	4,253	
Pregnancies	1,852	
. Births		1,158
. Miscarriages		290
. Pregnancies in progress		404
Donors	1,324	

and different interested medical disciplines such as gynecology, pediatrics, genetics, virology and endocrinology. The directors are physicians in biological science(10 centers), gynecology and obstetrics(2 centers), urology(1 center), or endocrinology(1 center).

The physical plant is provided to CECOS by the Hospital Center and the personnel are hired either by CECOS directly or by the Hospital for CECOS. Even though CECOS is an independent operation within the Hospital Center, there are close links between the two which are defined by written agreement.

The budget of a Center is independent of the hospital's. Its income is derived mainly from charges for paillettes, that is frozen semen for AID, and services such as spermiograms and semen cryopreservation, the latter in cases of autopreservation or artificial insemination with husband's semen(AIH). Fees are established in accordance with a not for profit policy. Financial support has also come from the Ministry of Health since the inception of CECOS in order to facillitate its establishment(approximately 25% of the total budget for the first three years).

The budgetary and managerial autonomy of CECOS has allowed the Centers to respond to the needs of both hospital based and private practitioners. The centers are also independent of each other, there being no formal central organization or director. However, they have all been established and operate under the same guidelines and have the same objectives. These objectives are periodically discussed during Director's meetings. In order to further increase cooperation on an administrative, financial, technical and scientific level, the CECOS Centers have recently decided to create a federation.

Three functions have been defined for CECOS: (1) Semen preservation for AID; (2) semen autopreservation for AIH; and(3) research.

CECOS and AID

CECOS has developed an AID program with the Statistical Research Unit of the National Institute of Health and Medical Reserach (INSERM). This program includes donor recruitment, semen preparation, recording AID requests, verifying indications for semen preservation and artificial insemination, the selection and provision of semen for insemination, collection of data, and the use of findings to improve the efficacy of our procedures. Inseminations are performed either at the CECOS Center or by a gynecologist in hospital or private practice.

Semen Donation: The "nouvelle politique" of CECOS

In the practice of AID with fresh semen, the donor has been most
often young and single and has always been payed. In contrast, CECOS
has maintained a policy that the semen donation be simply that, a
gift for which no payment is received as is the case for organ donation. If the payment of a donor of fresh semen were justified by
the necessity of his convocation on a specific hour and day, this is
no longer the case. Semen banking now allows the donor to come to
the Center at his convenience with only reimbursement for transportation, if necessary.

The selling of semen can lead to abuses as has occurred with
blood donation. In fact, the argument that paying donors increases
the availability of semen is false in the respect that it tends to
make it morally less attractive to many men and permits the public
to become disinterested in the problem. The solution to problems of
donor recruitment, we feel, lies in the acceptance by the public of
a responsibility in this area of human need.

A second CECOS principle concerning the donation is that it be
made by a couple. Only married men less than 50 years of age who
have one or more normal children and have the consent of their spouses
are accepted as donors. This requirement offers several advantages.
First, there is an additional guarantee of donor fertility as well
as a lower risk of hereditary disease. Furthermore, there are significant moral and psychological benefits: Opinions have often been
voiced that artificial insemination falls into the realm of adultery
due to the role played, more or less consciously, by the donor. By
replacing the notion of "the donor" by that of "the couple donor" and
replacing the notion of "woman receiver" by that of "couple receiver",
the image of adultry as well as the accessory role of AID are greatly
attenuated.

The third principle concerning semen donation is in regard to
its repitition. In artificial insemination with fresh semen, donors
were used for long periods and often for a large number of women.
In certain cases, this created substantial risks of consanguinity.
In CECOS, only a limited number of ejaculates, usually 5 or 6 are taken from a given donor during a brief period of about 1 month. On
the first visit, a careful study of the donor is carried out which
includes personal and family medical history, a physical examination,
establishment of morphotype and semen examination. Only those candidates who have a sperm count of at least 50 million per ml, 50%
normal forms and, after freezing, 40% motile spermatozoa are accepted
as donors. Once accepted, a karyotype is performed and arrangements
are made to obtain a stock of about 100 doses (0.25 ml each) which
normally requires 5 or 6 ejaculates. Appointments are made at the
convenience of the donor who is never again solicited for a semen

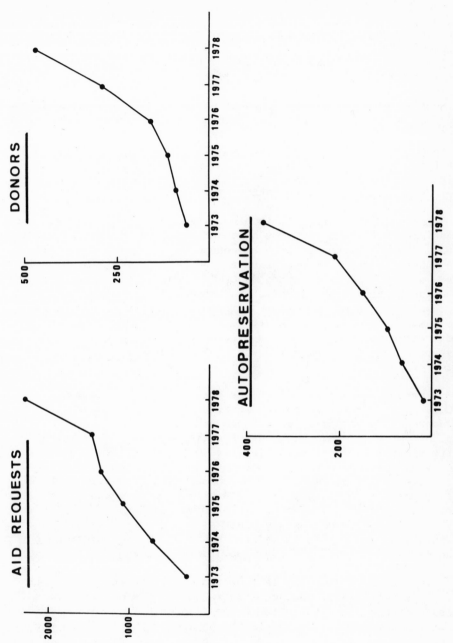

FIGURE 2. Evolution of CECOS activity from 1973 to 1978

donation. It should be added that semen donations have been accepted
from individuals not meeting the above criteria but their semen is
used only for research purposes.

This new policy of CECOS, therefore, is characterized by a non-
paid donation, a couple's donation and a limited donation. This policy has the additional advantages of being able to be presented
openly to the public and used to elicit both public support and participation. Nevertheless, it could be feared that a rule of non-
payment would limit the development of AID. This has not been our
experience in CECOS since donations have kept pace with semen de-
mands(Figure 2). However, a continual recruitment effort has been
necessary since the demand for AID has constantly increased. For
the first six years, CECOS has had a total of 1,324 donors.

Indications and Contra-Indications for AID

The indication for AID is established by CECOS. The couple requesting AID is sent to CECOS by a referring physician or consults
CECOS directly. The Center then conducts an inquiry concerning
the couple in order to establish an indication for AID which is
based on criteria established by CECOS. The center also maintains
the responsibility of establishing the morphotype for donor couple
matching and giving the couple information on the AID treatment
program, particularly in regard to the delay before treatment begins
and treatment organization and procedures. To present, only couples
have been accepted, unmarried women and homosexual "couples" having
been refused.

There are several indications for artificial insemination in
CECOS. The primary indication is irreversible male sterility, that
is secretory azoospermia which does not arise from a curable hypo-
gonadotropism or anexcretory azoospermia which is not surgically
correctable. The indication in these cases is evident but CECOS is
receiving more and more requests as a result of spermatozoa insuf-
ficiencies(oligozoospermia, asthenozoospermia, teratozoospermia).
Such cases are not accepted for AID unless other means of improving
their fertility, including trials of semen enrichment for AIH, have
failed. If there remains any doubt as to the irreversibility of the
sterility, semen examinations are repeated and the referring physician is asked to evaluate the couple more thoroughly.

The second indication is the presence of genetic risks, that
is, the likelihood of the husband transmitting a dominant hereditary
disease or contributing to the expression of a recessive disorder.
In such cases, the Center seeks the advice of a genetician who evaluates the significance of this risk and the possibility of prenatal
diagnosis. More rarely, AID has been considered indicated in cases
of Rh incompatibility with severe isoimmunization of the woman or
for problems of ejaculation.

The evaluation of the couple is completed by an interview with a psychiatrist working with the Center. The purpose is not to judge the motivation for the couple's request but rather to simply reveal cases of psychological pathology. Rejections on the basis of this interview are rare. In the great majority of cases, the value of the interview lies in the opportunity it affords the couple for deeper reflection regarding their motivations and concerns.

The reasons for refusing a request for AID are, therefore, quite varied: Unproven male sterility, female infertility or psychological disorders. The percentage of couples refused, however, remains low. Out of a total of 6,385 requests received in 6 years at 7 Centers, only 290 or 4.6% have been denied.

Semen Freezing and Utilization

The same cryopreservation technique has been adopted throughout CECOS: A cryprotector medium with a glycerol and egg yolk base, semen packaging in 0.25 ml straws or paillettes, rapid(7 min.) freezing and storage in liquid nitrogen.

The choice of donor semen used for an insemination is based not only on the morphotypes and blood types(ABO and Rh) of the husband, but also of the wife. The principal here is to avoid introducing a character which does not exist in either partner.

The Insemination Procedure

The inseminations are carried out by gynecologists either in CECOS or by those in hospital or private practice. There is no distinction made by CECOS between physicians in hospital and private practice.

In all cases, the gynecologists are required to respect a protocol which includes, in particular, insemination with only one semen dose in each of the first two cycles. This procedure is carried out in order to permit assessment of factors affecting success, both female(insemination timing, condition of the cervix, hormonal equilibrium) and male(number and quality of spermatozoa). Beginning with the third insemination cycle, the gynecologist is free to increase the number of inseminations and doses used. In cases of multiple insemination, the paillettes used contain semen from the same donor and from the same ejaculate.

If an insemination is to take place outside of the CECOS Center, the semen is picked up and transported by the couple in small containers of liquid nitrogen which will keep the paillettes for 5 days. When it is time to perform the insemination, the paillette is removed from the liquid nitrogen and allowed to thaw for a few minutes at room temperature. After cutting-off one end of the paillette, it is placed in an insemination device with which the semen can be slowly injected directly into the cervix.

Collection and Analysis of Data on AID

CECOS has centralized all information on donors, requesting couples, inseminations, associated gynecological treatment, occurrence and evolution of conceptions and the condition of the child at birth. This information is codified for computer processing. At the first Center, CECOS at Paris-Bicêtre, all data has been treated in this matter from the Center's inception. For each donor and each woman, dual records are kept. One which is nominal is maintained at the Center during the treatment phase, the other which is prepared for computer analysis and is anonymously identified by a coded number is transmitted to the Statistical Research Center. This has the advantages of making a large amount of data readily accessible for evaluation and research and maintaining anonymity which is very important to both donors and receivers. Computer processing also permits comparison of results obtained by a Center according to the gynecologist who performs the insemination since they are also identified by a code number.

The evolution of the number of requests received per year by the different Centers is presented in Table 2. The Centers in Paris are the most active according to this index, being responsible for 43% of the requests in 1978. Certain results of CECOS are shown in Table 3 but they cannot be used for extensive analysis since this requires an evaluation based upon rates per cycle as discussed elsewhere in this volume by Schwartz (page 200).

AUTOPRESERVATION FOR AIH

When a man is to undergo sterilization, either voluntary as by vasectomy or involuntary as in treatment for cancer, preservation of his semen allows him to retain the possibility of having children. This activity involved   for all of CECOS from 1973 to 1978 a total of 903 cases: 469(52%) for vasectomy and 434(48%) for a sterilizing treatment.

The problem posed in these cases is similar to that in certain fertile men, the quality of their semen is not adequate for cryopreservation. This is especially the case for cancer patients whose semen quality is poor, probably as a result of their disease. Of these patients, only about 40% meet established criteria for cryopreservation which are described by Czyglik and David in this volume (page 598).

Finally, semen enrichment techniques and cryopreservation have been employed in an attempt to improve oligozoospermic semen for AIH. This procedure has progressed little since oligozoospermia is most often accompanied by asthenozoospermia. Hence, the additional loss of motility resulting from freezing completely removes the fertilizing capacity of this semen.

JURIDICIAL PROBLEMS

Presently in France, there are no laws or government regulations concerning artificial insemination. Existing legislation in regard to paternity actually gives the husband the possibility of disavowing the child produced by AID. Legislation has recently been proposed and is now being considered by the Senate. Furthermore, the Ministry of Health is studying a group of proposed Sperm Bank regulations: Requirements for creation, regulation of functions, fee setting, etc.

Finally, a new problem has arisen as a result of autopreservation: The request for *post-morten* insemination. What should a Center do if a woman whose husband has stored his semen requests insemination after his death? For the moment, it has been decided by CECOS that requests for autopreserved semen will be honored only when made by the man. Therefore, his semen cannot be given to another person including his wife unless he is alive. This problem should also be considered in future legislation.

CONCLUSION

The French CECOS system is still undergoing development. Each year its activity increases: As shown in Figure 2, there was a 30% increase in AID requests, semen donations and AIH requests from 1977 to 1978. Certain Centers have reached a limit of maximum desirable activity which has been determined to be about 600 new requests for AID and 300 to 400 autocryopreservations per year. Therefore, it is necessary to plan new Centers: Based upon current demand, there is a need for one sperm bank per 2 to 4 million inhabitants. For France, this means an increase from the present number of 14 to a total of about 20 Centers. This evolution should be progressive and accompanied by reinforcement of the links among Centers. In parallel, CECOS hopes to improve communication on an international level, that is, with centers in other countries with similar activities. The First Symposium on Human Artificial Insemination and Cryopreservation is the result of this desire.

REFERENCES

1. Chosson, J., Caderas de Kerleau, J., Merger, R., Hartemann, J.
    and Louyot, S.   Etude medico-sociale de l'insémination arti-
    ficielle.   Bul. Fed. Soc. Gyn. et Obst. de langue française,
    1 bis:309, 1957.

PRESENT STATUS OF DONOR INSEMINATION IN BELGIUM

Robert Schoysman and Andrée Schoysman-Deboeck

Fertility Department
Academic Hospital V.U.B.
Brussels, Belgium

It is impossible to determine today who performed the first donor insemination(AID) in Belgium, our colleagues who were thought to be interested in this technique being no longer alive. One can state, however, that it is most unlikely that any donor insemination took place in Belgium before the second world war. It is probable that it was first practiced in the mid-1940's or early 1950's. There are no data available since the cases were obviously very few and since the general consensus of doctors in our country in those days was most certainly hostile to the principle of donor insemination. Therefore, those very few who actually handled some cases would not have published their results. Even so, it is estimated that up to the mid-1950's, roughly one hundred pregnancies were obtained by this technique. It also must be taken into consideration that these cases were few, not only because of doctors' negative attitudes, but also because of a very low number of demands. Indeed, in the 1940's and 1950's, adoption was not as difficult as it is today and there-fore, the need for AID was not so acute when infertility in a couple was due to a male factor. Furthermore, due to traditionalism and lack of information, the acceptance of AID by the public was very limited.

We began performing donor insemination in the beginning of 1956. This took place at the University of Brussels and although this in-stitution was known for its more open and undogmatic approach to problems of this kind, there was obviously ill-feeling about this activity. However, demands were received, examined, and eventually accepted at a very slowly increasing rhythm of 2 or 3 more cases per year.

AID was only done with fresh semen. Over the years the activity steadily grew and by the end of the 1960's, some 70 pregnancies had been obtained. The demands were then coming with such a frequency that it was no longer possible to meet them with fresh donor semen and in 1970 we organized the first liquid nitrogen sperm bank in Brussels. At that time, Andrée Schoysman-Deboeck gradually took over the activity of freezing semen and performing the donor insem- inations and we had become more and more interested since from a bio- logical and human point of view the results obtained were very favor- able. As will be presented in another paper, the sperm bank has allowed us to have to date over 900 successes with AID. For the above-mentioned reasons of ill-feeling about AID, this first sperm bank was organized in private practice, but today there is also a second sperm bank at Brussels Free Flemish University.

In the meantime, other colleagues had become interested in AID, Professor O. Steeno from the Flemish University of Louvain, who started donor insemination some ten years ago, has close to 300 preg- nancies so far, a remarkable achievement since he only uses fresh semen.

In 1977, Dr. F. Comhaire at the University of Ghent, organized a liquid nitrogen sperm bank. We have no precise information on the actual results but less than 50 pregnancies seem to have been ob- tained so far. The University of Liege also has a sperm bank, but it is presently only in its initial stages although some pregnancies have been obtained as we have been informed by Professor R. Lambotte. It is certain that a few colleagues do perform donor inseminations in their private practice. Their patients come to them having been disappointed by the long waiting lists at the too few clinics which perform AID on a large scale. There are no precise data on the number of successes they have obtained but one can reasonnably assume there are no more than a few dozen per year. There are, however, two exceptions: One colleague (Dr P. Devroey) has obtained 125 pregnan- cies with fresh semen and another colleague, over 30 pregnancies with both fresh and frozen semen.

CONCLUSION

The total number of successes obtained by AID in Belgium can be estimated to be 2000 pregnancies and it is very unlikely that private practice or unpublished results will greatly increase that figure. Considering that the yearly number of demands for a popula- tion of 10 million like Belgium lies between 500 and 600, present facilities and structures are wholly insufficient and it is imper- ative that more gynecological centers with an interest in infertil- ity organize sperm banks.

The prejudice and reluctance towards AID, so strong some 25 years ago, have gradually though not entirely disappeared. Many colleagues with open hostility towards AID have been very favorably impressed by the happiness of the couples, the high rate of demands for a second baby by the same technique, and the strikingly low percentage of psychological disturbances and eventual divorce. To our knowledge, there has never been a legal complication in a case of AID in our country.

Finally, the Clergy(Belgium has a majority of Catholics in its population), opposed to AID on the theological grounds, has shown through the advice of many of its priests an open-minded approach to this problem in many cases. This indicates a sincere interest in respecting a couple's personality within the boundaries of their moral rules.

ARTIFICIAL INSEMINATION AND SPERM BANKS:

THE CANADIAN EXPERIENCE

Jacques E. Rioux and C.D.F. Ackman

Department of Obstetrics and Gynecology
Centre Hospitalier de l'Université Laval
Quebec, Canada

Department of Urology
McGill University
Montreal, Canada

The first artificial insemination in Canada was performed in 1968. We have calculated that there have been at least 1500 births by artificial insemination over the last decade. There are currently about fifteen nonprofit university affiliated fertility centers which practice artificial insemination. Four of these centers possess a liquid nitrogen bank and use frozen semen. The reasons generally cited for using these techniques are: The difficulty in recruiting donors; an inability to grant certain requests for insemination because the ideal donor could not be found; and in certain cases, desire to improve the husband's semen as in the case of oligospermia, where the aim is to accumulate split ejaculate.

The Husband

The husband's semen is very rarely used, particularly if it is significantly deficient with respect to any one of the parameters considered to be essential (number, motility, morphology). Indeed, using the husband in these cases always yields poor results. On the other hand, if the husband's semen is satisfactory, it is used for intrauterine insemination when the wife presents an insurmountable cervical problem or when antibodies exist in the cervical mucus. None of the centers inseminate with a mixture of the husband's semen and that of a donor. This is sometimes requested by a husband whose spermiogram reveals questionable fertility. We always advise

against it.   Indeed, certain centers even request the husband to
abstain from sexual relations or else to use a condom during the
insemination period.

Donors

Most of the centers(80%) use medical or dental students or students from other schools of the university. The other centers recruit their donors amongst the hospital personnel or nurses' husbands or, better still, amongst husbands of pregnant or recently delivered patients. In short, most donors are not married and have
never given proof of fertility. They are remunerated.

Donor Selection. Most of the centers follow an almost identical
line of conduct: For a man to be accepted as a donor, the following
procedures must be performed: (1) Semen analysis with results in
the upper normal range; (2) semen culture revealing the absence of
pathogenic bacteria; (3) interview with medical history including
precise information about his family, obtained with the help of a
genetic check-list; (4) medical examination, with normal findings;
(5) blood grouping; (6) V.D.R.L.; (7) SMA-12; and (8) karyotyping.

It is to be noted that women inseminated several times during
the same cycle do not always receive semen from the same donor. This
is, however, very clearly explained.

The Recipient Couple

In most cases, the couple is married or else living together
in a rather stable way. However, single women are accepted for
insemination.

When sterility has been diagnosed in the man, one of two courses
of action can be pursued. On the one hand, insemination of the woman can be attempted immediatly on the assumption that she is potentially fertile. Investigations are performed only in the event
of failure. On the other hand, the woman can be investigated immediatly and insemination attempted only if she is presumed to be
fertile. Most of the centers require only a diphasic basal temperature curve and an endometrial biopsy as proof of ovulation, completed by a normal hysterosalpingogram.

The artificial insemination consent forms used by the centers
are generally rather complete. First, all the information pertaining to the donors can be found. Then, the patient is warned that
the inseminations may not lead to pregnancy. The number of cycles
during which insemination is performed is limited in some centers:
after six good cycles that is, with presumption of ovulation and
best possible timing of insemination without pregnancy, the patient

is withdrawn from the insemination program. Lastly, it is recalled that if a pregnancy does occur, it is subject to all the advantages and drawbacks of a normal pregnancy. More precisely, it has been found that miscarriages, ectopic pregnancies and congenital malformations do not occur more frequently in pregnancies resulting from artificial insemination.

Matching Criteria

The criteria governing selection of a donor for a recipient couple vary from one center to another and also in function of donor availability. An effort is made to match eye and hair color and to find compatible blood groups except of course in cases of rhesus incompatibility.

Techniques

Most of the centers practice intracervical insemination with a Palmer cannula. Some perform only direct intravaginal insemination with a syringe. On both cases, inseminations are most often carried out by nurses trained in gynecology. Lastly, certain centers practice intrauterine insemination when the indications make it necessary.

Results

The centers which use only fresh semen report pregnancy rates varying from 60 to 80%. The difference of 20% is due either to better selection of women before insemination or to the presence of associated pathological conditions such as anovulation or tubal obstructions treated surgically in an attempt to achieve fertility by insemination. The centers which use only frozen semen report a lower success rate: 20 to 40%. Lastly, at least 30% of women who have become pregnant by artificial insemination return for a second or even a third pregnancy.

Records

All the centers keep complete records of the recipient couples. In most cases, these are hospital records which are kept for many years, in accordance with each province's laws.

In general, no effort is made by the insemination center to evaluate the product of conception. Most centers advise the patient to give birth elsewhere. Thus, if the couple wants to keep the insemination secret, this makes it much simpler. The patient is requested to notify the center after the birth in order to furnish details of the pregnancy and the delivery as well as the baby's sex and general condition.

On the whole, records of the donors are poorly kept. They are discarded after only a few years, and most of the centers say they cannot identify the donor used for a given couple. This reticence seems to result from the fear that if donors felt threatened because they could be identified, they would be much harder to find.

Legislation

At the present time, there is none. It has been proposed that the husband's signature be required, since it seems to be generally agreed that a document signed by husband and wife recognizing the use of artificial insemination makes the child legitimate and prevents the husband from ever being able to disown him. The Canadian government has created a Royal Commission to study the problems related to and caused by the use of the very simple technique known as artificial insemination. The report of this commission will soon be submitted to the government, which will be able to take inspiration from it in formulating legislation. Furthermore, it will serve as a guide for centers currently engaged in artificial insemination and for those which would like to be. Such standards will also become necessary if a court case ever arises in which the quality of an act of insemination is in question.

CONCLUSION

Artificial insemination as currently practiced in Canada renders a great service. Unfortunately, there is no uniformity among the various centers performing it because no law exists in this domain. The members of the Royal Commission hope that their report will enable the legislators to formulate a law which will not check existing practices or future innovations.

PRESENT STATUS OF AID AND SPERM BANKS IN SWITZERLAND

A. Campana [*], U. Gigon [**], F. Maire [***],
G. Szalmaj [****] and H. Wyss [*****]

[*] Ospedale Distrettuale "La Carita", Locarno
[**] Hôpital Universitaire de Bern, Bern
[***] Hôpital Cantonal de Liestal, Liestal
[****] Hôpital Cantonal de St. Gallen, St. Gallen
[*****] Hôpital Universitaire de Basel, Basel
Switzerland

The first Swiss semen bank for artificial insemination by donor (AID) using liquid nitrogen as freezing agent and glycerol as protective medium was set up at St. Gallen in 1970. There are now 5 AID centres in Switzerland(Figure 1) sharing the following characteristics: (1) The insemination centre is in a public gynaecological clinic; (2) insemination is performed only at the hospital where the semen bank is situated; and(3) the 5 insemination centres belong to the Swiss Work Group for Artificial Insemination which was set up in 1977 for the purpose of co-ordinating the activities of the centres, standardizing working methods and carrying out scientific programs on a joint basis.

Selection of Donors

Donor selection is done in the Bern, St. Gallen and Liestal centres by the gynecologist performing the insemination and in the Basel and Locarno centres by the gynecologist and the geneticist. All the centres share the following criteria for acceptance of potential donors: Social motivation for donating semen; normal psycho-intellectual state; normal genetic screen; normal clinical and laboratory tests including those for syphilis and gonorrhoea; sperm count of more than 40 x10^6 spermatozoa/ml with normal motility and morphology; and age of donor between 20 and 40.

At the last meeting of the Swiss Work Group for Artificial

35

FIGURE 1.   AID centres in Switzerland

Insemination, the geneticist, Dr. Bühler, put forward a genetic test
plan for donors(Table 1).   The plan has already been adopted by the
Basel and Locarno clinics.

The most controversial point is whether or not a karyotype is
performed.   Dr. Gigon of Bern, for example, does not request the donor's karyotype but suggests that all women conceiving after AID
have their amniotic fluid tested.   The problem is an extremely interesting one because, apart from the genetic applications, there
are considerations of a legal(documentation of the research done on
the donor), an economic(cost of performing a karyotype), and a moral
nature(acceptance of termination of the pregnancy on the woman's part
in the event of a positive prenatal diagnosis).

Until such time as the legal problems raised by AID are finally
clarified, it seems to us advisable to proceed as follows: Carry
out genetic screening, including karyotype, for all potential donors;
and suggest amniocenteses to all women conceiving through AID.

Population Genetics and the Number of Children from One Donor

This problem has been studied in our group by the geneticist
Dr. Moser.   His conclusion is that the risk of in-breeding occurring in future generations is extremely low, even if a single donor
fathers 10 or more children, that is with the condition that individuals
procreated by means of AID are distributed evenly among the population.   In practical terms, the problem as it concerns Switzerland

TABLE 1. *Genetic screening for potential donors*

---

1. Genealogical research

2. Age(< 40 years)

3. Exclusion of high-risk professions

4. Exclusion of medicine or drug users

5. Karyotype

6. Chromatopsia test

7. Audiometry

8. Blood pressure measurement

9. Urine tests

10. Perspiration test

11. (Prenatal diagnosis for pregnancy following AID).

---

is governed by two factors: (1) A donor gives his semen for a period usually not exceeding 1 year, an average of 3 to 4 ejaculates being collected per month; and (2) a significant proportion of the couples requesting AID come from other countries, notably Italy at Locarno, Germany at Basel, and Austria at St. Gallen.

In view of the limited period during which semen is collected from a donor and the geographical distribution of the couples requesting AID, we have no problem as far as the number of children that may be fathered by one donor is concerned. This allows us when necessary to utilize the semen of several donors in an insemination cycle and to safeguard the anonymity of the procedure. In no case, however, is the identity of the donor mentioned on the insemination record.

Criteria for Choice of the Donor

The only criterion of choice of the donor common to all the Swiss centres is the couple's blood group.

At the Locarno and St. Gallen clinics, the choice also takes account of the physical characteristics of the couple. In Bern, on the other hand, the ejaculates of donors having the same blood group are mixed so that it is impossible to select a donor on the basis of the couple's physical characteristics.

Semen Bank

It should first be pointed out that the use of fresh or frozen semen varies among the Swiss centres. Basel, for example, is currently performing only fresh semen inseminations, while the centre using the highest percentage of frozen semen is St. Gallen with 85% (Table 2).

For freezing we use a container with liquid nitrogen, a protective medium with egg yolk, glycerol, glucose aqueous solution, and sodium citrate, in a 1:1 concentration with the semen, it is stored in 0.5 cc. paillettes.

Technique of Insemination

Between 0.5 and 1 ml of semen is injected for each insemination. Normally insemination is achieved by means of the Finkentscher-Semm cap. An average of 2 or 4 inseminations are made per cycle at intervals of 24 to 48 hours.

TABLE 2. *Type of semen used in AID*

	Fresh semen	Frozen semen
Basel	100%	0%
Bern	90%	10%
Liestal	25%	75%
Locarno	40%	60%
St. Gallen	15%	85%

TABLE 3. *Figures for pregnancies following AID in Switzerland*

Basel	60
Bern	454
Liestal	70
Locarno	151
St. Gallen	566
Total	1301

Figures for pregnancies following AID

There was a total of 1,301 pregnancies following AID achieved in the 5 AID centres in Switzerland by the end of February, 1979 (Table 3).

The centre with the highest percentage of pregnancies was St. Gallen, with 43.5% followed by Bern with 34.9%.

The Swiss Work Group for Artificial Insemination

This is an interdisciplinary work group linking all the Swiss AID centres and made up of gynaecologists, andrologists, geneticists, biologists, biochemists, veterinarians from animal insemination centres, psychologists, and lawyers.

The setting-up of this group which has been operating for a year and a half undoubtedly represents the beginning of a new phase in the practice of AID in Switzerland.

Besides bringing together at a national level all the gynecologists practicing AID in public hospitals, it also brings together in an active capacity representatives of the various disciplines involved in the problem of artificial insemination.

PRESENT STATUS OF AID AND SPERM BANKS IN DENMARK

Paul E. Lebech

Department of Obstetrics and Gynecology
Frederiksberg Hospital
Copenhagen, Denmark

Twelve years ago only a few births following artificial insemination with donor semen(AID) had been recorded in Denmark(population 5.1 million), while today the number exceeds 1000. Interest
in AID continues to increase and the response may be assessed in
different ways. About 33,000 couples of a fertile age marry each
year. Almost 10% of them are expected to be infertile and of this
percentage the cause is male infertility in about one-third to one-
half. On the basis of interviews with such couples, we estimate
that about half of them wish to utilize AID which means about 500
couples a year. Furthermore, there must be some accumulation from
previous years, and of course a number of couples want more than
one child by AID.

Calculations of the use of semen portions and an estimate of
the number of inseminations performed annually at present(based upon
data from the largest clinics) indicate that 500 to 1000 couples are
treated each year. But it was not until the use of deep-frozen human
semen was systematized that the insemination could be carried out
in several centres in all parts of the country. The use of deep-
frozen semen solved a number of practical problems relating to the
employment of fresh semen. It obviates the risk that the donor and
patient might be in the same building at the same time and thereby
avoids problems of discretion as well as the necessity of having a
sufficiently large panel of donors to make sure that donor semen was
available at all times.

After the first sperm bank at Frederiksberg Hospital had been
operating for a few years,[1] and its obvious advantages substantiated,
similar banks were gradually established in connection with other

gynecological departments. Recently, a sperm bank has been established in Copenhagen which delivers semen to clinics all over the
country. As a result, AID is now performed as a routine procedure
in practically all gynecological units. Three units still use mainly fresh semen and a few have their own sperm bank. In most places
the waiting time has been reduced to less than one year and in some
hospitals to a few months.

Apart from the technical problems, to which a reasonable solution has been found, certain legal and ethical problems still accom-
pany AID. In Denmark and other Scandinavian countries, there is no
present legislation on artificial insemination.

In 1953 a Commission appointed by the Danish Ministry of Justice issued a Report concerning a special law on artificial insemination.[2] This Report has never been made into an act, but it affords an excellent orientation concerning the legal problems involved
in AID. It is possible to establish that a doctor in a Danish institution is entitled to carry out AID. There are no rules or laws
to prevent the doctor, woman, husband, or the donor from participating. A couple wishing insemination must submit a written request
to the doctor. It is emphasized in the Commission Report that the
doctor must select a donor and he must prevent the woman's and her
husband's identity from becoming known to the donor and *vice versa*.
In general, these are the rules followed in practice today.

It was pointed out in the Report that central registration of
children born after AID was possible. Some of the judicial and medical members of the Commission felt that legislation on AID details
might make matters more difficult rather than easier for all parties
concerned.

The child's legal status today is perhaps somewhat uncertain,
but this problem can arise only in cases where the husband or com-
peting heirs later try to prove that the child cannot be the husband's. There is no legal precedent in Denmark for such cases since
legal proceedings have never been instituted after AID. Inciden-
tally, such proceedings will rarely, or never, serve the child's
interests, and in the opinion of several Danish judges, it is quite
possible that such a case would be dismissed by the court. The donor's legal status is also somewhat in doubt, but it must be clearly
pointed out to him that his collaboration does not entail any obligations on his part. According to the Commission Report an action
cannot be brought against the donor as long as the general *pater est*
rule of the law protects the child.

Here too, the use of sperm banks in which the donor can be recorded by a number can ensure his anonymity, even in an extreme situation. Presumably, it is not necessary to legislate in this field,

but in my opinion it is most important to secure legitimacy for the
child. It should be sufficient in this regard to establish that
the husband has given his permission for this procedure. Owing to
these problems we have not yet consented to inseminate unwed women.

In Scandinavia there have been several conference panel discussions on AID attended by doctors, clergymen, laywers, and geneticists. There has not been any official reaction from the Church.
Occasionally certain fundamental religious objections have been
raised, but on the whole the attitude of the clergy has been extremely understanding.

From various quarters, int. al. from donors(but never from
geneticists), the risk of consanguinity and its risk of an increased occurrence of heritable chromosomal anomalies has been questioned. This risk is exceedingly small with the frequency of children born through AID at present.

Even though a donor can be used for 20 pregnancies, calculations show that in Denmark consanguinity because of AID can arise
at most 2 or 3 times in each century.

In the course of the past few years the public has been well
informed of the practice of AID and of its legal and ethical problems through mass media presentations. This has, in fact, acted
to increase interest in AID, especially since at present, the chance of adopting a child is very small. AID still presents many problems, especially of a psychological and social nature which must
be clarified in the future.

REFERENCES

1. Lebech, P.E. Banques de sperme humain. Fécondité et Stérilité
        du Mâle. Paris, 1972.

2. Betaenkning om en saerlig lovgivning om kunstig befrugtning:
        Justitsministeriet. Copenhagen, 1958.

AID AND SPERM BANK

DEVELOPMENT IN ISRAEL

J. Barkay and H. Zuckerman

Department of Obstetrics and Gynecology
Central Emek Hospital
Afula, Israël

Judaism is very keen on family purity, and thus artificial insemination is subject to many prohibitions, not just in regard to
the donor, which I will later clarify, but also in regard to the
way semen is collected since the "spoiling" of semen is forbidden
by the Torah.

According to Jewish law, AIH is permitted if it is the only
way fertilization can be obtained. AID is a very complex problem and
it is completely forbidden if the donor is Jewish. This raises the
possibility that some day a man might marry his half-sister, which
is an incestual act. The child would be considered illegitimate. AID,
if the donor is not Jewish, is less condemned. It is permitted
because marriage between a Jewish woman and a gentile(non-Jewish)
is not recognized and the child is considered to belong only to the
mother. This means that not only is the child not considered a
bastard, but he is accepted as a complete Jew and is fit to fulfill
any ritual role. For the conservative Jewish population which continues to keep the customs and traditions of the religion and of
course for the rabbinical courts, acceptance of this Jewish law
makes AID treatment possible in Israel without difficulty.

Insemination in Israel has mostly been practiced in private
clinics making control of any kind quite impossible. Institution-
alized insemination was, until recently, almost non-existent and
there was a great need for establishing such an institution. According, we have developed a sperm bank at Afula Hospital.

The aim of our cryobank was not only to carry out freeze preservation of donor semen, but also freeze preservation for husband semen. This has been done in cases of malignancy(the semen

should be collected and preserved before radiation) and today we
are preserving the collected semen of more than 45 patients after
seminoma, lymphogranulomotosis, etc., from all parts of the country.
Two children have been born to present by this means.

Semen can also be preserved before prostatectomy or vasectomy,
after accidents resulting in paraplegia with diminished fertilizing
capacity, in dangerous professions or high risk occupations, as, for
example, workers in a radiation environment or construction workers
who, through falls or other accidents, are prone to testicular injury. Other candidates are men in military service such as pilots:
Today, all the invalid military patients with problems of fertility
are concentrated in Afula.

Previously frozen and stored semen also makes it possible for
insemination during ovulation in the absence of the husband and last,
but not least, the cryopreserved semen is very useful for medical
experiments, pooling, concentration and selection of X and Y chromo-
some-bearing spermatozoa, electronic microscopic studies, etc.

In 1974, we published the preliminary paper of our freezing
method and in 1978 we completed our work on our further developed
device for human semen freezing(Figure 1) by which the preparation
of the semen and the freezing process are reduced to a simple procedure, requiring about 5 minutes presently. The instrument itself
is based on the principle of evaporation of liquid nitrogen which
acts as a refrigerant for the freezing plated, controlled by a ther-
mostat(Figure 2). Rapid rate freezing can be performed for pellet
production and slow rate freezing for paillettes(Figure 3). A high
degree of isolation of each sample is made possible by inter-
changeable freezing plates(figure 4). Freezing of the samples
is accomplished at an initial temperature of -80°, with storage at
-196°. The protective medium has remained almost unchanged since
our preliminary report: The ratio between the semen and protective
medium is 1 ml to 0.66 ml with the protective medium being composed
of prefabricated Difco egg-yolk(40%), a 3% sodium citrate solution
(40%), glycerol(10%) and streptomycin. The freezing process has been
reduced in the last few years to 5 minutes since we have omitted
unnecessary prefreeze cooling at 5° for 15 minutes. The recovery
index for the thawed spermatozoa is from 50 to 60%.

We tried continually to find a way of improving motility of
the frozen spermatozoa after the thawing, and in 1977 we began to
add frozen caffeine pellets to the frozen semen pellets in the proportion of 1:5.   The caffeine solution which we prepare for
freezing in pellet form consists of 80 mg pure caffeine pulver mixed
with 10 ml of Hartman infusion solution(7 m/M final concentration).

We have succeeded in raising the motility of the thawed

FIGURE 1. Semen freezing apparatus

FIGURE 2. Freezing plate of semen freezing apparatus
and pellet formation

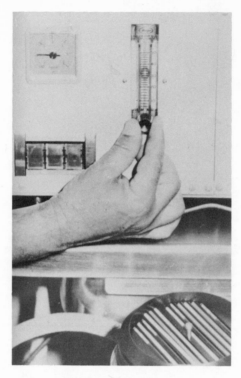

FIGURE 3.   Adjustment of freezing rate and special plate
for freezing paillettes(lower right)

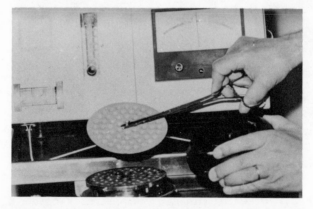

FIGURE 4.   Method of changing the freezing plate

TABLE 1. *Comparison of insemination results for spermatozoa having or not having been treated with caffeine (Male fertility institute of Central Emek Hospital, Afula)*

Type of insemination	No. of patients	Delivery		Abortion		Current Pregnancies		Total pregnancies		Pregnancies (%)
		No. of patients	Cycles of insemination	No. of patients	Cycles of insemination	No. of patients	Cycles of insemination	No. of patients	Cycles of insemination	
1974-76 without caffeine										
AID	46	18	115	2	10	7	50	27	165	58.6
AIH	10	1	9	1	8	2	16	4	33	40
Total	56	19	124	3	18	9	66	31	198	55.4
1976-78 with caffeine										
AID	68	37	162	4	18	6	24	47	204	69.1
AIH	22	8	40	1	6	2	10	11	56	50
Total	90	45	202	5	24	8	34	58	260	64.4

semen and the fertilizing capacity by 10%. The results of the past
four years are presented in Table 1.

At present we are the only sperm bank in Israël but in the
future another sperm bank is being planned at the University of the
Negev in Beer Sheva. We intend to cooperate with that center and we
hope to be able to work together on the many problems for which solutions are still being sought. We are also planning, after the
peace agreement in the Middle East, a co-ordination and scientific
cooperation with our colleagues in the Fertility Centers of neigh-
boring countries, especially at the University of Cairo, which we
hope will be of mutual scientific benefit.

REFERENCES

1. Steinberg, A. Artificial insemination as viewed by the Halacha.
        (Hebrew). Book of Asya. pp. 133-136.

2. Ericson, R.J. Isolation and storage of progressively motile
        human sperm. Andrologie 9, 1:111-114, 1977.

3. Barkay, J., Zukerman, H. and Haiman, M. New practical method
        of freezing and storing human sperm and a preliminary report
        on its use. Fertil. Steril., 25:399, 1974.

4. Barkay, J. and Zukerman, H. Further developed device for human
        sperm freezing by the twenty minute method. Fertil. Steril.,
        29:304, 1978.

5. Barkay, J. and Zukerman, H. Effect of caffeine on increasing
        the motility of frozen human sperm. Fertil. Steril., 28:175,
        1977.

ARTIFICIAL INSEMINATION AND SEMEN BANKS IN ITALY

Vincenzo Traina

Contrattista Universitario
Bari, Italy

One cannot ignore that a considerable amount of criticism has been made of artificial insemination. The strictly negative pronouncement of the Catholic Church along with the impending rigour of the law have caused Italian gynecologists to perform it with extreme caution.

Indeed, contributions in the field of homologous insemination may be regarded as insignificant[1-4] while contributions regarding insemination with donor semen is restricted essentially to the work carried out by Prof. G. Traina[5,6] (figure 1). When, as far back as 1943, he reported the positive results he had obtained in a few cases, the response was one of severe criticism and disagreement. However, he carried on with his work. Only in 1974, during the 3rd Updating Course on Sterility in Married Couples which was held in Palermo was it possible to mention the work done from 1949 and after.[7] This work was reported extensively in subsequent conferences and publications.[8,13]

After the crime of adultery, which until then had offered a much debated opportunity of banning AID in Italy, was eliminated from our Law in 1969, it appeared obvious that our legislation contained no provision either defining the treatment as a crime or prohibiting and punishing it. Thus, the doctor giving the treatment does not commit any crime. Still, he must be fully aware of the responsibility resting upon him and must comply with the principles of deontology.

It is my personal feeling that the future development of artificial insemination in our country will be much the same as it has been with other social issues such as divorce and abortion for which

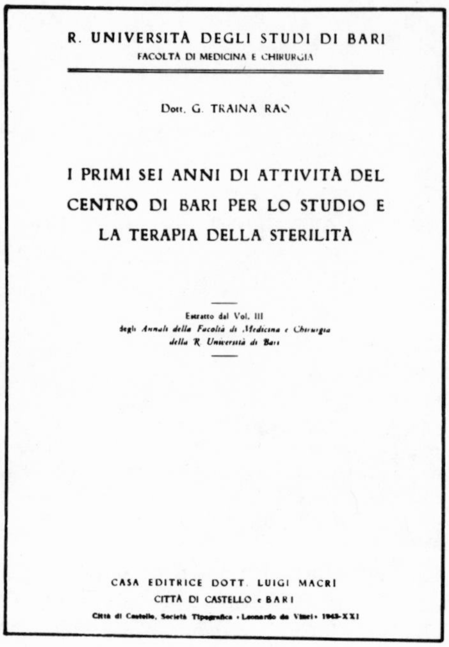
R. UNIVERSITÀ DEGLI STUDI DI BARI
FACOLTÀ DI MEDICINA E CHIRURGIA

Dott. G. TRAINA RAO

I PRIMI SEI ANNI DI ATTIVITÀ DEL CENTRO DI BARI PER LO STUDIO E LA TERAPIA DELLA STERILITÀ

Estratto dal Vol. III
degli *Annali della Facoltà di Medicina e Chirurgia della R. Università di Bari*

CASA EDITRICE DOTT. LUIGI MACRI
CITTÀ DI CASTELLO e BARI
Città di Castello, Società Tipografica «Leonardo da Vinci» 1943-XXI

FIGURE 1. The first paper in Italy(1943) presenting results on AID

a positive solution has been found after long and painstaking efforts. As divorce and abortion, AID appears to be one of the requirements of a new society as is unquestionably shown by the many pressing demands reaching our Centre from all over Italy(Figure 2) on the part of infertile couples who want to have children and often belong to very humble social classes.

Regarding the semen banks(Figure 3), I feel obliged to mention Lazzaro Spallanzani[14] who first succeeded in preserving human semen by means of freezing as early as 1776. It was again another Italian (Figure 4), Paolo Mantegazza,[15] Professor in Pathology at Pavia, whose marvellous intuition led him to suggest the establishment, in 1866, of an "iced" semen depository for veterinary use, who rather prophetically declared "...it will then become possible to perform artificial fertilization with "iced" semen, transported from one country to another at high speed. It might even be that a husband who has died on a battle-field can fecundate his own wife after he has been reduced to a corpse and produce legitimate children after his death...".

An important step forward was taken a century later(in 1949),

FIGURE 2.   Number of women treated in 1977-1978 in the
different districts of Italy

when glycerol was first added to protect the spermatozoa from the
lethal effects of the freezing process. After semen preservation
was achieved, it was only a small step to the creation of semen
"banks".

Whereas efficient banks have been established in the U.S.A.
and many European countries, particularly France, in Italy AID is
still conducted with extreme caution and the fact that semen banks
have been established in other countries has stimulated rather severe criticism.

SPERM BANKING: OUR EXPERIENCE

We have been able to create a bank which has been in operation
for almost a year. Our organization has been established within a
privately owned hospital and we have been working with the utmost
care, availing ourselves of the experience of our colleagues abroad.

In addition to acquiring material for our studies, our purpose
was to be able to perform AIH by enriching oligospermic ejaculates

 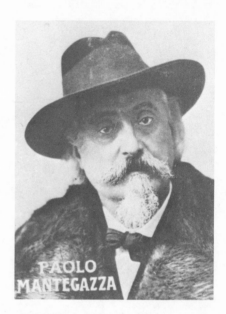

FIGURE 3.   Lazzaro Spallanzani   FIGURE 4.   Paolo Mantegazza

and by banking semen for cases of voluntary induced sterility.   Our donor selection process and techniques of AI as well as our results are described elsewhere in this volume

The Donor File

   Through the cooperation of the Andrology Department of the Post Graduate Medical School at the University of Pisa and certain specialists in Italy, we have developed a Donor File which permits all information on the donor, medical and family history, data on personal characteristics, semen analysis, etc., to be coded.   This information is kept at the semen bank and is accessible only to the physician in charge.

CONCLUSION

   To date, we have encountered no legal difficulties.   The Italian law, like that of certain other countries, contains no provisions in respect to AI, the subject being ignored altogether.

It should be noted, however, that the semen bank has only served our own purposes and has not been advertised. It would be desirable to develop legal provisions such that would help avert difficulties and dangers which might arise from an uncontrolled spreading of AID: Such legal provisions should envision the creation of properly organized centers, offer full guarantees on the origin and preparation of the semen, and provide adequate legal protection for the child.

REFERENCES

1. Alfieri, E.   La fecondazione artificiale nella donna. Clinica Nuova, 1:209, 1945.

2. Bailo, P.   Limiti medico-morali per l'attuabilita della fecondazione artificiale.   Min. Med., 2:41:42, 1950.

3. Bocci, A.   La fecondazione artificiale umana.   Convegno della Sez. Piemontese della Soc. Ital. Med. Soc.,   Salice Terme, 28-6-59, Corriere Sanitario, a. VI, n. 8, 1959.

4. Tommasi, C., Coghi I. and Custo, G.   Validita dell'inseminazio ne artificiale omologa nel trattamento della sterilita coniugale. Riv. Ost. Gin., 24:257, 1969.

5. Traina, G.   Considerazioni sulla fecondazione artificiale della donna.   Progressi di terapia, n. 3, 1943.

6. Traina, G.   I primi sei anni di attivita del Centro di Bari per lo studio e la terapia della sterilita.   Ed. Macri, Citta di Castella, 1943.

7. Traina, G.   L'inseminazione artificiale.   Comunicazione al 3° corso sulla Sterilita Coniugale.   Palermo, 24-27 April 1974.

8. Traina, G.   Inseminazione artificiale mediante donatore (AID) nel trattamento della sterilita coniugale.   Risultati in 241 casi.   Min. Gin., 29:745, 1977.

9. Traina, G. and V.   L'inseminazione artificiale omologa (AIH) nel trattamento della sterilita.   Min. Gin., 30:1147, 1978 (in coll.).

10. Traina, V.   Le banche del seme.   Sessuologia, 1:37, 1977.

11. Traina, V.   L'inseminazione artificiale umana.   Minerva Medica. Torino, 1977.

12. Traina, V.   L'inseminazione artificiale in Italia.   La Riforma Medica, 91-92:307, 15 Nov. 1977.

13.   Traina, V.   Le banche del seme all'estero.   La Riforma Medica.
      91-92:244, 31 Oct. 1977.

14.   Spallanzani, L.   Osservazioni ed esperienze intorno ai vermi-
      celli spermatici dell'uomo e degli animali.   Opuscoli di
      fisica animale e vegetale, Modena, 1776.

15.   Mantegazza, P.   Fisiologia sullo sperma umano.   Rend. Reale
      Ist. Lombardo, 3:183, 1866.

THE FIRST SPERM BANK IN SPAIN:

ORGANIZATION AND FIRST YEAR RESULTS

Simon Marina

Hospital de la Santa Cruz y San Pablo
Barcelona, Spain

The first human semen bank was set up in Barcelona by the author. It is a private center which opened in January, 1978.

The bank was created due to the large demand for artificial insemination with donor semen (AID) by Spanish couples whose cause for sterility could be attributed to the husband. Spanish civil legislation does not refer to AID so there have been no legal diffi- culties encountered to date.

Donors

Donors have consisted of university students, mostly in medicine, between 18 and 30 years of age who have been recruited through ad- vertising at the universities. Most are bachelors and all are clear- ly informed about the destination of the semen. Once the conditions are known, 95% accept being semen donors.

Personal and familial investigations are carried out basically to detect pathologies of possible hereditary transmission (hyper- tension, diabetes mellitus, epilepsy, mental disease, headaches, etc.). Infectious diseases of the donor with possible transmission through the semen (viral hepatitis, gonorrhea) are also considered. General physical examination (weight, size, hair and eye, color, cardiopulmonary auscultation, abdominal palpation) and a genital examination (testes, penis, epididymis, vas deferens and prostate is performed. The blood group is determined (ABO and Rh - anti D - factor) and an Australia antigen is tested for when there is a history of viral hepatitis.

The conditions of semen collection including an abstinence

57

of 4 to 7 days and examination of the semen including cytomorphology
are standardized in our laboratory. Acceptable semens have counts
greater than 70 million/ml, grade 3 motility, 70% normal forms and
no spermatozoa agglutination.

Of 94 prospective donors, 50(53%) were rejected due to a
genital abnormality such as cryptorchidism or poor quality semen.

Accepted donors receive 1000 ptas for each semen sample and
are allowed to donate once a week. Total anonymity is guaranteed.
The motivations of the donors are three: Economic compensation, the
wish to know whether they were fertile and the wish to contribute
to the solution of the problem of sterility in couples without
children(20% were blood donors). Some samples were donations preceding a vasectomy.

Couples

All inseminated women have been married and the husband has
been determined to have a negative fertility prognosis. Information
on AID is always given to the couple. It is suggested that they
postpone the decision if either has the slightest doubt. They are
informed about donor selection, the insemination procedure, risks,
probabilities of success, the legal and religious aspects(Pius XII
and the Catholic church forbade it in 1949) and the cost.

The somatic data of the husband are obtained(weight, size,
hair and eye, color) as well as the blood group(ABO, and Rh -
anti D) of both wife and husband. No psychological study is performed and no document is signed.

For the time being, we have received no request of AID from
single women. Some couples have wished to bring the semen of a relative for insemination but they have been rejected. If the woman
is more than 40 years of age or if she suffers from some important
disease with hereditary basis, our present attitude has been to not
perform AID.

Freezing Technique

The freezing technique is that of Drs R. Schoysman and A.
Schoysman-Deboeck[1] which incorporates a glycero-egg yolk-citrate
medium with a final glycerol concentration of 7%. The pH is adjusted
to 7.2 to 7.4 and no antibiotics are added. The semen is mixed with
cryoprotector medium in a proportion of 2 to 1 during 10 minutes.
Straws of 0.5ml are filled by aspiration(IMV, l'Aigle-France), closed
and placed in a container of liquid nitrogen where they remain stored.
Frozen samples are thawed and spermatozoa motility studied. A motility of 50% is required for use in AID. Semen culture is performed
to detect gonococci.

The transport is made in small containers full of liquid nitrogen, with an autonomy of 3 days(TCB 4 L'Air Liquide). At the present time, samples for AID are supplied to 8 gynecologists (all from Barcelona).

For the selection of the sample, the blood groups of the couple and the weight, size, hair and eyes colouring of the husband are taken into consideration. The Spanish population is rather homogeneous considering these phenotypic data so that sufficient semen samples can be obtained without having too many donors. At the present time, insemination can be carried out without delay.

Insemination

The thawing technique, selection of days, patterns and number of inseminations per cycle, the placing of the cervical cap and the hormonal induction of ovulation are aspects completely decided upon by the gynecologist.

The cost of the semen samples for the first cycle is 15,000 ptas (about 3 or 4 straws). During the next months, the cost is 10,000 ptas per set.

RESULTS

The results are reported in Tables 1, 2 and 3. Out of 103 inseminated women, 27 pregnacies have been obtained

TABLE 1.

Inseminated women	103
Pregnancies(1 twin)	27
Births(all normal)	5
- Males	3
- Females	2
Abortion	1

TABLE 2. *Pregnancies compared with the number of inseminated cycles*

Cycle	Pregnancies
1st	8
2nd	7
3rd	6
3 months	21
4th	0
5th	1
6th	3
6 months	25
7th	2
TOTAL	27

TABLE 3. *Pregnancies compared with ag*

Age (years)	Inseminated	Not pregnant	Pregnant
Less than 25	9	7	2
From 25 to 30	52	37	15
From 30 to 35	30	20	10
More than 35	12	12	0
TOTAL	103	76	27

REFERENCES

1. Schoysman, R. and Schoysman-Debroek, A. Results of donor insemination with frozen semen. In: Sperm action, Proy Repro. Biol. Vol. 1. I.O. Hubinout, ed. , Karger, Basel, 1976, pp. 252.

HUMAN SEMEN BANK AT THE SPANISH SOCIAL SECURITY HOSPITAL

José A. Portuondo and Abel D. Echanojauregui

Service of Obstetrics and Gynecology
Ciudad Sanitaria "Enrique Sotomayor"
    de la Seguridad Social
Cruces-Bilbao, Spain

INTRODUCTION

The first Spanish human semen bank was created in Barcelona, in January 1978, by S. Marina, MD. The first Spanish human semen bank established in a Social Security Hospital was at the Ciudad Sanitaria de la Seguridad Social "Enrique Sotomayor" Cruces-Bilbao in 1978. The lay press has dedicated several issues to the human sperm bank, which still is a novelty in this country.

There is no law regulating donor artificial insemination in Spain. Practicing artificial insemination with donor is not against the Constitution, but according to the General College of Physicians and Doctors, medical practice should be kept within general ethical principles.

MATERIAL AND METHODS

Pre-Enrolement for Infertility

Two consecutive semen analyses of the husband are performed before non-reversible male infertility is concluded. We no longer perform testicular biopsy in cases of azoospermia because of poor therapeutic value. Female fertility is fully evaluated according to the minimal procedures established by the American Fertility Society. Basal body temperature is recorded during at least 3 cycles to estimate ovulation.

Hysterosalpingography is performed on the 8th to 12th day of the cycle to prove tubal patency. A 24 hour urinary pregnandiol assay is used to evaluate progesterone production. Endometrial biopsy is performed on the 22nd to 23rd day of the cycle for the diagnosis of ovulation and corpus luteum function. In our series, a routine laparoscopy is scheduled for the 23rd day of the cycle to rule out endometriosis, pelvic adhesions and anovulation.

Finally, an agreement is signed by both husband and wife to discharge the doctor who performs the AID of medical responsibility. A one half hour personal interview is held with each couple by a staff doctor in order to ascertain that AID is the most suitable procedure in their particular case.

Human Semen Banking

Donors. Three donor sources are usually accepted: Donors from the infertility or Family Planning Clinics, who are motivated through a previous contact with doctors (one third of our donors), donors from the general population and donors from the University (two thirds of our donors, travel expenses are usually paid).

In our hospital donors are selected through a complete history and general physical examination to rule out a serious present disease. Personal characteristics of blood group and Rh test, height and weight and color of hair and eyes are noted. Donor semen analysis is performed within an hour of production, and a freezing-thawing test is done in order to check post-thaw motility. Donor karyotyping is carried out in 15-20% of the cases and we intend to perform it routinely.

Semen Banking: Two cryoprotector media are mainly used in our semen bank: a glycerol-egg yolk-citrate mixture with a final concentration of 7% glycerol (Table 1) or a 15% glycerol Lopata's semen diluent[1] (Table 2). The semen mixed volume to volume with medium is placed in 2ml ampoules and quick frozen in 8 minutes. A liquid nitrogen refrigerator (Union Carbide, England, LR10) is used for samples storage. Thawing is performed keeping the semen samples at room temperature for half an hour or diping the ampoules in tap water for 10 minutes.

Insemination Procedure

Donor and husband characteristics are matched as much as possible. Donor blood type and Rh are matched either to the husband or wife. Both fresh and frozen semen are used in our AID program. It is injected through a plastic Millex cervical cup. Two inseminations per cycle with one day in between are performed near the time of ovulation. Timing of ovulation is estimated by careful

TABLE 1. *Protective Medium*

For 100ml:			
	Glucose	1.98g	
	Citrate	1,72g	
	Water	49	ml
	Glycerol	21	ml
	Egg yolk	30	ml

This mixture is heated at 56°C for 30 minutes.
Then 2g. of glycocol are added and the pH is
adjusted between 7.2 and 7.4, no antibiotics
are added.

TABLE 2. *Compounds used for preparing the
          semen diluent*

Coumpound	Concentration	
NaCl	5.3	gm/liter
KCl	0.35	gm/liter
KH_2PO_4	0.05	gm/liter
$NaHCO_3$	3.0	gm/liter
$CaCl_2 \cdot 2H_2O$	0.3	gm/liter
$MgSO_4 \cdot 7H_2O$	0.05	gm/liter
Sodium Pyrubate	0.036	gm/liter
Sodium Lactate	2.4	gm/liter
Glucose	1.0	gm/liter
SPPS[a]	2.0	gm/liter
HCl (1N)	1.0	gm/liter
Penicilin G	100,000	IU/liter
Streptomycin Sulfate	100,000	µg/liter

examination of the cervical mucus, the length of the cycle and previous basal body temperature charts.

When needed, ovulation induction with either Clomiphene or
HMG+ HCG is carried out. When Clomiphene is used, inseminations
are done 5 and 7 days after the Clomiphene regimen is terminated.

CONCLUSION

This is the first human semen bank located in a Social Security Hospital in Spain and has been operating since November, 1978. Both fresh and frozen semen are used. Donor sources are both the Infertility Clinic and students of the Medical School. Two inseminations per cycle are usually performed and frequent ovulation induction with Clomiphene is used. There is a two month waiting list and there is no charge for the procedure. In the first 8 months of the program there have been several pregnancies and no complications have been encountered.

REFERENCES

1.   Lopata, A., Patullo, M.J., Chang, A. and Briam, J. A method
        for collecting motile spermatozoa from numan semen. Fertil.
        Steril., 27:677, 1976.

ORGANISATION OF SPERM BANKS

ON A NATIONAL BASIS

David W. Richardson

MRC Unit of Reproductive Biology
Edinburgh, Scotland

INTRODUCTION

There has been a considerable increase in the demand for artificial insemination with donor semen (AID) in several European countries during the past 5 years. In Great Britain there was an increase
of one third between 1976 and 1977. This rise in requests for AID
is mainly due to the striking decrease in the availability of children
for adoption due to the liberalization of the abortion laws   and
effective contraception.

In view of the substantially increased demand for AID, several
countries have considered establishing a nationwide system of semen
banks. This presentation will consider the organisation and operation of such banks on a national basis.

FACTORS INFLUENCING THE ESTABLISHMENT
OF A NATIONAL SYSTEM OF SEMEN BANKS

There are at least five principal factors which would influence
the organisation of a nationwide network of semen banks. These include
the financial resources designated for the service and the personnel.
The size and area of the country and the geographic distribution and
size of population are major factors, as well as whether the country
has a private or government-financed health care system. The communication network within the country is important, particularly its
transportation system.

A single national semen bank with several small satellite banks

has obvious merit and may well be feasible for countries with an
area of approximately 40,000 square kilometres and a population of
5 million ; in fact Denmark has such a system. We face problems of
a different magnitude when we consider larger countries such as
France with an area 12 times that of Denmark of the United Kingdom
and West Germany with 1i times the population of Denmark (Table 1).
In addition, the population distribution shows marked variation from
country to country. These considerations make it highly unlikely
that any common scheme for AID services would fulfil the requirements for each European country, consequently we may expect to see
each country developing quite different formats for its AID services.
These differences will be accentuated because the countries have
differing forms of health care, some being based on a private system
and others on a governmental health service. My proposals concerning sperm bank organisation are directed towards the United Kingdom,
but it is hoped they will be pertinent to other countries.

ADVANTAGES AND DISADVANTAGES OF
A NATIONAL SYSTEM OF AID CENTRES

The principal benefits of a national system of AID centres would
include the adoption of standardised protocols pertaining to patient
and donor selection. Each centre would have the facilities to carry
out detailed seminal analysis and to cryopreserve and store semen.
The stringent quality control of the semen processing should ensure
uniformly high standards being maintained which in turn may improve
the success rate.

The current problems of donor recruitment should be minimized
and a panel of donors established that would encompass as wide a
variety of characteristics as possible, in order to improve the
"matching" of donor to husband. The donors should include men from
as many ethnic groups as possible. A national network should facilitate the inter-centre exchange of semen. It should facilitate
follow-up of the children and their families if desired.

TABLE 1. *Area and population of selected European countries*

Country	Area (km^2)	Population (millions)
Denmark	43,000	5
Netherlands	36,000	13
United Kingdom	244,000	56
France	551,000	53

The system must include at least one research section which would concentrate on optimising semen cryo-preservation methods and the evaluation of the potential fertility of semen together with research upon clinical and endocrinological topics allied to infertility and AI. Staff from the regional banks would have the opportunity to work at the research section for certain periods. Disadvantages of a national system would include the loss of "local" control over the selection of donors and possible difficulties associated with the bureaucratic management of such a network.

THE ORGANISATION OF AN AID SERVICE

It is unlikely that a nationwide AID system would have direct government backing, and in Britain some respected or independent body would appear best fitted to develop the system.

The Royal College of Obstetricians and Gynaecologists, London, has organised two study groups in the past three years to examine the status of artificial insemination. It also set up a sub-committee to make recommendations concerning AID in Great Britain. Some of these recommendations will be incorporated during consideration of the organisation of an AID service.

GENERAL CLINIC ARRANGEMENTS

It was recommended that ideally patients should not have to travel more than 80 miles (130 km) or for longer than 3 hours for treatment.

If possible the AID service should operate on a seven day per week basis. The service would undoubtedly benefit from being associated with a comprehensive sub-fertility clinic. This would mean that counselling, patient investigation and treatment was carried out by the staff actually involved in the AID service.

PATIENT AND DONOR ASSESSMENT

The clinical assessment of referred patients should be based upon the protocol proposed by the WHO Task Force for the investigation of the infertile couple.

If AID is recommended and the couple have been thoroughly counselled and given sufficient time to reach a mature and responsible decision, they should not have to wait for longer than 6 months before starting AID treatment.

The Royal College of Obstetricians and Gynaecologists have

produced a booklet for couples considering AID and also a consent form drafted by their legal advisors.

Coded record systems should be used to identify the recipients, the donors and their semen and its use in treatment. No records should be kept which identify and link the donor and recipient by name, and the strictest confidentiality is essential regarding patient records and notes.

The Royal College sub-committee recommended that potential donors should be interviewed by medical members of the team involved in the AID service. They emphasised that adequate numbers of donors should be recruited before patients were accepted. It was considered that donors should satisfy the criteria shown in Table 2.

Donors should be told to report any symptoms of, or contact with infectious deseases. Donor semen should be checked for gonococci, and if frozen semen is being used, no semen should be issued for AID until the culture test for gonococci is known to be negative.

THE INFRA-STRUCTURE OF
A NATIONWIDE SYSTEM OF AID CENTRES

A system based upon regional centres would be best suited to the United Kingdom with its population of 56 million and the basic structure would involve a three tier system (Table 3).   The principal component would be a series of 10-12 regional centres, systematically and strategically located throughout the United Kingdom. Each centre could serve about 5 million people.

At present there are a number of established centres which could form the framework for this regional system. These main centres would recruit and select the donors, screen the semen, carry out all the semen freezing and provide the major storage facilities. They would use and approved protocol for semen preservation, and all

TABLE 2. *Guide lines for selection of donors*

---

1. No personal or family history of inheritable disorders.

2. No personal history of potentially transmissable infection.

3. Reasonable intelligence.

4. Acceptable physical appearance.

5. Responsible attitude.

TABLE 3. *The organisation of a national AID system*

Tier	Component
Tier 1	Regional centres (10-12)
Tier 2	Subsidiary satellite banks (city/town)
Tier 3	Individual unit or clinic bank

semen evaluation and processing records would be their responsibility. The second tier would incorporate an arrangement of subsidiary satellite storage tanks, situated in the towns where AID centres are located and each tank would be capable of holding semen from a least 6 donors. Requests for semen from the individual clinic or unit bank, the third tier in the system, would have to be placed two weeks in advance of requirement. The specimens would be sent in a returnable transporter tank having a "holding" life of 7 days. Each consignment of donor semen would be accompanied by a coded donor description and details of the semen, and prior to the despatch of the specimens, a senior staff member must check the accompanying documentation.

SEMEN CODING AND INVENTORY

In the regional centres the minimal information recorded upon each stored semen would be the donor code, the date of the specimen, and the number of semen units. A wall chart system would be used to record the day to day use of specimens, whilst a master card or computerised system would be used for management of the inventory of reserve semen stocks. Semen would be stored in a minimum of two tanks with each donor allotted a specific location. The specimens would be coded and distributed so as to obviate the possibility to mis-selection of donor semen. Clearly marked sections of the tanks or different coloured-coded tanks would house semen from different ethnic groups. All tanks would have a sensor-warning system to monitor the levels of liquid nitrogen.

Each clinician or AID center would be requested to report their results once every three months to the regional bank. The report forms upon each patient would include as a minimum, the information shown in Table 4.

A single collation unit would be set up which would keep a master coded registry of donors and their characteristics. This unit would also receive the results from each regional centre to enable comprehensive records to be kept and the results of AID to be analysed. This data would provide valuable clinical and biochemical

TABLE 4. *Patient information to be returned*
          to collation centre

---

1. Patient code

2. Ovulation assessment result

3. Number of inseminations and donor code

4. Dates of insemination

5. Method of insemination

6. Post-thaw motility of semen

7. Outcome of inseminations.

---

information upon the optimal parameters for predicting ovulation
and timing insemination, and basic information with regard to fertilization and gamete physiology. For example, studies to evaluate
the efficacy and characteristics of semen after extended storage
could be pursued. When certain donors had achieved three pregnancies,
straws of semen from the proven specimens would be designated for
re-assessment after 1, 3, 5 and 10 years. Semen from a minimum of
20 donors would have to be evaluated for statistical validity. Incorporated into the date retrieval system would be a programme to
monitor the numbers and outcome of pregnancies achieved by each donor.
This facility would permit semen from donors, who have achieved a
certain number of pregnancies, to be distributed to different regions
of the country.

STAFF

Each regional centre would probably require a staff of 4 or 5
consisting of a clinician in charge, a graduate biologist, a technician and one or two administrative staff. A medical social worker
would undoubtedly add considerable expertise to the service, though
he or she may form part of the team within the individual clinic.

In England, one area health authority has established a regional AID service. The experience gained from this model may serve as
the basis for a nationwide network.

CONCLUSION

The demand for AID is increasing markedly and it would appear
that "private" semen banks will not meet the demands in Great Britain.
The best potential solution to this need is probably to set up a

regionally based system of AID centres funded through the National Health Service but initially organised through the auspices of the Royal College of Obstetricians and Gynaecologists of London.

ADDENDUM

This paper presents the personal views of the author, and does not represent the official policy or views of the Medical Research Council.

THE USE OF MINICOMPUTERS IN SPERM BANK MANAGEMENT

E. Vendrely, P. Dhont, M.O. Alnot,
A. Delezoide and C. Da Lage

Centre d'Etude et de Conservation du Sperme
    de Paris-Necker
Paris, France

Computer evolution over recent years has led to a very significant reduction in their size and cost. Manufacturers are even
offering to the general public models whose capabilities are on a
par with computers considered powerful a decade ago. With new lan-
guages making communication with the machine clear and simple,
programming can be mastered relatively quickly. It is possible to
record on magnetic tape(a cassette or, better still, a minidisk) a
system with thousands of entries. The considerable space and the
speed with which data can be retrieved provide ample justification
for the use of this technology. Management programs as well can
be preserved in this way and utilized by staff having little knowledge of computer science with a negligible risk of error.

We undertook the project of transferring all the CECOS-Necker
records into a small memory individual computer which is simple to
use. These records concern the semen donors, the couples requesting
AID and the data required for monitoring storage of frozen semen
paillettes(straws).

The management of the bank involves the choice of a donor whose
characteristics match those of the couple making a request as well
as the recording of paillette arrival and departure.

MATERIAL AND METHODS

Computer

The machine used is a Wang 2200 B type PCS II minicomputer.
Very compact, it groups in one console the central management unit,

73

a command keyboard, a cathode screen and a double system for reading flexible minidisks.

The central unit consists essentially of a central memory divided into two parts: A random access memory(RAM), immediately available to the user, with a capacity of 16 K octets(i.e., 16 000 words of 8 bits); and a read only memory(ROM), not directly available, allowing the use of a hundred or so command instructions and mathematical and logical functions.

A modified basic language is used for communication between the user and the machine. It allows manipulation of series of alphabetic and numeric characters. This language uses instructions in English but permits the operator to speak with the computer in his own language.

The command keyboard is, on the whole, comparable to that of a typewriter and can even be used as one. However, shifting to upper case produces complete basic language instructions, which considerably accelerates programming and facilitates dialogue. Another part of the keyboard is comprised of numerical keys corresponding to mathematical function, as on an ordinary desk calculator.

The cathode screen can display 16 64-character lines.

Each disk, 13/4 cm in diameter, can record 90 K octets of data corresponding to records or to programs, both of which, moreover, can be stored on the same disk and be retrieved through their title in the catalogue zone.

Lastly, a rapid print out(120 characters/second) is attached to the PCS II console and makes it possible to have access to all indispensable information as well as considerably facilitating the writing and use of programs.

Previous CECOS Management System

Two types of records were used in the past:

For the Donor, whose identity is strictly confidential, a card showed: Identification number, ethnic group, blood group(ABO and Rh), physical characteristics(weight, height, eye color, hair color and texture), identification number for each ejaculate, number of paillettes obtained from each ejaculate, average number(in millions) of motile spermatozoa per 0.25 ml paillette.

For the Couple, the records consisted of cards containing the following information:

. Front. First and last names of husband and wife and wife's
maiden name, address, telephone number, name of referring physician and characteristics of husband and wife(ethnic group,
birth date, blood group, physical traits).   If the couple
had referred a donor to the sperm bank, his number is clearly
entered on the card so as to prevent his semen from being
assigned to this couple.

. Back. Dates of insemination, number of cycles of insemination,
number of the ejaculate assigned and number of paillettes
used for each insemination and result of each cycle of insemin-
ation(success and failure).

The management of the bank involved the choice of a donor to
match the couple making the request as well as the keeping of day-
to-day records of the identity and number of paillettes taken from
the sperm bank.

New Computerized Management

Computerizing the management of CECOS-Necker required six programs and three data stores, the latter for day-to-day use as well
as for statistical research studies.

The programs developed are of two types: Creation or modification of data stores and retrieval of stored information.   It goes
without saying that other programs can be created at a future date.

Data entry programs. Three in number, each has a name(Donor,
Couple or Bank) which is automatically entered in the catalogue zone
of the minidisk, making almost instantaneous retrieval possible.
The aim of the Donor program is to enter the characteristics of new
donors. The Couple program does the same for couples who are to
receive artificial insemination. The Bank program permits entry of
technical information required to locate the paillettes in the
storage containers.

These three programs permit access to the corresponding data
stores. They have the same basic structure, each one having three
parts. The beginning of the program asks the question: Creation
of a new data store or modification of an existing one? If the
second alternative is chosen, the computer is asked to read back
the data store disk before going on. The data entered is then
placed in the central memory. The second part of the program permits entry of information not yet recorded in the store relating
to donors, couples or paillettes. A correction subprogram requests
display, for example, of all the characteristics of a donor stored
in the central(RAM) memory. If an error is found, the program can
be temporarily interrupted. Correction is immediately followed by

the reading back of the data and their display. When there is neither an error nor a change to be made, the program returns automatically to start to await entry of another item. If the operator
wishes, a paper print out of this data can be obtained, either to
be placed in a library or to be used later to permit more rapid
comparison of donor and couple characteristics. When all the information has been entered into the central memory, the user requests
storage on the minidisk and the program ends.

   The Donor program enters into memory the following data: Four
      identification number, ethnic group, blood group(ABO and Rh),
eye color, hair color and texture, height.

   The Couple program enters, for each member of the couple, the
same data as that of the Donor program, and in addition, their dates
of birth. The identification number has five figures, the first two
corresponding to the year of the first visit and the last three to
the order or registration. The fact that the identification numbers
in the Donor and Couple programs have a different number of digits
avoids all confusion between them.

   The Bank program is used to enter all the characteristics of
each paillette: Color of paillettes and tubes containing them(to
locate them in the containers); number of paillettes obtained for
each ejaculate; average number(in millions) of motile spermatozoa
per 0.25 ml paillette; number of couples already assigned to a given paillette; and number of pregnancies and miscarriages corresponding to a given ejaculate(each donor is limited to five pregnancies).

   Data Stores. They correspond to matrices of alphanumerical
words, each element of which(letter, number or symbol) has two meanings, one inherent and the other determined by its place in the
word. The matrix dimension used is governed by the size of the computer's memory. For our machine, this is small, so each alphanumerical matrix has had to be limited to 50 couples, 255 donors or 100
paillettes. Nevertheless, the possibility of reading in succession
numerous matrices on one or two minidisks while only one at a time
is stored in the memory means that the quantity of information which
can be retrieved is considerable. The central memory of the PCS II
contains only 16 K octets, but the current state of progress in this
field will certainly make much larger memories available in the near
future without significant cost increase.

   Data management programs. There are three such programs. The
first("AFF-COU" from the French for "couple assignment") searches
the list of couples for the one whose five-figure identification
number has been called and transfers it to the central memory. The
program is then rased from the(RAM) memory. The second("AFF-DON",
from the French for "donor assignment") transfers the Donor data

store to the central memory and extracts from the list of donors
the one(s) possessing several characteristics in common with the
couple. When a donor has been chosen, a third program("AFF-BAN",
from the French for "bank assignment") searches the Bank data store
for the characteristics of the paillettes corresponding to the donor
chosen and displays them on the screen.

The most complex program is the one which assigns a donor to
a couple. It permits comparison of all the phenotypic characteristics of the legal father with those of each donor. When the entire
Donor data store has been read, the identification number of those
possessing one to six characteristics matching the father's is shown
on the screen. Of course, if the phenotypes are equivalent(six
characters in common), the problem is simple. All that remains to
be done is to check that there are a sufficient number of paillettes
in the bank corresponding to this or these donors and to assign one
of them to the couple. If the match is imperfect(five or four characteristics in common, four seems to be the minimum acceptable
number), the number of characteristics in decreasing order must be
selected on the keyboard. When this has been done, the phenotype
of the donor(s) is displayed on the screen and the physician chooses
the one which seems to him most suitable, judging essentially in
terms of the phenotypic characteristics of the husband or sometimes
of the wife. Referring to the couple's characteristics, the physician can thus choose the most suitable donor from those selected
by the computer.

All the characteristics are not of the same importance for this
choice. Some are essential, such as ethnic group and Rh factor(to
prevent immunological accidents). On the other hand, the ABO blood
group of the donor may be different from that of the father when its
genetic combination with that of the mother will lead to a phenotypic
result which could have occurred naturally. The other characteristics of hair color(five categories, ranging from blond to black),
hair texture(straight, curly or kinky), and height are used to make
the best choice possible taking into account both the husband and
wife's phenotypic characteristics, that is when no donor is available
who has six characteristics in common with the husband.

The identification number of the donor chosen is then noted and
entered when requested by the AFF-BAN program. The identification
numbers of this donor's ejaculates are then displayed on the screen.
The ejaculate finally selected depends on the number of couples to
whom it has already been assigned, the number of paillettes still
available and the AID cycle under way(since a given donor is used
at most for only three consecutive cycles; in case of failure, the
donor is routinely changed).

Screen display, or better still, paper print out, of the

location characteristics of the paillettes sought makes it possible
to identify them quickly and easily in the storage container. The
use of the print out unit allows preservation, for each AID act
performed, of records on the characteristics of the couple, the
donor and the paillettes.

DISCUSSION

Using a minicomputer presents numerous advantages. Foremost
is that of the ability to create data stores rapidly, with instantaneous check by screen display, thus enormously reducing the risk
of typographical errors. Another is that of very rapid search of
large data stores, which could formerly only be done manually.

By freeing the physician from the meticulous and delicate task
of data manipulation, the computer returns to him his proper role
in the final decision once the range of choices has been reduced.
Printed data can now be collected automatically, which considerably
reduces the risk of error since the degree of compatibility between
the donor and the legal father is now known with absolute certainty.

In addition, someone unfamiliar with computers can very easily
use such a machine once the basic instructions have been mastered.
However, this raises the important problem of the confidential nature of donor and couple records. Accordingly, the data stores
should be accessible only to authorized persons. Confidentiality
is much more effectively protected when the data are stored on magnetic tape rather than on written cards, since access to the information recorded can be obtained only through use of a "key" composed
of an alpha-numerical code almost impossible to discover accidentally.

On first glance, the main disadvantage of computerization lies
in the cost of the equipment. However, the price of presently
available small computers is in fact falling rapidly. These machines,
moreover, can serve many purposes in the center, whether for managing
other data stores or for calculations and statistical analysis.

In conclusion, computerization of sperm bank management considerably increases efficiency and reliability. The development of
minicomputers has brought this technology into reach for any laboratory, given the decrease in size and price of the machines and
the fact that they can be used by a staff which, while qualified,
is not really specialized in this domain.

The spread of computerized management to more sperm banks also
promises to make data centralization possible in the future. This
will make it easier to have full knowledge of all requests made and
paillettes available. Coordination of CECOS activity, at least on

a national level, would have a positive effect on the handling of couples requesting insemination.

REFERENCES

1. Belaisch, J.   Insémination avec sperme congelé.   Gynécologie, 27:157-159, 1976.

2. Bertholus, J.R.   Le secret.   Echanges, 115:36-37, 1972.

3. Borg, V.   L'insémination artificielle.   Contraception, Fertilité, Sexualité, 3:309-315, 1975.

4. David, G.   Les banques de sperme.   Fertilité orthogénie, 5:317-319, 1973.

5. David, G.   Les banques de sperme en France.   Arch. Fr. Pédiat. 32:401-404, 1975.

6. Netter, A.   Banques de sperme.   Actualités gynécologiques, Paris, Masson, 63-67, 1974.

7. Rioux, J.E., Cloutier, D., Mailhot, J. and Valet, J.P.   Insémination artificielle et utilisation d'une banque de sperme à la consultation de stérilité du C.H.U.   Union méd. Canada, 103:477-481, 1974.

ESTABLISHMENT OF A CENTRAL SEMEN BANK IN DENMARK

SUPPLYING 22 GYNECOLOGICAL DEPARTMENTS

N.C. Nielsen[*] and K.B. Hansen[**]

Gynecology Department, Bispebjerg Hospital
Copenhagen, Denmark
University Hospital
Arhus, Denmark

In Denmark, artificial insemination with donor semen (AID) using using frozen semen has so far been used only to a limited extent. The explanation seems to be that the various gynecological clinics have not had access to a sufficiently large semen laboratory which could check the quality of the ejaculates supplied and the reliability of the technique used. This requirement for a central semen bank was met by the Laboratory of the Copenhagen Health Service General Practitioners which houses the largest analytical semen laboratory in the country.

Among the Danish population there is not only an increasing acceptance of AID, but also a demand for this treatment in cases of childlessness due to greatly reduced fertility in the male. This is reflected by the existence of a waiting period of up to two years in clinics which have practiced AID with fresh semen and is due to the fact that only a few departments outside of Copenhagen have performed donor insemination. Therefore, the women from the entire country have had to go to one of the very few centers for treatment, a procedure which is expensive and inconvenient. Accordingly we felt it necessary to establish a central semen bank.

Anticipating that similar demands will arise in several countries, we think that it is reasonable to describe the establishment of a Central Semen Bank for serving gynecological departments throughout Denmark, and to a lesser extent those in Norway and Iceland.

It is obvious, and has indeed been amply demonstrated, that the better the quality of semen, the higher the conception rate. Since the conception rate seems to be lower with frozen than with fresh

81

semen, we felt that we could accept only ejaculates having optimal
cellular qualities.

As noted in Table 1, we defined optimal cellular qualities as:
A spermatozoa concentration above 80 million per ml, abnormal spermatozoal heads and non-motile spermatozoa not exceeding 30%, and excellent motility. Furthermore the ejaculate had to be of a volume exceeding 2 ml to afford a reasonable number of portions for insemination. In addition to the optimum semen qualities in the fresh ejaculate, it was demanded that motility remain excellent after a
freezing trial and that number of non-motile spermatozoa after thawing not exceed 50% (Table 2).

Such a strict selection of potential donors ought to make it
possible for all the 0.5 ml portions of semen delivered by the Semen
Bank for insemination to contain at least 10 million spermatozoa of
excellent motility and acceptable morphology. This was secured by
freezing the total ejaculate in portions of 0.5 ml and on the next
day, thawing one of the portions to check it for the above mentioned
characteristics. It was soon apparent that the establisment of a
donor panel fulfilling the ejaculate criteria required a very large
number of candidates.

Initially about 200 donors, mainly university students, applied.
On routine semen testing in the laboratory, it was found that 25%
fulfilled the demands of optimum quality for the fresh ejaculate.
After trial freezing of these donors' semen, only half preserved an
acceptable spermatozoa motility. This is due to the phenomenon
described by Pedersen and Lebech:[2] In spite of normal morphology
an ejaculate is not necessarilly suitable for freezing. The donors

TABLE 1. *Minimum requirements for donor semen*
          before freezing

Sperm conc.	> 80 mill/ml
Non-motile	< 30%
Abnormal heads	< 30%
Motility	excellent

TABLE 2. *Minimum requirements for donor semen after freezing*

Sperm. conc.	> 80 mill/ml
Immobile	< 50%
Abnormal heads	< 30%
Motility	excellent

who proved to have well suited semen were examined in order to make sure that they were mentally and physically healthy. In Table 3, the specific items in the medical history that we have focused on are pointed out. In Table 4, items included in the objective analysis of the donors are shown. Finally, the psychic performances of the applicants were evaluated. At this point, the donor panel had been reduced to about 10 to 15% of those, who had originally applied. Based upon these and the next 300 applicants who were evaluated, it appears that only about 10-15% of the candidates can be expected to be suitable, according to our criteria. All ejaculates supplied are currently checked to assure that the criterion of 10 million spermatozoa of excellent motility and normal morphology per portion of semen is maintained. The calculations based upon the analytical observations are performed by means of EDP.

Table 5 illustrates the change in a single semen quality variable, namely the concentration of motile spermatozoa for 250 semen samples collected over a 1 year period. That this running control of the ejaculates is fundamental is clearly illustrated in Figure 1 where the variations of three qualities, spermatozoa concentration, motility before freezing and motility after freezing, are indicated for one donor during a 12 month period. The freezing method used is essentially that described by Perloff et al.[3] which is simple and affords good results.

Figure 2 shows the location of the gynecological departments in Denmark which receive their supplies from the Central Semen Bank in Copenhagen. Two methods of transport are used. Within the area of Metropolitan Copenhagen, where the semen can be sent to the departments within one hour, it is ordered by telephone and transported in a car, thawing en route. When the semen is to be used outside this area, it is transported in liquid nitrogen. About 50 straws are forwarded at a time since the departments are able to maintain the nitrogen level in the transport containers. The capacity of these is such that it is necessary to fill them up about twice a week. This makes it possible to transport the semen by car in Denmark, and by air to Norway.

TABLE 3. *Factors sought in medical history*
of donors

. Serious familial hereditary disease
  (somatic, psychiatric).

. Uro-genital disease incl. venereal.

. Fever during the last six months.

TABLE 4. *Objective analysis of the donors*

. Height, weight, body build.

. Hair color, eye color, race.

. Blood group(rhesus), WR, GR.

. Karyotyping.

. By interview, psychic performance.

TABLE 5. *Variation in semen samples collected*
during one year(n = 250)

Sperm. conc.	81 $\pm$ 29 mill/ml
Motility before freezing	62 $\pm$ 23 mill/ml
Motility after freezing	41 $\pm$ 17 mill/ml.

    The use of AID offers several advantages. First, the ejacul-
ates can be evaluated by the semen analysis laboratory. Also, as
the period of the ovulatory cycle during which insemination may result in pregnancy spans only a few days, it is of utmost importance
to be able to obtain semen at this optimal time. Furthermore, patients consider it essential that the donor is as similar to their
husband as possible in regard eyes and hair color and body build.
In certain cases it is also necessary to consider the blood group.
In practice, all of these conditions can be fulfilled only by the
use of frozen semen.

    For obvious reasons complete anonymity must be assured. This
is also fulfilled by the use of semen from a central bank, where

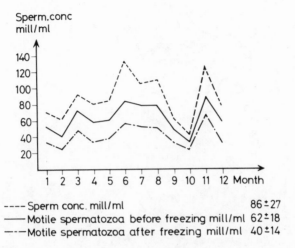

----Sperm conc. mill/ml   86±27
——Motile spermatozoa before freezing mill/ml 62±18
—·—Motile spermatozoa after freezing mill/ml 40±14

FIGURE 1. Variation of three semen characteristics for one donor over a 12 month period

much time may elapse between the collection of the ejaculate and its use.

In addition, when using frozen ejaculates from a semen bank, the result of a bacteriological culture of the semen is available before its use. The importance of this factor is emphasized by the fact, that Neisseria gonorrhoeae can survive deep-freezing to - 196°C.[4] We have unfortunately been able to confirm this. When the bank was being established, three women were infected with gonorrhoeae after insemination with semen from the same donor. Two developed salpingitis and one arthritis of the knee. N. gonorrhoeae were cultivated from stored frozen semen delivered by that donor. We now perform bacteriological control for N. gonorrhoeae on every ejaculate. This possibility does not exist when fresh semen is used for AID.

Since each gynecological department decides upon the indications for AID, the result for the whole country is difficult to assess. To estimate the reliability of the freezing method and a possible unfavorable influence of the transport, we selected as a reference clinic the University Hospital in Arhus which is about 300 km from

FIGURE 2.   Location of gynecological departments in Denmark

Copenhagen. The indication for using AID in this department is that
the husband has azoospermia, severe oligospermia, or a greatly reduced motility. As a rule, this assessment is based upon at least
three semen samples.

Insemination was performed on 43 women, all of whom could be
considered fully fertile according to comprehensive fertility studies. As shown in Table 6, 31 pregnancies occurred in a maximum
treatment period of 9 cycles. This corresponds to a conception rate
of 73%. The mean treatment period before conception was 3.7 cycles,
while the mean period of insemination for all subjects was 5.0
cycles. Four of the pregnancies terminated in miscarriage whereas
22 patients have delivered normal children, and five are still pregnant. The pregnancies occurred after varying periods of treatment:
One fourth conceived in the first cycle and half of the patients
within three months.

TABLE 6. *Results of AID in 43 normal women*

Pregnancies:	31(72%)
22 Normal children	
4 Miscarriages	
5 Still pregnant	
Treatment cycles:	
Maximum	9.0
Mean for all women	5.0
Mean for those pregnant	3.7

Of course, the advantages pointed out for the use of frozen semen must be considered in terms of the conception rates obtained by the use of fresh and frozen semen respectively. On the basis of the literature and our own results, the advantages of frozen semen seem to outweigh its possibly somewhat lower pregnancy rate. Moreover, it is not only possible, but probable, that future results can be improved by advances in freezing techniques, and perhaps also by more reliable methods of excluding donors whose semen cannot tolerate freezing. Finally, it should be emphasized that the establishment and maintenance of a central semen bank supplying frozen semen will be necessary if the entire population is to have equal access to this treatment. Procuring suitable donors and simultaneously maintaining complete anonymity is difficult, if not impossible, outside the largest cities.

REFERENCES

1. Lebech, P.E. Fécondité et Stérilité du Mâle, Masson et Cie, Paris, p. 349, 1972.

2. Pedersen, H. and Lebech, P.E. Fertil. Steril., 22:125, 1971.

3. Perloff, W.H., Steinberger, E. and Sherman, J.K. Fertil. Steril., 15:501, 1964.

4. Sherman, J.K. and Rosenfeld, J. Fertil. Steril., 26:1043, 1975.

SPERM BANKS AND DONOR RECRUITMENT IN FRANCE

Dominique Le Lannou, Bernard Lobel
and Yves Chambon

Centre d'Etude et de Conservation du Sperme
    (CECOS), Rennes
Rennes, France

INTRODUCTION

In France, sperm banks(Centres d'Etudes et de Conservation du Sperm: CECOS) operate in accordance with two main principles formulated by Georges David:[1] "All sperm donations must be given voluntarily without payment and the donation must come from a couple who has had one or more children". These principles were aimed at removing the clandestine cloak from semen donation and recasting the image of the donor in a healthier light, free from any sense of shame. These worthy aims, however, added considerably to the existing problems of donor recruitment. Only by a greater awareness of these problems and by greater efforts to overcome them will it be possible for sperm banks in France to continue functioning in strict adherence to the two principles.

The first sperm bank in France began operating in 1973. Since then 1,200 donor couples have been recruited by the 14 banks now functioning. Over the same period, some 6,500 couples have sought AID treatment. Figure 1 shows the steady rise in demand for this treatment over the years.

METHODS OF DONOR RECRUITMENT

A study was undertaken to determine not so much the reasons or motives prompting a couple to make a semen donation but rather the factors contributing to the final decision to donate. Donors were found to fall into four distinct groups(Table 1, Figure 2).

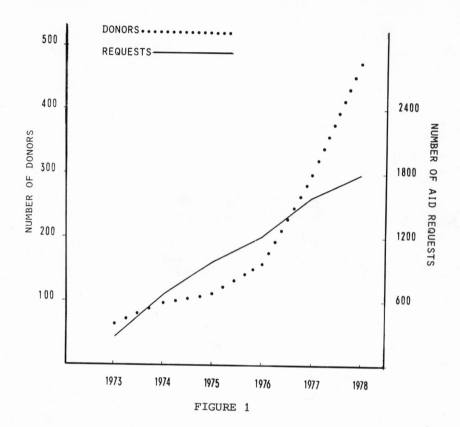

FIGURE 1

Unsolicited Volunteers. After hearing about sperm bank activities from mass media sources, these couples spontaneously volunteered their assistance. They have accounted for 29% of donating
couples since 1973. Over the years the number of such donors has
not grown: In fact, they constitute a declining proportion of the
donor population, of which they made up 70% in 1973 but only 18%
in 1978.

Contacts Among the Medical Profession. These couples, most of
them working in some area of medicine, were contacted directly
by sperm bank teams. They account for 17 per cent of donors and
provided the main source of sperm donations during the first year
of operation.

Donors Responding to Pleas by AID Candidates. First resorted
to in 1976, this method of recruitment has proved the most effective,
providing 34 per cent of donating couples at the start and 50 per
cent in 1978. Donors are generally relatives or close friends of
couples seeking AID treatment who were encouraged to seek volunteers

TABLE 1. *Number of donor couples according to recruitment method from 1973 to 1978*

	1973	1974	1975	1976	1977	1978	Bilan
Unsolicited volunteers	44 (70%)	49 (51%)	45 (40%)	47 (29%)	72 (24%)	89 (19%)	346 (29%)
Medical worker contacts	8 (13%)	31 (32%)	30 (26%)	40 (25%)	55 (19%)	43 (9%)	207 (17%)
Referred by gynecologists	0 (13%)	3 (3%)	4 (3%)	15 (9%)	13 (5%)	13 (3%)	48 (4%)
Refered by AID candidates	1 (2%)	1 (2%)	14 (12%)	41 (26%)	114 (39%)	239 (50%)	410 (34%)
Vasectomy	8 (13%)	12 (13%)	20 (18%)	18 (11%)	33 (11%)	61 (13%)	152 (13%)
Other	1 (2%)	0	1 (1%)	0	7 (2%)	29 (6%)	38 (3%)
Total	62	96	114	161	294	474	1201
No. of AID request	278	671	999	1279	1558	1794	6565

themselves because of the sometimes very long time taken by sperm banks to find suitable donors. Naturally, the AID candidates are told that the donors they provide will not be used for their own individual treatment but rather that their help in solving the recruitment problem gives them priority on the waiting list of couples seeking AID.

There are, it is true, dangers in this approach. Some AID candidates may feel pressured or even blackmailed into providing donors, "otherwise we won't get treatment". Other couples, eager or desperate to cut down the waiting time, may be tempted to break the secret of their decision, and afterwards may regret having done so. This approach, therefore, should only be recommended to couples whose views on the secrecy of treatment do not conflict with its implications.

The study showed that 10 per cent of AID candidates contacted their relatives and close friends with a view to stimulating recruitment.

Vasectomy Patients. Although officially unrecognized, vasectomy

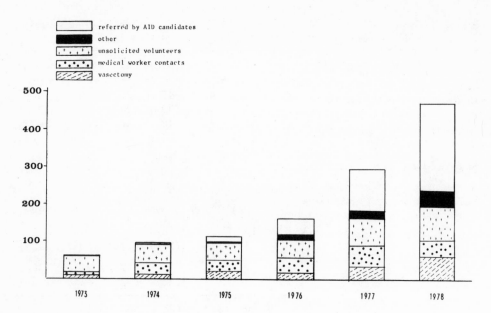

FIGURE 2. Donor couples according to recruitment method (CECOS)

or voluntary male sterilisation is on the increase in France. It is becoming increasingly common for surgeons to recommend semen preservation to their vasectomy patients, in view of a possible later use by the patients themselves who are encouraged to visit a sperm bank where they are given information about semen donation. Currently one out of three vasectomy patients becomes a donor.

TABLE 2. *Vasectomy candidates*

	1973	1974	1975	1976	1977	1978	Bilan
Number of vasectomy candidates requesting preservation	8	35	48	76	97	131	395
Number of vasectomy candidates requesting preservation and agreeing to become a donor	8	12	20	18	33	61	152

TABLE 3. *Donor selection*

Number of donors interviewed in CECOS	1201
Number of "acceptable" donors	747(62,2%)
Number of rejected donors	454

Cause of donor rejection:	
Genetic abnormality	15(1,25%)
Karyotype abnormality	20(1,7 %)
Poor semen quality	130(10,8 %)
Poor freezing tolerance	128(10,7 %)
Failure to return	132(11,0 %)
Other	29(2,4 %)

TOTAL	454

DONOR SELECTION

To reduce risk to a minimum, donor selection is extremely strict in French sperm banks(CECOS). Only 62 per cent of prospective donors are accepted. Of donors initially interviewed, 11 per cent fail to return to make their donation, possibly through inadequate motivation. Twenty-seven per cent of donors are rejected either for poor semen quality before or after freezing(21,5 per cent) or more rarely for genetic or other reasons.

ESTIMATED NUMBERS OF DONORS REQUIRED

Despite recruitment difficulties and restrictive selection criteria, can the sperm banks satisfy the demand for AID treatment? In estimating the number of donors needed to meet this demand, three points must be considered: Less than 50 per cent of women seeking AID achieve pregnancies in the best results so far reported; no more than 5 pregnancies are allowed for a given donor in order to avoid the risk of consanguinity; and donor selection gives a donor acceptance rate of about 60 per cent. Theoretically, the number of donors required can be calculated as follows:

$$\text{Number of donors} = \text{Number of AID requests} \times \frac{50}{100} \times \frac{1}{5} \times \frac{100}{60} =$$

$$\frac{\text{Number of AID requests}}{6}$$

This formula gives the minimum number of donors required, since all variables cannot be calculated. It is not certain, for example, that a total of 5 pregnancies can be achieved with each donor. In 1978, therefore, 1,800 requests for AID treatment called for the recruitment of a minimum of $\frac{1,800}{6} = 300$ donors. In fact, 470 donors were enrolled.

Without being overoptimistic, then, sperm banks in France can be said to be well on the way to achieving their double aim: On one hand, to meet the demand for artificial donor insemination and on the other, to foster greater public acceptance of AID by providing maximum conditions of safety and reliability.

CONCLUSIONS

The recruitment of donor couples for AID still presents difficulties. Nevertheless, despite their strict adherence to basic principles and thanks to continuous efforts to increase public awareness of their activities, CECOS are exceedingly well equipped to meet current demands for artificial donor insemination.

REFERENCES

1.   David, G.   Les banques de sperme en France.   Arch. Fr. Pédiatr. 32:401, 1975.

HISTORICAL SYNOPSIS OF HUMAN SEMEN CRYOBANKING

Jerome K. Sherman

Department of Anatomy
University of Arkansas for Medical Studies
Little Rock, Arkansas

Since history does not change, much of the information in this brief historical synopsis of human semen cryobanking has been previously presented except for a bit of up dating with current events and predicting of the future.

PAST HISTORY (1776-1964) (Table 1)

Spallanzani in 1776 was perhaps the first to report observations on the effects of freezing temperatures on human spermatozoa, and Montegazza in 1866 was the first to suggest banks for frozen human semen. During the period of 1938 through 1945, it was observed that some human spermatozoa could survive freezing and storage at temperatures as low as 269° below 0°C. The possibility of preservation by freezing of significant numbers of spermatozoa for prolonged periods subsequently arose from the successful use of glycerol as a cryoprotective agent with bovine spermatozoa in 1949 and 1950.

The emphasis of attempts at cryopreservation, though, was placed upon semen of farm animals, with the coincident neglect of research on developing technics for man. It was not until 1953 and 1954 that reports of successful research with human semen at "Dry Ice" temperatures, along with the first demonstration that frozen-thawed human spermatozoa were capable of fertilization and induction of normal embryonic development, were made by the author and associates. About 25 births resulting from frozen human semen were reported in the next 9 years.

The valid question was asked in 1963 as to why, after the

TABLE 1. *Development of human semen cryobanking(1776-1964)*

Date	Contributor	Contribution
1776	Spallanzani	First low-temperature observations.
1866	Mantegazza	First suggestion of frozen semen bank.
1938	Jahnel	-269°C survival; storage at -79°C
1940	Shettles	Individual variation, aging, and thawing.
1942	Hoagland and Pincus	Vitrification principle; foam freezing.
1945	Parkes	Survival better in greater volumes.
1949	Polge, Smith and Parkes	Glycerol as cryoprotective agent.
1953-55	Sherman	Freezing rates; glycerol; preservation.
1953-55	Bunge, Keettel and Sherman	First progeny from stored spermatozoa; dry ice method.
1954-59	Keettel et al.	Sixteen births with stored spermatozoa.
1958-59	Sawada et al.	Six births with stored spermatozoa.
1962-63	Sherman	Survival factors; banking applications; nitrogen-vapor technique.
1964	Perloff, Steinberger and Sherman	Four births with nitrogen-vapor technique.

introduction in 1953 and 1954 of a simple "Dry Ice" preservation method which maintained fertilizing capacity and resulted in normal progeny, many banks for frozen human semen were not established and applications reported.

The answer proposed was that perhaps the methods or religious and legal practice, and certainly the medical practitioners, were not ready for a program of evaluative application of human semen preserved by freezing.

Following the evaluation of various cryobiologic factors after 1960, the author employed liquid nitrogen at a temperature of 196° below 0°C. to develop a simple, efficient and clinically proved method for preserving human spermatozoa by freezing. Semen pretreated with glycerol was frozen in the vapor of liquid nitrogen, and subsequently stored in the same container. An average cryosur-

vival of 70%, based upon the number of moving cells, was realized.
No further loss during frozen-storage for periods up to 1 year was
noted after thawing. Four normal births were reported in 1964 from
initial clinical application of this method.

RECENT HISTORY (1964-1976)

Some highlights in research and clinical application are seen
in Tables 2 and 3.

In 1972, as in 1964, one had reason to ask why there had not
been considerably more activity in human semen banking, especially
in view of improvements since 1963 both in frozen-storage methodology and in medical acceptance, as well as the increased clinical
use of donor insemination with fresh semen. It was the author's
contention that conditions in medical practice, especially the requisite demand for clinical application of frozen-stored semen and
the economic balance of time and effort, still were not conducive
to favorable development after 1964. As predicted in 1964, low
temperature research on human spermatozoa had not been a serious
concern of the cryobiologist. Investigative effort toward uncovering
factors associated with cryoinjury and cryoprotection of human semen
had been slight compared to the parallel period in the early developmental history of bull semen banking. Impetus, demand and financial
support for research and development have been the salient factors
in accounting for the accelerated applications of frozen-stored bovine semen in cattle breeding. Introduction of cryoprotection with
glycerol in 1949 was the impetus, while efficient genetic improvement of livestock provided the demand. The vital requisite funding
came from commercial breeders who foresaw the enormous economic mar-
ket for semen banks in improvement of livestock through artificial
breeding with semen from select bulls.

Glycerol, the impetus for banking bull semen, had been used
routinely in small scale cryopreservation of human semen for about
two decades, but clinical demand as well as financial support from
any source, governmental or private, was wanting or inadequate.
Clinical results as of 1976 are summarized in Table 4.

CURRENT STATUS

The establishment of much publicized commercial cryobanks in
about 1972 in the United States was based primarily on the reasonable expectation that millions of men would elect to store their semen as so called "fertility insurance" prior to undergoing vasectomy
in population control. This has since proved to be an unrealized
expectation, the economically important absence of which has slowed

TABLE 2. *Development of human semen cryobanking(1964-present)*

Date	Contributor	Contribution
1964	Sherman	DMSO unsuitable(Toxic) as cryoprotectant.
1968	Iizuka et al.	More births from semen with egg yolk extender.
1968	Ackerman	Metabolic effects: Temperature shock, freezing-thawing.
1969	Matheson et al.; Trelford and Mueller	Births from semen stored in plastic straws.
1969	Fjallbrant and Ackerman	Fertility after 3-YR storage; mucus test.
1968-70	Ackerman and Sod-Moriah	Stability of DNA, Hyaluronidase level and citric acid in frozen storage.
1972-73	Sherman	Normal progeny from semen stored over 1 OYR.
1974	Sherman and Char	Motility and Y chromosome fluorescence unaltered after 13 YR or frozen storage.
1974	Barkay, Zuckerman and Heiman	Pellet freezing of diluted semen; births
1976	Sherman	About 1,500 births worldwide; fewer abnormalities and abortions than in normal population.

considerably the growth of commercial banking. There are now about
a dozen commercial and university-based banks in the United States,
15 national banks in France, and probably fewer than a dozen other
notable cryobanks throughout the rest of the world, including those
in Austria, Belgium, Brazil, England, Denmark, Israel, Japan, Spain
and Sweden. Based on incomplete surveys and personal contacts, with
full appreciation of limitations in coverage, an estimate in 1978
of over 3,000 births from the clinical use of frozen stored human
semen was considered conservative. Currently the figure is over
5,000. As noted, normal births have resulted from semen stored for
over ten years, and there is no evidence of mutagenic effects of
cryobanking. To the contrary, the percent of abnormal progeny is
considerably below that of the normal population. Even the abortion
rate appears slightly below the normal level. Emphasis today still
is on cryobanking for AID, but the recent awakening interest in

TABLE 3. *Research on frozen human semen(literature since 1964)*

. Nitrogen vapor technique confirmed as superior.

. Liquid nitrogen storage confirmed as superior.

. No motility loss after 3 to 10 years frozen-storage.

. Diluents compatible with frozen-storage and fertility.

. 5-10% glycerol best cryoprotective agent.

. DMSO as cryoprotective but more toxic than glycerol.

. Latent cryoinjury phenomenon proved to be real.

. Metabolic and ultrastructural cryoinjury of many semen.

. No cryoinjury of fertility enzyme(Hyaluronidase).

. Genetic material(DNA) unchanged in 1 1/2 years frozen-storage.

. No cryoinjury of citric acid metabolism.

. Fertility maintained(cervical mucus penetration test) after 3 years frozen-storage.

(See Sherman, 1973, for details, Table 2).

TABLE 4. *Births from frozen-stored human semen[a] up to 1976[22]*

No. of normal children born	1,464
No. of abnormal children born	11
No. of spontaneous abortions	113
No. of pregnancies still unreported as births	71
Longest period of cryopreservation of fertility	
Asia(Iizuka, Japan)	13 mo
Europe(Lebech, Denmark)	5 yr
United States(Sherman)	$10\frac{1}{4}$ yr
Before international shipment(Sherman United States)	6 yr

[a]Pregnancies for births reported followed, on the average, a protocol of two inseminations of 0.5 to 1 ml of semen in each of four cycles, aside from results of one clinician, who routinely inseminates 14 times per cycle.

certain applications of AIH with unique related benefits of cryobanking have stimulated more activity in AIH with cryobanked human
semen in both research evaluation and the clinical practice of infertility. It has also emphasized the limitations of semen quality
in realizing the potential afforded by these applications in infertility therapy, along with the coincident need for improving upon
both the quality of semen used for AIH and the attendant methods for
its frozen-storage.[40]

Successful cryobanking extends and enriches the attributes of
artificial(therapeutic) insemination of fresh semen in infertility
therapy and population control to include applications shown in
Table 5. There is evidence of growing international interest in
semen cryobanking, as can be seen in Table 6.

Recently, the establishment of the American Association of
Tissue Banks has provided a peer group mechanism for requisite stability and quality control in cryobanking of transplants, including
human spermatozoa(Table 7). Some of the categories covered in proposed standards include those listed in Table 8.

THE FUTURE

Human semen cryobanking should continue to develop in an un-
spectacular but progressive manner throughout the world. A break-
through in achieving one hundred percent cryosurvival of spermatozoa, if realized, will not accelerate its growth significantly, as
applications of cryobanking in clinical practice are self-limiting
and existing methods are adequate for their implementation. I predict, however, that there will be a more intense interest in cryobanking for AIH, primarily in pre-therapy storage and in job related
pre-exposure storage as protection against both deliberate and

TABLE 5. *Applications of semen cryobanking*

. Timed multiple inseminations for AIH and AID.

. Storage, pooling, concentration for AIH.

. Storage after *in vitro* improvements for AIH.

. Retention of fertilizing capacity in absence, death or hazard
  exposure of husband or donor.

. On demand AID, with wide selection of traits.

. Pre-vasectomy storage.

. Pre-Therapy storage.

TABLE 6. *Recent contributors to cryobanking of human semen*

Country	Contributor
Belgium	Schoysman and Schoysman
Brazil	Nakamura et al.
England	Wooley; Richardson
France	Czyba; David; Emperaire; Guerin; Jondet
Germany	Bregulla; Glender; Schill
Israel	Barkay; Zuckerman
Norway	Ulstein
Spain	Anselmo
Sweden	Friberg; Gemzell
USA	Alexander; Dmowski; Ericsson; Paulson.

TABLE 7. *American Association of tissue banks*

1. Incorporated in June 1976.

2. First national meeting May 1977.

3. Objectives of AATB:

   A. To promote scientific and technical knowledge concerning procurement, processing, storage, transplantation and evaluation of cells, tissues and organs for clinical and research use.

   B. To establish codes and standards for cell tissue and organ preservation used for clinical and research purposes.

accidental exposure to environmental agents which may compromise fertility or, even worse, compromise development of normal progeny. In addition, more research emphasis will be directed at improving the quality of spermatozoa prior to cryobanking and insemination in attempts at increasing fertilizing capacity of relatively infertile semen.

Efforts of the American Association of Tissue Banks (AATB) and of other such organizations will prevail in the establishment of peer group devised standards or guidelines for cryobanking. This

TABLE 8. *Categories of standards for semen cryobanking proposed by the American Association of Tissue Banks.*

1. Missions and goals

    a. General
    b. Specific

2. Organizational considerations

    a. General
    b. Facilities and equipment
    c. Personnel
    d. Organizational procedures
    e. Records
    f. Quality control

3. Acquisition of tissues

    a. Ethical/legal considerations
       . Biomedical ethics
       . Medico-legal aspects
    b. Selection criteria-donor
       . Personal history
       . Physical history
       . Rejection
       . Genetic history
    c. Procurement

4. Processing, preservation and storage of tissues

    a. Semen analysis-screening
    b. Semen cryobanking
    c. Quality control

5. Distribution

6. Fiscal considerations.

will occur first on a national and then perhaps on an international level to insure the efficacy and safety of cryobanking in realizing its worthwhile clinical applications in benefiting mankind.

REFERENCES

Ackerman, D.R. The effect of cooling and freezing on the aerobic and anaerobic lactic acid production of human semen. Fertil. Steril., 19:123, 1968.

Ackerman, D.R. Hyaluronidase in human semen and sperm suspensions subjected to temperature shock and to freezing. J. Reprod. Fertil., 23:521, 1970.

Ackerman, D.R. and Sod-Moriah, U.A. DNA content of human spermatozoa after storage at low temperatures. J. Reprod. Fertil. 17:1, 1968.

Barkay, J., Zuckerman, H. and Heiman, M. A new practical method of freezing and storing human sperm and a preliminary report on its use. Fertil. Steril., 25:399, 1974.

Bunge, R.G., Keettel, W.C. and Sherman, J.K. Clinical use of frozen semen; report of 4 cases. Fertil. Steril., 5:520, 1954.

Bunge, R.G. and Sherman, J.K. Fertilizing capacity of frozen human spermatozoa. Nature, London, 172:767, 1953.

Fjallbrant, B. and Ackerman, D.R. Cervical mucus penetration *in vitro* by fresh and frozen preserved human semen specimens. J. Reprod. Fertil., 20;515, 1969.

Friberg, J. and Gemzell, C. Inseminations of human sperm after freezing in liquid nitrogen vapors with glycerol or glycerol-egg-yolk-citrate as protective media. Amer. J. Obst. Gynec., 116:330, 1973.

Hoagland, H. and Pincus, G. Revival of mammalian sperm after immersion in liquid nitrogen. J. Gen. Physiol., 25:337, 1941-42.

Iizuka, R. and Sawada, Y. Successful inseminations with frozen human semen. Jap. J. Fertil. Steril., 3:1, 1958.

Iizuka, R., Sawada, Y. and Koi, H. Medical analyses and sociological side lights of heterologous artificial insemination. Jap. J. Fertil. Steril., 13:79, 1968.

Jahnel, F. Uber die widerstandsfahigkeit von menschlichen spermatozoen gegenuber starker kalte. Klin. Wschr., 17:1273, 1938.

Keettel, W.C., Bunge, R.G., Bradbury, J.T. and Nelson, W.O. Report of pregnancies in infertile couples. JAMA, 160:102, 1956.

Keettel, W.C. Personal communication, 1959.

Kleegman, S., Amelar, R.D. and Sherman, J.K. Roundtable: Artificial donor insemination. Med. Aspects Hum. Sex.; 4:85, 1970.

Lebech, P.E. Banques de sperme humain. Fecond. Steril. Male, Paris 349, 1972.

Mantegazza, P. Sullo sperma umano. Rendic. Reale Inst. Lomb, 3:
183, 1866.

Matheson, G.W., Carlborg, L. and Gemzell, C. Frozen human semen for
artificial insemination. Amer. J. Obstet. Gynec., 104:495,
1969.

Parkes, A.S. Preservation of human spermatozoa at low temperatures.
Brit. Med. J., 2:212, 1945.

Polge, C., Smith, A.U. and Parkes, A.S. Revival of spermatozoa after
vitrification and dehydration at low temperatures. Nature,
London, 164:666, 1949.

Perloff, W.H., Steinberger, E. and Sherman, J.K. Conception with
human spermatozoa frozen by nitrogen vapor technic. Fertil.
Steril., 15:501, 1964.

Sawada, Y. The preservation of human semen by deep freezing. Int.
J. Fertil., 9:525, 1964.

Sherman, J.K. Freezing and freeze-drying of human spermatozoa.
Fertil. Steril., 5:357, 1954.

Sherman, J.K. Temperature shock in human spermatozoa. Proc. Soc.
Exp. Biol. Med., 88:6, 1955.

Sherman, J.K. Improved methods of preservation of human spermatozoa by freezing and freeze-drying. Fertil. Steril., 14:49,
1963.

Sherman, J.K. "Banks for frozen stored human spermatozoa". In:
Proceedings of the Eleventh International Congress of Gene-
tics, Vol. 1, Geerts, S.J. and V. Abeelen, J.H.F., edts,
New-York, MacMillan, pp. 273, 1963.

Sherman, J.K. Research on frozen human semen: Past, present and
future. Fertil. Steril., 15:485, 1964.

Sherman, J.K. Low temperature research on spermatozoa and eggs.
Cryobiology, 1:103, 1963.

Sherman, J.K. Dimethyl sulfoxide as a protective agent during freezing and thawing of human spermatozoa. Proc. Soc. Exp. Biol.
Med., 117:261, 1964.

Sherman, J.K. Long-term cryopreservation of motility and fertility
of human spermatozoa. Cryobiology, 9:332, 1972.

Sherman, J.K. Unpublished results, 1972.

Sherman, J.K.   Synopsis of the use of frozen human semen since 1964:
     State of the art of human semen banking. Fertil. Steril.,
     24:397, 1973.

Sherman, J.K.   Clinical use of frozen human semen. Transplant Proc.
     8:165, 1976.

Sherman, J.K.   Banks for frozen human semen, current status and
     prospects. In: The integrity of frozen spermatozoa,
     Washington, D.C., National Academy of Sciences Publ., pp.
     78-91, 1978.

Sherman, J.K.   Cryobanking of semen in AIH. In: Homologous arti-
     ficial insemination and male sub-fertility, Emperaire J.C.
     and Hafez E.S.E. eds, New York, Elsevier, North Holland
     Biomedical Press, in publication, 1979.

Sherman, J.K. and Bunge R.G.   Observations on preservation of human
     spermatozoa at low temperatures. Proc. Soc. Exp. Biol. Med.
     82:686, 1953.

Sherman, J.K. and Char, F.   Stability of Y chromosome fluorescence
     during freeze-thawing and frozen-storage of human spermato-
     zoa. Fertil. Steril., 25:311, 1974.

Shettles, L.B.   Respiration of human spermatozoa and their response
     to various gases and low temperatures. Amer. J. Physiol.,
     128:408, 1940.

Spallanzani, L.   Opuscoli di Fisca. Animale, e Vegetabile, Opuscolo
     II. Osservazioni, e Sperienze Intorno ai Vermicelli Sperma-
     tici dell'Uomo e degli Animali. Modena, 1776

Trelford, J.D. and Mueller, F.   Observations and studies on the
     storage of human sperm. Canad. Med. Ass. J., 100:62, 1969.

QUANTITATIVE ULTRASTRUCTURAL MODIFICATIONS

IN HUMAN SPERMATOZOA AFTER FREEZING

Denise Escalier and Jean-Pierre Bisson

Centre d'Etude et de Conservation
   du Sperme at Paris-Bicêtre
Kremlin-Bicêtre, France

INTRODUCTION

Observations of decreased spermatozoa motility after freezing have motivated investigations attempting to identify ultrastructural cell damage from this procedure. As a result, lesions to the plasma membrane, acrosome and certain flagellar elements have been documented.[1,7,10,12] However, these studies have been performed on spermatozoa frozen in cryoprotector media. Therefore, their findings are the result of a dual process: Cryo-aggression and cryo-protection. A better understanding of these two processes as well as the effect of the cryoprotector medium alone without freezing is needed and may lead to improved efficacy of semen cryopreservation. Of the studies that have approached the problem in this way,[8,9] none have quantified their results.

This study will assess the ultrastructural characteristics of spermatozoa from the same ejaculate under four different conditions: In seminal plasma after ejaculation; after freezing without cryoprotector medium, and in cryoprotector medium before and after freezing. A unique aspect of this study is the method of observation which permits objective quantification of lesions, and thus valid statistical analysis.

MATERIALS AND METHODS

Semen Collection and Preparation

The semen of four donors was used. The ejaculates were characterized as a group by the following values: Sperm count > 40 million/

ml, motility > 70%, abnormal forms < 40%.[3] Specimens were collected
after 3 days of abstinence. After 1/2 hr of liquifaction at 37°C,
each ejaculate was divided into four equal test portions. One por-
tion(P1) serving as a control was left at 37°C for 30 minutes without addition of cryoprotector medium and then placed at ambient temperature. A second portion(P2) to be used for studying the effect of
the cryoprotector medium was diluted with an equivalent volume of
this medium(20 ml of egg yolk, 15 ml of glycerol, 1 g of glycerine,
100,000 I.U. of penicillin, 1.3 g of glucose and 1.6 g of citrate in
100 ml of medium). The solution was left at 37°C for 30 minutes and
then exposed to ambient temperature. A third portion(P3) used for
the study of cryo-aggression(freezing without protector medium) was
placed in 0.25 ml paillettes and then rapidly frozen in liquid nitrogen. The fourth portion(P4) was used to study cryoprotection
(freezing with cryoprotector medium). It was first diluted volume
to volume with cryoprotector medium, placed in 0.25 ml paillettes
and then frozen using the same procedure as with P3. After 20 minutes in the liquid nitrogen, P3 and P4 were thawed at room temperature.

Electron Microscopy

Each sample was fixed by adding 2 volumes of a 4% glutaraldehyde
solution. After centrifugation, the pellet was treated with 2% osmic
acid and then embedded in araldite. These sections obtained with an
ultramicrotome were stained with uranyl acetate and lead citrate and
then examined with an electron microscope(Sopelem) at 75 KV.

The sections were all analysed blindly by the same investigator
in that they were not identified according to the portion from which
they were taken. Only those sections providing incidences of spermatozoa structures that could be used for evaluation were retained.
For each portion of the ejaculate, an analysis was made of 30 sagital
head sections including the implantation plate; 30 middle piece
sections, consisting of 15 longitudinal sections from the implantation plate to the annulus and 15 transverse sections; and 30 principal piece sections consisting of 15 longitudinal sections 3 to 5
microns in length, and 15 transverse sections at two spaced locations,
one proximal and the other distal. Therefore, data for each of the
4 different semen conditions were obtained through the analysis of
120 spermatozoa heads, middle pieces and principal pieces. This
analysis was systematically performed in that each sample was evaluated according to a special form which consisted of a list of all
the spermatozoa abnormalities observed in a qualitative pilot study.
The list(Tables 1, 2, 3) included 54 head, 64 middle piece and 39
principal piece modifications. The modifications, which were precisely defined, required only a positive or negative response as
to their presence.

TABLE 1. *Ultrastructural modifications of components of the head*

Head lysed

Unstable Plasma Membrane

    absent
    discontinuous
    vesicular
    granular
    wavy
    swollen

Stable Plasma Membrane

    absent
    discontinuous
    wavy
    swollen
    granular

Acrosome

    asymetrical
    destroyed
    vesiculated
    borders not parallel
    not parallel to nucleus
    enlarged
    thinned
    density
      . high
      . low
      . heterogeneous
    external membrane
      . absent
      . granular
      . discontinuous
      . vesicular
      . wavy
    internal membrane
      . absent
      . granular
      . discontinuous
      . wavy

Post Acrosomal Cap

    absent
    abnormal
    contour indistinct
    discontinuous
    detached

Nucleus

    deformed
    condensation
      . abnormal
    one large vacuole
    multiple vacuoles
    inclusions
    nuclear membrane
      . indistinct
      . absent
      . discontinuous
      . swollen

Nuclear ring

    dissociated

Posterior nuclear space

    absent
    enlarged
    open
    heterogenous
    wall
      . swollen
      . thinned
      . granular.

TABLE 2. *Ultrastructural modifications of middle piece components*

Middle Piece - lysed

Flagella   - coiled.

Cytoplasmic excess

 absent
 large
 small
 vacuolar
 granular
 lipid droplets

Plasma membrane

 absent
 discontinuous
 wavy

Implantation plate

 contour indistinct
 discontinuous
 not parallel to nucleus
 diameter abnormal
 dissociated

Centriole

 abnormal
 contour indistinct

Mitochondria

 dispersed
 high number
 low number
 discontinuous external membrane
 irregular internal membrane
 architecture indistinct
 contents
  . heterogeneous
  . darkly stained
 form
  . rounded
  . dilated
  . flattened
 cristae
  . Peripherally placed
  . dilated
  . variable thickness
  . narrowed

Mitochondria(cont.)

 membrane space
  . enlarged
  . variable width
  . narrowed
 membrane densification
 membrane space density
  . high
  . granular
 cristae density
  . high
  . granular
 matrix density
  . low
  . granular
 inclusions
 clear spaces
 empty

Axoneme

 abnormal
 deformed
 disorganized
 tubules
  . > 9
  . < 9
 indistinct contour
 peritubular densification
 radial spokes
  . indistinct
  . absent
 matrix dense

Coarse fibers

 absent
 excess number
 reduced number
 separated from tubules
 decreased density
 doubled

Anulus

 indistinct
 absent.

TABLE 3. *Ultrastructural modifications of principal piece components*

Principle piece - lysed

Flagella   - coiled

Plasma membrane

    absent
    discontinuous
    irregular
    swollen
    granular

Axoneme

    absent
    deformed
    contour indistinct
    tubules
      · N > (9 + 2)
      · N < (9 + 2)
    radial spokes
      · indistinct
    matrix
      · dense
      · granular
      · enlarged
    peritubular densification

Coarse fibers

    absent
    contour indistinct
    disposition abnormal
    number
      · > 9
      · < 9
    fibers separated from tubules
    density
      · low
      · heterogeneous

Fibrous sheath

    contour indistinct
    discontinuous
    circumferential strands
      · massed
      · dissociated
    thickness
      · increased
      · reduced
      · variable
    density
      · low
      · heterogeneous
    granular contour

Longitudinal columns

    absent
    indistinct
    increased volume
    contour indistinct.

Statistical Analysis

The total number observations of each lesion in the 4 ejaculates combined was used to compare the experimental portions (P_2, P_3, P_4) to the control portion (P_1) using a weighted difference (D) which was calculated as follows:

$$D = \frac{|S(P_x) - S(P_1)|^2}{S(P_1)}$$

where $S(P_x)$ = The sum of a lesion in an experimental portion (P_2, P_3, P_4), and

$S(P_1)$ = The sum of a lesion in the control portion.

The greater the weighted difference for a structural lesion, the greater the number of lesions in the experimental as compared to the control portion. Since the test yields a result about 2.5 times greater and is more conservative than a Chi square test, a difference of 10 was considered to be significant. Therefore, only differences greater than 10 have been reported.

RESULTS

The total of the differences according to structure for each experimental portion (Table 4) is highest for P_3, that is, those semen portions frozen without cryoprotector medium. This total is somewhat less elevated for semen frozen with cryoprotection (P_3). The differences for samples to which only cryoprotector medium had been added (P_2) were only about half those for P_2.

Tables 5, 6 and 7 present the differences for each lesion according to substructure between the 3 experimental portions and the control portions. Spermatozoa exposed to cryoprotector medium alone demonstrate only minor morphological modifications, which involve primarily the acrosome and mitochondria (Table 5). However, when spermatozoa in this medium were frozen, somewhat greater modifications in the acrosome and mitochondria were noted and the flagella was also affected (Table 6). Freezing without protector medium resulted in severe structural changes which included the nucleus (Table 7). Finally, in all experimental portions, an increase in flagellar coiling was noted.

TABLE 4. *Total of weighted difference for modifications observed*
in each major structural element of the spermatozoon
according to the three experimental conditions(P_2, P_3, P_4)

Structure	P_2 37°C in cryoprotector medium	P_3 -196°C in seminal plasma	P_4 -196°C in cryoprotector medium
Head	587	1,392	707
Middle piece	167	1,397	234
Principle piece	77	791	675
Total	831	3,580	1,616

TABLE 5. *Effect of cryoprotector medium alone on spermatozoon
structure. Results are given as the weighted difference
for all ejaculates between spermatozoa in seminal plasma
(P_1) and those in cryoprotector medium(P_2) before freezing*

Plasma membranes

    Head
      . unstable plasma membrane
        . absent   32.4
        . swollen   20
        . discontinuous 16 [+]
      . stable plasma membrane
        . absent   10.6

Post acrosomal cap

    contour indistinct   55.6

Posterior nuclear space

    granular wall   115

Middle piece

    implantation plate
      . contour indistinct 36.5
    centriole
      . contour indistinct 108

Acrosome

    internal membrane
      . granular   180
    external membrane
      . granular   72.2
    density heterogeneous 65.3
    destroyed   20.5

Mitochondria

    membrane space
      . variable width   72.2 [+]
    contents
      . heterogeneous   12.1

Cytoplasmic excess

    granular   21.8 [+]
    vacuolar   13.5 [+]

Flagella - Middle piece

    axoneme
      . contour indistinct 11.5 [+]
      . peritubular
        densification   10.3
    fibrous sheath
      . density heteroge-
        neous   30 [+]
      . granular contour   25
      . coiled   12.1

[+]Modification more frequent in the control(P_1) population.

TABLE 6. *Cryoprotection: The effect of freezing on spermatozoon*
structure in the presence of cryoprotector medium. Re-
sults are given as the weighted difference for all eja-
culates between spermatozoa in seminal plasma (P_1) and
those frozen in cryoprotector medium(P_4)

Plasma membranes

head
. unstable plasma memb.
. swollen   34.5
. absent   20.4
. stable plasma memb.
. wavy   20.1
principle piece
. swollen   16.0

Post acrosomal cap

absent   15.1

Acrosome

density
. heterogeneous   231.2
internal membrane
. wavy   114.2
borders not parallel   68
enlarged   64.2
vesiculated   42.6
external membrane
. wavy   37.9
density
. low   31.1
destroyed   10.0

Mitochondria

content heterogeneous   96.8
architecture indistincte 59
membrane densification 39.2
contents darkly stained 17.2
membrane space
. narrowed   10.0

Middle piece

axonene
. contour indistinct   11.7

Principal piece

axoneme
. contour indistinct   105.8
. peritubular
densification   20.0
radial spokes
. indistinct   16.1
matrix
. granular   13.5

Coarse fibers

granular contour   176.3
density
. heterogeneous   49.4
circumferential strands
dissociated   12.5

Flagella

coiled   16.6

TABLE 7. *Cryoagression: The effect of freezing in seminal plasma on spermatozoon structure. Results are given as the weighted difference for all ejaculates between spermatozoa in seminal plasma before(P_1) and after freezing(P_3)*

Plasma membranes (P.M.)		Mitochondria	
head		empty	480.2
. unstable P.M.		dilated	336
. absent	131.0 [+]	membrane densification	168.2
. wavy	12.6 [+]	membrane space	
. stable P.M.		narrowed	62.5
. absent	88.2	architecture indistinct	61.5
. wavy	37.5	contents heterogeneous	25.1
. discontinuous	10.8	discontinuous external	
middle piece		membrane	24.2
. discontinuous	69.0	dispersed	12.8
principal piece			
. discontinuous	32.6	**Cytoplasmic excess**	
		large	20.1 [+]
Post acrosomal cap		granular	18 [+]
		vacuolar	12.9 [+]
contour indistinct	63		
absent	40.5	Middle piece	
		axoneme	
Nuclear ring		. contour indistinct	62.7
dissociated	63	. radia spokes	
		indistinct	13.2
Nucleus		matrix density	
membrane		. low	10.5
. swollen	26.2		
. discontinuous	19.5	**Principal piece**	
condensation		axoneme	
. abnormal	21.5	. contour indistinct	450.6
		. matrix enlarged	48.7
Implantation plate		. peritubular	
		densification	46.8
contour indistinct	20.1	coarse fibers	
		. contour indistinct	450.6
Acrosome		. density low	52.9
vesicular	280.0	fibrous sheath	
external membrane		. granular contour	24.0
. discontinuous	135.2	. variable thickness	12.0
. absent	39.2		
. wavy	37.9	**Flagella**	
destroyed	112.0		
borders not parallel	94.1	coiled	13.5
internal membrane			
. discontinuous	66		
. wavy	10.2		

[+] Modification more frequent in the control P_1 population.

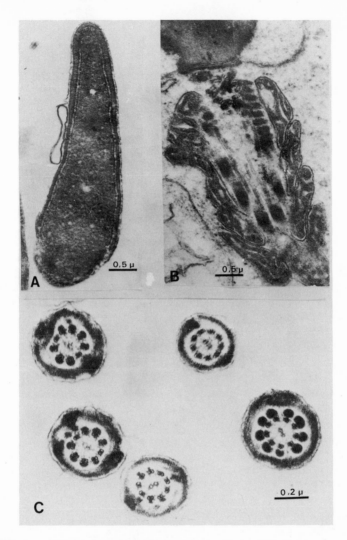

FIGURE 1. Ultrastructural aspects of spermatozoa in cryoprotector medium without freezing(P_2)

A. Longitudinal section of a head. The unstable plasma
    membrane is discontinuous; the internal acrosomal mem-
    brane is granular; the sub-acrosomal space is heterege-
    neous.

B. Longitudinal section of a middle piece. The mitochon-
    dria have a membrane space of variable width and the
    crista are clearly visible.

C. Transverse sections of principal pieces. The axoneme-
    tubule complex is dense and the fibrous sheath has a
    granular contour.

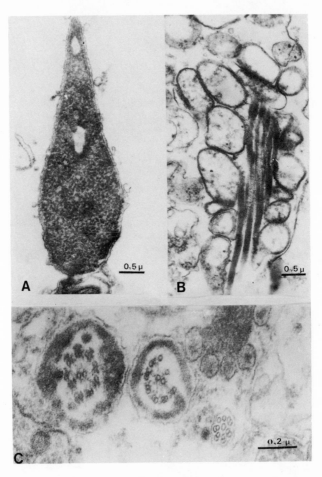

FIGURE 2. Ultrastructural aspects of spermatozoa after
freezing in seminal plasma(P_3)

A. Longitudinal section of a head. The unstable plasma
    membrane is absent; the post-acrosomal cap is indi-
    stinct; the acrosomal external membrane and acrosomal
    contents are missing; the nucleus is of diminished
    density; the nuclear membrane is discontinous.

B. Longitudinal section of a middle piece. The mito-
    chondria are empty and dilated, and have a narrowed
    membrane space.

C. Transverse section of a principal piece. The plasma
    membrane is discontinuous and wavy; the axoneme and
    coarse fibers have indistinct contours; the fibrous
    sheath is discontinuous and has a granular contour.

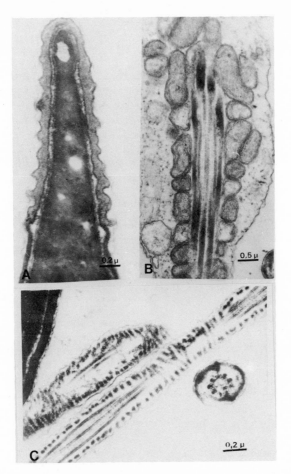

FIGURE 3. Ultrastructural aspects of spermatozoa after
freezing in cryoprotector medium(P_4)

A. Longitudinal section of a head(anterior part). The
    unstable plasma membrane is swollen and wavy. The
    limiting membranes of the acrosome are wavy and their
    borders are not parallel; the acrosomal contents are
    heterogeneous and are of decreased density.

B. Transverse section of a middle piece. The architecture
    of the mitochondria is difficult to distinguish and
    their contents are heterogeneous.

C. Two longitudinal sections and one transverse section
    of principal pieces. The plasma membrane is wavy; the
    fibrous sheath has a granular contour and is heteroge-
    neous; the axoneme and coarse fibers have indistinct
    contours; the matrix is granular.

DISCUSSION

Experimental Technique

In order to eliminate the occurrence of artefacts due to the electron microscopic technique, the results used in this study have been obtained by comparing spermatozoa subjected to different conditions to those from the same ejaculates acting as controls, the latter having been maintained at 37° after collection. Both were fixed by the same method but in fact, the conditions of fixation were not always strictly identical: P_1(control) and P_3(frozen without dilution) contained only spermatozoa and seminal fluid, whereas P_2(medium only) and P_4(frozen with medium) contained cryoprotector medium. This resulted in a certain dissimilarities in regard to cell concentration, substances in contact with the cells and osmotic tonicity of the medium. This limitation, however, affects only the interpretation of the lesions observed, not the reality of their existence.

Effect of the Medium

A medium is used with the objective of protecting the spermatozoa but is itself the source of certain lesions. These lesions are more pronounced in the head where they involve primarily the plasma membrane and the acrosome. The special fragility of this zone, which disappears during the acrosomal reaction before fertilization, is well known.[6] Wooley[13] has also reported these types of lesions after the simple addition of cryoprotector medium. It has been proposed that this is due primarily to the effect of glycerol.[8,12]

With only exposure to the medium, the integrity of the middle piece is well maintained. Flagellar structures are also little affected. Even though there were a certain number of coiled flagellae, this phenomenon is typical of spermatozoa placed in any artificial medium, especially if there are changes in osmotic conditions.[5] These findings are on the whole compatible with the fact that the percentage of motile forms is only slighty decreased in the presence of the medium.[4]

Protector medium and Cryo-agression

Freezing without protection has long been known to cause the death of spermatozoa as it does for any other cell. Previous studies have pointed out the severity of damage to the mitochondria and acrosome, but this was not quantified.[1,7] Modifications of both the external membrane and contents of the acrosome have been reported by Schill.[12] Furthermore, Pedersen, in a more thorough study, found that lesions of the acrosome were dominant,[10] but he also noted lesions of mitochondria and the coarse fibers. The present study has revealed that lesions to the spermatozoa are generalized but affect most the nucleus and two flagellar structures, the axoneme and the fibrous sheath.

CONCLUSION

The primary value of quantifying spermatozoa morphological alterations in cryopreservation techniques is to establish an order of induced lesions according to structure. In this study, the spermatozoal structures most frequently affected by freezing in cryoprotector medium were, in decreasing order, the acrosome, coarse fibers, fibrous sheath, mitochondria and axoneme.

From the results of this study, it is evident that the methods of cryoprotection presently available are of limited efficacy and, thus, research must continue in this area. In order to evaluate new methods, it seems imperative to use a methodical system, such as the check list developped for this study, in order to quantify observed structural lesions.

REFERENCES

1. Behrman, S.J. Freeze preservation of human spermatozoa in liquid nitrogen vapor. Schweiz, Z. Gynäk. Geburtsh; 2:307-313, 1971.

2. Bostrom, K. and Rubin, S.O. Destruction of spermatozoa in freeze-thawing of human semen. Scand. J. Urol. Nephrol., 7:120-122, 1973.

3. David, G., Bisson, J.P., Czyglik, F., Jouannet P. and Gernigon, C. Que doit comporter l'examen du sperme ? Comment en interpréter les résultats ? Feuillets de Biologie, XV:76, 1974.

4. David, G. and Czyglik, F. Tolérance à la congélation du sperme humain en fonction de la qualité initiale du sperme. J. Gyn. Obst. Biol. Repr., 6:601-610, 1977.

5. Drevius, L.O. and Eriksson, H. Osmotic swelling of mammalian spermatozoa. Experimental Cell Research, 42:136-156, 1966.

6. Fawcett, D.W. The structure of the mammalian spermatozoon. Int. Rev. Ctyol., 7, 1958.

7. Friberg, J. and Nilsson, O. Motility and morphology of human sperms after freezing in liquid nitrogen. In: "Current Problems in Fertility", Ingelman, Sundberg and Lunell, eds. Plenum Press, New-York-London, 1971.

8. Jones, R.C. Fertility and infertility in mammals in relation to sperm structure. In: The Biology of male gamete. J.G. Duckett and P.A. Racey, eds. Academic Press, London, pp. 343-365, 1975.

9. Matheson, G.W., Carlborg, L. and Gemzell, C. Frozen human semen for artificial insemination. Am. J. Obst. Gynec., 104:495-501, 1969.

10. Pedersen, H. and Lebech, P.E. Ultrastructural changes in the human spermatozoon after freezing for artificial insemination. Fertil. and Steril., 22:2, 1971.

11. Pedersen, H. The human spermatozoon. Dan. Med. Bull., 21 suppl. 1:3-36, 1974.

12. Schill, W.B. and Wolff, H. Ultrastructure of human sperm acrosome and determination of acrosin activity under conditions of semen preservation. Int. J. Fertil., 19:217-223, 1974.

13. Woolley, D.M. and Richardson, D.W. Ultrastructural injury to human spermatozoa after freezing and thawing. J. Reprod. Fert., 52:389-394, 1978.

COMPARISON OF CRYOPROTECTION TECHNIQUES:

A LIGHT AND ELECTRON MICROSCOPY STUDY

Robert F. Harrison and Brian L. Sheppard

T.C.D. Department of Obstetrics
    and Gynaecology
Rotunda Hospital
Dublin, Ireland

INTRODUCTION

The conveniences of freeze preserved human semen for artificial insemination outweigh for many clinicians the fact that frozen semen appears to be between 15-25% less effective in producing pregnancy than similar quality inseminated fresh whole semen.[1-2]

An extensive literature search failed to reveal the optimum method of cryo-preservation. Different rates of freezing and thawing are employed and various materials have been selected as the cryo-protective diluent additive, even criteria for measurement of effectiveness vary from department to department.

In order, therefore, to obtain the best results for our own patients when it was decided to set up facilities for cryo-preservation at Chelsea Hospital for Women, London, and subsequently at the T.C.D. Department of Obstetrics and Gynaecology in Dublin, an initial controlled trial of the two most commonly used methods of cryo-preservation was set up. The aim of this study was not only to try and discover which method gave the best results in our hands as judged by the imperfect criterion of post-thaw motility viewed through a light microscope, but also to use the greater discernability and diagnostic potential of the scanning electron microscope at our disposal. In the past, cryo-injuries have been related to both the method[3] and the rate of cooling.[4] These consist of ultra-structural damage to the acrosome and the mitochondria.[5] It was hoped that by building in sufficient controls it might be possible to discover changes in morphology unseen by light microscope, changes that could account for the superiority of one particular method of preparation and perhaps even suggest why freeze storage reduces motility, life span and fertilization capacity of human spermatozoa samples.[6]

MATERIEL AND METHODS

Semen

Fresh masturbation samples of semen were collected from nine fertile volunteers and a full semen analysis performed. Specimens were halved and the relevant cryo-protective diluents added, either a complex cryo-protective medium in a one to one ratio[7-8] (containing 3.2 grams trisodium citrate, 2.2 grams fructose in 100 ml to which is added 28 ml of glycerol; stored at minus 20°C until day of experiment when 18 ml is unfrozen and 7 ml hen's egg yolk is added) or analar grade glycerol[9] and mixed gently to an amount of 10% of the total semen volume.

Samples were left for five minutes at room temperature and each was further subdivided and placed in four suitably coded and marked plastic ampoules.[10] After standing for one hour at minus 20°C and being suspended in liquid nitrogen vapour for eight minutes, they were then lowered for storage into the liquid nitrogen container at minus 196°C.

Samples from each volunteer were removed from storage for further examination at one hour, one day, one week and one month intervals after freezing. The post-thaw motility was re-assessed using light microscopy by the same observer using a sliding scale after slowly thawing the specimen for 15 minutes at 37°C.

Electron Microscopy (JEOL 50A)

For this study, the fresh sample and one unfrozen at one month was used. In order to include all necessary controls for each subject, eleven samples were prepared for viewing (Table 1). Washing and suspension was in a sodium cacodylate solution with a pH of 7.4 and when necessary centrifugation was carried out at 500 r.p.m with a room temperature of 37°C for two intervals of 20 minutes.

A drop of each sample was fixed in osmium tetroxide (1.3%) in 0.67 molar sodium cacodylate for 30 minutes at 4°C. After removal of the fixative by filter paper capillary action, a staged dehydration with 100% acetone was performed at 10 minutes intervals between each stage. The cover slips were then mounted on specimen stubs and sputter coated with gold film for viewing.

TABLE 1. *Flow sheet of specimen preparation for electron microscopy*

Specimen	Procedure
1.	Control pre-treatment
2.	Control pre-treatment + buffer
3.	Control pre-treatment + buffer, wash and resuspend
4.	Pre-freeze complex medium
5.	Pre-freeze complex medium, wash and resuspend
6.	Pre-freeze glycerol medium
7.	Pre-freeze glycerol medium, wash and resuspend
8.	Post freeze complex medium
9.	Post-freeze complex medium, wash and resuspend
10.	Post-freeze glycerol medium
11.	Post-freeze glycerol medium, wash and suspend
12.	Buffer suspension Na Cacodylate

All the specimens were scanned blind(BLS) to a magnification standard of 1500 times and representative areas photographed with a detail magnification of 4000 times.

RESULTS

Light Microscopy Study

Table 2 shows that in no case did the addition of the diluent alter the initial motility assessment but in practically all the post-thaw stages, the cryo-survival rate was greater with the complex medium. Certainly, a variability in freezability[11] was present, especially when the initial motility was low. The cryo-survival rate was lower, especially when only glycerol was added. The subjectivity of measuring motility using the light microscope, even by the same observer, is illustrated by case 2A(Table 2) where motility appears to increase after one month compared to the one hour value. However, in all the other cases the trend established at one hour was maintained.

The superiority of the complex medium is demonstrated in Figure 1 which shows curves for the mean cryo-survival rate. The most

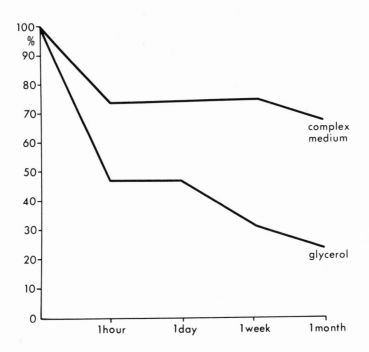

FIGURE 1. Human spermatozoa cryo-survival rates for glycerol
and complex medium as a function of the period of frozen stor-
age. Cryo-survival= $\dfrac{\text{Post-thaw motility} \times 100}{\text{Pre-freeze motility}}$

significant fall occurs by one hour. This provides a useful quick
and accurate way of assessing freezability potential, a subject of
great importance to those in the commercial cryo-preservation field
where variability and freezability may not always be appreciated
by potential customers such as those undergoing vasectomy, medical
or surgical castration or those who may wish to procreate after
their own death.

Electron Microscopy

As shown in Table 3, two distinct features emerged from the
Electron Microscopic study. It was evident there was a highly significant increase in disruption of the acrosomal part of the seminal
head in specimens where glycerol alone was used for cryoprotection
in comparison to all the specimens before freezing and to those which
had been frozen with the complex medium. This no doubt accounted for
the decrease in motility. It is extremely unlikely that such spermatozoa could retain viability and fertilization potential.

The second consistent feature was the presence of tail coiling
in all the specimens that had been centrifuged. This has been seen

TABLE 2. *Comparison of a complex cryoprotective medium(A) and a glycerol medium(B) before and after different freezing periods based on spermatozoa with purposeful progressing motility*

Volunteer	Medium	Pre-freeze motility(%)	Post-thaw motility(%)			
			1 hour	1 day	1 week	1 month
1	A	60%	60%	60%	60%	40%
	B	60%	40%	30%	30%	10%
2	A	40%	10%	40%	40%	25%
	B	40%	5%	10%	5%	5%
3	A	30%	30%	30%	30%	30%
	B	30%	10%	10%	5%	5%
4	A	40%	40%	25%	25%	30%
	B	40%	20%	20%	10%	5%
5	A	60%	50%	50%	50%	50%
	B	60%	30%	40%	20%	25%
6	A	25%	10%	10%	10%	10%
	B	25%	10%	10%	5%	5%
7	A	50%	50%	40%	40%	40%
	B	50%	25%	30%	25%	25%
8	A	50%	40%	40%	40%	40%
	B	50%	40%	40%	30%	20%
9	A	30%	10%	10%	10%	10%
	B	30%	>5%	5%	>5%	5%

TABLE 3. *Electron microscope abnormal findings*

Specimen	Mean Motility(%)	Main abnormal findings
1	60	
2	60	
3	40	Looped tails
4	60	
5	30	Looped tails
6	60	
7	20	Looped tails
8	60	
9	20	Looped tails
10	30	Head disrupted
11	5	Head disrupted

in other species[12-13] and ascribed to osmotic disturbance of the plasmalemma. However, human spermatozoa are thought to be independent of the effect of glycerolation on permeability and the distribution of these results makes it more likely that the tail coiling phenomenon in this case is a physical consequence of or reaction to prolonged circular motion. However, whether this process is reversible is doubtful and the possible effect on fertilization potential can be seen by the drop in mean percentage of motility in these cases (Table 3).

Extremely high magnifications are necessary for such lesions to be seen. This unfortunately is a disadvantage in that only one or two spermatozoa can be viewed at one time making accurate enumeration of results, so easy with the light microscope, impossible. Extreme care is needed in the preparation of specimens to avoid artifacts and many controls need to be built into each study. Clearly at present, the electron microscope's best use is complimentary to that of the light microscope in studies such as this where the superiority of an egg yolk citrate mix as cryo-protective agent over glycerol is not only demonstrated, but the damage caused by cryo-injury and perhaps even by centrifujation is shown as well.

ACKNOWLEDGEMENTS

To Miss J. Stedronska, Seminology Laboratory, Chelsea Hospital for Women and Miss Phillipu, for their technical help on the light microscopy part of the study.

Results of this study have in part been presented at the World Congress on Fertility and Sterility, 1978, Miami, USA.

REFERENCES

1. Behrman, S.J. In: Techniques of artificial insemination in progress in infertility. Behrman S.J. and Kistner R.W., eds. Little Brown & Co, Boston, pp. 717, 1968.

2. Sherman, J.K. Research on frozen human semen, past, present, future. Fertil. and Steril., 15:5, 1964.

3. McGann, L.E. and Farrant, J. Survival of tissue culture cells frozen by a two step procedure at minus 196°C N° 1 holding temperature and time. Cryo-biol., 13:261, 1976.

4. Rudiger, H., Wohler, W., von Bohmer, H. and Passarge, E. Cooling velocity and cell recovery. Nature, 254:361, 1975.

5. Friberg, J. and Nilsson, O. Motility and Morphology of human sperms after freezing in liquid nitrogen. In: Current problems in fertility, Ingleman-Sundberg A. and Lunnell N.O., eds., Plenum Press, New York, 1971.

6. Sherman, J.K. Improved methods of preservation of human spermatozoa by freezing. Fertil. Steril., 14:49, 1963.

7. Richardson, D.W. Artificial insemination in the human. In: Modern trends in human genetics, n° 2, Emery A.E.H. ed., Butterworths, London, pp. 404, 1975.

8. Sadlier, R.F.M.S. The preservation of mammalian spermatozoa by freezing. Lab. Pract., 15:413, 1966.

9. Newton, J. Current status of artificial insemination in clinical practice, in: Proceedings of the 4th study group on artificial insemination. Brudenell, M., McLaren, A. and Short, R. Symonds, M., eds. Royal College of Obstetricians and Gynaecologists. pp. 25, 1976.

10. Harrison, R.F., Stedronska, J. and Evans, P. A marking instrument for use in cryo-preservation. Brit. Med. J., 2:6028, 1976.

11. Beck, W.W. and Silverstein, I. Variable motility recovery of
     spermatozoa following freeze preservation. Fertil. and
     Steril., 26:63, 1975.

12. Bakst, R. and Sexton, T.J. Fertilizing capacity and ultra-
     structure of fowl and turkey spermatozoa before and after
     freezing. Reprod. Fertil., 55:1, 1979.

13. Drevius, L.O. Permiability of the bull sperm membrane, in: Func-
     tional anatomy of the spermatazoon. Afzelius B.A., ed.,
     Pergamon Press New York, pp. 373, 1975.

EFFECT OF CRYOPRESERVATION ON ACROSOMAL

PROTEIN OF HUMAN SPERMATOZOA

Karl H. Broer

Department of Obstetrics and Gynecology
University of Cologne
Cologne, West Germany

INTRODUCTION

The spermatozoa coating antigen(SCA), lactoferrin, exists in various body fluids, including seminal plasma and cervical mucus. The highest level is to be found in the seminal plasma. Lactoferrin can be demonstrated by the immunofluorescence technique and is present on the spermatozoa in the acrosomal region.[1]

A statistically significant higher percentage of spermatozoa heads are coated with lactoferrin in semen specimens with normal spermatozoa morphology than in those containing spermatozoa with atypical configurations.

Using lactoferrin fluorescence as a marker, we investigated the amount of SCA during *in vivo* migration of spermatozoa through cervical mucus and after the cryopreservation procedure as well.

MATERIALS AND METHODS

Human ejaculates were obtained from 13 fertile patients consulting the infertility unit. The wives of these patients were subjected to the fractional post-coital tests. Semen samples and the material obtained from the external and internal os(within two hours after intercourse) were smeared on slides. Following this, FITC(Fluorescein-iso-thiocyanate) labelled antilactoferrin gamma-globulin, obtained from rabbits(Behring AG, Marburg, W. Germany), was used in immunofluorescence studies on lactoferrin. The percentage of lactoferrin positive spermatozoa heads was calculated after

131

counting a minimum of 300 spermatozoa on each slide.

To determine the specificity of the influence of LF-positive spermatozoa, a comparative investigation was done after spermatozoa passage through a serum albumin column.[3,4] Additionally, cryopreservation using the Behrmann-Sawada medium and the pellet method was performed. After storage in liquid nitrogen(MV: 93 days) and thawing, the spermatozoa were smeared on slides and stained in the same manner as the untreated samples.

The FITC labelled rabbit gammaglobulin fraction(donated by Behring Werke A.G., Marburgh, W. Germany) served as a control for the ejaculate.

RESULTS

Both before and after *in vivo* penetration, the lactoferrin related fluorescence could be clearly localized in the acrosomal region and was easily distinguished from other fluorescent lacto-ferrin particles in the cervical mucus(Figure 1). The proportion of LF-positive spermatozoa heads in the ejaculates before the *in vivo* penetration ranged between 48.8% in the serum filtration study, 50.9% in the post-coital study and 51.9% in the cryopreservation

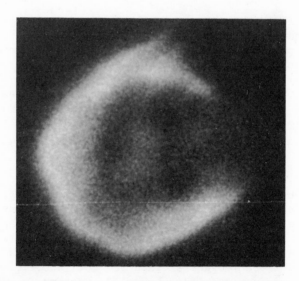

FIGURE 1. Fluorescence in the acrosomal region of a spermatozoid

study. The slight differences are due to individual variations and
to different days of investigation and investigators.

There was a significant decrease after *in vivo* penetration in
LF-positive spermatozoa heads in the semen samples: From 50.9%
(± 7.8%) before penetration to 39.8% (± 11.7%) at the external os
and down to 19.1% (± 10.1%) at the internal os (Table 1).

The filtration assay according to Ericsson[3] did not show any
significant influence on the percentage of LF positive spermatozoa
(Table 2).

The cryopreservation procedure resulted in a statistically
significant (t= 3.480) decrease of the amount of LF-positive spermatozoa (Table 3). The specificity of the anti-lactoferrin-gammaglo-
bulins was demonstrated by the controls which had 1.9% (± 1.2%) LF
positive spermatozoa after adding FITC labelled rabbit gammaglobulin.

DISCUSSION

The presence of lactoferrin on the spermatozoal head is strongly correlated to head morphology, i.e. the percentage of LF-positive
spermatozoa in samples with morphologically normal heads is double
that in samples with abnormal heads, as demonstrated in a previous
study.[2] This may be related to normal function of the acrosomal
region which is equiped with several proteins that are more likely
to be found in normally configurated spermatozoa heads. Whether
lactoferrin or other coated proteins are needed for the fertilization procedure is not yet clear.

During the *in vitro* penetration of spermatozoa into preovulatory
cervical mucus, lactoferrin is partly removed as demonstrated in a
recent investigation.[5] A similar phenomenon takes place during
in vivo migration through the cervix uteri as shown by the above
described results was obtained by the fractional post-coital tests.

These washing effects do not completely eliminate all the lactoferrin content. The remainder might be removed during the migration
through the upper cervical region upon which post-coital tests are
now being undertaken.

SCA does wash off after spermatozoa filtration through serum
albumin, which suggests an additional specific mechanical SCA washing
effect of the cervical mucus.

The meaning of the partial removal of SCA from the spermatozoa
during *in vivo* or *in vitro* penetration through cervical mucus is
not fully understood and may possibily be part of the capacitation

TABLE 1. *Effect of ovulatory cervical mucus on spermatozoa coating antigen(lactoferrin) during "in vivo" penetration through cervix uteri(fractional post-coital-test)*

Semen sample	Sperm count (x10⁶/ml)	Motility (% Normal)	Morphology (% Normal)	Cervical score (Insler)	Lactoferrin positive spermatozoa in ejaculate (%)	Lactoferrin positive spermatozoa at external os level(%)	Lactoferrin positive spermatozoa at internal os level(%)
1	80	75	76	11	58	50	19
2	63	79	68	12	56	49	28
3	70	75	72	11	52	41	10
4	108	80	75	12	52	53	30
5	102	70	70	9	31	8	19
6	76	70	81	11	52	40	23
7+	112	75	72	12	62	45	6
8	54	83	72	12	48	46	3
9+	92	57	68	11	50	48	45
10	110	68	76	10	53	38	30
11	95	80	72	11	49	35	20
12+	76	70	74	9	45	29	11
13	88	78	80	11	45	36	38
MV($\pm$SD)	86.6($\pm$18.6)	83.8($+$6.8)	74.5($+$4.0)	11	50.9($+$7.8)	39.8($\pm$11.7)	19.1($\pm$10.1)

+Cryopreserved.

TABLE 2. *Percentage of lactoferrin-fluorescence positive human spermatozoa heads after passage through human serum albumin.*

Semen sample	Semen analysis			Lactoferrin positive spermatozoa					
	Sperm count (x10⁶/ml)	Motility (%)	Morphology (% normal)	Ejaculate No +/total	%	After 70.5% HSA passage No. +/total	%	After 17.5% HSA passage No. +/total	%
1 c	71	83	75	41/121	33.8	54/177	31.0	22/86	26.0
2	97	81	79	177/315	56.1	120/226	53.0	84/159	52.8
3 c	117	76	74	76/193	39.3	55/143	38.4	33/102	32.0
4	107	80	82	396/675	58.6	35/60	58.0	40/67	59.7
5	45	73	78	152/285	53.3	108/195	55.3	146/268	55.0
6 c	104	83	72	56/120	46.6	126/341	37.0	62/212	29.0
7 c	9	36	47	110/284	38.5	46/116	39.6	33/106	31.0
8	23	74	65	163/344	38.6	109/198	55.0	123/202	60.8
9	27	72	76	117/208	56.2	96/188	51.0	182/345	52.7
10	112	71	57	198/418	47.3	237/395	60.0	40/67	59.7
11	75	80	60	304/574	52.9	161/307	52.4	102/192	53.4
12	101	74	82	179/346	51.7	158/308	51.2	207/192	55.7
13	11	72	76	126/242	52.0	63/124	50.8	61/104	58.6
				Mean: 48.8 (±8)		48.6 (±9)		(48.2 (±13.2)	

$|t = 0.178|$

TABLE 3. *Percentage of lactoferrin-positive human spermatozoa before and after cryopreservation*

Semen sample	Sperm count (x10⁶/ml)	Before cryopreservation			After cryopreservation	
		Motility (%)	Morphology (% normal)	LF-positive (%)	Motility (%)	LF-positive (%)
1	71	83	75	53.3	51	33.8
2	117	76	74	47.3	50	39.3
3	104	83	72	48.6	61	46.6
4	9	36	47	47.3	21	38.5
5	105	84	72	54.2	52	41.6
6	115	78	80	52.1	46	44.5
7	112	75	72	62.5	48	50.0
8	92	57	68	49.9	40	45.1
9	76	70	74	51.2	51	50.8
10 EPID	86	80	72	2	52	1
11 EPID	40	60	62	1	38	1
Mean:		70%		51.9(±4.6) [t= 3.480]	46%	43.3 (±5.5)

process. The slight, but significant decrease of the lactoferrin content on the spermatozoal head after freezing in liquid nitrogen leads us to conclude that the procedure may partly destroy the protein pattern of the acrosomal region.

References

1. Broer, K. H., Hirschhäuser, C., Dauber, U. and Baudner, S.
   The function of Lactoferrin in relation to sperm head morphology.
   IRCS Med. Sci., 5: 116, 1977.

2. Ericsson, R. J. and Glass, R. H.
   Isolation of progressively motile sperm from infertile men.
   Fertil. Steril., 28: 330, 1977.

3. Broer, K. H. and Dauber, U.
   A filtering method for cleaning up spermatozoa in cases of asthenospermia.
   Int. J. Fertil., 23: 234, 1978.

4. Broer, K. H., Dauber, U., Hermann, W. P. and Hirschhäuser, C.
   The presence of Lactoferrin on the human sperm head during in vitro penetrations through cervical mucus.
   IRCS Med. Sci., 5: 362, 1977.

BIOCHEMICAL MODIFICATIONS OF FROZEN SEMEN

Jean-François Guerin, Yves Menezo
and Jean-Claude Czyba

Centre d'Etudes et de Conservation du Sperme
   (CECOS), Lyon
Lyon, France

INTRODUCTION

The preservation of human semen in liquid nitrogen is now a common practice which has permitted a considerable extension in the application of artificial insemination, and whose advantages are now well proven. However, there is one major problem with the cryo-preservation of human semen: The incontestable drop in fertilizing capacity. Several authors have correlated this with the reduction in motility of a sample after thawing which is, indeed, more marked for human semen than for the majority of domesticated species(especially cattle). It would, however, seem clear that post-thaw motility is not a sufficient criterion of fertilizing power of a frozen semen sample. According to Behrman "The post thaw motility of a frozen preserved semen is not a determinant or index of its subsequent fertility".[3] In addition, certain frozen semen samples appear to loose all their fertility capacity even though residual motility is good.

Several authors have described changes in the energy metabolism of spermatozoa after freezing,[1,2,3,19] and other studies, particularly on bovine spermatozoa, demonstrate modifications in the activity of certain enzymes, notably GOT and hyaluronidase.[5,6,12,13,17] These two enzymes were also studied in frozen human spermatozoa by Graham et al.[11] but otherwise little is known about the modification of enzymatic activity of human spermatozoa by freezing.

As a preliminary study, we examined the possibility that freezing might have harmful consequences on the seminal plasma which could then influence the gametes. Cryo-preservation causes several physico-chemical disturbances, particularly to macromolecules, and the

motility and metabolism of the spermatozoa may well be influenced
by protein factors present in the seminal plasma.[9-20] We studied the effects of freezing and thawing on the energy metabolism
of the spermatozoa by measuring their respiratory activity, an in-
dicator of oxidative metabolism, and by estimating the activities
of a large number of enzymes. The use of a semi-quantitative analytical system allowed us to study the activities of 65 different
enzymes on samples before and after freezing.

MATERIALS AND METHODS

Ejaculates were obtained from healthy donors, and complete
spermiograms were performed. The samples were allowed to stand for
30 minutes then diluted with an equal volume of a standard cryo-
protective medium containing 10% glycerol(final concentration), egg
yolk, sodium citrate, glycine, and glucose as described by Ackerman.[4]

Preparation of Samples

For studies on the effect of freezing on the seminal plasma
the mixture of semen and cryoprotection medium was divided into two
equal fractions which were centrifuged at 600 g for 10 min. Each
cell precipitate was resuspended in 2 ml of buffered Krebs-Ringer
solution. One of the supernatants was left at room temperature for
10 min while the other was frozen in liquid nitrogen, kept frozen
for a short time and then thawed at room temperature. After a further centrifugation, one of the cell precipitates was resuspended
in the untreated seminal plasma and the other in the frozen and thawed sample.

For studies on the freezing of the spermatozoa, the mixture of
semen and cryoprotection medium was placed in sealed straws of 0.25
ml capacity. These were then frozen in a horizontal position, usually in nitrogen vapors with two intermediate stages[10] but at times in
a programed freezing apparatus as previously described.[7] After the
storage period, the straws were removed from the liquid nitrogen and
allowed to thaw at room temperature.

Motility

The percentage motility was initially estimated by careful
observation under a phase contrast microscope. At present we use
a spermokinemeter(SKM100) which uses the optical Doppler effect to
provide precision measurements of the percentage of motile forms
and the mean characteristic instantaneous velocity of the population
at 37°C.[8-14]

Oxygen Consumption

Oxygen consumption was measured by a polarographic method using a Clark electrode in a chamber at 37°C. The true respiratory activity of the spermatozoa was obtained by subtraction of the oxygen consumption of the mixture of seminal plasma and cryoprotector medium prepared by high speed centrifugation from that of the total sample.

Measurement of Enzyme Activity

Spermatozoa were resuspended in hypotonic solution and submitted to brief sonication. This homogenate was centrifuged at high speed and the supernatants were used for enzyme testing. A semi-quantitative colorimetric method (API ZYM: API system, Montalien-Vercien, France) allowed the simultaneous estimation of 65 enzyme activities (8 dehydrogenases, 19 hydrolases and 38 amino-peptidases) [13-19] and a precise spectrophotometric method based on the elevation of optical density associated with the reduction of NADP was used for accurate measurements of activities of two enzymes, glucose 6-phosphate dehydrogenase (G6PD) and 6-phosphate gluconate dehydrogenase (6PGD).

Statistical Tests

Results were compared using the pairs test derived from Student's test.

RESULTS

The results concerning the effect of freezing seminal plasma on the unfrozen motility and oxygen consumption of unfrozen spermatozoa from 13 donors are summarized in Table 1. The characteristic instantaneous velocity is identical for the two samples, and the slight reduction in percentage motility and in oxygen consumption are not significant.

The effects of freezing and thawing on spermatozoa are shown in Table 2. The percentage motility is in general severely reduced after freezing and thawing. The residual motility was calculated using the classical formula:

$$\text{Residual motility:} \quad \frac{\text{\% motility after thawing}}{\text{\% motility before freezing}} \times 100$$

The mean value for the 20 samples tested was 38%, but the variations between individuals were considerable.

TABLE 1.   *Effects of seminal plasma freezing and thawing on motility and O_2 consumption of spermatozoa (velocity expressed as $\mu m/s$; O_2 consumption expressed as μl $O_2/10^8$ spermatozoa/hour). Values represent the mean of 13 measurements.*

	Untreated seminal plasma	Frozen seminal plasma
Motility(%)	47	43
Mean velocity	52	52
O_2 consumption	4,6	3,4

TABLE 2.   *Effects of deep freezing on motility, O_2 consumption, and enzyme activities in thawed spermatozoa. (O_2 consumption expressed as μl $O_2/10^8$ spermatozoa; enzyme activities expressed as $m.I.U./10^8$ spermatozoa). Values represent the mean of 20 measurements for percentage of motility and O_2 consumption, and the mean of 10 measurements for enzyme activities.*

	Before freezing	After thawing	% of recovery
Motility(%)	72	27	38
O_2 consumption	5.35	1.95	36
G6PD activity	4.30	1.39	33
6PGD activity	14.2	9.23	65

Oxygen consumption appears to be still more seriously diminished. The difference between the two samples is significant(p < 0.01) and remains so even when motile spermatozoa are considered alone(p < 0.02). The variability between individuals is also greater than that observed for motility, and the individual values of these measurements for the first 10 individuals tested(taken in order of their arrival at the clinic) are tabulated in Table 3.   It can be seen that for 4 individuals the respiratory activity virtually disappeared after freezing and thawing although the residual motility remained satisfactory.

Testing of the enzyme activities by the API ZYM technique showed that all hydrolase and peptidase activities detectable in fresh spermatozoa were preserved after freezing and thawing within the limits

TABLE 3. *Individual results concerning the effects of deep freezing on spermatozoa respiratory activity (ZO_2 denotes $\mu l\ O_2/10^8$ spermatozoa/hour).*

Donors	ZO_2 (before freezing)	$Z'O_2$ (after thawing)	$(Z'Z) \times 100$ (residual O_2 consumption)	Percentage of residual motility
I	10.8	7.3	68	40
II	3.3	5.8	176	45
III	8.7	0	0	30
IV	7.0	2.7	39	40
V	6.8	0.7	10	30
VI	8.2	2.9	35	50
VII	8.0	0.2	3	35
VIII	4.3	1.5	35	40
IX	5.4	0	0	30
X	2.7	0	0	20

of sensitivity of the method. Among the dehydrogenases, lactate dehydrogenase (LDH) appears to be unaffected (within our limits of sensitivity), while 6PGD and especially G6PD activity are markedly reduced after freezing and thawing. This reduction was consistently observed on over 50 samples and was independant of the freezing method used (programed apparatus or manual freezing in nitrogen vapors). These observations were confirmed by a precise spectrophotometric measurement of these enzyme activities for 10 donors (Table 2). For these cases, 65% of the initial 6PGD activity remains after freezing, but only 33% of the initial G6PD activity.

As with respiratory activity, we have observed that some. samples appear to loose all their G6PD activity after freezing and thawing. In order to determine whether the loss of activity was due to destruction of the enzyme or to leakage from the spermatozoon, we tested the enzyme activity of total samples (spermatozoa plus suspension medium) before and after freezing and thawing. No significant difference could be found between such samples and we conclude that the loss of activity corresponds to a leakage of enzyme from the spermatozoon to the surrounding medium under freezing conditions.

DISCUSSION

Deep freezing in liquid nitrogen does not appear to cause modifications in components of the seminal plasma which affect the metabolism of the spermatozoa. Neither motility nor respiratory activity are affected when spermatozoa are suspended in seminal plasma
which has been frozen and thawed in the presence of a cryoprotector
medium. Eliasson[9] and Trifunac et al.[20] have independantly demonstrated the presence of a factor present in the seminal plasma which
could depress the respiratory activity of spermatozoa. This factor
is thermolabile,[20] but does not appear to be affected by deep freezing.

In this study we show that there are several different levels
of alteration of the cell by deep freezing. The oxydative metabolism,
as reflected by oxygen consumption, is severely affected. This agrees
with the observations of Ackerman[1-2] who showed that freezing caused
a deviation of the metabolism towards the glycolytic pathway, and
confirms the results of Sawada et al.[19] although the spermatozoon
respiration was measured in a completely different manner. The total loss of respiratory activity in certain frozen samples is interesting and might in some way explain the loss of fertilizing power
of certain spermatozoa despite their rentention of a satisfactory
residual mobility.

Of all the enzyme activities tested, only those of the two dehydrogenases of the hexose monophosphate shunt appear to be diminished
after freezing, especially that of G6PD which may sometimes be no longer detectable . These two enzymes, and therefore the pentose pathway
are lacking in the spermatozoa of certain species, notably cattle.[16]
In human spermatozoa this metabolic pathway would appear to play an
important role: In the absence of appreciable biosynthetic reactions
in the mature gamete, it must serve to produce energy through ATP.[18]
If this function is disturbed as well as that of the oxydative pathway, it is not difficult to imagine that the fertilizing capacity of
the spermatozoa could suffer. The reduction in G6PD activity corresponds to a release of the enzyme into the surrounding medium.
These observations are in agreement with those on Ram spermatozoa[16]
in which the concentration of G6PD in the seminal plasma increases
after freezing, and those on human spermatozoa in which there is a
release of GOT, LDT, and hyaluronidase.[11]

It is well known that the effect of freezing on cell membranes
is to increase their fragility; since G6PD appears to be particularly
sensitive to this action, the measurement of its residual activity
might constitute a good estimation of the state of the plasma membrane and be a useful indirect morphological criterion of the effects
of freezing.

Our results show that the motility, respiration and G6PD activity are reduced by essentially the same percentage if one considers
the mean values (Table 2). We have, however, observed that these modifications were rarely of the same magnitude in an individual sample. This is not surprising since the the different lesions involved do not depend upon a single mechanism; the reduction in motility
more probably reflects a lesion in the flagellar mechanism than a
disorder of energetic metabolism, at least initially. The appreciation of the success of freezing a semen sample should therefore be
based upon several criteria rather than upon a single one (residual
motility being frequently the only measurement considered at the
present). In addition, attempts to improve the fertilizing power
of frozen semen should take into account all the different aspects
of cell alterations induced during freezing and thawing.

REFERENCES

1. Ackerman, D.R. Fructose utilization of human spermatozoa after
   cooling and freezing. Int. J. Fertil., 12:1-4, 1967.

2. Ackerman, D.R. Effect of cooling and freezing on the aerobic
   and anaerobic lactic acid production of human semen. Fertil.
   Steril. 19:123-128, 1968.

3. Behrman, S.R. Preservation of human sperm by liquid nitrogen
   vapor freezing. In: A. Ingleman-Sundberg and N.O. Lunell,
   eds. Current problems in fertility., New-York: Plenum
   Publishing Corp., 1971.

4. Behrman, S.J. and Ackerman, D.R. Freeze preservation of human
   sperm. Am. J. Obstet. Gynecol., 103:654-664, 1969.

5. Brown, K.I., Crabo, B.G., Graham, E.F. and Pace, M.M. Some
   factors affecting loss of intra-cellular enzymes from spermatozoa. Cryobiology, 8:220-224, 1971.

6. Crabo, B.G., Bower R.E., Brown, K.I., Graham, E.F. and Pace M.M.
   Extracellular glutamic-oxaloacetic transaminase as a measure
   on membrane injury in spermatozoa during treatment. In: A.
   Ingleman-Sundberg and N.O. Lunell, eds. Current problems in
   fertility, New York: Plenum Publishing Corp., pp. 33-38, 1971.

7.. Czyba, J.C., Pinatel, M.C. and Guerin, J.F. Preservation and
    storage of human sperm. Acta Med. Pol., 19:133-145, 1978.

8. Dubois, P., Jouannet, P., Berge, P., Volochine, B., Serres, C.
   and David, G. Méthode et appareillage de mesure objective
   de la mobilité des spermatozoïdes humains. Ann. Physiol.
   Biol. et Med., 9:1, 19-41, 1975.

9. Eliasson, R.   Oxygen consumption of human spermatozoa in semi-
    nal plasma and a Ringer solution.   J. Reprod. Fertil., 71:
    27, 385-389, 1971.

10. Emperaire, J.C. and Riviere, J.   La congélation du sperme hu-
     main normal.   J. Gyn. Obst. Biol. Repr., 3:215, 1974.

11. Graham, E.K. and Crabo, B.G.   Some methods of freezing and
     evaluating human spermatozoa.   In: The integrity of fro-
     zen spermatozoa.   Natl academy of Science, Library of Con-
     gress, 77:940-301, 1978.

12. Jouannet, P., Volochine, B., Deguent, P. and David, G.   Study
     of human spermatozoa motility parameters by scattered light.
     Prog. Reprod. Biol., 1:28-35, 1976.

13. Menezo, Y., Monget, D. and Guerin, J.F.   Diagramme enzymatique
     du spermatozoïde humain.   Application à l'étude in vitro des
     effets du chlorure de benzalkonium.   Contraception, Fertili-
     té, Sexualité, 7:208-211, 1979.

14. Murdoch, R.N. and White, I.G.   Studies of the distribution and
     source of enzymes in mammalian semen.   Austral. J. Biol. Sci.
     21:483-490, 1968.

15. Pace, M.M. and Graham, E.F.   The release of glutamic oxaloace-
     tic transaminase from bovine spermatozoa as a test method of
     assessing semen quality and fertility.   Biol. Reprod., 2:
     140-146, 1970.

16. Peterson, R.N. and Freund, M.   Profile of glytolytic enzyme
     activities in human spermatozoa.   Fertil and Steril., 21:2,
     151-158, 1970.

17. Sawada, Y., Ackerman, D. and Behrman, S.J.   Motility and respi-
     ration of human spermatozoa after cooling to various low
     temperatures.   Fertil. Steril., 18:6, 775-781, 1967.

18. Trifunac, N.P. and Bernstein, G.S.   Inhibition of the oxidative
     metabolism of human spermatozoa by a heat labile factor in
     seminal plasma.   Fertil. Steril., 27:11, 1295, 1976.

19. Guerin, J.F., Menezo, Y. and Czyba, J.C.   Enzyme profiles of
     human sperm and their modification after deep freezing.   Ar-
     chives of Andrology, Vol. 2, suppl. 1:33, 1979.

EFFECTS OF FREEZING ON SPERMATOZOA MOTILITY

Catherine Serres, Pierre Jouannet,
Françoise Czyglik and Georges David

Centre d'Etude et de Conservation du Sperme
(CECOS), Paris-Bicêtre
Kremlin-Bicêtre, France

INTRODUCTION

A decrease in spermatozoa motility is the most striking effect of semen freezing. Although motility is the semen characteristic which correlates best with fertility in bovines,[1] the same type of relation has yet to be demonstrated in man.[2-6] Nevertheless, the majority of investigators who have evaluated the effect of freezing techniques or frozen storage on the gamete have chosen motility as their primary parameter. This choice may be due, in part, to the simplicity of estimating motility by microscopic examination. Unfortunately, the examination of one drop of semen between a glass slide and coverslip is very subjective and can be the source of many errors. Accordingly, it is difficult to make valid comparisons among samples tested under different experimental conditions or in different laboratories.[7]

Laser Doppler Velocimetry(LDV) has permitted objective and rapid measurement of the number of motile cells in a spermatozoa population as well as the determination of their velocity distribution.[8] LDV is used in this study in order to quantify modifications in spermatozoa motility, particularly in respect to the influence of initial semen quality, dilution in cryoprotector medium and freezing and thawing procedures.

MATERIALS AND METHODS

The study consisted of two parts. The first was carried out
on a series of 90 ejaculates obtained from 48 men with proven fertility who wished to store their semen prior to vasectomy. Their semen
was tested for spermatozoa motility, modal velocity and velocity
distribution under the following conditions: In seminal plasma and
before freezing and after thawing in cryoprotector medium.

The second part of the study was performed with 5 ejaculates
from student volunteers which were evaluated for motility and vitality under the same three conditions described above.

All ejaculates were collected at the laboratory by masturbation
following a mean period of abstinence of 3.54 $\pm$ 0.13 days.

Freezing Technique

After 30 minutes of liquifaction at 37°C, the semen was diluted
volume for volume(1:1) with a cryoprotector medium containing gly-
cerol(15%), egg yolk, glucose and citrate.[2] The mixture was left
15 minutes at ambient temperature and then distributed into 0.25 ml
paillettes(straws). The paillettes were immediately frozen by placing them in a horizontal position in vapors of liquid nitrogen
(-60°C) for 7 minutes. They were then put into the liquid nitrogen
for storage.[9] Thawing took place on the same day by exposure for a
few minutes to ambient temperature.

Measurement of Motility

The laser doppler velocimeter is able to analyse variations
in the frequency of light scattered by motile spermatozoa. It is an
objective and rapid method which requires only a very small quantity
of semen.[8] An example of a frequency spectrum of scattered light
for one semen sample is given in Figure 1. Each frequency of the
spectrum corresponds to a density of spermatozoa for which the relationship between velocity and the frequency of scattered light
is explained by the Doppler effect.[8] Thus, it is possible to plot
the velocity distribution of a spermatozoa population through the
point by point derivation of the spectrum frequencies. The number
of motile forms is related to the density of the spectrum.

For raw human semen, the spectrum of scattered light lies under
100 Hz and is nearly always exponential, corresponding to a unimodal
Poisson-type velocity distribution.[10] In this case, the semi-log-
arithmic expression of the frequency spectrum yields a straight line,
the slope of which represents the mode of the velocity distribution.
This mode has been termed the characteristic velocity(Vc).

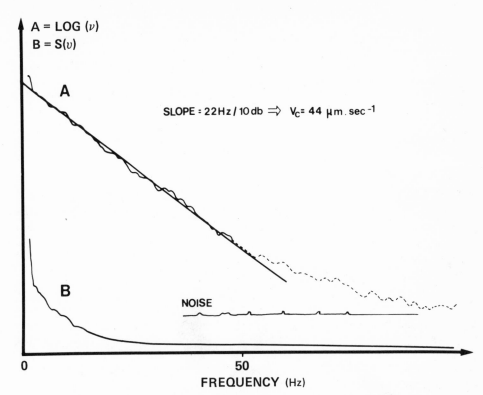

FIGURE 1. Frequency spectrum of scattered light for one
semen sample expressed directy(B) and logarithmically(A).

LDV measurements are made on a small portion of the semen which
is placed into a 100 μm deep well with a volume of 17 mm^3 in a block
of optical glass. All measurements are performed at 37°C.

Measurement of Vitality

Five ejaculates were studied for vitality. Measurements were
carried out on samples of raw semen and semen in cryoprotector medium both before and after freezing.

A 50 μl portion of spermatozoa sample was mixed with 50 μl of
a 0.5% ethidium bromide solution and 20 μl of a 0.00025% acridine
orange solution. This results in fluorescent staining of the spermatozoa; the living cells are colored red and the dead cells, green. For
each measurement, 200 cells were counted.

RESULTS

Semen freezing after dilution in cryoprotector medium did not cause any modification of the frequency spectrum of scattered light which remained exponential in all cases(Figure 2). This signifies that the unimodal Poisson-type velocity distribution remained unchanged under the conditions of this study(Figure 3). Only the slopes of the semi-logarithmically plotted spectra were found to vary which corresponds to differences in the number and velocity of the motile spermatozoa. Therefore, it is possible to compare their characteristic velocities(modal velocity) under different experimental conditions.

As shown for one ejaculate in Figure 2, the dilution in cryoprotector medium does not change the percentage of motile spermatozoa(74% versus 77%) but does result in an increase of characteristic velocity(75 μ/s versus 59 μ/s). Conversely, after thawing, there is a large drop in the percentage of motile spermatozoa(45%) whereas the characteristic velocity is little changed(69 μ/s).

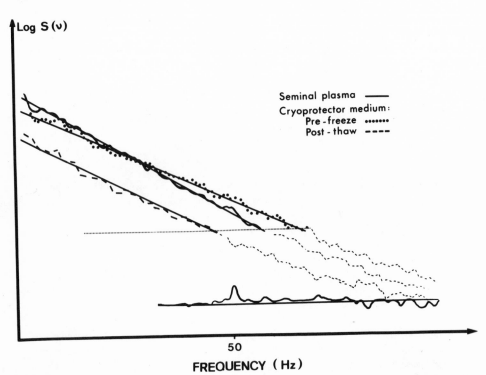

FIGURE 2. Frequency spectra for one semen sample in seminal plasma and before freezing and after thawing in cryoprotector medium.

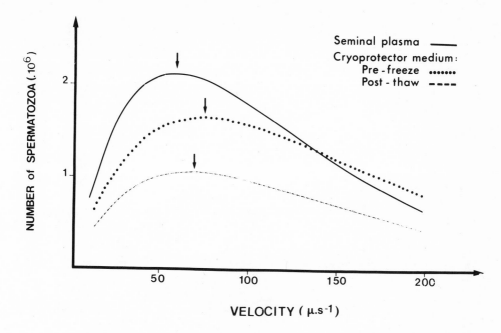

FIGURE 3. Velocity distributions for the spectra
presented in Figure 2.

Spermatozoa Motility

The percentage of motile spermatozoa in the 90 ejaculates
studied are presented in Figure 4. The mean motility is 77% $\pm$ 1.8
in seminal plasma, 65% $\pm$ 1.9 in cryoprotector medium and 41% $\pm$ 2.1
after thawing. The motility recovery rate(MRR), that is the percentage of motile spermatozoa recovered after freezing, was determined as follows:

$$ MRR = \frac{\text{\% Motile spermatozoa after thawing}}{\text{\% Motile spermatozoa in seminal plasma}} $$

For the 90 ejaculates tested, the MRR varied from 0.10 to 0.95
and the mean MRR was 0.53.

The MRR was not correlated with the length of abstinence prior
to semen collection($r = 0.08$). However, it was correlated with certain other semen variables: Sperm count ($r = 0.39$, $p < 10^{-4}$, percentage of normal forms ($r = 0.42$, $p < 10^{-2}$), percentage of motile

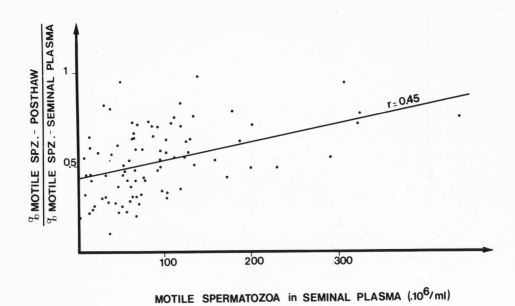

FIGURE 4. Percentage recovery for motile spermatozoa (MRR) as a function of initial motility.

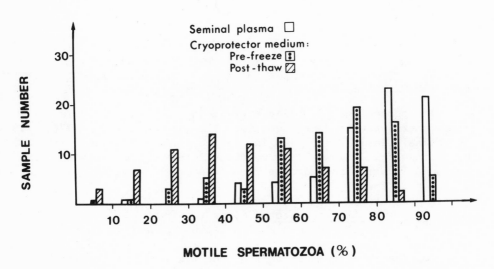

FIGURE 5. Distribution of the 90 ejaculates studied as a function of the percentage of motile spermatozoa in seminal plasma and before freezing and after thawing in cryoprotector medium.

spermatozoa($r = 0.45$, $p < 10^{-5}$), and concentration of motile spermatozoa($r = 0.45$, $p < 10^{-5}$)(Figure 5).

The two stages of the freezing procedure can be considered separately: The MRR after dilution in cryoprotector medium but before freezing was not correlated to the initial concentration of motile spermatozoa($r = 0.058$), whereas there was a correlation between the initial concentration of motile forms and the post-thaw MRR($r = 0.42$, $p < 10^{-4}$).

Characteristic Velocity(Vc)

The results for the Vc are presented in Figure 6. In the seminal plasma, the mean Vc was 57 µ/s $\pm$ 1.84. There was a significant increase in Vc after dilution in cryoprotector medium(67 µ/s $\pm$ 1.66, $p < 0.01$) which disappeared after freezing(59 µ/s $\pm$ 1.76).

As for motility, the proportion of Vc recovery or Vc recovery rate(VRR) can be calculated as follows:

$$VRR = \frac{Vc \text{ after thawing}}{Vc \text{ in seminal plasma}}$$

For the population studied, the mean VRR differed little from 1. However, there was a marked within group variability(0.49 to 1.47). Individual VRR results were not found to be correlated with either spermatozoa concentration in seminal plasma(Figure 7) or the initial Vc($r = 0.17$).

Evolution of Motility and Vitality

Assessments of motility and vitality as a function of time and medium were made on 5 ejaculates which presented different percentages of motile forms and different initial Vc levels in seminal plasma. In order to compare the results for different experimental conditions, the ratio of experimental to initial seminal plasma values was determined. In seminal plasma alone, there was a regular and progressive decrease in the percentage of motile forms; this decrease being 15% at 1 hour, 25% at 4 hours(Figure 8). Dilution in cryoprotector medium results in an immediate 15% decrease in the percentage of motile forms after which the evolution of motility loss parallels that of the seminal plasma. Spermatozoal vitality is little modified under the same conditions.

After thawing, there is a marked decrease in vitality which is 40% lower than that observed in seminal plasma. The decrease in the percentage of motile spermatozoa after thawing is of the same order, at least for the first 30 minutes. After 30 minutes, motility is lost at a greater rate than in unfrozen samples.

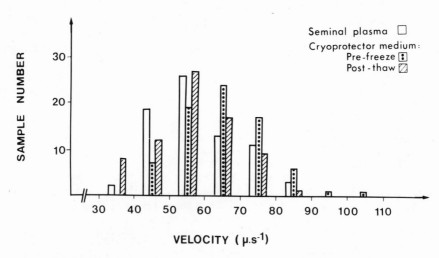

FIGURE 6.   Distribution of the ninety ejaculates as a
function of characteristic velocity in seminal plasma and
before freezing and after thawing in cryoprotector medium.

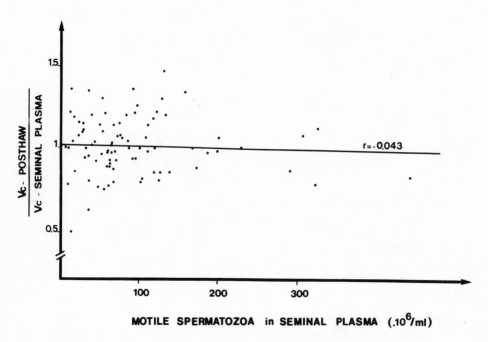

FIGURE 7.   Proportion of post-thaw recovery of motile
spermatozoa as a function of initial concentration in
seminal plasma

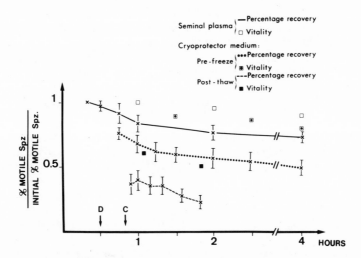

FIGURE 8. Evolution of the percentage recovery for spermatozoa motility and vitality as a function of time under different conditions: In seminal plasma, and before freezing and after thawing in cryoprotector medium(D denotes dilution and C, freezing).

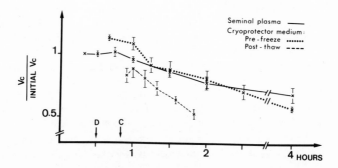

FIGURE 9. Evolution of the characteristic velocity as a function of time in seminal plasma and before freezing and after thawing in cryoprotector medium.

As for the Vc, it is stable in seminal plasma for the first
hour but then decreases progressively to two-thirds of its initial
value(69%) after 4 hours, dilution in cryoprotector medium causes
the Vc to rise initially, but this is followed by a decrease in the
Vc which is more rapid than that for spermatozoa in pure seminal
plasma. After thawing, the drop in Vc is both early and marked.

DISCUSSION

This study has confirmed that the freezing of semen results in
a large drop in the percentage of motile spermatozoa as has been
described by many authors. The decrease in motility was par-
alleled by a decrease in the proportion of living spermatozoa.
Through laser Doppler velocimetry(LDV), it has been possible to demonstrate that the velocity distribution and modal velocity(Vc) of
a spermatozoa sample is stable in the first 15 minutes after thawing.

The post-thaw recovery rates for motile spermatozoa after freezing reported by different investigators are quite variable but their
studies were not uniform in regard to subjects studied, freezing
techniques and measurement methods. In this study in fertile men,
a mean recovery rate of 53% was obtained.

Two questions are raised by the above observations: (1) What
is the role of technical conditions; and(2) are all the spermatozoa
affected in the same way by freezing? In regard to technical conditions, dilution in cryoprotector medium resulted in a decrease in
motile forms, an increase in velocity but little or no change in
vitality. The modifications of motility and velocity may have been
due to a "dilution effect" as described by White[11] and analysed by
Freund and Wiederman.[12] The latter authors found, however, that motility did decrease at high dilutions. Conversely, Matheson et al.[5]
consistently observed 10 to 20% drops in motility with dilutions of
only 1/2(1:1).

The initial increase observed in modal velocity(Vc) may simply
have been due to the semen's dilution. However, it was followed by
a decrease in Vc that was at a greater rate than in seminal fluid,
thus suggesting that the cryoprotector medium compromises spermatozoa survival. Regardless, it is the cryoaggression which has the
most detrimental effect on spermatozoa motility. Freezing results
in definitive cellular lesions as reflected by the decrease in vitality, the amplitude of this decrease being identical to that for
motility. The deleterious effect of cryoaggression is also reflected
in the fact that a semen with a similar pre-freeze and post-thaw
motility will show a much more rapid drop in motility with time after
thawing.

The large heterogeneity among ejaculates suggests that semen characteristics may have a role in the observed modifications. In this study, the recovery rate of motile spermatozoa varied from 0.10 to 0.95, an observation that has been made by others.[13-17] Large variations were also noted in the recovery of the modal velocity(0.49 to 1.47). To understand the reasons for this variability and to identify the semen characteristics which will permit one to predict the response to freezing are goals of all those involved in human semen cryopreservation. The responsibility of genetic factors has been evoked[18] but Beck and Silverstein[13] have shown that the recovery rate can be quite variable from one ejaculate to the other in the same person. There is no unanimity regarding the semen characteristics which correlate best with freezing tolerance: For certain investigators it is the percentage of motile spermatozoa and the sperm count[9,17] whereas for others, none of the semen characteristics are looked upon as good indices.[1,14,19]

In this study, the recovery rate for motile spermatozoa, the MRR,was best correlated with the fresh semen concentration of motile cells and the percentage of motile and normal forms. In fact, figure 5 shows that it was especially above 100×10^6 motile spermatozoa per ml that the MRR became significantly better; in the range of 0 to 100×10^6 and at times for identical values, MRR variability was quite high. Therefore, it would appear that other yet identified semen factors.

On the practical side, it appears necessary to test each ejaculate by thawing a paillette and determining the MRR. This approach would be particularly indicated in cases of autocryopreservation preceeding vasectomy[19] or sterilizing treatment[20] as is presently being practiced.

The processing of the semen in cryopreservation, that is the temperature patterns of freezing and thawing and the type of cryoprotector medium(concentration of glycerol and additives), appear to have an important influence on the results.[12,13,15,18,21] The rapid and progressive modification of spermatozoa motility observed in this study when left in contact with the cryoprotector medium suggests that the duration of the manipulation is an important factor. Although Sherman[18] has shown that 30 minutes of incubation with glycerol gives results which are no worse than with only a few seconds of incubation, others,[5,6,21] have stressed the importance of minimizing the time between ejaculation and freezing.

Another time factor is the period between thawing and insemination. Even though the percentage of motile spermatozoa was found to be stable in the 30 minutes after thawing, the Vc was found to drop rapidly. Therefore, carrying out insemination in the 10 or 15 minutes following thawing as suggested by Rubin[15] would seem advised.

CONCLUSION

Cryopreservation of human spermatozoa resulted in a 47% decrease in the percentage of motile forms. Two-thirds of this decrease was due to cryoaggression and one third to dilution in cryoprotector medium. The high variability in the post-thaw recovery of motile spermatozoa with different ejaculates indicates that each must be tested after thawing. There is no evidence that the analysis of fresh semen allows one to predict freezing tolerance.

Future studies on cryotolerance must take into account the time elapsed between ejaculation or thawing and measurements as well as the nature of the cryoprotector medium and the degree of semen dilution. Also, measurements should be made using objective techniques rather than microscopic methods.

REFERENCES

1. Graham, E.F., Schmehl, M.K.L., Evensen, B.K. and Nelson, D.S. Viability assays for frozen semen., Cryobiology, 15:242-244, 1978.

2. Behrman, S.J. and Sawada, Y. Heterologous and homologous insemination with human semen frozen and stored in a liquid nitrogen refrigerator. Fertil. Steril., 17:457, 1966.

3. Bunge, R.G. and Sherman, J.K. Fertilizing capacity of frozen human spermatozoa. Nature, 172 767, 1953.

4. Friberg, J. and Gemzell, C. Inseminations of human sperm after freezing in liquid nitrogen vapors with glycerol or glycerol-egg-yolk-citrate as protective media. Am. J. Obstet. Gynec., 116:330-334, 1973.

5. Matheson, G., Carlborg, L. and Gemzell, C. Frozen human semen for artificial insemination. Am. J. Obst. Gynec., 104:495-501, 1969.

6. Sawada, Y., Ackerman, D. and Behrman, S.J. Motility and respiration of human spermatozoa after cooling to various low temperatures. Fertil. Steril., 6:775-781, 1967.

7. Van Duijn, C., Van Voorst, C. and Freund, M. Movement characteristics of human spermatozoa analysed from kinemicrographs. Europ. J. Obstet. Gynec., 4:121-135, 1971.

8. Dubois, N., Jouannet, P., Berge, P., Volochine, B., Serres, C. and David, G. Méthode et appareillage de mesure objective de la mobilité des spermatozoïdes humains. Ann. Phys. Biol. et Méd., 9:19-41, 1975.

9. David, G. and Czyglik, F. Tolérance à la congélation du sperme humain en fonction de la qualité initiale du sperme. J. Gyn. Obst. Biol. Repr., 6:601, 1977.

10. Jouannet, P., Volochine, B., Deguent, P., Serres, C. and David, G. Light scattering determination of various characteristic parameters of spermatozoa motility in a serie of human sperm. Andrologia, 9;36-49, 1977.

11. White, J.G. The effect of some seminal constituents and related substances on diluted mammalian spermatozoa. Aust. J. Biol. Sci., 7:379, 1954.

12. Freund, M. and Wiederman, J. Factors affecting the dilution freezing and storage of human semen. J. Reprod. Fertil., 11:1-17, 1966.

13. Beck, W. and Silverstein, I. Variable motility recovery of spermatozoa following freeze preservation. Fertil. Steril., 26:863, 1975.

14. Emperaire, J.C. and Riviere, J. La congélation du sperme humain normal. J. Gyn. Obstet. Biol. Reprod., 3:215-222, 1974.

15. Rubin, S.O., Andersson, L. and Bostrom, K. Deep-freeze preservation of normal and pathologic human sperm. Scand. J. Urol. Nephrol., 3:144-150, 1969.

16. Silbert, J.A. Large scale preservation of human semen. Cryobiologie, 9:556-558, 1972.

17. Smith, K.D. and Steinberger, E. Survival of spermatozoa in a human sperm bank. JAMA, 7:774-777, 1973.

18. Sherman, J.K. Freezing and freeze-drying of human spermatozoa. Fertil. Steril., 5:357-371, 1954.

19. Jouannet, P., Jardin, A., Czyglik, F., David, G. and Fourcade, R. Conservation du sperme et vasectomie. Séminaire d'uro-néphrologie, 5:113-120, P. Küss et M. Legrain Eds, Masson, Paris, 1979.

20. David, G. and Czyglik, F.   Indications néphrologiques de la
    conservation du sperme.   <u>Séminaire d'uro-néphrologie</u>,
    94, 1979.

21. Menkin, N.F., Lusis, P., Zaikis, J.P. and Rock, J.   Refrigérant
    preservation of human spermatozoa.   II factors influencing
    recovery in oligo and euspermie semen.   <u>Fertil. Steril.</u>, 15:
    551-527, 1964.

SEMEN FREEZING IN 0.5 AND 0.25 ML STRAWS

Jean-Claude Emperaire*
and Françoise Czyglik**

*Centre de Physiopathologie de la Reproduction
    et de la Sexualité Humaine
Hôpital Xavier Arnozan
Pessac, France
**Centre d'Etude et de Conservation du Sperme
    (CECOS), Paris-Bicêtre
Kremlin-Bicêtre, France

It is striking to note that the evolution of improvements
brought about in human semen freezing have followed, with a long
delay, the results of veterinary research on animal breeding, mostly
in the cattle. The use of liquid nitrogen, for instance, as a cooling agent for human semen, appeared only in 1963;[1] at this time, the
semen was still dispensed in glass ampules, although the plastic
straw had been used in cattle breeding for at least ten years.[2] Up
to 1973, no work involved the so-called fine straw of 0.25 ml in volume which has been used with cattle since 1965.[3]

The 0.25 ml straw has replaced the 0.5 ml straw in veterinary
insemination for several reasons, the main ones being a better sperm-
atoza recovery rate as well as improved insemination results;[4] the
1.2 ml straw had already been discarded in favor of the 0.5 ml straw
for the same reasons.[5] The reduction of the insemination dose would
also appear to be of great interest in a country where the donor
problem is acute, providing clinical success rates are comparable.

The present study using human semen was undertaken to compare
the spermatozoa recovery rate for 0.25 and 0.5 ml straws after freezing with liquid nitrogen. To our knowledge, this is the first study
of its type in man.

MATERIEL AND METHODS

Semen was collected at the laboratory by masturbation. After liquefaction at room temperature, a sample was taken for evaluation of concentration, vitality, initial (prefreeze) motility and morphology. The semen was then mixed one to one by volume with Ackerman protective medium.[6] The final glycerol concentration of the mixture was 7 to 7.5%. After an equilibration period of 15 to 20 minutes at room temperature, the mixture was dispensed into both 0.25 and 0.5 ml straws which were sealed at both ends. In this study, there were 31 ejaculates, 23 normal and 8 oligo-asthenospermic, which produced a total of 186 straws (93 of each type). An Air Liquide RCB 60 T was used for both freezing and storing the straws. The freezing process was a fast, one step cooling method described for both the 0.5 ml[7] and the 0.25 ml[8,9] straws. Both types of straws from the same ejaculate were frozen in the same operation and at the same time. Taken at room temperature, the straws were placed horizontally for 7 to 10 minutes in the nitrogen vapors at a distance above the liquid nitrogen surface of 8 cm (temperature - 150°C) for the 0.5 ml straw, and of 20 to 25 cm (temperature - 60°C) for the 0.25 ml straw. Afterwards, they were plunged directly into the liquid nitrogen where they were stored.

The straws were thawed simply by exposure to room temperature for 10 minutes. Both types of straws from the same ejaculate were evaluated at the same time; double-blind measurement of the post-freeze motility was performed by the same two technicians.

RESULTS

Figure 1 shows the temperature variations of the mixture within both types of straws during the freezing and the thawing processes.

Figure 2 shows the spermatozoa recovery rate (SRR) with both types of straws. Although the SRR appears higher for the 0.5 ml straw, statistical analysis failed to reveal a significant difference.

DISCUSSION

The plastic straw is the most widely used container for semen preservation throughout the world because of easy manipulation, handling, labelling and storage. It facilitates the insemination procedure since it can be used in a specially designed syringe.

The size of the straw has been progressively reduced in veterinary insemination. Early straws held 1 ml, but were rapidly

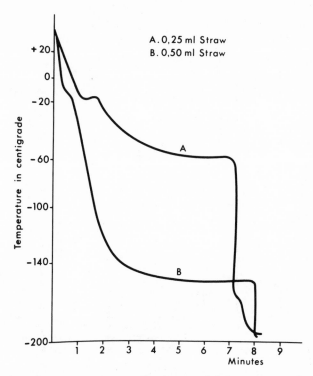

FIGURE 1.   Temperature variations within straws during freezing.

replaced by the 0.5 ml straw which gave equivalent efficacy.   The fine straw has been preferred to the large one in veterinary insemination for 15 years for two mean reasons: (1) It has been shown that only some 300,000 live spermatozoa are needed to impregnate a cow, though the bull semen holds above 700×10^6 spermatozoa per ml;[10]   (2) the post-thaw motility of bovine semen has proven better when frozen in fine straws than in large ones, probably because of a better and faster temperature distribution within its contents.[11]

With normal human semen, the spermatozoa recovery rate using this freeze-thaw procedure has been reported to be 58 to 69% with the 0.5 ml straw[6,7,12,13] and around 60% with the 0.25 straw;[6] in this latter study on freezing tolerance, the SRR with 0.25 ml straws depended upon prefreeze characteristics, even when in normal range.   The recovery rate was higher when the concentration of the ejaculate exceeded 50 million spermatozoa per ml; it also positively correlated both with prefreeze motility, being higher when above 65%, and with morphology, being higher when there were more than 60% normal forms.[9]   These findings agree with those that had been published earlier for the 0.5 ml straw and other containers.[14,15,16]

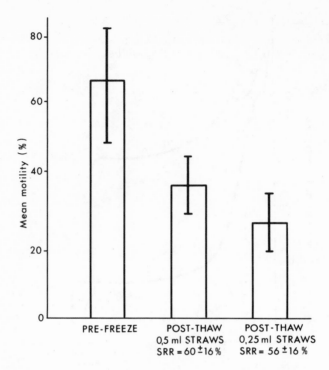

FIGURE 2. Pre-freeze motility and post-thaw spermatozoa recovery rate(SRR) for 0.5 and 0.25 ml straws in 31 semen specimens. Students't test: P = 0.7, non-significant.

The present double blind study did not reveal a significant difference in SRR between the two types of straws, and on this basis, the fine straw appears at least as satisfactory as the large one.

In terms of ability to achieve fertilization, the fine straw has proven to be more efficient in large bovine studies.[17] In humans, no such comparative study is available. Data reported in the literature are difficult to assess, since most studies are more concerned with the variable of female partner fertility. Furthermore, the presentation of results differs from one author to the next: Dropouts, for instance, are not always taken into account. With these qualifications in mind, the pregnancy rate ranges from 50 to 60% for the 0.5 ml straw with 90% of the pregnancies occuring with six insemination cycles.[12,18,19] Those studies performed with the 0.25 ml straw have yielded similar results according to our calculations from their raw data.[8,20]

It has been stated that 25 million motile spermatozoa per 0.5 ml straw are necessary for an acceptable conception rate.[19] As just mentioned, however, comparable results have been obtained with the

0.25 ml straw which contains about 10 million motile spermatozoa. Therefore, it appears that the same pregnancy rate can be maintained despite a reduction of the insemination volume and, thereby, the number of spermatozoa, a hypothesis supported by animal studies.[10]

CONCLUSION

This study has shown that there is no significant difference in cryotolerance between spermatozoa frozen in 0.5 ml and 0.25 plastic straws based upon post-thaw recovery of motile forms. Although clinical studies have reported similar results in artificial insemination using semen frozen in either 0.5 or 0.25 ml straws, none have compared the fertilizing capacity of these two straws directly and thus equivalent efficacy is presently presumptive.

REFERENCES

1. Sherman, J.K. Improved methods of preservation of human spermatozoa by freezing and freeze-drying. _Fertil. Steril._, 14: 49, 1963.

2. Cassou, R. Congélation du sperme du taureau conditionné en paillettes de matière plastique. _CR Soc. Biol._, 144:486, 1950.

3. Emperaire, J.C., Hurpy, R. and Riviere, J. Congélation comparée des spermes humain et bovin. Application à la mise au point d'une méthode de congélation du sperme humain en paillettes fines. _J. Gyn. Obst. Biol. Repr._, 20:707, 1973.

4. Jondet, R. Influence de la réduction du volume de la dose de sperme congelé et de sa teneur en spermatozoïdes sur la fécondation des vaches inséminées artificiellement. _Proc. VI° Cong. Int. Reprod. Anim. Insem. Artif._ Paris, 2:1061, 1968.

5. Jondet, R. Advances in semen preservation. In: _Artificial breeding of farm animals,_ The Irish genesiology Society, Dublin, p. 87, 1967.

6. Behrman, S.J. and Ackerman, D.R. Freeze preservation of human semen. _Amer. J. Obstet. Gynecol._ 103:654, 1969.

7. Empereraire, J.C. and Riviere, J. La congélation du sperme humain normal. _J. Gyn. Obst. Biol. Repr._ 3:215, 1974.

8. Czyglik, F. La conservation du sperme humain par congélation et ses applications. _Gynécologie_ 27:147, 1976.

9. David, G. and Czyglik, F.   Tolérance à la congélation du sperme humain en fonction de la qualité initiale du sperme.   J. Gyn. Obst. Biol. Repr., 6:5-601, 1977.

10. Jondet, R.   Fertilité et nombre minimal de spermatozoïdes en insémination artificielle bovine.   CR Soc. Biol. 163:12-2678, 1969.

11. Meryman, H.T.   The freezing process.   In: Recent research in freezing and drying, Parkes A.S. and Smith, A. Ed., Blackwell Scientific Publications, Oxford, G.B., p. 320, 1960.

12. Lebech, P.E.   Banques de sperme humain.   In: Fécondité et Stérilité du Mâle, C. Thibault Ed., Masson et Co., Paris, France, p. 349, 1972.

13. Matheson, G.W., Carlborg, L. and Gemzell, C.   Frozen human semen for artificial insemination.   Amer. J. Obstet. Gynecol., 106:495, 1969.

14. Sawada, Y. and Ackerman, D.R.   Use of frozen semen.   In: Progress in infertility.   Behrman, S.J. and Kistner, R.W. Ed., Little Brown and C°, Boston, p. 731, 1968.

15. Smith, K.D. and Steinberger, E.   Survival of spermatozoa in a human sperm bank.   Effects of long term storage in liquid nitrogen.   JAMA 223:7-774, 1973.

16. Ulstein, M.   Fertility, motility and penetration in cervical mucus of freeze-preserved human spermatozoa.   Acta Obstet. Gynec. Scand. 52:205, 1973.

17. Cassou, R.   Unpublished data.

18. Ansbacher, R.   Artificial insemination with frozen spermatozoa. Fertil. Steril. 29:4-375, 1978.

19. Matthews, C.D., Broom, T.J., Crawshaw, K.M., Hopkins, R.E., Kerin, J.F.F. and Svigos, J.M.   The influence of insemination timing and semen characteristics on the efficiency of a donor insemination program.   Fertil. Steril., 29:375. 1978.

20. Schwartz, D., Mayaux, B.A., Martin-Boyce, A., Czyglik, F. and David, G.   Donor insemination: Conception rate according to cycle day in a series of 821 cycles with a single insemination.   Fertil. Steril., 31:226, 1979.

SURVIVAL OF HUMAN SPERMATOZOA AFTER

FREEZING WITH DIFFERENT TECHNIQUES

Jan Friberg

Department of Obstetrics and Gynecology
Downstate Medical Center
Brooklyn, New York, U.S.A.

In comparison with the extensive use of frozen semen in veterinary medicine, farily slow progress in the cryopreservation of human semen has been seen over the past ten years. The primary reason for this is probably the reduced conception rate that is being observed with frozen semen in comparison with fresh semen.[1,3] There is also some evidence that certain women cannot conceive with frozen-thawed semen whereas they easily conceive with fresh semen. These disadvantages have called for continued investigation in order to improve the techniques for freezing of human spermatozoa.

There are principally two different techniques for the freezing of human semen currently being used. In the method introduced by Sherman,[9,10] semen and glycerol are mixed in the proportion of 10 to 1. The freezing is performed in vapors of liquid nitrogen. We have called this the "direct" freezing method. In the method of Behrman and Sawada,[2] semen is mixed in the proportion 1 to 1 with a glycerol-egg yolk-citrate buffer. We have exclusively used French straws, or "paillettes", as containers for both the freezing of semen and its handling during insemination.

The temperature variation during the freezing procedure is quite marked as shown in Figure 1. In Sherman's method, the paillettes are kept in liquid nitrogen vapors for 8 minutes and then lowered down into the liquid nitrogen. Because of the narrowness of the opening of our liquid nitrogen container, the paillettes were frozen in vertical position. The semen sample is quickly super-cooled to -15°C. As the sample starts to freeze, the temperature rises to -8°C and then falls off very quickly. In the lower part of the paillette, which is close to the surface of liquid nitrogen the temperature goes down to -110°C. In Behrman-Sawada's freezing method,

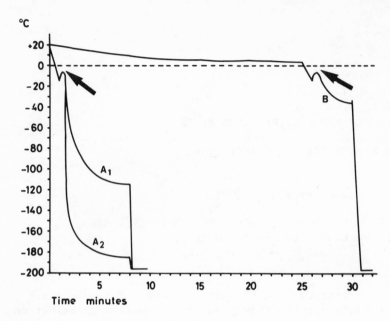

FIGURE 1.   Temperature variation of semen during freezing :
A. Sherman's or the "direct" method, A_1 being the curve for
the semen in the lower portion of the paillette closest to
the liquid nitrogen and A_2 that for the upper portion of the
paillette.
B. Behrman-Sawada's or the gradual method.
The arrow indicates the range of heat diffusion.

the semen sample is kept at +4°C for 20 minutes and temperature
equilibrium is reached in about this time. The specimen is then
moved to a vessel containing alcohol at -40°C where it is kept for
5 minutes before it is lowered into liquid nitrogen.[7] In this method the temperature changes show approximately the same pattern as
in the "direct" freezing but takes slightly longer.

The temperature rise during room temperature thawing of a semen
sample is shown in figure 2. The same pattern is seen irrespective
of whether the semen was frozen with glycerol or glycerol-egg yolk
citrate as a protective medium. Near -8°C the curve levels out for
about 1 1/2 minutes after which the temperature continues to rise.
During this plateau, the semen sample thaws. Investigation has
indicated that room temperature is superior for thawing as compared
to a +37°C water bath or a +4°C waterbath.[7]

Spermatozoa frozen without a protective medium are severely
damaged and lack progressive motility. The most pronounced damage

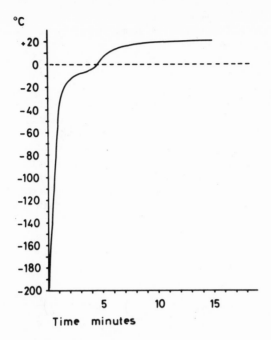

FIGURE 2. Temperature rise during room temperature
thawing of a semen sample from -196°C.

in these spermatozoa as observed in transmission electron microscopy
is incurred by the mitocondria which are swollen and in some instances ruptured. The acrosome has also been noted to be wrinkled
and ruptured. After freezing with a protective medium, the mitocondria retain better their normal morphology. With glycerol as a
protective medium, the acrosome is much more wrinkled than when
glycerol-egg yolk-citrate has been used. Our impression, therefore,
is that freezing of spermatozoa according to Behrman-Sawada causes
less damage than freezing with Sherman's method.[4]

Although post-thaw spermatozoa motility in some studies appears
to have a poor correlation with fertilizing capacity of the semen
sample, it is still probably the best single parameter to use in
order to evaluate how well a freezing technique works. We have
compared the effect of different freezing methods and the effect
of glycerol and glycerol-egg yolk-citrate on the post-thaw motility
of different donor semen samples. In this study the motility of
a fresh semen sample was followed for 12 hours. Aliquots of the
same semen sample were frozen according to Sherman[9] and Behrman-
Sawada.[2] In addition, aliquots of the specimens were also frozen
according to Sherman but with glycerol-egg yolk-citrate as the protective medium and according to Behrman-Sawada but with glycerol
as the protective medium. After thawing, spermatozoa motility was

followed at room temperature for 12 hours. Surprisingly, great variations were observed within the same donor's semen sample when it had been frozen according to the different methods. Figure 4 shows a donor semen sample with an 80% retained motility of the spermatozoa after freezing and thawing. No major variations were observed between the different freezing methods. Figure 5 shows for one semen sample a 50% motility reduction for all the methods as compared to the fresh semen. In other semen samples, motility varied and was quite good after direct freezing but was almost nil after gradual freezing. The use of different protective media also seems to have an influence on the results.[6] These findings were relatively constant when different ejaculates from the same donor were tested on repeated occasions and indicate that several freezing methods have to be used in order to get an optional post-thaw motility of the spermatozoa for a given donor.

I SEMEN:GLYCEROL(10:1) RAPID FREEZING IN LIQUID NITROGEN VAPORS (SHERMAN METHOD)		III SEMEN:GLYCEROL-EGG YOLK-CITRATE(1:1) GRADUAL FREEZING $(+4° \to -40° \to -196°$ C) (BEHRMAN-SAWADA METHOD)
	C CONTROL FRESH SEMEN	
II SEMEN:GLYCEROL(10:1) GRADUAL FREEZING $(+4° \to -40° \to -196°)$		IV SEMEN:GLYCEROL-EGG YOLK-CITRATE(1:1) RAPID FREEZING IN LIQUID NITROGEN VAPORS

FIGURE 3. Different techniques used for evaluation of motility of human spermatozoa after freezing in liquid nitrogen.

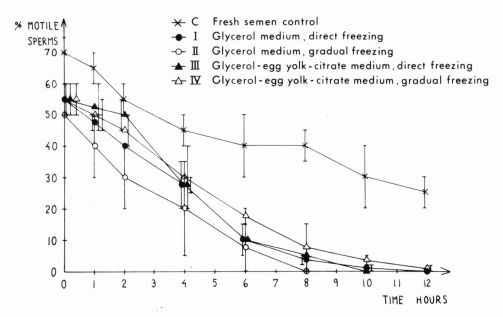

FIGURE 4. Motility of a semen sample after freezing in liquid nitrogen. All techniques tested show approximately an 80% retained motility and a 12 hour *in vitro* survival.

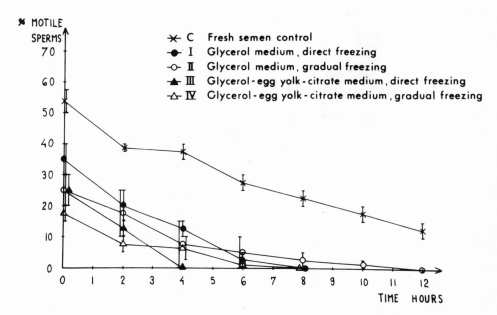

FIGURE 5. Motility reduction of 50% in a semen sample frozen in liquid nitrogen.

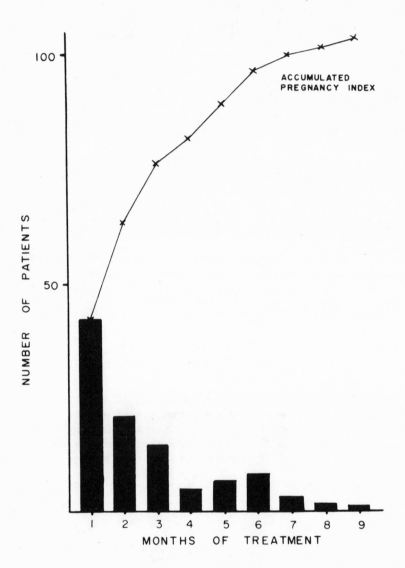

FIGURE 6. Number of months(treatment cycles) prior to conception. The cumulative pregnancy index is represented by the curve.

The ability of glycerol or glycerol-egg-yolk-citrate to protect spermatozoa during direct freezing was also investigated in
clinical trials: 83 patients were inseminated with frozen semen
during 93 ovulatory cycles in which glycerol was used as a protective medium and during 94 cycles in which glycerol-egg-yolk-citrate
was used as the protective medium. When glycerol was used, 10 conceptions occurred but with glycerol-egg yolk-citrate, we had 16
conceptions.[5] Statistically, there is no difference between these
two groups but we have to remember that considerably higher concentrations of spermatozoa were used with glycerol as a protective
medium since the semen sample is diluted 10 to 1 with glycerol whereas the semen mixed with glycerol-egg-yolk-citrate is diluted in the
proportion of 1:1. In this study we also examined the patients 24
hours after insemination for surviving spermatozoa in the cervical
mucus. With both glycerol and glycerol-egg-yolk citrate as protective medium, a few surviving spermatozoa were noted in 60% of the
patients, but no correlation of surviving spermatozoa with subsequent pregnancy was noted.[5]

Our use of frozen semen has resulted in 103 conceptions giving
90 live births. Figure 6 indicates the number of months used
for the insemination before pregnancy occurred. It can be seen
that about 75% of all pregnancies occurred within the first 3 months
of treatment and 94% within 6 months of treatment.[6] When one considers the significance of such figures, insemination with frozen
semen should probably only be done for 6 months; then fresh semen
should be used.

Of the ninety normal children, 42 were boys and 48 girls.
Thirteen pregnancies ended with spontaneous abortion which is the
expected frequency of spontaneous abortion in a Swedish population.[8]

REFERENCES

1.   Behrman, S.J. and Ackerman, D.R.   Freeze preservation of human
        sperm. Am. J. Obstet. Gynecol., 103:654-664, 1969.

2.   Behrman, S.J. and Sawada, Y.   Heterologous and homologous inse-
        minations with human semen frozen and stored in a liquid
        nitrogen refrigerator. Fertil. Steril., 17:457:466, 1966.

3.   Carlborg, L.   Some problems involved in freezing and insemination
        with human sperm. In: A. Ingelman-Sundberg and N.O. Lunell,
        Eds, Current problems in fertility, pp. 23-27, Plenum Press,
        New York, 1971.

4. Friberg, J. and Nilsson, O. Motility and morphology of human
     sperms after freezing in liquid nitrogen. In: A. Ingelman-
     Sundberg and N.O. Lunell Eds., Current problems in fertility,
     pp. 17-22, Plenum Press, New York, 1971.

5. Friberg, J. and Gemzell, C. Inseminations of human sperm after
     freezing in liquid nitrogen vapors with glycerol or glycerol-
     egg-yolk-citrate as protective media. Am. J. Obstet. Gynecol.
     116:330-334, 1973.

6. Friberg, J. and Gemzell, C. Sperm freezing and donor insemina-
     tion. Int. J. Fertil., 22:148-154, 1977.

7. Matheson, G.W., Carlborg, L. and Gemzell, C. Frozen human semen
     for artificial insemination. Am. J. Obstet. Gynecol., 104:
     495-501, 1969.

8. Petterson, F. Epidemiology of early pregnancy wastage. Scandi-
     navian University Books. Stockholm, 1968.

9. Sherman, J.K. Improved methods of preservation of human sperm-
     atozoa by freezing and freeze-drying. Fertil. Steril., 14:
     49-64, 1963.

10. Sherman, J.K. Research on frozen human semen. Past, present,
     future. Fertil. Steril. 15:485-499, 1964.

CLINICAL USE OF HUMAN SEMEN

AFTER LONG-TERM STORAGE

Stanley Friedman

Department of Obstetrics and Gynecology
UCLA School of Medicine
Los Angeles, California, USA

The single pregnancy, following insemination of human semen which had been frozen and stored for 10 years, is often cited to indicate that such long-term storage is efficacious. To my knowledge, however, there is no published data concerning the clinical and practical aspects of long-term storage of human sperm. With an anticipated proliferation of semen banks, and an anticipated increase in the number of men having vasectomies, it is important to gather whatever information is currently available about long-term storage of human semen. With this information, some predictions may be made about the clinical usefulness of this technic, problems attendant to it may be identified, and avenues of research to ameliorate such problems may be suggested.

The Tyler Medical Clinic established a sperm bank in 1969. The primary objective of the bank was to facilite AID for women with infertile husbands. However, urologists in Southern California who learned of the existence of the bank, began to refer men for storage of sperm prior to vasectomy, or prior to treatment for genital cancer which would result in sterility. Later, men were referred prior to therapy for other forms of malignancies, such as Hodgkin's disease, or prior to the use of drugs for other major diseases which might render them infertile. Without actively seeking such candidates for long-term storage, within 10 years, 335 men deposited specimens for possible future use (Table 1): 182 were prevasectomy, 153 pre-therapeutic sterilization. The number of semen specimens obtained from each man varied from 1 to 8. Many of the specimens were divided into 2 aliquots prior to storage.

Only 3 couples returned postvasectomy for AI (Table 2). The pre-freeze counts and motility were within normal limits. The letters

175

TABLE 1. *Semen storage*

	Prevasectomy	Pre-cancer Therapy
Number (1969-1978)	182	153
Current (Feb 1979)	137	128

are our method of grading the degree of motility and forward progression. "A" and "AB" are considered normal with excellent to good forward progression ; "B" and "C" are abnormal with poor or no forward progression or very sluggish movement. Post-thaw motility varied considerably. One conception occurred with a 7-year old specimen with a single insemination. Motility of this thawed specimen was quite good. The other two couples each had only 2 cycles of AI, without success.

Nine couples returned after therapeutic sterilization(Table 3). The first 8 had cancer therapy, the 9th had received a drug for the treatment of severe arthritis. Pre-freeze counts and motility for the cancer patients averaged 40 million with 50% motility, somewhat below normal limits. This suggested that the underlying disease probably was affecting spermatogenesis. In our experience, pre-freeze motility of 50% carries a poor prognosis, and this was borne out here. The post-thaw motility averaged 25% and there were no pregnancies in this group. The specimens of two of the men were mailed out of the city to other physicians who performed the AIs and we have no follow-up information on the post-thaw specimens of the results of the AIs. We presume there were no pregnancies.

In order to learn more about the effects of long-term storage, specimens from men who had broken contact with the Clinic were thawed. In regard to this, I think it appropriate to comment on the

TABLE 2. *AI with prevasectomy specimens*

Pt.	Years of Storage	Pre-freeze Count	Pre-freeze Motility	Post-thaw Count	Post-thaw Motility	Pregnancy
RC·	7	80	75AB	65	45AB	Yes
JL	1 1/2	60	60A	60	15AB	No
EL	1/3	?	40AB	?	30B	No

TABLE 3. *AI with pre-cancer therapy specimens*

Pt.	Years of storage	Prefreeze		Post-thaw		Pregnancy
		Count	Motility	Count	Motility	
KK	3	50	60AB	55	15B	No
GH	2	20	40AB	*	*	No
RS	1 1/2	10	20B	5	20B	No
SB	1	?	60AB	100	20AB	No
JM	1	60	50AB	*	*	No
CA	1	60	60AB	70	25AB	No
FW	1	70	75AB	70	45AB	No
CJ	1/2	10	45AB	10	20AB	No
EM	2	60	60AB	?	50B	No

* Specimens used by other physicians

contractual arrangements entered into between the Clinic and these
men. Before accepting semen for storage, a form is signed by the
donor absolving the Clinic of any responsability should the semen
be destroyed, spoiled, or lost. The donor also agrees co pay an
annual storage fee, now $40.00. The fee is the same regardless of
the number of specimens per donor. Should the fee not be paid, and
the donor fails to respond to further requests for payment, the specimens may be discarded. In actual practice, we have only discarded
58 of the 335 specimens, despite the fact that many more storage
payments are outstanding. The legality of our contract is questionable, never having been challenged, and therefore we are not overly
aggressive in discarding specimens.

Nevertheless, we have discarded a number of specimens and recently we took motion pictures of some of those which had been stored
for long periods. We had not heard from the donors of these specimens in a number of years and efforts to contact them were unsuccessful. About 15 such specimens were thawed after 6 to 7 years of
storage.

The results of long-term storage were unpredictable. Some specimens maintained good motility, most others did not, although initial
motilities were comparable. The motility of specimens from the same
donor showed significant variations. Because of this unpredictabi-
lity, it is important not to oversell the concept of "vasectomy

insurance" as is being done by some commercial semen banks in the United States. When semen is being deposited, one must emphasize that long-term storage is not a guarantee that fertility can be preserved with current technology.

LIMITS OF LONG TERM SEMEN CRYOPRESERVATION

Georges David and Françoise Czyglik

Centre d'Etude et de Conservation du Sperme
  (CECOS), Paris-Bicêtre
Kremlin-Bicêtre, France

The problem of long term cryopreservation of semen in man is of particular concern in preventive autocryopreservation which finds its indications in men about to undergo vasectomy or a treatment which carries a risk of sterility. In such cases, it is necessary to have assurances that the fertilizing capacity of the frozen semen will be maintained for many years. Despite the importance of this problem, it has been considered in only two studies.[1,2] However, these studies used only motility as a criterion and their results were contradictory.

The objective of this study is to assess the consequences of semen cryopreservation on both motility and fertilizing capacity for periods up to 5 years.

MATERIALS AND METHODS

For the study of motility, 68 ejaculates from as many fertile men were used: 63 being AID donors and 5 about to undergo treatment carrying a risk of sterilization.

Fertilizing capacity was the object of two studies. The first explored short-term fertilizing capacity, that is during the first year of cryopreservation: A comparison was made between the mean success rate per cycle for 874 semen doses stored for 6 months or less and 445 doses stored for 6 to 12 months.

Unfortunately, it was not possible to continue studying fertilizing capacity in this manner beyond 12 months due to the rapid turn-over of semen doses held by the Sperm Bank. However, a certain

179

number of paillettes from ejaculates giving pregnancies are set
aside in order that women requesting a second pregnancy can be
treated with the same ejaculate. Therefore, only these women could
be used for the second study which concerned long-term fertilizing
capacity of cryopreserved semen. Since it was decided to use the
mean number of cycles necessary for conception as the mode of evaluation, only 51 women who actually achieved a second pregnancy were
included. They were divided into 2 groups: 25 who had conceived
with semen stored for 1 to 3 years and 26 who had conceived with
semen stored for 3 to 6 years. These two groups were then compared.
It was not possible to compare the first and second pregnancy treatment periods since for technical reasons, different ejaculates had
been used with most patients in the cycles preceeding their first
pregnancy.

                                RESULTS

     The 68 ejaculates used for the study of motility had the follow-
ing pre-freeze characteristics: A mean sperm count of 116 x10^6/ml
(SD = 72.6) and a mean of 71.9%(SD $\pm$ 9.1) motile forms. After one
day of storage, there was a post-thaw motility of 46.4%(SD $\pm$ 12.4).
A second evaluation made after 5 to 6 years of storage revealed a
post-thaw motility of 43.2(SD $\pm$ 12.2). There is no significant difference in these results.

     In regard to fertilizing capacity in the first year of storage,
the mean success rate per cycle was 10% for both the 874 doses stored
less than 6 months and the 445 doses stored for 6 to 12 months. As
to long term fertilizing capacity, the 25 second pregnancies obtained
with semen stored for 1 to 3 years and the 26 obtained with semen
stored 3 to 5 years were achieved in a mean of 2.9($\pm$ 2.1) and 2.8
($\pm$ 2.4) cycles respectively.

                               DISCUSSION

     This study has demonstrated stability in spermatozoa motility
for up to 5 years. This is in agreement with the findings of
Sherman[1] on 25 ejaculates freeze stored for 10 years: Even though
he found individual variations in motility, the mean percentage of
motile forms did not differ significantly with time. However,
Steinberger[2] has reported a substantial decrease in motility beyond
3 years of storage and after 5 years he found that motility was only
20% of the pre-freeze value. He also found that the loss of motility was quite variable according to the sample. High quality semen
with an initial motility of 60 to 89% and a sperm count of 40 to
200 million/ml showed a much smaller decrease in motility with time.

The principle concern in cryopreservation, of course, is the semen's ability to give a pregnancy and this has never been systematically studied. Sherman[1] has simply reported 3 pregnancies(2 normal births and 1 miscarriage) obtained with semen stored for 10 years, a result that has never been equaled, much less surpassed. Therefore, it may very well be that these were exceptional cases. The results of the present study indicate that the fertilizing capacity of cryopreserved semen is maintained for at least 5 years since: (1) No significant difference in the success rate per cycle was found between the first and second 6 month periods in the first year of storage for 68 ejaculates; and(2) similar delays for a second pregnancy were observed for 25 women inseminated with semen stored 1 to 3 years and for 26 women inseminated with semen stored 3 to 5 years. Although it has not been possible to compare the ejaculates used in the studies on short-term(< 1 year) and long-term(1 to 5 years) storage as explained in Materials and Methods, the remarkable stability observed in fertilizing capacity within each of these periods strongly suggests that it spans both.

The findings of this study are felt to justify semen autopreservation as an approach to men facing sterilization but with one reservation: It is possible that poorer quality semen will not demonstrate the same stability in fertilizing capacity. Accordingly, further studies are needed not only to determine the efficacy of semen preserved for more than 5 years but also to evaluate stability as a function of semen quality.

REFERENCES

1. Sherman, J.K. Synopsis of the use of frozen human semen since 1964: State of the art of human semen banking. Fertil. Steril., 24-397, 1973.

2. Smith, K.D. and Steinberger, E. Survival of spermatozoa in a human sperm bank. Effects of long-term storage in liquid nitrogen. JAMA, 223-774, 1973.

THE ROLE OF CRYOBANKING IN ARTIFICIAL INSEMINATION

J. Barkay and H. Zuckerman

Central Emek Hospital
Afula, Israel

The idea of sperm banking originates from Mantegazza[1] who in 1866 proposed the establishment of a sperm bank which might be useful in different ways ; for instance in the case of a soldier whose sperm could be preserved before going to war and could be used by his wife to have progeny, even after his death. The realisation of this idea had to wait almost a hundred years until Sherman originated the slow rate method of freezing human semen, which proved to be effective and has been in use ever since.

The use of freeze preservation of human sperm has played an important role in the field of reproduction in the last decade. Furthermore the application of cryobanking can be of vital importance : (1) In cases of malignancy the sperm can be collected and preserved before radiation ; (2) before prostatectomy ; (3) before vasectomy ; (4) in cases of dangerous professions which can be injurious to male fertility ; (5) after accidents resulting in paraplegia accompanied by decreased fertilizing capacity ; and (6) in cases where the homologous insemination has failed. In the latter case, services of a sperm bank are psychologically more easily accepted by the couple in despair by suggesting a mixture of frozen sperm of husband with the preserved donor sperm from the bank. According to our experience this method has a great psychological effect, and even the most intelligent of our patients cling to it like a drowning person.

The freezing process has also been used in experiments on the concentration and separation of oligo-asthenospermic semen. The freeze preservation of the pooled split ejaculate is not a new method. Although it is possible to preserve the concentrated part of the semen sample in most cases of oligospermy, there has been no evident solution for those with asthenospermy.   There have been recent

183

experiments to improve the quality of asthenospermic frozen sperm :

. Filteration by glasswool columns which separate debris (immobile and agglutinated spermatozoids) from the good spermatozoids with penetrating ability. The filtered semen can be frozen and after thawing, it will have increased motility.[2]

. Separation of fast moving spermatozoids in human serum albumen
  (HSA). A Pasteur pipette is filled halfway with HSA, and above
  that with semen in the same quantity. After half and hour, the
  best motile spermatozoids penetrate the HSA which can be centri-
  fugated and prepared for freezing. In this way, it is possible
  to obtain frozen semen with very good motility.[3] Ericson proved
  that spermatozoids obtained by this method, can be separated
  X or Y chromosome bearing types. Therefore it is possible to
  influence the sex of the embryo.[4]

. Another method that gives good results is a combined filteration and concentration of the spermatozoa by a milex filter.
  The device is filled with semen and after filtration, it is
  aspirated back with the same quantity of protective medium.
  This concentrated material is ready for cryopreservation.[5]

. All of the above methods are still in the experimental stage
  and not currently used routinely.

. In 1977, Barkay and Zuckerman reported on the effect of caffeine
  on the motility of frozen sperm. This method seems to give
  good results and during the last year has been a technique used
  routinely by several centers. Our observations suggest that it
  improves semen fertilizing capacity.[6] We hope that in the future, it will be possible by the aid of the above mentioned
  methods to develop a new way, which will solve the problem of
  AIH with cryosperm also in cases of astheno spermy.

FREEZING TECHNIQUES

     In 1963, Sherman described a very simple slow-rate freezing
method,[7] Cans with ampules containing semen are suspended over the
vapors of liquid nitrogen, the freezing temperature of which is
-80°C (Figure 1). The cans are then submerged in the liquid nitrogen container, lowering the temperature to -196°C. The principle
of this method is still in use.[8,9]

     The freezing system incorporating automatic equipment is based
on the use of vapors of liquid nitrogen.[10] The entire system, although
efficient, proved to be so complicated and expensive that only large
centers could use it (Figure 2). The semen with the protective medium
can be prepared in ampules or in straws as recommended by Cassau and

FIGURE 1. Liquid nitrogen container construction and demonstration of slow rate freezing technique. Preserved semen in ampules is a suspended over liquid nitrogen vapors.

FIGURE 2. Laboratory with automatic freezing system.

Jondet in 1964[11,12] at a temperature of -80°C. The storing is also
in liquid nitrogen at -196°C (Figure 3).

In 1964, Nagasa and Niva presented a very simple rapid rate
freezing method in pellet form by dripping the sperm mixture on the
dry ice block at -75°C[13] (Figure 4). The pellets are stored in liquid nitrogen. This method is not ideal for human sperm freezing,
because the isolation technique is not perfect and semen residues
may remain on the dry ice and mix with other samples. Also, there
may be problems in obtaining daily supplies of dry ice. Therefore,
this technique is practical only for large veterinary centers.

In 1974 and 1978, Barkay and Zuckerman developed an apparatus
which was intended to concentrate on the advantages of the previously mentioned methods[14,15] (Figure 5). Using this method, it is possible to produce pellets by rapid freezing in liquid nitrogen vapors.
Complete separation and isolation of the semen samples is also possible. The same device can also be used for slow rate freezing with
straws (Figure 6). This method is simple, handy and quick to operate
and can be used for freezing even only one sample of semen, if required. Therefore, it is a method for small hospitals.

FIGURE 3.   Liquid nitrogen storage container

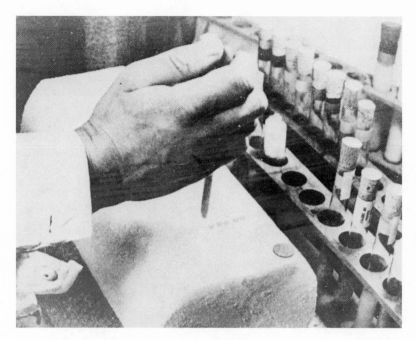

FIGURE 4. Rapid rate semen freezing technique: Pellets
are formed by placing drops of prepared semen on dry ice

All methods for sperm preservation known today have a common
fault : the decrease in motility of spermatozoids caused by crystal-
lization and respiratory shock during the freezing process. Professor Lebech from Copenhagen recently informed the author about his
successful experiments in developing a slow rate freezing method
using straws which in a first step are cooled to -80°C in an alcohol
bath, thereby eliminating the crystallizing effect and increasing
the recovery index.[16]

FIGURE 5. Rapid rate semen freezing device (Barkay and Zuckerman)

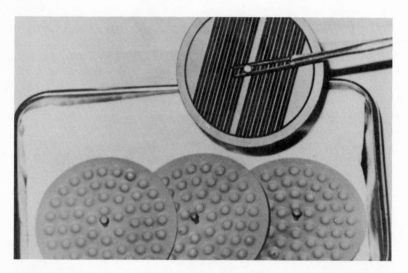

FIGURE 6. Three teflon coated pellet molding disks and one disk designed for freezing semen in straws

REFERENCES

1. Mantegazza, J. Fisiologia Sullo Spermo Umano. Rendic., Real
    Instit. Lomb., 3:183, 1866.

2. Paulson, J.D. A glass wool column procedure for removing extra-
    neous material from the human ejaculate. Fertil. Steril.
    28:178, 1977.

3. Ericsson, R.J. Isolation and storage of progressively motile
    human sperm., Andrologia, 9 (1), 111-114, 1977.

4. Glass, R.H. Sex preselection. Obst. Gynec., 49:122, 1977.

5. Comhair, F. Personal Communication. Gent., 1978.

6. Barkay, J. and Zuckerman, H. Effect of caffeine on increasing
    the motility of frozen human sperm. Fertil. Steril., 28:175,
    1977.

7. Sherman, J.K. Improved methods of preservation of human sper-
    matozoa by freeze drying. Fertil. Steril., 14:49, 1963.

8. Sokol, K. Prospective Praxis-Zevgungs Vorsorge, Sexualmedizin
    1: 152-155, 1972.

9. Lebech, E. Banques de Sperme Humain Fecondité at Sterilité,
    Dumale, Paris, 1973.

10. Behrman, S.J. and Sawada, Y. Heterologous and homologous in-
    semination with human semen frozen and stored in a liquid
    nitrogen refridgerator. Fertil. Steril., 17:457 1961.

11. Cassov, R. La méthode des paillettes en plastique adaptée à
    la généralisation de la congélation. Fifth International
    Congress of Animal Reproduction and Artificial Insemination,
    Trento 4:463, 1964.

12. Jondet, R. Congélation rapide du sperme de Tauren conditionné
    en paillettes. Fifth International Congress of Animal Re-
    production and Artificial Insemination, Trento 4:410, 1964.

13. Nagase, H. and Niwa, T. Deep freezing bull semen in concentra-
    ted pellet form. Fifth International Congress of Animal
    Reproduction and Artificial Insemination, Trento 4:410, 1964.

14. Barkay, J., Zuckerman, H. and Heiman, M. A new practical me-
        thod of freezing and storing human sperm and a preliminary
        report on its use. Fertil. Steril. 25:399, 1974.

15. Barkay, J. and Zuckerman, H. Further developed device for human
        sperm freezing by the twenty-minute method. Fertil. Steril.,
        29:304, 1978.

16. Lebech, P. Personal communication, Jerusalem, 1978.

THE EFFICACY OF NATURAL INSEMINATION:

A COMPARATIVE STANDARD FOR AID

Henri Léridon

Institut National d'Etudes Démographiques
Paris, France

In order to measure the effectiveness of sterility therapy of whatever type, it is necessary to have a reference for comparison. Of course, if it were certain that all the couples undergoing treatment were absolutely sterile, any success obtained, even after years of effort, could be attributed to the effect of the treatment. However, this is not the case in practice. For example, women seeking help for fertility problems who receive hormone medication are most likely not sterile but merely subfertile, the aim of the treatment being to shorten the time required for conception to a more nearly normal duration. Measurement of the efficiency of the method used therefore presupposes the possibility of comparing the results obtained after treatment to values observed in a "normal" population.

For AID, this is all the more obvious. In this technique, the spouse thought to be responsible for the couple's sterility(the husband) is replaced by a donor chosen from a male population with normal fertility. It must therefore be possible to compare the success rate of a series of inseminations with the probability of insemination after a compare number of acts of intercourse between two fertile partners.

THE TIME REQUIRED TO CONCEIVE AND FECUNDABILITY

It so happens that demographers have long been interested in evaluating this probability. To do so, data must be obtained on the time required to conceive, i.e., the period elapsing between the time when a woman starts to be exposed to the risk of conceiving and the time when conception occurs. In practice, the determination of this period poses problems of observation at both beginning and

end. On the one hand, there are only two "natural" situations
which introduce women to the risk of conception: Marriage, on condition that this signifies the beginning of sexual relations and
that no contraception is employed(this was formerly the case in most
populations, and continues to be true in much of the third world);
and cessation of contraception when the couple desires a child, on
condition that the date of cessation can be unambiguously determined
and that it is not followed by a period without sexual relations,
as will be seen below.

On the other hand, it is not conceptions which are reported,
but rather pregnancies, more or less recent, or even births. The
date of conception is always calculated retrospectively with varying
accuracy. What is more important, an unknown proportion of early
spontaneous abortions can increase the apparent calculated time required to conceive.

If these problems are assumed to be solved, how is the monthly
probability of conception, or fecundability calculated from the time
required to conceive? If all couples could be supposed to have the
same fertility, the problem would be simple. Let p be the probability
and N the total number of couples "at risk", then during the first
month, the number of conceptions would be pN; during the second
month, $p(1-p)N$; during the third month $p(1-p)^2 N$, etc. This takes the
form of a geometric distribution, and the average period m is related
to p by: $m = 1/p$. The number of conceptions therefore decreases
each month, but the proportion of couples still at risk who conceive
each month remains equal to p. Now, in reality this is not the case,
for if a group of couples is observed from marriage on, the risk of
conception decreases each month. In the data analyzed by P. Vincent,[1]
the risk of conception was :

. 22% in the first month of marriage

. 18% after three months without conception

. 14% after six months without conception

. 12% after one year without conception.

It is clear that the most fertile women conceived most quickly
and that with time, the group of women still at risk of a first
conception came to comprise only those who were less fertile.

Consider this example: Women having had at least nine living
children, who can hence readily be assumed to have had little recourse to contraception, especially in the early days of marriage,
must have an above average fecundability. Certainly none of them
were sterile or subfertile. Now, as has been seen, their monthly

risk of conception did not exceed 22%, and the average time required to conceive was greater than 5 months.

Coming back to the problem of the heterogeneity of couples, since the first model proposed(a geometric distribution) is not suitable, another must be found. Let us therefore assume that fecundability varies from one couple to another, choosing, for example, a distribution function of a known type for which the parameters will be estimated by using the distribution of times required to conceive (a more detailed explanation of the estimation methods can be found elsewhere[2,3]). Selected results are given in Table 1.

It can be seen that average fecundability is on the order of 0.2 to 0.3 and the time required to conceive varies between 4 and 10 months. These results were obtained mainly for women of about 25; some of the studies cited have shown that fecundability increases from puberty to 20-25 and falls rapidly after 35.

The importance of exact determination of the beginning of the period of exposure to the risk after cessation of contraception can be seen from the data of Spira et al.:[6] To the average time required to conceive, equal to 4.9 months, a "waiting time" of 2.7 months was added. This may partially explain the difference between the times required to conceive observed for populations 3 and 4 in Table 1.

TABLE 1. *Fertility and time required to conceive with natural insemination.*

Population	Average fecundability (Probability of conception per month) p	Average time required to conceive m	Average time required to conceive in a homogeneous group[a] m'
1. French families[1] (9 children)	0.234	5.54 months	4.28 months
2. Hutterites(U.S.A)[4]	0.252	4.75 months	3.97 months
3. Americans[5] (after contraception)	0.144	10.03 months	6.94 months
4. Paris region[6] (after contraception)	0.29	4.9[b] months	3.45 months

[a]The time that would have been observed if the fecundability of each couple had been equal to the average fecundability of the group(m"=1/p)
[b]To this time was added a "waiting time" of an average of 2.7 months between the date of cessation of contraception and the date at which the women said they began unprotected intercourse.

EFFECTIVE FECUNDABILITY, APPARENT FECUNDABILITY, TOTAL FECUNDABILITY

The value obtained for the fertility obviously depends on whether or not pregnancies not leading to live births are taken into account. If only live births are considered in populations 1 and 4 (Table 1) and the contribution of pregnancies lasting only a few months is ignored in calculating the "time required to conceive", the value measured is that of "effective fecundability". This is inevitable when purely retrospective data are used and the women are not questioned. If pregnancies leading to spontaneous abortion (usually at 3-4 months) or still birth are taken into account, the apparent fecundability is measured populations 3 and 4 in Table 1.

If all spontaneous abortions, including those occurring in the first weeks, could be detected, the conception rate would be much higher. It is well known that the number of miscarriages cited in surveys or recognized by women themselves represents only a small proportion of total intrauterine mortality. It is not, therefore, the real risk of conception or total fecundability that is being measured, but this is of no great matter for our subject, since the aim of AID is to give women children born alive!

At best one can measure the frequency of pregnancies lasting at least two weeks after conception, i.e., in existence at the date of the first absent menstrual period (the earliest date at which pregnancy tests can be performed). This recognizable fecundability may be more than one-third higher than the effective fertility.

THE RISK OF CONCEPTION ON DIFFERENT DAYS OF THE CYCLE

An implicit tenet on which the preceding discussion is based must now be considered. In addition to indicating the necessity for the couples observed not to avoid conception by any means, the corollary requirement that these couples must not seek to conceive by increasing their frequency of intercourse or by limiting intercourse to the fertile part of the cycle must also be mentioned.

Thus far we have been using the menstrual cycle as a unit of time without being concerned with the exact time of conception within this period. However, the risk of conception varies greatly with the day of the cycle, from nil at the beginning and end to maximal close to ovulation. Until Barrett and Marshall's studies,[7] little effort was made to calculate the risk attached to each day of the cycle, and only indirect calculations were used to estimate the duration of the fertile period. These authors used temperature curves on which the women noted the days on which intercourse took place in order to calculate, using a single model, the probability of conceiving on each day of the cycle as defined relative to ovul-

TABLE 2. *Probability of conception on different days of the cycle.*[7]

Day	Probability
5th before ovulation	0.13
4th before ovulation	0.20
3rd before ovulation	0.17
2nd before ovulation	0.30
1st before ovulation	0.14
1st after ovulation	0.07
(Other days: Values not significantly different from zero)	

ation. The results are shown in Table 2, from which it can be seen that this probability never exceeds 30% on any day and is significantly different from zero on only 6 days. Schwartz has reported at this symposium that the results obtained by a single artificial insemination per cycle measure up very satisfactorily to Barret and Marshall's estimations. (page 213).

TABLE 3. *Monthly probability of conception (fecundability) for different frequencies of intercourse.* *

Intercourse/6 days	Probability
1	0.17
2	0.31
3	0.42
4	0.53
5	0.61
6	0.68

*From Barrett and Marshall's data.[7]

But couples do not necessarily limit themselves to a single act of intercourse during the fertile period, particularly if they are trying to conceive. If the daily probabilities of Table 2 are combined purely mechanically, assuming them to be independent, the results obtained are shown in Table 3, from which it can be seen that the overall risk of conception rises very rapidly with the frequency of intercourse. For an average frequency, i.e., one or two acts of intercourse every 6 days (4-8 per cycle), the monthly fertility obtained is of the same order as that cited above: 0.2 to 0.3 For higher frequencies, available data (for AID in particular) do not reveal as rapid a rise in fertility, which seems to imply that the model is then no longer satisfactory.

REFERENCES

1. Vincent, P. Recherches sur la fécondité biologique, I.N.E.D.-P.U.F., Travaux et Documents n° 37, Paris, 1961.

2. Leridon, H. Human fertility. The basic components. Univ. of Chicago Press, Chicago and London, 1977. Aspects biométriques de la fécondité humaine, I.N.E.D.-P.U.F. Travaux et Documents n° 65, 1973.

3. Sheps, M. and Menken, J. Mathematical models of conception and birth. Univ. of Chicago Press, Chicago and London, 1973.

4. Majumdar, H. and Sheps, M. Estimation of a type I geometric distribution from observations on conception times. Demography, 7-3:349-60, 1970.

5. Potter, R.G. and Parker, M.P. Predicting the time required to conceive, Population studies, 18-1:99-116, 1964.

6. Spira, A., Ulmann, B. and Heard, I. Fécondabilité après différents modes de contraception. Commun. au Colloque sur la Contraception, Paris, 1-2 mars 1979. A paraître dans les Collections de l'I.N.S.E.R.M., 1979.

7. Barrett, J.C. and Marshall, J. The risk of conception on different days of the menstrual cycle. Population Studies, 23-3:455-61, 1969.

MODE OF EVALUATION OF RESULTS IN ARTIFICIAL INSEMINATION

D. Schwartz and M.J. Mayaux

Unité de Recherches Statistiques de l'INSERM
Villejuif, France

INTRODUCTION

Improved effectiveness in artificial insemination would result from the comparison of studies incorporating different treatment techniques. However, this is difficult to do presently. In studies published to date, the characteristics of the patient populations are different in regard to ethnic background, age distribution, means of selection, etc. To a certain extent, it is possible to minimize or take into account such differences. However, it is essential that the methods used to analyse the data provide indices which have the same meaning. Such a standardized approach has been used in other fields as for example in the evaluation of survival or the effectiveness of contraceptive methods. On the contrary, in artificial insemination diverse indices are currently in use and most are misleading. Even though calculated in the same manner from one study to the other, they do not have the same meaning. This is particularly true for the overall success rate. This index adopted by practically all investigators makes the serious mistake of relating the number of successes to the number of women treated. In fact, this unit, the woman treated, is without meaning when one does not take into account the number of treatment cycles since they can vary greatly for numerous reasons. Other indices less frequently used have the same deficiency. One is the number of cycles needed to conceive and another is the "cumulative success rate" when based only upon those women conceiving.

The purpose of this paper is to first point out the deficiencies of several traditionally used indices as well as the reasons for these deficiencies, and then to present valid indices of true comparative value.

197

The methods of evaluation to be proposed will be demonstrated using the results of a study carried out by the sperm bank at Bicêtre Hospital(CECOS, Paris-Bicêtre), France, or by using hypothetical examples. The Bicêtre study, described in another paper,[1] included all patients treated during the first five years of the bank's operation and will henceforth be referred to as the "model study". In our presentation, all insemination cycles beyond the 12th have been excluded from the calculations for the sake of simplicity.

CLASSIFICATION OF PATIENTS

A physician or a clinic, sperm bank or other facility desires to make an assessment of results obtained over a certain period terminating on a given date t.

First, it is necessary to precisely define for each patient the cycles retained for the assessment: It is essential that all and only those insemination cycles occurring during this period be included.

The patients must then be classified. On the date t, a woman must fall into one of the following four categories: (1) Lost to follow up at cycle i: Women for whom the result at the ith(last) cycle of insemination cannot be obtained; (2) success at cycle i: Women conceiving at the ith cycle of insemination. For purposes of standardization, the criteria of conception must be established. In the model study, at least 21 days of hyperthermia and a positive immunological test were used to confirm pregnancy; (3) dropouts at the end of cycle i. Women who declared that they were discontinuing treatment and; (4) open cases at the end of cycle i: Women do not drop out but for whom the cycle(i + 1) of insemination had not yet taken place at the date t.

A problem is presented by those patients who have not declared that they are dropping out but for whom there has been a long delay since their last insemination cycle. By convention, those cases for which this delay exceeded one year were classified as dropouts.

The classification of the subjects into these four categories according to insemination cycle(Table 1) provides all the necessary data but is not very meaningful *per se*. It is from this data, however, that both analytic and synthetic evaluations can be made.

TABLE 1. *Classification of patients*

Cycle no.	No. of patients	No. of lost to follow up.	No. of succes- ses.	No. of dropouts at end of cycle.	No. of open cases at end of cycle.
1	1188	9	120	35	45
2	979	14	114	41	36
3	774	9	75	39	54
4	597	8	61	25	42
5	461	2	43	33	26
6	357	2	30	27	32
7	266	5	15	18	21
8	207	2	19	8	28
9	150	2	11	7	11
10	119	2	9	6	15
11	87	0	7	5	5
12	70	1	7	1	6
Total	5255 (patients x cycle.)	56	511	245	321

ANALYTIC EVALUATION: RATES PER CYCLE

Four basic rates can be determined for the first insemination cycle using the data in Table 1 taken from the model study(1188 patients: 9 lost to follow up(LF), 120 successes(S), 35 dropouts (DO), 45 open cases(OC)).

The lost to follow up rate for the 1st cycle is 9/1,188= 0.8%.

The success rate based upon those patients not lost to follow-up is 120/(1,188 − 9)= 10.2%.

The dropout rate based upon those patients remaining at the end of the 1st cycle is 35/(1,188 − 9 − 120)= 3.3%.

The open cases rate based upon those passing to the second cycle is 45/(1,188 − 9 − 120 − 35)= 4.4%.

By continuing in the same manner cycle by cycle, four rates
are obtained for all cycles. The results(Table 2) represent a complete analytic evaluation of the data obtained and allow one to determine whether or not the rates varied and if so, to what degree
for the 1st to 12th cycle. Even though Table 2 does not provide a
synthetic evaluation of a facility's performance, it contains all
the elements necessary for this evaluation which aside from its inherent value is sufficient reason for its being established.

TRANSITION TOWARDS SYNTHETIC EVALUATION:

CALCULATION OF MEAN RATES

The simplest approach is to express the rates of each subject
category for the totality of the 12 cycles. Two situations could
exist. First suppose that the probability of an event(sucess, dropout, etc.) is the same for each of the 12 cycles   This would initially appear to be the case for the model study since the rates
of each category differ little from the 1st to 12th cycle. Under
such circumstances the probability of an event can be estimated
using the totals indicated on the bottom line of Table 1(5,255
patients x cycles, 56 LF, 511 S, 245 DO, 321 OC) as follows :

for LF: LF = 56/5,255 = 1.1%

for S :   S = 511/(5,255 - 56) = 9.8%

for DO: DO = 245/(5,255 - 56 - 511) = 5.2%

for OC: OC = 321/(5,255 - 56 - 511 - 245) = 7.2%.

This procedure relating the number of cases for each event to the
number of patient x cycles associated with that event is analogous
to that proposed by Pearl[2] to quantify the effectiveness of a contraceptive technique. It is not difficult to show that this type
of calculation is one of weighted means for the rates of each of
the 12 cycles, the weight given to each cycle rate being proportional to the number of cases it is based upon: Maximum for the 1st
cycle and then decreasing with successive cycles. The four rates
thus obtained are presented in Table 2. Now, let us suppose that the
probability of an event varies from one cycle to the other. In natural production, for example, it is known that the success rate
decreases cycle by cycle because of the progressive elimination of
the most fertile women.[3] With such variation of the probability,
the mean rate retains a practical value in summarizing the 12 cycles
but it does not allow an appreciation of the evolution with time.
Moreover, it must not be calculated by the preceding method since
more weight is given to the initial cycles than to the later cycles.
Accordingly, it is necessary to proceed by calculating the ordinary
(unweighted) mean from the rate for each of the 12 cycles.

TABLE 2. *Rates per cycle(%)*

Cycle no.	1	2	3	4	5	6	7	8	9	10	11	12
Lost to follow-up	0.8	1.4	1.2	1.3	0.4	0.6	1.9	1.0	1.3	1.7	0.0	1.4
Successes	10.2	11.8	9.8	10.4	9.4	8.5	5.7	9.3	7.4	7.7	8.0	10.1
Dropouts at end of cycle	3.3	4.8	5.7	4.7	7.9	8.3	7.3	4.3	5.1	5.6	6.3	1.6
Open cases at end of cycle	4.4	4.4	8.3	8.4	6.8	10.7	9.2	15.7	8.5	14.7	6.7	9.8

SYNTHETIC EVALUATION

Two misleading indices. The overall success rate and the number of cycles necessary for conception.

The overall success rate(OSR), the most commonly employed index
is the most deceptive. For the model study, Table 1 shows that during the period involved, there were 1,188 patients treated of which
there were 511 successes. These two figures have a certain inherent
value. However, the OSR which is the number of successes over the
number of patients treated(OSR = 511/1,188 = 43%) leads one to believe that the "effectiveness" of the facility is 43 successes for
every 100 women treated. In fact, it is evident that such an "effectiveness" depends not only upon the success rate per cycle but
also upon the number of insemination cycles for each woman which varies markedly for numerous reasons. This can be illustrated using
certain examples.

First, imagine that a gynecologist inseminates 100 women for
up to 12 cycles if necessary without cases of OF, DO or even OC since
an assessment would not be made until the last woman had had her last
treatment. Suppose now that the success rate is 10% for each of the
12 cycles. One obtains thus:

cycle no.	1	2	3	4	5	6	7	8	9	10	11	12
Number of women treated	100	90	81	73	66	59	53	48	43	39	35	31
Number of successes	10	9	8	7	7	6	5	5	4	4	4	3
Cumulative success rate	10	19	27	34	41	47	52	57	61	65	69	72

If the gynecologist assesses his results he will have an OSR of 10%
after the 1st cycle; 19% after the 2nd cycle; and so on up to 72%
after the 12th cycle. Between the rates of 10% and 72%, the only
difference is the time elapsed. In reality, the situation is more
complicated since the patients will have variable treatment periods.
Thus, the success rate for the patient population will have values
ranging from 10% to 72% in relation to the treatment time distribution. Consequently, the OSR can be greatly influenced by the number
of LF, DO and OC patients.

Take now the example of a facility in continual service which
makes an assessment at time t. If the rates for LF, S, DO and OC
are nearly constant from the 1st to the 12th cycle, it would be
possible to calculate the OSR from the rates per cycle using a simple formula *(page 203). Certain problems are revealed by applying
this formula to the results of 3 hypothetical studies for which the
different rates per cycle and the OSR are :

	LF	S	DO	OC	OSR
Study 1	0%	10%	0%	0%	72%
Study 2	10%	10%	10%	10%	29%
Study 3	0%	3%	0%	0%	29%

In studies 1 and 2, the success rate per cycle is the same but the OSR differs considerably because of the large number of patients in the second who did not complete 12 cycles for different reasons. Conversely, studies 2 and 3 have the same OSR even though the success rates per cycle are quite different.

These examples point out well how misleading the OSR can be as an index for evaluating the effectiveness of insemination techniques.

The other frequently used index is the mean number of cycles necessary for conception. For the previously mentioned gynecologist treating 100 patients without cases of LF, DO or OC, the mean number of cycles needed for conception(n) would be for an assessment after:

1 cycle(10 successes)
$$n = 1$$

2 cycle(19 successes)
$$n = \frac{1 \times 10 + 2 \times 9}{19} = 1.5$$

12 cycles(72 successes)
$$n = \frac{1 \times 10 + 2 \times 9 + \dots + 12 \times 3}{72} = 5.3$$

Accordingly, the index varies between 1 and 5.3 cycles on the basis of time alone. In reality, the situation is further complicated by the fact that patients have treatment times differing for numerous reasons and the index for such a patient population would have values ranging from 1 to 5.3 depending upon the distribution of treatment times. Therefore, this index is greatly influenced by the number of LF, DO and OC patients and would be as misleading as the OSR.

Cumulative rates. Instead of expressing effectiveness which depends upon both treatment technique and events limiting treatment

---

* Calculation of the OSR: The OSR, as a function of the rates for LF, S, DO and OC, is:

$$OSR = S \times \frac{1 - R^{12}}{1 - R} \quad \text{with } R = (1 - LF)(1 - S)(1 - DO)(1 - OC).$$

In the model study, for example, if the weighted mean rates calculated above are used in this formula(LF= 1.1%, S= 9.8%, DO= 5.2%, OC= 7.2%), an OSR of 43% is obtained which is the value previously determined.

time as a single index, cumulative rates can be used to quantify two
types of effectiveness; one based on the hypothesis that interfering
events do not exist whereas the other takes these events into account.

    a.   The theoretical success rate aims at estimating the proba-
bility of success in i. cycles (i = 1, 2,..., 12) of a patients who
continues treatment up to the ith cycle if conception has not occurred.   The success rates (S_i) can be successively calculated from
i= 1 to i= 12 as will be shown for the model study but transposed
to a basis of 1,000 women.   Using 1,000 women as opposed to the
1,188 actually treated does not change the results since they are
expressed in the form of percentages but does simplify the calculations.

    The calculation is based upon the previously determined success
rates per cycle which were 10.2%, 11.8%, 9.8%... for the 1st, 2nd,
3rd, ... cycles (Table 2).   Using these rates, we first calculate
the number of successes for 1,000 women in the 1st cycle which would
be 1.000 x 10.2% or 102.   Accordingly there remain at the beginning
of the 2nd cycle 1,000 - 102 or 898 women for whom there were 898 x
11.8% or 106 successes which leaves 792 women to be treated in the
3rd cycle.   The number of successes for the 3rd to 12th cycles can
be calculated in the same manner (Table 3).

TABLE 3.   *Theoretical cumulative success rates (without dropouts).*
          Life table.

Cycle no.	Number of patients	Rate of success (%)	Number of successes	Cumulative rate (per 1000)	Cumulative rate (%)
1	1000	10.2	102	102	10.2
2	898	11.8	106	208	20.8
3	792	9.8	78	286	28.6
4	714	10.4	74	360	36,0
5	640	9.4	60	420	42.0
6	580	8.5	49	469	46.9
7	531	5.7	30	499	49.9
8	501	9.3	47	546	54.6
9	454	7.4	34	580	58.0
10	420	7.7	32	612	61.2
11	388	8.0	31	643	64.3
12	357	10.1	36	679	67.9

This method is a slightly modified form of that developed for
actuarial assessments of survival[4,5] from which comes the designa-
tion of "Life table" for Table 4 and "actuarial rates" for the S_i
rates.

The precision of the S_i rates is based upon their variances.[*]
For the model study, the 95% confidence limits were 47% $\pm$ 3% and
68% $\pm$ 5% at 6 and 12 cycles respectively.

The successive values of S_i are reported in F.igure 1. It can
be noted that the delay prior to reaching a 50% success level(median
delay is 7 cycles).

b.   The various <u>effective cumulative rates</u> have the objective
of taking into account the actual DO rate and if desired the LF rate.
Here we will consider only DO rate and if desired the LF rate.   Here
we will consider only DO based upon the assumption that there would
be no LF cases.

The effective <u>cumulative success rate</u> is designed to estimate
the probability of success in i cycles(i = 1, 2, ... 12) for patients
following treatment until the ith cycle unless they had succeeded
or dropped out, the DO rate after each cycle being that which pre-
vails for the study in question.   These success rates(S_i) can be
calculated successively from i= 1 to i= 12 by establishing a life
table which takes into account the proportion of DO after each cycle.
Therefore, by considering the success rates in the model study at
each cycle(10.2%, 11.8%, etc.) as well as the DO rates(3.3%, 4.8%,
etc. according to Table 2), we obtain for an initial 1,000 women,
1,000 x 10.2% or 102 successes and for the 898 remaining, 898 x 3.3%
or 30 DO.   Thus for the 2nd cycle there are 898 - 30 or 868 women
which gives 868 x 11.8% or 102 successes.   At this point, there remain 868 - 102 or 766 women of which 766 x 4.8% or 37 are DO; the
calculations continue accordingly until the ith cycle(Table 4:
Cumulative rates expressed in thousandths for brevity).   The S_i rates graphically expressed(figure 1) show, in particular, a median
delay of 9 cycles.

---

[*]The formula to be used to calculate the variance is given by references 5 and 6:

$$\text{Var } S_i = (1 - S_i)^2 \; \frac{S_1}{N_1(1 - s_i)} + \cdots\cdots + \frac{s_i}{N(1 - s_i)}$$

where s_i is the success rate of cycle i and N_i the number of patients beginning the cycle minus the number lost to follow-up.

TABLE 4. *Effective cumulative rates (with dropouts). Life table.*

No. of cycle	Number of patients	Rate of success (%)	Number of successes	Remaining cases	Rate of dropouts (%)	Number of dropouts	Cumulative rates per 1000 Successes	Cumulative rates per 1000 Dropouts
1	1000	10.2	102	898	3.3	30	102	30
2	868	11.8	102	766	4.8	37	204	67
3	729	9.8	71	658	5.7	38	275	105
4	620	10.4	64	556	4.7	26	339	131
5	530	9.4	50	480	7.9	38	389	169
6	442	8.5	38	404	8.3	34	427	203
7	370	5.7	21	349	7.3	25	448	228
8	324	9.3	30	294	4.3	13	478	241
9	281	7.4	21	260	5.1	13	499	254
10	247	7.7	19	228	5.6	13	518	267
11	215	8.0	17	198	6.3	12	535	279
12	186	10.1	19	167	1.6	3	554	282

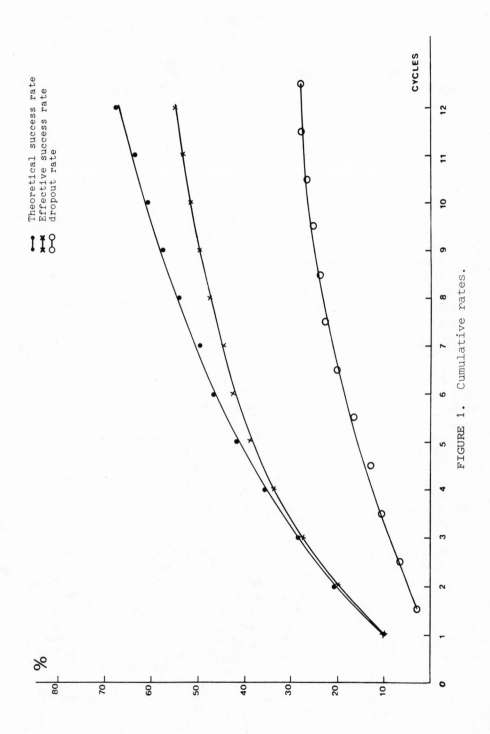

FIGURE 1. Cumulative rates.

The cumulative dropout rates presented as well as the success
rates both in the life table(Table 4) and graphically(Figure 1) indicate the DO probability in i cycles of insemination. This is important information from a practical aspect but it cannot be obtained directly from the raw data. Say for example that there was a
dropout rate for 12 cycles of 21%(245/1.188 according to Table 1)
would present the same problems as indicated for the OSR.

The effective cumulative success rates which take into account
not only DO but also LF could be calculated as well by the life
table technique. However, because of the uncertainty concerning
the LF cases in AID, this calculation will not be presented.

c. Commentary on cumulative rates. All the cumulative rates
presented in this paper clearly express varied and valuable aspects
of an assessment at i cycles. These aspects for 1,000 women who
have completed treatment without the occurrence of LF cases are the
expected numbers for: a) Success if no patient had dropped out;
b) DO taking into account the actual DO frequency; and c) success
taking DO into account. After 6 cycles in the model study, for
example, these numbers are 469 successes for (a), 203 DO and 427
successes for (b) and (c) respectively. The number of successes
on an effective basis, that is taking into account DO, is only
slightly lower than that on a theoretical basis which ignores dropouts because the mean DO rate is low(5%). By using this method we
have been able to obtain a complete assessment after each cycle but
the rates yielded are meaningful only under certain assumptions
concerning the LF, DO and OC patient groups.

The first assumption involves the LF patients. These are
ignored in the calculation of all the rates which could induce a
bias if the results of their inseminations were not comparable to
that of the other patients. Furthermore, the effective rates presented here describe a situation in which there are no LF cases.
Thus, these rates are meaningful only if the proportion of LF cases
were minimal.

The second assuption involves the OC patients who are also
ignored in all rate calculations. This does not introduce a bias
since these patients are in principle comparable to the others,
their histories terminating simply because of an observation period
which was too short. In fact, the situation is somewhat more complex. The women who declare at the end of cycle i that they are
not dropping out but have not requested insemination for several
months may actually be dropouts. In the model study, it was decided
to classify them as dropouts when the time since the last request
reached 1 year. Therefore, there were a certain number of OC patients
remaining with whom there had been no contact for several months.
There are probably dropouts included among them and thus there is

undoubtedly an underestimation of the DO rates and in turn an over-estimation of the effective cumulative success rate. This overesti-mation is very low if the proportion of OC patients is low.

The third assumption concerns dropouts and the calculation of theoretical rates. Dropouts were not taken into account in these calculations. In order not to induce a bias, it is necessary that the women who drop out are comparable to those who continue but such an assuption could be contested. As the number of failures increases the decision on whether to continue or drop out becomes more and more influenced by factors which argue against fertility: The mul-tiplying and repetition of exploratory tests, age, etc. It is thus quite likely that dropouts are somewhat less fertile than those who continue. Accordingly, the theoretical rates will be slightly over-estimated to increasing degrees from the 1st to 12th cycle. Under the extreme hypothesis that all the women dropping out are sterile, the cumulative theoretical rate would be equal to the effective rate.

ASSESSMENT OF WOMEN CONCEIVING

Several authors have made synthetic or analytic evaluations considering the women who had conceived as a separate group.

One evaluation is the distribution of pregnancies among the different cycles: In the model study in which 511 pregnancies were confirmed, 120 occurred in cycle 1, 114 in cycle 2, etc., for which the pregnancy rates would be respectively 120/511 or 23%, 114/511 or 22%, and so forth to 7/511 or 1% at the 12th cycle. These rates, the total of which equals 100%, decrease as expected from the 1st to 12th cycle simply because of the fact there are fewer and fewer patients after each successive cycle. These rates have no value in making comparisons between studies. Furthermore, they have often been termed as cycle success rates which creates confusion with the previously discussed rates per cycle.

Other authors have established a life table restricted to those women who had conceived. This method applied to the model study would consider the 511 women conceiving as the initial study group of which 391 remained after the 120 successes of the first cycle, 277 after 114 successes in the 2nd cycle, etc. This table gives the success rate per cycle and the cumulative rates which could be mistaken for theoretical cumulative rates since only successes have been considered and DO, OC and LF cases have been ignored. For example, the success rate for the first cycle which is also the cu-mulative success rate for the first cycle would be 120/511. However this rate is based on 511 pregnancies, a number which is dependent upon the number of LF, DO and OC cases and thus is not comparable between different studies. We encounter here the same difficulty as with the OSR, but these rates are particularly misleading since the sophisticated presentation makes them appear valid. Furthermore, they can create confusion for the correct rates.

CONCLUSION

This paper has shown that evaluations of results in artificial insemination have been carried out using various procedures, only a few of which have the same meaning from one study to another and thus permit comparisons. If this review has not been exhaustive, it has at least pointed out the reasons for which an index may be misleading. All the indices which consider the total number of pregnancies without taking into account the number of treatment cycles are completely without comparative value since the number of cycles depends upon multiple non-explicit factors for which the frequency varies for each study. The per cycle and actuarial rates calculated on the basis of the entire population and not only on pregnant women avoid this problem and permit valid comparisons. If their calculation appears somewhat long or complicated, this is because one calculates simultaneously several different aspects of the assessment at cycles 1, 2, 3, etc. The presentation of the calculations in Tables 3 and 4 in conjunction with the detailed explanation in the text should enable one to quickly familiarize himself with the reasoning behind the calculations and their execution which actually involves only the basic mathematical operations of addition, subtraction, multiplication and division !

REFERENCES

1. Schwartz, D., Mayaux, M.J., Martin-Boyce, A., Czyglik, F. and David, G. Donor insemination: Conception rate according to cycle day in a series of 821 cycles with a single insemination. Fertil. Steril., 31:2, 1979.

2. Pearl, R. Contraception and fertility in 2.000 women. Human Biol. 4, 3:363-407, 1932.

3. Leridon, H. Human Fertility. The basic components. The University of Chicago Press., 1973.

4. Berkson, J. and Gage, R.P. Calculation of survival rates for cancer. Proc. Staff Meetings Mayo clin., 25:270, 1950.

5. Schwartz, D., Flamant, R. and Lellouch, J. L'essai thérapeutique chez l'homme. Editions médicales, Flammarion, Paris, 1970.

6. Major Greenwood. A report of the natural duration of cancer. Reports on P.H. Med. Subjects, 33:1-26, 1926.

RESULTS OF AID FOR A FIRST

AND SUCCEEDING PREGNANCIES

Georges David, Françoise Czyglik,[*]
Daniel Schwartz[**] and Marie-Jeanne Mayaux[**]

[*] Centre d'Etude et de Conservation du Sperme
     (CECOS), Paris-Bicêtre
   Kremlin-Bicêtre, France

[**] Institut National de la Santé et de la
     Recherche Statistique
   Villejuif, Paris

INTRODUCTION

From the time of its opening on January 1, 1973 until January 31, 1978, the Centre d'Etude et de Conservation du Sperme de Paris-Bicêtre was involved in the treatment of 1188 women by AID. Inseminations were carried out with cryopreserved semen according to a treatment protocol which called for, in particular, a single insemination for the first two AID cycles. This study will compare the results for the first series of treatments (reported elsewhere[1]) to successive series carried out for a second or third pregnancy.

MATERIALS AND METHODS

Patients

Women were accepted into the AID program only after irreversible sterility in the husband due to azoospermia or severe spermatozoal insufficiency was confirmed. At the time of the first insemination the average age of the women was 29.7 ± 4. After a first pregnancy, 136 women were treated a second time and of these, 16 were treated again for a third pregnancy.

Donors

The semen donors were under 45 years of age and married, had the permission of their spouses, had one or more normal children and had agreed to a free donation. They were carefully interviewed in order to determine the risk for the transmission of a hereditary disease. They were also submitted to a clinical examination as well as a serological test for syphilis and a karyotype.

Freezing Technique

All semen was collected at the Center through masturbation after a recommended abstinence of three days. After liquefaction, a fraction was subjected to the following measurements ; volume, sperm count and percentage of both motile spermatozoa and normal forms. Only semen with a sperm count of 50 million per ml or higher with at least 50% motile and 50% normal forms was retained.

The ejaculates were prepared and frozen as follows: They were diluted by an equal volume of cryoprotector medium(in 100 ml ; 20 ml of egg-yolk ; 15 ml of glycerol ; 1.3 g of glucose ; 1.15 g of sodium citrate ; 1 g of glycine; 50 mg of streptomycin and 100,000 I.U. of penicillin) ; left for 15 minutes at room temperature ; distributed into 0.25 ml plastic straws(paillettes) ; rapidly frozen in a horizontal position in vapors of liquid nitrogen at approximately -60°C for about 7 minutes ; and then stored in liquid nitrogen in a vertical position.

Thawing was accomplished by placing the paillette at room temperature after removal from the liquid nitrogen.

A fraction was thawed on the same day the semen was collected in order to evaluate tolerance to freezing ; this freezing tolerance test(FTT) is considered positive when the number of motile spermatozoa is greater than 50%. When lower than 30%, the FTT is considered negative. Between 30 and 50%, the FTT is positive only if a *in vitro* cervical mucus penetration test is positive.

Treatment Evaluation

Couples requesting AID were required to make a formal application to the program after an initial consultation. The delay between acceptance and the beginning of treatment was variable according to the availability of semen. In the majority of cases, this delay was about 1 year.

The data on each couple and donor were transmitted under anonymous conditions to the Unité de Recherches Statistiques for coding

and computer analysis. The temperature curves were carefully interpreted for each cycle with several aspects including temperatures,
days and durations being noted.

Treatment Evaluation

     The patients were placed in one of four categories on the date
of assessment(January 31, 1978) as described by Schwartz and Mayaux
elsewhere in this volume(pg 198). These categories were: (1) Lost
to follow-up (patients for whom no data had been received since the
last insemination cycle, the results of which were not known); (2)
Success based upon 21 days of hypertherma and clinical or serological
confirmation of pregnancy, regardless of its out come ; (3) Dropouts
(women who had declared their withdrawal from the AID program);
(4) and open cases(patients whose next treatment cycle had not yet
taken place on January 31, 1978). In regard to open cases, if there
had been a long delay, that is, greater than one year since the last
AID treatment, the patient was classified as a dropout rather than
an open case.

     From the distribution of cases according to category, the suc-
cess rate as well as other more descriptive indices have been determined. The latter include: (1) Rates per cycle of success, open
cases and dropouts ; (2) mean rates of success and dropouts for all
cycles ; and (3) cumulative success rates according to the life
table method. For the latter, a distinction was made between the
effective success rate which takes dropouts into account and the
theoretical success rate which ignores dropouts.

     These calculations have been made for two treatment series:
Treatments for a first pregnancy(1188 women) and treatments for a
second or a third pregnancy which were grouped(142 women).

                              RESULTS

Series 1: Treatment for a first pregnancy

     As reported in another study,[1] the overall results(Table 1)
included a success rate of 45%, a miscarriage rate of 17% and a sex
ratio of 1.03. The results per cycle are given in Table 2; those
for the first 12 cycles being given individually, and those for
all cycles after the 12th being given as a group. The mean success
rate per cycle was 9.8% for the first 12 cycles.

     The rates for successes, dropouts and open cases per cycle
are given in Table 3. From these, the cumulative success rates,
both theoretical and effective, were calculated(Table 4). The
median delays for conception(time at which 50% of the population

TABLE 1. *Overall results of AID for patients seeking a first pregnancy(series 1) and those seeking a second or third pregnancy(series 2)*

Series	No. of patients	No. of pregnancies	No. of births Single	No. of births Multiple	No. and Sex of children	Pregnancy interrupted	Pregnancies in progress
1 (1st pregnancy)	1188	529 (44,5%)	346	18	382 { 193 / 188	82 miscarriages 4 ectopic pregnancies 1 therapeutic abortion	78
2 (2nd and 3rd pregnancy). (2nd: 136) (3rd: 16)	152	82 (54%)	62	1	64 { 29 / 35	14 miscarriages 1 therapeutic abortion	3

TABLE 2. *Classification of patients seeking a first pregnancy (series 1)* [1]

Cycle No.	No. of patients	No. of lost to follow-up	No. of successes	No. of drop-outs at end of cycle	No. of open cases at end of cycle
1	1188	9	120	35	45
2	979	14	114	41	36
3	774	9	75	39	54
4	597	8	61	25	42
5	461	2	43	33	26
6	357	2	30	27	32
7	266	5	15	18	21
8	207	2	19	8	28
9	150	2	11	7	11
10	119	2	9	6	15
11	87	0	7	5	5
12	70	1	7	1	6
Total	5255 patients x cycle	56[1]	511[2]	245[3]	321
> 12	55	0	18	7	30

[1] Permits calculation of the mean lost to follow-up rate per cycle: 56/5255 = 1.1%.

[2] Permits calculation of the mean success rate per cycle: 511/5255 -56 = 9.8%.

[3] Permits calculation of the mean dropout rate per cycle: 245/5255 - 56 - 511 = 5.2%.

TABLE 3. *Rates per cycle for patients seeking a first pregnancy (series 1)*

Cycle No.	1	2	3	4	5	6	7	8	9	10	11	12
Lost to follow-up	0.8	1.4	1.2	1.3	0.4	0.6	1.9	1.0	1.3	1.7	0.0	1.4
Successes(%)	10.2	11.8	9.8	10.4	9.4	8.5	5.7	9.3	7.4	7.7	8.0	10.1
Dropouts at end of cycle(%)	3.3	4.8	5.7	4.7	7.9	8.3	7.3	4.3	5.1	5.6	6.3	1.6

TABLE IV. *Cumulative rates for patients seeking a first pregnancy (Series 1).*

Cycle No.	1	2	3	4	5	6	7	8	9	10	11	12
Theoretical rate(without dropouts)(%)	10.2	20.8	28.6	36.0	42.0	46.9	49.9	54.6	58.0	61.2	64.3	67.9
Effective rate(with dropouts)(%)												
- Successes(%)	10.2	20.4	27.5	33.9	38.9	42.7	44.8	47.8	49.9	51.8	53.5	55.4
- Dropouts(%)	3.0	6.7	10.5	13.1	16.9	20.3	22.8	24.1	25.4	26.7	27.9	28.2

had conceived) under theoretical and effective conditions were 7 and 9 days respectively.

Series 2:   Treatment for a 2nd or 3rd pregnancy

The overall success rate was 59% and the miscarriages occurred in 17% of those conceiving(Table 1). Cycle by cycle assessment revealed mean rates per cycle of 16.3% for successes, 1.3% for open cases and 4% for dropouts(Table 5).

DISCUSSION

A previous study[1] on the same population of women seeking a first pregnancy demonstrated that age has an important influence on the result of AID: The mean success rate per cycle dropped from 13.8% for women 25 or under to 5.3% for those over 35 years of age. However, these results must be interpreted cautiously since childless older women may constitue a population with a subfertility that is independent of age. For instance, such women may have husbands in whom it is not possible to confirm whether or not infertility is or always has been complete: A man with oligozoospermia or asthenozoospermia, as opposed to one with azoospermia, may be capable of fertilizing a highly fertile woman. Thus with time couples of this type would be less and less likely to present for AID as compared to those in which the woman is subfertile. In effect, the subfertile woman could be said to have been selected by time. However, even if there is such a selection, this does not change the fact that in AID, the prognosis is closely linked to the age of the woman. Accordingly, it is important to explore male fertility as early as possible in order not to unecessarily compromise the prognosis by delaying the initiation of AID.

In the present study, a second important factor, the result of previous AID treatment, has been shown to affect success. The success rate per cycle for women receiving AID for a first child was 9.8% whereas for women being treated in order to have a second or third child, it was 16.3%.

The influence of age and previous AID results on the success of an AID treatment have not been previously studied to our knowledge. Of 15 published studies on AID with cryopreserved semen, only 5 include more than 100 cases(Table 6). Furthermore, their results are usually expressed in terms of an overall success rate, that is the percentage of pregnancies obtained. This index, as shown by Schwartz (pg. 202) cannot be used for valid comparisons.

Four authors have presented data on a per cycle basis from which it was possible to calculate, if not already given, the

TABLE 5. *Classification of patients seeking second and third pregnancies*

Cycle No.	No. of patients	No. lost to follow-up [*]	No. of successes[*]	No. of dropouts at end of cycle [*]	No. of open cases [*]
1	152	$2_{1.3}$	$31_{20.7}$	$1_{0.8}$	$10_{8.5}$
2	108	$2_{1.8}$	$19_{17.9}$	$2_{2.3}$	$11_{12.9}$
3	74	0	$8_{10.8}$	$4_{6.1}$	$8_{12.9}$
4	54	0	$8_{14.8}$	0	$3_{6.5}$
5	43	0	$6_{13.9}$	$5_{13.5}$	$4_{12.5}$
6	28	$1_{3.6}$	$2_{7.4}$	1_4	$3_{12.5}$
7	21	0	1	3	2
8	15	1	3	1	4
9	6	0	1	0	1
10	4	0	1	0	0
11	3	0	2	0	0
12	1	0	0	0	1
Total	509	6	82	17	47

Mean success rate per cycle = 16.3%
[*]Percentages are denoted by the subscripts.

TABLE 6. *Results of AID in previously published studies*

Authors and references	No. of women	No. of successes	%	Authors and references	No. of women	N° of successes	%
Keetel et al. 1956[2]	26	9	34.6	Barkay et al. 1974[11]	11	6	54.5
Behrmann et al. 1966[3]	28	12	42.9	Cottinet et al. 1974[12]	55	18	32.7
Behrmann et al. 1969[4]	68	19	42.9	Ravina and Schneider 1974[13]	48	23	47.9
Matheson et al. 1969[5]	7	3	42.9				
				Millet et al. 1974[14]	60	25	41.7
Carlborg 1971[6]	76	22	28.9				
				Jondet et al. 1975[15]	266	120	45.1
Lebech 1972[7]	114	59	51.8				
				Ledward et al. 1976[16]	16	6	37.5
Tyler 1973[8]	278	137	49.3				
				Matthews 1976[17]	77	37	48.1
Steinberger and Smith 1973[9]	59	36	61.0				
				Friberg et al. 1977[18]	-	103	
Friberg and Gemzell 1973[10]	83.26	26	31.3	Friedman 1977[19]	227	91	40.1
				Bromwich et al. 1978[20]	214	82	38.3

success rate per cycle: 15.4% for Jondet et al. [15] 14.7% for
Lebech,[7] 9.6% for Friedman,[19] and 5.1% for Bromwich.[20] Such wide
variation may be due to differences of techniques either in cryopreservation or insemination. The composition of the study popu -
lations in regard to age distribution and the proportion of women
having already had a pregnancy may also have influenced the results
as discussed above. Since the populations were not well defined,
the validity of any comparisons must remain questionable.

The results of this study point out the necessity of accurately
defining the study populations, especially in terms of age and the
proportion of previous pregnancies. It is also clear that the analysis of data on AID must be carried out using a uniform method such
as that proposed by Schwartz and Mayaux(pg 197) if comparisons among
studies are to be possible.

REFERENCES

1. David,G., Czyglik,F., Mayaux,M.J., Martin-Boyce, A. and
       Schwartz,D.   Artificial Insemination with frozen semen :
       protocol method of analysis and results for 1188 women.
       To be published in Brit.J.Obst.Gynaec.,1980

2. Keetel,W.C., Bunge,R.G. and Bradbury,J.T.   Report of pregnan-
       cies in infertile couples. J.A.M.A., 160 : 102,1956

3. Behrman,S.J. and Sawada,Y.   Heterologous inseminations with
       human semen frozen and stored in a liquid nitrogen refri-
       gerator. Fertil.Steril. I7 : 457, I966

4. Behrman,S.J. and Ackerman,D.R.   Freeze preservation of human
       sperm. Am. J.Obstet.Gynecol. 103 : 604, 1969

5. Matheson,W., Carlborg,L. and Genzell,C.   Frozen human semen
       for artificial insemination. Am.J.Obst.Gynecol.,I04 : 495,
       1969

6. Carlborg,L.   Some problems involved in freezing and insemina-
       tion with human sperm. In : Current Problems in Fertility,
       Ingelman-Sundberg A. and Lunnel,N.O.,eds. Plenum Press,
       New York, 1971

7. Lebech,E.   Banques de sperme humain.Fécondité et stérilité du
       mâle - Acquisitions récentes. Masson, Paris pp 349, 1972

8. Tyler, T. The clinical use of frozen semen banks. Fertil.Steril
       24 : 413, I973

9. Steinberger,E. and Smith,K.D. Artificial insemination with fresh or frozen semen, J.A.M.A. 223 : 778, 1973

10. Friberg,J.and Genzell,C. Inseminations of human sperm after freezing in liquid nitrogen vapors with glycerol or glycerol-egg-yolk-citrate as protective media. Am.J.of Obst. Gynecol. 116: 330, 1973

11. Barkay,J., Zuckerman,H. and Helman,M.
A new, practical method of freezing and storing human sperm and a preliminary report on its use. Fertil.Steril., 25: 39, 1974

12. Cottinet,D., Gagnaire J.C., Lansac,J.and Thirion,A. Utilisation du sperme congelé dans l'insémination artificielle avec donneur. Gynécologie, 6: 133,1974

13. Ravina,J.J. and Schneider,M.C. Insémination artificielle avec sperme conservé de donneurs. La Nouvelle Presse Médicale,3: 1359, 1974

14. Millet,D., Jondet,N. and Netter,A. L'hétéro-insémination par le sperme humain congelé: Premiers résultats de l'hôpital Necker. J.Gyn. Obst.Repr., 3: 903,1974

15. Jondet,M., Millet,D., Coruau,J.,Picaud,C.and Netter,A. Utilisation du sperme congelé pour l'insémination humaine hétérologue. Gynecologie 26: 285,1975

16. Ledward,R.S., Grich,J.,Sharp,P. and Cotton,R.E. The establishment of a programme of artificial insemination by donors semen within the national health service. Brit.J. Obst.Gynaec. 83: 907-920, 1976

17. Matthews,C. Current status of A.I. in clinical practice. Proceeding of the fourth Study group of the Royal College of Obstetricians and Gynaecologists, 26-27: 38,1976

18. Friberg,J. and Genzelle,C. Sperm freezing and donor insemination. In. J. Fertil., 22 : 148-154, 1977

19. Friedman,S. Artificial donor insemination with frozen human semen. Fert. Steril. 28: 1230, 1977

20. Bromwich,P., Kilpatrick,J. and Newton,J.R. Artificial insemination with frozen donor semen. Brit.J.Obst.Gynaec. 85: 641, 1978

ARTIFICIAL INSEMINATION WITH FROZEN HUMAN SEMEN: 227 CASES

Stanley Friedman

Department of Obstetrics and Gynecology
UCLA School of Medicine
Los Angeles, California, USA

This study describes the experience of an infertility practice which maintains a frozen semen bank as its primary source of AID. Two hundred and twenty-seven women began AID between January 1st and December 31st, 1974, and the study ended March 31st, 1976. Thus, the study period covered a relatively short duration, 27 months, during which time personnel, patient and donor selection, technics and adjunctive therapy did not vary. During these 27 months, 97 patients conceived for an overall pregnancy rate of 41.9%.

The indications for donor insemination are given in Table 1. Many wives of oligospermic men had months of husband inseminations before AID. The pregnancy rate was consistent, regardless of the indication for AID.

Table 2 gives the influence of age and previous fertility on AID. There was no significant difference in pregnancies among the various age groups nor did a history of prior fertility significantly affect the success rate, although there is a trend to increased numbers of pregnancies in women with demonstrated fertility.

It seemed that women in certain particularly stressful occupations, such as school teaching, comprised a large part of our practice, and were particularly resistant to infertility treatment. It was also felt that cigarette smoking might have an adverse effect on fertility treatment, or that as a sign of stress, it could serve as a marker of those resistant to such treatment. As indicated in Table 3, neither of these beliefs were substantiated by any significant differences in pregnancy rates.

TABLE 1. *Indications for AID.*

Indications	No of patients
Vasectomy	67
Azoospermia	67
Oligospermia	87
Genetic	6

Additional causes of infertility, as expected, significantly lowered the pregnancy rate(Table 4). Furthermore, there is probably a greater difference between these figures than is indicated here, since some patients who were thought to be normal and did not conceive, were not laparascoped and had probably also additional causes for infertility.

TABLE 2. *Influence of age and gravidity on AID.*

	No of patients	No of pregnancies (%)
Age		
< 25	62	24(38.7)
25-30	124	51(41.1)
31-35	35	14(40.0)
> 35	6	2(33.3)
Gravida		
0	150	54(36.0)
1	50	27 ⎤
2	21	8 ⎟ (48.1)
3	5	2 ⎟
> 3	1	0 ⎦

TABLE 3. *Influence of occupation and smoking on AID.*

	No. of patients	No of. pregnancies(%)
Occupation		
Homemaker	88	34(39)
Teacher	23	9(39)
Healthcare	17	7(41)
Other	95	39(41)
Daily cigarette usage		
None	132	50(37.4)
< one pack	23	8(34.8)
One pack	30	14(46.7)
Two packs	11	4(36.4)
> two packs	1	1(100)

TABLE 4. *Influence of additional infertility factors on AID.*

	No. of patients	No. of pregnancies(%)
No additional factors	174	81(46.6)
Additional factors	53	10(18.9)
Tubal disease	19	3
Anovulation	11	2
Endometriosis	6	2
Cervical factor	6	1
Other	11	2

Table 5 gives the overall results of the present study, the number of patients inseminated each cycle, the number and percentage of pregnancies per cycle, and in the last column, the cumulative pregnancy rate.

When a woman begins AID, she first wants to know "How long will it take me to get pregnant?" The possibility of failure has not crossed her mind. But after 3 or 4 months, she will ask "What are my chances of ever getting pregnant?" or "How long should I continue to try?" A satisfactory answer to these questions is not available.

One way to answer would be to state that 58% of all pregnancies will occur in the first 3 cycles and 85% will have occurred within 6 cycles. This still does not tell a woman what her particular chances are.

One could use the percentage of pregnancies per cycle to answer these questions. However, there is no real trend here, no matter how many months of inseminations. Indeed, the highest percentage occurred in the eleventh month. This high success rate can be partly explained by the fact that 2 of the patients here underwent laparoscopy after 6 to 8 months of unsuccessful inseminations. At laparoscopy, endometriotic lesions were found and cauterized, and then after another 3 to 5 months of inseminations, pregnancies occurred.

TABLE 5. *Pregnancies per month of insemination.*

Month of insemination	No. of Pts	No. of pregnancies	% Pregnancies cycle	Cumulative pregnancy rate (%)
1	227	23	10.1	24.2
2	182	23	12.6	48.4
3	133	10	7.5	59.0
4	108	10	9.3	69.5
5	81	8	9.9	77.9
6	67	7	10.4	85.3
7	49	3	6.1	88.4
8	33	3	9.1	91.6
9	26	2	7.7	93.7
10	18	1	5.6	94.7
11	15	5	33.3	100.0
12	8	0	0.0	

Neither the cumulative pregnancy rate, nor the incidence of pregnancies per cycle, nor the overall pregnancy rate takes into consideration a factor which has a marked influence on the success of AID: The large number of dropouts.

Table 6 gives the number of patients inseminated per month, the number of dropouts per cycle, and in the last column, the cumulative dropout rate after subtracting those who conceived. To our chagrin, 37% of unsuccessfully inseminated patients quit after only 3 months, and two-thirds after 6 months. That the dropout rate obviously will effect the success rate must be impressed upon couples beginning AID.

Table 7 gives the most reasonable figures to present to those who want to know what their ultimate chances are. It gives the cumulative pregnancy rates, corrected for dropouts, in women who persist in AID for these numbers of cycles. This method of calculating pregnancy rates can be carried to an extreme. For example, if every patient but one should drop out after 15 cycles, and the last one in the study conceived in the 16th cycle, one could claim a 100% pregnancy rate in patients who persisted in AID for 16 cycles. This method has been criticized for this reason. But, if one limits themselves to a more reasonable number of insemination cycles, such as 9 or 12, this gives the most meaningful prognostic information to an individual couple.

TABLE 6. *Dropounts per month of insemination.*

Month	No. of Pts.	No. of pregnancies	No. of Dropouts	Dropouts/ cycle(%)	Cumulative dropout rate (%)
1	227	23	22	10.8	10.8
2	182	20	26	16.4	26.5
3	133	10	15	12.2	36.8
4	108	9	17	17.3	49.7
5	81	8	6	8.2	56.2
6	67	7	11	18.3	66.4
7	49	3	13	28.3	73.8
8	33	3	4	13.3	78.1
9	26	2	6	25.0	83.3
10	18	1	2	11.8	85.3
11	15	5	2	20.0	89.9
12	8	0	3	37.5	92.1

TABLE 7. *Pregnancy rates corrected for dropouts.*

Months of inseminations	Pregnancy rate (%)
3	31.3
4	40.2
6	57.5
9	78.8
11	92.2

These figures include the patients with additional infertility factors. Elimination of that group would yield a 67.4% conception rate in normal women having more than 3 cycles of AID.

Furthermore, we inadvertently underestimate our pregnancy rate because of our failure to follow up the results of every insemination. I had made this statement when I presented some of this material several years ago. At that time, we had 91 pregnancies from this series. Since then, we learned of 4 more pregnancies when patients in this series returned to us after having conceived and delivered without our knowledge and wished to embark upon another series of AID. We assume that there are others who have conceived without letting us know about it. Thus the efficiency of the follow-up should be considered when comparing success rates.

Frozen semen has certain advantages over fresh semen. A large donor pool permits a matching of the husband's physical characteristics that is not possible when one relies upon fresh samples. There is no limit to the timing and number of inseminations. Semen from the same donor can be used as often as needed in a given patient, and should a thawed specimen be unsatisfactory, other specimens from the same donor are available, assuring a consistency in the quality of the semen. If it is felt necessary, any specimen can be cultured for gonococcus before freezing.

There are no known disadvantages to the use of frozen semen. Although one would expect a higher rate of success with fresh specimens, this is not always borne out by a careful comparison with such series. There is a higher incidence of pregnancies with fresh specimens in the first two cycles. Thereafter, the rate of success seems to be similar with fresh and frozen specimens, and after 6 or more months, there is little difference in the cumulative pregnancy rate. Perhaps, with frozen semen, the ability to time the inseminations more precisely, to do the inseminations more often, and to use only semen with a good count and motility, may overcome the advantages of fresh specimens.

Some authors have arbitrarily limited the number of cycles of insemination in the belief that if a pregnancy does not occur within this set limit, usually 6 cycles, there is little hope of success with continued inseminations. I do not think there is any data to support these limitations, especially if a laparoscopy has ruled out additional infertility factors. We have one patient, not in this series, who conceived on her 24th cycle of inseminations carried out over a 3-year period. We have patients who conceived within 6 cycles, had children, returned for repeat inseminations, and took 16 to 18 cycles to conceive again. As long as the patient and her husband have the emotional stamina to persist in treatment, we offer it to them.

A disturbing finding was the large number of couples who did not persist in treatment. We do not know if this dropout rate is limited to AID patients, or if it is characteristic of all patients undergoing infertility treatment. For a while, we thought that the cost of AID was a significant cause for the dropout rate. However, in Czechoslovakia, which has a national health service, the dropout rate was virtually identical to ours, suggesting that cost might not be a factor.

I would like to say a few words about AIM, that is, the mixing of donor semen with that of the semen of an oligoasthenospermic husband. This practice has been severely criticized for two reasons. One reason is the belief that a couple that insists upon this, has not accepted the fact that the husband is infertile. This somehow renders them psychologically unprepared or unfit for a pregnancy from donor insemination, and also might put the offspring at some psychologic risk in the future. I am not a psychiatrist and I cannot answer this except to say that there is no evidence to substantiate this hypothesis. Having witnessed many couples having successful AIMs, we have been unable to detect any behavioral differences in these couples compared to couples having AID. The second reason for condemning AIM is that it may be counterproductive. Some seminal specimens from oligospermic husbands have been shown to contain antibodies which might interfere with normal semen function. When this was reported, it was rather alarming, because it had been our policy to perform AIM at the couple's request. Therefore, we reviewed the efficacy of AIM in these same 227 patients whom I have just presented. In our original study, we did not differentiate between AID and AIM.

Table 8 gives the results of this investigation. Thirty-four patients requested AIM and 13 conceived. Seven who failed to conceive after AIM changed to AID and 2 conceived. One hundred and ninety-three patients had AID alone and 80 conceived. There were

TABLE 8.   *Comparison of AIM and AID.*

	No.	Pregnancies (%)
AIM	34	13 (38.2)
AID	193	80 ⎤
AIM → AID	7	2 ⎦ (41.0)

no significant differences between the AIM and AID groups with regard
to age, prior fertility, and additional infertility factors.   The
conception rates between groups were not significantly different.
The pregnancy outcome, pregnancy rates per cycle of AI, and dropout
rates were also similar.

This study does not disprove the hypothesis that semen of infertile men may be harmful to normal semen.   Perhaps there might
have been more conceptions by not performing AIM.   Nevertheless,
our success rate is comparable to those reported by others who do
not perform AIM, and only by offering it will some couples find donor insemination acceptable.

RESULTS OF AID IN 865 COUPLES

Andrée Schoysman-Deboeck, Mireille Merckx, Luc Segal,
Marcel Vekemans and Nadine Verhoeven

Fertility Department
Academic Hospital VUB
Brussels, Belgium

The data reported here are purely clinical with all the short-
comings inherent to retrospective case studies.

Our series of patients are not homogeneous. We have been using
fresh semen samples whenever possible or frozen semen samples when
necessary in a given cycle or in a given patient for different cycles. Furthermore, the selection of patients for AID probably changed as our experience grew. It is also different now than some eight
years ago due to the fact that the waiting time increased from just
1 or 2 months to 18 or 24 months. Finally, some husbands were azoospermic while others were severely oligospermic and some of the
wives had gynecological problems reducing their fertility.

An AID treatment or an AID series in this report denotes the
total number of cycles and the necessary number of inseminations in
each cycle until a pregnancy is obtained or the patient gives up.
The data include all cases treated and all cycles in which at least
one insemination was performed whether or not the insemination appeared valid after the end of the cycle and whether or not a pregnancy was achieved. Only terminated patients are considered with
those still under therapy being excluded. It is important to mention all patients and all cycles in overall results because problems
such as delayed ovulation, anovulation, misinterpretation of the
B.B.T. chart, discouragement of the patients and even lack of availability of adequate semen or of the doctor himself are inherent to
the practice of AID.

As shown in Table 1, 1121 treatments have been performed in

TABLE 1. *Number of AID cycles and number of pregnancies obtained.*

Number of pregnancies for each couple	Number of couples	Number of AID treatments	Number of pregnancies obtained
0	181 (20.9%)	181	0
1	480 (55.5%)	499	480
1	461 (53.3%)	461	461
1 but not 2	19 (2.2%)	38	19
2	176 (20.2%)	353	352
2	175 (20.2%)	350	350
2 but not 3	1 (0.11%)	3	2
3	25 (2.9%)	75	75
4	2 (0.23%)	8	8
5	1 (0.11%)	5	5
TOTAL	865	1121	920

865 couples. A total number of 920 pregnancies has been obtained
in 684 couples, 181 having no sucess at all. Only in special cases
where the efficacy of a given technique was being assessed have the
figures been corrected and cycles that could not have given any
results been discarded.

The Duration of AID Treatments

As in ordinary fertility problems, time is a very important
factor in AID. The number of cycles needed to achieve a pregnancy
as well as the duration of treatments before dropping out in this
series of cases is summarized in Table 2 and represented in Figure
1.

First, the failures will be considered in some detail. There
were 201 treatments performed which gave no result: 181 prior to
a first pregnancy, 19 prior to a second and 1 prior to a third.
These failures may be divided as follows:

. No information. In 39 cases(19%) no information was received
  after the last AID. Most of these cases are spread over the
  first four cycles of therapy. Some, as learned by experience
  with similar cases, may have achieved a pregnancy and return-
  ing later to ask for a second child, having considered the
  first success as normal and of no interest for the doctor.
  However, most of were probably not very motivated for AID and
  wished to forget everything about it.

. Impossible for practical reasons. In 21 cases(10,4%), further
  AID was not practical since the patients had problems such as
  living too far away(Italy, North Africa, Zaïre), having had
  to move abroad. In some cases it was discontinued because of
  severe disease or accident to a member of the family. These
  cases occurred mostly during the first 6 or 7 cycles.

. Gynecological problems. Twenty patients(10%) had a gynecological problem such as reduced tubal patency, post-myomectomy
  status, treated endometriosis, anovulation, cervical canal or
  mucous alteration, etc. Just 4 of them appeared at a second
  laparoscopy to be definitely sterile but the other cases might
  have expected a pregnancy. These patients gave up AID and
  were often encouraged to do so between the 4th and the 24th
  cycle of treatment.

. Older women. Forty two patients(21%) dropped the treatment
  because they were nearing or over 40 years of age. These patients are spread over all cycles but the majority were treated
  for a minimum of 10 cycles. Several requested a second pregnancy and one a third. It is obvious that these cases

TABLE 2. *Number of pregnancies obtained for each number of AID cycles.*

Number or cycles	Number of pregnancies	% of successes				
1	205	18.28				
2	152	13.56	42.63			
3	121	10.79		62.06		
4	79	7.04				
5	85	7.58	19.43			
6	54	4.81			75.52	
7	40	3.57				
8	30	2.68	7.76			
9	17	1.51		13.46		
10	24	2.14				
11	18	1.60	5.7			
12	22	1.96				
13	9	0.80				80%
14	4	0.35				
15	5	0.44				
16	7	0.62				
17	4	0.35				
18	5	0.45				
19	7	0.62				
20	3	0.26				
24	2	0.18				
26	1	0.09	5.1			
27	3	0.26				
28	1	0.09				
29	1	0.09				
33	1	0.09				
38	1	0.09				
40	1	0.09				
56	1	0.09				
60	1	0.09				

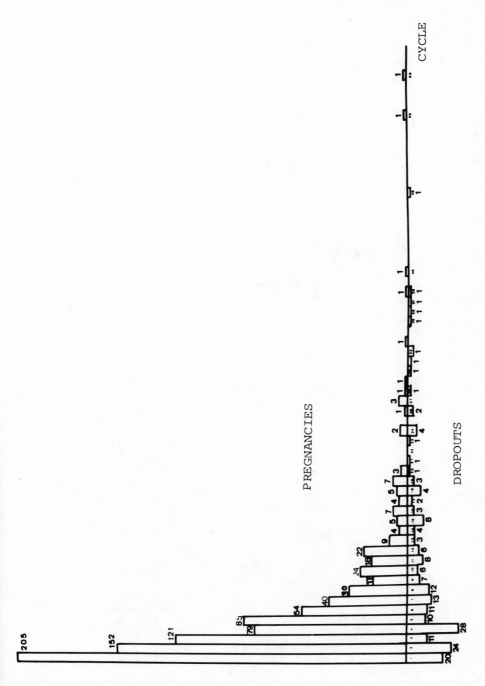

FIGURE 1.   Number of pregnancies and number of dropouts per treatment cycle.

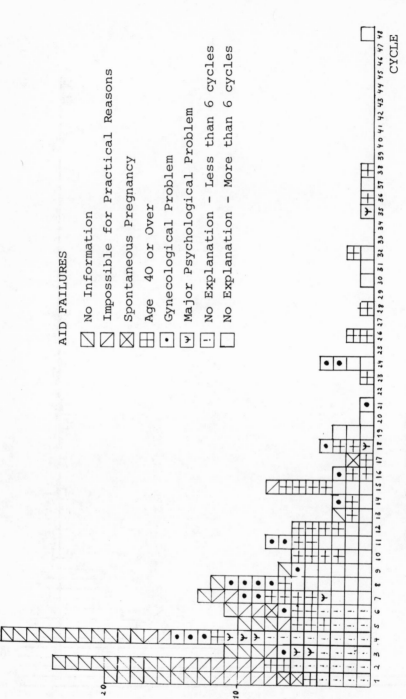

FIGURE 2.   AID failures per cycle.

represent real problems and the main question is how humanly
justifiable it is to start at all under such circumstances.

. Spontaneous pregnancy. Four patients(2%) became spontaneously
pregnant, 2 after having had one previous cycle of AID, 1 after
six AID cycles and 1 after seventeen cycles. The same frequen-
cy(2%) of spontaneous fertility in the waiting list patients
indicates that 1 or 2% of the pregnancies considered to be the
results of AID in this series could be due to the husband.

. Discouragement. There were 34 patients(14%) who dropped AID
treatment after 1 to 6 cycles, 5 of them with a psychological
problem such as depression or marital conflict. Most of these
patients were considered to be poorly motivated or, as was the
case some 8 to 10 years ago, poorly informed about the possible
duration of AID treatment. As the waiting list has grown longer and patients receive accurate information about the results
obtained with AID in our group, the number of such cases has
dropped dramatically. There were 41 cases in which AID was given up after more than 6 cycles without any gynecological
explanation for the failure.

In conclusion, the failures of AID are a very heterogenous
group and it is impossible to state how many cases are actually
failures of the technique. Accordingly, it seems extremely important to carefully inform the couples before starting AID about what
is possible and what might be difficult. They must be assured that
as long as there is no medical problem, their decision is always
best and will be respected and supported. Although we deplore a
very long waiting list, it appeared after several years that such
a delay is a natural way of revealing motivated couples. The problem of older women is a very painful one and long cycles of failure may be more depressing than a negative recommendation to the
initial request for AID.

Within the group of patients having obtained a pregnancy, the
duration of some treatments has also been a matter of concern.
Therefore, it was very important to know the normal distribution
in time of pregnancies occuring in the human population. The work
of Lestaeghe et al. indicates that the conception probability in
the normal fertile population is of about 20% for each cycle of
exposure.

Figure 2 shows that about 50% of the couples have a pregnancy within 3 cycles; 6 out of 1000 have to wait for more than
two years to get theirs. Comparison with Figure 1 shows a definite
similarity of distribution of the pregnancies obtained by AID.

In order to compare our results with natural reproduction,

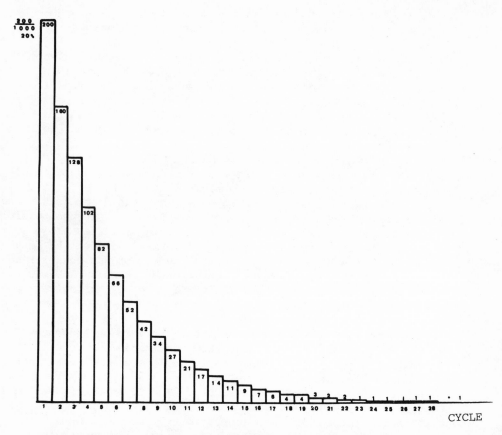

FIGURE 3. Number of cycles to obtain pregnancy in a
population with a conception probability of 0.20.

we calculated for successful patients the rate(Table 3) and chance
(Table 4) of pregnancy for each cycle. Table 5 indicates the probability obtained for all cycles in our series, including all dropouts. As long as the figures are high enough to be significant,
the chances are equal to about 20%, which is close to that observed
in the normal fertile population. Thus, we could say that AID gives
roughly the same results as natural reproduction. Although the
chances of obtaining a pregnancy seem to get smaller with time,
they are certainly promising enough to continue the treatment in
the small percentage of patients involved.

The total number of cycles of AID performed among all the patients of this group is 6207(average value for pregnancy: 6.74
cycles). The total number of cycles among the patients with a pregnancy is 4513(average value for pregnancy: 4.9 cycles). The
average number of inseminations per cycle is 2.

TABLE 3. *Distribution of the obtained pregnancies for each AID cycle.*

Number of cycles	Number of pregnancies	Percent of total pregnancies			
1	205	22.28			
2	152	16.52	51.95%		
3	121	13.15			
4	79	8.58		75.64%	
5	85	9.25	23.69%		
6	54	5.87			92.02%
7	40	4.34			
8	30	3.26	9.44%		
9	17	1.84		16.38%	
10	24	2.60			
11	18	1.95	6.94%		
12	22	2.39			
13	9	0.98			
14	4	0.44			
15	5	0.55			
16	7	0.77			
17	4	0.44			
18	5	0.55			
19	7	0.77			
20	3	0.33			
24	2	0.22			
26	1	0.11	± 0.11%		
27	3	0.33			
28	1	0.11			
29	1	0.11			
33	1	0.11			
38	1	0.11			
40	1	0.11			
56	1	0.11			
60	1	0.11			

A. SCHOYSMAN-DEBOECK ET AL.

TABLE 4. *Chances of pregnancy for each treatment cycle for the 911 women who achieved a pregnancy.*

Number of cycles	Number of AID treatments	Number of pregnancies	Percent of pregnancies
1	911	207	23.4
2	707	149	21.0
3	558	119	21.32
4	439	78	17.76
5	361	84	23.26
6	277	54	19.49
7	223	40	17.93
8	183	29	15.85
9	154	17	11.03
10	137	24	17.51
11	113	18	15.92
12	95	22	23.16
13	73	9	12.33
14	64	4	6.25
15	60	5	8.33
16	55	7	12.73
17	48	4	8.33
18	44	5	11.36
19	39	7	17.95
20	32	3	9.37

In the fertile group the average of 4.9 cycles for a pregnancy may seem high compared with some data in the literature. But very often the studies described are limited to a definite number of AID cycles. It is easy to show that if the AID treatment is limited to 12 cycles, the average number of cycles to obtain a pregnancy becomes 3.9, but if the treatment is stopped after 6 cycles, pregnancy is obtained after an average of 2.8 cycles.

TABLE 5. *Chances of pregnancy for the first 20 AID cycles for all patients treated.*

Cycles	Cases treated	Number of pregnancies	Percent of pregnancies	Dropouts
1	1121	205	18.29	20
2	896	152	16.96	24
3	720	121	16.80	11
4	588	79	13.43	28
5	481	85	17.67	10
6	386	54	13.99	11
7	321	40	12.46	13
8	268	30	11.19	12
9	226	17	7.52	7
10	202	24	11.89	6
11	172	18	10.46	8
12	146	22	15.07	6
13	118	9	7.63	3
14	106	4	3.77	3
15	99	5	5.05	8
16	86	7	8.14	3
17	76	4	5.26	2
18	70	5	7.14	4
19	61	7	11.47	3
20	51	3	6.0	1

The evolution of the pregnancies after AID is summarized in Table 6. Based upon the results, several remarks are justified:

. The number of miscarriages out of the number of terminated pregnancies (712) is 121 or 16.8%. This figure, at the upper limit of normal, must be considered carefully because among our patients, all miscarriages including very early ones, are registered. Moreover, about 100 unended pregnancies are older than 4 months and will no longer result in miscarriages. This brings the total percentage of miscarriages to 14.9%.

TABLE 6. *Evolution of the pregnancies obtained by AID.*

	Living children					Premature dead	Still-born	Ectopic	Mis-carriages	Malformations Anomalies
	(Still) Unknown	Boys	Girls	Sex?	Multiple pregnancies					
Fresh semen (148)	24	52	43	2	1 twins	1 1 twins	3	1	19 (15.32%)	1 premature boy alive, almost blind
Frozen semen (415)	114	107	120	5	5 twins 1 triplet	1	1	2	59 (including) (1 mole) (19.60%)	1 congenital sacro-iliac luxation. 1 lacrymal duct malformation. 1 agenesia of adrenal glands in one of the triplets (died after two days). 1 mongoloid boy. 1 cleft palate (like the mother).
Mixed Semen (342)	69	103	111	–	9 twins 1 triplet	–	3	1	43 (15.75%)	1 microphtalmia (living) 1 syndactylia 2 tces 1 Fallot heart disease 1 mongoloid girl 1 forearm malformation 1 meningocoele (operated and well)
Unknown (fresh or frozen)	–	7	5	1	–	1	–	–	1	–
TOTAL (920)	207	269	279	8	15 twins 2 triplets	4	7	4	122 (17.11%)	

594 children.

. The high frequency of multiple pregnancies(in our series about 2.63% of all cases   compared with 1.25% in our population) is certainly related to the rather frequent medical induction of ovulation. Nevertheless, the 2 pairs of twins prematurily born and dead were real twins.

Again, the problem of older women and the occurence of miscarriages after at times long term AID as well as the age limit for starting treatment have been a matters of concern.   In Table 7, the frequency of miscarriages as related to the patient's age on all well documented cases is reported.   The total number of cases is still low but the trend after 37 years of age seems to be rather unfavorable.

Fearing that our data would be influenced by the fact that some of the husbands are not azoospermic but only severely oligospermic(less than 4-5 million spermatozoa/ml.) and convinced as we are that the sub-fertile man unmasks the sub-fertile woman, we compared the percentage of pregnancies obtained in each cycle in the two

TABLE 7. *Percentage of miscarriages according to age.*

Age	Number of pregnancies	Number of miscarriages	Percent of miscarriages
22	7	0	0
23	9	3	33.3
24	32	3	9.4
25	34	4	11.8
26	47	6	12.8
27	60	11	18.3
28	76	6	7.9
29	86	8	9.3
30	62	12	19.3
31	52	9	17.3
32	43	5	11.6
33	44	6	13.6
34	37	1	2.7
35	34	4	11.7
36	25	3	12
37	17	1	5.9
38	17	5	29.4
39	12	2	16.6
40	3	3	100
41	1	1	100
42	1	0	0

groups of couples. Between these 2 groups of patients there is no significant difference. We may only conclude that the oligospermic patients admitted in this AID series react as azoospermic men.

Since the beginning of our experience, 3 main modifications in the AID treatments have been progressively introduced and deserve comment:

. Cervical insemination versus peri-cervical insemination with cervical cap. We have compared for all patients having achieved a pregnancy the results obtained in all cycles with intra-cervical insemination and the results observed in all cycles where a cervical cap was used.

. Frenquency of insemination. At first, the inseminations started on the first possible ovulation day as indicated by a previous study of the B.B.T. Chart and length of the cycle were repeated every day. Later, since the post-insemination tests were generally very good after 24 hours, as well as for practical reasons, the inseminations were repeated only every 2 days.

TABLE 8. *Comparison of the percentage of pregnancies obtained after each number of cycles in women with azoospermic husbands and in women with oligospermic husbands.*

Cycle number	Pregnancies(%) Azoospermic husbands	Pregnancies(%) Oligospermic husbands
1	25	23.8
2	15.6	17.1
3	12.9	9.6
4	9.1	5.4
5	8.7	8.4
6	6.6	7.9
7	4.7	4.6
8	2.8	5.8
9	0.7	2.9
10	2.1	3.6
11	1.9	1.7
12	3.3	2.1
13	0.9	0.8
14	0.7	0.8
15	0.9	0.4
16	0.5	-
17	0.9	0.4
18	0.2	0.8
19	0.6	1.2
20	0.2	0.4

TABLE 9. *Results of intra-cervical inseminations with and without use of a cervical cap.*

Method of insemination	Number of cycles	Number of pregnancies	Percent of pregnancies
Intra-cervical	2012	338	16.80%
Cervical cap (Semm)	2063	525	25.44%

The comparison of cycles with daily insemination to cycles with insemination every 2 days is summarized in Table 10. The cycles with only one insemination resulted from the decision not to repeat a second insemination one or two days later. The use of only one insemination corresponded to the occurrence of a good quality of cycle where the time of ovulation was easy to foresee. We have no explanation for the seemingly illogical "best" results with inseminations repeated every 2 days as opposed to every day but can advance 2 hypotheses: (1) The daily insemination whether intra-cervical or with a cervical cap is somewhat irritating to the cervix and this fact reduces the chances of success of succeeding inseminations; and (2) the patients and the doctors are more relaxed when they have to organize an appointment every 2 days instead of every day, especially as many of the patients had to travel long distances and were unable to arrive before 5 or 6 p.m.

Stimulation of Ovulation

Difficulty foreseeing ovulation for AID can be partially overcome by induction of ovulation in the vast majority of patients. Nevertheless, it is obvious that the treatment used must be safe without daily monitoring of hormonal balance. Two types of stimulation have been used. Among women who ovulate but have irregular cycles or show poor estrogen impregnation before ovulation, the following treatment according to Taymor, has been used: from day 8 to 12, 150 I.U. of HMG; on day 13 and if necessary 15 or even 17, 5000 I.U. of HCG. Clomiphene (50 to 100 mg. a day) from day 1 to 5 or 2 to 6 has been administered for short luteal phases and more recently in cases of irregular cycles. The results of these treatments are briefly presented in Table 11.

The percentage of pregnancies in these difficult cycles is about the same as in normal patients. The good results obtained with Clomiphene should be verified in a larger group and for a long er period as it has not yet been used enough to include resistant

TABLE 10. *Comparative results of inseminations repeated every day or every two days.*

Frequency of the AID	Number of cycles	Number of pregnancies	Percent of pregnancies
Once in a cycle	928	165	17.78
Every day	1106	183	16.54
Every 2 days	2028	524	25.83

TABLE 11. *Results obtained after regulation of cycles by HMG/HGC or Clomiphene.*

Stimulation	Number of cycles treated	Pregnancies obtained	
HMG/HCG (after Taymor)	957	192 (20.06%)	still unknown 20 (16.9%) miscarriages 31 normal babies 132 twins 9 pairs (6.3%)
Clomiphene	280	79 (28.21%)	still unknown 46 miscarriages 4 (12.12%) normal babies 25 twins 3 pairs⎤ triplets pair ⎦ 13.8%

or difficult cases. More difficult cases of anovulation were treat
ed by higher doses of HMG/HCG but of course under laboratory control. One birth of triplets was observed in a amenorrheic woman
without spontaneous ovulation who was treated under cycle-monito-
ring with extremely high doses of HMG/HCG. Another occured in a
woman who had received 50 mg of Clomiphene.

Although it is impossible to separate the real effect of these
3 technical modifications, the data seem to indicate some improvement with each.

CONCLUSION

Briefly, the results of AID in a large group gave a least one pregnancy in 80% of all couples. The number of failures can certainly be reduced by better instruction of the patients either to prevent them from despair after just a few cycles, or to inform them about the possibility of AID before they reach 40 years of age. Although AID is not very complicated from a technical point of view, it is sometimes practically and psychologically difficult for both patients and doctors. The result in invaluable: A child.

ACKNOWLEDGEMENT

To all donors whose names will for ever remain secret, our thanks; without their dedicated gifts, our program would not be possible.

ARTIFICIAL INSEMINATION WITH FROZEN SPERMATOZOA:

RESULTS FROM 1967 TO 1978

P.E. Lebech and G. Detlefsen

Department of Obstetrics and Gynecology
Frederiksberg Hospital
Copenhagen, Denmark

INTRODUCTION

Artificial insemination with donor semen (AID) has in recent years been de-dramatized and in Denmark at least, it is now accepted by the population as well as by many members of the medical profession as a reasonable possibility in the treatment of childlessness. It is important, therefore, that couples who wish to utilize AID should have a reasonably easy access to this treatment and the greatest possible chances of success. They should also be assured that the semen used, which they are entirely unable to check, is derived from men having physical and mental qualities of an acceptable standard.

Semen selection is facilitated by the use of frozen semen stored in so-called sperm banks. This makes it possible to even select the donors by a number of other criteria, e.g. color of hair and eyes, height, blood group, etc. Moreover, it is possible to inseminate the same woman with semen from the same donor on several consecutive days and through several menstrual cycles.

At Frederiksberg Hospital, Copenhagen, we have had a sperm bank with frozen semen which has been in continuous operation since 1967.

From 1972 to 1973, the freezing technique was modified, and we started associating more intensive hormone therapy with AID in the hope of improving the results.

MATERIAL AND METHODS

Donors

All the donors are young students, either from universities or colleges. The selection and examination of the donors were according to guidelines previously published.[1] We have had no difficulty in procuring donors whose payment has increased in step with inflation. Today it is 100 Danish kroner per ejaculate (about 20 U.S. dollars).

Freezing Technique

Only donors with an entirely normal spermiogram are used. Freezing and thawing tests are performed and the quality is assessed on the basis of the spermatozoa concentration, the number of immobile and "dead" spermatozoa (after vital staining), the mean motility (in seconds per mm based on the mean of 50 spermatozoa) and lifespan in hours.

Only ejaculates which after freezing and thawing contain 40% or more motile or living spermatozoa and in which the mean motility is less than 42 sec/mm and the lifespan unchanged are accepted by the bank and later used for insemination.

Technique of Preparation

The medium is prepared beginning with 150 ml of sterile egg yolk and 150 ml of sterile distilled water which are mixed and then centrifuged at 20,000 x g for 10 minutes. The supernatant (50% egg yolk) is inactivated at 68°C. A 60ml portion of this egg yolk preparation is mixed with glycerin (21ml), sodium citrate (1g), fructose (0.5 g), streptomycin (0.3 g) and water (up to 100 ml). The pH is 7. One part of this medium is added to 2 parts of fresh semen under aseptic conditions at room temperature with cautious stirring (magnetic stirrer). Immediately after mixing, spermatozoa suspension is drawn into plastic straws, sealed with wax and placed horizontally in a thermos bucket at -30°C for 9 minutes and then at -80°C for 10 minutes, after which it is transferred directly into liquid N_2. Thawing is done at room temperature immediately before use.

In the first part of the study (1968-1969) the same freezing technique was used except that the medium contained phosphate buffer at pH 7.4 and 8% glycerin.[1] About 60% of the ejaculates met the criteria and could be used.

Patients Selection

All couples had been investigated in the Fertility Clinic and when it was found that there was irreversible sterility in the male, the possibility of AID was considered.

After a waiting period of about two years, all the couples were invited for an interview, together as well as separately. When insemination was decided, there was usually a waiting period of two or three months before treatment was started. None of those who accepted or were accepted for AID after the interview discontinued treatment or dropped out.

Before AID was instituted, the women were investigated according to our usual procedures: Basal temperature curve and hormone work-up, hysterosalpingography or laparoscopy, and analyses of cervical mucus.

The patients studied from 1972 to 1978 may be divided into 3 groups: Group I comprised of 117 women who were found to be normal through our investigations; group II includes 51 women with anovulation or severe oligomenorrhea; and group III consists of 14 women with a history of surgery for occluded tubes or uterine malformations.

Of the husbands, 62% had aspermia, 37% had greatly reduced quality of sperm at repeated spermiograms. There were two men with normal fertility but one was a carrier of Down's syndrome and the other was Rhesus positive while his wife was Rhesus immunized. Of the 182 women, 18 have given birth to two or more children.

The early part of the study from 1968-1972 included only women who had exhibited normal conditions or slight variations in the menstrual cycle with only one having had a history of tubal plastic surgery.

Insemination Procedure

Before treatment was instituted, the women had recorded a basal temperature curve for at least two cycles. These curves were also recorded throughout the entire period of insemination and submitted at the beginning of each menstrual period. On the basis of these curves and serum progesterone determinations, it was attempted to fix the probable time of ovulation. The women were told to present themselves a day or two before expected ovulation and the cervical mucus was examined.

Cervical Mucus Analysis

Using a special syringe furnished with a standardized capillary tube, mucus was aspirated and its elasticity assessed on the basis of the vacuum in the syringue(measured in μl) required to fill the capillary tube with 60 μlof mucus .[1] The capillary tube was sealed with wax at both ends and sent directly to the laboratory where the sperm penetration test of Kremer[2] was performed. In some cases, this was done with the same spermatozoa with which the woman was to be inseminated. The motility of the spermatozoa in the column of cervical mucus at 37°C and in 100% humidity is read after 15 min. and stated in mm.[3]   The result is available in 20 min. while the woman is waiting. If the mucus was optimal, the insemination was performed.

     Group II who were anovulatory or had considerable variations in their menstural cycles were treated with 100 mg clomiphene citrate daily for four days, followed by 6000 IU human chorionic gonadotrophin (HCG) on day 14 or at an optimal time. Other women have been stimulated with human menopausal gonadotrophin (HMG) with simultaneous determinations of the serum estradiol followed by treatment with HCG. The inseminations were carried out at optimal times and in most cases daily until basal temperature curves, charges in cervical mucus, or progesterone analyses showed that ovulation had occurred.

     As a matter of principle, all patients were offered AID for 6 cycles but quite often we waived this restriction and continued for another few cycles.

     For each insemination, 0.5 ml semen was used and second period of the study, we used a cervical cap as recommended by Jondet.

                              RESULTS

     Figure 1 gives the age distribution of the women for the two periods of 1968 to 1972 and 1972 to 1978. There were no statistically significant differences between the two study periods.

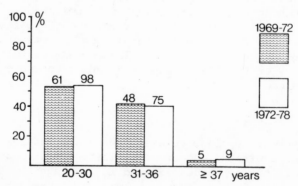

FIGURE 1.   Age distribution of 296 women in two studies for AID.

TABLE 1. *Sperm penetration in the cervical mucus at the time of insemination resulting in pregnancy.*

	Penetration <24mm/15min.	Penetration 25-39mm/15min.	Penetration >40mm/15min.
Group I			
% of pregnancies	27,3	72,1*	87,8*
Total	11	68	41
Group II			
% of pregnancies	57.1	66.7	50.0
Total	14	27	14

* Pregnancy rate significantly higher than for women with lower penetration(p= 0.001).

TABLE 2. *Elasticity in the cervical mucus at the time of insemination followed by pregnancy.*

	Elasticity 600mkrl.vacuum	Elasticity 800mkrl.vacuum	Elasticity 1000mkrl.vacuum
Group I			
% of pregnancies	70.1	81.0	75.0
Total	77	21	8
Group II			
% of pregnancies	59.5	71.4	60.0
Total	42	7	5

No significant differences observed.

The result of the sperm penetration test for the cycle in which conception occurred is shown in Table 1. According to the present findings, the conception rate was significantly higher for women with a sperm penetration exceeding 25 mm /15 min. The chances of pregnancy rise with increasing sperm penetration. This did not apply to the woman of group II (stimulated with clomiphene or HMG).

Table 2 illustrates a similar study of the elasticity of the cervical mucus at the time when the woman conceived. There is no correlation between the conception rate and elasticity at a 600, 800

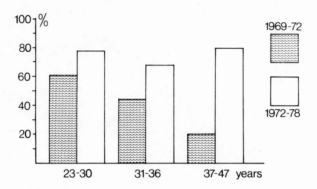

FIGURE 2. Correlation between pregnancy rate and age in
the first study 1969-72 and in the second study 1972-78.

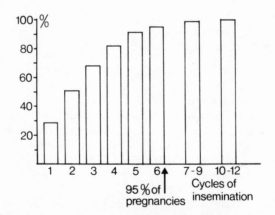

FIGURE 3. Cumulative percentage of pregnancies in relation to the number of months of insemination.

or 100 μg vacuum. At an elasticity exceeding 1000 μg, insemination
was usually not performed since under such conditions there is low
or no spermatozoa penetration. Therefore, changes in elasticity below a 1000 μg vacuum are not useful as a criterion for timing insemination. In practice, however, successful insemination can be expected
only at a penetration of 25 mm/15 mn or over.

Figure 2 presents the conception rate and age in the two periods.
There is no statistically significant difference in the conception
rate between the age groups. Figure 3 presents the cumulative pregnancy rate in relation to the number of insemination cycles. It can
be seen that 29% conceived in the first cycle and the number increased
regularly during the subsequent months so that 95% of those women who
eventually conceived had done so after the 6th treatment cycle. In
other words, by continuing the treatment beyond 6 cycles, it is possible to obtain at most a 5% increase in the conception rate.

Table 3 presents the conception rate in groups I, II and III.
It is apparent that the results are equally favorable in all three
groups. It is reasonable, therefore, to try treating all infertile
women with a sterile partner if AID is decided upon.

Table 4 which presents a survey of the two study periods, shows
a significantly higher pregnancy rate for 1972 to 1978 during which
significantly fewer inseminations were needed to obtain a pregnancy.

Table 5 presents the outcome of the pregnancies. The abortion
rate was 20.6%(the same in both periods). The sex ratio was 51%
girls to 49% boys. Three of the infants had malformations. A girl,
whose mother had been stimulated with clomiphene, had sirenomelia
and hydrocephalus and two infants had unilateral pes equinovarus.
All the other infants were normal. Of the three twin pregnancies,
one occurred in group I and two in group II(hormone stimulated).

TABLE 3. *Results of AID with frozen spermatozoa.*

	Group I "Normal"	Group II[a] Oligo- amenorrhoea	Group III Tubal occlusion, uterine abnormal- ities(surgery)
No. women	128	57	15
No. pregnancies	94	35	10
% pregnant	73	61	67

[a] All treated with clomiphene citrate or gonadotropins(HMG, HCG).
No significant differences in pregnancy rate observed among
groups.

TABLE 4. *Results of AID with Frozen spermatozoa.*

AID period	Women	Cycles per pregnancy	Inseminations per pregnancy	Pregnancy rate(%)
1969-1972	114	6,8	19,5	51.7
1972-1978	200	5.4	8.3	69.5

The number of inseminations are significantly lower and the pregnancy rate significantly higher for the 1972 to 1978 period.

TABLE 5. *Pregnancy outcome.*

	Number	%
Normal deliveries	153	76.9
Twins	3	1.5
Ectopic pregnancy	1	0.5
Abortions	41	20.6
Legal abortion	1	0.5
Total	199	100

DISCUSSION AND CONCLUSION

We have not yet carried out a systematic follow-up of the parents and children but we have maintained contact with practically all of them and they have spontaneously reported their joy in the children. There have been no negative reactions.

We have planned, and the parents have accepted, a follow-up study when the children are about 14 years of age. At that time it may be presumed that most of the theoretically possible familial problems will have occurred.

The two periods of 1968 to 1972 and 1972 to 1978 are not entirely comparable since a number of conditions were different.

In our opinion, the selection of donors and the freezing technique have not had any detectable influence upon the more favorable results in the later period when the conception rate was almost 70%, a result as good as that obtained with fresh semen(5). We

feel that the main reason for the improved results in the later period which included a larger proportion of sub-fertile women was
the more accurate fixing of the ovulation time by hormone, basal
temperature curve and in particular, cervical mucus analysis. Therefore, it would seem that better results are obtainable by the use
of frozen spermatozoa if the insemination is done shortly before
ovulation occurs.

The abortion rate at almost 20% was the same in both periods.
This is higher than Behrmann's[6] but at the same level as that reported by Jondet[7] and others.[8] Ten of the women who aborted during
their first pregnancy have subsequently delivered viable infants
after a second series of treatments.

We conclude that frozen semen can be used with favorable results and that a sperm bank should be among the facilities at the
disposal of a modern fertility clinic.

REFERENCES

1. Lebech, P.E. Les banques de sperme humain. In: Fécondité et
       Stérilité du Mâle, Paris, 1972.

2. Lebech, P.E., Svendsen, P. and Ostergaard, E. The effects of
       small doses of gestagen on the cervical mucus. Int. J. Fer-
       til., 15:65, 1970.

3. Kremer, J. A simple sperm penetration test. Int. J. Fertil
       10:209, 1965.

4. Jondet, M., Millet, D. and Netter, A. Adaptation d'une Cap
       cervicale pour l'insémination artificielle. J. Gyn. Obst.
       Biol. Reprod., 4:141, 1975.

5. Detlefsen, G. and Starup, J. Erfaring med donorinsemination i
       430 tilfaelde. Ugeskr. Laeg., 139:2264, 1977.

6. Behrman, S. and Ackerman, D.R. Freeze preservation of human
       sperm. Amer. J. Obstet. Gynecol., 103:654, 1969.

7. Jondet, M. Congélation du sperme humain. Bull Acad. de France,
       49:373, 1976.

8. Sherman, J.K. Synopsis of the use frozen human semen since 1964.
       Fertil. Steril., 24:397, 1973.

ARTIFICIAL INSEMINATION WITH FROZEN DONOR SEMEN:

RESULTS IN 604 WOMEN

Didier Millet [*] and Michel Jondet [**]

[*] 9 Avenue Franco Russe
[**] Fondation de Recherche en Hormonologie
Paris, France

We founded a unit of semen storage and artificial insemination
in 1973 at the Hôpital Necker in Paris (Dr Netter's Department),
where a technique of semen freezing in liquid nitrogen has been
used.[1] After checking the fertilizing ability of this stored semen[2]
we conducted inseminations until 1977.

MATERIAL AND METHODS

Semen Packaging. The conditions of selection and storage
of semen have been published elsewhere.[1] It will only be mentioned
that semen is packaged in 0.25ml straws.

Indications for Insemination. Insemination was indicated in
99% of cases where husband's infertility was concerned: In 1 case
out of 6, it was the result of an excretory azoospermy. Other cases
included secretory azoospermia, oligozoospermia, asthenozoospermia
and severe teratozoospermia with infertility for over two years.
In only 1% of cases was the indication of genetic origin: Either
rhesus incompatibility with maternal isoimmunisation having resulted
in severe accidents or true deleterious paternal chromosomic aber-
ration.

Previous Gynecological Check Up. Examinations required for wom-
en in order to appreciate their potential fertility are: Hysterography, basal body temperature curve during 3 cycles, estradiol and
plasma progesterone at day 6 of the thermal plateau, a detection of
antitoxoplasmic and antirubellic antibodies (with vaccination in   ·
case of negative response).

Insemination Procedure. The first insemination day was chosen
according to the thermic curve of the preceding cycle: the last
presumed day of hypothermia(or the preceding one) was retained. The
size of the cervix cervical opening, amount of cervical mucus and
mucus viscosity were rated from 0 to 3. Insemination was performed
only when the cervix was well opened, had an abundant mucus and had
good spinnbarkeit(10 cm), that is to say with a cervical score between 6 and 9.

Part of the straw was instilled on cervical mucus in the cervix and the rest deposited in the cervical cap placed previously on
the cervix. This cap that we designed[3] can easily be penetrated for
the insemination by means of a cruciform incision. A volume of air
equal to that of the injected semen escapes simultaneously without
aspiration being necessary. When the gun is drawn out, the cap
shuts spontaneously ensuring complete sealing. This method results
in good contact between the mucus and spermatozoa. Moreover, time
is gained by limiting decubitus to a few minutes. Insemination was
repeated daily as long as morning temperature did not increase and
the cervical score remained satisfactory. On the average, 2 to 3
inseminations per cycle were performed.

Ovarian Stimulation Treatments. In cases of luteal insufficiency, we first used HCG: 3 injections of 5000 I.U. during the luteal
phase. In case of too wide a variation in the ovulation date, clomiphene was used at a dosage of 100 mg daily from day 2 to day 6 of
menstruation which reduced unfavorable effects on cervical mucus.

In case of anovulation we used the same drug alone or followed
by HCG. If this treatment failed we provoked ovulation with HMG
and HCG. Cervical mucus insufficiency was first treated with clomiphene alone or rarely with clomiphene followed by oestrogens in
the preovulatory phase; in case of failure, 150 I.U. HCG was injected
each day from day 7 to day 12 of the cycle. A titration of plasma
estradiol was made on day 13 and the HMG dose was modified according to the result.

RESULTS

During four years, 604 women were inseminated during a total
of 2411 menstrual cycles. Without taking into account possible
conceptions which could be interpreted as being due to the presence
of a corpus luteum of 16 to 20 days duration, we recorded 342 conceptions, confirmed by laboratory studies. Conception occurred in
56.6% of the cases.

In 48 cases, early or late abortion was observed. There were
2 cases of ectopic pregnancy. Three twin pregnancies were recorded.

At the present time, 107 males and 118 females have been born which gives a 0.9 sex ratio, slightly lower than normal.   Two children were still-born as a result of gravidic toxemia.   Out of the 225 births, 4 malformations were observed: a trisomy 21(the mother was 41 years old), a case of club foot, a hip subluxation and a tracheal abnormality.

DISCUSSION

We shall consider parameters which may affect the insemination data.

Age of the Patients.   The patients were divided into 4 age groups(Table 1).   The conception rate was relatively stable from 20 to 34 years with a slightly higher abortion rate in the youngest group.   Above 35 years, the conception rate decreased markedly. This apparent decrease in fertility seems at this age to be partly associated with a more frequent organic pelvic pathology.   This fact should not exclude these patients from insemination.   However before starting insemination, further studies are necessary.   One must not hesitate to resort to coelioscopy to diagnose any genital pathology and treat it if possible.

Initial apparent fertility.   Existence of functional ovarian pathology, oligomenorrhea or even amenorrhea, or luteal insufficiency do not alter the results(Table 2).   Induction of ovulation is practiced at the same time as insemination.   With induced ovulation, insemination can be easily performed with maturity of the follicle at the time of HCG injection: the results are sometimes amazingly fast.

Existence of uterine organic abnormalities as malformation, adenomyosis, myomas and, most importantly of tubo-peritoneo-ovarian pathology such as endometriosis or infection sequellae affect the

TABLE 1.   *Influence of age.*

Age	No. of women	Conception rate (%)	Abortion rate (%)
20-24	76	56.6	25.6
25-29	281	62	14.4
30-34	181	57	13.5
after 35	66	32	9.5

TABLE 2. *Results of AID in women with gynecologic abnormalities.*

	No. of women	Pregnant (%)
Functional abnormalities		51.06
Anatomical abnormalities		
uterus	103	41
fallopian	39	36
Normal	415	63

results more seriously. Treatment of these kinds of pathology must take place just before insemination to give a maximum chance to these women. This maximum lies in the year following treatment which requires close collaboration with the surgeons.

Choice of Insemination Day. In 81 out of 241 cycles, we performed only a single insemination. The timing of this insemination revealed that a better conception rate was obtained on the day of minimal temperature or on one of the two preceding days.[4] On the contrary as soon as the thermal increase began, the conception rate decreased. This confirms what is known regarding the role of the cervix and cervical mucus as a reception site and their influence on sperm survival, the latter being regularly distributed to the uterus and oviducts from cervical crypts.[5]

Results in Relation to the Cycle. In the first six months, 90% of pregnancies were obtained. Even so, it is necessary to improve this score to ensure that less fertile women become pregnant. We observed as Schoysman et al.[6] that the conception rate is relatively stable from one cycle to another. Indeed there is no privileged cycle. However conception rates are better in the first 3 cycles. This may be attributed to the fact that the more fertile women are more likely to be fertilized at the beginning. One also notices that at the beginning of inseminations, ovarian and cervical functional disturbances are rather rare (Figure 1).

Deficiency in cervical mucus and shifts in ovulation appear later. They are a consequence of anxiety, or progressive lassitude in these patients because of repeated failures. With these later cycles, conception rates decrease slightly. They increase again towards the 9th or 10th cycle. This increase is not due to chance, but is the result of the treatment for these functional disturbances.

Effect of Ovarian Stimulation Treatment. We decided to use the ovarian stimulation treatment only when necessary and not

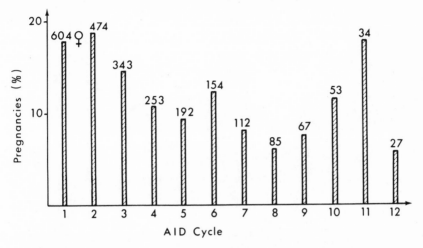

FIGURE 1. Pregnancies occuring per cycle of AID.

routinely. As the cycles progress, the percentage of women treated at the same time of insemination increases. It reaches 80% at cycle 7 (Figure 2). These treatments allow correction of ovulatory disturbances and cervical insufficiency. We carry them out for half cycles. Half of the pregnancies can be in part attributed to these treatments (Table 3) which are not considered to involve supplementary risks.

We observed 2 cases of severe ovarian hyperstimulation which occured in amenorrheal women given this treatment, an effect unknown to us in menstruating women. Out of the 3 cases of twin pregnancies, only one could possibly be attributed to the use of clomiphene, the other two being spontaneous. In this group where most women present only transitory functional problems induced by the conditions of insemination, the physiological hypothalamo-hypophyso-ovarian regulations are certainly much less disturbed than in amenorrheal women. This would explain the rarity of incidents in menstruating women.

A few authors have referred to a problem of increased abortion associated with chromosomal aberrations[7] and to malformations following treatments with ovulation inducers.[8] We did not observe such facts: The rate of spontaneous abortion represented 15.2% of untreated conceptions and 12.8% of conceptions following treatment. Malformations seem to be incidental; a longer series would be necessary to draw any conclusions.

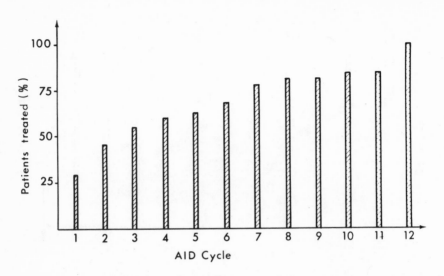

FIGURE 2. Women treated in the pregnant group per cycle.

Effects of coelioscopy. In the case of failure to conceive
following 6 to 8 cycles with insemination seemingly performed under
good conditions, we suggest a coelioscopy completed by a test of tubal permeability with methylene blue and a biopsy curettage of the
endometrium. This was done 53 times. In 22 cases the examination
did not reveal any abnormality and was followed by a pregnancy in
54% of the cases. Pregnancy was rapidly obtained (1 to 4 cycles
following examination). In 31 cases, pelvic pathology not detected
by clinical examination and hysterography was revealed. A specific
treatment could sometimes be undertaken, but the rate of success was
lower at 24%.

Use of coelioscopy seems to be of value. It has two purposes:
(1) Diagnosis of an unknown pathology; (2) a guide for treatment.
In this way the situation can be assessed before deciding to discontinue inseminations. If coelioscopy is normal, it helps to eliminate
doubt in the mind of the practictioner and patient. Moreover, this act
may have therapeutic value because it may rapidly be followed by
pregnancy in many cases. This suggests several factors: disagglu-
tination of the fimbriae of the abdominal ostium and renewal of the
endometrium which is often dystrophic or hyperplastic and could
counteract nidation.

Number of motile sperm deposited. We showed that a relationship
exists between conception rate and the sperm number deposited during
each cycle (Table 4). In 1494 cycles, we found a significant relation (p < 0.001) which confirms the logical hypothesis as well as

TABLE 3. *Influence of treatments on conception and abortion rates.*

	No. of cycles	Pregnancy(%)	Abortion(%)
Without treatment	1,030	15.5	15
With treatment	1,058	14	16.5
Clomiphene	285	13	10.5
Clo+ HCG	280	16	27
HCG	328	13	16
HMG	65	12	0
HMG+ HCG	100	16	12.5

TABLE 4. *Influence of the number of motile spermatozoa inseminated.*

No. of total cycles studied	476	499	519
No. of motile sperm. inseminated per cycle(Million)	2-15	16-25	Sup. 26
Conception rate(%)	12.8	15.2	18.5

the few studies showing a correlation between pregnancy and spermiogram quality.[9]

It would be interesting to determine the optimal spermatozoa number to be deposited in a cycle in order to understand the insemination pattern better(which remains too uncertain) and to improve the results which although satisfactory still need to be improved.

REFERENCES

1. Jondet, M. and Netter, A. Organisation d'une banque de sperme humain. Quelques problèmes. Gynécologie, 24:141-144, 1973.

2. Millet, D., Jondet, M. and Netter, A. L'hétéro-insémination par le sperme humain congelé. Premiers résultats de l'Hôpital Necker. J. Gyn. Obst. Biol. Reprod., 3:903, 1974.

3. Jondet, M., Millet, D. and Netter, A. Adaptation d'une cap cervicale pour l'insémination artificielle humaine. J. Gyn.

Obst. Biol. Reprod., 4:141, 1975.

4. Cludy, I. Insémination artificielle avec donneur. Aspects cliniques et psychologiques. A thesis in Medicine, Univ. Paris V, 1977.

5. Hafez, E.S.E. Gamete transport. In: Human reproduction , Hafez and Evans, Eds., Harper and Row, Hagerstown, pp. 85, 1973.

6. Schoysman, R. and Schoysman-Deboeck, A. Results of donor insemination with frozen semen. In: Sperm action Progr. Reprod. Biol. , Vol. 1, Karger Ed., Bâle, pp. 252, 1976.

7. Boue, J.G. and Boue, A. Increased frequency of chromosomal anomalies in abortions after induced ovulation. Lancet, 1:679, 1973

8. Alberman, N. Fertility drugs and contraceptive agents. In: "Towards the prevention of fetal malformations", Scrimgore ed., Edinburgh, pp. 91, 1978.

9. Smith, K.D., Rodriguez-Rigau, L.J. and Steingerger, E. Relation between indices of semen analysis and pregnancy rate in infertile couples. Fertil. Steril., 28:1314, 1977.

RESULTS OF HETEROLOGOUS INSEMINATION AT

THE UNIVERSITY OF BERNE GYNECOLOGY CLINIC

Ulrich Gigon and R. Haldemann

Gynecology Clinic
University of Berne
Berne, Switzerland

INTRODUCTION

Heterologous insemination in cases of androgenic sterility and genetic disease is an alternative to adoption. Many married couples in whom there exists androgenic sterility or genetic problems are doubtful concerning the personal characteristics of an adopted child; they believe that a heterologous insemination creates better psychological and genetic conditions than adoption for happy parenthood. In probably every country in Europe, the legal aspects are still to some extent unresolved. In accordance with Art. 256 of the Swiss Code of Civil Law, however, a husband has no just cause for complaint if he has agreed to the effecting of procreation through a third party. It is, of course, still unclear whether a child possesses its own right of appeal, if it has not been established that it is legally the child of the presumed father. In spite of the unclear legal situation and the moral-theological problems, the number of married couples desiring artificial insemination is increasing rapidly.

We report here on the results achieved with 605 married couples who were treated at our clinic between 1974 and 1978. The indications for heterologous insemination are presented in Table 1.

METHOD

In 591 cases, infertility of the husband, confirmed by biopsy or by chromosome examination, was the indication for the insemination. Genetic disease in families desirous of having children is

267

TABLE 1. *Male indications for AID.*

Infertility

  · Confirmed by two semen analyses and in certain
    cases by biopsy of the testis or karyotyping.

Genetic

  · Autosomal-dominant disorders such as Rhesus
    incompatibility with a homozygous Rh-positive
    father, myotonia dystrophica, osteopsathyrosis,
    etc.

  · Autosomal-recessive, such as cystic fibrosis,
    Werdnig-Hoffmann syndrome, cystic degeneration
    of the kidneys, etc.

  · Chromosome abnormalities such as mongolism due to
    translocation.

a relatively new indication. Cases that we have treated include one
presenting with Rhesus incompatibility(a homozygous Rhesus-positive
father), one with familial myotonia dystrophica, seven with cystic
fibrosis and five with a Werdnig-Hoffmann syndrome. The attention
of the couples must, of course, be drawn to the fact that with autosomal recessive disorders, no tests of heterozygoty for the donor
of the semen exist as yet. In cystic fibrosis, for instance, where
the occurrence of the pathological gene in the population is frequent,
the risk of transmission is about 2% even with AID.

Extensive organic or endocrine investigations on the wife are
only carried out(See Table 2) if the history is suggestive. No genetic examination of the woman is made; hysterosalpingography or
laparoscopy is only carried out after two insemination cycles have
been unsuccessful. In cases of women with oligomenorrhea, the usual
hormone investigations are made.

The selection of the donor is made in accordance with the criteria shown in Table 3. No heredopathia, malformations, mental diseases or diabetes appear in the anamnesis. No determination of the
karyotype is made. However, only young donors are considered so as
to minimize the risk of mutations. The problem of blood groups has,
we think, been solved by the fact that no groups B or AB occur in
our body of donors. With 00 or BB constellations of the married couple concerned, we use semen of blood group 0 donors.

Centrally stimulating agents such as Clomiphene and Gonadotro-
pine are employed fairly generously for the inducing and timing of
ovulation so that success may be achieved as quickly as possible thus,

TABLE 2. *Examination of the wife prior to AID.*

. No genetic investigation.

. Basal temperature curve for 1-2 months.

. Hysterosalpingography or laparoscopy after two cycles without conception, FSH, 17-beta-oestradiol and prolactin determinations in cases of oligomenorrhea.

TABLE 3. *Selection of donors.*

Anamnesis

. No heredopathia, no malformations, no insanity and no diabetes in the family.

Age

. Under 35 (Few spontaneous mutations).

Intelligence

. Students.

Character

. Socially suited.

at least in terms of time, keeping the strain on the couple to a minimum. In general, we perform three inseminations at 72, 48 and 24 hours before the anticipated ovulation. The fresh or cryogenically preserved semen is placed paracervically by means of a portio cap according to Semm. The inseminations are carried out systematically every day, as stated above, until ovulation has taken place. With delayed ovulation cycles, or in cases of women with oligomenorrea, up to 7 or 8 inseminations within the same month are frequently required.

RESULTS AND DISCUSSION

The results obtained at our clinic are shown in Table 4.: 454 conceptions occurred among the 605 women treated; the overall conception rate was thus 74%. If the couples still under treatment are not counted, as well as the cases where insemination was discontinued because of anatomical defects, the pregnancy rate would be even better. We do not share the view of several authors that

TABLE 4. *Results of AID interventions carried out at*
the Gynaecological Clinic of the University
of Berne(1974- October 1978).

No. of conceptions in 605 cases	454	= 74 %
. Live births	271	
. Delayed pregnancies proceeding normally	99	
. Multiple pregnancies(twins)	15	= 3.3%
. Abortions(incl. 1 ectopic pregnancy and 1 vesicular mole).	59	= 13 %
. Intrauterine deaths	4	= 0.9%
. Malformations(1 of twins)	7	= 1.3%

inseminations should be discontinued after the sixth unsuccessful
insemination cycle since successes occurred in our group even after
12 to 20 cycles of treatment. The quite high rate of 3.3% twin
pregnancies is no doubt due to the generous use of an ovulation in-
ducer. The abortion rate of 13% lies just above the rate to be
expected from the population as a whole; in four cases intrauterine
death occurred; seven children were malformed.

Abortions, intrauterine deaths and especially malformations
are particularly painful disappointments for the married couple concerned. These cases of failure are broken down in Table 5. From
this Table, it is seen that out of 454 pregnancies, 70 i.e. 15.2%
were abnormal. In two cases, a true umbilical knot was responsible
for intrauterine death; in one case, the baby died *in utero* due to
eclampsia. The abnormality in another case was shown to be due to
a double heterozygous beta-drepanocytosis of the mother. Among the
malformations, we observed one epispadias, one talipes equinovarus,
one defect of the interventricular septum and one omphalocele or
myelomeningocele in twins, the embryos dying in the 20th week of the
pregnancy. From routine antenatal amniocentesis, we were able to
detect two chromosome abnormalities in sufficient time(16th week
of pregnancy). They consisted of one trisomia and one translocation
17-P-19-Q. Abortion was induced in both cases by means of intramuscular injection of 15-methylprostaglandin.

Pregnancies following heterologous insemination are at greater
risk in our opinion and call for watchful treatment. In Table 6,
the minimum requirements for the supervision of these pregnancies
are shown. In every case of successful heterologous insemination,
we recommend, irrespective of the age of the mother, early amniocentesis for antenatal chromosome analysis and for determination

TABLE 5. *Analysis of the abnormal pregnancies following AID.*

<u>Conceptions</u>	454
<u>Early and delayed abortions</u>	59
<u>Intrauterine deaths</u>	4

. True umbilical knots(2 cases)

. Eclampsia(1 case).
. Double heterozygous beta-
  drepanocytosis of mother(1 case)

<u>Malformations</u>	7

. Epispadias(1 case)

. Talipes equinovarus(1 case)

. Defect of interventricular septrum(1 case)

. Omphalocele or myelomeningocele
  in twins(2 children)

. Trisomia(1 case)[*]

. Translocation 17-P-19-Q(1 case)[*]

Total.. 70 = 15.2%

[*]As a result of antenatal chromosome analysis, it was possible to abort by means of 15-methyl-PG(intramuscular) in both cases.

TABLE 6. *Indispensable investigations during pregnancies following successful AID.*

. Amniocentesis in the 16th week of pregnancy with antenatal chromosome analysis and determination of alpha-fetoprotein.

. Ultrasonic investigations.

. Rh-prophylaxis with Rh-negative women following early amniocentesis and post partum.

. Search for antibodies with Rh-negative women.

of alpha- fetoprotein so that chromosomal problems or spinal malformations necessitating interruption of pregnancy may be recognized
early.   Since most malformations arise *de novo*, determination of
the karyotype of the foetus is certainly to be preferred to the
karyotype determination of the woman and the donor.

In all cases with Rhesus-negative women, a routine search for
antibodies must of course be made, and the Rhesus prophylaxis with
Rh-negative women must be carried out after early amniocentesis as
well as *post partum*.

RESULTS OF AID WITH FRESH AND FROZEN SEMEN: 488 CASES

Giovanni Traina and Vincenzo Traina

Contrattista Universitario
Bari, Italy

INTRODUCTION

The University Centre for the Diagnosis and Treatment of Sterility, Bari, Italy, has had a long standing interest in artificial insemination.   Under the direction of Giovanni Traina,[1-2], patients are known to have been treated by artificial insemination as early as 1943.   Previous results have been published elsewhere.[3-4]

MATERIALS AND METHOD

Fresh semen was used until the early months of 1978 and frozen semen through the end of December, 1978.   Altogether, 488 women received treatment.   Of these, 247 were treated in 1977-1978.   The increased activity in the latter two years is due to the fact that as our work became known: a growing number of requests reached the Center from all over Italy.   The establishment of a semen bank has also been a factor since it appears to be the only possible means of having large amounts of semen readily at hand.

To present, 230 pregnancies have been obtained, 111 of these in the last two years.   There were 24 cases in which women requested another pregnancy and became pregnant a second time, another two obtained a third pregnancy.

Insemination is done intracervically after evaluating the basal body temperature chart and the cervical mucus and it is repeated for 1 to 13 months, sometimes with the administration of drugs to stimulate ovulation.

Donors were selected among university medical students, men from the area surrounding Bari with the help of social workers, and persons consulting the Family Planning Unit. The donors were not paid but some have been reimbursed for their expenses.

Once the psycho-physical qualities of the candidate has been established, his family and medical histories are carefully taken in order to determine if there exist any familial or congenital disorders. Thorough clinical and laboratory examinations are also carried out. Furthermore, we feel that an evaluation by a geneticist is essential since he is often able to discern characteristics indicative of morphogenetic defects which may otherwise not be perceived. A karyotype completes the genetic evaluation.

All data on the donors is recorded on special coded forms and the confidentiallity of the donor is assured.

RESULTS

The number of conceptions per cycle are presented in Table 1: 76.52% of the pregnancies were obtained within the first three months and 93.48% within the first 6 months. Treatment efficacy seems to be restricted to 6 to 9 insemination cycles after which there must be a reevaluation. However, each couple presents individual problems and it may be reasonable to continue the treatment further in certain cases as is demonstrated by the rather exceptional example of a woman whom we had been treating for 12 years and had been submitted to a number of clinical and laboratory investigations during that time until eventually she became pregnant.

In order to obtain the total 230 pregnancies, 643 cycles were necessary, giving a mean value of 2.79 cycles per pregnancy. For the results of the first six cycles, the mean value was 2.43.

DISCUSSION

The percentage of pregnancies for all 488 patients treated with AID was 47.13%. This percentage may seem comparatively low, but it should be noted that prior to 1976, the patients receiving the treatment were not prepared to take the matter seriously enough and that AID treatment has since received a more general acceptance. Additionally, the ability to diagnose ovulation at that time was less accurate which probably accounted for a certain number of failures.

It should also be noted that the data of the last two years include women that were still undergoing treatment on December 31, 1978: Out of 247 patients, 80 had been treated less than 3 months

TABLE 1. *Results of artificial insemination with donor.*

Number	Up to December 1976 241 women			January 1977 to December 1978 247 women			Total 488 women		
	I	II	III	I	II	III	I	II	III
	Pregnancies		Success rate(%)	Pregnancies		Success rate(%)	Pregnancies		Success rate(%)
	Per cycle	Total		Per cycle	Total		Per cycle	Total	
1	25 (21.00%)	25 (21.00%)	10.37	47 (42.34%)	47 (42.34%)	19.03	72 (31.30%)	72 (31.30%)	14.75
2	28 (23.52%)	53 (44.53%)	21.99	28 (25.22%)	75 (67.57%)	30.36	56 (24.35%)	128 (55.65%)	26.23
3	33 (27.73%)	86 (72.26%)	35.68	15 (13.51%)	90 (81.08%)	36.34	48 (20.87%	176 (76.52%)	36.06
4	8 (6.72%)	94 (78.99%)	39.00	9 (8.11%)	99 (89.19%)	40.08	17 (7.39%)	193 (83.91%)	39.55
5	4 (3.36%)	98 (82.35%)	40.66	1 (0.90%)	100 (90.09%)	40.49	5 (2.17%)	198 (86.08%)	40.57
6	11 (9.24%)	109 (91.59%)	45.23	6 (5.40%)	106 (95.49%)	42.91	17 (7.39%)	215 (93.48%)	44.05
7	2 (1.68%)	111 (93.27%)	46.06	2 (1.80%)	109 (97.30%)	43.72	4 (1.74%)	219 (95.22%)	44.88
8	5 (4.20%)	116 (97.47%)	48.13	2 (1.80%)	110 (99.10%)	44.53	7 (3.04%)	226 (98.26%)	46.31
9	3 (2.52%)	119 (100.00 %)		1 (0.90%)	111 (100.00%)		4 (1.74%)	230 (100.00%)	
	Women treated 6 months Success: 86.23%			Women treated 6 months Success: 94.87%			Women treated 6 months Success: 90.20%		

N.B. The percentages of columns I are, compared with the total of the pregnancies, the successes obtained with reference to treatment cycles.
. The percentages of columns II are, compared with the total of pregnancies, the result of the addition of the successes obtained during treatment months.
. The percentages of columns III are the successes obtained with reference to the number of women treated.

and 11 less than 6 months. If only the group of women treated for
at least six months is considered, the percentage of pregnancies
for both series is as high as 90,20%, but for the years 1977-1978,
it is 94,87%(Table 1). Pregnancies were obtained in about 70% of
the women younger than 25 years, 50% between 26 and 35 and about
20% older than 36 years.

Nineteen miscarriages were recorded(8.26%) but 80% of the women
who had aborted successfully finished a second pregnancy after a new
treatment. The percentage of miscarriages was similar to that of the
general population. The age of the women was not especially significant with the largest number of miscarriages occurring in the 26
to 30 year old group. Neither ectopic nor twin pregnancies were
observed. No negative effect was recorded with regard to the babies
born through AID.

Apart from semen factors, it would appear that failures are
essentially related to the following: (1) An altogether too short
insemination treatment due to hasty termination of the patient's
treatment; (2) a decision of couples living a long distance from
the Center to leave before the monthly treatment cycle had been concluded; (3) difficulties in the evaluation of the ovulation period.

REFERENCES

1. Traina, G. Considerazioni sulla fecondazione artificiale della
        donna. Progressi di terapia, n° 3, 1943.

2. Traina, G. I primi sei anni di attivita del Centro di Bari per
        lo studio e la terapia della sterilita. Ed. Macri, Citta
        di Castello, 1943.

3. Traina, G. Inseminazione artificiale mediante donatore(AID) nel
        trattamento della sterilita coniu gale. Risultati in 241
        casi. Min. Gin. 29:745, 1977.

4. Traina, V. L'inseminazione artificiale umana. Ed. Miner va
        Medica, Torino, 1977.

PHYSICAL AND MENTAL DEVELOPMENT

OF CHILDREN BORN THROUGH AID

Fumio Mochimaru, Hirohisa Sato,
Toshifumi Kobayashi, Rihachi Iizuka

Department of Obstetrics and Gynecology
Keio University School of Medicine
Tokyo, Japan

INTRODUCTION

Artificial insemination with donor semen(AID) is the major technique employed in the therapy of couples with infertility seeondary to severe oligospermia and azoospermia. Over the past deeade, there have been favorable changes in public, legal and medical attitudes towards AID. Significant progress in research, both basic and applied, has contributed to these changes. There still remains however a lack of critical evaluation on the genetic adequacy or stability of progeny resulting from cryopreserved human semen which seems to be one of the major arguments against clinical use of frozen human semen.

Our first report on physical and mental development of children born following AID with frozen semen was made in 1968.[1] Emphasis of clinical results, however, remains valid in discussing various problems on AID which have been raised.

MATERIALS AND METHODS

Prior to initiation of donor insemination, the three concerned parties, doctor, husband and recipient, must be evaluated. All our donors are medical students of the university. On assigning donor semen, we take only the blood type and rhesus characteristic of each donor into account since the Japanese are homogeneous race.

All couples are interviewed together and undergo a routine

277

infertility evaluation to identify any other pathology. They are
required to release us from liability for unpredictable accidents
before their registration.

Procedures employed for freeze preservation of human semen are
illustrated in Figure 1. With the dry-ice method, human is frozen
at minus 79 degrees C., while with the liquid nitrogen technique,
freezing temperature can be set at minus 196 degrees C. The latter
has been found to provide a more stable temperature than the former.

Before freezing, semen and a protective medium(K-S Medium) are
mixed in the proportion of one to one. K-S medium consists of:
(1) Egg-yolk, 25% by volume; (2) glycerol, 15% by volume; (3) a
mixture of 5% glucose aqueous solution in the proportion of two or
three(66%) ; and, for each milliliter of the mixture, (4) 1 mg. of
penicillin or erythromycin and (5) 20 mg. of glycine are added.

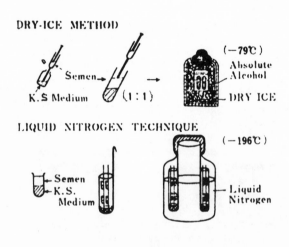

DRY-ICE METHOD

Semen
K.S Medium (1:1)

(−79℃)
Absolute Alcohol
DRY ICE

LIQUID NITROGEN TECHNIQUE

Semen
K.S. Medium

(−196℃)
Liquid Nitrogen

K-S Medium

1.	Egg-Yolk	25ml
2.	Glycerol	15ml
3.	2 %Glycine	2grm.
4.	2.9% Sodium Citrate Aq.	40.6ml
5.	5 %Glucose Aq.	17.4ml
6.	Penicilline or Erythromycin	500mg/ml

FIGURE 1. Procedures for frozen storage of human
spermatozoa.

As a rule, a half milliliter of semen is poured into the uterine cavity. Insemination is performed on those days immediatly preceeding ovulation which usually can be anticipated by means of a basal body temperature(BBT) chart and cervical mucus and vaginal cytosmear analysis. After insemination, the patient is asked to remain on her back with her legs extended for 30 minutes.

The data on physical development of children born following AID with frozen semen were collected through a letter questionnaire and an evaluation of mental development which was performed with the assistance of a psychologist.

RESULTS

The physical development of 133 children born through AID with frozen semen was evaluated on the basis of body length and weight and compared with those of children born naturally. Figure 2 shows their body lengths plotted against age. Their body weights are depicted in the same fashion in Figure 3. It was revealed that physical development of children born from AID with frozen semen tended to be somewhat better than that of the controls.

The mental development of children born from AID with frozen as well as fresh semen was evaluated. Fifty-four children on whom the examination could be performed were divided into two groups according to age: One of forty children 2 1/2 years of age or older, and the other of 14 children under 2 1/2. The former group was examined for intelligence quotient(I.Q.) by the Binet method as modified by Tanaka, the latter for development quotient(D.Q.) by the method of Tsumori and Inage. In this series, 9 children born from AID with frozen semen were included.

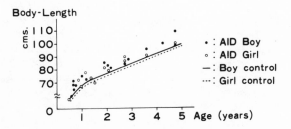

FIGURE 2. Physical development of AID babies born from frozen semen(I).

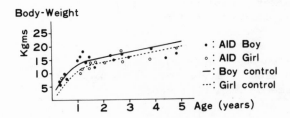

FIGURE 3.   Physical development of AID babies born
from frozen semen(II).

The I.Q. distribution of the 40 children as shown in Figure 4.
ranged from 84 to 148 with a mean of 111.7.   The 14 children under
2 1/2 years of age which included 6 from frozen semen were examined
for D.Q.   As shown in Figure 5 in which representative values are
spaced in the same manner as those for I.Q., most of the cases fell
between 100 and 110.

Thus mental development of children born following AID, whether
with fresh or frozen semen, was found to be superior to that of
those born naturally.

DISCUSSION

In 1909, the first report of a birth from AID appeared in the
literature.   In Japan, the first report of a baby from AID was in
1951 by our clinic which later introduced a technique for freeze
preservation of human spermatozoa for insemination which incorporated a specific preservative(K-S medium).   In 1958, 4 pregnancies
from frozen AID were reported for the first time in Japan by our
clinic.   The number of patients who have become pregnant to present
has reached 191.   However, little attempt to evaluate the physical
and mental development has been made in the past.   As far as we have
been able to ascertain in a search of the literature, we can find
only two other reports, one by Jackson and the other by Kleegman
et al., which are consistent with our findings.

Although the development of children from frozen AID appeared
to be superior to that of the controls, there still remains a lack
of the critical evaluation on genetic adequacy or stability of

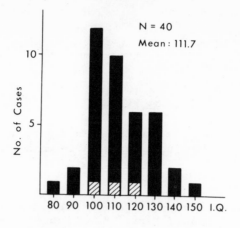

FIGURE 4. Intelligence quotients(I.Q.).

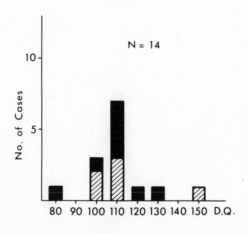

FIGURE 5. Development quotients(D.Q.).

progeny resulting from cryopreserved human semen, especially following long term storage. Although this sample is not large enough to
justify conclusions, our results, from a clinical point of view,
support the practice of AID with frozen semen.

REFERENCES

1. Iizuka, R. et al. The physical and mental development of chil-
        dren born following artificial insemination. Int. J. Fertil.
        13:24, 1968.

2. Ando, K. and Iizuka, R. Clinical evaluation of artificial in-
        seminations. Presented at the Annual Meeting of the Japan-
        ese Association of Fertility and Sterility, 1963.

3. Bunge, R.G. and Sherman, J.K. Fertilizing capacity of frozen
        human spermatozoa. Nature, 172:767, 1953.

4. Iizuka, R. and Sawada, Y. Successful insemination with frozen
        pooled human semen. Jap. J. Fertil. & Steril., 3:241, 1958.

COMPARISON OF RESULTS OF AID WITH FRESH AND FROZEN SEMEN[*]

Emil Steinberger, Luis J. Rodriguez-Rigau
and Keith D. Smith.

Department of Reproductive Medicine and Biology
University of Texas Medical School at Houston
Houston, Texas 77025 U.S.A.

INTRODUCTION

The use of frozen semen for AID has gained wide acceptance and a relatively large number of pregnancies have been reported following the use of this technique.[1] A number of reports dealing with either fresh or frozen semen use in AID have been published.[2-6] Some authors have attempted to compare the published results for the two types of semen and concluded that the pregnancy rates are either similar or slightly lower when frozen semen is employed.[3,6,7] Actually, the reported data are difficult to evaluate. One has to compare results obtained by different groups of investigators practicing in various parts of the world, treating different populations of infertile couples and utilizing different technical and therapeutic approaches. Such comparisons are at best difficult. However, in several reports the same groups of investigators compared results with each type of semen and also concluded that pregnancy rates are indeed similar or only slightly decreased when frozen semen is used.[8-10] While pregnancy rate is one of the most important parameters used in the evaluation of efficacy of AID, it is not the only measure. The number of cycles of insemination required for pregnancy to occur should also be considered when comparing the effectiveness of AID with fresh and frozen semen. In this communication, AID results obtained with fresh and frozen semen in a relatively large group of women are compared with respect to both pregnancy rate and number of insemination cycles required for pregnancy to occur. In addition, the influence of the recipient's fertility state on the outcome of the AID is also evaluated.

[*]This study was supported by Departmental funds.

283

MATERIALS AND METHODS

A group of 148 allegedly fertile women referred for AID was studied. Ten women in whom bilateral tubal disease was diagnosed on initial evaluation were excluded. Ovulatory function in each of the remaining 138 women was evaluated as previously described[11-14] prior to the initiation of AID. Treatment of ovulatory dysfunction, when indicated, was initiated prior to AID. The techniques used for timing of ovulation, insemination, evaluation of sperm survival in cervical mucus and cryopreservation of semen in liquid nitrogen have been published.[9,11,15,16] The details of protocol and of the procedures for donor selection and semen collection have been similar to those used previously.[9]

In this group of 138 women, 185 attempts for conception were undertaken. For this study, an attempt for conception is defined as the total number of cycles of insemination required for pregnancy to occur or for the patient to elect to discontinue further inseminations. Thus, some patients experienced more than one attempt for conception, each involving one or more cycles of insemination. Pregnancy was attempted once in 102 women, and two or more times in 36 women. Each recipient was assigned to receive inseminations with fresh or frozen semen on the basis of anticipated availability or lack of availability of fresh semen from a donor matching the physical characteristics of the male partner, but no attempt was made to limit inseminations in each recipient to only fresh or only frozen semen. Nevertheless, only fresh or only frozen semen was used in most recipients and, in those cases where both types of semen were utilized, either fresh or frozen semen was used in the majority of insemination cycles. Consequently, we were able to divide the 185 attempts at pregnancy into two groups: Those where predominantly fresh semen was used and those where predominantly frozen semen was utilized. Results (pregnancy rates and number of insemination cycles required for pregnancy to occur) in these two groups were then compared. In addition, since all insemination cycles were performed with either fresh or frozen semen, the results were analysed with respect to the number of pregnancies occurring during cycles where only fresh semen or only frozen semen was utilized. The number of insemination cycles per pregnancy with fresh or frozen semen were then compared.

Finally, the group of recipients was subdivided on the basis of normal or abnormal ovulatory activity. Pregnancy rates and number of insemination cycles required for pregnancy to occur in these two subgroups of recipients were calculated and compared.

RESULTS

Comparison of Results of AID with Fresh and Frozen Semen

A total of 133 pregnancies resulted from 185 attempts for conception in 138 women, a pregnancy rate of 71.9%. A total of 974
insemination cycles were required in the course of the 185 attempts
to achieve 133 conceptions, a rate of 1 pregnancy for every 7.4 AID
cycles (Table 1). In the 133 successful attempts, 534 cycles of
insemination were performed, a rate of 1 pregnancy for every 4 AID
cycles. In the 52 unsuccessful attempts, 440 cycles of insemination
were performed, an average of 8.5 cycles per attempt for conception.

Of the 133 pregnancies, 89 occurred in cycles of insemination
where fresh semen was used and 44 in cycles where frozen semen was
utilized, an average of 4.9 cycles/pregnancy with fresh semen and
12.3 cycles/pregnancy with frozen semen for the entire group of
185 attempts (successful and unsuccessful). If only the 133 successful attempts are considered, the averages were 2.4 cycles/pregnancy
with fresh semen and 7.2 cycles/pregnancy with frozen semen.

When the results were analyzed on the basis of whether individual recipients were inseminated predominantly with fresh or predominantly with frozen semen, only a slightly higher pregnancy rate
was observed when predominantly fresh semen was used. On the other
hand, the number of insemination cycles required for pregnancy to
occur was more than double when predominantly frozen semen was used
(Table 2).

Influence of Ovulatory Dysfunction on the Results of AID
with Fresh and Frozen Semen

Of the total of 974 insemination cycles, 258 were performed in
recipients with normal ovulatory activity, and 716 in women with
ovulatory dysfunction. The distribution of cycles of insemination
with fresh and frozen semen in these groups and the occurrence of
pregnancy are summarized in Table 3. The smallest number of AID
cycles/pregnancy was observed in recipients with normal ovulatory
function inseminated with fresh semen, and the largest in cases with
ovulatory dysfunction receiving frozen semen. Table 4 summarizes
the results when only the 133 successful attempts for pregnancy
were considered. As found for the entire group, the use of frozen
semen in recipients with ovulatory dysfunction was associated with
a significantly higher number of AID cycles/pregnancy.

When the results were analyzed on the basis of whether individual recipients, with normal or abnormal ovulatory function, were
inseminated predominantly with fresh or frozen semen (Table 5), the
following was observed :   (1) In recipients with normal ovulatory

TABLE 1. *Pregnancy rates in relation to the use of fresh or frozen semen in individual cycles of insemination.*

Type of semen used in AID	Successful attempts (n=133)			Unsuccessful attempts (n+52)	Total attempts (n+185)	
	Cycles	Pregnancies	Cycles/pregnancies	cycles	Cycles	Cycles/pregnancies
Fresh semen	216	89	2.4	218	434	4.9
Frozen semen	318	44	7.2*	222	540	12.3*
Total	534	133	4.0	440	974	7.4

* $p < 0.001$ (χ^2 test).

TABLE 2.   *Pregnancy rates and number of insemination cycles after AID with predominantly fresh or frozen semen in individual recipients.*

Type of semen used for AID	Attempts	Pregnancies	Pregnant (%)	Pregnant AID cycles	Not pregnant AID cycles
Predominantly fresh	112	85	75.9	2.8 ± 0.3	5.9 ± 0.7
Predominantly frozen	69	44^a	$63.8^{n.s.}$	$6.3. \pm 0.6^{**}$	$11.2 \pm 2.2^{*}$
Total	185	133	71.9	4.0 ± 0.4	8.5 ± 1.1

[a]women inseminated predominantly with frozen semen who conceived during an insemination cycle where fresh semen was used were excluded.

ns not significant (X^2 test).

[*]$p < 0.05$ (Student's t test).

[**]$p < 0.001$ (Student's t test).

TABLE 3.   *Influence of ovulatory dysfunction on the results of AID with fresh or frozen semen in individual cycles of insemination for the entire group (185 attempts for pregnancy).*

Ovulatory function	Cycles		Pregnancies		Cycles/Pregnancies	
	Fresh	Frozen	Fresh	Frozen	Fresh	Frozen
Normal	116	142	41	26	2.8_a	5.5_c
Abnormal	318	398	48	18	6.6_b	22.1_d
Total	434	540	89	44	4.9	12.3

X^2 tests : a < b ($p < 0.001$), c < d ($p < 0.001$), a < c ($p < 0.025$), b < d ($p < 0.001$).

TABLE 4. *Influence of ovulatory dysfunction on the results of AID with fresh or frozen semen in the 133 successful attempts for pregnancy.*

Ovulatory function	Cycles		Pregnancies		Cycles/Pregnancies	
	Fresh	Frozen	Fresh	Frozen	Fresh	Frozen
Normal	86	107	41	26	2.1$_a$	4.1$_c$
Abnormal	130	211	48	18	2.7$_b$	11.7$_d$
Total	216	318	89	44	2.4	7.2

χ^2 tests : a = b (p < 0.10), c < d (p < 0.001), a < c (p < 0.025), b < d (p < 0.001).

activity, the pregnancy rate following insemination predominantly with fresh semen (86.7%) was not significantly different from the pregnancy rate observed after insemination with predominantly frozen semen (81.3%), but the average number of AID cycles necessary for pregnancy to occur was lower when fresh semen was used (2.0 cycles with fresh semen and 4.2 cycles with frozen semen) ; (2) the presence of ovulatory dysfunction resulted in both decreased pregnancy rates and prolongation of the time required for pregnancy to occur ; (3) the lowest pregnancy rate and the highest number of AID cycles/pregnancy was observed in recipients with ovulatory dysfunction inseminated predominantly with frozen semen (48.6% and 9.3 cycles, respectively).

Comparison of Data Calculated on the Basis of Individual Cycles of Insemination with Data Calculated on the Basis of Individual Recipients

The number of AID cycles per pregnancy calculated on the basis of individual cycles of insemination (either with fresh or frozen semen) was compared with the number of AID cycles per pregnancy calculated on the basis of groups of recipients inseminated predominantly with fresh or frozen semen (Table 6). The striking similarity of the results strongly suggests that the data based on the groups of recipients inseminated predominantly with either fresh or frozen semen reflect the true distribution of pregnancies which occurs after insemination with either type of semen exclusively.

DISCUSSION

Artificial insemination with donor semen (AID) has become an accepted, widely utilized, and effective procedure for therapy of

TABLE 5. Pregnancy rates and number of insemination cycles necessary for pregnancy to occur after AID with predominantly fresh or frozen semen in recipients with normal or abnormal ovulatory function.

Ovulatory function	Attempts		Pregnancies		Pregnant (%)		AID cycles ($\bar{X} \pm SE$)	
	Fresh	Frozen	Fresh	Frozen	Fresh	Frozen	Fresh	Frozen
Normal	45	32	39	26	86.7	81.3	$2.0 \pm 0.3_a$	$4.2 \pm 0.3_c$
Abnormal	67	37	46	18	68.7	48.6	$3.4 \pm 0.4_b$	$9.3 \pm 1.5_d$
Total	112	69	85	44	75.9	63.8	2.8 ± 0.3	6.3 ± 0.6

Student's t tests : a < b (p < 0.01), a < c (p < 0.001), c < d (p < 0.005), b < d (p < 0.001).

TABLE 6.   *Comparison of pregnancy rates calculated on the basis of individual cycles of insemination (with fresh or frozen semen) or on the basis of individual recipients inseminated predominantly with fresh or frozen semen.*

Type of semen used for AID	Ovulatory function	AID cycles pregnancies	
		Calculated on the basis of individual cycles of insemination.	Calculated on the basis of individual recipients
Fresh	normal	2.8	2.7
	abnormal	6.6	6.3
	mean	4.9	4.6
Frozen	normal	5.5	5.5
	abnormal	22.1	21.6
	mean	12.3	12.2
Mean (Fresh + Frozen)		7.3	7.4

infertility in couples where the male partner is sterile, has a genetically transferable disorder or suffers with "severe oligospermia".[1-10,17,18] When techniques for cryopreservation of human semen were developed,[15,19-21] it was hoped that this technique would aid the physician practicing AID, and in certain instances, that it would be advantageous to the recipient.[22] The question facing investigators engaged in the study of AID was to determine whether the use of frozen semen is as safe, effective and efficient as the use of fresh semen. Unfortunately, most reports dealing with this question were based on experience with either fresh or frozen semen and on the comparison of results with those previously published by other investigators.[1,6] Only a few reports are available where the same group of investigators used both fresh and frozen semen in their practice, and was able to compare the results of AID with both types of semen in the same patient population.[8-10] In the study presented here, an attempt was made to extend our prior observations on the comparison of results of AID with the two types of semen, and to include an additional parameter, the female factor. The results reported here confirm our prior conclusions made on the basis of a study involving a smaller group of patients,[9] that utilization of frozen semen does not result in a markedly different pregnancy rate

but in a definite increase in the number of insemination cycles nee-
essary for pregnancy to occur.

The parameters used to evaluate the efficacy of AID have to be
clearly defined in order to appropriately analyze the results. If
only pregnancy rates are considered, in other words, the percent of
all women that become pregnant regardless of the number of insemination cycles necessary for conception to take place, no marked differences between the efficacy of fresh and frozen semen are seen. The
pregnancy rates achieved with both types of semen in our patient population are similar to those reported by other investigators.[1,8]
However, when the results are analyzed on the basis of the number of
insemination cycles necessary for pregnancy to occur, marked differences are observed between fresh and frozen semen. Women who
conceived after insemination with frozen semen required more than
twice the number of AID cycles than women who conceived after inseminations with fresh semen. These data permit us to conclude and to
advise the patient that, if all other factors are equal, the chances
for pregnancy to occur are similar when either type of semen is used
but that the time necessary for pregnancy to occur will be longer if
frozen semen is utilized. It must be emphasized, however, that these
conclusions are only applicable for either a large random group of
women, or for women with normal ovulatory function. When ovulatory
dysfunction is present in the recipient, the use of frozen semen again
delays the occurence of conception but is also associated with a diminished pregnancy rate. These results illustrate the important
interaction between the fertility potentials of each partner which
influences the overall fertility potential of the couple as a unit.
If the fertility potential of both partners is high, pregnancy rates
are high and conceptions occur promptly ; when either a female or a
male factor is present, conception is delayed. If both male and
female factors are present conception is delayed and pregnancy rates
are decreased (Table 7).

TABLE 7.   *Pregnancy rates and number of cycles necessary for
conception to occur in the presence of female and male
factors.*

Male factor	Female factor	
	Absent (normal ovulatory function)	Present (ovulatory dysfunction)
Absent (fresh semen)	87.7% pregnancy in 2.0 + 0.3 cycles	68.7% pregnancy in 3.4 + 0.4 cycles
Present (frozen semen)	81.3% pregnancy in 4.2 + 0.3 cycles	48.6% pregnancy in 9.3 + 1.5 cycles

Some of the conclusions derived from this study must be tempered with caution since we dealt with groups of women inseminated predominantly, rather than exclusively, with either fresh or frozen semen. However, it should be emplasized that in most women more than 90% of inseminations were performed exclusively with fresh or with frozen semen. All pregnancies in women inseminated predominantly with fresh semen occurred in cycles where fresh semen was used. In the group of women inseminated predominantly with frozen semen, four conceptions occurred in cycles where fresh semen was used. These were excluded from the computations (Tables 2 and 5). In an attempt to further analyze the date derived from the division of the patient population into the two groups (predominantly fresh or predominantly frozen), we calculated the results on the basis of the use of either fresh or frozen semen in individual cycles rather than in individual recipients (Tables 1, 3 and 4). This permitted an analysis of pregnancies occurring exclusively from insemination with either fresh or frozen semen. The average number of insemination cycles per pregnancy derived from this analysis was then compared with the number of insemination cycles per pregnancy obtained on the basis of the analysis of the two groups of women (Table 6). The striking similarity of the results strongly suggests that the data derived from the evaluation of the groups of women inseminated predominantly with either type of semen reflect true differences, most likely due to the utilization of the two types of semen for AID.

REFERENCES

1. Sherman, J.K. Clinical use of frozen human semen. Transplant Proc. (Suppl. 1), 8:165, 1976.

2. Behrman, S.J. Techniques of artificial insemination. In : S.J. Behrman and R.W. Kistner, eds., Progress in Infertility, 1st Edition, Little, Brown and Co., Boston, p. 717, 1968.

3. Strickler, R.C., Keller, D.W. and Warren, J.C. Artificial insemination with fresh donor semen. N. Engl. J. Med. 293:848, 1975.

4. Chong, A.P. and Taymor, M.L. Sixteen years experience with therapeutic donor insemination. Fertil Steril., 26:791, 1975.

5. Koren, Z. and Lieberman, R. Fifteen years experience with artificial insemination. Int. J. Fert. 21:119, 1976.

6. Friedman, S. Artificial donor insemination with frozen human semen. Fertil. Steril., 28:1230, 1977.

7. Ansbacher, R. Artificial insemination with frozen spermatozoa.

Fertil. Steril., 29:375, 1978.

8. Behrman, S.J. and Sawada, Y. Heterologous and homologous in-
    seminations with human semen frozen and stored in a liquid-
    nitrogen refrigerator. Fertil. Steril., 17:457, 1966.

9. Steinberger, E. and Smith, K.D. Artificial insemination with
    fresh or frozen semen. A comparative Study. J.A.M.A.,
    223:778, 1973.

10. Sulewski, J.M., Eisenberg, F. and Stenger, V.G. A longitudinal
    analysis of artificial insemination with donor semen. Fertil.
    Steril., 29:527, 1978.

11. Perloff, W.H. and Steinberger, E. *In vivo* survival of sperma-
    tozoa in cervical mucus. Am. J. Obstet. Gynecol., 88:439,
    1964.

12. Smith, K.D., Rodriguez-Rigau, L.J. and Steinberger, E. The
    infertile couple : working with them together. In :
    A.T.K. Cockett and R.L. Urry, eds., Male Infertility Workup,
    Treatment and Research. Grune and Stratton, New York, p.211,
    1977.

13. Smith, K.D., Rodriguez-Rigau, L.J. and Steinberger, E. Relation
    between indices of semen analysis and pregnancy rates in
    infertile couples. Fertil. Steril., 28:1314, 1977.

14. Steinberger, E., Smith, K.D., Tcholakian, R.K. and Rodriguez-
    Rigau, L.J. Testosterone levels in female partners of in-
    fertile couples. Am. J. Obstet. Gynecol., 133:133, 1979.

15. Steinberger, E. and Perloff, W.H. Preliminary experience with
    a human sperm bank. Am. J. Obstet. Gynecol., 92:577, 1965.

16. Smith, K.D. and Steinberger, E. Survival of spermatozoa in a
    human sperm bank. Effects of long-term storage in liquid
    nitrogen. J.A.M.A., 223:774, 1973.

17. The American Fertility Society. Artificial Insemination : An
    accepted Medical Technique. The American Fertility Society,
    Birmingham, Alabama, 1978.

18. Beck, W.W. A critical look at the legal, ethical and technical
    aspects of artificial insemination. Fertil. Steril., 27:1,
    1976.

19. Bunge, R.G. and Sherman, J.K. Fertilizing capacity of frozen
    human spermatozoa. Nature, London, 172:767, 1953.

20. Iizuka R. and Sawada, Y.   Successful inseminations with frozen
     human semen.   Jap. J. Fertil. Steril., 3:4, 1958.

21. Perloff, W.H., Steinberger, E. and Sherman, J.K.   Conceptions
     with human spermatozoa frozen by the nitrogen vapor techni-
     que.   Fertil. Steril. 15:501, 1964.

22. Kleegman, S., Amelar, R.D., Sherman, J.K., Hirschhorn, K. and
     Pilpel, H.   Artificial donor insemination (roundtable).   Med.
     Aspects. Human Sexuality., 4:85, 1970.

CLINICAL COMPARISON OF FRESH AND FROZEN SEMEN

Andrée Schoysman-Deboeck and Robert Schoysman

Fertility Department
Academic Hospital V.U.B.
Brussels, Belgium

Different laboratory tests presently available can be used to obtain a fair amount of information on the quality of semen.

Comparisons of fresh and frozen semen in various *in vitro* tests are of great value, but the true test for semen is its ability to fertilize and to give a pregnancy. Therefore, it appeared of great interest to compare the results obtained with fresh and frozen semen in a single AID study.

First, the only possible comparison in this work is between fresh semen and semen frozen by the technique used in our laboratory. The reported results should not be interpreted to infer that other freezing and storing methods give better or poorer results.

The frozen semen is treated and stored as follows: Within the hour after ejaculation or if possible immediately after liquefaction, the volume of the ejaculate is measured; after checking the sample for the number of spermatozoa and motility, it is diluted with half its volume of the protective medium(Table 1).

This protective medium is similar to those classically described but is more concentrated and allows dilution of the semen with 50% of its volume instead of with an equal volume. The final mixture of protective medium and semen contains 7% glycerol.

After mixing the semen with the diluant solution for about 10 minutes, the semen solution is aspirated in 0.5ml plastic straws (from I.M.V., L'Aigle). The straws are sealed with a special sealing powder from the same manufacturer, identification marks are

TABLE 1. *Protective medium.*

For 100 ml	Glucose	1.98	g
	Citrate	1.72	g
	Water	49	ml
	Glycerol	21	ml
	Egg yolk	30	ml

This mixture is heated at 55°C for 30 minutes. Then 2g of glycocol are added and the pH is adjusted between 7.2 and 7.4. No antibiotics are added.

written on the straws, and the freezing is carried out horizontally in a liquid nitrogen container (RCB 60, l'Air Liquide) about 8 cm above the liquid nitrogen level for 8 minutes. Afterwards, the straws are dipped in the liquid nitrogen of the container for storage. Thawing is accomplished by agitating the plastic straws in water at 20-24°C for one minute. One dose of 0.5 ml frozen semen is utilized for each insemination.

In this AID study, fresh semen was used whenever possible and the insemination performed within three hours after collection. A volume of 0.5 ml fresh semen per insemination was used and this fresh semen was also placed in plastic straws. The difference between 0.5 ml of fresh semen and an identical volume of the same semen frozen was at once obvious. The fresh semen sample contains, when acceptable for AID, at least 70% of good motile spermatozoa at a concentration of about 80 tc 120 million/ml.

The frozen sample, diluted by 1/3 and loosing at least 20% of its motility after freezing and thawing, contained only about half the number of motile spermatozoa as the fresh semen. When only one insemination is necessary in one cycle, it is easy to know whether the observed result is due to fresh or frozen semen, but when inseminations have to be repeated, successive inseminations may be performed either with fresh or frozen samples from the same donor. Such cycles of AID with more than one insemination in which both fresh semen and frozen semen are used cannot be included in a comparative survey. We have considered these cycles as performed with mixed semen. It must be emphasized here that we never mix fresh and frozen semen for a single insemination. The fact that several cycles of AID in one woman are performed with fresh, frozen or mixed semen samples prohibits the formation of a group of women always inseminated with fresh and a group always inseminated with frozen semen.

One donor's semen is used to give no more than 6 to 10 children. Therefore, the series of inseminations done with each donor's semen are too small to compare the results obtained by use of his fresh, frozen or mixed semen in women whose normal fertility and normal length of AID treatment can only be assessed by statistical consid- erations on a great number of cases. The normal variations in concentration and motility of the different semen samples of a same donor add to the confusion.

In spite of all these difficulties and with the conviction that no definitive results could be expected, we tried to compare the results obtained clinically with both types of semen: (1) In all AID cycles resulting in pregnancy and (2) in all first cycles of AID treatment with, of course, cycles of no possible value or those poorly documented being discarded.

RESULTS

Fresh semen seems to give about 5% more pregnancies than fro- zen semen(Table 2).

Since cycles included in the comparison for all cycles was extremely variable, we tried to compare the results obtained with fresh and with frozen semen in the first cycle of AID treatment. These groups were also heterogenous, but probably in a different way. All first AID treatment cycles were reviewed including fer- tile patients, failures and patients still under treatment whose first cycle gave no result. A total number of 1256 first cycle AID resulted in 204 pregnancies(Table 2). The same superiority of fresh semen(about 4%) was again observed. In this comparison, however, the results obtained by using mixed semen are somewhat lower than for all cycles.

In AID, the percentage of miscarriages in pregnancies with frozen semen was 19.6%(Table 3). If that figure is corrected by the number of unended pregnancies longer than 4 1/2 months, it

TABLE 2. *Results of AID with fresh or with frozen semen for all cycles.*

Type of semen	Number of cycles treated	Number of pregnancies	Pregnancies(%)
Fresh	610	148	24.26
Frozen	2027	415	20.07
Fresh & Frozen (Mixed)	1449	342	23.6

TABLE 3. *Results of AID with fresh or frozen semen in the first AID cycles.*

Type of semen	Number of first cycles	Number of pregnancies	Pregnancies(%)
Fresh	225	43	19.11
Frozen	654	101	15.44
Fresh & Frozen (Mixed)	377	60	15.91

becomes 16.2%. Under the same conditions, the percentage of miscarriages in pregnancies obtained by fresh semen varies between 15.3%
and 13.9%.

It is interesting to observe that for over a period of years
in which 300 pregnancies were obtained by AID, the percentage of
miscarriages in pregnancies obtained with frozen semen always remained somewhat higher than those obtained with fresh semen. No
difference was observed as far as frequency and types of malformations between the two groups. The incidence of malformations were
in fact not different from those observed in the normal population.
The date indicate that frozen semen seems to be somewhat less fertile than fresh semen and may be related in some way to a higher
incidence of miscarriages.

If we consider the fact that the inseminations were performed
with doses of frozen semen containing half the amount of motile
spermatozoa than the doses of fresh semen, it must be concluded
that spermatozoa stored in liquid nitrogen are still clinically of
excellent quality. It is quite possible that in both cases we used
a number of motile spermatozoa in excess of what is really needed.
If so, the fertility of frozen spermatozoa could be somewhat slightly altered. We hope that the teams working with doses of 0.25 ml
for each insemination will provide more information on this point.
In order to better compare fresh and frozen semen, we intend in
the future to use inseminations doses of 0.25 ml of fresh semen and
compare this with doses of 0.50 ml of frozen semen.

In conclusion, even if frozen semen may be somewhat less effective than fresh semen when used as described, this difference
is not so great as to negate its practical advantages. We were able
to obtain 99 children after AID with fresh semen while use of frozen
semen gave, in a shorter period, 245 children and played a part in
the conception of 234 others. Even if we are convinced that the
results with fresh semen are somewhat superior, we do not in practice have to choose between what is good and less good, but rather

TABLE 4. *Evolution of the pregnancies obtained by AID.*

	594 living children				Multiple pregnancies	Prema-ture	Premature dead	Still born	Ectopic	Miscarriages	Malformations Abnormalities
	Not yet known	Boys	Girls	Sex?							
Fresh Semen (148)	24	52	43	2	1 twins	1	1 twins	3	1	19 (15.32%)	1 premature alive almost blind.
Frozen Semen (415)	114	107	120	5	5 twins 1 triplet	-	1	1	2	59 (including 1 mola). (19.6%)	1 congenital sacro-iliac luxation. 1 lacrymal duct malformation. 1 agenesia of adrenal glands in one of the triplets(died after two days). 1 mongoloid boy. 1 cleft palate(like the mother).
Mixed Semen (342)	69	103	111	-	9 twins 1 triplet	2	-	3	1	43 (15.75%)	1 microphtalmia (living). 1 syndactylia (2 toes) 1 fallot heart disease. 1 mongoloid girl. 1 forearm malformation. 1 meningocoele (operated and well).
Unknown (Fresh or Frozen) (15)	-	7	5	1	-	-	1	-	-	1	
Total (920)	207	269	279	8	15 twins 2 triplets	3	4	7	4	122 (17.11%)	

between what is possible(frozen semen) and what is impossible(fresh semen from a tall red-headed man with type B Rh- blood on Easter Monday).

ACKNOWLEDGEMENTS

We are grateful to Mr. Cassou from I.M.V. L'Aigle who has helped us with his equipment and his enthusiasm, to Mr. Ledent, from L'Air Liquide, Belgique, who started our sperm bank with us and to the maintenance personnel from L'Air Liquide and from the Akademisch Ziekenhuis V.U.B. for having helped us keep under all circumstances a high liquid nitrogen level.

Most of all we are indebted to Mrs. Jenny Van Hecke, medical secretary, who contributed greatly in smoothing out many impatient calls from doctors and patients with ever renewed understanding patience and efficiency. Her frequent retyping of texts is only a small part of her valued collaboration.

THE FEMALE FACTOR IN AID

Emil Steinberger, Luis J. Rodriguez-Rigau
and Keith D. Smith

Department of Reproductive Medicine and Biology
University of Texas Medical School at Houston
Houston, Texas, U.S.A.

INTRODUCTION

Sufficient information has accumulated in the literature to permit the conclusion that a complicated interaction between the fertility potentials of each partner determines a couple's fertility.[1,6] Artificial insemination with donor semen (AID) is one of the techniques utilized to overcome the presence of a severe male factor. AID is practiced usually after a relatively brief evaluation of the female, primarily directed towards exclusion of major disturbances (E.G. tubal disease, anovulation). The analysis of the data obtained in this type of patient population is frequently utilized for the assessment of the efficacy of AID. The recipients are considered as a homogeneous group as far as their fertility potential is concerned. The success rates of AID reported in the literature vary greatly ; pregnancy rates as low as 40% and as high as 80% have been reported.[7,8] It is difficult to compare the various reports. Not only do the techniques of insemination and quality of the donor semen probably vary in the different reports but also, and more importantly, the makeup of the recipient population is most likely heterogeneous, being a function of the extent of evaluation and therapy of the AID recipients.

In the study reported here, the female partners of a large group of infertile couples referred for AID were extensively evaluated prior to initiation of inseminations. When indicated, treatment of the female was instituted prior to initiation of AID. The efficacy of AID in this group of couples was analyzed in light of the presence or absence of a female factor. Results were then compared with

301

observations made in a group of infertile couples who did not opt
for AID, where no male factor was present and where a female factor
was diagnosed and treated. Finally, the data were also analyzed
longitudinally (1964-1979) in order to investigage the possibility
that the AID results could have been influenced by changes in our
ability to diagnose and treat fertility disturbances in the female
during this period.

MATERIALS AND METHODS

Study Populations

   AID Group. 148 infertile couples referred for AID in the
course of the past 15 years compose this study group. The female
partners had usually received preliminary screening by the referring
physician. Nevertheless, in all cases they were extensively evaluated by our team prior to initiation of AID. The diagnostic procedures were directed primarily towards evaluation of the possibility
of uterine or tubal disorders, ovulatory dysfunction, cervical factors, and general medical or endocrine disturbances. The details
of these diagnostic procedures have been previously described.[3,4,6,9]
In 10 cases bilateral tubal disease was diagnosed and these were
excluded. In the remaining 138 couples, 185 attempts for pregnancy
utilizing AID were carried out ; of these, 79 were performed in women
with normal ovulatory function and 106 in females with ovulatory
dysfunction. The techniques and procedures used for insemination
and donor selection were previously described.[10]

   Non AID Infertile Group: 126 infertile couples in whom no AID
was performed, but where the female partners had ovulatory disturbance, composed this study group. Both partners were evaluated as
previously described.[3,4,6,9] The diagnostic evaluation of the female
was the same as that utilized in the AID group. In 7 cases bilateral tubal disease was diagnosed ; these were excluded.

Therapeutic Management

   In the non-AID infertile group, all female partners were treated.   In the AID group, those females in whom ovulatory dysfunction
was diagnosed were treated prior to initiation of AID, and where
indicated, treatment was continued during the cycles of insemination.
When no ovulatory disturbance was detected, AID was carried out
without additional therapy. The therapy of ovulatory dysfunction
included the use of estrogens, prednisone, clomiphene citrate, human
menopausal gonadotropin, human chorionic gonadotropin, thyroid hormone and wedge resection of the ovaries.

   The AID group was composed of patients seen during a period

which spanned 15 years (1964-1979). During this time marked changes
in diagnostic and therapeutic capabilities occurred and consequently,
the management was not uniform. In view of this, we arbitrarily
divided the AID population into two subgroups, those seen prior to
and those after 1971 because in our practice prior to 1971, a number
of diagnostic techniques were not routinely utilized (e.g. determination of plasma hormone levels, advanced radiographic techniques,
laparoscopic examination, etc.) and certain therapeutic modalities
were used only on an investigative basis in a limited number of patients.

RESULTS

AID Population. There were 133 conceptions from 185 attempts
at pregnancy giving a pregnancy rate of 71.9%. The incidence of
pregnancy after the first cycle of insemination was 20.5% (38 pregnancies), after the fourth cycle 51.4% (95 pregnancies) and after
the tenth cycle 67.0% (124 pregnancies). The remaining 9 pregnancies, bringing the total number to 133 (71.9% pregnancy rate) occurred subsequent to more than 10 AID cycles. Of the 133 conceptions, 28.6% occurred after a single cycle of insemination, 71.4%
after 4 cycles and 93.2% after 10 AID cycles. The remaining 6.8%
of the pregnancies required more than 10 cycles of insemination
(Table 1).

A modest decrease in pregnancy rate (not statistically significant) was observed when ovulatory dysfunction was present in the
AID recipient (Table 2). A dramatic difference between the results
in the two groups of recipients (those with normal and those with
abnormal ovulatory function) was noted when the average number of
AID cycles required for pregnancy to occur was compared (Table 3).
In women with normal ovulatory activity who conceived, 2.9 cycles
were required for pregnancy to occur. In women with ovulatory abnormalities, 5.2 cycles were required. In unsuccessful attemps
for pregnancy, an average of 8.5 insemination cycles were performed.

Pregnancy rates and number of insemination cycles in cases seen
prior to and after 1971 were compared (Tables 4 and 5). Although
the overall pregnancy rates were similar (71.4% before and 72.4%
after 1971), a significantly higher number of insemination cycles
was required for pregnancy to occur in cases seen prior to 1971
(5.2 cycles before and 2.8 after 1971). In AID recipients with
normal ovulatory activity seen after 1971, the number of insemination
cycles required for pregnancy was the lowest (1.4 cycles). The largest number of AID cycles necessary for pregnancy to occur and the
lowest pregnancy rate were noted in AID recipients with ovulatory
dysfunction treated prior to 1971 (51.2% pregnancy rate in an average
of 8.8. insemination cycles). Treatment of ovulatory dysfunction

TABLE 1. *Analysis of pregnancies and dropouts by cycle of insemination.*

Cycle of insemination	No. of attempts	No. pregnancies	Monthly pregnancy rate (%)	Cumulative pregnancy rate (%)	No. of dropouts	Monthly dropout rate (%)	% of total pregnancies
1st	185	38	20.5	20.5	2	1.1	28.6
2nd	145	20	13.8	31.4	7	4.8	43.6
3rd	118	23	19.5	43.8	3	2.5	60.9
4th	92	14	15.2	51.4	5	5.4	71.4
5th	73	10	13.7	56.8	7	9.6	78.9
6th	56	7	12.5	60.5	6	10.7	84.2
7th	43	6	14.0	63.8	3	7.0	88.7
8th	34	1	2.9	64.3	3	8.8	89.5
9th	30	3	10.0	65.9	1	3.3	91.7
10th	26	2	7.7	67.0	4	15.4	93.2
Total	185	133[a]	-	71.9[a]	52[b]	-	100.0[a]

[a] 9 pregnancies occurred after more than 10 cycles of insemination (11-31 cycles)
[b] 11 attempts were discontinued after more than 10 cycles of insemination(11-43 cycles).

TABLE 2. *Pregnancy rates in the AID group related to the presence or absence of ovulatory dysfunction.*

Ovulation function	Attempts	Pregnancies	% Pregnancy
Normal	79	67	84.4
Abnormal	106	66	62.3[n.s.]
Total	185	133	71.9

n.s. not significant (χ^2 test).

after 1971 resulted in significant improvement of these results (70% pregnancy rate in 3.4 insemination cycles.)

Non-AID infertile population. Ovulatory dysfunction was treated in the female partners of 119 infertile couples who did not opt for AID and whose male partners were not treated. A direct relationship between the motile sperm count of the husband and the pregnancy rate was observed (Table 6). The incidence of pregnancy ranged from 33% in couples whose male partners' motile sperm counts were below 5 million/ml to 70% when motile sperm counts were above 100 million/ml. The average duration of treatment of the female partners required for pregnancy to occur was 5.5. months.

TABLE 3. *Number of cycles of insemination related to the presence or absence of ovulatory dysfunction.*

Ovulatory function	Attempts		AID cycles ($\bar{x}\pm SE$)	
	Pregnant	Not pregnant	Pregnant	Not pregnant
Normal	67	12	2.9 ± 0.3	5.2 ± 1.2
Abnormal	66	40	5.2 ± 0.6[*]	9.5 ± 1.4[n.s.]
Total	133	52	4.1 ± 0.4	8.5 ± 1.1

[*]$p < 0.001$ (Student's t test)
ns not significant(student's t test).

TABLE 4. *Comparison of pregnancy rates related to ovulatory function in patients seen before and after 1971.*

| | Total group | | Ovulatory function | | | |
| | | | Normal | | Abnormal | |
	Attempts	Pregnancy (%)	Attempts	Pregnancy (%)	Attempts	Pregnancy (%)
Before 1971	98	71.4	55	87.3	43	51.2
After 1971	87	$72.4^{n.s.}$	24	$79.2^{n.s.}$	63	$69.8^{n.s.}$

n.s. not significant (χ^2 test)

TABLE 5. *Comparison of the number of AID cycles necessary for pregnancy to occur related to ovulatory function in patients seen before and after 1971.*

| | Total Group | | Ovulatory function | | | |
| | | | Normal | | Abnormal | |
	Pregnancies	AID cycles	Pregnancies	AID cycles	Pregnancies	AID cycles
Before 1971	70	5.2 ± 0.6	48	3.5 ± 0.4	22	8.8 ± 1.6
After 1971	63	$1.8 \pm 0.3^{**}$	19	$1.4 \pm 0.2^{*}$	44	$3.4 \pm 0.4^{*}$

*$p < 0.005$ (Student's t test).
**$p < 0.001$ (Student's t test).

TABLE 6. *Pregnancy rates in a group of 119 non-AID infertile couples where ovulatory dysfunction*
was treated in the females and no treatment was offered to the males, related to duration
of treatment and the male factor.

Motile sperm count (million/ml)	Couples	Pregnancies	Pregnancy (%)	Duration of treatment (months)	
				Pregnant	Not pregnant
< 5.1	18	6	33.3	3.0 $\pm$ 0.6	5.7 $\pm$ 1.2
5.1 - 10.0	18	5	27.8	3.8 $\pm$ 1.7	12.8 $\pm$ 2.3
10.1 - 20.0	17	9	52.9	7.9 $\pm$ 2.8	8.9 $\pm$ 1.9
20.1 - 40.0	28	16	57.1	5.6 $\pm$ 1.4	10.8 $\pm$ 1.7
40.1 - 60.0	20	12	60	6.6 $\pm$ 1.9	6.8 $\pm$ 1.4
60.1 - 100.0	8	5	62.5	5.4 $\pm$ 2.0	16.3 $\pm$ 9.8
> 100.0	10	7	70.0	4.0 $\pm$ 1.1	10.7 $\pm$ 5.5
Total	119	60	50.4	5.5 $\pm$ 0.7	9.7 $\pm$ 0.9

Comparison of Results of Treatment of Ovulatory Dysfunction
in the AID and the Non-AID Populations.

        In the AID subgroup where ovulatory dysfunction was treated, the
pregnancy rate was 62.3% and 5.2 cycles of insemination were required
for pregnancy to occur.   The results are strikingly similar to those
achieved by treatment of ovulatory dysfunction in the female partners
of those non-AID couples where the motile sperm count (MSC) of the
male partner was above 10 million/ml (59% pregnancy rate in 6 months
of treatment) or above 40 million/ml (63% pregnancy rate in 5.6.
months), in other words, when apparently no male factor was present
(Table 7).

                                    DISCUSSION

        Artificial insemination with donor semen (AID) is often the
procedure of choice for treatment of infertility in couples where a
severe male factor is present.[11,13]   Frequently, the females do not
receive extensive diagnostic evaluation or treatment prior to AID.
If no conception occurs, either the patient or the physician may
become discouraged prior to further evaluation of the female.   The
lack of conception in these patients is considered as an "insemination
failure".   Theoretically, the AID failure rate in a perfectly normal
female, assuming proper donor selection and adequate insemination
technique and timing, should approach zero and no more than one insemination cycle should be required for pregnancy to take place.
Keeping this in mind, we paid particular attention to the evaluation
and treatment of women referred for AID, and in this report analyzed
the AID results in relation to the reproductive system status of the
recipients.

TABLE 7.   *Comparison of pregnancy rates and duration of
           treatment necessary for conception to occur in
           the AID population with ovulatory dysfunction
           and in the non-AID infertile population where
           no male factor was considered to be present.*

Population	Pregnancy (%)	Months of treatment until occurrence of pregnancy
AID group	62.3	5.2 ± 0.6
non-AID group		
MSC[a] > 10 million/ml	59.0	6.0 ± 0.7
MSC[a] > 40 million/ml	63.2	5.6 ± 1.1

[a]MSC : Motile sperm count.

No patients with bilateral tubal disease or other serious anatomical abnormalities of the reproductive tract were included in this
study. When ovulatory dysfunction was present, no matter how minor,
it was treated. In most cases this resulted in apparent normaliza-
tion of ovulatory activity. Thus, theoretically we were dealing with
a group of "fertile" women. The overall pregnancy rate, however, was
considerably less than 100% (72%) and the average number of AID cycles
necessary for pregnancy to occur was considerably more than one (4.1).
It is of interest to note that pregnancy rates reported in the literature are not only considerably less than 100% but they also vary
anywhere from 40% to 80%.[7,8,14,16] In our group of patients the failure rate of 28% could conceivably be considered as the "insemination
failure rate" as it is frequently described in the literature.

When one takes under consideration, in addition to the overall
pregnancy rate, the other data presented in this communication, the
above conclusion becomes questionable. When the AID group in which
recipients showed ovulatory dysfunction was compared to a non-AID
group of infertile couples in which the female partner also showed
ovulatory disturbance but no male factor was present, the pregnancy
rates and the duration of treatment required for conception to take
place were noted to be similar. In both groups the diagnosis of
ovulatory dysfunction was made by the same team of physicians using
similar methodology and the same therapeutic approach. This suggests
strongly that the failure rate was due to a female factor in both
groups, and that our diagnostic and therapeutic techniques are probably not sufficiently sophisticated to detect and correct all abnormalities in the female that may be associated with diminished
fertility. This is further illustrated by comparison of the results
achieved prior to and after 1971 in our population of patients.   Improvement in the diagnostic and therapeutic techniques employed after
1971 was reflected by significant increase in the pregnancy rate and
decrease in the number of insemination cycles necessary for pregnancy
to occur. When one considers the group of AID recipients evaluated
after 1971 and looks at the subgroup in whom no abnormalities were
detected, the number of AID cycles required for pregnancy to occur
was noted to be close to the theoritical unity (1.4). Consequently,
it appears that the hypothesis that the fertility potential of the
recipient is the major determinant of AID failure is valid when all
other parameters (quality of semen, insemination technique, timing,
etc.) are adequate.

REFERENCES

1. Steinberger, E. and Steinberger, A. The testis, basis and cli-
       nical aspects. In : H. Balin and S. Glasser, eds, Repro-
       ductive Biology, Excerpta Medica, Amsterdam, p. 133, 1972.

2. Van Zyl, J.A., Menkveld, R., Van W. Kotze, T.J., Retief, A.E. and Van Niekerk, W.A. Oligospermia : a seven-year survey of the incidence, chromosomal aberrations, treatment and pregnancy rate. Int. J. Fertil. 20:129, 1975.

3. Smith, K.D., Rodriguez-Rigua, L.J. and Steinberger, E. The infertile couple, working with them together. In : A.T.K. Cockett and R.L. Urry eds., Male Infertility, Workup, Treatment and Research. Grune and Stratton, New York, p. 211, 1977.

4. Smith, K.D., Rodriguez-Rigau, L.J. and Steinberger, E. : Relation between indices of semen analysis and pregnancy rates in infertile couples. Fertil. Steril. 28:1314, 1977.

5. Rodriguez-Rigau, L.J., Smith, K.D. and Steinberger, E. Relationship of varicocele to sperm output and fertility of male partners in infertile couples. J. Urol., 120:691, 1978.

6. Steinberger, E., Smith, K.D., Tcholakian, R.K. and Rodriguez-Rigau, L.J. Testosterone levels in female partners of infertile couples. Am. J. Obstet. Gynecol. 133:133, 1979.

7. Friedman, S. Artificial donor insemination with frozen human semen. Fertil. Steril. 28:1230, 1977.

8. Koren, Z. and Lieberman, R. Fifteen years experience with artificial insemination. Int. J. Fertil, 21:119, 1976.

9. Perloff, W.H. and Steinberger, E. *In vivo* survival of spermatozoa in cervical mucus. Am. J. Obstet. Gynecol. 88:439, 1964.

10. Steinberger, E. and Smith, K.D. Artificial insemination with fresh or frozen semen. A comparative study. J.A.M.A. 223: 778, 1973.

11. The American Fertility Society. Artificial Insemination. An accepted medical technique. The Americain Fertility Society, Birmingham, Alabama, 1978.

12. Behrman, S.J. Techniques of artificial insemination. In : S.J. Behrman and R.W. Kistner eds., Progress in Infertility, Little, Brown and Co., Boston, p. 720, 1968.

13. Beck, W.W. A critical look at the legal, ethical and technical aspects of artificial insemination. Fertil. Steril., 27:1 1976.

14. Chong, A.P. and Taymor, M.L. Sixteen years experience with
     therapeutic donor insemination. Fertil. Steril., 26:791,
     1975.

15. Ansbacher, R. Artificial insemination with frozen spermatozoa.
     Fertil. Steril., 29:1978.

16. Sulewski, J.M., Eisenberg, F. and Stenger, V.G. A longitudinal
     analysis of artificial insemination with donor semen. Fertil.
     Steril., 29:527, 1978.

THE MALE FACTOR IN AID REQUESTS: 558 CASES

A. Mattei,* M.G. Mattei,** P. Laugier,* J.F. Mattei,*
B. Conte-Devoix * and R. Roulier *

 * Centre d'Etude et de Conservation du Sperme(CECOS).
** Centre de Génétique Médicale, C.H.U. Timone
    Marseille, France.

Sperm banks, in addition to being beneficial in other ways,
facilitate recording and centralization of AID requests. Since the
Marseille CECOS center was opened four years ago, about 10% of the
requests addressed to us have been refused, either because the
couple's sterility was entirely attributable to the wife or because
the husband's subfertility could be successfully treated(hypogona-
trophic hypogonadism, excretory azoospermia, varicocoele). There
were 558 requests granted, 551 of which were prompted by male sterility judged to be irreversible and 7 by genetic abnormalities or
Rhesus incompatibility.

The homogeneity of this series of 551 cases is based on the
irreversible nature of the sterility. Series of this type can serve
as a reference in the study of male subfertility which is often more
difficult to diagnose and explain.

MATERIALS AND METHODS

A team of 3 physicians examined 558 patients and their wives
in a sterility clinic. Examination of the husband was conducted
in order to eliminate unjustified requests and to determine the
nature of the disorder responsible for the sterility. Examination
of the wife sought to identify factors causing sterility or hypofertility and to decide on the treatment required before or during
insemination.

As is shown in Figure 1, examination of the husband included

313

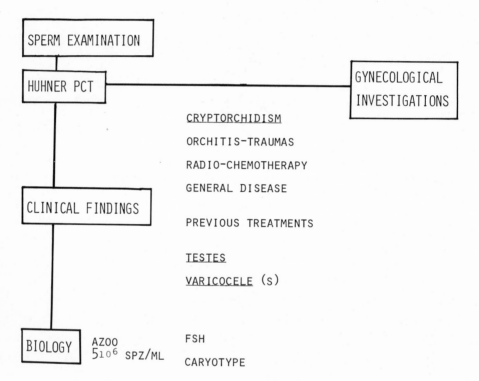

FIGURE 1.   Steps in an andrologic evaluation.

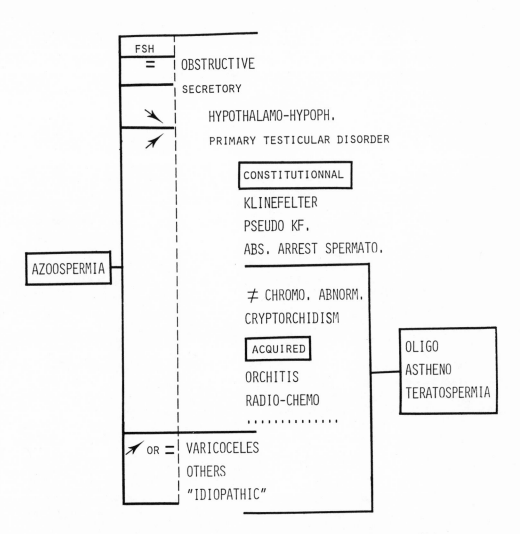

FIGURE 2.   Classification of factors of male sterility

clinical and laboratory investigations; the latter include, in addition to a spermiogram and spermocytogram performed according to the method of David et al.:[4] (1) Radioimmunological determination of serum FSH in cases of azoospermia and oligospermia (under 10 million sperm/ml); and (2) karyotyping for these cases, as well as for cases of asthenospermia and idiopathic teratospermia.[8]

COMMENTS

Since, during our first three years of operation, patients came from southern France, Spain, Italy and North Africa and their sterility was sometimes of long standing, it was not always possible to obtain all the information that could be desired, particularly as far as surgical procedures performed years earlier were concerned.

Although karyotypes were routinely performed whenever linefelter's syndrome was suspected, they could not be done as often as we would have liked because the genetic laboratories working with us first had to meet our demands for karyotypes of donors and women to receive AID.

As far as hormone assays are concerned, the radioimmunological serum FSH titer, measured by our laboratory from the end of the first year on, appears to us to be necessary and sufficient for investigation of male sterility and subfertility.[10,11] In hypoganadotrophic hypogonadism, a normal or subnormal value is observed, with a weak LHRH response; but the diagnosis is already suspected on the basis of clinical signs of hypogonadism. A higher than normal FSH value is found when spermatogenesis is irreversibly pertubed which in cases of azoospermia and severe oligospermia is a good argument for AID. In excretory azoospermia, a normal FSH value is found. Thus, in azoospermia with normal testicular volume, the FSH titer distinguishes between excretory (normal FSH) and secretory (high FSH) types, rendering unnecessary testicular biopsy which we now perform only during operations for excretory azoospermia and varicocoele or when genetic abnormalities are suspected.

LH assay is of much interest: It is normal in most cases, high in some cases where the FSH titer is high, and normal or low in hypogonadotrophic hypogonadism.

Prolactine levels are usually normal. An explanation could not be found for a slight elevation found in 90% of the cases of oligospermia or secretory azoospermia; clinical trials with bromocryptine were not effective.[12] It is rare, when a case of male sterility is being investigated, that a large adenoma with very high prolactine levels is discovered.

Testosterone levels are lowered only in cases of hypogonadotrophic hypogonadism; such results are found in conjunction with
clinical hypogonadism and lowered LH and FSH levels, or the rare
cases of hypogenital Klinefeter's syndrome.

CLASSIFICATION OF MALE STERILITY (FIGURE 2)

Classification is possible when the etiology and pathogenesis
of the sterility have been completely determined.[1,6,7] In almost
half the cases "idiopathic forms", no cause is found. In most other
cases, pathogeneses remains poorly understood (varicocoeles). The poor
factors to which subfertility is attributed can also be presented
by apparently normally fertile individuals. Inversely, some sterile patients present several subfertility factors. For these
reasons, any classification is imperfect, tentative and based on
a mixture of clinical observations and laboratory results.

It is therefore preferable to speak of subfertility factors
rather than of causes of sterility; and to adopt the principle of
an open classification in order to integrate all these factors,
several of which may be presented by a given individual, without
seeking to ascribe to them an order of importance.

When an individual presents several subfertility factors,
however, the fertility prognosis cannot be considered favorable;
this situation constitutes a good argument for AID.

RESULTS AND DISCUSSION

Overall Results

Figure 3 shows that cryptorchism is frequent (20% of all cases);
its incidence being the same as that of absent and arrested spermatogenesis. The incidence of idiopathic forms is 20% for absent
and arrested spermatogenesis and 14.1% for oligo/astheno/terato-
spermia. The frequency with which two or more factors are found
in association in the same individual is shown in Tables 6 and 7.

Comparison with an "Unbiased" Series of Sterile and Subfertile
Male Patients (Figure 4)

This series consists of 441 patients seen for investigation
of an infertile couple where the results of the postcoital test
were poor or negative after optimization of the cervical mucus.
It excludes men who requested AID from the outset but includes those
to whom AID was suggested after investigation and treatment where
appropriate.

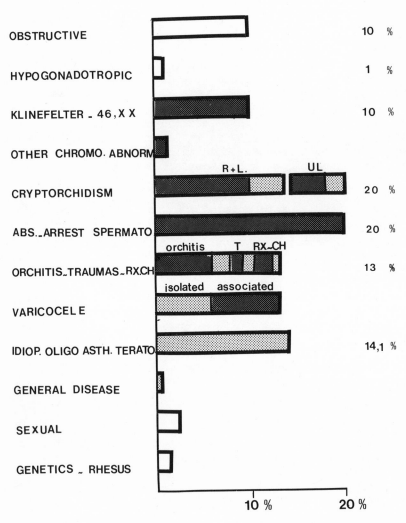

FIGURE 3. Hypofertility factors observed in 551 men consulting for AID.

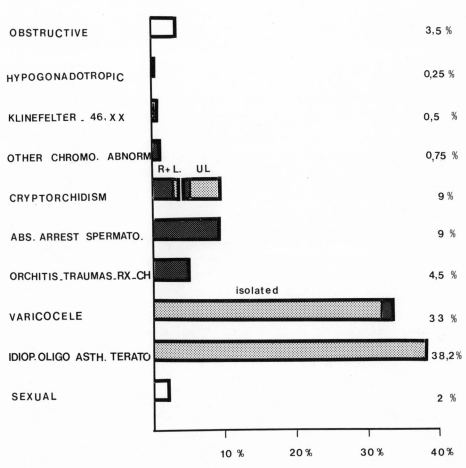

FIGURE 4. Hypofertility factors in 440 men consulting for sterility.

In this study, cryptorchism was observed in only 9% of the cases as was arrested and absent spermatogenesis, while the proportion of varicocoeles(33%) and idiopathic oligospermia(38.2%) were higher.

Excretory Azoospermia

Of the 56 cases of excretory azoospermia, 34 were congenital and 7 acquired(6 infections, 1 traumatic), while the etiology of the other 15 could not be determined(operations performed previously, records unobtainable).

Hypogonadotrophic Hypogonadism

This disorder was present in only 1% of these cases for two reasons: This condition is infrequent; and in this disorder, only treatment with HMG-HCG is highly effective, satisfactory virilization being obtained in all cases.

In 2/3 of the cases, spermatogenesis was compatible with the possibility of obtaining pregnancy and thus only 1/3 of these individuals had reason to request AID.

Karyotype Abnormalities(Table 1)

Klinefelter's syndrome was observed in 10% of these cases of irreversible sterility. Its incidence in this study, as in all others published to date[2,3,6-8] is obviously higher than that observed in the population as a whole(1.2%). Two of the 49 patients affected were chromosomal mosaics.

Seven patients presented a 46 XX karyotype. Morphologically, they ressembled the patients with Klinefelter's syndrome, except that testicular hypotrophy and secondary signs of hypogonadism are less pronounced.[5,13]

Only 3 cases presented with 47 XYY karyotypes, although the incidence of this sex chromosome imbalance is estimated to be comparable to that of Klinefelter's syndrome. This discordant observation is probably due to the fact that many men who present this abnormality do not seek help for infertility since some present satisfactory fertility while others have serious personality problems which keep them from leading normal lives socially and from marrying.[9]

The incidence of other chromosomal anomalies is probably underestimated in this series because, while karyotyping was performed whenever Klinefelter's syndrome was suspected clinically, it could not be carried out in all the other cases where it would have been desirable for reasons already cited.

TABLE 1. *Chromosome abnormalities found in 67 of 551 men consulting for AID.*

Chromosome abnormality	Number
. Klinefelter	79
47 XXY (47)	
46 XX/47 XXY (1)	
46 XY/46 XX/47 XXY (1)	
. 46 XX	7
. 47 XYY	3
. 45 X	1
. Y structural abnormalities	5
45 X/46 XY dic. (1)	
46 XY q- (2)	
46 XY/46 XY 2 q^h (1)	
46 XY inv(p+ q-) (1)	
. Autosomic abnormalities	2
46 XY transloc. 13, 15 (1)	
46 XY transloc. 10, 11 and q23, q25 (1)	

A history of cryptorchism, presented by less than 1% of the general population, was recorded in 20% of our patients(Table 2). In 70%, it was bilateral and associated with azoospermia; the other 30% presented severe oligospermia. Another subfertility factor was associated in 25% of the cases: (1) An excretory disorder due either directly to the cryptorchism or to surgery; (2) hypogonadotrophic hypogonadism(25% of published cases); (3) Klinefelter's syndrome or 46 XX(10% of published cases).

Absent or arrested spermatogenesis was diagnosed in 109 patients (20% of the cases). Twenty presented testicular atrophy but normal karyotypes. This corresponds to the pseudo-Klinefelter's syndrome described by Nelson. Distinguishing microscopicly among pseudo-Klinefelter's syndrome, "Sertoli cell only" syndrome and arrested spermatogenesis has been superseded by the radio-immunological determination of FSH titers. A high FSH level gives a diagnosis of secretory idiopathic azoospermia involving disruption of primary spermatogenesis and renders unnecessary testicular biopsy, whose usefulness is further limited by the fact that there exist intermediate forms of the three major histological types, which have not, moreover, been proven to be different in nature.

TABLE 2. *Associated hypofertility factors found in men presenting*
          with cryptorchism.

	Number
Cryptorchism: 111 men(20%)	
Bilateral	75
- Azoospermia (52)	
- Oligospermia(14)	
Unilateral(Right: 17, left: 19)	36
- Azoospermia (22)	
- Oligospermia(14)	
Associations: 27 men	
Obstructive disorder	1
Hypogonadism	2
47 XXY	5
46 XX	2
Orchitis	5
Torsion	4
Radiotherapy	1
Varicocele	1

TABLE 3. *Factors of hypofertility associated with varicocele which*
          was discovered in 72 of 155 men(13%) consulting for AID.

	Number
Varicocele: 72 men	
Left	40
Bilateral	31
Right	1
Operated	14
Associated factors: 44 men	
Obstructive azoospermia	4
Hypogonadotrophic	1
Klinefelter	5
Other chromosome abnormalities	3
Cryptorchism	7
Absentor arrested spermatogenisis	16
Orchitis	5
Torsion	1
Radiotherapy	1
Idiopathic azoospermia	1

The incidence of associated excretory anomalies is certainly higher than that recorded, as patients with high FSH levels no longer undergo either testicular biopsy nor surgical exploration. Associated varicocoeles were observed in 16 patients; no causal relationship could be established.

Varicocoeles (Table 3)

Varicocoeles were found in 72 patients, 14 of whom underwent surgery. In 28 patients, this was the only abnormality observed whereas another subfertility factor was associated in 44. These findings confirm the idea that, in many patients, sterility cannot be attributed solely to a varicocoele. It shoud rather be looked upon either as an epiphenomenon, as a factor aggravating another known or unknown cause of diminished spermatogenesis, or else as the agent responsible for potentially irreversible lesions which then progress antonomously independent of the factor which induced them.

CONCLUSION

Aside from the 7 cases of genetic anomalies (1.2%) and the 13 cases of sexual dysfunction (2.3%), it was male sterility diagnosed as irreversible which motivated both the couples' request for AID and the Marseille CECOS Center's acceptance. This paper presents an analysis and an open classification of the various factors discovered: History of cryptorchism (20%); absent or arrested spermatogenesis (20%); Klinefelter's syndrome and 46 XX (10%); traumatic or radiochemotherapeutic sequellae (13%); varicocoele (13%) ; idiopathic form (14%); excretory disorder (10%); and hypogonadotrophic hypogonadism ((1%).

The frequency of both cryptorchism and the association of several subfertility factors in the same patient should be stressed. The value of a high serum FSH level in evaluating modifications of spermatogenesis is also worthy of note.

REFERENCES

1. Les aspects cytologiques, étiologiques et pronostiques des infertilités masculines. Tentative de classification à propos de 1303 cas. La Nouvelle Presse Médicale, 5:1678-1682, 1976.

2. Bourrouillou, G., Colombies, P., Blanc, P., Grozdea, J. and Pontonnier, F. Anomalies chromosomiques chez les hommes stériles. Etude chez 241 sujets. La Nouvelle Presse Médicale., 7:3777, 1978.

3. Chandley, A.C., Edmond, P., Christies, S., Gowans, L., Fletcher,
    J., Frackiewicz, A. and Newton, M. Cytogenetics and infert-
    ility in man. I. Karyotype and seminal analysis. Results
    of a five-year survey of men attending a subfertility clinic.
    Ann. Hum. Genet., Lond. 39:231, 1975.

4. David, G, Bisson, J.P., Jouannet, P., Czyglik, F., Gernigon, Cl.,
    Alexandre, CL. and Dreyfus, G. Les tératospermies. In:
    Fertilité et Stérilité du Mâle, Masson, Paris, pp. 81-102,
    1972.

5. de La Chapelle, A. Nature and origin of males with XX sex
    chromosomes. Amer. J. Hum. Genet., 24:71-105, 1972.

6. Dixon, R. and Buttram, V. Artificial insemination using donor
    semen: A review of 171 cases. Fertil. Steril., Feb.:130,
    1976.

7. Dubin, L. and Amelar, R.D. Etiologic factors in 1294 consecu-
    tives cases of male infertility. Fertil. Steril., 22:469-
    474, 1971.

8. Kjessler, B. Facteurs génétiques dans la subfertilité mâle
    humaine. In: Fertilité Stérilité du Mâle., Masson, Paris,
    pp. 205-225, 1972.

9. Noel, B., Quack, B., Durand, Y. and Rethore, M.O. Les hommes
    47 XYY. Annales de Génétique, 4:223:235, 1969.

10. Roulier, R., Mattei, A. and Franchimont, P. Intérêt et limites
    du dosage de FSH et LH avant et après stimulation par LH-RH
    dans les stérilités et hypogonadismes masculins. Ann. Endocr.
    Paris, 37:407:424, 1976.

11. Roulier, R., Mattei, A., Duvivier, J. and Franchimont, P. Mea-
    surement of gonadotrophins, testosterone, Δ 4 androstenedione
    and dihydrotestosterone in idiopathic oligospermia. Clin.
    Endocr., 9:303-311, 1978.

12. Roulier, R., Mattei, A. and Franchimont, P. Prolactin in male
    reproductive functions, In: Progress in Prolactin Physio-
    logy and Pathology., Robyns, C. and Harter, eds, Elsevier/
    North-Holland, Biomedical Press, 1978.

13. Vague, J., Guidon, J., Mattei, J.F., Luciani, J.M. and Angeletti,
    S. Les hommes à caryotype 46 XX. Ann. Endocr., Paris, 38:
    311-321, 1977.

EVALUATION OF FEMALE FERTILITY BEFORE AID

A. Bremond,* D. Cottinet** and J. Lansac ***

*Clinique Gynécologique, Hôpital Edouard Herriot
Lyon, France
**Centre d'Etude et de Conservation du Sperme(CECOS)
Hôpital Edouard Herriot
Lyon, France
***Clinique Gynécologique et Obstétricale
Centre Hospitalier Régional de Tours
Tours, France

The results of artificial insemination with donor semen(AID)
have been reviewed by one of the authors(J. Lansac). For all the
French Centers of artificial insemination, the overall pregnancy rate
is 43.5%(Table 1). At the Center of Lyon, it is 40%. This rather
low success rate has occurred despite the selection of women under
35 years of age and without an infertility factor. The reasons for
refusing a couple AID are shown on Table 2. The major cause was
male infertility which was not sufficiently documented but the rate
of female infertility factors was also rather high.   In our center
the selection has been the same as indicated in Table 2. We have
evaluated at the gynaecological clinic of Hospital Edouard Herriot
the influence of sub-clinical factors affecting the pregnancy rate
in AID.

MATERIALS AND METHODS

We have selected at random 78 records of couples attending the
clinic for problems of male infertility. The investigator knew
nothing about the results of AID. Anything which could indicate that
a pregnancy was obtained by AID was removed from the medical records
since we had observed in a previous study that when the observer knew
negative results had been obtained, he often found a reason for the
failure of AID.

325

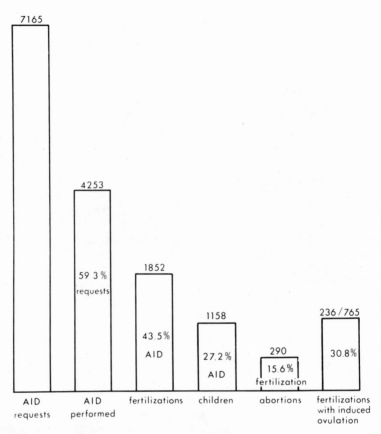

FIGURE 1. Results collected from all French Centers from their opening to 31.12.1978

For each patient, the information included age, previous pelvic surgery, pattern of menstrual cycle, pattern of body temperature, hysterogram and semen analysis(oligospermia or azoospermia). We also noted if the patient lived near of far from the clinic(less or more than 100 kilometers).

In this group of patients 38 of the 78 became pregnant.

RESULTS

Among the factors studied, many do not appear to influence the results of AID: (1) Results are the same whether the husband has an azoospermia or an oligospermia(Table 3); (2) when the menstrual cycle is regular, the pregnancy rate is 49.1%; when it is

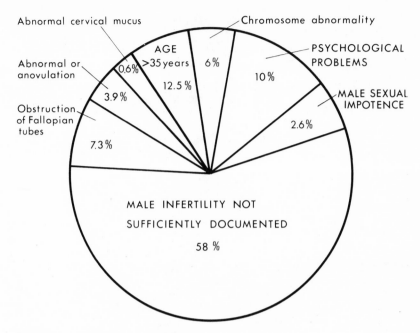

FIGURE 2. Study of 150 medical records of couples not
accepted for AID(CECOS of Grenoble, Lille, Lyon, Nancy,
Rennes, Toulouse and Tours).

irregular, the pregnancy rate is 45.4%(Table 4) but this difference
is not significant; (3) no difference was noted between the pattern
of body temperature curves for three cycles before AID and those for
successful cycles.

The pregnancy rate is higher when the patient lives no more
than 100 kilometers from the clinic(Table 6), but the difference
is not significant. For patients less than 30 years age, the pregnancy rate is 54.2% but only 31.5% after 30(Table 7).

We found better results when there was no history of pelvic
surgery(appendectomy or gynecological surgery)(Table 8). Even with
normal hysterograms only 4 patients became pregnant among 14 patients
with previous pelvic surgery. The hysterograms showed in all cases
at least one normal Fallopian tube but 18 patients had minor ab-
normalities(endometrial hyperplasia, small cervical polyp or obstruction of one Fallopian tube with the other being normal). The pregnancy rate was 52.5% with a perfect genital tract and 33.3% when
there was one minor abnormality(Table 9).

TABLE 3. *Success rate of AID according to the sperm count.*

	Azoospermia	Oligospermia	Unknown	Normal
Pregnant	24 = 48%	7 = 41.1%	7	0
Not pregnant	26 = 52%	10 = 58.9%	3	1

TABLE 4. *Menstrual cycle pattern and outcome of AID.*

	Menstrual cycle	
	Regular	Not regular
Pregnant	28 = 49.1%	10 = 45.4%
Not pregnant	29 = 50.9%	11 = 54.6%

TABLE 5. *Results of AID according to the body temperature pattern.*

	Basal body temperature records before AID			
	Normal	Short luteal phase (< 12 days)	Ovulating day not regular (≥ 6 days)	More than one abnormality
Pregnant	19	5	12	2
Not pregnant	19	5	13	0
Total.......	38	10	25	2

TABLE 6. *The pregnancy rate and distance patient lives from Center*

	< 100 kilometers	≥ 100 kilometers
Pregnant	23 = 56.1%	15 = 40.5%
Not pregnant	18 = 43.9%	22 = 59.5%
	CHI Square: 1.93 N.S.	

TABLE 7. *Age and AID success rate.*

	< 30 years of age	≥ 31 years of age
Pregnant	32 = 54.2%	6 = 31.5%
Not pregnant	27 = 45.8%	13 = 68.5%
	CHI Square: 3.14 (0.05 < p < 0.1)	

TABLE 8. *History of pelvic surgery and AID.*

	Previous pelvic surgery	No previous pelvic surgery
Pregnant	4 = 28.6%	34 = 53.1%
Not pregnant	10 = 71.4%	30 = 46.9%
	CHI Square: 3.05 (0.05 < p < 0.01)	

The final success rate was 65.8% in the group of patients less than 31 years of age with no history of pelvic surgery and a normal hysterogram. In the other cases, it was only 29.7%(Table 10).

DISCUSSION

In spite of a rigorous clinical selection, the patients referred to our clinic for AID needed to be rechecked since many minor infertility factors in women may escape the first gynecologist.

TABLE 9. *Hysterogram and AID.*

| | Hysterogram | | |
	Normal	Minor abnormality	Unknown
Pregnant	31 = 52.5%	6 = 33.3%	1
Not pregnant	28 = 47.5%	12 = 69.7%	0

CHI Square: 2.85(0.05 < p < 0.1)

TABLE 10. *Results of AID and presence or absence of gynecological factors.*

	At least one of these factors: - age over 30 years - previous pelvic surgery - minor abnormalities on hysterogram.	None of these factors
Pregnant	11 = 29.7%	27 = 65.8%
Not pregnant	26 = 70.3%	14 = 34.2%

Chi Square: 11.74(p < 0.001)

One may think that in infertile men, the seminal fluid may exert adverse effects of the fertilizing ability of the donor's semen in AID. In these cases, it was advised to use contraceptive condoms in order to avoid contact between the husband's semen and the cervical mucus. Furthermore, it is possible that the fertilization may result from the husband's spermatozoa in cases of oligospermia. These two factors could explain the same pregnancy rates in the cases of azoospermia or oligospermia.

That no difference in success rate is observed whether the menstrual cycle is regular or not, may be explained by the treatments carried out in cases of abnormalities. In Table 1, one can see a 30.8% fertilization rate with induced ovulation. When the patients live far from our center, the pregnancy rate with AID is lower. Although this difference is not significant, it is evident that AID is more difficult to perform.

We do not feel that AID should be carried out in women over 35 years of age. Our pregnancy rate was 54.2% for those under 30 and 31.5% for those over 30. Although it is not reasonable to refuse AID to all patients over 30 years of age, this factor must be taken into account in evaluating the fertility of the woman.

Previous pelvic surgery can leave pelvic sequelae and we think that gynecological laparoscopy must be carried out in these cases even if the hysterogram appears to be normal. The minor abnormalities observed on the X-Ray must be corrected medically or surgically prior to AID.

Since AID is expensive for the couple and for the community, semen donors are difficult to obtain and failure difficult to accept, we feel that it is necessary to make a rigorous selection among the women requesting AID. By considering age, personal medical history, hysterogram and laparoscopy, it may be possible to predict cases with little hope of success.

It is possible to determine cases with a poor prognosis by taking into account the results of the first three treatments with AID and studying basal body temperature, spermatozoa in cervical mucus and psychological behavior. In patients with a good prognosis, AID is pursued for more than six cycles.

ACKNOWLEDGEMENT

The authors would like to thank the Doctors E. Claraz, G. Robert and N. Saunier for their assistance.

IMPORTANCE OF INSEMINATION TIMING AND FREQUENCY IN AID

Daniel Schwartz,* Marie-Jeanne Mayaux,* Vincent Heuche,*
Françoise Czyglik,** and Georges David **

* Unité de Recherches Statistique de l'Institut National
  de la Santé et de la Recherche Médicale,
  Villejuif, France
** Centre d'Etude et de Conservation du Sperme(CECOS)
  de Paris-Bicêtre
  Kremlin-Bicêtre, France

INTRODUCTION

From a practical as well as theoretical point of view, it is
evident that a knowledge of the optimal timing and frequency for artificial insemination would be quite valuable. Accordingly, a study
on women undergoing artificial insemination with donor semen(AID)
was carried out in order to determine success rates for different
days of the menstrual cycle. These success rates which were based
upon the results of single insemination cycles were then compared
to those for multiple insemination cycles.

Previous findings have been published elsewhere;[1] this paper
reports on a much greater number of cycles.

MATERIALS AND METHODS

The women included in this study were being treated with AID
by their gynecologist who obtained frozen semen samples in paillettes
from the Centre d'Etudes et de Conservation du Sperme(CECOS)
at Bicêtre Hospital. The regulations and criteria of CECOS, Paris-
Bicêtre are outlined below :

. Definition of subjects: Generally couples in which the husband
  presents a proven and irreversible sterility (azoospermia or
  oligospermia), the wife being presumed fertile.

. Selection of donors: Married men of less than 45 years of age
who have one or more children and no history of congenital or
hereditary disease in their family. Donors are not paid and
the consent of the wife is required.

. Semen collection and criteria: Semen specimens are collected
at C.E.C.O.S. by masturbation after a recommended 3 day abstinence. An assessment of thawed semen is carried out on the
same day in order to determine freezing tolerance. Ejaculates
with 50% or more motile forms after thawing are retained. Those
having between 30% and 50% motile forms are used only if their
ability to penetrate the cervical mucus *in vitro* is good.

. Protocol: Gynecologists and couples were to respect to the
extent possible a protocol designed to permit scientific evaluation of AID. The essentiel elements in the protocol concerning insemination and data analysis are as follows:

- An initial observation period during which the basal body
temperature(B.B.T.) curves are recorded for at least 3 cycles
in order to determine the "low point"(defined below) which is
presumed to correspond to the best day for insemination.

- A second period designated as controlled insemination. During
a maximum of two cycles, a single insemination by the intra-
cervical administration of one dose is carried out without associated gynecological treatment.

- An unrestricted period follows if conception has not occurred.
During this period, no limitations are placed on the number and
mode of inseminations or the association of other therapeutic
measures.

- Documents on couples and donors are transmitted in anonymous
form to the Centre Statistique where a computer analysis is
performed.

- B.B.T. curves are interpreted by one of three persons, all
having been trained to analyse the curves in the same manner.
The curves are selected randomly in such a way that curves of
one patient are not read in succession. They are then analysed
blindly, the reader being unaware of whether or not insemination
had been practiced during the cycle.

- Several measurements are made on each B.B.T. curve of which
the principal is the "zero" point or "low point"; that is, the
last day of low temperature as defined by Vincent.[2] B.B.T.
curves upon which this point can not be defined are classified
as "illegible".

- Insemination is considered a "success" when a 21 day hyperthermic plateau is followed by clinical or hormonal confirmation
of conception (regardless of the outcome of the pregnancy).

The present study is based on data collected in the first 5
years of operation of CECOS Paris-Bicêtre (Feb. 1, 1973 to Jan. 31,
1978). During this period, 1188 women were treated for a total of
6040 cycles including 2928 cycles with only one insemination (1132
under controlled conditions and 1796 under unrestricted conditions).

RESULTS

The study is based principally on 1132 controlled insemination
cycles. For these cycles, the success rate was 11%. B.B.T. curves
were available for 1012 of the cycles but only 850 were legible.
The success rate for these 850 cycles was 13%, the distribution
being as follows: No successes were observed for 101 inseminations
occurring outside the period of minus four (- 4) to plus two (+ 2) days
as calculated from the zero point day; the success rate for the remaining 749 cycles within this period was 14% over all but varied
according to the day as indicated in Table 1 and Figure 1a.

According to the Chi square test, these rates are significantly
different in an overall comparison (p = 0.05). There appears to be
an optimum period from day - 3 to day 0 with a mean rate of 17%
whereas outside of this period, the mean rate is 8%. In the optimal
period, two maxima at days - 1 and - 3 seem to exist but are not significant. It would be worthwhile for purposes of comparing populations to define the mean day of success that one would obtain in a
series of single insemination cycles equally distributed among all
days considered. This mean $\overline{d}$ can be estimated from Table 1 as
follows:

$$\overline{d} = \frac{(-4) \times 0.08 + (-3) \times 0.17 + \ldots + (+ 2) \times 0.08}{0.08 + 0.17 + \ldots + 0.08} = - 1.2$$

Also studied were 1796 cycles of unrestricted insemination but
in which there were, in fact, only single inseminations. Among
these, 1243 had legible B.B.T. curves for which the success rate was

TABLE 1. *Success rate according to day (controlled insemination).*

Day	- 4	- 3	- 2	- 1	0	+ 1	+ 2
Success	8%	17%	13%	21%	15%	9%	8%
(Patients)	(38)	(72)	(90)	(146)	(226)	(125)	(52)

9%. A distribution of these cases showed no success for 177 insemination cycles outside the period of days −3 to +2 whereas the success
rate for the remaining 1066 cycles which was 10% overall again varied
according to the day as indicated in Table 2 and Figure 1b.

TABLE 2. *Success rate according today (unrestricted insemination).*

Day	− 3	− 2	− 1	0	+ 1	+ 2
Success	6%	11%	7%	13%	11%	9%
(Patients)	(78)	(131)	(200)	(412)	(170)	(79)

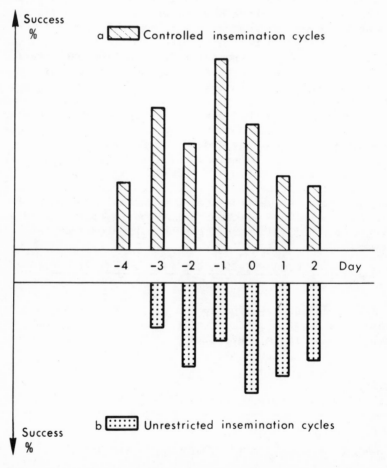

FIGURE 1. Success rate according to insemination day for
controlled (a) and unrestricted (b) insemination cycles.

It does not appear possible to identify an optimum day in this 6 day interval. Other differences from controlled insemination cycles include a lower success rate(10% versus 14%, p < 0.01), a one day delay in the beginning of the fertile period(day − 3 versus − 4), a later suggested maximum(day 0 versus − 1) and a later mean day of success(−0.3 versus − 1.2).

Finally, the success rate for multiple insemination cycles in the unrestricted period was studied by determining the success rate as a function of the number of inseminations(Table 3). In addition, expected values of success were calculated using a mathematical model which expresses the probability of success for multiple insemination cycles on day i, j, etc. as a function of the probability of success for a single insemination on the corresponding day.[3]

DISCUSSION

Of the few studies on the optimal day for artificial insemination reported in the literature, there are none in which the data or statistical methods could be considered sufficient for a valid conclusion as to the "best" day for insemination. A study by Haman on 440 women receiving artificial insemination showed a greater number of conceptions for day 13.[4] Strickler et al. observed in 45 conceptions a maximum for what was considered to be the ovulation day as judged by B.B.T. curves.[5] However, these two studies included cycles with multiples inseminations and the day of fertilization chosen by the authors was that which they considered the most probable thus resulting in an overestimation for those days.

Based upon single insemination cycles, a maximum number of conceptions was found to occur on day 14 by Behrman for 68 conceptions,[6] two days before the middle of the cycle by Torrano and Murphy for 153 conceptions,[7] and at the middle of the cycle by Raboch and Mellan for 100 births.[8] However, these authors considered only the number of successes on a given day and not the success rate. Thus, the number of successes was greatest for those days on which inseminations were performed the most frequently, that is, those considered *a priori* the best. These studies, therefore, do not permit the definition of an optimum day.

TABLE 3. *Success rate as a function of the number of insemination per cycle(unrestricted insemination).*

Number of inseminations	1	2	3	4
Number of cycles	1280	1143	481	122
Observed rate	10%	13%	17%	16%
Expected rate	10%	14%	16%	16%

The present study first examined controlled single insemination cycles without supplementary gynecological treatment. A fertile period was determined to exist between four days before(- 4) and two days after(+ 2) day zero, the day on which the "zero point" was observed on the B.B.T. curve. Within this fertile period, there appeared to be a 4 day optimal period from day - 3 to day 0 which perhaps included one(day - 1) or two(days - 1 and - 3) best days. The success rate for this optimal period was clearly superior to that of the fertile period(17% versus 8%).

From a practical standpoint, the fact that the optimal period terminates on day 0 would argue against inseminating too late. In this study, the day by far the most often utilized for insemination was day 0, but it does not appear to be any better than the 3 preceding days, especially day - 1, in regard to success. Furthermore, if one attemps to inseminate on day 0, there is a risk of it being performed too late, that is, on a day when the fertility is diminished or even nil.

The study of unrestricted insemination cycles yielded slightly different results: There was a shorter period of fertility(day - 3 to day + 2) during which the fertility was only fair and there was no apparent "best" day. Nevertheless, the results do not contradict those for the controlled period and would reinforce a strategy of inseminating early rather than late in the fertile period.

A second very practical question concerns the value of multiple inseminations as opposed to single inseminations within the fertile period. The results of this study clearly show that although the probability of success may increase with two or even three inseminations, a point is quickly reached beyond which further inseminations have little or no effect.

From a theoretical point of view determination of a fertile period and especially the most fertile days would contribute greatly to the understanding of certain mechanisms of fertilization. It should first be emphasized that the length of the fertile periods observed in this study are not necessarily those for a given woman or for a given cycle in which the fertile period may actually be shorter. Each cycle possesses a fertile period occurring near the time of ovulation but the fertile periods observed in this study result from a distribution of individual periods as well as a distribution of errors arising from the estimation of the ovulation day from B.B.T. curves. Better timing of ovulation, now available through echography,[9] is necessary in order to calculate the distribution of individual fertile periods from which the length of survival of the gamets could be deduced.

In regard to fertile periods, it is also interesting to compare controlled and unrestricted cycles. The unrestricted insemination cycles have several particularities, the principle being that there is often concomitant gynecological treatment. These cycles which had a lower success rate were associated with a shorter fertile period and a mean day of success closer to day 0 than the controlled cycles, even though the semen utilized was the same. One explanation could be that the female genital environment in these cycles is less favorable to the survival of the spermatozoa.

Also of theoretical interest are the results concerning the success rate as a function of the number of inseminations per cycle since close agreement was found between observed and expected values, the latter obtained by means of a mathematical model. Such models, if verified by other studies, should, beyond their explanatory value, allow one to approach the following practical questions: To what extent will efficacy be improved by carrying out two or more inseminations per cycle, by augmenting the number of spermatozoa per dose, or by combining these two procedures?

REFERENCES

1. Schwartz, D., Mayaux, M.J., Martin-Boyce, A., Czyglik, F. and David, G. Donor insemination: Conception rate according to cycle day in a series of 821 cycles with a single insemination. Fertil. Steril., 31:226-229, 1979.

2. Vincent, B. Atlas des courbes thermiques. Ed. 4, C.D.I.C. Nantes, 1964.

3. Schwartz, D., Macdonald, P.D.M. and Heuchel, V. Fecundability, coital frequency and the viability of ova. To be published in Population Studies, vol. 34-2, 1980.

4. Haman, J.O. Therapeutic donor insemination: A review of 440 cases. California Med., 90, 130, 1959.

5. Strickler, R.C., Keller, D.W. and Warren, J.C. Artificial insemination with fresh donor semen. New Engl. J. Med., 293, 848, 1975.

6. Behrman, S.J. Artificial insemination. Fertil. Steril., 10: 248, 1959.

7. Torrano, E.F. and Murphy, D.P. Cycle day of conception by insemination or isolated coitus. Fertil. Steril., 13:492, 1962.

8.   Raboch, J. and Mellan, J.   Cycle day of conception by a single
     therapeutic donor insemination.   100 births.   Intern. J.
     Fertil., 11:281-283, 1966.

9.   Renaud, R., Dervain, I., Macler, J., Ehret, C. and Spira, A.
     Ultrasound monitoring ovulation.   Lancet, 1:665, 1979.

THE SERIAL ASSESSMENT OF GRAAFIAN FOLLICLE

GROWTH BY ULTRASONIC MEANS FOR TIMING AID

J.F. Kerin, G.B. Young, M.M. Lees,
S. Lawson, A.A. Templeton and O.T. Baird

Department of Obstetrics and Gynaecology
University of Edinburgh
Edinburgh, Scotland

INTRODUCTION

The application of ultrasound to measure Graafian follicle growth in spontaneous and induced ovular menstrual cycles in women has been described by Hackloer et al.[1,2] and Ylöstalo et al.[3] They were able to demonstrate a good correlation between incremental follicular growth and increasing oestrogen levels in peripheral venous blood. Their methods were adopted to measure the daily follicular growth in the ovaries of women undergoing donor artificial insemination (AID) with cryopreserved semen. Preliminary results have been described[4]: It was found that insemination could be timed to the day before and the day of rupture of the dominant Graafian follicle with a considerable degree of precision. There is increasing evidence that these are the optimal days for insemination in a menstrual cycle if the lowest cycle to conception ratio (recognizable fecundability) is to be achieved.[5]

METHOD

Each woman was seen daily from day ten of the menstrual cycle until there was ultrasonic evidence of ovulation and corpus luteum formation. Daily assessments of the cervical score,[4] 24 hour urinary total oestrogen and pregnanediol estimation and the assessment of follicle growth by ultrasound were made. Apart from the ultrasonic evidence of ovulation, it was also confirmed by a luteal level of pregnanediol in a 24 hour urine collection made one week following the day of ovulation.

From day 10 of the menstrual cycle, each ovary was scanned using

341

a "Sonicaid" multiplanar, B-Scanner. The full bladder technique as described by Hackeloer[1] was used. The uterus could be readily identified as a midline structure and the ovaries outlined as longitudinal scans were made laterally to the left and then to the right of the midline. The ovaries tended to lie in a symmetrical position adjacent to the posterior wall of the distended bladder. The Sonicaid has a high quality flicker free gray scale. Three focused transducers, 2.5, 3.5 and 5.0 Mhz,are available. A caliper system capable of measurement in millimeters and based on the velocity of sound; 1564 metres/second was used. Gating and magnification systems are also included as standard components of this machine.

From a series of 72 scans carried out on a daily basis from the midfollicular to the early luteal phase in 12 menstrual cycles, an appreciation of ovarian size, the active ovary containing the dominant follicle and the surrounding population of follicles greater than 7 mm in diameter could be identified.

RESULTS

The day of the maximal cervical score in a previous study has been shown to occur on the day of the serum luteinizing hormone (LH) peak (day 0) and that the peak serum oestradiol-17β level occurs 24 hours prior to this.[6] As shown in Figure 1, the peak urinary total oestrogen concentration occurred between day -1 and 0, the cervical score was maximal on day 0 and maximal follicular size was found to occur between day 0 and +1.

It was possible to identify the dominant Graafian follicle at least three days prior to ovulation. It was most unusual for any sister follicles to obtain a diameter of more than 14 mm in diameter in spontaneous ovular cycles. However, it was not unusual to detect three to four follicles between 5 to 14 mm in diameter in the ovary containing the dominant follicle as well as in the opposite ovary. These follicles exhibited day to day growth changes which were much less dramatic than the rapid growth of the largest preovular follicle. This dominant follicle reached an average peak diameter of 23 $\pm$ 3.6 mm between day 0 and +1. In all cases the follicle ovulated within 24 to 36 hours of reaching this diameter and on day +2 an outline of the early corpus luteum could be seen. In most cases the corpus luteum could be identified by its serpiginous outline and reduced size (collapsed follicle).

AID TIMING

The women undergoing AID were inseminated from the moment the dominant follicle reached a diameter of 2.0 centimetres until the earliest evidence of corpus luteum formation as assessed by ultrasound

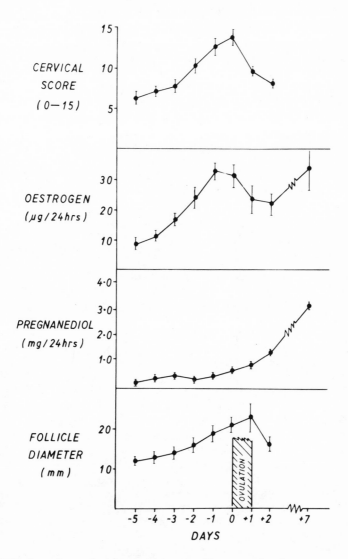

FIGURE 1. Correlations between the cervical mucus score (0- 15), urinary total oestrogen(ug/24 hours) and follicle diameter(mm). Results are expressed as a mean + SEM. Day 0 was designated the day of maximal cervical score.

measurements. This usually meant insemination was carried out over two to three days. When more data are available and pregnancy rates have been assessed, it may be sufficient to inseminate on the day the follicle reaches this diameter and/or the day afterwards. It would be appear from the small series of cycles studied that these optimal days are days 0 and +1 to +2 in relation to the LH peak in peripheral venous blood.

From a logistical point of view it was possible to perform an adequate ultrasonic scan of a woman's ovaries and measure the family of follicles to the nearest millimetre in 10 to 15 minutes. The women did not find the procedure unpleasant and when a clear explanation of the aims of the procedure was given, these well motivated women become quite interested in this visual demonstration of their reproductive cycle.

DISCUSSION

It has been demonstrated that ultrasound can be used to define the immediate preovular follicle and that as a result, artificial insemination can be timed just prior to and following ovulation. Furthermore, it has been confirmed that a good correlation exists between follicular growth, the cervical mucus score and urinary oestrogen and pregnanediol excretion.

The application of ultrasound to measure the cyclical follicular and luteal events which take place in spontaneous and induced ovular cycles would appear to have a great deal to offer in terms of gaining more fundamental information about ovarian function and its control. In the field of *in vitro* fertilization the immediate preovular follicle could be defined and localized prior to aspiration of the follicular fluid and ovum under laparoscopic control. Both Hackeloer[1] and Ylöstalo[3] have used this method to track follicular growth following induction of ovulation with gonadotrophins or clomiphene. Our initial work in this field indicates that ultrasonic tracking of follicular growth may be more accurate than serial oestrogen estimations in detecting minor degrees of hyperstimulation when using either clomid or gonadotrophin therapy. Therefore, the ovulating dose of HCG can be withheld and hopefully the incidence of multiple pregnancy be further reduced. Finally, the ultrasonic tracking of abnormal follicular growth and correlating this with hormonal changes will be invaluable in disorders of ovulation and also in following follicular and luteal responses to prospective drugs and hormones used in an attempt to restore normal ovarian function.

REFERENCES

1. Hackloer,   B.J.   The ultrasonic demonstration of follicular
    development during the normal menstrual cycle and after
    hormone stimulation. Proc. of the Int. Symp. on Recent Ad-
    vances in Ultrasound Diagnosis : Excerpta Medica Int. Cong.
    Series N° 436, October, 1977.

2. Hackloer,   B.J., Fleming, R., Robinson, H.P., Adam, A.H. and
    Coutts, J.R.T. Ultrasound assessment of follicular growth :
    A new technique for observation of ovarian development.
    Int. Symp. on the Functional Morphology of the Human Ovary,
    Glasgow, Scotland, 1978.

3. Ylöstalo, P., Rönnberg, L. and Jouppila, P. Simultaneous moni-
    toring of the growth of the ovarian follicle with ultrasound
    and oestrogen assays during ovulation induction. Third
    Reinier De Graaf Symp., Maastricht, The Netherlands, 1978.

4. Kerin, J.F. Determination of the optimal timing of insemination
    in women. Artificial insemination : Proc. of the Royal
    College of Obstetricians and Gynaecologists, Sutton Bonnington,
    England, March, 1979.

5. Matthews, C.D., Broom, T.J., Crawshaw, K.M., Hopkins, R.E.,
    Kerin, J.F.P. and Svigos, J.M. The influence of insemina-
    tion timing and sperm characteristics on the efficiency of
    a donor insemination programme. Fert. Steril., 1979 (In
    Press).

6. Kerin, J.F.P., Matthews, C.D., Svigos, J.M., Makin, A.E.,
    Symons, R.G. and Smeaton, T.C. Linear and quantitative mi-
    gration of stored sperm through cervical mucus during the
    periovular period. Fert. Steril., 27:1054, 1976.

ECHOGRAPHIC STUDY OF OVULATION

R. Renaud,[*] I. Dervain,[*] J. Macler,[*] E. Ehret,[*]
A. Spira,[**] S. Plas-Roser,[***] and C. Aron[***]

[*]Service de Gynécologie Obstétrique
Faculté de Médecine de Strasbourg
Schiltigheim, France.
[**] Unité de Recherches Statistiques, Inserm,
Villejuif, France.
[***] Institut d'Histologie,
Faculté de Médecine de Strasbourg
Strasbourg, France.

In 1975 Hackloer[3,4] and the authors[8,9,10] reported the possibility of visualizing echographically the pre-ovulatory follicle.
Practical applications in the surveillance of ovulation-induction
treatments and the techniques of artificial insemination demanded
a more precise knowledge of the dynamics of normal follicle development. The present work comprises a study of follicle growth and
disappearance as observed by echography. At the same time, basal
temperature curves, plasma hormone levels and cervical changes were
followed to situate the chronology of ovulation. These indirect
parameters of ovulation were later correlated with the direct observation of follicle growth and ovulation by echography.

MATERIALS AND METHODS

Ten healthy women volunteers, between 24 and 28 years of age,
with regular menstrual cycles were studied for a total of 18
cycles. They were taking neither oral contraceptives nor other hormones. The following investigations were carried out:

. Echography: A Kretz Technik gray-scale ultrasonic apparatus
with a 2 MHz transducer was employed for these studies. Record-
ings were made when the bladder was full. The ovaries were
located by repeated parasagittal and transverse B-scans.

Echography was performed at 7 PM on the 8th, 10th and 12th
through 19th day of the cycle(and lasted between 10 and 20 minutes).

. Basal body temperature: Rectal temperature was recorded on
waking(approximately 7 AM). The curves were interpreted inde-
pendently by a center of artificial insemination after random
mixing with 50 other menothermic curves.

. Serum hormone measure: Blood was drawn at every echographic
session. The level of plasma LH was determined on the 5th and
12th through 15th day of the cycle. Plasma 17 β estradiol levels were measured on the 8th through 15th day of the cycle.
Determinations of all hormones were made on the 19th day of the
cycle. All determinations were performed by radio-immunoassay.

. Cervical score: The appearance of the cervix and mucus was
evaluated by speculum examination at each echographic session.
A score from 1 to 12 was noted in accordance with the criteria
established by Insler.[5]

In this study, only those cycles with an unambiguious B.B.T.
curve and a definite mid-cycle peak in LH and 17 β estradiol levels
were considered in the results. Only 10 cycles fulfilled these conditions. Of these 10 cycles, only 9 had been evaluated for cervical
score(1 woman being a virgin), and only 8 showed a significant rise
in the level of progesterone.

RESULTS

Echographic Image

Round, clear, cyst-like sonolucent bodies were seen bulging
from the surface of the more echogenic ovary. They were easily spot-
ted and were first seen when their diameters were between 0.8 and
1.0 cm(when not circular, diameter was recorded with respect to the
largest diameter measurable) (Figures 1, 2, 3, 4, 5).

Charactoristics of Echographic Images

Figure 6 and Table 1 reveal that growth was progressive. The
day of echographic disappearance is considered as day ECO. A sufficient number of measurements were available for only 4 days prior
to disappearance of the images. No significant differences of rate
of growth were found from woman to woman when these results were
statistically adjusted to a linear model. The average rate of growth
was 3 mm per day from the time the echographic image was first visible. Repeated measurements performed in only one cycle, however
revealed the existence of a phase of rapid growth in the ten hours

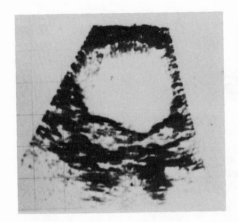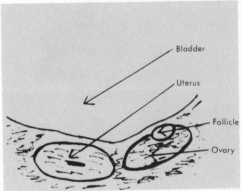

FIGURE 1. Follicle at 0.8 cm in diameter: Transverse B-scan.

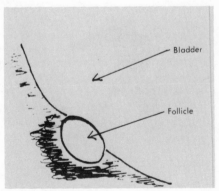

FIGURE 2. Follicle at 2 cm in diameter: Parasagittal B-scan.

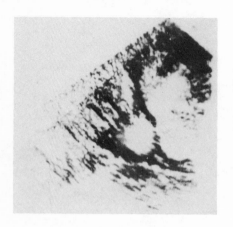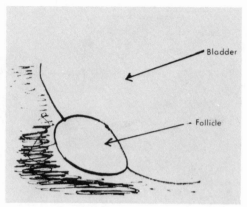

FIGURE 3. Follicle at 3 cm in diameter: Parasagittal B-scan.

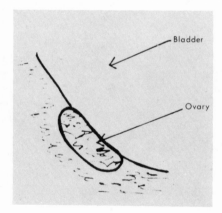

FIGURE 4. Post-ovulatory ovary: Parasagittal B-scan.

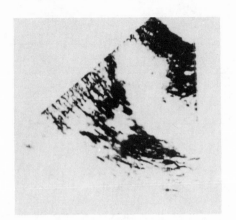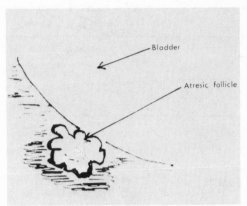

FIGURE 5.   Atresic follicle: Parasagittal B-scan.

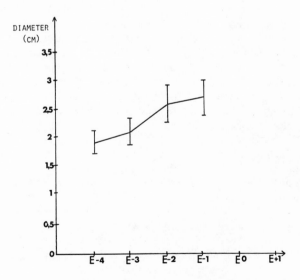

FIGURE 6.   Average growth of echographic image during
the four days before its disappearance(E 0).

TABLE 1. *Average diameter of echographic image on the 4 days prece-*
          ding the day of disappearance(Day EC 0).

	EC-4	EC-3	EC-2	EC-1	EC 0
Average diameter (cm)	1,9 ± 0.2	2.1 ± 0.2	2.6 ± 0.3	2.7 ± 0.3	0

immediately preceding disappearance of the echographic image. At
7 PM on day D O the diameter was measured at 20 mm. At 10 AM, the
next morning(D + 1) the diameter was 26 mm and increased to 33 mm
5 hours later. By 7 PM, the echographic image was no longer visible.
(The significance of this rapid growth is unknown).

Disappearance of Echographic Image with Respect to Other Indices

    BBT: (Table 2). Theoretically, ovulation occurs on the last
day of the hypothermic phase. This is designated in this study
as Day TO . In 4 cycles, the echographic image disappeared for 5
on day T + 1 and for 1 on day T - 1.

    Since temperatures were recorded early in the morning and the
echographic examination was made in the evening, the moment of
disappearance of the echographic image with respect to the BBT
could only be determined within 24 hours(± 12 hours). Frequently
repeated measurements, carried out for only one cycle, permitted a
more precise determination. In that case the echographic image
was seen to disappear between 8 and 12 hours on the first day of
the hyperthermic plateau, day T + 1.

    Level of LH: The day of maximum LH level was taken as the
point of reference. Table 3 shows that the echographic image disappeared on that day in 3 of the cycles, and on the following day
in the remaining 7 cycles.

    Level of 17 β estradiol(Table 4) :   The day of maximum 17 β
estradiol level was used as the reference point. Table 4 reveals
that in 3 cycles, the echographic image disappeared on that day.
In the remaining 7 cycles the image was no longer visible 2 days
after the maximum 17 β estradiol value.

TABLE 2. *Day of disappearance of echographic image with respect to the last day of the hypothermic phase of the BBT Curve (Day T 0).*

Day of image disappearance	T-1	T O	T+1	Total
Number of cycles	1	4	5	10

TABLE 3. *Disappearance of echographic image with respect to the day of maximum LH level (Day LH 0).*

Day of image disappearance	LH O	LH + 1	Total
Number of cycles	3	7	10

TABLE 4. *Disappearance of echographic image with respect to the day of maximum 17 β estradiol level (Day ES 0).*

Day of image disappearance	ES O	ES + 1	ES + 2	Total
Number of cycles	3	0	7	10

Level of progesterone (Table 5): The beginning of the rise in progesterone levels was taken as the reference point. In 2 of the 8 cycles studied, the disappearance of the echographic image coincided with this day. In 4 cycles it was no longer seen on the day following the beginning of the rise, and in the remaining 2 cycles it was no longer visible 2 days after the initial rise. In all cycles, then, the level of progesterone began to rise at the time of or before the echographic image disappeared.

Insler Cervical Score (Table 6): In 4 of the 9 cycles studied, the echographic image disappeared on the day of the maximal cervical score. In the remaining 5 cycles, the echographic image was no longer visible the following day. In all cases, the echographic image disappeared within 3 days from the time the cervical score reached a value of 8 (Table 5).

TABLE 5. *Disappearance of echographic image with respect to day marking the rise in progesterone level(Day PG 0).*

Day of image disappearance	PG-1	PG 0	PG+1	PG+2	Total
Number of cycles	0	2	4	2	8

TABLE 6. *Disappearance of echographic image with respect to the day of maximum cervical score(Day CS 0).*

Day of image disappearance	CS 0	CS + 1	Total
Number of cycles	4	5	9

TABLE 7. *Disappearance of echographic image with respect to the day marking a cervical score of 8(Day CS 8).*

Day of image disappearance	CS 8	CS 8+1	CS 8+2	CS 8+3	Total
Number of cycles	2	2	2	1	7

DISCUSSION

Pelvic echography performed during the period before ovulation permits the visualisation of echolucent structures that are localized latero-uterinely in the vicinity of the ovaries. The size and growth caracteristics of these cyst-like structures with their sudden disappearance in mid-cycle are highly suggestive of pre-ovulatory follicles.

This work enables us to be unequivocal about the nature of the echographic images seen. Hormone and other indirect measures reveal that the disappearance of the structures coincides remarkably well with that of supposed ovulation. In all cycles the peak levels of 17 β estradiol and LH, and the rise of progesterone precede or correspond with the moment of disappearance of the echographic images. The time delay is within 48 hours for 17 β estradiol and progesterone and not more than 24 hours for LH. These images therefore are most assuredly those of pre-ovulatory follicles(Figure 7).

Technically the visualisation of these pre-ovulatory follicles poses little problem for an experienced operator. The follicles were first seen when their diameter was between 0.8 and 1 cm. The growth of the follicles was linear at 0.3 cm per day attaining a diameter of 2.7 $\pm$ 0.3 cm before disappearing. These results are in basic agreement with those of Hackloer,[4] Rönnberg[11] and Kerin.[6] That a rapid increase in follicle size(volume) occurs in the ten hours immediately preceding ovulation is suggested by our results but is not definitive at this time.

Although in most cycles studied a single follicle was observed on the surface of the ovary, in 4 cases 2 follicles, 1 preceding the other, were visualized. The first follicle grew to a diameter of 1.8 - 2 cm after which it disappeared and was followed by the appearance of the second follicle. The exact significance of this is unclear. In 2 cases, this phenomenon was accompagnied by 2 different peaks in 17 β estradiol and raises the possibility that a synergy may be necessary among several follicles in order that one may arrive at maturity.[2] It is difficult to reconcile this with the notion that atresic follicles have only a negligible hormonal secretion.[1,7] These ideas will be explored in a future publication(Figure 8).

From a practical point of view, echography has many advantages. It is a completely non-invasive technique that can be easily repeated without the inconvenience of multiple blood drawings. Furthermore, results are immediate which eliminates the often long delay of

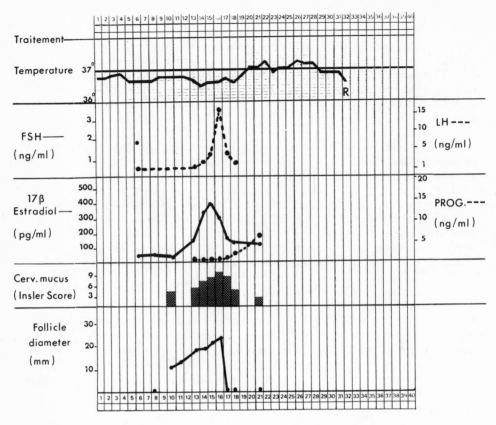

FIGURE 7. Correlation of BBT, plasma hormone levels, cervical score, and follicle diameter in a normal menstrual cycle.

hormone studies. By providing an actual measure of follicle growth and disappearance, echography acts essentially as a reference point for estimating the reliability of other indirect methods of detecting ovulation. Finally, in the energy and frequency range habitually used in diagnostic explorations, ultrasound has been shown to be without harmful effect on mammalian tissue and growing cells. Present experience with what is now almost routine echographic examination in the early weeks of pregnancy confirms the complete innocuousness of this method.

This feature makes echography a method of choice in at least 2 clinical applications. By providing an immediate view of the number and size of pre-ovulatory follicles, echography may be invaluable in the monitoring of ovulation-induction techniques. Treatment could be modified so as to respect as much as possible the normal physiological caracteristics of follicle growth and thereby minimize the

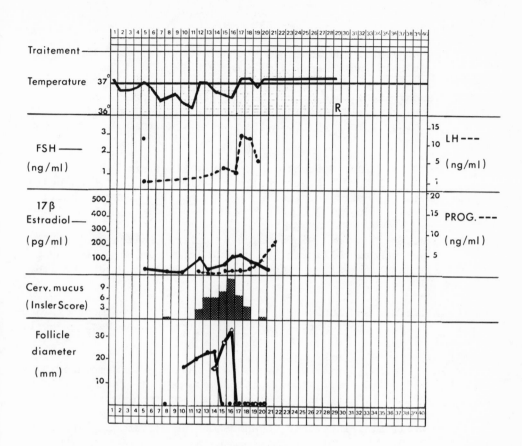

FIGURE 8. Correlation of BBT, plasma hormone levels, cervical score, and follicle diameter in a normal menstrual cycle with two follicles; only one is ovulatory but two differents peaks in 17 β estradiol are observed.

risk of multiple pregnancy and ovarian hyperstimulation, both easily and precociously detected by echography. Finally, echography may find an important place in determining the optimal moment to begin artificial insemination. For the present, the current practice of inseminating when the cervical score reaches 8 seems most judicious as demonstrated in this study by the fact that in all cycles, ovulation occurred within the 3 days following this event.

REFERENCES

1. Couts, J.R.T.   Hormone production by the ovary.   Clinics in
   Obstet. and Gynec., 3:63:83, 1976.

2. Franchi, L.L.   The ovary: Development structure and temporal
   changes.   In: Scientific foundations of Obstetrics and Gynecology., Philipp, E.E., Barnes, J., Newton, M., Eds., London,
   159-166, 1977.

3. Hackloer, B.J., Nitschke, S., Daume, E., Sturm, G. and
   Buchholtz, R.   Ultraschalldarstellung von Ovarveränderungen
   bei Gonadotropinstimulierung.   Geburtsh. u. Frauenheilk.,
   37:185-190, 1977.

4. Hackloer, B.J. and Robinson, H.P.   Ultraschalldarstellung des
   wachsenden follikels und corpus luteum im normalen physio-
   logischen zyklus.   Geburtsh. u. Frauenheilk., 38:163-168,
   1978.

5. Insler, V. and Lunenfeld, B.   Diagnosis and treatment of functional infertility.   In: Infertility, Grosse Verlag, Berlin,
   1978.

6. Kerin, J.F., Young, B., Lees, MM., Lawson, S., Templeton, A.A.
   and Baird, D.T.   The serial assessment of graafian follicle
   growth by ultrasonic means for timing donor artificial insemination presented at International Symposium on Human
   Artificial Insemination and Semen preservation. Paris, April
   1979.

7. Lunenfeld, B., Kradem, L. and Eshkol, A.   Structure and function
   of the growing follicle.   Clinics in Obstet. and Gynec.,
   3:27-39, 1976.

8. Macler, J., Schumacher, J.C. and Renaud, R.   La surveillance
   échographique de l'induction de l'ovulation.   Symposium
   International d'Echographie Obstétricale, Paris, April
   1977.   pp. 467-468, Paris, 1979.

9. Renaud, R., Macler, J., Ehret, C., Jacquetin, B. and
   Schumacher, J.C.   Apport de l'échographie dans la surveil-
   lance de l'induction de l'ovulation.   IVème Colloque de la
   Société Française pour l'Application des Ultrasons à la
   Médecine et à la Biologie, Paris, December 1977.

10. Renaud, R., Jacquetin, B., Ehret, C., Macler, J., Dervain, I.,
     Plas-Roser, S., and Aron, C. La surveillance échographique
     de l'induction de l'ovulation. Société Nationale de Gynec.
     Obst., Paris, Oct. 1977. In: Gyn. Obst. Biol. Repr., 7:746-
     749, 1978.

11. Rönnberg, L., Ylöstalo, P. and Jouppila, P. Ultrasound to time
     stimulation. Lancet, 1:669, 1978.

METHODS AND RESULTS FOR REGULATED OVULATION

IN ARTIFICIAL INSEMINATION

Thomas Katzorke, Dirk Propping and Peter F. Tauber

Department of Obstetrics and Gynecology
University of Essen Medical School
Essen, West Germany

INTRODUCTION

The major part of the female population which desires artificial insemination by donor (AID) can be characterized by the ovulatory cycle pattern at the first visit. Only a small group of patients present the problem of irregularity or anovulation at the beginning of AID therapy. In our experience during the last three years, this group represents approximately 20% of all our female patients.

Our presentation concerns exclusively the group of women who present as so called "normal females" to the physician but exhibit abnormalities in the regulation of their cycles in successive courses of insemination therapy (Tables 1 and 2). For these patients "ovulation timing" is required. We define ovulatory cycle irregularity as a variation in ovulation day of at least ± 3 days as compared to the previous cycle or as the occurrence of frequent anovulation. Insemination is usually performed two or three times at daily intervals during the period of the midcyclic LH-peak in order to ensure that the most fertile time of the cycle is covered. Even so, the best success rates are only about 60% and it takes an average of at least two or three months to achieve pregnancy.

In most cases, this daily check-up program is impracticable since the patients live too far away from the insemination center. Of our AID patients, only 10% come from Essen, a large town with a population of 700,000 while the remaining 90% come from distances further than 50 km. Due to this problem of accessibility as well as to legal restrictions which limit AID to only a small number of facilities, it was the aim of our group to see the patients who could undergo

361

TABLE 1. *Spontaneous change in the ovulation day of more than*
± 3 days including anovulation with AID.

	Regular ovulation	Irregular ovulation
Essen[a] (N = 58)		
Before AID	46 (79%)	12 (21%)
During Insemination cycles 1-6	29 (50%)	29 (50%)
Lyon[b] (N = 59)		
Before AID	33 (56%)	26 (44%)
During insemination cycles 1-3	15 (25%)	44 (75%)

[a] Sterility Unit, University of Essen.
[b] Czyba et al.(1978),[2] Lyon, France.

TABLE 2. *Spontaneous changes in ovulation of more than ± 3 days*
including anovulation under serial AID treatment in 46
women.

		No. of cases per insemination cycle					
	Cases (%)	1	2	3	4	5	6
Irregular or anovulation	37%	6	3	1	2	2	3
Pregnancy	37%	6	6	3	1	1	0
Cycle apparently normal but no pregnancy	26%						

artificial insemination only once or twice in a given cycle and to
perform the insemination on days when there was a high probability
of ovulation. This procedure requires an insemination service which
operates seven days a week.

Generally it appears that the emotional problems generated by
the procedure of AID are considerable. Approximately 30% of the

women become anovulatory or ovulate poorly during the insemination
cycles and need stimulation or regulation. This affects to a
greater extent the older patients(Table 3) and couples with a longer
duration of infertility(Table 4).

Delays in ovulation and subsequent temperature shift have been
observed in patients undergoing AID.[1] Insemination timing which
is solely based on the analysis of previous basal body temperature
records frequently fails therefore. Daily examinations of cervical
mucus for ferning and spinbarkeit at midcycle is time-consuming,
subjective, and inconvenient for the physician. It also increases
the emotional and financial burden for the patient.[2]

TABLE 3. *Percentage of irregular or anovulatory cycles and age*
(N= 58).

	Age (Yrs)	Regular Ovulation	Irregular Ovulation
Before AID	20-25	11.6%	16.7%
	25-30	62.8%	50.0%
	30-40	25.6%	33.3%
After AID	20-25	17.2%	15.8%
	25-30	62.1%	31.6%
	30-40	20.7%	52.6%

TABLE 4. *Percentage of irregular or anovulatory cycles and*
duration of infertility(N= 58).

	Years of infertility	Regular Ovulation	Irregular Ovulation
Before AID	0-2	25.6%	16.6%
	2-5	37.2%	41.7%
	5 and more	37.2%	41.7%
After AID	0-2	31.0%	15.8%
	2-5	31.0%	31.6%
	5 and more	38.0%	52.6%

Due to the episodic secretion of LH, even the day of the LH-peak cannot be identified with certainty unless frequent serial assays are performed. If the LH-peak day can be identified, however, it is the day with the highest fertility rate (Table 5). No correlation seems to exist with the day of BBT rise (Table 6).

The patients in this study ranged from 20 to 40 years of age and had been infertile from one to ten years. Prior to insemination, complete infertility check-ups had been performed in all cases including physical examination, hormonal status, hysterosalpingography and in some cases diagnostic laparoscopy for proof of tubal patency. AID therapy was done in previously normal cyclic women with fresh semen through intracervical administration. For ovulation timing beginning with the first insemination cycle, either clomiphene, HMG-HCG or a potent stimulatory analogue of LH-RH were used.

Clomiphene

According to Klay,[2] clomiphene was used with success in ovulatory women: (1) To produce predictable and regulated ovulation; (2) to allow time to schedule the inseminations when office personnel and donors were readily available; (3) to improve the pregnancy rate and (4) to decrease the emotional and financial burdens of repeated AID failures. With 50 mg clomiphene given over 5 consecutive days and 2 inseminations performed at 5 and 7 days after completion of clomiphene treatment, 16 pregnancies were achieved in 17 women. The temperature rise after clomiphene administration usually occurs 6 to 9 days after completion of the 5 day course; days 5 and 7 were therefore optimal for insemination.

We used the same regimen in the majority of patients with a constant administration of clomiphene from days 5 to 9 and inseminations with fresh semen at days 14 and 16. Of 42 women, 22 became pregnant after 6 insemination cycles. Ovarian hyperstimulation did not occur in any case (Table 6).

TABLE 5. *AID conceptions and day of insemination according to the LH-peak.*

	Insemination day (LH peak= 0)					
	-2	-1	0	+1	+2	+3
N= 17[a]	-	2	12	3	-	-
N= 28[b]	-	0-5	23	0-5	-	-

[a] Infertility Unit University of Essen
[b] Matthews et al., 1978.

TABLE 6. *AID conceptions and day of insemination according to the
"ovulation day" as determined by the BBT curve.*

	Insemination day (BBT ovulation= 0)					
	-2	-1	0	+1	+2	+3
N= 17[a]	2	-	4	5	4	2

[a]Infertility Unit, University of Essen.

HMG—HCG

Ovulation inductions with HMG/HCG were done according to Berger
and Taymor[3] with minor modifications. For induction of ovulation at
a predictable time, each patient received human menopausal gonado-
tropins (HMG, Pergonal 500, Serono Laboratories, Freiburg, West
Germany) in five consecutive daily injections of two ampules (= 150
IU LH and FSH) on days 8 to 12 of the menstrual cycle. To trigger
ovulation, 10,000 IU of human chorionic gonadotropin (Pregnesin,
Serono Laboratories, Freiburg) were administered on day 13. Insemination was performed on days 11 and 13. The results showed a cumulative pregnancy rate at 6 months of 64%. All pregnancies occured
in the first 4 treatment cycles (Table 7). Following this method but
with an additional 6,000 IU HCG on day 13, Berger and Taymor achieved
a 55% pregnancy rate. All conceptions occurred within the first
three cycles of insemination treatment.

The results suggest that ovulating patients with a planned
course of "low dose" gonadotropin therapy are not exposed to an undue risk, and that estrogen monitoring is probably not necessary to
avoid ovarian hyperstimulation. Five and six day courses of HMG
treatment have been performed without estrogen monitoring[4] with
the shorter course of HMG being the more effective. It is safe even
without estrogen monitoring although this may increase the effectiveness of this treatment. One disadvantage of this method of
ovulation timing is the necessary collaboration of a physician at
the patient's home-town to perform the intramuscular injections.
In addition, this therapy is expensive.

Longacting Stimulatory LH-RH Analogue

The analogue used by us was D-Ser (TBU)[6] -EA[10] -LH-RH (HOE 766,
Burserelin, Hoechst AG, Frankfurt, West Germany), which is 20 to
170 times more effective in causing prolonged release of LH, FSH
and 17β-estradiol in women with normal gonadal function as compared
to the natural LH-RH decapeptide.[5]

TABLE 7. *Clomiphene timing of ovulation in normaly cyclic women and results of AID.*

Agent	No. of cases	Conceptions per insemination cycle						Results
		1	2	3	4	5	6	
Clomiphene 50 mg on days 5-9. Insemination Days 14+ 16[a]	42	9 (21.4%)	5 (11.9%)	5 (11.9%)	1 (2.4%)	1 (2.4%)	1 (2.4%)	52.4% pregnancy rate 4 abortions 1 X twins
Clomiphene 50 mg from day 4, 5 or 6 of the cycle for 5 days, insemination on days 5 and 7 after completion[b]	17	10 (59%)	4 (23%)		2 (12%)			94% pregnancy rate 2 X twins 2 abortions.

1 dropout after 2 cycles

[a] Sterility Unit, University of Essen.
[b] Klay, L.J., 1976[5]

Twenty-eight healthy women between 20 to 32 years of age with ovulatory cycles of 27 to 30 days were investigated. The patients received the analogue conveniently as a nasal spray. A daily dosage of 87 µg or 174 µg (resorption quotient 1-4%) was administered at day 13 of the cycle to provoke the LH-peak.   AID was performed on day 13. This treatment caused ovulation at days 14 or 15 in 85% of the cases.[6] The pregnancy rate with the two different dosages was 62% and 73% respectively (Table 8).

Application of the analogue at day 13 led to a high release of LH and FSH, both being significantly different from the levels in untreated patients. No significant differences were found in the estradiol-levels, however, although all cervical parameters indicated sufficient estrogenic stimulation.

It is difficult to reach any conclusion as to the relative efficacy of LH-RH and its analogues versus placebo as a trigger of ovulation[7] since ovulation may be imminent or have already occurred.

TABLE 8.   *HMG/HCG timing of ovulation in normally cyclic women.*
           Results of AID.

Agent	Total cases	Treatment period	Number of pregnancies						Outcome of pregnancies
150 IU LH+FSH days 8-12 10,000 IU HCG day 13 Insemination days 11 + 13[a]	22	6 cycles	14(63.6%) Per cycle						12 births 2 abortions
			1	2	3	4	5	6	
			8	4	1	1	0	0	
150 IU LH+FSH days 8-12 6,000 IU HCG day 13 Insemination days 11 + 13[b]	20	3 cycles	11(55%)						10 births (2 twins) 1 abortion.
150 IU LH+FSH days 7-12 6,000 IU HCG days 14 Insemination days 12 + 14[c]	8	3 cycles	2(25%)						

[a] Infertility Unit, University of Essen.
[b] Berger and Taymor, 1971.
[c] Taymor and Jittivanich, 1978.

Our results demonstrate the ability and efficacy of the LH-RH analogue HOE 766 to produce ovulation when given on day 13 of the
cycle with a high pregnancy rate being achieved in combination with
AID treatment without hyperstimulation or the occurrence of multiple
pregnancies.

CONCLUSION

      Even with a history of regular ovulatory cycles, approximately
30% of women start to ovulate irregularly or infrequently under serial insemination procedures. Physical or hormonal parameters for
ovulation detection are time-consuming and occasionally impracticable, particularly when the patient lives far from the insemination
center. It therefore becomes important not only to detect, but to
predict the time of ovulation so that a single properly timed insemination can yield a pregnancy. The overall pregnancy rate of 73%
achieved through three different treatment regimens for ovulation
timing suggests that usually no monitoring is required. When ovulation was not regulated by treatment, the pregnancy rate was only 37%.
In both instances, however, 90% of the pregnancies were achieved
within the first 3 cycles(Tables 9, 10). It is rather difficult to
evaluate the efficacy of a given treatment schedule for ovulation
regulation. In our experience, best results have been achieved
with the analogue. Nevertheless, the decision for ovulation timing
in a certain patient should be individualized being based upon various parameters such as case history, psychological character of
the patient and her response to AID treatment. Since spontaneous
ovulations may always occur, one must avoid inducing an alteration
of the menstrual cycle which otherwise would have been spontaneously
normal.

TABLE 9. *LH-RH ovulation timing with LH-RH Analogue D-SER(TBU)^6-EA^{10}*
         in normally cyclic women and results of AID.

Agent	Total cases	Pregnancies per Insemination cycle						AID result
		1	2	3	4	5	6	
87 µg analogue intranasally on day 13, insemination on day 13.	13	3	2	–	2	1	–	8 pregnancies (61.5%) 2 abortions
174 µg analogue intranasally on day 13, insemination on day 13.	15	5	2	3	1	–	–	11 pregnancies (73.3%)

TABLE 10. *Pregnancy rate in 6 consecutive AID cycles: Results of two untreated groups and one regulated group.*

Patient group	Insemination cycle					
	1	2	3	4	5	6
Clomiphene, HMG/HCG or analogue regulated[a] (N = 55)	45.5% (25)	23.6% (13)	20.0% (11)	5.5% (3)	3.6% (2)	1.8% (1)
Untreated[a] (N = 17)	35.3% (6)	35.3% (6)	17.6% (3)	5.9% (1)	– –	5.9% (1)
Untreated[b]	27.6%	12.1%	22.4%	24.1%	6.9%	3.4%

[a]Infertility Unit, University of Essen.
[b]Czyba et al., Lyon, France, 1978.

TABLE 11. *Pregnancy rates after 6 consecutive cycles of AID associated with different agents for regulating ovulation in normally cyclic women.*

Agent	Total cases	Cumulative pregnancy rate after 6 insemination cycles
Untreated	46	17(36.9%)
Clomiphene 50 mg days 5-9	42	22(52.4%)
HMG/HCG 150 IU LH + FSH days 8-12 10,000 IU HCG day 13	22	14(52.4%)
LH-RH analogue 87 µg day 13	13	8(61.5%)
LH-RH analogue 174 µg day 13	15	11(73.3%)

REFERENCES

1. Czyba, J.C., Cottinet, D. and Souchier, C. Perturbations de
        l'ovulation consécutives à l'insémination artificielle avec
        donneurs (AID). J. Gyn. Obst. Biol. Repr., 7:499, 1978.

2. Klay, .J. Clomiphene-regulated ovulation for donor artificial
        insemination., Fertil. Steril., 27:383, 1976.

3. Berger, W.J. and Taymor, M.L. Combined human menopausal gona-
        dotropin therapy and donor insemination. Fertil. Steril.,
        22:787, 1971.

4. Taymor, M.L. and Jittivanich, B. Ovulation regulation with HMG
        for artificial insemination. Proceedings of the 1st Int.
        Symposium on Artificial Insemination, Bordeaux, Ed. J.C.
        Emperaire and A. Audebert, pp. 26-30, 1978.

5. Dericks-Tan, J.S.E., Hammer, E. and Taubert, H.D. The effect
        of D-Ser(TBU)6 -LH-RH-EA^{10} upon gonadotropin release in nor-
        mally cyclic women. J. Clin. Endrocrinol. Metab., 45:597,
        1977.

6. Katzorke, T.H., Propping, D., Tauber, P.F. and Ludwig, H.
        Programming of ovulation with a new LH-RH analogue (HOE 766;
        D-Ser(TBU)6 -EA^{10} -LH-RH) for artificial insemination. V°
        European Congress on Sterility and Fertility, Venice, Octo-
        ber 2nd/6th, 1978.

7. Reyes, F.I., Winter, J.S.D., Rochefort, J.G. and Faiman, C.
        Luteinizing hormone releasing hormone as an ovulation trigger
        in regularly ovulating women; problems in assessment of ef-
        ficacy. Fertil. Steril., 28:1175, 1977.

GENETIC ASPECTS OF ARTIFICIAL INSEMINATION

Jean Frezal and M. Briard

Clinique de Genetique Medicale
Hôpital des Enfants Malades
Paris, France

It is possible to identify three groups of characteristics which
are under the control of genetic factors whose prevalences are shown
in Table 1. The first group is that of monofactorial characteristics
obeying Mendel's laws. Mc Kusick recently collected 1364 known and
1447 probable examples in the latest edition of his catalogue published in 1978 (Table 2).[1]

The second group is that of multiple malformative syndromes with
mental retardation, governed by chromosomal anomalies which are very
rarely transmissible. Lastly, in the third group, both heredity and
environment contribute to the realization of the characteristic, and
it is often very difficult to ascribe to each its proper share of
importance. The interaction of several genes appears to be involved
(polygenic heredity). Many congenital malformations are found in
this group (Table 3).

This article considers successively the genetic aspects of
donor choice, genetic indications for artificial insemination and
the genetic follow-up of pregnancies resulting from artificial insemination.

Donor Choice

A donor must satisfy certain criteria: He must not present
any definite or possible hereditary physical or mental abnormalities. Thorough genetic screening must have eliminated the possibility of his carrying an abnormal gene which could be transmitted.
This includes dominant genes with variable penetrance (those whose
characteristic effect is not observed in all carriers) and genes

TABLE 1. *Prevalence of hereditary diseases in groups of 1000 children studied between 0 to 8 years of age.*

	1 a*	1 b*	2**
Genetic disorders	1.8	2.3	9.9
dominant	0.6	0.8	7.0
recessive	0.9	1.1	2.5
sex-linked	0.3	0.4	0.4
Chromosomal anomalies	1.6	2.0	5.8 [§]
Congenital malformations	35.8	42.8	24.0
Other multifactorial disorders	15.8	47.3	
Total	55.0	94.4	
Non hereditary disorders	6.0	27.0	
Total	61.0	121.4	

* Trimble and Doughty, British Columbia[4]
  a. minimum estimate
  b. maximum estimate
** Carter, C (UK)
  § Average frequency observed in 6 series collected by Evans[2] after deduction of balanced alterations(18%).

TABLE 2. *Frequency of monofactorial genetic characteristics.*

	Known	Possible
Autosomal dominant	736	753
Autosomal recessive	521	596
X-linked	107	98
Total	1364	1447

TABLE 3. *Frequencies of certain hereditary diseases in a series of 756,000 births.*[4]

	Frequency of type	Frequency of category
Nerve and Muscle		1/150
. Anencephalia, Spina bifida, Hydrocephalia	1/700	
. Epilepsy	1/500	
. Mental retardation	1/400	
. Myopathy	1/9000	
Skeleton		1/150
. Hip dislocation	1/700	
. Clubfoot	1/300	
Eyes		1/170
. Strabismus	1/200	
Heart and Vessels		1/200
. IAC	1/1500	
. IAV	1/700	
Face and Neck		1/500
. Cleft lip and palate	1/600	
Digestive and Annexial Organs		1/500
. Pyloric stonesis	1/1000	
External Genital Organs		1/500
Ears		1/700
. Deafness	1/1100	
Metabolism		1/1000
. Phenylketonuvia	1/18000	
. Viscidosis	1/5000	
. Diabetes	1/2000	
Kidneys and Urinary System		1/1000
Endocrine Glands		1/4000
. Hypothyroidism	1/800	
Blood		1/6000
. Hypo- and agammaglobulineuria	1/16000	
. Hemophilia	1/15000	

responsible for characteristics with delayed clinical manifestations such as multiple intestinal polyposis, which is seen before the age of 40 in only half its potential victims, and Huntington's chorea, a degenerative disease of the nervous system which begins after 40 in 50% of all cases.

Karyotyping. This is a routine test in the potential donor.
Nevertheless, this examination clearly does not constitute a guarantee of genetic health. This fundamental fact should be stressed as
it is not sufficiently well-known. The karyotype of a potential donor proves only that he does not carry any balanced chromosomal abnormalities, the presence of which would disqualify him, despite the observation of Evans et al. in a random survey(as opposed to a study
based on families of malformed infants) that Robertsonian as well as
reciprocal translocations carry a small malformative risk(t 14-21
translocations excepted).

Tests for Recessive Genes. Heterozygous carriers of genes which
are responsible for autosomal recessive characteristics when present
homozygously pose a delicate question. In fact, such genes are uni-
versally present, though estimates vary as to their average number
per person. However, cases in which one such gene can be recognized
as present in a given individual are exceptional. It is worth stres-
sing that routine screening for heterozygotes is an illusion, except
for qualitative protein abnormalities and certain enzymatic abnormalities in particular racial groups; these points will be treated later
in greater depth.

Results of these tests are meaningful only when they are performed on close relatives of homozygous individuals, that is, patient's families, and not when carried out on the population at large.
In other words, subnormal enzymatic activity, while significant if
observed in the father of a patient, does not in any way suggest, if
found in a randomly selected individual, that he is heterozygous for
the gene which controles this activity. In fact, if the gene is rare,
such an individual has a very high probability of being homozygous
for the normal allele. It is therefore clear that such examinations
should be carried out only in very special circumstances. In certain
cases, the family history orients the investigation. Even if our
autosomal recessive characteristic is found in the family, the potential donor can only rarely be diagnosed as being heterozygous.
This is particularly uncertain in cystic fibrosis, the most common
of recessive diseases, and impossible in infantile muscular atrophy,
another relatively common one. In other cases, the fact that the
donor belongs to a particular racial group serves as a guide. For
example, a hemoglobin study, which is easy and reliable enough to
perform for every donor, is indispensable only for those from Mediterranean countries and tropical regions. A study of the hexosami-
nidases, the deficit in which, in homozygous individuals, is responsible for GM2 gangliosidosis(Tay-Sachs disease), must be carried out
in Lithuanian and Russian Jews.

Risk of Recessive Disease. Subjects heterozygous for a harmful
gene cannot be eliminated from the group of donors because such genes
are carried by all individuals. It is therefore hardly necessary to

eliminate persons who are known to be heterozygous for such a gene.
It would even be possible to envision a kind of exchange of semen
(of course anonymous) between men who have fathered a child with a
recessive disease. When genes are rare, the probability that the
wives are heterozygous for two of them is minute and such a procedure
would therefore carry no particular risk. It goes without saying
that the risk increases if the gene's frequency is high; if this is the
case, either the donor must be eliminated or it is necessary to verify, if possible, that the recipient is not heterozygous for the
same gene.

    Donor Age. The last question concerns the donor's age, since
the frequency of certain mutations has been observed to increase
with the father's age. In our opinion, this increase is too slight
to be taken into consideration.

Genetic Questions

    Artificial insemination performed because of a genetic risk must
be discussed in terms of its very special context. The essential
point is that the husband is fertile. If he carries an abnormal
characteristic, the fact that his wife is resorting to artificial
insemination cannot fail to have psychological consequences for each.
If the couple, threatened with the risk of another accident, decides
not to have any more children, the wife may well react very badly to
the conflict between her self-imposed sterility and her desire for
other children.

    If both parents are responsible for an autosomal recessive char-
acteristic their child has been found to carry, artificial insemination destroys the equilibrium of the family. If could be feared
that the husband will feel that he could father a normal child with
another woman, which may make one wonder about the couple's stability.
From this point of view, using the husband as a donor, as was proposed
above, should be seriously considered.

    Before artificial insemination is agreed to, serious thought
should be given to the situation into which a child so conceived
is likely to be born when one or both of the parents or one or more
children in the family is handicapped. Consideration should also be
given to the problems which may arise when the child grows up and
may be looked upon as a carrier capable of transmitting a hereditary
characteristic in the light of the family history of his blood relatives. This raises the question of the confidential nature of the
child's origins.

    The indication for AID can only be present if the characteristic
motivating the request is definitely hereditary and present either in
the father, for an autosomal dominant characteristic, or in both

members of the couple, for an autosomal recessive one. It is therefore necessary that the wife's fertilization by a donor carry no
particular risk. This eliminates most congenital malformations,
whose etiologies are uncertain and for which a change of donor cannot be guaranteed to reduce the risk of recurrence which is statistically small.

Artificial insemination does not seem to us to be desirable if
the parents already have a normal child or if the couple is not
married(we have received such a request). This procedure should
be reserved for cases in which the risk concerns a severely han-
dicapping but not immediatly lethal disease.

Lastly, fertilization by a fertile husband must be prevented
once artificial insemination has been performed. The fact that the
couple are pretending, so to speak, to have created the child together, makes this a real risk.

Genetic Follow up of the Pregnancy

It is essential to recall that the couple cannot be guaranteed
that the child conceived by artificial insemination will be normal,
no matter what precautions, which have been considered somewhat
illusory, have been taken. The couple must be informed that the risk
of having a sick, malformed or handicapped child in this case is no
different from that which accompanies every conception: This means
between 2 and 3% of which 1/10 to 1/5 pose significant medical problems.[3] This notion is particularly important in artificial insemination, and still more so when it is performed for genetic reasons.

It must be added that the means at our disposal only very rarely
permit prenatal diagnosis of an abnormality. It is, of course, possible to perform amniocentesis and check for chromosomal abnormalities
by karyotyping or for neural tube malformations by alphafetoprotein
assay of the amniotic fluid. After the fourth month, real time
echotomography can be used. However, there is no objective reason
for performing these examinations, any more than there could be for
doing so for any other pregnancy, since the risks are the same for
all women of the same age. If the circumstances of the insemination
lead to these investigations being pursued, the couple must be told
of their limitations since the great majority of malformations cannot
be detected during pregnancy.

This article has considered the problem only from the couple's
point of view, which is as it should be. After all, the effect of
artificial insemination on the genetic structure of the general population is doubtless negligible or even inexistent as long as each
donor is responsible for only a limited number of fertilizations.

REFERENCES

1. Mc Kusick, V.A. Mendelian inheritance in man, Vol. 1, The Johns
    Hopkins University Press, Baltimore, 1, 1978.

2. Evans, J.A., Canning, N., Hunter, A.G.W., Martrolf, J.T., Ray, M.,
    Thompson, D.R. and Hamerton, J.L. A cytogenetic survey of
    14,069 newborn infants. III. An analysis of the signifi-
    cance and cytologic behavior of the Robertsonian and reci-
    procal translocations. Cytogenet. Cell. Genet., 20;96-123,
    1978.

3. Mc Keown, T. Human malformation. Brit. Med. Bull. 32:1-3, 1976.

4. Trimble, B.K. and Doughty, J.H. The amount of hereditary disease
    in human populations. Ann. Hum. Genet., 38:199-209, 1974.

POPULATION GENETICS AND AID

Hans Moser

Genetic Counseling Service
University Department of Pediatrics
Berne, Switzerland

GENERAL REMARKS AND DEFINITIONS

The main objective in human genetics is to study variability in man, and the smallest system from which variability may arise is 2 different genes(or allels) for a given locus on a chromosome pair. The two-allele system responsible for cystic fibrosis(CF), a recessive hereditary disease, is shown in Figure 1: If the relative gene-frequency is p or 1/40 for the(pathological) CF-allel and q or 39/40 (or virtually 1) for its normal counterpart, we shall expect the following relative frequencies for the 3 possible genotypes in the population: 1/1600(p^2) for the patients with CF, about 1/20($2pq$) for heterozygotes(or carriers) and somewhat less than 1(q^2) for homozygote, normal individuals. These relative frequencies will remain constant for dozens of generations because there is an equilibrium between new mutations or unknown heterozygote-advantages and the gene-loss by an almost zero fertility-rate for CF-patients.

Population genetics as a sub-discipline of human genetics deals with natural or artificial influences which may shift the genetic equilibrium and therefore change the relative gene frequencies within our "gene-pool"(Figure 2). The removal of selection disadvantages due to therapeutic progress, e.g. in phenylketonuria and hemophilia, may raise the respective gene-frequencies, whereas the removal of a selection advantage for heterozygotes, e.g. eradication of malaria, will lower the gene frequencies for sickle cell anemia and other hematological disorders. Similar situations are connected with modern human behaviour, such as greater "mobility" which will lower the inbreeding rate or specific family planing situations among which AID may now be included.

379

Relative frequencies	
Genes	Genotypes
$p_{CF} = \dfrac{1}{40}$ $q_{(norm.)} = \dfrac{39}{40} \ (\sim 1)$	Patients: $p^2 = \dfrac{1}{1'600}$ Heterozygotes: $2pq \sim 2 \times \dfrac{1}{40} \sim \dfrac{1}{20}$ "Normals": $q^2 \sim 1$
$p + q = 1$	$(p + q)^2 = 1$
" constant for each generation "	

FIGURE 1.   Genetic equilibrium in cystic fibrosis(CF).

NON-SPECIFIC INFLUENCES OF AID ON THE GENE-POOL

The number of requests for AID, still mainly for reasons of male sterility, is increasing continuously since it is now almost impossible to adopt a child. We may, therefore, expect a fair number of children to be produced anonymously by one donor, but born to different mothers.

Then, of course, the question arises as to what would be expected number of unintentional marriages between half-sibs in the next generation since the offspring of these matings would be at greater risk for recessive diseases than those born to marriages between cousins. Before calculating this proportion let us make the following assumptions:

- The proportion(P) of live births by AID in a given population will be 1%(10^{-2}). Thus, they will number N/100 where N is the total number of live births per year for the population(in Switzerland, N= 70,000 and N/100= 700).

- The annual number of offspring by the same donor will equal 10 (donors being replaced after 6 to 12 months). Thus, the annual number of donors required(D) would equal N/100/10 per year or; D= Nx 10^{-3} ($\sim$ 70 in Switzerland).

- The number of marriages per year in the next generation(M) will be $\leqslant$ N/2 ($\sim$ 30,000 for Switzerland).

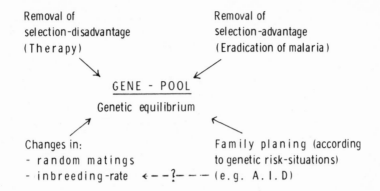

FIGURE 2. Influences of population genetics on the gene-pool due to therapeutic or preventive medical measures and to changes in social behavior or attitudes towards family planing.

Accordingly, the following calculations can be made :

. The expected annual number of marriages between AID individuals(A):

$A= MP^2 \leqslant N/2x\ 10^{-4}$ ($\sim$ 3 couples in Switzerland).

. The expected annual number of half-sib marriages(H):

$H= A/D \leqslant \dfrac{N/2x\ 10^{-4}}{Nx10^{-3}} \leqslant \dfrac{1}{20}$ (independent of N).

Therefore, we obtain a very small number(less than 1) of half-sib marriages in 20 years, a finding which is independent of population size since N cancels out in the equation. Even if we assumed the mean number of AID offspring per donor to be 50, the expected event of a half-sib marriage is still less than 1 in 5 years. This is much lower than the consanguinity or even the incest rates in any population.

INFLUENCES OF AID ON SPECIFIC GENETIC EQUILIBRIUM

Effects on genetic equilibrium could be expected if AID is more frequently performed for genetic reasons. As can be seen in Figure 3, AID may be indicated for the 3 main types or modes of inheritance: autosomal-dominant(if the male spouse is the affected one), auto-somal-recessive(after the birth of an affected child, e.g. cystic

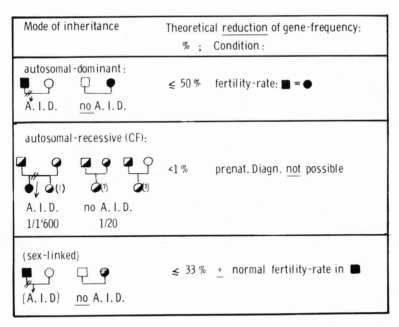

FIGURE 3. Influences of AID for genetic problems on specific gene-frequencies.

fibrosis) or sex-linked, dominant or recessive(again if the male spouse is affected). The main beneficial effect of AID is the lowering of recurrence risks. In cystic fibrosis this risk decreases from 25% to less than 2%.

According to population genetics, there will be a long term reduction of specific gene frequencies but this will differ strongly depending upon the mode of inheritance and the conditions mentioned on the right of Figure 3 such as male fertility-rates in patients with autosomal-dominant or sex-linked diseases, the possibility of prenatal diagnosis, etc. In dominant or sex-linked conditions, the reduction of specific gene frequencies is even more outstanding(theoretically up to 50% and 33% respectively) than in autosomal-recessive disorders(less than 1%) because here, more than 98% of the gene-pool is maintained in heterozygous individual who will only exceptionally marry an identical carrier.

The gene frequency reductions are independent of the number of AID offspring per donor, even if the latter cannot be excluded

as a carrier of the pathological gene in question by a specific
heterozygote test(in case of autosomal-recessive diseases).

CONCLUSIONS

As to the non-specific population genetic influences of AID,
our considerations are of course purely speculative since in order
to facilitate our calculations, we assumed simplified conditions,
such as random distribution of AID offspring, etc. These conditions may vary according to the present or future practice by the
different AID clinics or services, such as the selection of donors,
their mean number of successful inseminations, or the time after
which they would be replaced by new donors.

From our calculations, however, we may conclude that even under
unfavorable conditions, the expected increase of consanguinous
marriages in the future generation due to unintended half-sib-
matings is negligible when compared to the actual consanguinity
or even incest rate. These conclusions are well in accordance with
Rasmuson[1] who stated that the extremely slight increase of the
consanguinity rate should not be considered as an objection to AID
for childless couples.

There is an increasing amount of AID performed for genetic reasons which is mainly requested by couples with a child suffering
from an autosomal-recessive disease. AID is a genuine alternative,
if not superior, to adoption because of its anonymity as well as
for various psychological reasons. Besides their beneficial reduction of the individual genetic risk from 25% to almost zero, they
will also theoretically lower the frequency of different pathological genes in the population, an effect which would be measurable
at least in some dominant diseases such as Huntington's chorea or
myotonic dystrophy.

REFERENCE

1. Rasmuson, M. Genetiska risker vid heterolog insemination.
    Läkartidningen, 72:2042-2043, 1975.

ARTIFICIAL INSEMINATION AND CONSANGUINITY

Albert Jacquard[*] and Damien Schöevaërt[**]

[*] Institut National d'Etudes Démographiques, Paris, France
[**] Centre d'Etude et de Conservation du Sperme
(CECOS), Paris-Bicêtre. Kremlin-Bicêtre, France

One of the fears produced by the more widespread use of artificial insemination in our species concerns a very "loaded" concept
or, rather, word: Consanguinity. The reasoning is simple: Individuals born unknowingly of the same father, a donor whose semen was
used to inseminate their mothers, are in danger of meeting and bearing children together; such couples, and their children, would
therefore be "consanguineous."

From a biological point of view, the only consequence of this
consanguinity would be an increase in the probability of the births
of homozygous individuals. This increase can be evaluated precisely.
Consider a locus corresponding to a certain Mendelian character, i.e.
one controlled by a pair of genes(such as ABO and MN blood groups,
cystic fibrosis, PTC tasting ability, etc.). This locus is occupied
by several genes of different types, which correspond to different
categories or alleles such as the alleles A, B and O in the ABO
system. A population may be described by the frequency p_i of various
alleles (a_i). In such a population, the probability that a child
born of an unrelated mother and father will be homozygous$(a_i a_i)$ is
equal to the square of the allele's frequency.

$$P_{ii} = (p_i)^2 \qquad (1)$$

This result, which may seem "purely mathematical", is in fact
in perfect agreement with observed data. Whenever the frequency
of an allele and that of the corresponding homozygotes can be measured, relation(1) is found to be very valid within sampling errors.

When the father and mother are related, relation(1) is no longer
satisfactory. In the case that concerns us here, in which the two

385

members of the couple have the same father (p), the reasoning is as
follows. The genes received by the child C may both result from
the reproduction of one of the genes possessed by his other grand-
father P'. The probability of this event occurring is 1/8 (1/2 for
P transmitting to C the gene received from P' x 1/2 for P' transmitting the same gene to both P and M).

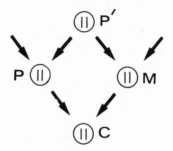

In this case, the child is homozygous, with a probability for having
the genotype $a_i a_i$ equal to the frequency pi of the allele a_i. If
the child does not receive both genes from P', formula (1) remains
valid. Therefore :

$$P_C \ (a_i a_i) = \frac{1}{8} \ pi + \frac{7}{8} \ pi^2$$

$$= pi^2 + \frac{1}{8} \ pi \ (1 - pi) > pi^2$$

     For example, for cystic fibrosis, pi is of the order of 2/100;
hence Pii = 4/10,000. The risk of homozygosity, hence the risk of
disease, since the gene is recessive, is thus multiplied by 7.

     Thus it is certain that "half-sibling" parents increase the
risk of appearance of recessive diseases. Conscious of this risk,
the AID center has sought to reduce it by decreasing the probability
of the formation of such unknowing half-sibling couples by limiting,
at times very strictly, the number of descendants allowed for one
donor. However, because of the scarcity of donors, such a limitation may seriously hinder the functioning of such centers.

     How can a relation be formulated between a population's con-
sanguinity and the use of artificial insemination as described by
the proportion of women inseminated(w) and the number of descendants of each donor? It happens that this question can be answered
easily, by using a formula which relates the increase in the mean
consanguinity of a population with each generation to the number
of men and women, and the means and variances of the number of their
children:

$$1 - \alpha_g = \left[1 - \frac{1}{2Ne}\right]\left[1 - \alpha_{(g-1)}\right] \tag{2}$$

where Ne is given by:

$$\frac{1}{Ne} = \frac{1}{4\left(N_m - \frac{1}{\overline{x}m}\right)}\left[\frac{Vm}{\overline{x}_m^2} - \frac{1}{\overline{x}_m} + 1\right]$$
$$+ \frac{1}{4\left[N_f - \frac{1}{\overline{x}f}\right]}\left[\frac{Vf}{\overline{x}f^2} - \frac{1}{\overline{x}_f} + 1\right] \tag{3}$$

where :

α_g represents the probability of both genes of an individual
generation g being indentical;

N_m, N_f, the number of men and the number of women;

xm, xf, the mean numbers of their children;

Vm, Vf, the variances of the numbers of their children.

The introduction of artificial insemination increases the means
$\overline{x}m$ and $\overline{x}f$ of the numbers of children, and increases the variance V_m
of this number for men while decreasing the variance V_f for women.
It has been shown (1) that the overall effect of these changes is to
decrease the parameter N_e and hence, to increase the rate of increase
in consanguinity. The decrease in N_e is given by:

$$\Delta N_e = \frac{w}{4}\left(x + \frac{V}{x} - 3\right)$$

This variance turns out to be minimal even when the number
of children per donor is large. In a population where p = 1/100,
i.e., where 1 out of 1,000 births results from artificial insemination, and where the mean value of x is equal to 10 with a variance
of 10, the genetic mass is decreased by only 2%. The time required
to attain 0.10 consanguinity, at 106 generations in a general population of 500, is reduced to 104 generations by the use of artificial
insemination. The overall danger is therefore negligible. However,
it may take on much greater proportions if the population using
artificial insemination constitutes a truly isolated subgroup. The
danger would then arise less as a direct consequence of this technique than as a consequence of an increase tendency towards isolation.

REFERENCES

1. Jacquard, A., Schoëvaërt, D. Insémination et consanguinité.
        Ann. Génét. 19:229-231, 1976.

CHROMOSOME STUDIES IN 1942 WOMEN BEFORE

ARTIFICIAL INSEMINATION WITH DONOR SEMEN

J.F. Mattei,[*] M.G. Mattei,[*] N. Moreau,[**]
M. Guichaoua,[***] A.M. Bolcioni,[****] and A. Mattei[****]

[*]Centre de Génétique Médicale
Hôpital des Enfants de la Timone
Marseille, France.
[**]Laboratoire d'Histologie et d'Embryologie,
Lyon, France.
[***]Laboratoire d'Histologie, Embryologie et Génétique
Faculté de Médecine de la Timone
Marseille, France.
[****]Centre d'Etude et de Conservation du Sperme(CECOS)
Marseille, France.

INTRODUCTION

The frequency of chromosomal abnormalities in the general population, underestimated for quite some time, is beginning to be better understood since the introduction of routine chromosomal analysis during epidemiological investigations. It is currently accepted that out of every 140 live births, one neonate displays a balanced or unbalanced chromosome abnormality.[1,2]

Taking into account these observations and in order to minimize the risk of malformed offspring, genetic evaluation including chromosome studies was performed in 1042 women prior to artificial insemination with donor semen(AID).

MATERIAL AND METHODS

Karyotyping was performed in 1042 women by examining peripheral blood lymphocyte cultures. In every case, 15 mitoses were analyzed by R-banding after mild heat denaturation according to Dutrillaux and Lejeune.[3] In cases where a structural abnormality was detected, complementary investigative techniques were employed(C, G and N banding, and specific staining of the secondary constriction of chromosome q). Detection of an aneuploid cell led to analyzing 30 or 50 additional mitoses, whereby diagnosis of mosaicism was made only after 50 mitoses had been examined with at least 3 cells displaying the same aneuploid configuration(Figure 1). Marker chromosomes were identified according to the criteria defined by Lubs and Ruddle[4] and Orye.[5]

RESULTS

A normal karyotype was found in 975 women(93.57% of cases); marker chromosomes without obvious pathological significance were observed in 46 women(4.42% of cases). A chromosome abnormality was displayed by 21 women thus representing 2.01% of the cases(Table 1).

Chromosome variants(Table 2) included in particular acrocentric chromosomes whose short arms, secondary constriction or satellite were found to be more or less enlarged(Table 3). Abnormal lengthening of the secondary constriction involved chromosome 1 in one case, chromosome 9 in three cases and chromosome 16 in four cases. In two women an abnormally fragile chromosome 2 was observed as evidenced by frequent breaks or gaps in the zone 2q14. Finally, a

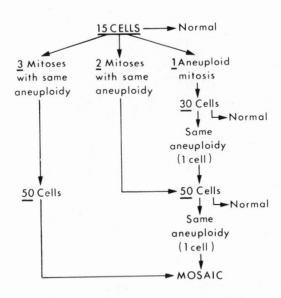

FIGURE 1.   Detection of Mosaicism.

pericentric inversion of chromosome 9 was seen in ten cases, the same breakpoints being consistently involved(9p11q12).

Regarding the observed chromosome abnormalities(Table 4), two cases presented a small supernumerary metacentric chromosome which was impossible to precisely identify; however, N banding showed that the extra chromosome contained satellites on both ends and thus probably corresponded to an isochromosome containing the short arms of an acrocentric chromosome(Figure 2).

Two women presented a pericentric inversion of chromosome 2, with breakpoints at 2p12q14 in one case and 2p11q13 in the other (Figure 3). A Robertsonian translocation was encountered in 3 cases |t(13, 14); t(13, 21); t(14, 15)|. Fourteen women were found to have an abnormal number of chromosomes: In one case a triple X karyotype was observed whereas the 13 other women presented a more or less complex mosaicism containing a dominant 46, XX clone in all 13 cases (Table 5).

TABLE 1. *Chromosome studies in 1042 women before artificial insemination.*

Karyotype	No.	%
Normal	975	93.57
Variant	46	4.42
Abnormal	21	2.01

TABLE 2. *Chromosome variants(1,042 karyotypes before A.I.).*

Type	No.	%
Acrocentrics	26	2.50
Secondary constrictions (1, 9, 16)	8	0.77
Constitutional fragility	2	0.19
Pericentric inversion of 9	10	0.96

TABLE 3. *Acrocentric variants(1,042 karyo-*
types before A.I.).

	Variations			
Chromosomes	p+	s	ss	p-
13	1			
14	1	2	1	
15	2	2	1	1
21	4	3		
22	3	4		1

TABLE 4. *Chromosome abnormalities(1,042 karyo-*
types before A.I.).

Abnormalities	No.	%
Extra metacentric	2	0.19
Abnormal sex chromosome no.	14	1.34
Pericentric inversion of chromosome no. 2	2	0.19
Robertsonian translocation	3	0.29

TABLE 5. *Abnormal gonosome number(1,042*
karyotypes before A.I.).

Abnormalities	Number
47, XXX	1
46, XX/47, XXX	9
45, X/46, XX	2
45, X/46, XX/47, XXX	2
TOTAL	14

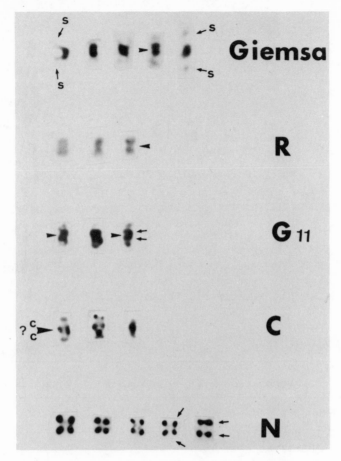

FIGURE 2.   Small extra-metacentric chromosome.

DISCUSSION

The results lead us to consider the frequency of chromosome abnormalities and the significance that should be attributed to such
findings during genetic counselling, especially in the case of marker chromosomes and pericentric inversions.

The patients examined in this study were unique in that all were
phenotypically normal adult women who underwent investigation due
to the sterility of their husbands.   Theoretically, the frequency
of chromosome anomalies in such persons should be lower than in the
general population.   Surprisingly, we found a significantly higher
incidence of chromosome abnormalities compared to results of other
studies(Table 6).[6] This higher frequency might be accounted for by

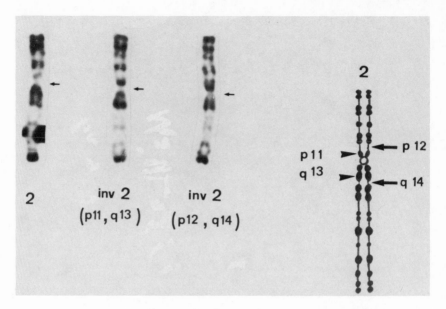

FIGURE 3. Pericentric inversion of chromosome 2.

TABLE 6. *Reported frequency of abnormalities.*

Population	Number	% Anomalies
Neonates	56,952	0.62
7-10 year old (Patil et al., 1977)	4,342	0.48
Women (present study)	1,042	2.01

biased recruitment, i.e. the presence of a chromosomal abnormality in the wife may have accentuated male hypofertility. However, this hypothetical explanation does not seem probable since exhaustive investigation of the husbands revealed the presence of true male sterility in all cases. On the other hand, the significantly in-creased frequency in the present study could be related to method-ological differences. Indeed, in epidemiological investigations, banding studies are not performed routinely which may in turn lead to non-recognition of certain structural rearrangements (representing 0.32% of the anomalies in the present study): Additionnaly, analysis of a very small number of mitoses may cause one to miss many mosaics. The higher frequency of abnormalities in the present study thus seems directly related to exhaustive examination of all the karyotypes in regard to cell number and identification of chromosomes with a diagnostic rather than epidemiological orientation. Although we examined a large series of women, it seems premature to attempt to establish frequencies based on detection of 21 cases of chromosome abnormalities. More studies of this type must be performed if frequencies are to be determined.

Since the first studies of human karyotypes, investigators have attempted to identify the presence of certain morphological chromosome variants. This notion of "variant" or "marker" chromosomes is still rather imprecise and possible relationships between morphological chromosome variants and phenotypic abnormalities are widely debated due to the reported frequency of marker chromosomes in the general population.[7] It is currently acknowledged that chromosome variants are most often found in phenotypically normal individuals. This has led to their being considered "normal variants" whose transmission from generation to generation occurs according to Mendelian inheritance. However, recent progress in techniques of chromosome identification now allow distinctions to be made among the different markers and such cytogenetic heterogeneity suggests that prudence is needed when interpreting such images. In regard to genetic counselling, it thus seems reasonable to evaluate the risk for malformed offspring in terms of "risk factors" and not in terms of chromosome rearrangements as is the case in translocations. Accordingly, the presence of marker chromosomes should not be considered a contraindication to artificial insemination nor an indication to perform amniocentesis.

Pericentric inversions constitue a difficult problem during genetic counselling since the theoretical data and follow-up studies needed to estimate the reproductive consequences of inversion are lacking.[8] The frequency of the classic pericentric inversion of chromosome 9, involving breakpoints 9p11q12, ranges from 1 to 1.5% according to previous studies (0.96% in the present investigation) and the incidence of this inversion does not seem to be significantly higher in a population of encephalopathic or malformed patients. Consequently, this abnormality can be considered a minimal risk factor and to our knowledge does not constitute a clear indication for amniocentesis. However, this is not the case when inversion involves the other autosomes. Although these pericentric inversions do not apparently express themselves clinically in most cases, the risks of having malformed offspring are indeed very real, arising from recombinant aneusomy, positional effect or interchromosomal effect.[9] In a population of mentally retarded patients, Breg found inversions to be 14 times more frequent than in the general population.[10] It thus seems reasonable to perform amniocentesis when routine evaluation in women reveals the presence of a pericentric inversion other than the classical inversion of chromosome 9.

In conclusion, two points merit emphasis. First, routine

karyotyping of women prior to artificial insemination appears to be necessary. Indeed, when a woman who is confronted by her husband's sterility accepts AID, it is indispensable from a human and medical standpoint to bring together the conditions allowing pregnancy to occur, to reach term and to produce a normal child. With this notion in mind and cognizant of the limitations involved, routine chromosomal analysis seems justified and our results add further weight to this point of view. Secondly, in the case of chromosomal abnormalities, a hypothetical risk of malformation must be considered thus raising the question of whether or not early amniocentesis should be carried out. Our approach is to perform early amniocentesis in abnormalities of chromosome number, supernumerary chromosomes, translocations and pericentric inversions other than those involving chromosome 9. On the other hand, the presence of so called "marker" chromosomes or pericentric inversions of chromosome 9 are not considered an indication for such investigation. Only long term evaluation based on population studies and clinical experience from medical genetics centers will be able to confirm the appropriateness of this approach.

REFERENCES

1. Hamerton, J.L., Canning, N., Ray, M. and Smith, S. A cytogenetic survey of 14,069 newborn infants. I. Incidence of chromosome abnormalities. Clin. Genet., 8:223-243, 1975.

2. Hook, E.B. and Hammerton, J.L. The frequency of chromosome abnormalities detected in consecutive newborn studies - differences between studies - results by sex and by severity of phenotypic involvement. In: Population Cytogenetics, Ernest B. Hook and Ian H. Porier, eds. Academic Press, pp. 63, 1977.

3. Dutrillaux, B. and Lejeune, J. Sur une nouvelle technique d'analyse du caryotype humain. C.R. Acad. Sci., 272:2638, 1971.

4. Lubs, H.A. and Ruddle, F.H. Chromosome polymorphism in american negro and white populations. Nature, 233:134, 1971.

5. Orye, E. Satellite association and variations in lenght of the nucleolar constriction of normal and variant human G chromosomes. Humangenetik, 22:299-309, 1974.

6. Patil, S.R., Lubs, H.A., Kimberling, W.J., Brown, J., Cohen, M., Gerald, P., Hecht, F., Moorhead, P., Myrianthopoulos, N. and Summitt, R.L. Chromosomal abnormalities ascertained in a collaborative survey of 4,342 seven and eight year old children: Frequency, phenotype and epidemiology. In:

Population Cytogenetics, Ernest B. Hook and Ian H. Porier, eds. Academic Press, pp. 103, 1977.

7. Friedrich, J. and Nielsen, J. Chromosome studies in 5,049 consecutive newborn children. Clin. Genet., 4:333-343, 1973.

8. Giraud, F., Mattei, J.F., Mattei, M.G. and Ayme, S. Les inversions péricentriques: A propos de 47 observations. J. Génét. hum., 27:109-122, 1979.

9. Ayme, S., Mattei, M.G., Mattei, J.F. and Giraud, F. Abnormal childhood phenotypes associated with the same balanced chromosome rearrangements as in the parents. Hum. Genet., 48: 7-12, 1979.

10. Breg, W.R. Euploid structural rearrangements in the mentally retarded. In: Population Cytogenetics .
     Ernest B. Hook and Ian H. Porier, eds, Academic Press, pp.99, 1977.

PROBLEMS RELATED TO REQUESTS FOR AID AND

PSYCHOLOGICAL ASSISTANCE OFFERED TO COUPLES

Marie Chevret

Centre d'Etude et de Conservation du Sperme
    (CECOS), Lyon
Lyon, France

INTRODUCTION

The presence at the Lyon CECOS of a psychology team of three
members, 2 psychologists(a woman and a man) and a woman physician,
allows psychological assistance to be offered to couples having
problems at any time during the course of their quest for artificial
insemination with donor semen(AID) or with husband's semen(AIH).
Between January and September 1978, 24 couples were seen by the
psychology team. Described herein is the type of assistance given
the therapeutic effects obtained and the results one can hope for
in brief therapeutic encounters.

The Couples

The social class of the couples was similar to that of the population consulting the center(7 professionals, 9 middle class,
8 laborers or small business employees). The only significant common factor for couples coming to the center was their proximity to
the center. Only couples living in Lyon or less than 60 km away
came for several interviews.

The couples were self referred since they had acted on the offer for help given them routinely at their first interview. Six
came on the advice of the gynecologist, either private or team, four
on the advice of other team members(biologist, secretary) and four
on the advice of the psychologists after the first routine interview.

The request for help occured at different points of the AID
program. In 12 cases, therapy took place before insemination and
was sometimes continued through the first few cycles. The reasons

for the request varied: Anovulatory amenorrhea(1 case), habitual
taking of tranquilizers for long periods which was deemed dangerous
for the future pregnancy(2 cases), communication problems in the
couple and which had become unbearable, most often for the woman
(3 cases) and doubts and ambivalent feelings regarding AID(4 cases).

During insemination, among the reasons for consultation were
depression which followed 3 or 4 unsuccessful trials(5 cases), poor
communication with the physician(2 cases), reemergence of ambivalent
feelings about the procedure(2 cases), and severe phobia during AID
(1 cases).   Only 2 cases were followed up after insemination.   One
woman became severely depressed after the death of the foetus at
the 8 month of pregnancy with total loss of self-esteem and an inability to cope with the loss of the child.   A deaf woman of 26, the
wife of a deaf-mute, who refused to "hear" that the inseminations
were terminated, kept constantly coming back and attempted to manipulate the team through relatives.   She refused all psychological
assistance which might point out reality to her and listens only
to her general practitioner who allegedly tells her that direct
inseminations into the fallopian tubes is 100% successful.   We were
unable to stop this vicious cycle and the woman is presently depressed.

From a study of those 24 cases, several noteworthy observations
can be made:

. Couples who request help spontaneously are not the ones most
  disturbed by insemination.   Their request often indicates an
  ability to clearly assess their situation as well as a strong
  motivation, since many couples give up their quest.

. Some requests are of a seeking nature: "It does not work, the
  gynecologists say there is nothing wrong and it must be psychological, so here we are...".   The couples(4 cases) communicate little verbally and tend to present many somatic symptoms:
  fatigue, abdominal pain... etc.   For them we always chose relaxation therapy as the means of communication and help.

. From a psychodynamic point of view, these individuals often
  still show much involvement with their childhood in their com-
  munications(18 out of 24 cases).   We heard secrets concerning
  their own birth, a distant and idealized father or a distant
  and rejected father, an unhappy childhood, an overattachment
  to mother or clearly stated oedipal conflicts.

. The core problem for these couples in contrast to fertile ones
  is the unavoidable confrontation between two aspects of the wish
  for a child.   Reality of biological procreation in these cases
  compels these couples to follow a coherent, rigidly structured,

obsessive procedure such as taking the temperature every morning. This is difficult for couples who, prior to their wish
to have a child, did not bother with contraception and left
things to chance: "We were careful, but anyhow it would not
have been catastrophic at that point". It is the impact of
reality with the fantasized aspects(necessarily conflictual
for them) of the wish for a child which produces anxiety in
them. The triggering factor may be the beginning of inseminations: "Will I be able to conceive even though I feel depressed and am still undecided?" or, "after failure of the
first few cycles could I be sterile?". Furthermore, the procedure of insemination, with its rigid compulsory aspects and
its failures reactivates guilt feelings in the husband toward
his wife and vice versa. Excessive altruism in one member of
a couple towards the other leads to failures in communication,
each member hiding his disappointments to protect the other.

For preventive purposes, we would like to point out that some
couples are especially in need of help and attention from the team
since their conflict not only relates to male sterility and the re-
nouncement of biological offspring, but also raises the whole problem of the risk of death with a concreteness which give those
fantasies a very strong impact on their thoughts. These are the
cases in which there are genetic reasons for insemination, where the
male has to give up natural paternity since it would result in malformation or death. "In my dreams, I populate the earth with mons-
ters", said one man.

Couples in which one member has a severe disease such as cancer, where the threat of death is a very prominent fantasy(in contrast with cases of accidental paraplegia for instance, where death
is not a threat), are especially fragile: Each member is closed
within his secret about that threat which is never expressed in the
couple. In these cases, recurrent miscarriages and of pregnancies
with death in utero, lead to fantasies of "giving death rather than
giving birth". These couples have to be especially carefully liste-
ned to by the team and referred for psychological help as soon as
they express that wish.

Interviews or relaxation with the woman alone, interviews with
the couple, couple relaxation, interviews with husband and interviews
with the woman; all these types of help can be offered.

The first or first few interviews which are used to evaluate
the request for help and the types of conflicts raised always take
place in the presence and with the agreement of the spouse with
whom the type of assistance offered is discussed. Couple interviews
occur in the presence of a male psychologist if it seems necessary
to balance the communication between the spouses. Some interviews

TABLE 1. *Types of assistance.*

Mode of assistance	Number of cases	Number and Rate
. Interviews or relaxation for the woman alone	11	8-10 sessions,1 every two weeks.
. Interviews or relaxation for the woman alone and Interviews with the couple	6	4- 6 sessions,1 every two weeks; 2- 3 sessions, 1/month.
. Interviews with the couple	5	4-6 sessions, 1/month or every two weeks.
. Couple relaxation	1	10 sessions.
. Interviews with woman . Interviews with husband	1	10 sessions,1 every two weeks. 4 semaines.

take place outside CECOS with a male analyst, a regular collaborator
with the CECOS program. Three women were referred to an outside
woman analyst: One case each of a psychogenic amenorrhea, a severe
phobic reaction and a severe depression after the death of a foetus.

The type of contract, psychotherapeutic interviews or relaxation with the couple or individual on a weekly or biweekly basis,
are decided upon after the preliminary interviews which are used to
assess psychodynamic factors and the capacity for mobilizing and crea-
ting new emotional investments as well as clarifying the request
for help, that is often situation specific and not related to global
psychopathology. Thus, the usual contract is for short term therapy with a possibility, however, of reevaluating needs for longer or
more profound therapy. Relaxation techniques are offered to individuals whose usual modes of communication are somatic rather than
verbal, or to those whose complex and meandering verbalizations serve
mostly defensive purposes. Help is offered within the setting CECOS
itself which allows us to bypass the anxiety producing psychiatric
setting and which also forces the members of the team to confront
the two worlds of reality and fantasy involved in the procedure.
Couples are not charged, all therapy being reimbursed by national
health insurance as part of the treatment for sterility. Should
one then assume, as does Mme Audras, quoted in Reboul's thesis,
that patients somehow feel obliged to find other ways of repaying
their debt ?: "They pay in nature".[16]

Our aim is to listen with a psychotherapeutic ear; not to change the patient's personality or to help them solve all their unconscious conflicts, but rather to help them understand and accept the facts of male sterility, the facts and constraints of insemination and the possibility of failures, as well as to help them reorganize their defense and coping mechanisms in a more flexible fashion. Our attitude of persmissiveness is the initial contract: "This is a place where you may talk about everything you experience, feel or think about insemination and all that you say will be confidential."

An essential feature of our therapeutic attitude is that we do not have a real or factual stake in the wish for a child as does the gynecologist who performs the insemination or as does the CECOS biologist. Our gratification does not derive from the birth of a child but from helping patients formulate, verbalize and communicate their own wishes. Our own desire is not for the couple to have a child, but for the couples to cope with their lives and the reality of their situation, complicated as it may be by their sterility and all its attending difficulties.

RESULTS

Among our 24 cases, we have:

. 7 pregnancies - 1 case required interviews up to the 5th month.

. 1 anovulatory amenorrhea.

. 4 decisions in favor of AID.

. 2 reestablishments of communication in the couple without, as yet, a decision on AID.

. 2 giving up the wish for a child.

. 1 total failure of our intervention.

. 3 considering themselves as improved.

. 2 presently in psychoanalytic therapy.

. 1 adoption.

. 1 still continuing interviews.

The nature of the results is obviously difficult to assess. The factors we attempted to evaluate are: Improvement of depression, increased emotional control and better coping with life and its problems. In fact, patients themselves assess the results in terms of a deeper awareness of the situation. At the end of the contract, it is always in those terms that they evaluate their improvement: "Now, I can give up wanting a child", or "Now I can decide to start the inseminations", or "I am going to start a course of psychotherapy since I am confused about whether or not I want a child".

Our own evaluation leads us at times to consider the giving up of the wish for a child as a good result and a successful conception as a poor result.

REFERENCES

1. Amnon David, M.O. and Dalia Avidan, M.A. "Artificial insemination donor: Clinical and psychologic aspects". Fertil. and Steril., 27:528-532, 1976.

2. Benedek, T. "Parenthood as development phase". J. Amer. Psycho-anal. Assn., 7:389-417, 1959.

3. Benedek, T. "The organization of the reproductive drive". Int. J. Psycho-anal., 41:1-15, 1971.

4. Chevret, M. Le vécu de l'insémination artificielle. Lyon, Thèse de Médecine, 1977.

5. Czyba, J.C. and Cottinet, D. Perturbations de l'ovulation consécutive à l'insémination artificielle avec donneur. Confrontations psychiatriques, 1978.

6. Czyba, J.C. and Chevret, M. La stérilité masculine: Histoire du couple stérile de la manifestation du désir d'enfant à la réussite de l'insémination artificielle avec donneur. Cahiers médicaux, 3:1517-1520, 1978.

7. Czyba, J.C. and Chevret, M. Typical history of the involvement of the sterile couple with AID. 5th European Congress of Sterility and Fertility., Venice, 2-6 Octobre 1978.

8. Czyba, J.C. and Chevret, M. Psychological Reactions of couples to artificial insemination with donor sperm. Int. J. of Fertil. (to be published).

9. Fedida, P., Philbert, R. and Canet Cl. Psychoanalyse et Relaxation. Essai théorique et pratique d'un groupe de contrôle pour la relaxation. Rev. Méd. Psychosom., n° 1, 1972.

10. Gerstel, G. A psycho-analytic view of artificial insemination. Amer. J. Psycho ther   , 17:64-77, 1963.

11. Guyotat, J. Psychothérapies médicales: Aspects théoriques, techniques et de formation (Tome 1). Situations de pratique médicale (Tome 2), Masson, 1978.

12. Levie, L.H. An inquiry into the psychological effects on parents of artificial insemination with donor semen. Eugen. Revue, 59:97-105, 1967.

13. Nijs, P. Aspects psychosomatiques de l'insémination artificielle. Cahiers de sexologie clinique, 12:261-272, 1976.

14. Mises, R. and Semenov, G. Problèmes psychologiques liés à l'I.A.D. Confrontations psychiatriques, 16:219-235, 1978.

15. Pasini, W. La dimension psychologique de l'insémination artificielle hétérologue. Contracept. Fertil. Sexual., 2:309-312, 1975.

16. Reboul, J. Analyse d'entretiens avec des femmes dites stériles. Thèse pour obtenir le grade de Docteur en Biologie humaine, Novembre 1978.

17. Sapir, M., Reverchon, F. and Prevost, J. La Relaxation: Son approche psychanalytique. Dunod, Paris, 1977.

18. Watzlawick, P., Weakland, J. and Fisch, R. Changements paradoxes et psychothérapie. Seuil, Paris, 1975.

PSYCHO-DYNAMIC DISCUSSIONS WITH COUPLES REQUESTING AID

Giuseppe d'Elicio, Aldo Campana and L. Mornaghini

Service of Endocrinology and Gynecology
Ospedale Distrettnale di Locarno
Locarno, Switzerland

INTRODUCTION

The findings reported here are the results of psychological consultations with couples requesting AID at the Sterility Centre of La Carità Hospital, Locarno. There were 21 couples who presented themselves during the period Octobre 1978 to January 1979.

The objective of the study is to evaluate certain problems showing a meaningful correlation with the request for artificial insemination. We have tried to determine the following: The couple's sexual understanding in relation to the diagnosis of sterility and the choice of AID; which of the partners first considered insemination as a possibility; and respective attitudes to AID and adoption. Spontaneous comments on AID were elicited as frequently as possible.

METHOD

The method used was that of the semi-standardized clinical discussion. The couples arrived at the psychological discussion stage after an initial interview with the gynecologist. The psychological discussion may be divided into 3 phases: An initial free-expression phase, with the material that emerges being treated in the same way as associative material; a second informative phase during which the couple's questions are answered; and the collection of standardized data.

RESULTS

Standardized data

    The time elapsing between the marriage and the diagnosis of
sterility was, on the average, 3 1/2 years with a range of 6 months
to 11 years. The time elapsing between the desire to have children
and the diagnosis of sterility was, on average, 2 1/2 years, with
a range of 6 months to 10 years.

    An average of 6 months elapsed between the diagnosis of steri-
lity and the receipt of information about AID which ranged from 0
to 2 years (0 referring to cases in which information about AID was
communicated simultaneously with the diagnosis of sterility). Thirteen couples considered adoption as a possibility whereas 8 rejected
it *a priori*; an actual request for adoption had been made by 3 of
the 21 couples.

    The information about AID came from the mass media in 9 cases,
from a gynecologist in 8 cases, and from other sources in 3 cases
(acquaintances), and in 1 case from a general practitioner. Information acquired from the mass media was always supplemented by the
gynecologist or urologist in attendance. The suggestion to try AID
originated with the husband in 12 cases, with the wife in 5 cases,
and jointly in the 4 remaining cases.

    Sexual understanding before the diagnosis of sterility was
said to be satisfactory in 19 couples and unsatisfactory in the
other 2. Following the diagnosis, the frequency of intercourse
dropped sharply in 4 cases, dropped somewhat in 6 cases, and remained
unchanged in 11 cases. The quality of intercourse underwent a change
for the worse following the diagnosis in 10 cases; in 11 cases, it
remained unchanged. In addition, the couple's equilibrium underwent
a perceptible crisis in 13 cases; the remaining 8 couples experienced
no great change.

    The topics that spontaneously formed the subject of questions
and answers by the men on the one hand and by the women on the other
are as follows in descending order of frequency:

. By the men: Donors, anonymity, resemblance, technique of semen conservation, technique of AID.

. By the women: Very frequent questions concern the technique of
  AID, revealing fear of the consequences (malformations, problems
  during pregnancy and labor), the fear arising out of a conception that is not natural. Then come questions to do with moral
  problems, psycho-prophylactic advice, doubts about resemblance,
  details concerning anonymity and the choice of donor.

REFLECTIONS ON THE FREE-DISCUSSION

SESSIONS AND CONCLUSIONS

The free discussions were not recorded in their entirety. The notes taken after the discussions, which constitute our first-hand material, cannot be presented in full for obvious reasons. We shall nevertheless report, together with certain findings that emerged, the conclusions.

The object of the present study, as already mentioned, was to investigate the kind of motivation that prompts people to ask for AID. Toward this end, we concentrated our attention on what we regard as four significant points. The first has to do with the changes in the couple's sexual understanding after they learn of the diagnosis of sterility and the relationship that exists between these phenomena and the choice of AID. Half the couples spontaneously reported a drop in the frequency and quality of sexual intercourse following the diagnosis of sterility. Allowing for the fact that many couples were ill at ease on the subject of their sexual understanding, this result can be considered erroneous by default.

Furthermore, 13 of the 21 couples stated that they had experienced or were experiencing a crisis of greater or lesser severity following the diagnosis of sterility. There was much talk of a confusion between sexual potency and reproductive potency. We have particularly observed that frustration of the wish to have children rendered sexuality pointless, as it were, there by killing desire. In other words, learning of sterility does not directly bring about a drop in or seizing-up of sexuality; rather it is the disappointment arising out of the frustration of the desire to have children that diminishes sexual interest and weakens sexual desire. In fact most of the couples concerned re-established successful erotic relations once solutions of the problem of having children, rather than the problem of sterility, had been looked into.

Another question which we looked into was which partner mainly supported or had first become convinced of the advisability of AID: Remember that this decision crops up at a difficult time, usually during the crisis that follows the diagnosis of sterility. Often the partners support each other during the decision-making process; both consider the possibility over a period of greater or lesser duration, though without mentioning it, always waiting for the other partner to bring it up. Most often it is the husband who makes the first suggestion, possibly because in the majority of cases the problem is felt to be particularly his. As far as the woman is concerned, she is afraid of hurting him or provoking some unexpected reaction by broaching the subject of AID. It is probably the fears of the wife that lead to the decision being taken by the husband. We often had the impression that the wife had done everything in her power to persuade the husband to suggest AID.

The third question is that of the relationship between AID and adoption. Theoretically adoption was considered by 13 of the 21 couples, but only 3 had actually asked for it. In most cases, the desire to have a child of one's own is greater than that to have an adopted child.

There are several conscious and well-known motivations that lead people to prefer AID to adoption. These are that the child who is born as a result of AID is at least the natural offspring of one of the partners, there is an experience of pregnancy, there are no bureaucratic problems and none of the publicity, waiting, and possible discrimination as a result of the necessary social investigations required in cases of adoption.

These considerations do not, however, get to the bottom of the problem of what prompts people to ask for AID. Certainly from the emotive point of view, AID has the undoubted advantage of masking socially the problem of sterility. This is a point that may give rise to controversy. It could be argued that the need to deny sterility to other people and to manipulate this undoubted reality expresses a failure to work out the problem personally and consequently a certain emotional immaturity.

Out of 21 couples, 13 said they had been through a more or less serious crisis period and that the decision to request AID had emerged as the final outcome of that crisis. A desire to conceal sterility socially is certainly present, but it does not automatically mean that the personal and marital problem of sterility is being denied. Moreover, many statements made during the discussions reveal an attempt to make good the deficiencies in the couple. AID is looked on as a kind of cement capable of consolidating an existing marital bond that sterility has impaired.

The allusion to the couple seems to us to be of particular importance. It is the couple more than the individual that is affected by sterility, and it is within the couple that motivation to request AID springs most tangibly to life. Individually, many of the people who consulted, particularly the men, could possibly have accepted or denied completely the problem of sterility. In the interaction of the couple, none of that was possible. AID constituted a personal solution to a problem experienced by the couple. Adoption, on the other hand, appears as a social solution to the couple's problem.

The last point concerns the sort of information about AID asked for most frequently during these discussions. Men are mainly preoccupied by the problems of the donor, of anonymity, and of resemblance. Women, in asking for information about the technique of AID,

express fears or doubts about possible foetal malformations or dis-
functions or other problems during pregnancy and labor. Information
about the technique of insemination finally raised moral problems
and the question of the right to anonymity.

The interpretation of these findings and of the family circumstances behind them makes it necessary for us to make contact with
the unconscious. We do not in this brief exposé wish to get involved
with problems relating to the unconscious. Of course sterility is
connected with infant fears of castration and the Oedipus complex.
Thus, it tends to mobilize the defence mechanisms used to tackle
the Oedipal conflict. All these questions and particularly the
emotive key and the style in which they have been asked reveal that
they originate in the curiosity, guilt, and fear of punishment that
typify the problems of the infant unconscious. It would be amazing
if all this did not come out under such circumstances. In this
connection, we would only say that clear and precise information given to the couple in an atmosphere of professional competence can
in our opinion help to keep fantasies as far as possible in their
proper place, even if it certainly does not banish the kind that
people dream every night.

IS THERE A RIGHT TO AID ?

Bernard Poyen, Jean-Claude Penochet,
André Mattei and Michele Choux

Centre d'Etude et de Conservation du Sperme
  (CECOS), Marseille
Marseille, France

We do not intend to enter into a discussion upon the usefulness
or necessity of legislation, but taking our clinical experience as
a starting point, we wish to stimulate reflection upon the validity
of the psychopathological criteria upon which our acceptance or
refusal of a request for AID is based.

When the C.E.C.O.S. were first set up, the practice of holding
a voluntary psychological interview was instituted. This practice
has since become systematic. Amongst the aims of this interview,
besides helping, preparing and giving the couple an opportunity for
deeper reflection, the psychologist was more or less implicitly
expected to make a final choice. Up till this moment, both psychiatrists and psychologists have either refused this role of representing a protective barrier, or taken a particularly hedged
position which in fact came down to avoiding making a decision.

There are two psychiatrists at the Marseille CECOS, one
since 1974, the other since 1975 who have been conducting interviews
in collaboration with the same marriage guidance counsellor. We
have now dealt with 450 cases which represent all the couples interviewed between February 1974 and December 1978, that is to say over
a five year period. The number of refusals based on psychological
criteria is 8, about 2%. This small number of observations enables
us to report here the clinical details.

In the first two cases, one of the two partners presented clear
evidence of a psychotic structure: In case n°1, it was that of a
paranoia of the husband on the verge of having delusions. He
insisted on keeping a constant watch on his wife within the

consultation premises and the doctors were included in his mistrust.
"You never know what goes on around corners" he said. The intellectual level of his wife was low, and she stated that if she had
been aware of her husband's sterility, she would not have married
him. In case n°2, the husband had suffered an acute psychotic
decompensation sometime after he was informed of his sterility
which had required a month's hospitalisation. The direct link
could be seen through the delirious themes of persecution and paternity which he had expressed. The wife, for her part, was suffering from serious phobia whose symptoms had been provoked by her
husband's illness.

In two other cases, it was a question of neurotic symptomato-
logy on the husband's side which seemed to hide a deeper personality
disturbance. The third case was that of a man who had undergone a
voluntary vasectomy against the advice of psychiatrists and psychologists. He had decided to undergo a vasectomy at the time of his
first sexual relations at the age of 28 when he had become aware of
a horrifying fact, he could engender a son who would ressemble his
own father, a father who he had hated and detested. The only
escape from this implacable idea which assailed him, together with
a host of obsessional symptoms was the voluntary interruption of
his offspring by rejecting concretely the paternal image.

In case 4, the husband was suffering from a neurosis with various phobia. The symptoms which had appeared at the moment his
sterility became known had forced him to give up his work and to
stay at home. His anxiety was such that the psychiatrists had even
attempted electro-shock therapy. The patient insisted that we make
a small incision in his abdomen before inseminating his wife so that
he could show the scar to his parents in order to prove that a
surgical operation had removed his sterility.

In cases 5 and 6, the two husbands were suffering from Klinefelter's syndrome. In both cases, our refusal was based not only
upon the very low intellectual level, but upon its association with
other aggravating factors; for couple 5, a lack of social integration which came from a hysterical and hypochondric pattern of behaviour and for couple 6, the instability and incompatibility of
partners.

In the last two cases, our refusal was similarly based on several factors. The husband being over 50, the weakness of motives
and the low intellectual level. In case n°7, the wife had warned
her husband that she would leave him if he refused to let her be
inseminated, or if the insemination failed. In case n°8, there
were already two children, each born of previous marriages. The
husband had broken off all contacts with his own child, but on the
other hand made his wife's daughter believe he was her real father.

We suggest a discussion of the right to AID based on three points: Do we have the right to refuse, when should we refuse, how should we refuse ?

Do we have the right to refuse? Our experience confirms the small number of pathological cases among couples requesting AID. There nevertheless remain these few cases which raise the problem of contra-indications. It has been said that there are no indications in the field of AID, only requests for AID. There are, nonetheless, calls for help and suffering, psychological conditions for which AID is always indicated.

In the case of a clear pathological state, the child will be worse as a cure than the illness, and it would also bear a heavy burden. This medical act involves our responsibility, and it is dangerous to avoid the problem by arguing that if the couple had not been sterile, they would not have sought our help. In our activity as psychiatrists, we are too often the passive witnesses of catastrophes for us not to be able to say no when the opportunity presents itself. But it is fair to point out that we are then in the position of an expert which is difficult to reconcile with our therapeutic or advisory role.

When should we refuse? If the matter is relatively easy to decide in a clear pathological situation, it is much less so in disputable cases which do not present clear contra-indications but simply poor indications, frequently due to numerous forms of neuroses. In this situation we are no longer certain of the soundness of our position: the problem is that of the possibility of predicting consequences in the realm of psychopathology.

From the point of view of predicting, the situation is rendered more complex by the interactions which take place between the mother, the father and the expected child. In a way, it is necessary to anticipate for all three. The need for a thorough investigation thus makes itself felt, a need which has begun to be satisfied. However, the impossibility of drawing all the consequences from this investigation, in an area where the unconscious plays so large a role is also apparent. Will it be necessary to follow them through the second generation before anything becomes certain as some theories assert?

How to refuse. This is a difficult question and one which can not have a simple reply when one considers the different nature of each couple. "Shifting the request" is not always easy in a situation that is far from being analytical. Should we justify our refusal, tell the truth or invoke physical reasons ? In any case it is necessary from the beginning to clearly explain to the couple that our acceptance is by no means automatic. A suitable attitude to these problems will only be adopted after a broad debate within CECOS.

It should allow us to clarify our position in the face of the upheav-
als   which AID provokes, both in the traditional role of the doctor
and in the exercise of medical authority.

Along this last line of thought concerning the ethics of medical authority in AID, we would like to bring forward some points that
seem important to us for the debate. The act of insemination is
technically simple and ultimately does not require any special qual-
ification.   The actual work of C.E.C.O.S. is not strictly medical, it
is biological. In spite of that, no one has yet contested the
doctor's place, no one has questionned his right to practice AID.
Probably this is because we consider the doctor better placed to
apply this particular technical act. But in our opinion, it is
incorrect to consider AID as a conventional therapeutic act: is it
not suprising that faced with an illness of the husband, we practice
a medical act on the wife to finally cure the couple? We can then
imagine two possible attitudes. In the first, the doctor wants to
remain a neutral technician who only practices the transfer of the
semen from the donor couple to the receiver couple without any other
consideration except biological. C.E.C.O.S. exists only as an
instrument between the two couples. In the second attitude, the
doctor feels ethically responsible for this act. He immediately
considers AID as a medical act which enables him to avoid asking
himself if this attitude is right or not. Naturally, he gives indications and contra-indications according to the scientific and medical data and according to our culture. Thus, he has the right to
say no. Or course, the couple also claims its right to AID and we
are engaged in a moral battle where the rights of each are opposed
and where we cannot arbitrate because of a lack of criteria.

We said that we are responsible for 2% of contra-indications
in the AID program. This proves that we are on the side of those
who consider AID as a medical act. But the scientific knowledge
that we have today is so poor in regard to prediction in the field
of psychopathology that it is easy to imagine that the percentage
can vary from 0% to 100% in function of the theoritical predjudices
or originality of the psychiatrist. It is not simple to know what
new therapeutic contract we have undertaken: A play with five
actors; the donor couple, the receiver couple, C.E.C.O.S., the society and the child. Each participant has his rights and duties,
that is a moral contract with other members of the group which shows
the complexity of the problem. Let us try casting the play:

. The donor couple is in a position to insist upon the good use
  of its donation and thus exclusively for AID(not for experimen-
  tation for example). It can also insist upon secrecy and being
  absolved of responsibility for the future, whereas it has a
  moral duty not to hide any of its history or even its motivations and to accept medical testing.

- Among the moral rights of the receiver couple, we must include the right to secrecy, the right to information on the benefits and risks of the AID, the guarantee of being treated with maximum care which implies a duty not to hide anything from the center.

- As for the doctor, he guards the right to apply the conscience clause. It is his moral right, but he also has the duty to respect the contract made with the donor who himself trusts the doctor in order that the child have a good environment. He must practice AID under the best technical and psychological conditions and foresee all the consequences of this birth.

- The society acting as producer and actor remains the real trustee. It must in a certain way say whether it agrees or not with AID and one way to do so is to create legislation. If the society promotes AID, it must give material means, and above all moral means, to all participants in order that it be carried out under the best conditions.

- Remaining is the expected child, bearer of hope and fear, the child is present/absent, marvellous/terrifying. He is fragile, an heir. He is the object of the dreams and desires of fairies, both good and bad, who have been bending over him, even before the coming to the cradle. This king child to whom we can give all rights but no obligations.

Establishing the rights and dutes of each other and using our own criteria for decision will be our best guarantee against some malicious wizardry, or at least against an arbitrary or dangerous attitude that will prevent the happy ending of this human tragicomedy.

HANDLING OF SECRECY BY AID COUPLES

Christine Manuel, Marie Chevret
and Jean-Claude Czyba

Centre d'Etudes et de Conservation
   du Sperme(CECOS), Lyon
Lyon, France

We have focused our attention on the problem of secrecy ever since the CECOS Center at Lyon initiated its research on the psychological aspects of AID.[1] None of the authors who previously cited secrecy as a problem in AID involvement[2] have studied systematically either the specific ways in which secrecy is dealt with by couples, or the psychological and social factors related to the ways of handling secrecy; we have therefore attempted to perform an objective descriptive study.

METHODS

We performed routine, preliminary, semi-directive interviews centered on secrecy with 72 couples requesting AID at the Lyon-CECOS Center. Every couple was interviewed by two psychologists (a man and a woman) for one and one half hours. The couples were told of our psychological research project. Our attitude was neutral, but empathetic. We asked the couples about their choice "to tell or not to tell", "who to tell", "not to tell what and why"... We refused to give specific advice about secrecy, asking the couples to rely on their own discretion, but at the same time, encouraging them to "share their concerns with us".

All couples accepted, often with great relief, to share with us many of their concerns about secrecy and the problems raised by its handling, thus confirming the Czyba's and Chevret's[1] observation on the importance of secrecy in the couple's way of coping with AID.

We never intended to use the inverviews to obtain psychopathological data, such as anamnestic relationships with parents, but told
the couples that we were willing to see them again, at any time, for
psychological help, advice and/or relaxation if they felt the need.

All information was gathered on "study data outlines" which we
have designed and included data obtained from administrative records
(i.e. demographic, socio-professional, medical) or from interviews,
not only about secrecy, but also about the emergence and evolution
of the wish for a child, the reactions to infertility, reasons for
choosing AID, and the problems arising from this "special way of
having a baby".

In each case, we obtained details on :

. The pattern of interpersonal communication of the secret(the
  "link of secrecy" as defined by Zempléni,[3] i.e.: Who was meant
  to be the target of the couple's secret(i.e. the people who
  were meant not to gain any knowledge about it) ; and who were
  the possible recipients of the secret(i.e. those to whom it
  might be confided or revealed, wholly or partly)?

. The precise content involved in the secret.

. The modes of communicating, or not communicating[3] the secret:
  Not communicating, i.e. preserving secrecy, either by retention
  (the secret remains untold), denial, lying(as defined by the
  couple, or one of the spouses), or simulation(i.e. conveying
  false, or partial information in order to create a "pseudo
  reality" for others, to deceive or delude them, this term was
  borrowed from Baudrillard[4] to describe a frequent aspect of
  secrecy in AID); or communicating, i.e. sharing the secret by
  confiding it in a secure confidential setting, by revealing it,
  directly or indirectly, in complex emotional situations, such
  as "confessing" it or "acting-out" the revelation, or by leak-
  ing, i.e. through behaviour patterns which are consciously
  aimed at preserving the secret, but which in fact indicate the
  very presence of secretiveness and involuntarily point out
  some of it's content.

FUNCTIONS OF SECRECY

Secrecy cannot be dealt with in a simple behavioral fashion
because it is a very complex pattern which can only be evaluated in
relation to the unique psychodynamics of each couple. However, we
can identify its protective functions on three levels:

. On an intrapsychic level: The specific ways of dealing with secrecy represent defenses against various and often unconscious conflicts reactivated by AID, infertility and the wish for a child. A psychoanalytic point of view is necessary for a more complete study on this level.[5,6]

. On a relational level: Secrecy reflects an adaptation for dealing with social and familial pressures, which are always interpreted according to intrapsychic factors. Because of pressures for conformity, it protects the couple or one of the spouses from rejection, guilt or dependency.

. On an evolutional level: Secrecy has a dynamic function, the effects of which will only be manifested in the future, as described by Khan,[6] these effects being on the future child as well as the parents.

Despite the protective function of secrecy, its preservation may have a high psychological price: If the very deep and legitimate need to communicate and share has to be defended against constantly, the secret itself may become a toxic and burdensome factor which is related, at times, to mood or behavioral disturbances, and even to more severe symptoms, such as paranoid fears, projection and isolation.

When the need for telling can be satisfied by "confidential sharing", in a secure setting, where the risks of misunderstanding, rejection or eventual revelation to the child are reduced(for example with physicians, members of the CECOS team, or other AID couples) the secret can be better preserved, or more easily shared in other circumstances.

TYPOLOGY

In an attempt to classify attitudes and behaviours towards secrecy, we used a double criterion: The target and the content of the secret.

We observed that 77% of the couples choose "absolute" secrecy, whose target is "everybody". Only 23% consider it normal to share "AID" specific content to different degrees. Among those wishing for an "absolute" secret, the contents included are: AID only(25%); AID and male infertility(20%); AID, male infertility and even the couple's sterility problem(32%).

But more, in fact, reveal or confide AID to at least one person (physicians excepted), including 48% among those who wish an "absolute" secrecy on this point. Many more share contents other than AID(78%). Of those who do not want to reveal the husband's sterility problem to anyone, most confide it to at least one person in

their families. In fact, only half of the couples wanting complete
anonymity in AID actually achieve it.

We have described 4 types of attitudes, equally represented in
our population(Table 1). This classification has helped us to discover common problems raised in each group and to confirm certain
hypotheses. It clearly shows that there is no "ideal way" of dealing
with secrecy: Each type has its problems and risks.

SOCIOCULTURAL FACTOR

Our population was divided by us into three "classes" or socio-
cultural(S.C.) levels according to two criteria: (1) The socio-
economic class(based on professional data); and (2) the cultural
setting and educational level. We relied on psychosociologists who
emphasize the role of educational factors in social differences.[7]
In our "upper class" there was a high representation of medical, para-
medical and educational professions, mostly among the wives.

Figure 1 shows the relationships between S.C. class and the
type of secret: It is suggested that the higher the S.C. class, the
easier the sharing of the secret. No significant link could be found
between S.C. class and Type II and III. We suggest that these results can be interpretated as social differences in the patterns of
communication within families,[8] in patterns of self-disclosure[9] and
in sociolinguistic ability[7](see Table 1, "problems raised").

We explored the relationship between S.C. class, donor recruitment by couples and secrecy. Because of the lack of volunteer donors during the past year(in the CECOS Centers, the donors have to
be father of at least one child and they are not renumerated), pressure was exerted on the couples by the Center to help in finding
donors. This donor's semen is not used for the couple's insemination. Couples who find a donor have "priority" for AID; They wait
3-6 months whereas the other couples up to 1 year depending upon
the number of requests and the donors recruited.

Secrecy is the most frequent reason for the "impossibility" of
recruitment; 31% of the couples estimate recruitment impossible for
them. However, 69% of the couples believe that there is some "possibility" of recruitment, either through physicians, through general
conversations on AID and the need for donors, or even by possibly
sharing of their secret. Nevertheless, not all have succeeded or,
indeed, even attempted.

Figure 2 shows that the higher the S.C. class, the more the
couples believe it possible to find donors and the greater the number donors found. There is also a qualitative effect of the S.C.

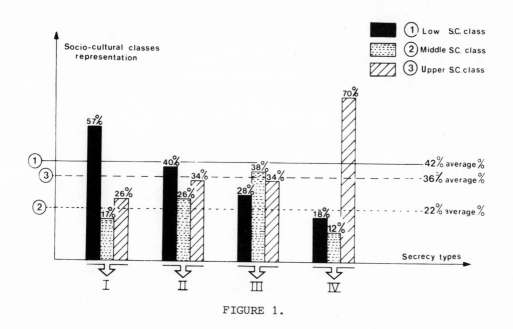

FIGURE 1.

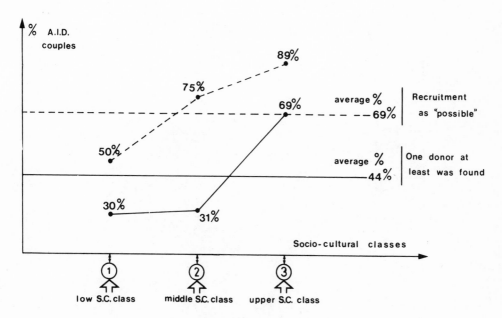

FIGURE 2.

TABLE 1. *Types of handling secrecy.*

	Type I	Type II	Type III	Type IV
Number	23	15	18	16
Content	Couple sterility + male infertility + AID.	Male infertility IAD.	AID	AID
Target	Everyone	Everyone	Everyone	- Non intimitates : 74% - Some intimitates: 28%
AID recipient	No one : 33% Donor only: 36%	No one : 14% Donor only: 48%	No one : 15% Donor only: 31%	Exclusive Non exclusive
Modes of communication	*Denial* of the wish for a child: 60% Retention; Leaking; Simulation: 40%	*Simulation* Medical treatment of the wife : 80%	*Confidence:* 55% simulations: Medical treatment of the husband : 60%	*Complex* (function of the recipient).
Problems raised	Relationships with others.	Couples relationships. Husband's self-esteem/ wife's wish for a child.	Parenthood	Type I or II. More couples where husband is infertile.
Psychological risks (involved by secrecy).	Paranoid feeling. Isolation. Breakdown of defenses.	Conflicts in the couple. Husbands gaining by the secret at the expense of the wife.	Guilt "wish to confess". Need to share.	"Family secret" (pseudo secret): 25% Secrecy towards child.
Psychological help.	Difficult in severe cases.	Possible, especially for wives (relaxation).	Possible as early as the preliminary interview.	Variable.
Recruitment of donors.	Low(4 donors). Low risks of refusal.	High(9 donors). Without "risks of revelation".	Low, if related to the attempts(5 donors). Many refusals.	High, 3 found several donors. 9 found at least 1 donor.
Socio-cultural factor.	Link with "low S.C. group".	Without clear influence.	Without clear influence.	Link with "high S.C. group".

class: The "middle" class(office workers, shopkeepers, laborers, skilled workers) have more faith in their ability than actual success. Could this be due to the characteristics of their social setting or to the general fear of not being admitted to AID if they do not cooperate(at least verbally) in donor recruitment? The two factors are probably combined.

In the light of our findings, to grant AID only to couples who are able to find a donor would certainly create social discrimination, namely by either denying AID to socio-economically deprived couples or by requiring that they take risks for which they feel psychologically unprepared. On the other hand, the pressure on couples by CECOS to recruit donors results in some(16%) viewing the sharing of their secret as a positive event which helps them to handle secrecy and improves their ability to cope with AID.

Figure 3 suggests that the type of secret may function as an intermediate variable between S.C. class and donor recruitment. Surprisingly, Type II has a very good score in recruitment(few refusals) if we relate this to the deep narcissistic trauma to this husband known to be infertile. This can be explained by the deep concern of the husbands for their responsibility in the couple's sterility, a condition which motivates them to request AID and to carry out recruitment as a "reparation".[10] Often this is accomplished by means of an "exclusive secret pact" with another man, analogous to adolescent secret pacts.

SECRECY TOWARDS THE FUTURE CHILD

The effects on the child of the parent's ways of handling secrecy preoccupy many couples, particularly in Types II and III.

In Type I and II, secrecy was the reason to choose AID rather than adoption(73% and 80% of the couples, respectively). With AID, it is possible not to tell the child and/or the relatives, no one would know that he is not ours, so he would be more ours". Another reason is that in AID, the husband's sterility and couple's sterility problem would be hidden by the childbirth: "We could be like others".

In Type III and IV, different modes of handling secrecy towards the child are conceived by the couple at the interview(preliminary to AID): Table 2 shows the results of our inquiry at this point for all couples.

All couples fear that an emotional trauma may be incurred by telling, and many consider that the timing of revelation is very important. Only one couple considered early telling as good. The

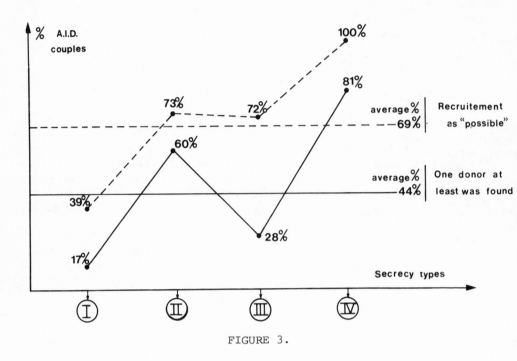

FIGURE 3.

others think that it could damage the child to be told of his AID
origin at an early age "when he could not understand" but consider
that they could   possibly (or certainly) reveal AID to the child
later.

These views are related to a general deep concern for the future child among these couples. They are in agreement with Wiener's
findings[11] on trauma caused to adoptees by being told of their
adoption at an early age which he described in his clinical psychoanalytic experience. Like Wiener,[12] the couples believe that the
best time to reveal his origin to the child is during his adolescent
or a young adult years.

For certain couples, of all types, secrecy towards the child is
not of immediate concern, since they are conscious of the great number of AID failures: About 50% of patients become pregnant.
There is no evident medical or biological reason for the 50% failure
rate. These couples cannot really believe in their future parenthood
because they fear that their hopes will not be realized: "If we can
have a child, we'll see later". Others think that their position
on this problem may change after the child has become a reality,
being a function of their relationships with him, his characteristics, and changes in social attitudes toward AID. Many relate their

TABLE 2. *Modes of handling secrecy with the child.*

Absolute Secrecy (44 couples)	Eventual Sharing (28 couples)
Reasons for secrecy	Agreement between spouses: 16 couples.
. With secrecy, the child is more "ours"(all).	. "Perhaps we may tell him, but not at an early age": 10 couples.
. It could worry the child to "be different".	."Certainly we will tell him later, not at an early age". 5 couples.
. The child could "bear a grudge toward us".	
. Everyone would know about the husband's infertility.	."Certainly, as soon as possible". 1 couple.
Prefer AID to adoption 30 couples	Disagreement between the spouses 12 couples.
. AID better than adoption because of secrecy towards the child: 30 couples(all).	. Wives only wish to tell the child "some day", husbands never": 9 couples
. Refusal of adoption because of the obligation to "tell the child": 28 couples.	. Husbands only wish to tell the child "some day", wives never": 3 couples.

decision to keep AID secret to public rejection of AID, especially in rural, lower class, or mediterranean settings(North-Africa, Italy, etc.).

Four couples who shared their secret "only"(!) with their entire family reject the idea telling the child and deny any risks of revelation by relatives. These couples have almost paranoid fears concerning "strangers" to the family(neighbors, friends at work) "who are bad people". This "family secret" seems to be a high risk factor[13] and we hope that follow-up study allows us to evaluate and possibly prevent its real consequences. These couples have no others particularities: They have no psychiatric or social pathology.

We agree with Mises[10] who considers that a positive point has been reached psychodynamically in the acceptance of AID by the husband when he believes that the child can know his origin "some day" without dramatic consequences for either him or the child.

Nevertheless, we feel that it would be useless or even dangerous to give any kind of strong advice to the couples as is done in
adoption. This would not alter the unconscious psychodynamics involved in AID as in the wish for a child "despite" or because of
infertility. In fact, it would probably tend to increase fears of
persecution, guilt or dependancy and other   conflicts so frequent
among the couples who have to cope with this "special only way to
have a baby together". Psychological help may however have an
important preventive function if the couples can discuss and share
their problems at any time with members of the CECOS team trained
in psychology who do not perform the insemination themselves.

CONCLUSION

The principle of medical confidentiality in AID gives a couple
freedom of choice in the matter of secrecy but also puts the responsability of handling the secret on their own shoulders. All
couples are conscious of this particuliar aspect of AID parenthood.
This compels couples to come to face with the way they differ from
prevailing models of parenthood primarily in regard to the differences between "natural"(biological) and "symbolic"(social) father-
hood. This situation somehow creates a "free space";[6] a necessary
space for secrecy, where conflicts, fantaisies as well as social and
family pressures will arise and have to be solved. The possibility
of sharing the secret could help the couples deal with such unavoidable difficulties, and may play a preventive role regarding the secret's potential toxicity. The couple's freedom, however, has to be
preserved and should not be infringed upon by obligations either to
reveal the secret for donor recruitment and other reasons or to
conceal it by routine advice aimed at "protecting the child". The
conditions should be such that they allow the AID couples to be
"parents like others"; the very objective of their request.

REFERENCES

1. Czyba, J.C. and Chevret, M. Psychological reactions to AID.
      Int. J. Fertil.(in press).

2. Levie, L.H. An inquiry into the psychological effects on pa-
      rents of AID. Eugenic Rev., 59, 97-105, 1967.

3. Zempleni, A. La chaîne du secret. Nouvelle Revue de Psycha-
      nalyse, 14, 313-333, 1976.

4. Baudrillard, J. La précession des simulacres. Traverses, 10,
    3-39, 1978.

5. Margolis, G.J. The psychology of keeping secrets. Int. Rev.
    Psycho., 3, 291-196, 1974.

6. Khan, M. L'espace du secret. N.R.P., 9, 45-46, 1974.

7. Bernstein, B. Social class language and socialization. In:
    Gigliogli, P., ed., Language and social context, Middlesex
    Penguin Books, pp. 157-178, 1972.

8. Pitrou, A. Relations entre générations et insertion sociale.
    Thèse 3ème cycle, L.E.S.T., Aix, 1976.

9. Jourard, P. and Friedman, J. Self disclosure - an experimen-
    tal analysis of the transparent self. In: Wiley, ed.,
    New York, 1971.

10. Mises, R., Semenov, G. and Huerre, P. Problèmes psychologiques
    liés à l'IAD. Confrontations psychiatriques, 16:219-236,
    1978.

11. Wiener, H. On being told of adoption. The psychoanalytic
    Quart., XLVI:1-22, 1977.

12. Wiener, H. On when and wether to disclose about adoption.
    J. Am. Psychoanal. Ass., 26:324-337, 1978.

13. Guyotat, J. Processus psychotique et filiation. Confrontations
    psychiatriques. 16:191-217, 1978.

DIFFICULTIES ENCOUNTERED BY INFERTILE COUPLES FACING AID

Claude Alexandre

45, rue de Courcelles
Paris, France

The effect of AID on the dynamics of the sterile couple is still poorly understood; thus, we find it useful to report two cases of couples separating after deciding on an AID, and two other previously reported cases[1] of total marital sexual impotence appearing at the beginning of a pregnancy through AID.

- Case 1. Mr A..., 27 years old, married for 6 years, had been referred to us in 1974 for primary sterility by total astheno-spermia and marked teratospermia consisting mainly of a micro-cephalia with acrosome absence. Two years after we had deter-mined the incurability of their sterility, the couple, apparently close, reached a decision to try AID. However, one year later, when the date of the AID was set, Mrs A... arrived in tears to tell us that her husband had just started an affair and was leaving her.

- Case 2. Mr B..., 24 years old, married for a year, consulted us at the end of 1974 for irreversible primary sterility due to total isolated asthenospermia. Eighteen months after, he came, still alone, asking for information on AID. We suggested dis-cussing this in his wife's presence, whom we thus met for the first time. This interview clearly indicated a serious diver-gence between the requests of the two parties: for him, it was simply a means of palliating his sterility by imposing AID on his wife. She was especially concerned by the inadequacy of her sexual life and, in spite of her strong maternal desires, only wanted to consider AID after this problem had been resolved. In fact, she had never been satisfied by her husband due to his consistent premature ejaculations. Natives of a small south Tunisian village, they first met on the wedding night and were

431

married according to ancestral tradition which included the
ritual of the proof of defloration. Their moving to Paris a
few months after the marriage enabled Mrs B. to discover a
different way of life and express her desires. Because of
this conflictual situation, we referred the couple to a psycho-
analyst who, after a series of interviews, ascertained an intense emotional split: Mrs B asked for a less decisive feminine status, whereas her husband, unable to accept this situation, started drinking and became impotent. Therefore, we were
not surprised to learn of their separation.

. Case 3. Mr X..., 41 years old, has recently been referred to
us because of total sexual impotence. Married at the age of
29, he consulted for a sterility due to total asthenospermia
whose congenital nature was established. The incurability
of this sterility was apparently well accepted. After a few
months hesitation between adoption and AID, the latter was
agreed upon. Immediately following the first insemination,
sexual activity decreased progressively, ceasing totally in the
weeks following the certitude of pregnancy; no intercourse took
place for over two years. He seemed very attached to "his son",
now two years old, and had a strong desire for a second child
(his wife is once again pregnant through AID). Nothing in this
patient's background was predictive of his impotence. To the
contrary, a poor AID tolerance seemed probable in the following
case.

. Case 4. Mr Y..., at the age of two, underwent a right orchidectomy with irradiation for cancer. Overprotected by an anxious mother, he remained emotionally immature; his fragile
balance was upset four times in a stereotypic way by a compul-
sion to drink bringing on obesity and abnormal sexual behavior.
The first episode occurred suddenly at the age of 20 when his
father, bankrupt, found himself forced to sell the house where
he had spent his entire childhood and where his mother died of
cancer when he was 13. The discovery of his azoospermia at the
end of 1972, one year after his marriage at the age of 25, and
the death of his father the following year led him to start
drinking once again. This man was referred to us in 1974: We
stated that his sterility was incurable, which he seemed to
accept fairly well and two months later, he came back to discuss
adoption and to ask for help to give up drinking. For a year,
he did rather well and in 1975 decided that his wife should
have AID. We saw him again at the end of 1976, one again unbalanced after ascertaining his wife's pregnancy; this break
down, more serious than the earlier ones, manifested itself
by: A resumption of his alcoholism which brought on an auto-
mobile accident while drunk as well as increasing professional
difficulties; and a total sexual impotence with his wife whom
he described as too distinguished a woman for him to be able

to approach. It was as if since she had been pregnant, she became "other" and inaccessible. He tried to compensate for his
sexual failure with this "Saint" by meeting with prostitutes,
always after having drunk to give himself courage. We recommended psychotherapy which he abandoned after a few sessions.
Yet this man who considered himself quite attached to his wife
and "his" son who he was convinced resembled him wished to have
a second child.

Beyond obvious analogies, these cases present a certain number
of disparities as to the role of AID and the modalities of intolerance.

The Role of AID. Cases 1 and 3 are the most clear-cut and consequently, the most revealing since AID seems to have been the sole
factor triggering an otherwise unforeseen intolerance. In case 2,
AID was merely an opportunity for a woman who had long been too
dependant to speak out. Its role is more difficult to determine in
case 4; it seems, however, to have been more influential than the
other unbalancing factors.

Modalities of Intolerance. The splitting up of a couple, which
can be seen in the first two cases contrasts with the reorganization
of conjugal economy characterizing the two other couples: A total
conjugal impotence after determination of the pregnancy through an
apparently well-accepted AID, claims of a very strong attachment to
the wife and the child plus the desire for a second child, and the
wife's apparent acceptance of this situation.

DISCUSSION

How do we Interpret these Cases?

In every case, AID means for the woman an experience of pleasure and fertility, of being untied and of having a child from
"Nobody". For the man, it means accepting being replaced by "Nobody" and certifying with his name the tangible proof of his sterility.

The vicissitudes of the sterile couple facing AID, anticipated
at the creation of the Centre d'Etude et de Conservation du Sperme
Humain (CECOS) in France, confirm that the formal acceptance of AID
by the couple does not imply that there will be no further problems.
It is obvious that such an experience cannot possibly be neutral and
not upset at the unconscious level the economy of each member of
the couple. The possibility for a woman to envision the pursuit of
common life with a sterile and now impotent husband, and the prospect
of a second child, seem to testify to the importance of the mainte-

nance of a certain fiction in a couple with complementary needs;
this fiction is necessarily sustained by secrecy. Separation or
impotence would express the interdict bound to the new status of the
woman fertilized by another, that other being either "Anybody", in
which case the woman is soiled and fit for rejection, or "Nobody",
in which case the woman becomes sacred: The Immaculate Conception.

What does AID Mean for the Physician?

In a previous study,[1] we had considered that the remarkable
discretion of literature as to the vicissitudes of the sterile couple facing AID could be explained by the fact that the formation of
semen banks was still too recent. This interpretation is clearly
erroneous since AID's practice has been well-established.

We have been impressed by the ambivalent reaction provoked by
our last communication, as though it were shocking to destroy the
illusion that AID was a practice fully and always satisfactory. We
are equally impressed by the frequency with which the physician abandons his duty of neutrality to suggest and even advise AID as a pro-
thesis for sterility, an intervention which can lead to the man's
impotency. The failure of AID places him for a second time in a
situation of impotence whose denunciation is hard for him to tolerate.

The Future of AID

It is obvious that the fact of AID cannot now be questionned;
it seems to provide a satisfactory solution for numerous couples
and the process which brought about its official authorization is,
in any case, irreversible. Even though authorized, AID does not
actually escape secrecy. Although recognized by the medical community, often in spite of itself, and soon to be recognized by legislation, AID is not yet accepted because it runs against individual
fantasies as well as social and religious edicts.

It is extremely unlikely that a preliminary systematic psychological investigation[2] could produce predictive data. A long-term
psychoanalytical research on not only consulting couples but perhaps
also physicians involved in AID is necessary to understand its significance.

REFERENCES

1. Alexandre, C. De la difficulté d'être Saint-Joseph: le "Père"
        stérile face à l'IAD. Communication à la Société Nationale
        de Gynécologie et d'Obstétrique de France, 11:12, 1978.

2. Bissery, J., Semenov, G., Mises R. and Huere, P. Les couples
        demandeurs d'insémination artificielle par donneur(IAD).
        Revue de Médecine psycho-somatique, 20:172-178, 1978.

MODIFICATIONS OF FEMALE FERTILITY IN AID

DUE TO PSYCHOLOGICAL FACTORS

Anne Cabau

Service of Obstetrics and Gynecology
Hôpital Antoine Béclère
Clamart, France

Although the technique of artificial insemination with donor
(AID) is well known, its impact on female fecundity has been little
studied.

Between 1973 and 1978, we treated 70 infertile couples
in whom the main cause of infertility was a male factor. The women
underwent AID for 1 to 16 cycles. The overall pregnancy rate among
this group of patients was 44%, with a spontaneous abortion rate of
20% of established pregnancies. In 75% of these cases, pregnancy
was established with AID within one to four menstrual cycles. Ovulation in some cases was induced using Clomiphene citrate or Human
Menopausal Gonadotropins(HMG).

A number of modifications of female fertility have been observed among this series of cases which appear to be related to psychogenic factors. These modifications in fertility may be grouped into
two periods.

Period Preceding AID

Regularisation of the cycle occurred in some women whose menstrual cycle had been irregular previous to the time that infertility of the couple was diagnosed. Three women who had exhibited
infertility for periods of 2 to 6 years became pregnant(through intercourse) from their oligospermic and severely teratospermic husbands during the one-year waiting period prior to AID. Two of these
women had a second pregnancy one to two years after the birth of their
first child. In one case, we were able to verify that the quality
of the semen had not changed(it contained 70 to 80% abnormal sperma-

tozoa). In the second case, the quality of the semen had improved. We believe that the prospect of having a child with AID alleviated stress due to the infertility, thus permitting the woman to recover a normal menstrual pattern and normal fertility. These unexpected pregnancies are comparable to those sometimes seen after adoption, just before the date chosen for surgery for a varicocele, or before insemination with the husband's own semen.

Period During AID

We have often been surprised to observe significant modifications in cycle regularity shortly after failure of the first series of inseminations. In women not conceiving after 3 or 4 AID cycles, we have observed an increased incidence of modifications of the menstrual cycle (irregularity, anovulation and/or poor cervical mucus). Treatment of this "AID induced infertility" is particularly difficult because of the frequent lack of a mucus secretion response of the cervical glands to estrogen stimulation and the difficulty of inducing ovulation due to resistance of the ovary to Clomiphene or HMG.

In certain cases where AID failed and yet the cycles seemed to be normal, evidence of tubal spasm was obtained by uterotubal insufflation, hysterography and even during dye injection under laparoscopy. In some instances, this uterotubal spasm is probably the underlying physiological cause for the infertility, but it also appears to become manifested for the first time in certain women after they have failed to conceive with AID. In such cases, treatment of the spasm by psychotherapy seems more appropriate and more efficient than treatment with antispasmodics or tranquillizers.

A false diagnosis of tubal obstruction was made by hysterography and laparaoscopy in one of our patients who underwent 6 cycles of AID without success. A second laparoscopy performed just before operation revealed the presence of a spasm at the uterotubal junction. She became pregnant at the 8th cycle of AID after a through discussion of why she might wish to prevent conception through self-induced tubal spasms.

PSYCHOLOGICAL FACTORS

One factor common to all women who believe they are sterile is the stress created by failure to become pregnant. We observe this situation with increasing frequency because women are now programing children as they program contraception. Today, women imagine they can get pregnant as easily as they can prevent pregnancy. If conception does not begin in one to three cycles after discontinuing contraception, they become disappointed and anxious. In such cases, it appears that menstrual cycles sometimes become modified as did those of certain patients of ours after the failure of 3 AID attempts. In such instances, the women become infertile.

There are factors common to all women undergoing artificial insemination by donor or by husband: The obligation to follow a basal body temperature chart, to see one's doctor at precise dates and to miss work without being able to give an explanation since the infertility of the husband is kept as a secret, is felt to be a nuisance.

Anovulation or complete suppression of cervical mucus production occurred in some women who found it necessary to stay a few days in Paris by themselves because they lived too far from the clinic for day-trips or in women who came to Paris with their husbands for an entire week during a holiday and demanded a pregnancy of themselves that particular cycle.

Other factors seem to be more specific to AID. Our patients express fears of congenital abnormalities in their offspring, of dissimilarities between child and husband or fear of failure of conception. Secrecy concerning the husband's infertility and AID creates difficulties with family and friends. In cases where we had to suggest laparoscopy and to treat cervical mucus insufficiency or anovulation, our patients were relieved to be able to talk openly with their family of their "own" sterility. There are women who have such heavy guilt feelings towards their infertile husband that they find relief in going through a period of infertility before becoming pregnant. Other women harbor a desire to stay infertile either because they cannot accept the idea of having a child from a donor or because the maintenance of their sterility is necessary for the couple's equilibrium. All of these factors are responsable for the fact that so many women give up further attempts to conceive after 2 or 3 AID cycles without success.

CONCLUSION

Qualitative evidence from a series of infertility cases treated with AID suggests that psychosomatic factors may play an important role in the failure of conception in some instances. Much more extensive work towards understanding the psychosomatic factors associated with idiopathic infertility in general, and failure of conception after AID in particular, is very much needed.

NON-ORGANIC SEXUAL DISORDERS AS AN INDICATION FOR AID

Jean Tignol* and Jean Claude Emperaire**

*Service de Psychiatrie, University of Bordeaux
**Centre d'Etude et de Conservation du Sperme
        (CECOS), Bordeaux
    Bordeaux, France

It is well known that some non-organic male sexual disorders
are responsible, among other problems, for a couple's sterility.
Artificial insemination with donor(AID) or husband(AIH) semen may
appear today to the couple and the physician to be THE solution
for sterility. We intend to examine the quality of this solution.

MALE PSYCHOGENIC SEXUAL

DYSFUNCTIONS CAUSING STERILITY

There are two types: impotency to penetrate and anejaculation
Impotency to penetrate prevents the introduction of fecundating semen into the vagina by two mecanisms acting alone or together: impotence and ultra-premature(before penetration) ejaculation. It
is often reenforced by coinciding sexual problems(vaginismus, dyspa-
reunia, frigidity) of the female partner. The refusal to penetrate
without any apparent problem of sexual ballistics is very pathological when it is followed by a request for insemination. Impotency
to penetrate in those requesting artificial insemination(A.I.) is
usually primary and represents the masculin variant of the unconsum-
mated marriage. It is less well known than the feminine type due
to refusal or vaginismus. When it is secondary, that is occurring

439

after a certain length of time of normal sexual function, the request of AI is rare. The couple's desire is mostly to reestablish
its sexual function more so than its fecundity.

Anejaculation has two variants. In "classical" anejaculation,
the patient is unable to ejaculate when awake, whatever maneuvre may
be employed. In some rare cases, they cannot recall having ever ejaculated but in most cases nocturnal emissions have been experienced.

In incomplete anejaculation, the patient can ejaculate when
awake, usually through masturbation, but is unable to do so in coïtus.
Sometimes this dysfunction concerns only the patient's wife and not
other women. Like impotence to penetrate, anejaculation may be primary or secondary. When it occurs after normal sexual functioning,
it may be attributed to different circumstances (diseases, psychological problems...) among which is the couple's decision to interrupt contraception in order to have a child (a recent personnal case).
Anejaculation, contrary to classical conceptions and in the opinion
of Johnson[1] is a frequent problem : 2% of the French who were
interviewed for the Simon Report[2] stated that their sexual activity
was never completed by ejaculation. This statistic is confirmed
clinically : sperm banks have literally "drawn into their dens"
anejaculators who seek the answer to their wife's desire for a child.

                                 AID OR AIH

Borg believes that the problem is one of satisfying request for
a child through a palliative artificial technique[3] whereas other
authors such as Nijs[4] view impotence as a contraindication for A.I.
As a palliative procedure, AIH would seem more indicated than AID.
It is very easy to get semen from impotent men and from men who are
partial anejaculators by masturbation. It is also possible to obtain
semen with other anejaculators through acrobatics with a vibrator
or by recuperating nocturnal emissions in condoms not containing
spermicidal agents.[5] The sperm is usually of good quality contrary
to those with hypofertility. That is why AIH has much more success
in this case than others. One can even use self-insemination with
a syringe practiced by the couple itself without the presence of the
physician.[6]

Technically, AID should be reserved for the rare anejaculator
in whom it is impossible to obtain the semen by the above mentioned means. It is also indicated when a disorder of the spermatogenesis is found along with impotence or anejaculation. This situation is not exceptionnal (2 personal cases and three by Geboes and
Steeno[5]) and one approaches the usual indications of AID.

But one should not discuss the indications of A.I. without examining the possibilites of etiological treatment of sterility arising
from male sexual dysfunction.

EFFICIENT TREATMENTS FOR MALE

PSYCHOGENIC DYSFUNCTION CAUSING STERILITY

Treatments for psychogenic sterility have existed for some time but are often ignored.

Anejaculation . As early as 1837, Grimaud de Caux[7] discussed the recovery of a famous mathematician : he was made half drunk just before intercourse. In 1916, Abraham[8] cured two patients by psychoanalysis. For about fifteen years, many published works revealed frequent recoveries.[1,5,6,9-11]

In our opinion, more than 50% of cases should be curable by different psychotherapeutic techniques and primarily through couple psycho, psychoanalytic, behavioristic or composite therapy.

Impotence to penetrate . This has the same prognosis as primary impotency and includes cases of ultra-premature ejaculation which thus has very different prognosis than simple premature ejaculation, the prognosis for the latter being very good. Masters and Johnson[1] although unsatisfied by their relative success, cured more than one out of 2 of such patients (40,6% were failures).

We feel that there are two type of patients : young impotents, who search out medical advice early and are usually good candidates for brief individual psychotherapy with a psychoanalytical emphasis. On the other hand, older impotents, who consult late for advice regarding an unconsumated marriage are more responsive to couple psychotherapy with or without individual treatment. Their treatment is more difficult and the prognosis is generally poor.

Different authors have various opinions concerning the curability of anejaculation and impotency. For example, Mattei[13] seems to think that impotency would easily be cured through sex therapy whereas for anejaculation, it would be more difficult. Pasini[14] disagrees with Masters and Johnson and others as well as ourselves concerning the efficacy of couple psychotherapy in the treatment of anejaculation.

These controversies are probably due to various factors : different types of training of the therapists, different techniques identified by the same term (such as couple psychotherapy) and above all, different patient selection.

Impotency, ultra premature ejaculation and anejaculation are only symptoms, manifestations breaking through the underlying pathological configurations as the visible sign of the much larger and hidden part of the iceberg. Most people showing these symptoms present personality disorders that could be considered as either "neurotic" from a general point of view or "not too bad" on initial impression but a certain number are frankly pathological : structured classical neurosis, character neurosis, psychotic character not yet decompensated. For the latter in particular, treatment of the sexual problem is contraindicated as is A.I. because of the risk of decompensation. The percentage of these very pathological patients is difficult to estimate but in our study, they comprised at least 10% of 150 persons consulting for male sexual problems and 2 out of the 10 couples referred for A.I.

INDICATIONS FOR AI :

CERTITUDES, QUESTIONS, PROPOSITIONS

When AID is desired for organic problems, the accompanying psychological problems as shown by Mises[15] for instance, are already quite complex : "By using insemination, the team invokes its responsability and is according obliged to examine its objectives when the situation is highly pathological". It seems to us that AI for male psychogenic problems deserves the same remark. Aside from the child to be born, there is here the possibility of treatment of the sexual problem and the underlying pathology.

Children from AID are beginning to be studied systematically and are apparently doing well. However, their parents generally did not present any particular pathology. In the case of a father's sexual dysfunction being accompanied by evidence of parental pathology, the inseminator must realize he is giving a child to a pathological couple who will probable remain so As a matter of fact, the couple's demand for immediate AI before or in lieu of treatment of the sexual problem has the objective to satisfy the wife's desire for a child without disturbing the balance set around the husband's sexual problem. However, anejaculators and impotents seem rather different.

Anejaculators with few exceptions do not suffer greatly from their problem. They support themselves by having intercourse. Their wife is the more dissatisfied sexually and in regard to childlessness. One could think that AIH would not change the couple's balance, unless the husband feels left out because of the child. AID also raises the question of the donor. Whatever the outcome, the husband remains an anejaculator and the wife sexually dissatisfied.

On the other hand, impotents usually suffer a great deal from their virile inferiority which may be maintained or sometimes exploited unconsciously by the wife (AI is kind of a sinless conception). What will become of the child of an impotent father and what paternal role may that father assume ? Do not forget that he is giving up on himself, on becoming able to penetrate sexually. From this point of view, we could say that AI re-enforces impotency.

Certitudes

For us, certain things are clear. AI should not be practiced prior to serious treatment of the sexual disorder, especially since it is curable in more than 50% (we would even say 70%) of the cases. In fact, treatment often takes care of not only the symptom, but also can considerably improve the psychological function of both the patient and the couple. In practice, AI provides a too appealing means of circumventing the considerable resistance that couples and physicians have in dealing with any problems which concern psychogenesis and psychotherapy.

We have had to establish criteria for AID : We do not categorically refuse insemination but rather delay it. During this delay, we propose a very versatile psychotherapy program and begin as proof of our good faith examinations needed prior to AID but without rushing. By so doing, we have recently managed to begin 4 couples on psychotherapy (1 impotent, 3 anejaculators) ; one who is an anejaculator also presents with azoospermia and thus AID is planned. Two other couples (1 impotent, 1 anejaculator), however, have refused psychotherapy with one chosing immediate AIH and the other AID.

Questions

Are we going to practice AI when treatment of the sexual disorder has failed? Is the treatment correct? Should we try another therapeutic method? If psychotherapy has failed, is this the proof that the patient is "too ill" and thus that insemination is contraindicated? Who is to decide and on what basis?

Propositions

To seriously treat these complex problems necessitates a cooperation between inseminators and psychotherapists. Too often encountered are pious wishes, territorial conflicts and prejudices. Inseminators stay very close to the symptom and the demand. They are wary of the unconscious ; they have faith in action and progress. Psychoanalytically, trained psychiatrists on the other hand are more wary of progress and action and are hesitant to generalise quickly on what they know about the unconscious. At least, two objections can be made to the psychiatrist's reticence to use AI, even secondarily. The psychiatrist may be mistaken like anyone else and sometimes in life, people may find an original and creative adjustment to an ordinarily destructive neurosis.

To avoid both errors and abuses and to promote research, it would seem necessary that the treatment of sexual problems and AI should be handled by a team whose role would be that of a guide, for physicians who could present their difficult cases for advice without losing them. A collective evaluation of the indications of insemination would: (1) Avoid a single physician's presumption, the psychiatrist's included, having too great an influence; (2) allow cross checking and the determination of clinical references and criteria; and (3) make possible an extensive study of couples and eventually children of insemination.

Such a team is beginning to operate in Bordeaux under the guidance of J.C. Emperaire and the encouragement of Professeur Riviere, thus widening the collaboration already existing between the authors of this communication.

REFERENCES

1. Masters, W.H. and Johnson, V.C. Human sexual inadequacy, 1970, French translation : Les mésententes sexuelles, Laffont, Paris, 1971.

2. Simon, P. Rapport sur le comportement sexuel des Français. P. Charron et E. Julliard, Ed. 1972.

3. Borg, V. L'insémination artificielle. Contraception, Fertilité, Sexualité, 3, 5:309-315, 1975.

4. Nijs, P. Aspects psychosomatiques de l'insémination artificielle. Cahiers de Sexologie Clinique, 3:261-272, 1976.

5. Geboes, K., Steeno, O. and de Moor, P. Primary anejaculation : diagnosis and therapy, Fertil. and Steril., 26, 10:1018-1020, 1975.

6. Belaisch, H. Frigidité et impuissance dans les stérilités anorganiques. Congrès International de Sexologie Médicale, Paris, 1974.

7. Grimaud de Caux. 1837. Cité par Gellman.

8. Abraham, K. L'éjaculation précoce. In:Oeuvres complètes, Tome 2, Payot, Paris, 1966.

9. Held, R.R. Psychothérapie et psychanalyse, Payot, Paris, 1968.

10. Gellman, R. and Gellman, C. Contribution à l'étude de l'absence d'éjaculation. Cahiers de Sexologie Clinique, 4, 20:183-189, 1978.

11. Tignol, J. Insémination artificielle conjugale (I.A.C.) pour stérilité masculine de cause non organique. Communication au

1er Symposium International sur l'insémination artificielle intra-conjugale et l'hypofertilité masculine, Bordeaux, France, 6-7 mai 1978.

12. Tignol, J. AIH for sexual inadequacy, In: <u>Husband's artificial insemination</u>. 1 vol, Martinus ed., Hollande, (to be published).

13. Mattei, A., Bolcini-Aujard, A.M., Bouhaben-Sitri, M.C. and Roulier, R. L'insémination artificielle intra-conjugale peut-elle aussi retentir sur la psychologie et la vie sexuelle des couples? <u>Contraception, Fertilité, Sexualité</u>, 6, 10:655-658, 1978.

14. Pasini, W. Evaluation critique des thérapies du couple. <u>Congrès International de Sexologie Médicale</u>, Paris, 1974.

15. Mises, R., Semenov, G. and Huerre, P. Problèmes psychologiques liés à l'insémination artificielle par donneur. <u>Confrontations Psychiatriques</u>, 16:219-236, 1978.

ARTIFICIAL INSEMINATION AND THE GENETIC DEFECT CRISIS:

A REVIEW OF QUALITY CONTROL AND CRISIS MANAGEMENT

C.F.D. Ackman[*] and   Jacques E. Rioux[**]

[*]Department of Urology
McGill University
Montreal, Canada
[**]Department of Obstetrics and Gynecology
Centre Hospitalier de l'Université Laval
Quebec, Canada

INTRODUCTION

The positive aspects of artificial insemination are the subject of much enthusiastic attention by both patients and medical personnel involved. The spectre of a genetic crisis is frequently mentioned but seldom examined in detail. Although reasonable efforts are made by most competent clinics to screen out donor defects, it is inevitable that a genetic crisis will eventually arise in most clinics. In addition, a child born with congenital abnormalities will frequently have a dramatic impact on previously repressed psychological stresses or stresses associated with the act of artificial insemination. This article reports such a crisis and examines the implications of quality control for semen donors and the importance of a carefully planned group effort and a contingency plan for such an event.

Case Report

M.R., a 31 year old white female gravida one, delivered a fullterm infant with multiple congenital birth defects including a tracheo-bronchial fistula. The obstetrician and paediatrician in attendance were unaware of the artificial insemination nature of the pregnancy. The patient contacted a member of the artificial insemination clinic and tearfully reported the incident. The infant was transferred to a children's hospital where the genetic consultant to the A.I. program examined the child. The etiology

447

was eventually traced to a non-disjunction translocation defect and
the child expired five days following birth. The couple were immediately referred for genetic counselling to discuss the probable
cause of the disorder and whether or not the procedure of artificial insemination might have contributed to the problem. The likelihood of a recurrence in a subsequent child by a different donor was
also discussed. Karyotyping was done on the mother as well as the
child and the record of the donor was examined in detail. Repeated
and thoughtful supportive communication was maintained with the
couple during the subsequent weeks until it was felt that they had
achieved a satisfactory adjustment to the problem. In addition, a
discussion was held and the donor was informed of the situation because of the remote but not insignificant probability that he may
have been responsible in spite of previous normal pregnancies. There
is evidence that the implementation of a contingent crisis plan
played a major role in reducing the psychological trauma faced by
this couple.

Most artificial insemination programs, whether using live fresh
specimens or frozen semen banking, rely on young healthy male donors
for material. Most clinics have some form of screening but little
or no attention appears to have been paid to a uniformity of standards for acceptibility. There is a wide spectrum of opinion concerning what degree of screening should take place. It is recognized
that many geneticists will establish such stringent rules that virtually every donor will be excluded. At the other extreme, many
clinics have no screening process whatsoever. Because of implications of product liability, it is evident that some compromise standard of acceptable genetic screening should be established in this
field. It is also imperative that any reputable artificial insemination clinic have a strong liaison with a genetic counsellor for
both donor screening and for the management of genetic disaster.
After careful consideration, a set of genetic screening standards
was established by our clinic in the form of a questionnaire and a
consultation with the consulting geneticist.

Donor Screening

The initial step should be a carefully completed genetic information questionnaire prepared by a geneticist associated with the
project and containing genetic screening material. The questionnaire should be part of the donor consent form.

Genetic Criteria for the Selection of Donors

The donor should be healthy and in particular should not have,
or have had:

. Any non-trivial malformation such as: cleft lip, cleft palate, spina bifida cystica, congenital heart defect, congenital hip dislocation, congenital club foot, hypospadias.

. Any familial disease with a major genetic component in the etiology such as: asthma, diabetes mellitus, psychosis, epileptic disorder, hypertension, rheumatoid arthritis or a severe refractive disorder.

. Any non-trivial Mendelian disorder such as albinism, hemophilia, hemoglobin disorder, neurofibromatosis, tuberous sclerosis, hereditary hypercholesterolemia.

The donor should be examined for heterozygosity for any recessively inherited gene known to be prevalent in the donor's racial group and for which heterozygosity can be detected such as: Thalassemia and G6PD deficiency in Mediterranean races, sickle cell disease in Blacks, Tay Sachs disease in Ashkenazi Jews and French Canadians.

The donor's first degree relatives (parents, sibs, children) should be free of:

. Congenital malformations.

. Major psychoses, epileptic disorders, juvenile diabetes mellitus, early onset coronary disease (check out hereditary hypercholesterolemia).

. Non-trivial disorders showing Mendelian inheritance in the following categories: (1) Autosomal dominant or X-linked inheritance with age of onset distribution that extends beyond the donor's age, such as Huntington's disease, Landouzy-Dejerine dystrophy, retinitis pigmentosa; (2) autosomal dominant inheritance with reduced penetrance, such as Marfan's syndrome, retinoblastoma, Alport's disease; (3) autosomal recessive inheritance with a high frequency in the population or if the donor's sperm will be used for many inseminations, such as cystic fibrosis of the pancreas in Caucasians; and (4) a chromosomal rearrangement or inbalance if other than a proven trisomy, unless the donor is found to have a normal karyotype.

Note that the above criteria require a physical examination of the donor, a personal history and a family history, and that consultation with a medical geneticist may be useful in certain cases.

A thorough physical examination must exclude significant hypertension, diabetes, genetic defects, and any significant history of disease. Blood specimens should be examined for glucose, uric acid, cholesterol, hepatitis, and VDRL. Urinalysis and culture of semen

is also required prior to acceptance. While proven fertility is
preferred in donors, a minimum acceptable standard for useful specimens for artificial insemination has been set at 60 million/ml,
with normal morphology in excess of 60% and normal motility at two
hours in excess of 60%.

Additional Stress Factors in a Genetic Crisis
as a Result of Artificial Insemination.

It must be clearly recognized that hidden concerns and fears
exist in even the most thoroughly screened couples. Many women fear
that artificial insemination is in some form or another unnatural
and that the husband may have a limited acceptance of the concept.
Undoubtedly, many women fear that under severe stress the husband
may in fact reject the child as being not his. Also unless properly indoctrinated, many couples may have hidden fears about the
additional risk of artificial insemination as an additive cause for
genetic defects in childbirth. On the other hand, the husband may
have suppressed feelings about his role as the child's natural father and have devised a fragile but tolerable ego compensation mechanism.   The unexpected arrival of a child with genetic abnormalities may place severe stress on his relationship.

The Genetic Crisis Relief Plan

A carefully devised plan must place emphasis on two major problems. The couple plunged into this crisis is immediately in need
of strong psychological support and a sensitivity to many of the
hidden frustrations which may have emerged during the *post-partum*
period, and the ensuing grief and frustration. During the artificial insemination interview, the couple is made aware of the existence of such a possibility and the existence of the supportive
team effort should a disaster occur. On two occasions this had been
found to be a major contribution to the function of the team following the incident. In one case, a psychiatric consultation was
sought by the team which subsequently proved to be a major contribution.

The second major function of the crisis plan is the thoughtful
and thorough review of the genetic factors involved. If the baby
conceived by artificial insemination is born with a congenital malformation or inheritied disorder, the following steps should be
taken:

. Genetic counselling with the parents to discuss the probable
  cause or causes for the disorder, whether or not the procedure
  could have caused the problem, and the likelihood of a recurrence in a subsequent child by a different donor, etc.

. In the case of a chromosomal problem, it may be useful to obtain karyotypes and look for chromosomal polymorphisms that may indicate where the problem arose. For example, during oogenesis, spermatogenesis, or post-fertilization.

. If the condition is such that the donor's offspring are at an appreciably increased risk, particularly if a pre-natal diagnosis is available, consideration should be given to the donor's right to know this. Because of the additional stress involved in this function, careful consideration of all factors involved must be considered before such a decision is taken.

CONCLUSION

Couples seeking artificial insemination should be thoughtfully and carefully informed of the possibility of a congenital abnormality and given information with regard to the additional risk, if any, from the act of artificial insemination itself. In addition, the couples should be informed by the group of the existence and procedure of the plan in the event of a genetic crisis. The screening of donors should be such that thorough documentation of genetic screening is carried out with the full cooperation of the geneticist affiliated with the inseminating group. Careful consideration must be given to an immediate response in the event of an accident emphasizing support for the couple and thorough genetic screening and evaluation of all parties involved. Our experience in two cases has been rewarding and justified our effort involved in devising an efficient and thoughtful plan of action in dealing with this unpleasant but potentially very difficult period for couples undergoing artificial insemination.

EVALUATION OF AID DONORS : MEDICAL AND

PSYCHOLOGICAL ASPECTS. A PRELIMINARY REPORT

Piet Nijs, O. Steeno and A. Steppe

Institute of Familial and Sexological Sciences
Catholic Universty of Louvain
Louvain, Belgium

INTRODUCTION

In Louvain (K.U.L.), advice concerning AID is given by a team consisting of gynecologists, an andrologist, a urologist and a psychologist-sexologist.

All are members of the "Human Fertility and Sterility Unit", an interdisciplinary team, which has been studying problems of human fertility on a clinical and theoretical basis since 1969.[1]

The role of the psychiastrist-sexologist is to function as a counselor for the couple with fertility problems (for the mourning process of their biological sterility, the analysis of the desire for a child, the analysis of the partner-relationship, etc.). The sexologist offers the couple the possibility of reflection so that they can reach a suitable option: the positive choice of staying childless, of adoption, of becoming foster parents or, if the man is infertile, of AID.[2]

The psychiastrist-sexologist also admits and counsels the donor-candidates, those who wish to give sperm for artificial insemination. If they are married, both the man and his wife are interviewed.

This paper outlines a preliminary report of this psycho-pathological evaluation. After we have discussed our findings, an attempt will be made to formulate certain indications and contra-indications.

TABLE 1. *Donor marital status and age.*

	Number	X̄ Age
Unmarried	23	24 y. 2 m.
Married	3	
		28 y. 8 m.
Divorced	1	

Material and Methods

There were 27 donors analysed. Their characteristics are outlined below and in Table 1.

Seven candidates had a regular job. There were 3 accountants, 1 nurse, 1 family doctor and 2 university graduates. Twenty candidates were students: 12 in medicine, 4 in engineering and 4 in human sciences. As for the married candidates the mean duration of marriage was 5 years, 1 month and the average age of the wife was 27 years, 4 months. All the wives had a psycho-pedagogic profession. One couple has only 1 child and 2 couples had 3 children (each 1 twin).

Until now there has been no systematic, active recruitment of donors for donor sperm. People were informed about the existence of AID in Louvain by lectures and scientific publications. There was also one television program in May 1972: "The child of calculation".

Although no psychometric tests have been performed, all of the donors were believed to have an above average I.Q. as judged by their professional level.

To present, AID at Louvain has been done with fresh sperm, which requires the donors to be frequently available. Each time they are called in, they receive a financial compensation of about 25 dollars. For juridicial reasons, only donors over 21 are accepted. Other than a general and andrological examination, there is also a genetic examination (karyotyping included).

Initially, the psychiatrist-sexologist explores the motives of those who have decided to be donors. In this way he evaluates the quality and lucidity of the decision. The donors are invited to read two informative books including a book by Levie, which serves as good general introduction[3] and a booklet reporting a survey of the Louvain AID experiences.[4]

Clinical Findings

The results can be summarized as follows. Between the first impulse to be a donor and the first concrete step, there is an interval of a little more than 6 months. At least half of them had discussed their decisions with close friends or members of the family (brother, sister-in-law). Both the married and the engaged unmarried donors had discussed it with their partners. The other donors who were not engaged all planned to inform their eventual partners except for one who considered it superfluous since to him, AID was a purely physical act without any relation or "adultery" involved.

Direct encounters with fertility problems either in their own family or in their immediate environment (friends, neighbors) usually provides the motivation to become a donor. In the married couples, the idea was first the wife's whereas in the engaged couples, it was usually thought of first by the man.

The donors themselves come from large families and usually are either the eldest or youngest. The average number of siblings is 4 whereas their partners have 5 or 6. Two had a twin.

Concerning their own family planning, the number of children desired was high and clearly higher than the average in Belgium (3.6 versus 1.8).

In case of infertility, the donors preferred AID but adoption was also an acceptable choice. Five explicitly preferred adoption since this is better known and accepted. Adoption is also considered as an equally attractive alternative for both partners for which the risks for the woman (pregnancy, delivery) are smaller.

It is worth mentioning that the donors had clearly opted for a consciously planned parenthood which is not necessarily the case in a marriage. In their partner relationship, they were clearly family and child oriented, with both being oriented toward health care or education (nurse, teacher, psychopedagogist or pediatrician).

Five of the donors were concerned about the possibility of consanguinous marriages between their own children and their AID children. Three considered informing their adult children about donorship. Two donors, who were not engaged, were not opposed to marriage with an unmarried mother.

As to donor motivation , a socially helping attitude is predominant. In one way or another they have encountered the problem of infertility and would like to either share their own hapiness of being a parent or contribute to the happiness of unknown persons. Giving semen (and conception) is considered a minimum contribution

and is regarded as essentially physiologic when compared to parenthood
(experience of pregnancy, delivery, raising of children). Most feel
that being a donor is simpler than being an acceptor. They also
think it takes a longer time to decide on accepting AID than on becoming a donor.

In the donor's experience, there is a clear cut distinction
between giving sperm and giving up a child for adoption. The idea
of the wife or partner of being "a baby-maker" was not an acceptable
alternative except in one case.

Although more than half of the donors compare giving sperm to
giving blood or plasma (less than half are blood/plasma donors),
all confirmed that the distinction between the consequences of
these donations is so great that it had occupied them very seriously

The majority wished to know that they "have been able to share
happiness"by giving a pregnancy even though some wonder whether or
not this is a secret wish to propagate themselves. A minority did not
wish to know if the sperm had been used for research of for AID. They
considered it best to keep the donation of sperm as a gift (arela-
tional). Sperm was an essential physical link: "by my sperm, their
child will be created". Giving sperm is a neutral physical act that
once done is over for ever.

Some donors at first feel uncomfortable about the masturbation
involved this neutral act. Donors originating from a strict educational background clearly stress that for them masturbation was not
a self-centered pleasure but rather an indispensable step to help
others. Some regret somewhat that the sacred state of parenthood
(with conception) has to take place in a "cold clinical climate".
The female partners especially regret it.

All donors prefer to stay anonymous, very strongly stress
discretion and do not wish to know the receivers. They consider this
necessary in order to be able to keep their involvement on a technical, neutral level without personal (intimate, sexual) contact.

All donors consider sperm-donation as a "purposeful act", which
one must be able to justify at the time and thereafter, and against
which one ought not to have any moral or religious-ethical objections.
Sperm-donation is considered as giving "some part of my physical
being, without any further involvement of myself (or of the couple)
as a person". The majority spontaneously realize that they really
care that there be no handicapped children born as a consequence
of medical selection.

As a secondary motivation, a donor becomes certain of his own
fertility by means of a thorough examination. The financial compensation is usually considered as secondary when compared to the

consequences of the semen use. Yet with some, it is the concrete
motivation to take the first step or to continue. Concern has been
expressed that the financial compensation may give rise to a pre-
mium hunt, as is sometimes the case with blood or plasma donors.

Discussion and Conclusion

Although semen donation is a unique act, "a small effort" on
a neutral and biological level (an essential, physical link in procreation), the consequences are on an interpersonal level. The
limited acceptability of AID in our society greatly explains why
only a limited number of couples are donors. All donors realize
that an extensive interview with an expert is possible. Others are
surprised at such an exhaustive interview. Extensive information
or reading about AID are considered indispensable. Furthermore,
semen donation is considered a purposeful act, and cannot be carried
out while one is still in a transitional situation regarding parenthood.

The findings of this preliminary report allow us to formulate
some indications and contra-indications which provide an orientation
for the psychosexual evaluation of the donor candidates (couples).
As positive elements, we note that:

. A decision-making-process that has been growing for a least
  6 months between the donor and his partner, intimate friends,
  family or an expert seen in consultation.

. The decision must be taken with the necessary amount of lucidity so that motives of and consequences for all persons concerned are sufficiently clear.

. There is a socially open, helping attitude in general and
  especially towards unknown couples with fertility problems.
  This helping attitude must not keep one from accepting financial compensation which is a means of neutralizing AID.

. Besides the chronological adult age of 21 years, there is an
  adult attitude required that permits the donors to take an
  unequivocal point of view towards parenthood, a clear distinction being made between biological procreation and psychosocial
  parenthood.

. Adequate information about AID (reading, extensive consultation
  with an expert) must be occur beforehand.

As negative elements, the following are noted:

. All crisis situations that threaten a free choice: Neurotic
  feelings of inferiority after a broken relationship or doubts

about the relationship-ability and impotency due to problems
of sexual identity or masturbation(guilt-feelings). In this
case donorship serves both as a compensation to get children
in spite of the relationship-incapacity and as a sublimation
for masturbation problems(phantasies of omnipotence).

. Sexual dysfunctions in which the man is hypersexual in comparison to the libido of the woman limit the free choice to
  become a donor since the choice is based on the adaptation of
  the sexual rhythm of the partners.

. A persistent fear of a consanguinous marriage between their
  own children and an AID child(incestuous phantasies) even
  though they are aware of the remote probability of such an
  event.

. Being too affected emotionally by the infertility problems of
  friends or family to whom one wants to give a surrogate child
  (imaginary relationship with the acceptors).

. Masked depression or pronounced obsessionnal and hypochondria-
  cal character.

. Poor psychosocial adaptation(study, career, relationship).

. Financial need as the primary motive or an inappropriate curiosity for modern scientific procedures.

. Hereditary psychiatric disturbances(schizophrenia, maniaco-
  depressive psychosis, psychopathic disorders, etc).

    AID donorship requires a well-balanced adult decision, arrived
at slowly and with a truly healthy attitude toward parenthood.
Although our team does not demand the fertility of the donor to have
been proven by the possession of two healthy children, we find that
such a criterion(Schoysman, Brussels) is meaningful because in that
case the donors can personally realize the consequences *in vivo*.

REFERENCES

1. De Wachter, M. et al. Menselijke vruchtbaarheid en geboorten-
        planning. Het paar en zijn begeleidend team. Els. Sequoia
        Brussel, pp. 176, 1976.

2. Nijs, P. and Rouffà, L. AID Couples: Psychological and psycho-
        pathological Evaluation. In: The Family, H. Hirsch, ed.
        Karger, Basel, pp. 222-225, 1975.

3. Levie, L.H. Kunstmatige inseminatie bij de mens.; Querido, Amsterdam, pp. 126, 1966.

4. Nijs, P. (ed.) Donorinseminatie. Leuvense Cahiers voor Seksuologie 2. Acco, Leuven, pp. 71, 1971.

PSYCHOLOGICAL ASPECTS OF SEMEN DONATION

Patrick Huerre

Centre d'Etude et de Conservation du Sperme
    (CECOS), Paris-Bicêtre
Kremlin-Bicêtre, France

Semen donations have had to conform to the following conditions at Paris-Bicêtre CECOS since its opening:[1] They are not renumerated, thus semen donation is treated like organ donations;
they must come from a couple with at least one child; and the donor's wife must give her consent.

Mass media appeals have not resulted in sufficient donations
for the rapidly increasing demand and couples have had to wait a
year for AID. Later, it was suggested to applicants that eliciting
donations would decrease their waiting time, with the clear understanding that there would be no relation between the donation and
the semen used for their request. All necessary precautions are
taken to maintain the donor's identity secret and the donor is
unaware of the destination of his semen. Everything surrounding
appeals and requests for donations is revealed to be laden with
significations which reverberate between the donor and recipient.
The danger of being overwhelmed if one agrees too easily to the
initiatives of applicant couples, who might wage a campaign in favor of donations in a disquietingly activistic way, should be neither forgotton nor dismissed.

Each of these approaches supplied half the donors for a certain time. At present, the latter is definitely the predominant
recruitment method.

What is Said

A heavy silence, only occasionally replaced by personal fantasizing, hangs over this subject. Little or nothing is said about

461

it. Where do semen donations come from and how and why are they
made? It would be nice to know, but not much of an effort is made
to find out. It is interesting to note that studies of this subject are almost nonexistent(with the exception of a questionnaire
survey of the feelings of donors during the presumed conclusion
of pregnancy). Furthermore only the donation is usually mentioned,
never the donors: Sometimes one has the impression that, for
those who seek or "recruit" them, speaking about them would be like
divulging a secret. If they are not mentioned, it is rather as if
they did not exist; paternity is reduced to a medical "treatment".

What the Donors Say

In order to look at donor opinion, we invited them to speak
with us individually, and all accepted. We were able to see 45
donors for about an hour and a half each; some of them were accompanied by their wives. We explained to them the reason for our
invitation and asked them to speak freely about their decision in
order that we might find out and understand more about it.

At first, they tended to express themselves in banalities or
to be on the defensive. They had taken a step which benefited them
in ways we shall consider and they came to see us in order to understand their motivation. Jokes and self-styled puns were often very
revealing. In all cases, donors have little resemblance to their
literary, science fiction or film versions.

Who Are They?

They are all couples, have an average of two children and
their average age is 32. Professionally, they are varied, ranging
from the factory worker to the physician and engineer; middle management and students also being represented. However, socially
and professionally, they are predominantly above-average. From a
geographical point of view: 28 out of 45 live in Paris and surrounding areas, while 17 come from the rest of the country.

The initiative as regards the donation was taken: in 11 cases
out of 45, by both members of the couple; in 25 cases out of 45 by
the husband; and in 9 cases out of 45 by the wife. That is to say
that the initiative was taken mainly by the husband or the couple;
when it was the wife's idea, it was essentially the result of direct requests from women friends whose husbands were sterile.

Attitude towards secrecy with respect to family and friends:
31 out of 45 intended to maintain secrecy; with respect to their
children: 5 out of 45 intended not to speak about it.

On this point, an aspect which certainly counts a great deal

is the social and cultural context in which questions of sterility,
semen donation and AID are situated. This rather often conditioned
their answers to these questions. While few of the donors(14 out
of 45) intended to speak of the donation with family and friends;
most(40 out of 45) intended to reveal it to their children, basing
this decision on the projected regression of the resistances and
taboos still attached to male sterility and its treatment.

The solution envisioned if they were in the applicant's position was as follows: Only 19 out of 45 would choose AID; and only
14 out of 45 would prefer adoption. That is to say that, for this
group, making a donation served to be more of a response to a personal story than the reflection of conviction relative to advantages of artificial insemination. From a psychopathological point
of view, although it is difficult to make a diagnosis in this context, we found no significant psychiatric problems amongst the donors.

The problem of the children to be born from their donations is
rarely mentioned but when it is, the donors seem to be on the defensive. Very few wonder what will become of these children, maintaining a watertight distinction between their action and the birth
which will follow from it which they do not feel concerns them. They
merely sometimes fantasize about the chances of their children later
meeting those conceived through their donation.

How do they come to us?

The donors present themselves either in response to an appeal
in the media, or as the result of a request by a sterile couple
(28 out of 45): They would have never come otherwise.

Why do they come?

In one way or another the donors have all been made aware of
problems concerning conception or sterility either by personal experience or through family or friends. A recent event(media appeal,
meeting a sterile couple, etc..) triggered their offer.

What can be said?

The act of donating semen entails masturbation leading to orgasm.
For the donors, is this orgasm always synonomous with pleasure?
Some of them recall painful sensations accompanying ejaculation.
However, for a large number of them, the donation is the consequence
and lasting materialization of a pleasure.

The fantasies attached, when not forcefully repressed("I think
only of the donation") are directed away from the woman and an ill

advised eroticism; they are nothing if not noble. It is as if masturbation, a forbidden pleasure, is made possible or even valoriz-
ed by the semen it engenders and the consent of the woman who is normally excluded. Onan's action has changed its sense, since that
which was forbidden was the scattering of the seed: the action becomes a means towards procreation and hence justified in their opinion.

Some examples may make the connection between the donation and
the donors' lives clearer. One man is the father of an only son and
has no intention of having other children. He is the youngest
child of a large family and his mother was wont to say:"I did not
want the last two". For him, the donation is a way of having many
children, "like his son" of whom he is proud, without having actually to be responsible for them. He is very guilty about having only
one child while his mother speaks constantly of large families. His
wife was hesitant but agreed when he explained to her that these
children "would be wanted".

Another man is the father of three children, and his daughter
is faced with childlessness because her husband is sterile. He volunteered on her behalf "so that she could be happy and experience
pregnancy. "It was his daughter who took the initiative regarding
this, as he described his son-in-law as being "a decent fellow but
rather spineless: "she took things into her own hands", "her husband
is not a good producer". The assurance that this donation would in
no case be biologically destined for his daughter enabled this man
to play an active role, otherwise unthinkable, in the conception of
the child to come: he will merely be the one thanks to whom the
waiting time for AID will be shortered.

Other men have themselves known times during which questions
of sterility, descendants and procreation were of concern to them.
An only son presents a defensive, ironical front: "I saw far and
wide". He is very successful and has three children; for him, having
a lot of children is "success and an insurance against failure".
When he was 17, his parents revealed to him that they were not mar-
ried(his father was not yet divorced) and that he had a half-brother
and a half-sister.

Another donor's wife had been declared to be sterile; they
adopted a child, and the wife had a successful pregnancy some years
later. "I was on the receiving end and now I am in the position
of donating". The wife of another learned recently that she had
a half-sister.

Another couple had a daughter who died and cannot have any
more children without risking the repetition of the same accident.
They are now applicants for AID and the husband has volunteered to
be a donor.

Finally, it at times appears that a donation may be related to a latent homosexuality. Since certain donors are recruited by a sterile male friend("my friend asked me") who comes with him each time. The donor explains that he donates "for him" after having come up against the hesitations of his wife who felt dispossessed of "something which belonged to her".

Another expresses his feminine identification by a slip of the tongue when he explains that he is motivated by the sterility of a coworker of my husband(it was one of his wife's coworkers): "it happened through my wife" as if his wife served only as a go-between in this latent homosexual relationship.

Thus, for these donating couples, information about the pos-sibilities of making a donation and the acquiring of an active at-titude in this area are superimposed on a meaningful background which makes it possible to understand some aspects of their action, whether the motivation lies in the seeking of gratification or in ego reinforcement.   Since the donation is not renumerated, this is the only way in which the donors can be paid. The donation seems to be unpaid only in a material sense. In this connection, the frequent identification with the characteristics attributed to the semen plays a non negligeable role: "agile, vigorous, mobile, numerous".

In other instances, donation serves to efface a personal trag-edy or serve as balm for a wounded ego. In still other cases, a latent unconscious desire is allowed to be played out on an offi-cial stage in a way which is gratifying for the donating-"receiving" couple, these terms having, moreover, become familiar.

But in this action, the mecanisms briefly described here are never involved in an indispensable or necessary way, nor do they appear as a response to a morbid or anxiety provoking situation, which has never been the case. Rather, it is a question of a prof-fered and accepted possibility of reconciling a certain latent ex-pectation and demand on their part with the gratification supplied by the idea of "service rendered".

REFERENCES

1. David, G. Les banques de sperme en France.   Arch. Franç. Pediatr., 32:401, 1975.

FOLLOW—UP STUDY ON CHILDREN BORN THROUGH AID

Christine Manuel and Jean-Claude Czyba

Centre d'Etude et de Conservation
    du Sperme
Lyon, France

INTRODUCTION

The research of Czyba-Chevret on psychological aspects of AID[1] has indicated a need for the study of parenthood[2] in AID and the influence of AID on the child since he has reported a deep emotional investment of these parents in the child as well as a frequent desire for a second child by the same procedure.

Such a study appears feasable since the experience of our psychology team in 75 preliminary AID interviews and in many other interviews for help or advice to couples during or after inseminations has confirmed that transference and its pathogenic effects which certain authors have feared[3] do not occur if 3 precautions are taken: (1) The interviews are done only by members of the team who are <u>not</u> involved in the practice of AID; (2) the inverviewers should have an awareness of their own reactions and motivations, which may be obtained from personal psychoanalytic training and/or through constant team discussions; (3) the couples should be considered as responsible for their own choices and future, and should not be treated as "patients" or "study objects".

Research using the above approach done at CECOS-Lyon on the psychological aspects of AID since 1976 has been given constant support by the couples themselves. Most of them hope that the findings may lead to a better understanding and practice of AID as well as change the social and professional (especially medical) attitudes towards AID. This allowed us to plan a follow-up study on the development of AID children based on interviews with parents. During preliminary interviews, requests for the couple's cooperation after the birth of an AID child always received favorable responses.

Very few studies have been published to date on this subject and they are often insufficient as pointed out by Chevret.[4] The need for a more thorough study led us to attempt a follow-up study, using 3 criteria: (1) A scientific criterion by comparing the study group with a control group, and statistically analyzing qualitative data; (2) a theoritical criterion by studying not only the motor and intellectual development of the children (as done by Izuka[5]), but also their emotional and somato-psychic development according to psychogenetic[6] and psychodynamic[7] findings; and (3) a methodological and ethical criterion by attempting to reconcile the necessity of neutrality in the interviews with that of gathering as much objective data as possible.

Our contact with other CECOS Centers drew our attention to common ethical concerns among professional ones in AID settings. We therefore had to take these concerns into account for the design of our study.

Becoming involved in eugenics is a real temptation in AID. For the practitioners involved in "producing children", as AID may be perceived on a psychological level, there are always underlying feelings of <u>guilt</u> and <u>omnipotence</u> related to "being responsible" for the child's birth. The refusal to get involved in eugenics(which fulfills the responsibility to the utmost) always implies defenses againsts these feelings of either guilt or omnipotence. One form of resistance is a "refusal to know" what kind of children were born by AID. The other leads to an avoidance of follow-up contacts with the families of AID children. Figure 1 schematically represents these concepts and the link with our research design which was conceived with the objective of gratifying our wishes to know as much as protecting us against those very feelings of guilt and omnipotence. It is impossible to avoid all risks and thus it was necessary to break out of the vicious cycle of all-or-none solutions, either eugenics, or AID practice without any control over its outcome, which may be responsible for the relative lack of research in this field.

PURPOSE OF THE STUDY

Evaluation of AID Children

There were two objectives for this study. The first was to evaluate similarities and differences in our sample as compared to control groups. The AID children were compared with a random group of naturally conceived children and a group of children naturally conceived after a long period of unwanted infertility and medical treatment. Information was obtained in similar ways in the 3 groups and included: (1) Indicators on physical, psychomotor, emotional and intellectual development of the child at a given age; (2)

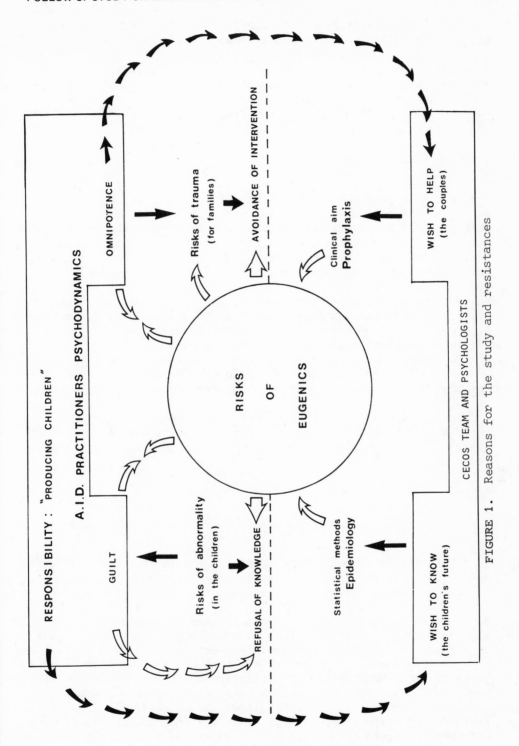

FIGURE 1. Reasons for the study and resistances

indicators on the parent-child relationship, patterns of up-bringing, gender role differenciation and patterns of involvment of the parents; (3) indicators on socio-cultural factors, life styles and living and working conditions of the family. The importance of these different variables was evaluated and compared within the 3 groups. A factorial analysis performed by a statistics team[8] in order to determine the presence and the importance of "high risk" factors and subjects.

Comparison Between Studies

The second purpose of the study was to confirm the results and hypotheses of previous studies. Better intellectual and motor developmental levels of AID children were reported by Izuka.[5] We shall attempt to verify these findings and estimate the relative part played by socio-cultural and emotional factors such as the overinvestment in these children by their parents, also mentioned by Izuka and reported by many authors.[9]

The particular psychodynamics of these children, about which there have been many publications, will be evaluated. Some authors[10] reported severe psychopathological effects; many others suggested, to the contrary, beneficial effects on parenthood.[11]

The protective function, or toxic effects of secrecy for the children and parents' ways of handling secrecy will be evaluated.

We plan to estimate in what way overinvestment in the children is related to the difficulties in satisfying the couple's wish for a child as well as its psychological effects on the child and parent-child relationship.

METHODS AND MATERIALS

This report is based upon certain preliminary results of an epidemiological survey of AID families now in progress. It consisted of routine, semi-directive interviews with both parents together in the presence of the child either in their home or at the CECOS Center as they preferred. All interviews were done exclusively by psychologists of CECOS when the children were 3 months, 18 months or 3 years of age. Thirteen families were included; 4 with children of 3 months, 3 with children of 18 months and 6 with children of 3 years of age. They represent a sampling which is hoped to be representative of the 60 families from three CECOS Centers presently entered in cross sectional and longitudinal surveys(Table 1). As is being done for the above surveys, the data recorded on "study date outlines" designed by a child psychologist in collaboration with an

INSERM research team. This team is specialized in public health epidemiology and had previously performed a longitudinal study on child
development in relation to various care patterns; we used their randomly selected population as a control group.[12]

RESULTS

We are well aware that the findings have no statistical value
and can only suggest certain trends. Nevertheless, we did confirm
the precociousness of AID children described by others in psychomotor as well as speech skills. None of the children showed any
noticeable retardation in development. Eight children acquired a
very early and surprisingly non conflictual sphincter control, both
bladder and rectal diurnal and nocturnal.

In all cases there was deep emotional investment by both parents for the child.

Seven children had psychosomatic disturbances clearly related
to the mother's anxiety. Fertility and pregnancy problems, such as
the length of the waiting period prior to conception, the risk of
miscarriage and the problems at child birth, were highly related to
this anxiety which continues during the first months of the infant's
life. The psychosomatic disturbances included an initial insomnia
and lasting sleep disturbances(3 cases), aerophagic colitis with
vomiting but without weight loss during the first month(1 case),
recurrent rhinitis(1 case), recurrent bronchitis(1 case) and con-
vulsion without neurological basis or crying apnea when surprised
or afraid[13](1 case). None of these disturbances affected the general health or physical and intellectual development of the children. In all cases they were well-tolerated by the parents.

We also observed an "over-involvment" of all fathers towards
their children. Most of the fathers seemed to have very "maternal"
behavior patterns: Even in the most conservatrive families in terms
of gender roles,[14] fathers took a large part in the physical nursing-
care of the child at the earliest age. Most of them had difficulty
(often greater than the mothers) in tolerating signs of frustration
on the part of the child as well as in setting up controls or limits.

Parents often express their gratification in terms of having
a child who is "loving" and "without grudges", the two most frequently cited qualities for children at the ages of 18 months and 3 years.
This is possibly related to their general refusal to reveal to the
child his origin. Their fear of traumatizing is associated with
a fear that the child may "bear a grudge" against them for "not

TABLE 1. *Children born after AID: Populations under study.*

Cross sectional: 77 children of the LYON-CECOS

    3 month   old children..........18

   18 month   old children..........24

    3 year   old children..........35

Children older than 3 years.........14 free interviews

Longitudinal study: 60 children (CECOS centers)

   LYON-CECOS   : 28

   MARSEILLE-CECOS   : 25

   GRENOBLE-CECOS   : 7

---

being like the others", upon learning of his origin. "The truth
is that it is <u>our child</u>" is the attitude most commonly expressed
by the parents: The truth of the desire is truer than the reality.

CONCLUSIONS

It would be as unfair to give our results an eugenic interpretation, as to justify malthusian politics, by observations of lags
in development related to socio-economic factors, the frequency of
school failures or the number of siblings.[15]

However, it is possible and even beneficial to use our results
for preventive purposes, provided complementary studies are performed. Retrospective studies to evaluate and compare various professional practices should also be done in the field of counseling,
selecting and interviewing potential parents(as in adoption, for
example).[16]

In any case, unless the rights and responsibilities of the couples are treated with the utmost respect, their parental role will
be deeply compromised. Research in this area could help to safeguard these rights and responsibilities, and provide more objective
information on AID for the general practitioner, the public and the
infertile couples.

REFERENCES

1. Czyba, J.C. and Chevret, M.   Psychological reactions of couples to AID. Int. J. Fertil.(in press).

2. Benedek, T. Parenthood as developmental phase. J. Am. Psychoanal. Ass., 1959, VII, 3:385-418.

3. Levie, L.H. An inquiry into the psychological effects on parents of AID. Eugenic Rev., 1967, 59:97-105.

4. Chevret, M. Le vécu de l'insémination artificielle. Thèse Doctor. Medecine, Univers. Lyon II, 1977.

5. Izuka, R., Sawada, Y. and Nishina, N. The physical and mental development of children born following artificial insemination. Int. J. Fertil., 1968, 13:24:32.

6. Gratiot-Alphandery, H. and Zazzo, R. Traité de psychologie de l'enfant. P.U.F., Paris, 1973.

7. Winnicot, D.W. The child and the family. Tavistock, London, 1975.

8. Crock, L. and Jacq, J. Methods of evaluating individual and collective factors related to suicide behaviour. Communication at the IXth International Congress of Suicide Prevention, Helsinki.

9. Farris, E.G. and Garrisson, M. Emotional impact of successfull AID. Obstr. Gynaecol., 1954, III, 19:19-20.

10. Gerstel, G.A. Psychoanalytic view of artificial insemination. Am. J. Psychotherapy, XVII, 1:64-77.

11. Mises, R. and Semenov, G. Problèmes psychologiques liés à l'IAD. Confrontations psychiatriques., 1978, 16:219-235.

12. Choquet, M. and Sacy, S. Epidémiologie appliquée à l'étude des facteurs de risques chez lenfant. Communication at IVth Congress of the French-British Ass. of Epidemiologists.

13. Kreisler, L., Fain, M. and Soule, M. L'enfant et son corps. P.U.F., Paris, 1974.

14. Khon, M.L. Social class and the exercise of parental authority. Am. Sociol. Rev., 1959, LXIX, 337-351.

15. Girard, A. and Bastide M. La stratification sociale et la dé-
     mocratisation de l'enseignement., <u>Population</u>, 1963, 455-457.

16. Wiener, H. On when and wether to disclose about adoption.
     <u>J. Am. Psychoanal. Ass.</u>, 1978, 26.

ATTEMPT AT FOLLOW-UP OF

CHILDREN BORN THROUGH AID

Gabriele Semenov, Roger Mises
and Jacqueline Bissery

Fondation Vallée
Gentilly, France

The data reported here are modest, since time does not yet
permit us to judge the eventual influence of artificial insemination
with donor semen(AID) on the personality development of the children
or to evaluate its effect on the evolution of family relationships.

These results concern 30 families, followed since the child's
birth, and a total of 31 children, one of the families having had
two. This number represents about 5% of the couples seen in psychological interviews preceding AID between 1973 and 1977, conducted
in conjunction with Kremlin-Bicêtre CECOS Center by the psychology
team at the Foundation Vallée. The percentage is small for two reasons: On one hand, the couples seen in preliminary interviews include a considerable number of subsequent failures and on the other
hand and perhaps more importantly, it seemed to us to be desirable
to leave as much as possible to the spontaneous actions of the parents. We were of course aware of the need to collect information
about what becomes of children born through AID but the fundamental
question was to what extent would asking to see these children be
advisable.

While the observation of very young children poses hardly any
problems for the child, the same is not same for their parents.
These couples have had to overcome considerable difficulties in order to realize their project of having a child. With this background
taken into consideration, would it not be harmful to solicit their
participation routinely in the absence of any request on their part?
To what extent would these parents feel fully authorized in their
role if we claimed the right to observe their children?

Without taking a definite stand with respect to the dilemna between te desire to observe the children and the risk of an untoward intrusion, we felt it would possible to ask the parents at the first interview to come back after the child's birth to share with us their experiences and opinions. However, there were very few parents who responded to our request. Despite the initial sincerity of their acceptance, the great majority of the families did not appear of their own accord.

In 1976, faced with this lack of information, we invited in writing a dozen randomly chosen couples whose children were about one year of age to share their experience with us. All responded to our request.

The number of couples who return of their own accord has increased over the last year. Still others come to ask for a second child.

At present, out of the 30 couples who have been followed up, 12 were invited, 9 came back of their own accord and 9 came back to ask for a second child. Nineteen of these couples brought their child(held proudly in the father's arms). The other eleven did not bring the child but spoke a great deal about him and showed us photographs.

The children ranged in age from 4 months to 3 1/2 years, but most of them were between 11 and 18 months at the time of examination.

With respect to their age, all the children showed advanced psychomotor development. They were well-balanced physiologically and none presented feeding or sleep problems. They enjoy a good emotional climate and a stimulating environment. On the whole, these are lively and active children who relate well to other people.

A case which illustrates these observations is that of a little girl who presented at birth a bilateral hip dislocation. She was put in a cast between the ages of 28 days and 2 months, then put into traction in an orthopedic service between 7 and 8 months and again put in a cast until she was 11 months old. When examined at the age of 13 months, her muscle tone and motor development were satisfactory. She walked with a little support and was beginning to talk . She was gay and eager to participate. Her parents had put themselves very much at her disposal(her mother had remained with her all during her hospital stay and her father went to see her every day). They were not over anxious, and their relationship with their daughter enabled her to emerge unscathed from the long ordeal.

For all 30 of the couples studied, the regression of the considerable anxiety presented at the first interview was remarkable.
They did not have an overprotective attitude towards their children.
Yet, these were very cherished children; many of them were breast
fed and the mothers tended to stop working (only one out of three
worked, whereas in a study of our first 100 cases seen before AID,
more than 80% of the women exercised a profession).

The fathers appeared to be especially fulfilled. The birth
had been intensely experienced by them and those who had been present stressed the happiness they felt. For them, the child's birth
clearly played a restorative role.

On the whole, the couples have evolved in a very favorable way,
except in one case. This couple, seen with their child, seemed
fine when the child was one year old, but the wife came back several
months later to speak about her difficulties: Her husband, who had
always been jealous, was becoming more and more so, watching her
and restraining her from going out. It would seem that fantasizing
about AID had aggravated his jealousy. This husband, moreover, had
seemed particularly anxious at the first interview.

One of the factors which pose psychological problems was found
to be the importance accorded to secrecy, although it had diminished
somewhat since the first interviews.

Despite the positive nature of this first evaluation based
on 30 couples, our experience is still too limited to allow as to
draw any conclusions. It would be important to know how these children evolve as they grow up: How will conflicts be experienced,
what will be the impact of secrecy on their way of relating to others
and on the development of cognition and ability to communicate?

Thus, the full cooperation of families with children from AID
would be very desirable for only a longitudinal study will make it
possible to answer these questions.

ARTIFICIAL INSEMINATION : IS THERE A MOVEMENT

TOWARDS A EUROPEAN LEGISLATION ?

Ferdinando Albanese

Directorate of Legal Affairs
Council of Europe
Strasbourg, France

The legal problems of artificial insemination in France and Great Britain are being discussed in other papers. I propose to deal with this subject in the 19 other member states of the Council of Europe and with the new moves towards harmonized legislation that have recently taken place in our organization.

From the legal point of view, artificial insemination raises two main groups of problems : The conditions under which artificial insemination is practiced ; and the effects of artificial insemination from the point of view of family law.

Present Legislation

With regard to its practice, it can be said that in Europe there is no legislation which specifically governs the administration of artificial insemination. Consequently, given the silence of the law, it is often difficult even to know whether it is permitted or forbidden. Case law, too, is sparse and, apart from one decision by the Padua Court of February 15, 1959 which held that a woman who had undergone insemination without her husband's consent was guilty of adultery, I know of no judicial decisions that have dealt with artificial insemination.

So far as the question of paternity is concerned, only three states in Europe have specific rules. In the Netherlands, Article 201 (1) of the Civil Code provides that a child born in wedlock is legitimate and that a husband who has given his consent to an act that may have resulted in the conception of the child has no right to repudiate the child's legitimacy. Under Article 1839 (3) of the Portuguese Civil Code, artificial insemination may not be relied on as the sole ground in an action to repudiate the legitimacy of the child if the spouse alleging artificial insemination consented to it. Article 265 (3) of the Swiss Civil Code states that a husband may not bring an action to repudiate the legitimacy of a child if he consented to conception by the act of a third party. In all other European states, however, it is possible to bring an action to repudiate the child's legitimacy. In some of them, not only the husband but also the mother, the child or any interested party may bring such an action.

Recommendation of the Council of Europe

The lack of specific legislation and the awareness that artificial insemination is increasingly being practiced in a number of member states have together prompted the Council of Europe to take up the matter to see whether a joint solution can be found to a problem which is taking the same form in all countries, and which, moreover, is now international in character since couples who are nationals of one state often go to another in order to obtain artificial insemination. With this in mind, an intergovernmental committee of experts was appointed to consider the matter and possibly prepare an appropriate legal instrument. I do not think I am revealing any secrets in saying that our experts immediately ran into opposition from some states, which felt that artificial insemination posed such problems, particularly of a moral, psychological and religious nature, that it was better not to legislate on the matter. The result of this opposition was that a Recommendation was drafted and not a Convention ; moreover, it is not a general recommendation but one that is addressed only to those states which at present intend to enact legislation. Consequently, the Recommendation's value lies solely in the quality of the solutions it proposes, not in any binding legal force.

The draft Recommendation on Artificial Insemination from the Council of Europe presented in this volume (see appendix) can now be examined by specialists outside governmental circles. This seems to be an extremely good occasion to evaluate its worth, especially since it is a draft which is amendable in that the European Committee of Public Health and the Committee of Ministers of the Council of Europe have yet to consider it.

Scope of the Recommendation

Before turning to the content of the Rules proposed in the draft Recommendation, I should like to say a few words about its scope of application *ratione personae*. As you can note from the draft, Article 1 provides that the Rules are to apply only to artificial insemination of a woman with the semen of an anonymous donor. Consequently, the Rules do not apply to artificial insemination with the

the semen of the husband, or artificial insemination with the semen
of the permanent companion of an unmarried woman. It should be noted
that Article 1 does not state expressly that artificial insemination
may be administered if the woman is unmarried. The Rules as a whole,
however, in particular Articles 3 and 5, indicate that such an operation is possible. This provision has given rise to a number of
difficulties. On one hand, it is said that the principle upon which
the Recommendation is based, namely to enable couples to have children in such circumstances that the child will appear to be theirs,
cannot be invoked in the case of an unmarried woman. Moreover, it
implies that artificial insemination ought to be used as therapy for
male sterility, and not as a means to permit an unmarried woman to
have a child. On the other hand, there are some who assert that, if
artificial insemination of a single woman were possible, it should
be possible for the child to establish natural paternity without
which there would be discrimination against such a child who unlike
other children born outside wedlock, would not be able to exercise
this right. Since Article 7 of the draft Recommendation prohibits
such a possibility, it follows that either artificial insemination
of a single woman should be forbidden, or an action to establish
paternity should be permitted.

Although they recognized the validity of this argument, the
Council of Europe experts felt it would be inadvisable to prohibit
artificial insemination of unmarried women since such a provision
would violate the now well-established principle in our Western ci-
vilisation that married and single women are equal under family law.
A compromise solution was found by a renvoi to domestic law. Under
Art. 2(1) which states that artificial insemination can be administered only when appropriate conditions exist for ensuring the welfare
of the child, it is left to domestic law to either prohibit artificial insemination of single women through the enactment of legislation or to leave it to the doctor to judge in each particular
case whether the fact that the woman is single is an "appropriate
condition".

Objectives of the Recommendation

The basic purpose of the draft is to provide legal protection
for five groups of persons : The donor, the husband of a married
woman requesting artificial insemination, the woman artificially
inseminated, the child born as a result of artificial insemination,
and the doctor under whose responsibility artificial insemination
is administered.

The donor is protected in so far as his semen may not be used
for artificial insemination without his express consent (Article 3)
(1), his identity must be kept secret (Article 5), and no relationship of affiliation between the donor and the child may be established
or proceedings for maintenance brought against him (Article 7) (2).

This last rule aroused strong opposition, particularly in countries where the right of every child to bring an action to establish paternity is constitutionally based and therefore in the nature of a fundamental right.

While I recognize the great merit of this principle, it seems to me that an exception should nevertheless be made in this case when one considers the two objectives in view : On one hand, the need to encourage donations of semen, for obviously few men would be prepared to offer their semen if proceedings for paternal affiliation might be brought against them ; now, we know that shortage of donors is the main obstacle to artificial insemination in all the countries ; on the other hand, the desirability of complete integration of the child with the couple receiving him, which precludes the establishment of natural paternity ; admittedly, the problem differs in the case of an unmarried woman, but in this event the need to attain the aforementioned objective would seem to preclude the establishment of paternity.

Protection of the woman who has requested artificial insemination and of her husband, if she is married, is provided by Article 3 of the draft Recommendation. This Article required the consent of all persons concerned, and the doctor responsible for the artificial insemination must ensure that such consent is given in an explicit manner. The Article does not impose a duty on the doctor to obtain the consent in writing, but leaves it to his discretion to obtain in advance evidence to be used in the event of dispute. The only requirement is that the consent must be explicit. Further provisions providing for any procedures to be followed by the doctor could of course be enacted under domestic law.

Other measures to protect the future mother are provided for in Articles 2, 4 and 5. Article 2 states that artificial insemination must be administered only under the responsibility of a doctor and Article 4 requires a certain number of appropriate medical examinations with a view to reducing the risk to the mother and future child. Article 5 provides for secrecy of the identity of all the persons concerned and of the operation itself.

These measures afford clear protection for not only the mother but also the child. The most important provisions for the benefit of the child, however, are those laid down in Articles 2 and 7 of the Rules appended to the Recommendation. Article 2 deals with the prerequisites for artificial insemination. Here, the Council of Europe experts felt that the Rules should not be too specific. The principle adopted was that of the "welfare" of the child, which means that artificial insemination must not be administered if the appropriate conditions do not exist for ensuring his welfare. I admit that notion is left rather "vague" since no attempt has been made to define it. However, this concept of "welfare of the child", if

interpreted in the light of medical practice in all countries, provides, in my view, sufficient guidance. For instance, artificial
insemination cannot exclusively be administered for a therapeutic
purpose to the mother (e.g., in case of neurosis), since the main
objective is the birth of a child in conditions as appropriate as
possible to ensure his future well-being. It was therefore thought
advisable not to list explicitly conditions such as psychological
stability of the couple, sufficient economic means, special requirements in the selection of donors (physical features, race, etc.),
since the solution of each case will depend on its special characteristics and also because any provision too specific in this field
risks being accused of "class" or "race" discrimination. The notion
of "welfare of the child", with regard to the special circumstances
of each case, permits a solution to all these problems and is, at
the same time, flexible enough to take into account unforeseen elements.

Of course, national legislation is free to enact more detailed
provisions in this regard but in the absence of any specific conditions it will be the responsibility of the doctor administering
artificial insemination to evaluate the "welfare" of the future
child. The most important provision for the legal protection of a
child born as a result of artificial insemination is, in fact, Article 7. This Article provides expressly that the legitimacy of the
child may not be contested on the sole ground of artificial insemination, if the husband has given his consent. Legitimacy may however
still be contested on other grounds, for example if artificial insemination in fact conceals an adulterous birth.

Lastly, the Rules appended to the Recommendation provide protection for the doctor. This protection is ensured, first, by making
artificial insemination "legal" and secondly, by safeguarding the
doctor's professional duty of secrecy. It should however be noted
that the rule as to anonymity is absolute only in so far as the identity of the donor is concerned. Secrecy as to the identity of the
woman and her husband and the fact of the operation may be subject
to an exception in the case of proceedings before a Court. One such
case is that of a husband who, after giving his consent to artificial
insemination contests the legitimacy of the resulting child. The
doctor may then disclose that artificial insemination did in fact
take place and that the husband consented to the operation.

One final provision, which has the general purpose of preventing
artificial insemination from becoming commercialized, is to be noted
in Article 6. This provides that no payment shall be made for donation of semen and that the work involved in receiving, treating and
conserving semen shall not be carried out for profit.

Lastly, the draft Recommendation seeks to achieve a balance between the various interests involved by proposing simple solutions which, we hope, will remove in the future the legal uncertainties and injustices of the present situation.

LEGAL ASPECTS OF AID

Douglas J. Cusine

Faculty of Law
Old Aberdeen AB 9 2UB
Scotland

It is not possible in the space of this article to dicuss all legal issues raised by Artificial Insemination by Donor (AID). I shall therefore confine my comments to those which arise out of the doctor/patient relationship but consider also the status of the child.

CONSENT

Clearly no doctor will inseminate a woman without her consent, but to be effective, the consent must be informed, i.e. the patient must be aware of any risks which AID involves. The important question is what risks should be mentioned. If the doctor mentions every risk inherent in a pregnancy, the patient may decide not to proceed, but equally, if he fails to mention some obvious risk, he may be considered negligent. It is not for a lawyer to say what risks should be mentioned although a court may eventually adjudicate on the issue. The safest course would be for the doctor to follow any course recommended by the leading members of his profession and I know that some groups of gynecologists, e.g. the Royal College Obstetricians and Gynecologists in the U.K., have produced a "check list". If a doctor could show that he had adhered to the standards laid down by his profession, I would doubt whether any court would criticize him.

So far I have mentioned only the woman, but it would be prudent to involve the husband at every stage. In the U.K., his consent is not required but reputable members of the profession will not countenance AID without it and will not give AID to other than married women. In some states, e.g. Oklahoma and California,[1] the husband's consent is required for the actual insemination. This is also the situation in the Council of Europe's Draft Resolution On Artificial

485

Insemination[2] which is discussed more fully by Mr. Albanese. In some other states, e.g. Georgia, the Netherlands and Switzerland,[3] the husband's consent is required before he will be regarded in law as the father.

It is not necessary in the U.K. or in any country which I have considered to obtain the consent of the donor's wife, but there is undoubtedly an ethical issue as to whether a wife ought to know about how her husband uses his procreative powers.

CONFIDENTIALITY

The most important aspect here is that of confidentiality since most donors will agree to participate in AID only if their identity remains a secret. In France, the Netherlands and Italy,[4] the law imposes a criminal sanction on those who disclose professional secrets, but there is no legislation in the U.K.[5] It is, however, an obligation imposed on doctors as was recognised in the Hippocratic Oath. Despite this, and any legislation, courts may require doctors to disclose professional information, if to do so would be in the public interest. If a doctor became involved in litigation, a court might require him to reveal the donor's name. The most likely situation is where it is suggested that the doctor has failed to do something and this failure has resulted in loss, injury or damage. This leads into a discussion of the doctor's responsibility.

THE DOCTOR'S RESPONSIBILITY IN LAW

By "doctor's responsibility", I mean what the law requires of the doctor in relation to those who might be affected by his actions. In AID, there are three persons who could be affected in this way. These are the donor, the patient and the child. There are two major requirements : one is the obligation of secrecy, already discussed, and the other is the obligation to prevent injury. That latter obligation is of great importance.

In the major legal systems, e.g. the U.K., U.S.A., France, Germany, Sweden and Australia,[6] the doctor is required to take reasonable care and failure to exercise that degree of care may amount to negligence and liability to anyone injured as the result. In this connection, the doctor is judged according to the standards of his profession and the question a court would ask would be "Would a doctor of reasonable competence have done what was done ?".

In carrying out the insemination, the doctor might injure the patient. This is highly unlikely, but what may happen is that the child is born mentally or physically handicapped and a suggestion might arise that the doctor had been negligent in that the donor had some defect which had been transmitted to the child.

Although the risk is theoretically present, it is probably slight in that the doctor will investigate the suitability of the donor. Obviously his semen must be of good quality but there has been considerable debate about what further tests or examinations should be undertaken. In the U.K., the Royal College of Obstetricians and Gynecologists will shortly be producing a booklet, giving the practitioner some guidance on this point and there is a screening procedure in the New York City Health Code,[7] but as far as I am aware, no country has legislation on this subject.

If it could be shown that the doctor had not adhered to the recommendations of his profession on screening and the child was injured as a result, then in many countries, e.g. U.K., U.S.A., France, the Netherlands and Australia,[8] the child would have a right of action. Some German States may make discretionary payments in such circumstances.[9] If , however, the doctor could show that he carried out all the tests recommended by the experts, a court would be unlikely to find that he was negligent.

STATUS OF THE CHILD

The status of the child born as the result of AID is a matter which naturaly concerns the husband and wife. The child's status is important because it determines inter alia how the birth should be registered and whether the child will succeed to the husband's estate.

There are a variety of approaches here. In some countries,[10] e.g. the U.K., Germany, Portugal and certain states in the U.S.A., a child born during a marriage is presumed to be legitimate, but it is possible to demostrate the contrary. If it could be shown that a child was conceived by AID, it would be illegitimate, but of course this would be difficult to prove. Many countries do not have this problem because they have abolished illegitimacy[11] and the English Law Commission has produced a Working Paper suggesting that the legal status of the incidents of illegitimacy be abolished.

Other countries, although only a few, have legislation specifically dealing with the AID child and all provide that if the husband has consented to the insemination, he is regarded in law as the father. Among these countries are the Netherlands, Switzerland and Portugal.[12] A similar bill was laid before the French Senate in October 1978.[13]

SUMMARY

It is convenient at this point to summarize the above points:

. The doctor must respect a donor's wishes to remain anonymous but he may be forced by a court to reveal the identity of the donor.

. The donor must be subjected to certain tests and it would be advantageous if there were some uniform agreement on what these tests should be.

. The doctor must advise the patient about the implications of AID and particularly about the risks which are involved. It would also be helpful if there were some uniform agreement on what risks should be mentioned to the patient.

. The doctor should take reasonable care to avoid injuring the resultant child but there may be no liability towards the child if he follows the procedure laid down by the members of his profession.

. Only a brief consideration can be given to the status of the child. It would be desireable if legislation were passed to ensure that the AID child was regarded as being the husband's child.

REFERENCES

1. Oklahoma Stat. Ann. title 10, Sections 551-553 (Supp. 1967), California Civil Code 7005, 1975, section 5.

2. Council of Europe. Information Bulletin on Legal Activities n° 1, June 1978, pp. 21-23.

3. Georgia Stat. 74-101. 1, Dutch Civil Code, Art. 201:1, Swiss Civil Code, Are. 256 (3).

4. French Penal Code, Art. 378, Penneau, J. La Responsabilité Médicale, Ch. 4., Eds. Sirey, 1977, Dutch Civil Code, Art. 272(1), Italian Civil Code, Art. 622.

5. Knight, B., Legal Aspects of Medical Practise, p. 5, (Churchill Livingstone, 1972); Glaiser, J. Medical Jurisprudence and Toxicology, 13th ed., pp. 52-55, (Churchill Livingstone 1973); D. v N.S.P.C.C., 1978, A.C. 171.

6. U.K., U.S.A., France, Germany, the Netherlands, Sweden, Australia, See Royal Commission on Civil Liability and Compensation for Personal Injury ("The Pearson Commission"), 1978, Cmnd. 7054, Vol. 3 (HMSO:London).

7. New York City Health Code, 1959, Art. 21:03-05

8. U.K. Report of the Scottish Law Commission on Antenatal Injury,
    1973, Cmnd. 5371 (HMSO:London) : Congenital Disabilities
    (Civil Liability) Act 1976 (for England and Wales). U.S.A.
    The Pearson Commission op cit. ch. 3 France : The Pearson
    Commission op cit. 4. The Netherlands: The Pearson Commission
    op cit. ch. 6. Australia : The Pearson Commission op cit.
    ch. 9. Aus

9. The Pearson Commission op cit. p. 113.

10. U.K. Clive, E.M. and Wilson, J.G. The Law of Husband and Wife
    in Scotland, 1974. W. Green & Son : Edinburgh. Cretney (SM)
    Principles of Family Law, 2nd ed. 1976 ch. 10. Sweet and
    Maxwell:London U.S.A. e.g. Louisiana, Maine, New York, Ohio,
    Wisconsin etc. Germany : Civil Code Art. 1591. Portugal Civil
    Code, Art. 1799.

11. Arizona Rev. Stat. Ann., 1956. Section 14-206. Oregon Rev. Stat.
    1963, Section 109.060 : Latin American.: Bolivia, Ecuador,
    Guatemala, Panama, Uruguay.

12. Dutch Civil Code, Art. 201:1. Swiss Civil Code, Art. 25 6 (3).
    Portuguese Civil Code, Art. 1799 also California Civil Code,
    Section 7005. Penal Code, Section 270. Oklahoma Sata, Ann.
    title 10, Sections 551-553 (supp. 1967).

13. Council of Europe. Information Bulletin on Legal Activities
    n° 2, February 1979, p. 22.

LEGAL STATUS IN FRANCE OF CHILDREN BORN AS A RESULT OF AID

Jean Mazars

Ministère de la Justice
Paris, France

In our legal system, paternity is generally established directly by the law: The father of a married woman's child is her hus-
band(Civil Code, Article 312), and the father of an illegitimate
child is the man who has recognized this child(Civil Code, Article
334-8). The biological truth is the determining factor in three
situations: When no legally valid act(neither marriage nor recognition) has established paternity, when the consequences of such
an act are denied in the name of biological truth(as in disavowing)
or when two legally valid paternity claims exist. Only in the case
of adoption does legal paternity directly contradict biological
fact, but the status of an adopted child is conferred by a judgment
and not by the volition of the parties concerned; the judgment, moreover, appears on the adopted child's birth certificate.

Artificial insemination with donor semen(AID) creates a situation to which these principles do not apply and paternity becomes
a fragile fiction since there is proof of its biological untruth.
Moreover, no endeavor is being made to exploit biological fact for
legal use. Thus, the law has great difficulty in dealing with the
consequences of AID. In practice, the absence of conflict is due
to the lack of claims for strict application of the law.

In this context, the first objective is to describe more explicitly the juridicial upheaval caused by AID. Secondly, an attempt
will be made to suggest means of alleviating the resulting difficulties.

UPHEAVAL DUE TO AID

As far as the legal status of the child is concerned, the problems created by AID concern essentially the domain of paternity since the maternal relation remains biologically unmodified by this fertilization technique. This would not, of course, be the case for a technique in which the fertilized ovum was not produced by the person who gives birth to the child.

In discussing the legal status of a child born as a result of AID, a distinction must be made between legally married couples and those who are not. The situation of the biological father, the donor, will be treated separately.

When the Couple is Married

The fundamental text here is Article 312 of the Civil Code: "The father of a child conceived during the subsistence of a valid marriage is the husband. Nevertheless, the husband may petition the court to disown the child, and this petition will be granted if the evidence is sufficient to prove that he cannot be the father". The problem raised by AID with respect to this law appears insoluble.

AID and the Law. AID creates a situation in which a child is born in wedlock, its conception having been desired by the husband (leaving aside the case in which his consent is not given), but the latter can be scientifically demonstrated not to be the father and is, moreover, the sole possible instigator of a petition to disown the child. Such a petition would inevitably be granted, what ever the previous intent of the husband, despite the fact that he had granted his assent to the procedure. It should be recalled that tacit or even explicit renunciation by the husband of his right to disown the child is impossible, since Article 311-9 of the Civil Code invalidates such a statement. A petition to disown can therefore always be entered and could only be accepted in this case. Such an action would transform the child's legal status from legitimate to illegitimate, with all the psychological, social and even juridicial consequences which such a change would involve.

The decision of the Supreme Court of Nice on June 30, 1976, followed from these arguments.

Attempts at Solution. It could be proposed that the husband adopt the child. But such an action would not make the adopted child completely the husband's, for the child would not have an ordinary birth certificate, and it would also reveal to a third party the absence of biological paternity. Furthermore, this measure can be taken only after birth and exclusively in response to the adopting party's request. Would it not then be preferable to

wait until the statute of limitation governing the petition to disown takes effect?

Another possibility would be to engage a countersuit against the
husband who petitions to disown a child to whose conception through
AID he had consented with a view to obtaining child support. Such a
contersuit might be based, for example, on Article 342 of the Civil
Code, according to which a mother may claim child support from any
person with whom she had sexual relations during the legal period
of conception. However, such an attempt would be ineffective since
the husband, in accordance with Article 342-4 of the Civil Code,
could prove that he could not be the child's father.

Could a countersuit be based on the moral obligation incumbent
to the husband due to this consent to AID? This would be very difficult, since it would be necessary to show that his consent went
beyond simple agreement to the procedure and included providing for
the child's needs. Also, in the absence of any specific text, it
would be necessary for his moral obligation to be transformed into
a civil obligation either by written agreement or by actions demonstrating intent, and a husband petitioning to disown a child would
not be likely to have pursued such a course.

An alternative might be to oblige the husband to pay damages
in compensation for the suffering incurred by the petition to disown. However, this would require proof of breach of contract, which
could exist only if it could be shown that the husband's consent to
AID implied a promise to provide for the child's needs, and such an
argument would be difficult to uphold. It should be noted that the
Court of Nice, in a decision made on February 23, 1977, consecutive
to the judgment cited above, refused to award either child support
or damages.

Under present law, it therefore follows that the husband retains sole control of the consequences of his consent to AID. This
constitutes an injustice as regards the child, who was born in accordance with the father's volition, only to be rejected by this same
volition and hence depvived of a father. The same injustice exists
in regards to the wife.

Thus, the juridicial status of the unborn child cannot be assured before conception, whatever precautions are taken. Couples
cannot escape this uncertain situation until the statute of limitations for petitions to disown goes into effect. Recall that in
France this occurs six months after the date of birth or the discovery of birth when the latter has been conceived(Article 316, Civil
Code).

Such a state of affairs, by the fact that it is not subject to

juridicial control from the beginning, is likely to impede the
development of AID.

When the Couple is not Married

What are the legal consequences of the man's consent to the
use of AID by his companion in this situation? None, under present
law, However, it is possible to recognize the unborn child and hence
establish legal paternity. Of course, recognition after birth
remains possible. Problems arise from two sources.

First, the fact that he has consented to AID does not oblige
the man to recognize the child. Indeed, he cannot in any way be
required to do so since he can always counter a paternity suit(sup-
posing the situation to be such that one can be undertaken) with
proof that he cannot be the child's biological father.

Secondly, such an act of recognition can never be binding,
since Article 339 of the Civil Code states that it can always be
contested by any interested party, including its author, and once
again paternity would be easy to disprove. However, in this case,
it would doubtless be possible to obtain damages from a man who
contested his own act of recognition. Thus, paradoxally, a child
born as a result of AID can be given better legal protection in this
context than when the couple is married; nevertheless, his status
remains open to attack.

The Donor

Under present law, nothing prevents attribution of paternity
to the donor. The only difficulty - but this is only a practical
problem and not an insurmontable one - lies in the protection of the
donor's identity as well as of the very use of AID by the confidential nature of the doctor-patient relationship.

If the donor's identity can be discovered, an unmarried mother
can initiate a paternity suit naming the donor if the latter has
left any written evidence which can be construed as unequivocal
proof of his role(Article 340, Civil Code). Do not physicians in
fact keep such documents?

If the act itself is known, the donor can engage a maternity
suit(Article 341, Civil Code), which he is certain to win if the
child is illegitimate or if, though legitimate, does not possess
legal status as such. Nothing, moreover, prevents him from marrying
the mother, who can then contest her ex-husband's paternity and legitimate the child born to her as a result of AID of which her new
husband was the source.

Thus, neither the donor nor the husband is safe from the sur-
prises that can arise from the application of juridicial rules which
did not foresee AID. The law may therefore have to be modified, as
that which is now in force seems incapable of providing a satisfactory solution.

SOLUTIONS

It is not our intention here to provide a catalogue of all possible solutions, but rather to formulate a proposition for the most
rapid means of achieving the objective: Minimization of the distinction between children born as a result of AID and those conceived by
natural fertilization. Adoption will not be considered because it
does not serve this purpose. Again, a distinction must be made between the situations of married and unmarried couples, and the position of the donor will once more be treated separately.

When the Couple is Married

The aim here is to prevent a husband who has consented to AID
from later disowning the child. However, he must still be allowed
to do so if it can be proven that the child was not born as a result
of AID.

A logical proposal is to make the husband's consent entirely
binding, the child becoming completely his, at least in the eye of
the law, this amounts to the introduction of a new source of legitimacy: The husband, though not the biological father, could then
assume legal paternity in advance and of his own volition. But no
further implications must be sought. While consenting to be the legal father of a child born as a result of AID, the husband must remain free to disown one who is not. This presupposes that, in case
of contestation, it can be shown whether or not the child was born
as a result of AID and hence that the donor's characteristics be
sufficiently identified or at least that means be left available for
obtaining such an identification until the statute of limitations
governing petitions to disown has gone into effect.

When the Couple is not Married

Here again it is a question of making consent to AID binding,
with the proviso that a woman is not required to obtain her companion's consent in order to avail herself of this procedure. Without
undue disruption of the law governing extramarital paternity, it would
be possible to authorize the initiation of paternity suits in cases
where a man has consented to his companion's recourse to AID and to
forbid contestation of recognition based solely on the fact that the
child was conceived through AID when consent to the latter has been

given by the recognizing party. It would doubtless be necessary in this case as well to preserve the possibility of proving that the child was not born as a result of the act of AID to which the legal father intended to give his consent, at least for the time during which a paternity suit may be initiated.

The Donor

AID, at least in the current view of the question, presupposes the existence of a very definite and impervious separation between biological and legal paternity. Since such a distinction does not exist in law at present, its creation appears desirable. This could be done by forbidding the establishment of legal paternity of a donor. The donor would then be protected from the initiation of paternity suits and the husband from donors' claims to his child. The wife would not be able to contest her husband's paternity, such an action requiring that the true paternity be established.

However, it must be realized that this innovation may face opposition from the growing claim that children have the right to know their true origins. This right is guaranteed by legislation in several countries; in France, for now, the demand is not sufficiently strong. In reality, what is involved is not so much paternity laws as the confidential nature of the doctor-patient relationship. A legal distinction can perfectly well be made between biological and legal paternity.

CONCLUSION

The legal problems raised by AID have not escaped the attention of jurists. A bill introduced to the French Senate by Senators Caillavet and Mezard attempts to provide some solutions. Its future remains uncertain.

In addition, although only AID has been discussed here, it should be noted that intraconjugal insemination, while raising generally simple questions, poses more serious ones in two cases: The artificial insemination of an unmarried woman using her companion's semen and that of a widow, using her late husband's semen. It can thus be seen that jurists will not lack for work in this area even if the problems discussed here are eliminated.

REFERENCES

1. Savatier, R. Le droit civil de la famille et les conquêtes de la biologie, Chronique, p. 33, Dalloz, 1948.

2. Merger, R. L'insémination artificielle. Semaine juridique,
      Doctrine n° 1389, 1957.

3. Nerson, R. Progrès scientifique et droit familial, Mélanges,
      Ripert, tome 1.

4. Nerson, R. L'influence de la biologie et de la médecine moder-
      nes sur le droit civil. Revue trimestrielle de droit civil,
      p. 661, 1970.

5. de la Marnierre, E.S. L'enfant éprouvette peut-il être désa-
      voué? Bulletin du Service Juridique de Protection de l'En-
      fance, p. 185, Septembre-Décembre 1977.

6. Mazen, N.J. L'insémination artificielle, une réalité ignorée
      par le législateur. Semaine juridique, Doctrine n° 2899,
      1978.

7. Harichaux, M and Ramu. Semaine juridique, Jurisprudence n°
      18597, 1977.

8. Huet, D. and Weiller. Jurisprudence, p. 45, Dalloz-Sirey,
      1977.

9. Nerson, R. Revue trimestrielle de droit civil, Jurisprudence
      française, p. 745, 1977.

10. Paillet, E. Gazette du Palais, 1er semestre, Jurisprudence,
      p. 48, 1977.

AID: AN OVERVIEW OF ETHICAL ISSUES

David J. Roy

Center of Bioethics
Clinical Research Institute of Montreal
Montreal, Canada

Artificial insemination by donor is not new. Familiarity with
this technique of human reproduction may lead some to believe that
all the major ethical and societal problems raised by this procedure have long since been resolved. This is not the case. Our task
at the moment is to review the major moral and ethical issues associated with AID. Part of this task calls for an identification
of the issues which have not yet been adequately resolved.

AID AND BASIC HUMAN VALUES

Human reproduction is an eminently social and profoundly interpersonal act. Techniques which modify traditional patterns of reproductive behavior inevitably introduce changes into the relationships and institutions designed to regulate and sustain that behavior
Such changes touch upon fundamental human values.

Artificial insemination by donor, though a relatively simple
technique, is by no means simply a technique. Fertilization without
sexual intercourse permits a separation of genetic from social fa-
therhood, a separation of a child's genetic and social identities,
and a separation of genetic communication which are integral components of human sexual intercourse. These separations affect the
biological and social origins of personhood, parenthood, marriage,
and the family. A hierarchy of human values cluster around these
relationships and institutions. These values have emerged slowly
and, indeed, not without pain and peril, over long periods of human history. For these reasons techniques that introduce changes
into these relationships and permit possible transformations of
these values raise questions of a moral and ethical nature.

MORALITY AND ETHICS

Values are expressions of what is really important in human living. As some things are more important than others, values do not exist in isolation. They are interrelated according to a hierarchy or an order of importance. A <u>moral</u> position expresses a stand on which values are most important or most fundamental in a given situation. A system of such positions is a <u>morality</u>. An <u>ethics</u> is ancillary to a moral position or to a morality. An <u>ethics</u> seeks to determine what conditions have to be fulfilled if a fundamental human value, or set of such values, are to be preserved and enhanced.

It is perhaps impolitic to mention that people frequently misconstrue the nature of moral and ethical reasoning. At one end of this spectrum of misconception, some will hold that absolute and unchanging principles deliver certain and clear conclusions about what we ought or ought not do. Others, at the other end of the spectrum, will argue, with almost complete relativity, that individual conscience, choice, or desire is the really only viable moral principle.

In fact, adequate judgments about moral and ethical acceptability are not reached in either of these extreme fashions.

Power, as we know, identifies what we <u>can</u> do. Morality and ethics attempt to define what we should do, less strongly, what we may do and, at certain boundary lines, what we should not do. Such definitions presuppose balanced and comprehensive considerations of human beings as complex patterns of many levels of need, desire, experience, functioning, and developmental goals. To narrowly base moral decisions on only one dimension of human existence is to court the risk of missing what is really important in human living.

Moreover, human beings are not individual islands unto themselves. Our relationships to one another are an integral part of the personal beings we are and continue to become. Living out these relationships generates a community and its institutions. A society and its institutions, in turn, shape our relationships to one another. So a morality and an ethics cannot ignore the structure of a community and the viability of its institutions on the assumption that spontaneous individual desires are laws unto themselves.

Time and cumulative human experience over extended periods of time are essential to moral and ethical reasoning. What appears highly desirable, in an individual instance and in the short run, may prove to be detrimental, even profoundly damaging, in the long run. Discerning what only appears to be good from what really is the individual and the common good is a function of morality and ethics. That is why morality and ethics demand that values, not simply the immediate objects of desire, be taken as the criteria of choice and decision.

Automatic appeals to a static image of human nature or of the nature of human sexuality and marriage will not favor the achievement of effective moral discernment. It is true that generations of human experience have revealed part of what is essential for balanced and healthy personal and societal development. But human nature, as well as the nature of any human reality reveals itself only historically, after a process of evolution. New ways of living human relationships ought not to be automatically rejected as being against human nature simply because these new ways have never been encountered before in human history. Conceptual analysis and thought experiments go only so far, usually not far enough. Effective moral discernment demands the real experiment of actual human experience.

Moral and ethical judgments, then, take time. Definitive moral and ethical judgments require the build-up of a history of experience. In the meantime, conditional and provisional moral judgments are usually possible, certainly respectable, and frequently represent the best we can do at a given moment. The experience of the present in an open, exploratory and critical relationship with the experience of past generations is really the only basis for ethical and moral judgments designed to preserve what should be preserved and further the achievement of what can be developed in the nature of human beings.

AID: MORAL AND ETHICAL CONSIDERATIONS

A number of conditions have to be fulfilled for AID to be morally acceptable in principle. A further set of conditions have to be met for AID to be ethically acceptable in fact. A number of questions identify these conditions in each case. The questions also formulate the key issues associated with AID as a technique of human reproduction.

AID: THE KEY MORAL QUESTIONS

The key moral questions with respect to AID are all various expressions of the over riding question as to whether or not AID can be judged to be acceptable in principle. This judgment will depend upon the answers we can reasonably give to at least the following questions:

. Does AID, as such, involve a dehumanization of human sexuality? For the husband? For the wife? For the donor?

. Does AID, as such, violate the integrity of the marital relationship of the receptor couple? Of the donor couple

. Does AID, as a method of human reproduction, permit an environment favorable to responsible parenthood and to the har-
  monious development of the child?

POSITIONS ON THE KEY MORAL QUESTIONS

AID and Human Sexuality

    Several of the leading Christian Churches have rejected AID
in principle as being against the institution of marriage and as
violating the natural law of human sexuality. We will concentrate
here on the charge that AID violates the structure of human sexuality.

    Masturbation. The less provocative aspect of this charge has
to do with how the semen is obtained from the donor. In traditional
Roman Catholic thinking, consciously stimulated ejaculation of semen is only justified within the context of a legitimate procreative act, that is, within the institution of marriage. Masturbation,
involving an interruption of this ordination to procreation has
been condemned as being against the natural orientation of the sex
act and, in the case of the male, against the natural orientation
or purpose of semen ejaculation.

    One is, of course, not committed to a public campaign in favor
of masturbation when one claims that there is another ethical per-
spective which can be taken on masturbation. An "act of masturbation" cannot be judged in isolation from its whole physiological,
emotional, and relational context. Is one going to be so unreali-
stic as to claim that ejaculation of semen outside the vagina during
the sex paly of a married couple is by definition masturbation(with
the wife's help, obviously) and hence against the natural law of
human sexuality? "Masturbation" in this context participates in the
love orientation and personal meaning of the entire sexual language
of this marriage. It is only one word in the entire sexual language
of this particular marriage.

    The ethics of masturbation- and this applies to all ethics-
has to be a context ethics. This is obvious and accepted with
respect to adolescent masturbation by anyone possessing any adequate degree of knowledge of adolescent physiology and psychology.

    What is the context of donor masturbation to obtain semen for
AID ? The ejaculation of semen is definitely destined for and directed to procreation in this case. The uniqueness of this context

is that the semen will be artificially injected into a woman who
is not the donor's wife. If this context is ethically unacceptable
or against the nature of human sexuality, then so will be the masturbation as one moment of this context. If the context should prove
ethically acceptable, then so also the masturbation. We are not
talking about an evil means for a good end in this entire matter.
We are talking about acts which take on their decisive moral or
ethical meaning from the context of which they are a part.

Depersonalization of Sex. The second charge against AID is
that procreation by this technique involves or leads to a deperson-
alisation and dehumanization of sexuality. The report, Artificial
Human Insemination(1943) of a commission appointed by the Archbishop
of Canterbury in 1945 considered AID to be a highpoint in the depersonalization of sex. The basic reason is that this technique
achieved procreation outside the context of human relationships.[1]
The same point is emphasized more explicitly in a recent Roman
Catholic texbook on medical ethics. The reference in the following
quotation is to AID: "This goes clearly against the divine plan
for the procreation of human life. It completely dissociates procreation from conjugal love. The end of procreation is to be realized according to human dignity which requires that new life be
the fruit of the intimate and exclusive marriage partnership of
love".[2]

It is true that with AID, the genetic communication responsible
for conception of a new human life is not an inner and constitutive
moment of the broader and personally richer communication achieved
in the language of sexuality by a man and woman who love and have
promised themselves to one another for life. The communication of
genetic information does not come from the husband, but, via the
doctor, from the donor. The sexual communication of love, trust,
promise and personal presence comes from the husband, not from the
donor of the sperm and genetic information.

Does this separation of genetic communication from love communication in the procreation of a child necessarily entail a depersonalization and dehumanization of sexuality, either in the case of
the donor or in the case of the married couple using AID? No, not
necessarily. The claim that AID "completely dissociates procreation
from conjugal love" is gratuitous, a priori with respect to the
actual experience of numerous AID couples, and, to the extent that
it is counter to this experience, basically false.

It need not always be, but very frequently is the case that a
married couple turn to AID procreation of a child not to "save their
marriage" but to fulfill it, and to fulfill the parenthood purposes
of their marriage. When adoption is not a possibility and a couple
turn to AID after full and honest discussion between themselves, with

the free and uncoerced consent of both husband and wife, with common purpose and shared hope, with an intensified promise to live for one another and together for the child-to-come, how can one justifiably say that AID is completely dissociating procreation from conjugal love? The genetic communication responsible for the conception of this child is not physiologically part of the act of sexual intercourse in which the partners express their love for one another. But that genetic communication becomes, by their free and shared choice, part of the conjugal love this couple expresses in sexual intercourse and in the whole pattern of their lives.

The purpose of these reflections is to seriously question the statement that AID, as such, that is, in principle, dissociates procreation from conjugal love. If AID did that, it would have to be rejected in principle. AID does involve a dissociation of the genetic communication necessary for procreation from the act of sexual intercourse between a husband and wife. However, when a desire for parenthood arises out of a husband and wife's conjugal love and, in the face of the husband's irreversible sterility and an impossibility of adoption, this couple turns to AID, then the anonymous genetic communication is taken up into their love and becomes part of the web of promise and fidelity binding these two people together and eventually to the child who will be born.

A similar pattern of reflection corresponding to a possible pattern of fact has to be made with respect to the donor. If the donor realizes and demands that the semen he is giving is being accepted by a married couple who love and are true to one another and who will embrace the child to be born into their love and into their future together, how can one say, despite the newness and uniqueness of this situation, that he is acting irresponsibly, that his donation of semen is dissociated from personal relationships and dissociated from conjugal love?

Obviously, and hopefully, his donation of semen is not part of a sexually expressed love for the woman involved. But this does not imply that the injection by the doctor of anonymously donated semen is necessarily and simply a technical and depersonalized from of human conception. A community of trust, understanding, human concern and various kinds of love is possible here as the determining, defining, and highly personal context of AID. This community begins with the married couple and encloses with varying degrees of affilation, the doctor, the counselor, and, indeed, the donor and his wife.

The personalization of semen donation, as will be briefly argued below, stands a greater chance if it is the gift of one couple to another. A student giving his sperm for $ 25.00 with no personal sharing, at a distance, of a couple's loving desire for a child and for parenthood is one thing. A married couple with children deciding to donate the husband's semen so that another couple may have a child is quite a different thing. The donation of semen can then be the expression of one loving couple's human concern for another couple.

The context described above should indicate that AID need not *per se* involve a depersonalization and dehumanizing of human sexuality. It may, but one cannot claim that it will do so automatically and in principle. That is why AID, from the point of view of the human and personal character of sexuality, need not and cannot be morally rejected in principle.

AID and Marriage

The report of the commission set up in 1945 by the Archbishop of Canterbury argued that AID could not be morally accepted because it "violates the exclusive union between husband and wife and involves a breach of the marriage."[3] Pope Pius XII expressed the same position in similar terms in 1949: "Only marriage partners have mutual rights over their bodies for the procreation of new life, and these rights are exclusive, non-transferable and inalienable".[4] AID is to be morally rejected, this statement argues, because it violates the exclusive, non-transferable and inalienable character of these mutual rights.

Do these positions truly reflect what happens to the structure of a marriage relationship when a couple turns to AID to bring a child into their marriage and transform their marriage into a family.

The marriage relationship, in Western Christendom and in many other cultures as well, most definitely involves the kind of exclusivity and totality mentioned in the two positions above. A marriage relationship begins in the mutual promise between a man and woman to live precisely this kind of relationship. Moreover, the promise is meant to be irrevocable, "until death do us part".

We have come to understand that the marriage relationship is not simply or even primarily contractual. The relationship involves and harbors the expectation of more than a bartering exchange of objects. The relationship begins in a promise of body and person which tends by its very logic to give a new and lasting shape to the marriage partner's whole life. A relationship which begins with a gift and gratitude and survives as a promise which reshapes one's whole life is a covenant relationship.

Covenant relationships are of several kinds. Marriage is a unique kind of covenant relationship precisely because of the exclusivity and totality of its sexual promise. Totality, because the

sexual promise of marriage encompasses many levels of communication.
The sexual language is rich and complex. In marriage that language
is a promise of genetic communication to bring about new human life.
But trust, belief, hope in the marriage partner, the union of one's
quest for personal identity and fulfillment with the like quest of
one's spouse, and unbounded and conditional acceptance of one's
loved spouse and a like gift of oneself - these are all moments of
the sexually embodied communication which constitute the marriage
relationship. Genetic communication is meant to be an expression
of one moment of this more comprehensive sexual communication and
promise one one's person. The marriage relationship calls for expression across the full register of the sexual expression of one's
being. The exclusivity of the marriage relationship means that this
full sexual communication of one's person is reserved for one's
spouse.

Adultery is what we generally hold to be such a profound violation of the marriage promise and of its sexual exclusivity and
totality as to signify a death or destruction of that relationship.
But AID, as such, is not adultery. It does not involve sexual intercourse between the wife and donor. It does not involve for that
reason the sexual communication between wife and donor of all of
those levels of personal self-gift which constitue the marriage
relationship. Genetic communication between wife and donor takes
place via AID, but that genetic communication does not employ the
sexual language.

This analysis really calls for further development. However,
enough has been said to meaningfully question whether AID as such
and in principle is such a serious violation of the marriage promise and the structure of the marriage relationship as to signify
a destruction of that relationship. AID does not demand or mean
that husband and wife transfer and alienate their mutual rights
over one another's body for the procreation of new life. The donor
is not being given a right over the wife's body,much less over her
person or her sexual communication of love and person. She reserves
this, by assumption, precisely for her husband.

AID procreation of a child does interfere with the exclusivity
and totality of the marital relationship on the level of genetic
communication. But it is difficult to say that this intervention
from a third party, willed and mutually accepted by the couple after
prolonged and open discussion together, constitutes a structural,
if not conscious or intentioned betrayal of the marriage promise.

It should be emphasized that our assumption here is that the
marriage partners turn to AID after they have already made a marriage promise which included the expectation of a child and of becoming a family. The decision for AID procreation of a child may

be seen, in the face of the husband's irreversible sterility and in
the absence of a possibility of adoption, as the expression of these
partners   taking up their marriage promise again and renewing it to
one another. The donor's genetic communication may be taken up
into this renewed promise and the carried to full familyhood by the
couple's continued exclusive and personally total sexual communication of themselves to one another.

Because this is in principle possible, AID should not be morally rejected in principle as involving a violation of the exclusivity and totality characteristic of the structure of the marital
relationship.

AID procreation of a child does involve an exception, a profound and weighty exception, to the normal structure of a marital
relationship. Indeed, procreation of the child to come is not
achieved via the husband's genetic communication with his wife.
On the other hand, it is no less true that the donor does not, by
reason of his communication of genetic material to this marriage,
obtain rights over the body, much less over the person of the wife.
AID procreation presents society with an exceptional form of marriage relationship. True. But the claim that such a marriage is
not, despite the couple's "good intentions", really a marriage is
gratuitous and unjustifiable. Too much personal and bodily exclusivity and totality can be retained in such a marriage to demand
its moral rejection in principle as a violation of the fundamental
structure of the marital relationship.

AID: THE KEY ETHICAL QUESTIONS

The moral acceptability of AID in principle does not mean that
AID is morally acceptable under any and all conditions. The following list of questions direct attention to some of the principal
conditions which have to be considered in elaborating the ethics
of AID.

. Should AID be considered to be purely a procedure of choice?
  Is it rather the case that AID should be considered as a reproductive procedure of last resort? More concretely, it is
  responsible to contemplate AID when adoption is possible?
  Should AID be considered to be a morally viable option only
  when adoption is not possible because of the non-availability
  of adoptable children?

. Should AID be considered only when it is a question of a married couple as the receiver of AID? Is a common-law marriage
  a sufficient guarantee of stability for the couple and for
  the family environment of the future child? Is AID to be con-

sidered a responsible choice in the case of a single woman of
avowed homosexual inclination?

. Under what conditions is a married couple to be considered a
responsible applicant for AID? Is the consent of both partners
required? Would the exerting of pressure of one partner on the
other be sufficient to make AID an irresponsible and unwise
decision for this couple? What degree of psychological balance
and maturity should be required of both partners? How is this
to be ascertained? Who is the judge? According to what criteria?

. Should the donor be a single man or a married man? A married
man who has already had children? Is the consent of the donor's
wife essential? Is anonymity essential? Without exception?

. There is general agreement that donors should not be haphazardly
accepted. They should be submitted to testing to assure the
quality of the sperm. How sophisticated should these tests
be?

. Should donors be paid for the offer of their semen? Does payment introduce an unacceptable commercial dimension to an activity which should remain in the domain of interpersonal gift
and gratitude. Is there a likelihood that the payment of donors will lead to an unacceptable number of unsuitable contributors?

. What arrangements are necessary to assure that the donor of
semen is acting with a maximum degree of responsibility with
respect to the child who will be born from his genetic contribution? One of the traditional objections to AID, it will be
recalled, is that the donor abandons all responsibility in an
area of human activity which demands a maximum of responsibility.

. Should there be a limit on the number of times a given donor
is used for AID?

. AID and Secrecy. The claim has been made that the necessary
secrecy involved in AID obliges the medical practitioner, the
husband and the wife, and the donor or donor couple to conspire
together to deceive the child and society as to the child's true
parentage and genetic identity. The claim here is that AID
necessarily involves a violation of truth, as in the case of
cover-up when a child is conceived via extra-marital intercourse. AID would involve an anti-factum violation of truth
which is willed and accepted in advance. This situation raises several questions: (1) Should the "secret" be kept from
the child? For how long?; (2) should the secret be kept from

the receptor couple's broader family?; realistically, can such
a secret be generally kept? and if not, is there not a risk
that the child will find out accidentally?; (3) if the child
is to be registered as the legitimate child of the receptor
couple, is it medically wise, from the point of view of medical genetics, that no records be kept of the child's true
genetic origins?; (4) if records were to be kept, primarily
for medical reasons, can anonymity be assured?; and (5) are
records necessary to assure eventual fulfillment of a child's
right to know his or her biological origins and if this right
exists and is recognized, how can the donor be protected
against future disturbance of his life?

. Does *post-mortem* artificial insemination, that is the use of
a man's frozen semen to fertilize his wife after his death,
respect the developmental needs of the child to be born? Is
this *post-mortem* AIH ethically acceptable only if the husband
has given his consent for such a use of his semen?

. Complaints have been expressed on the lack of adequate and
systematic follow-up studies of AID. Should AID couples and
their children be submitted to the potential disturbance that
could be caused by such studies? On the other hand, can we hope
for an adequate societal regulation of AID without the data
obtainable by such studies?

. Does the commercial cryobanking of human semen favor the logic
which would increasingly separate the reproduction of human
beings from the context of interpersonal love, from the context of promise, fidelity, and gratitude? Does the cryobanking
of human semen represent one step, via new developments in reproductive technologies, towards a literal production of human
beings, with eugenic motivation?

This listing of questions has focused attention on some of the
conditions which have to be considered to work out a proper ethics
of AID. The listing is not exhaustive. Moreover, a number of the
questions which have been identified still await an adequate answer.

AID REVISITED: RECENT EXPRESSIONS OF CONCERN

The claim that the debate about the ethics of AID seems now
to have been resolved is premature.[5] A number of major problems
still await adequate solution, at least in several countries highly
involved in human artificial insemination. Curie-Cohen et al.[6] and
Annas[7] have recently identified the most important of these problems.
They remain issues because the solutions proposed are still the
subject of debate. They are ethical issues because they touch upon

individual and social values of major importance.

The first problem arises from the lack of uniform standards
and policies to regulate the practice of AID. At least this is perceived as a problem in the United States. It is also a problem
in Canada. Annas[7] has interpreted one of the indications of the
Curie-Cohen survey as follows.

> "The results are disturbing. Besides pointing to a general
> lack of standards and the growing use of AID for husband with
> genetic defects and for single women, the findings tend to
> indicate that current practices are based primarily on pro-
> tecting the best interests of the semen donor rather than
> those of the recipient or resulting child".

A second problem centers on the screening of donors. The
Curie-Cohen study contains multiple indications that the screening
of donors is all too frequently haphazard, unstandardized and, even,
incompetent. "The screening of donors for genetic diseases is inadequate. A list of genetic traits needs to be established that can
be used routinely for screening donors... This screening should be
conducted by people trained in recognizing and evaluating genetic
traits".[6]

A third problem arises with the practice of using a number of
different donors for a single cycle or of mixing donor semen with
the husband's semen. There are sound genetic and social reasons
for avoiding this practice. It calls for regulation.

The multiple use of a donor defines a fourth problem. In many
areas no uniform policy exists to govern the maximum number of times
a donor will be used. The Curie-Cohen study concludes: "Guidelines are needed to limit the number of pregnancies produced by
a single donor."[6]

The keeping of records defines a fifth and difficult problem.
At present, "records on artificial insemination are woefully deficient".[6] Policies are required to determine what sorts of records
should be kept and how they should be kept to protect the interests
of all persons involved in AID.

                                  CONCLUSION

We already have a history of experience with artificial insemination by donor, with AID. That experience does not warrant a
moral rejection of AID in principle. Earlier positions which rejected AID as a depersonalization of human sexuality and as a violation of the marriage promise need to be reconsidered. There is

also little evidence available to indicate that marriages which turn to AID offer an environment which is not congenial to the healthy development of a child. Quite the contrary is true of many families which have AID children. There is also little evidence available to support the fear that AID is being used to promote a eugenic control of the population.

AID can be consistent with the high personal demands of human sexuality and with the exclusive and irrevocable promises of the marriage covenant. This means that AID should be morally acceptable in principle.

Nevertheless, a number of really significant problems associated with AID still await adequate solution. A clear public policy, designed to protect the various rights and interests subject to a potentially tragic clash, would be a major step towards assuring that AID is not only morally acceptable in principle, but also ethically acceptable in fact.

REFERENCES

1. Creighton, P. And Task force on human life, the Anglican Church of Canada. Artificial insemination by donor. A study of ethics, medicine and law in our technological society. Toronto, The Anglican Book Centre, p. 8, 1977.

2. Lobo, G. Current Problems in medical ethics. Allahabad: St Paul, 1975, p. 149.

3. Creighton, P. Idem.

4. Pius XII. Allocution au Quatrième Congrès international des médecins catholiques, 29 septembre 1949, Nouvelle revue théologique, juillet-août 1973, p. 769.

5. Artificial Insemination for all? Br. Med. J., 6188:458, 1979.

6. Curie-Choen, M., Luttrell, L. and Shapiro, S. Current practice of artificial insemination by donor in the United States. N. Engl. J. Med., 300:588-590, 1979.

7. Annas, G.A. Artificial insemination. Beyond the best interests of the donor. The hastings center report, 4:14-15, 1979.

PUBLIC OPINION ON AID AND STERILITY

Henri Leridon

Institut National d'Etudes Démographiques
Paris, France

Little data is available on the incidence of sterility at the present time, and what little there is is often difficult to interpret. The statistics quoted here are intended to provide the background for veiwing the opinions on sterility problems and possible solutions which were obtained mainly from responses to a dozen questions posed as part of the census conducted by I.N.E.D. in late 1976, using a representative sample of 2471 individuals. These questions were prepared in a cooperative effort involving the author, the psychosociology department of I.N.E.D.(A. Girard) and the Paris- Bicêtre C.E.C.O.S. Center(G. David and P. Huerre). Other aspects of this survey, together with the questionnaire used, were published in 1977.[1]

FIGURES ON STERILITY

Estimating the frequency of sterility in a population in which use of birth control is widespread is beset with many problems which will not be examined here. In the past, 5 to 6% of all couples in which the wife's age was 25(close to the average age at which women married at the time) were estimated to be definitively sterile.[2] There is every reason to think that the current frequency should be lower as a result of the substantial medical progress that has been made in both prevention and treatment of sterility.

In the 1978 I.N.E.D. survey which polled a representative national sample of 3000 women aged 20 to 45, one series of questions dealt with sterility and subfertility problems.[3] Some of the results are shown in Table 1. The women were asked to describe themselves in terms of a fertility scale consisting of four levels. Those whose response was either "I cannot have any more children" or "I don't think I can have any more children" were defined as "sterile". The results are therefore truly significant only for women who have had the time to attempt to have a child. Thus, in the 30 to 34 age group, 7 to 8% of the women classed themselves as sterile including those whose husbands were responsible for their childlessness, although this was rarely declared to be the case possibly, in part, because of the overly personal wording of the question and proposed answers as in "I cannot have any more children". The incidence of sterility was found to rise rapidly in the older age groups, but voluntary sterilization for contraceptive purposes accounts for part of this increase. When women who have undergone such surgery are excluded, the incidence of sterility can be estimated at 3% for the 30 to 34 age group and 8% for the 35 to 39 age group.

A good estimate of the incidence of persisting primary sterility appears to be provided by the proportion of women defining themselves as being both sterile and childless: Less than 1% of women under 30 and about 2% of those 30 to 39, which is extremely few. Secondary sterility was considered to be present when a woman with one or two children described herself as sterile, and this occurred in 2 to 3% of the 30 to 34 age group and 4 to 5% of the 35 to 39 age group. Women with a history of sterility who later gave birth (whether or not they were medically treated) should of course be included in all these estimates(work in progress).

Lastly, it can be noted that only 2 to 5% of the married women surveyed were childless after the age of 35.

PUBLIC OPINION ON STERILITY

The 1976 survey(which polled the population as a whole) indicated that the frequency of both childlessness and sterility tended to be over estimated. The percentage of couples remaining childless after at least ten years of marriage was estimated on the average to be 16%, which is two or three times the actual number. Furthermore, 54% of those polled indicated that this situation was "more often not intended" while 35% thought it "more often intended;" these findings would imply a frequency of over 8% for primary sterility, much higher than that shown in Table 1.

The husband is rarely believed to be solely responsible when the couple is sterile, as was shown by the answers obtained to the question: "When a couple cannot have children, it is most often in your opinion because of: The husband, the wife or both?" The responses were: The husband, 6%; the wife, 30%; both, 38%; don't know, 26%. That so many people claimed ignorance no doubt means that they were embarrassed by the subject. The fact that the

TABLE 1. *Sterile couples according to the age of the woman and the number of children already born (after study of INED-INSEE, 1978.3)*

	Age of the woman interviewed					All women
	20-24	25-29	30-34	35-39	40-44	20-44
Couples admitting sterility (%)	1.3	1.9	7.6	17.4	23.6	9.4
Couples sterile excluding contraceptive sterilizations (%)	0.8	1.3	3.1	8.4	17.2	5.6
Couples sterile and having no children (%)	0.1	0.3	1.8	2.3	3.3	1.5
Couples sterile having 1 or 2 children (%)	0.5	0.8	2.5	4.6	9.5	3.3
Women without children (married) (%)	35.6	11.1	8.1	2.6	5.4	11.2

majority of those who thought they knew the answer attributed the
responsibility to both partners should be considered keeping
in mind that this response has two possible meanings. Some who made
this choice intended it to signify that sterility often results from
the subfertility of both husband and wife rather than the sterility
of one alone, while for others, it provided a way to relieve the wife
of some of the responsibility without assigning it directly to the
husband. Yet others may have seen "both" as meaning "one as often
as the other," which is not dicernable from the question which only
provided an opportunity to avoid designating either husband or wife
as "more often" responsible. It is rather surprising that the same
response distribution was found for both women and men and varied
hardly at all with respect to the other parameters of the sample.

As for the ways by which a sterile couple may be able to have
a child, the survey chose to explore opinion on two: Adoption and
AID. Adoption was revealed to be a very acceptable alternative
since 77% of those polled thought that "for a couple unable to have
a child, it is good to adopt one", while 12% disagreed. These findings vary little from one socio-demographic group to another; at
most, acceptance was found to be greater in women than in men, in
younger than in older people and in more highly educated and higher
income groups.

Two out of three of those who opposed adoption gave as their
reason that the child "is not the real offspring of the couple."
This was also the response of 22% of those asked whether or not they
agreed that "a child's true parents are the ones who raise him; the
blood relationship is less important"(73% agreed). It is of course
true that in answering the second question those polled may have
had situations other than that of adoption in mind(for example,
foster children) and may also have been thinking of the conflicts
that sometimes arise between natural and adoptive parents.

PUBLIC OPINION AND AID

The topic of AID was presented in these terms: In a case in
which it is the husband who cannot have a child, it is also possible for the wife to have a child through artificial insemination
(fertilization without sexual relations), which can now be performed
using the semen of another man, who remains unknown to the couple,
is not renumerated and acts with his wife's accord and under medical
supervision.

Have you heard of this method? Yes: 79% ; No:. 19%; (Don't
know): 2% = 100%.

Thus, the method is widely known in all spheres, although it is not necessarily considered acceptable. A majority of those people who have heard of it think that "it is not a good solution": <u>Out of every 100 people polled, only 32 have heard of AID and think that "it is a good solution for a couple who definitely want to have a child and cannot have one otherwise</u>"(Table 2).

TABLE 2. *Opinions on AID(I.N.E.D. survey, November 1976, of people over 18).*

Have you heard of this method(AID)?	Yes	79%
	No	19
	No answer	2
		100

6a. If yes do you think this is a good solution for a couple determined to have a child that cannot do so otherwise?

	Yes	32
	No	39
	No answer	8
		79

6b. <u>If yes to 6a,</u> of the following reasons, which one seems to you to be the most important for your saying it is a good solution?"

. It allows the wife to really be a mother.	21
. Adopting a child is too long and complicated.	2
. As far as others are concerned, the child is really the couple's.	4
. In adoption, one does not have the child as soon as he is conceived.	1
. No answer.	1
	32

6c. <u>If no to 6b,</u> of the following reasons, which one seems to you to be the most important for not accepting this solution?

. The child would be only the mother's and not the husband's.	9
. The father would not be known.	3
. It would be like adultery.	3
. The donor might pass down undesirable traits.	5
. It is easy to adopt a child.	10
. It would be too difficult with respect to family and friends.	1
. Religious or moral beliefs.	3
. Another reason.	2
. No answer.	3
	39

For those who are in favor of the method, the decisive argument
is that "it permits the wife to really be a mother"(two thirds of
those in favor of AID or even more if another rather similar answer
is counted: "As far as others are concerned, the child is really
the couple's"). The negative version of this argument is used by
nearly one fourth of those who are against AID: "The child would
be only the mother's and not the husband's". The rest of those who
oppose AID cite genetic risk(transmission of undesirable characteristics), religions or moral beliefs or the too nearly adulterous
nature of the procedure, and prefer the more traditional solution
of adoption.

However, on the whole, AID and adoption are not seen as oppos-
ing alternatives. Fewer of those who were opposed to adoption were
in favor of AID than the number in favor of both adoption and AID:
19% as compared to 36%.

The importance attached to the blood relation plays a certain
role in the rejection or acceptance of AID. As mentioned above, 73%
of all those polled said they were "in agreement with the statement:
A child's true parents are the ones who raise him; the blood relationship is less important." But of those who disagreed, only 18%
approve of AID, as opposed to 37% of those who agreed.

To try to shed more light on reasons for hostility to or reserv-
ations about AID, two questions about the "technical" aspect of this
type of procedure were asked. People were requested to give their
opinions of the following two statements: (a) "Some scientific
experiments are dangerous; the ones concerned with "test tube babies"
are an example and can do no good for humanity", and (b) "When a
couple cannot have a child and yet are determined to have one, it is
normal for them to try every scientific and medical means possible
in order to do so". There were 65% who agreed with the second
statement, as compared with 24% who disagreed. Public opinion therefore considers it normal to use every medical technique available
which for us more or less included AID. However, scientific experiments in this area are not trusted: 56% approved of the first
statement, while 24% disapproved. While not formally contradictory,
these two attitudes seem to us to reveal a certain ambivalence about
techniques such as AID. Moreover, when these two questions are
considered together, the contradiction is revealed: A majority of
those who are worried by such scientific experiments approve the
use of "every scientific and medical means possible", just as do a
majority of those who are not. However, distrust of certain medical
techniques carries with it an unfavorable attitude towards AID.
Among those who find it normal to use every scientific and medical
means possible to have a child, 44% approve of AID, while of those
who do not agree with this concept, only 11% approve of AID.

In conclusion, the principle of AID seems to be widely known but is far from being widely approved, since only one out of three people knows about and approves of AID. The distrust of the others is based on a mixture of concern about the "artificial" nature of the procedure, the existence of the donor (from this point of view, the term "AID" is rather unfortunate since it stresses two of the main reasons for concern) and on a drawback which AID shares with adoption, namely that the child is not completely, at least biologically, the child of the couple.

It should be noted that this poll is two years "out of date" and since public opinion changes very quickly in this field, there is every reason to think that it is now more "liberal".

REFERENCES

1. Bastide, H. and Girard, A. Attitudes des Français sur la conjoncture démographique, la natalité et la politique familiale à la fin de 1976. Population, 32:519-554, 1977.

2. Leridon, H. Sur l'estimation de la stérilité. In the special edition: Hommage à Louis Henry. Population, 231-248, September 1977.

3. Leridon, H. and Sardon, J.P. Les pratiques contraceptives en France. Une enquête nationale I.N.E.D.-I.N.S.E.E. To be published in Population.

RESULTS OF AIH IN 1475 PATIENTS

H. Sato, T. Kobayashi, F. Mochimaru, R. Iizuka

Department of Obstetrics and Gynecology
Keio University School of Medicine
Tokyo, Japan

INTRODUCTION

It has been thirty years(1948) since we began performing artificial insemination with husband's semen(AIH) for the treatment
of infertility at our clinic and this method has unquestionably
become one of the most valuable therapeutic procedures in the
treatment of infertility.[1,2] Although many authors have reported
AIH to be effective,[3,4] others have expressed doubt regarding its
use in cases of oligospermia.[5,6] In our experience, the conception
rate with AIH has not improved as expected. Accordingly, we have
retrospectively analyzed the role of AIH in regard to indications, management of unsuccessful cases and improvement of semen
quality.

MATERIELS AND METHODS

The records of 9738 consecutive infertile couples seen between
April 1976 and December 1978 at the parenthood consultation clinic
in Keio University Hospital were reviewed. All patients had a minimum of two years of involuntary infertility and were examined
according to the following infertility check up: Semen analysis;
daily recording of basal body temperature(BBT); erythrocyte sedimentation rate(ESR); histological evaluation of the uterine endometrium; bacteriological culture of the menstrual flow for tuberculous
bacilli; patency test of the Fallopian tubes by means of Kimo-insufflation and hysterosalpingography; cervical mucus and vaginal cytosmear analysis;and post coital cervical mucous penetration test(PCT).

Of the 9738 patients, 1475 had AIH for the indications listed in Table 1. There were 1612 patients who had azoospermia or who failed to conceive with AIH because of severe oligospermia that were treated with donor semen(AID). Oligospermia was defined as a sperm count of less than 40 million/ml on at least two separate occasions and asthenospermia was defined as a sperm motility of less than 50%. These diagnoses comprised 70.2% of the patients that had AIH. Post-coital tests were performed 3 to 4 hours after coitus and defined as "poor" if fewer than 5 motile spermatozoa were seen per high power field. The couples who had passed all the examinations but suffered from infertility for over three years were classified as cases of unexplained infertility. When the woman had ovulation induced with human menopausal gonadotropin, we would at times perform AIH since ovulation was assured. Coital disorders included impotence, premature ejaculation, etc.

Inseminations were performed by the intrauterine method usually once or occasionally twice per cycle. After AIH, the patients received antibiotics for one day to avoid infections. The appropriate time for insemination was determined by examination of a BBT chart, the cervical mucus and a vaginal cytosmear.

There were 83 patients(5.63%) with oligospermia and/or asthenospermia in whom a split ejaculation technique was used in order to improve semen quality. The first portion was found in 71 out of 83 oligospermic patients to have a higher sperm concentration as well as

TABLE 1. *Indications for AIH in 1475 couples.*

Indication	Cases	%
.Oligospermia		
$< 1.0 \times 10^6$/ml	251	17.0
$1.0- 2.0 \times 10^6$/ml	268	18.2
$2.0- 4.0 \times 10^6$/ml	419	28.4
.Asthenospermia		
(motility < 50% normal density)	97	6.6
.Poor PCT	286	19.4
.Unexplained infertility	120	8.1
.Induced ovulation	18	1.2
.Coital disorders	16	1.1
Total	1475	100.0

better sperm motility than did the second portion, while the former had a smaller semen volume(1.43 ml) than the latter(3.36 ml). There were 79 patients with oligospermia ranging 4 to 40 million /ml as well as with asthenospermia ranging from 5% to 60% motility who were given kallikrein treatment. Kallikrein 200 KU, 400 KU or 600 KU was administered daily on an oral basis for a period of 6 to 12 months.

RESULTS

Of the 1475 patients included in this study who underwent AIH 16.4% became pregnant. The conception rates for each indication are listed in Table 2.

Although oligospermia and asthenospermia were 70.2% of all indications, pregnancy rate in these cases was only 10.3%. On the other hand a poor PCT was noted in 19.4% of all indicated patients but the pregnancy rate was 37.4%. The conception rates for induced ovulation and coital disorders were relatively high.

The relationship between conception and number of inseminations using the husband's semen is showed in Figure 1. More than 80% of all conceptions were obtained by the sixth cycle, after which the conception rate diminished rapidly.

TABLE 2. *Conception rate in 242 pregnancies following AIH in 1475 cases.*

Indication	No. of conceptions	Conception rate(%)
Oligospermia		
< 1.0 x10^6/ml	5	2.0
$1.0- 2.0$ x10^6/ml	25	9.3
$2.0- 4.0$ x10^6/ml	56	13.4
Asthenospermia (motility $< 50\%$, density: nl)	21	21.6
Poor PCT	107	37.4
Unexplained infertility	16	13.3
Induced ovulation	8	44.4
Coital disorders	4	25.0
Total	242	

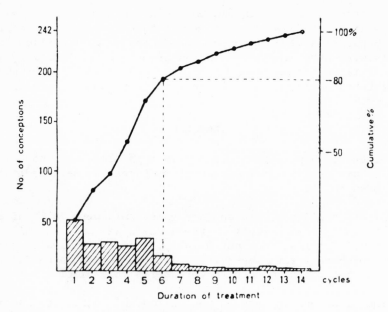

FIGURE 1. Relationship between conception and number
of inseminations using husband's fresh semen.

Split ejaculates were obtained in 83 patients, the first fraction being better than the second with regard to density and motility in most cases. Semen parameters and conception rate of the
whole semen and split ejaculate are compared in Tables 3 and 4.

The number of motile sperm was 8.3 million/ml in whole semen
and 13.5 million/ml in the first fraction of the split ejaculate;
a 63% improvement in spermatozoa motility was observed in the first
fraction. AIH with whole semen gave a conception rate of 10.3 whereas
it was 21.1% with split ejaculates.

There were 79 patients with oligospermia ranging from 4 to
40 million/ml and asthenospermia ranging from 5% to 60% motility
who were selected for kallikrein treatment. No clear response was
observed in 20 patients who were administered 200 KU/day or 600 KU/
day orally, respectively 62.5% and 40.9% of them showed a greater
than 50% improvement of spermatozoa density. Nine pregnancies occurred during and after 400 KU or 600 KU kallikrein treatment (Table
5).

TABLE 3. *Comparison of semen parameters and conception rate in whole semen and split ejaculate. Spermatozoa density ≤ 20 million/ml.*

	AIH cycles	Motile spermatozoa (million/ml)	Conceptions	Conception rate(%)	Motile spermatozoa in conception cycles (million/ml)	Mean AIH cycles
AIH: Whole Semen	136	8.3	14	10.3	10.3	3.9
AIH: Splite Ejaculate (1st portion)	38	13.5	8	21.1	17.8	1.4

TABLE 4. *Conception rate with split ejaculate.*

Spermatozoa density	Infertility period (years)	Patients	Conceptions	Conception rate (%)
A. Normospermia $\geq$ 40 million/ml	5.0	5	2	40.0
B. Oligospermia 20-40 million/ml	6.5	40	7	17.5
C. Oligospermia $\leq$ 20 million/ml	5.8	38	8	21.1
Mean value or total:	6.1	83	17	20.5

TABLE 5. *Effective cases and pregnant cases during and after kallikrein treatment.*

Dosage/day:	200 KU	400 KU	600 KU
Cases	20	40	19
Effective cases	6	25	8
Rate (%)	30.0	62.5	40.9
Conceptions	2	6	3
Rate (%)	10.0	15.0	16.7

DISCUSSION

The number of patients who come to our hospital has increased gradually. Many of them are directed to our hospital by other hospitals. Others have undergone partial treatment by other doctors. We usually performed the routine check-up in order to find out the exact cause of infertility.

It was revealed in our study that 1035 patients (70.2%) had AIH for reasons of partial or complex oligospermia and/or asthenospermia. Endocrine disorders, varicocele, genital infections and chromosomal abnormalities accounted for few of the cases of male infertility. Unfortunately, in a high percentage of infertile males, the causes of infertility could not be determined. When the sperm density was below 20 million/ml, the conception rate was especially poor. But

for other indications, particularly in cases of a poor PCT, the
conception rate was satisfactory. There is no question that AIH
is effective for these indications.

We usually performed AIH for six cycles. If conception did
not occur, we re-examined the patients according to the following
schedule: (1) Re-examination of the utero-tubal conditions; (2)
management of luteal insufficiency; (3) investigation of insemination method; and (4) improvement of semen qualities.

Tubal condition is likely to be poor if the patient had peri-
fimbrial adhesions, peritubal adhesions or endometriosis. Therefore,
we checked tubal condition by using a kimo-insufflation once every
three months. Luteal insufficiency was checked by BBT chart and if
insufficiency was noted, the patient was administered 3000-6000 IU
HCG once every two days for six days.

Insemination is a relatively simple procedure. The several different techniques of insemination are: (1) Intra-uterine; (2) intravaginal; and (3) intra-cervical. The intrauterine insemination
technique has been adopted in our clinic even though there is controversy over its adverse effects. There must be strict adherence
to using a limited amount of semen, otherwise the uterus often starts
contracting and the semen is expelled. Another potential problem
with this method is the possibility of acute pelvic inflammation
caused by the introduction of semen into the peritoneal cavity. For-
tunately, we have noted very few adverse effects of this method in
our thirty year experience.

A split ejaculate has been used when relatively high semen volume coexists with a low sperm count. The semen qualities of the
first fraction is superior to the whole semen, and the conception
rate is 21.1% versus 10.3% with whole semen.

According to recent reviews, kallikrein administration improves
semen qualities. A role for the kallikrein-kinin system in the
regulation of sperm motility and spermatogenesis has been demonstrated to some extent.[8] During and after kallikrein treatment, improvement of semen qualities and a good conception rate was observed.
AIH with split ejaculates or the administration of kallikrein resulted in an increase in the conception rate for patients with infertile semen in our study and thus these two methods are considered to be effective.

REFERENCES

1. Ando, K., and Iizuka, R.   Clinical evaluation of artificial
    inseminations.   Presented at the annual meeting of the
    Japanese Association of Fertility and Sterility in Tsu-
    City, 1963.

2. Notake, Y. and Iizuka, R.   Some medical evaluation of the re-
    sults of artificial inseminations performed at this parent-
    hood consultation clinic during the last 2 years.   Jap. J.
    Fertil. Steril., 13:332-336, 1968.

3. Moghissi, K.S., Gruber, J.S., Evans, S. and Yanez, J.   Homo-
    logous artificial insemination.   Am. J. Obstet. Gynecol.
    129:909-915, 1977.

4. White, R.M. and Glass, R.H.   Intrauterine insemination with
    husband's semen.   Obstet. Gynecol.   47:119-121, 1976.

5. Speichinger, J.P. and Mattox, J.H.   Homologous artivicial
    insemination and oligospermia.   Fertil. Steril.   27:135-
    138, 1976.

6. Nanley, W.C., Kitchin, J.D. and Thiagarajah, S.   Homologous
    insemination.   Fertil. Steril., 30:510-514, 1978.

7. Schill, W.B.   Influence of kallikrein on sperm count and sperm
    motility in patients with infertility problems.   In: Kinin-
    nogenase 2 (F.K. Schattaure Verlag, Stuttgart), pp. 129-146,
    1974.

8. Fritz, H.   The kallikrein-kinin-system in reproduction.   In: Ki-
    ninogenase 2, F.K. Schattaure Verlag, Stuttgart, pp. 9-14,
    1974.

AIH FOR SEMEN INSUFFICIENCY: 119 CASES

Claude Gernigon and Jean-Marie Kunstmann

Centre d'Etude et de Conservation du Sperme
(CECOS), Paris-Bicêtre
Kremlin-Bicêtre, France

The technique of artificial insemination with husband's semen (AIH) is far from new: It came into use more than a century before artificial insemination with donor semen(AID). It has been employed essentially in two indications: Problems related to sexual intercourse and semen abnormalities. The former are less common and constitute special cases which do not involve, in principle, semen abnormalities. The focus of this paper will be on semen insufficiencies for which the results in artificial insemination have long been mediocre. The development of *in vitro* techniques permitting the improvement of semen quality has placed this subject in a new light. Artificial insemination with such semen which may have a greater chance of success is no longer the principal therapeutic act; rather it is simply the necessary complement to the procedures carried out on the semen. The simplest improvement technique is the use of a split ejaculate which was extensively studied by MacLeod and Hotchkiss in 1942.[1] In recent years, several reports have been published on patients treated by AIH,[2-7] but the success rates have been rather variable. Criteria for patient selection have not always been rigorous or well-defined. The uneven nature of these studies prompted us to undertake a detailed analysis of 119 cases of severe semen insufficiencies treated by AIH, usually with semen enrichment.

MATERIALS AND METHODS

The average age of the husbands was 33; that of the wives, 30. The criteria used for selection were as follow:

Sterility lasting for at least 3 years; the average being 5

years: 49 couples(41%) had originally been referred for AID.

. For the women: Satisfactory tubal patency; negative post-
coital test with proof of *in vitro* mucus penetration after use
of a semen amelioration technique.

. For the men: A severe semen insufficiency classified according to
the presence or absence of oligozoospermia, asthenozoospermia
and teratozoospermia. Oligozoospermia was said to exist when
the sperm count was lower than 20 million per ml; when this was
the only abnormality found, the upper limit was placed at 10
million per ml. Asthenozoospermia was defined to be present
when motility after one hour was less than 40% and/or when
after 4 hours, secondary motility fell to less than 25%.
Teratozoospermia indicates that fewer than 50% normal forms
were observed.

The characteristics of the semen in the different groups are
shown in Table 1. The largest group was that which presented with
oligo-astheno-teratospermia(58.8% of the total).

The split ejaculate technique, the simplest used for semen improvement, was the one most frequently used. The first fraction
was employed for insemination after it had been verified to be the
richest. In two cases of oligozoospermia, centrifugation was used
to concentrate the spermatozoa. Serum albumin filtration using
Ericsson's technique[8] to permit selection of the more motile and
morphologically normal forms was applied in three cases in which
both asthenospermia and teratozoospermia were present. In two cases in which only asthenozoospermia was observed, the sperm count
being normal, an equal part of Tyrode's solution was simply added.
In seven cases, no enrichment technique was used.

Before AIH was begun, gynecological investigations were undertaken in order to determine whether any treatment might be required.
In 17 cases, evident ovulatory dysfunction prompted induction of
ovulation. The choice of the day for performing the insemination
was made on the basis of the temperature curve, the degree of cervical opening and examination of the mucus.

Approximately 1 ml of enriched or natural semen was used for
the inseminations. About 0.25 ml was introduced into the cervical
canal and the rest was put into a sterile plastic cap that was
placed in contact with the cervix. One to 3 inseminations were
performed during each cycle.

TABLE 1. *Distribution of cases according to semen abnormality and associated semen characteristics, the latter expressed as means ± one standard deviation.*

Semen Abnormality	Cases	Volume (ml)	Sperm Count (millions/ml)	Initial Motility(%)	Secondary Motility(%)	Normal forms(%)
Oligozoospermia	5 (4.2%)	5.2 ± 2.1	6.3 ± 3.6	58 ± 11	41 ± 12	53 ± 7
Asthenozoospermia	14 (11.8%)	4.1 ± 2.3	60.6 ± 36.9	40 ± 16	16 ± 9	57 ± 16
Oligo + Asthenozoospermia	15 (12.6%)	4.5 ± 2.1	11.7 ± 7.1	44 ± 11	20 ± 8	53 ± 5
Astheno + Teratozoospermia	15 (12.6%)	3.4 ± 1.9	83.0 ± 53.0	34 ± 13	17 ± 8	31 ± 9
Oligo + Astheno + Teratozoospermia	70 (58.8%)	4.5 ± 1.5	8.7 ± 5.3	36 ± 13	18 ± 13	30 ± 10

TABLE 2. *Use of methods of semen enrichment according to semen abnormality.*

Semen insufficiency	Cases	Enrichment method				
		Split Ejaculate	Concentration by centrifugation	Serum Albumin Filtration	Addition of Tyrode's solution	None
Oligozoospermia	5	3	2			
Asthenozoospermia	14	10			2	3
Oligo + Asthenozoospermia	15	14				1
Astheno + Teratozoospermia	15	8		3		4
Oligo + Astheno + Teratozoospermia	70	70				
Total	119	105 (88.8%)	2 (1.7%)	3 (2.5%)	2 (1.7%)	8 (5.9%)

RESULTS

There were 37 pregnancies obtained or 31% of the cases treated. In the group of 49 couples initially referred for AID because of particularly severe semen insufficiencies or chronic infertility, the success rate was 22%.

Results varied widely for the different indications(Table 3). The lowest success rate(24%) was found in the most serious cases, which were also the most numerous. There were cases in which oligozoospermia, asthenozoospermia and teratozoospermia were associated.

Results also differed depending on how the semen was processed. In the 7 cases in which no enrichment technique was used, 4 pregnancies were obtained. In the 3 cases in which serum albumine filtration was employed, there were no pregnancies. One of the two couples for whom centrifugation was carried out for oligozoospermia obtained a pregnancy, as did one of the two for whom Tyrode's solution was added for asthenozoospermia. In the group of 105 couples in whom split ejaculates were used, 30 pregnancies(28% success rate) resulted. Within this last group, the rates varied greatly with the different indications (Table 4).

In the 17 cases in which ovulation was induced, a 29% success rate was observed.

The fecundability defined as the success rate per cycle, is a better parameter to study than the overall rate. In this series, it was calculated only for the first 9 cycles(Table 5) since there were too few patients having more than 9 treatment cycles. During this period, 33 successes were obtained out of 790 insemination cycles, yielding an average success rate of 4.18%. Table 5 also shows the drop out rate for each cycle; 30 couples in all dropped out or an average per cycle of 3.79%. There were no couples lost to follow-up during the first 9 cycles.

Of the 36 pregnancies obtained, 7 ended in miscarriage(19%). Except for one premature birth, all infants were full-term; their average birth weight was 3145 g ± 401 g. No congenital malformations were observed.

DISCUSSION

A pregnancy rate of 31% was obtained for this series of 119 cases of semen abnormalities. However, this rate varied widely according to the semen abnormality. In the most severe cases, those presenting an associated oligozoospermia, asthenozoospermia and teratozoospermia, it was only 24% which is somewhat encouraging

TABLE 3. *Pregnancies obtained according to semen abnormality.*

Semen insufficiency	Couples treated	Pregnancies [*]
Oligozoospermia	5 (4.2%)	3
Asthenozoospermia	14 (11.8%)	5 (35%)
Oligo + Asthenozoospermia	15 (12.6%)	6 (40%)
Astheno + Teratozoospermia	15 (12.6%)	6 (40%)
Oligo + Astheno + Teratozoospermia	70 (58.8%)	17 (24%)
Total	119	37

[*] Percentages calculated only for groups with more than 10 cases.

TABLE 4. *Pregnancies obtained using a split ejaculate.*

Semen insufficiency	Cases	Pregnancies [*]
Oligozoospermia	3 (3%)	3
Asthenozoospermia	10 (9%)	3
Oligo + Asthenozoospermia	14 (13%)	5 (35.7%)
Astheno + Teratozoospermia	8 (8%)	3
Oligo + Astheno + Teratozoospermia	70 (67%)	17 (24%)
Total	105	30

[*] Percentages calculated only for groups with more than 10 cases.

TABLE 5. *Successes (pregnancies) and dropouts per cycle in the first 9 cycles.*

	CYCLE									Total
	1	2	3	4	5	6	7	8	9	
Cases treated	119	113	105	94	85	78	74	64	58	790 cycles
Successes	6	8	2	5	2	2	4	2	2	33 (4.18%)
Success rate per cycle	5	7	1.9	5.3	2.3	2.6	5.4	3.1	3.4	
Dropouts	0	0	0	9	4	5	2	6	4	30 (3.79%)
Dropout rate per cycle	0	0	0	4.5	4.7	6.4	2.7	9.4	6.9	

considering the definition of the group. A success rate of 22% was
achieved with those couples referred for AID(41% of the cases). However, the true significance of these results is impossible to determine without a control group.

The rates obtained per cycle permit a better evaluation and comparison of the results. The average success rate per cycle of 4.17%
is obviously smaller than that observed with AID, which is about 10%
in our experience (see p. 213).

The dropouts were relatively modest and none were noted before
the 4th cycle. This could be explained by the careful informing of
each couple before treatment was begun as to the necessity of per-
sistance over several cycles if they wished to have a reasonable
chance of success.

Comparison with previously published series is difficult for
several reasons. Some include patients with indications other than
semen abnormalities such as difficulties with intercourse or cervical
conditions. As far as semen insufficiencies are concerned, the distribution of oligozoospermia, asthenozoospermia and teratozoospermia
is not always cited, or else the selection criteria for these different groups and the semen processing techniques are very different.
Lastly, it is very often the case that only the overall results are
given and that these are expressed only in terms of the pregnancy
rate.

These factors explain the considerable differences observed
among published series (Table 6). Although calculating their average
overall success rate is admittedly arbitrary, the result, 23%, is
clearly far from negligible.

TABLE 6. *Results of previously published studies on AIH.*

Authors	Couples treated	Pregnancies
Ulstein[2]	35	10(28%)
Barwin[3]	20	11(55%)
Usherwood[4]	74	19(24%)
Steiman and Taymor[5]	40	9(22%)
Moghissi et al.[6]	60	9(18%)
Cohen and Delafontaine[7]	73	13(18%)
Total	302	71(23%)

For a better appreciation of the efficacy of AIH, the separate consideration of pure forms of semen insufficiencies is necessary, as well as the description of selection criteria and techniques used, particularly insofar as the semen is concerned. Furthermore, the results should be expressed as rates per cycle. Only if these conditions are met will it be possible to confirm the value of AIH in semen abnormalities suggested by the results of this study.

REFERENCES

1. Mac Leod, J. and Hotchkiss, R. The distribution of spermatozoa and of certain chemical constituents in the human ejaculate. J. Urol., 48:225, 1942.

2. Ulstein, M. Fertility of husbands at homologous insemination. Acta Obstet. Gynecol. Scand., 52:5, 1973.

3. Barwin, B.N. Intrauterine insemination of husband semen. J. Reprod. Fert., 36:101, 1974.

4. Usherwood, M.M., Halim, A. and Evans, P.R. Artificial insemina-(AIH) for sperm antibodies and oligospermia. Brit. J. Urol., 48:499, 1976.

5. Steiman, R.P. and Taymor, M.L. Artificial insemination homologous and its role in the management of infertility. Fertil. Steril., 28:146, 1977.

6. Moghissi, K.S., Gruber, J.S., Evans, S. and Yanez, J. Homologous artificial insemination. A reappraisial. Am. J. Obst. Gyn., 129:909, 1977.

7. Cohen, J. and Delafontaine, D. Intérêt de l'insémination avec éjaculat fractionné dans les stérilités du couple. Premier Symposium sur l'I.A.C. et l'Hypofertilité masculine. J.C. Emperaire and A. Audebert, eds. IARRH, Bordeaux, 1978.

8. Ericsson, R.J., Langevin, C.N. and Nishimo, M. Isolation of fractions rich in human Y sperm. Nature, 236:421, 1973.

AIH FOR CASES OF SPERMATOZOA

ANTIBODIES AND OLIGOZOOSPERMIA

M. McD. Usherwood

Department of Gynaecology
Stoke Mandeville Hospital
Aylesbury, Bucks, England

Because of poor results in treating subfertile men, a Clinic
was set up in 1972 at the London Hospital to provide practical therapies.   Included in the group was a gynaecologist and a urologist,
and this review is compiled as a result of their experiences.   Particular interest has been payed to patients with sperm antibodies and
oligozoospermia.

INDICATIONS

The indications for artificial insemination with husband's semen
(AIH) have been different for different authors and thus there can
be no absolute indications.   At the London Hospital AIH has been
used for the following reasons: Anatomical abnormalities of either
partner(especially male),retrograde ejaculation, sperm antibodies,
cervical mucus hostility, oligozoospermia, non-consummation of
marriage.

In terms of immunological causes of infertility, cervical mucus
hostility should be proven on the basis of a post-coital test(P.C.T)
in vitro and possibly using crossed cervical mucus hostility tests.
Whilst there is still a lot of discussion on the part played by
circulating spermatozoal antibodies, it may be that a significant
titre is the only demonstrable abnormality.   The method used can be
the Kibrick or Franklin-Duke method whilst fluorescent antibody
studies may demonstrate the exact site of antibodies on the spermatozoa themselves.   We have used a modified Kibrick test incorporating a serial dilution technique to observe agglutination(Table 1).

TABLE 1. *Modified Kibrick spermatozoa agglutination test.*

. 10 ml. of blood; spin down and separate serum.

. Decomplement serum at 56°C for 30 minutes.

. Make series of serial dilutions with isotonic saline
  1 : 4 to 1 : 64.

. Make positive and negative control samples.

. Add to each solution an equal volume of normal semen
  with density > 50 x 10^6/ml.

. Transfer to agglutination tube: Incubate at 36°C for
  2 hours.

. Check at 30 minute intervals for precipitation.

PREPARATIONS

Before arranging AIH, it is important that both partners are
fully prepared physically and psychologically. The investigations
needed for each should be designed so that there will be every hope
of the therapy succeeding. These tests can, of course, reveal an
indication for AIH, but they may also reveal factors which are not
immediately apparent.

The female's investigations need to include a detailed history,
particularly regarding her menses, previous operations and illnesses.
A full physical examination should precede any tests. These tests
should include a cervical smear, high vaginal swab, evidence of
ovulation by basal temperature chart, endometrial biopsy or plasma
progesterone levels, tests of tubal patency by either laparoscopy
or salpingography, spermatozoa antibody tests and post-coital tests
in vivo and possibly *in vitro*. If necessary it may be worth doing
serial estimations of follicle-stimulating hormone(F.S.H.), luteinizing hormone(L.H.) and prolactin levels. Laparoscopy is an important part of the investigations as it has been shown that conditions such as endometriosis and peritubular adhesions may be unde-
tected by other means. Thus in the series described by Usherwood
et al.,[16] there were several women who after laparoscopy stopped
having AIH. The optimal conditions can thus be achieved for the
women before embarking on a long-term course of AIH therapy.

The males need an equally comprehensive series of investigations
such as suggested by Halim et al.[7] A full history and physical
examination is basic. The investigations should include at least
two semen analyses on samples produced by masturbation, post-coital

tests and possibly spermatozoa mucus penetration tests, and sometimes hormone determinations of F.S.H., L.H. and prolactin. In
general, experience has shown that AIH is not worth embarking upon
where the semen analysis shows a spermatozoa density of less than
10 million per ml. and also a persistently low motility of less
than 30%. It is important to have an accurate assessment of the
man's spermatogenic capacity and to achieve this, a testicular biopsy and possibly a vasogram may be needed. If there is a reduced
sperm density or motility, then a variety of drug therapies can be
tried. The drug therapies used have included: Clomiphene citrate
50 mg. daily for 8/52, fluoxymesterone 5 mg. daily for 8/52, meste-
rolone, bromocriptine, arginine.

In general our experience has shown clomiphene citrate to be
most useful for increasing sperm density and fluoxymesterone in
cases with poor motility. In a few cases, bromocriptine has been
tried. It may be necessary to give one of these drugs at the same
time as performing AIH in order to maintain the sperm density at a
satisfactory level. Using these drugs, we have managed to offer
hope to many oligozoospermic men.

SPERMATOZOA WASHING

If there are demonstrable antibodies localised on the spermatozoa producing either head-to-head or tail-to-tail autoagglutin-
ation, then spermatozoa washing may be of value. It is also worth
doing if there are levels of circulating spermatozoa antibodies in
either partner greater than the equivalent of a Kibrick titre of 1
in 32. The method used at the London Hospital has been a volume
measurement of the fresh semen sample and a quick visual microscopic
analysis. An equal volume of phosphate buffered solution at a pH
of 7.2 is added. This is then centrifuged at 500 r.p.m. for 20
minutes. The supernatant is drawn off an another equal volume of
phosphate buffered solution is added before recentrifuging at 500
r.p.m. for 20 minutes. The supernatant is again drawn off and a
third equal volume of phosphate buffered solution is added. If necessary this can be repeated several times over. When the centrifugation is complete, the bolus of spermatozoa suspended in 1 ml.
of phosphate buffered solution ready for insemination. When there
are demonstrable levels of antibody, the partner is given a course
of prednisolone 5 mg. t.d.s. for two to three weeks immediately
prior to the insemination.[7] A similar method of therapy has been
suggested by Hendry et al.,[9] and Shulman, 1976.[12]

TECHNIQUE OF INSEMINATION

The technique of AIH can be one of several. The method chosen
in part depends on whether it is self-insemination using a Semm
cervical cap or doctor insemination. The Semm cap involves bathing
the cervix in a cervical cap full of semen, an intravaginal method.
The cap is attached by suction or is directly placed against the
cervix and then retrieved after the insemination. The alternative
method of doctor insemination has been to use the cervico-vaginal
method, which has proved comfortable to the patients and had few
side-effects.

The personnel doing the inseminations and the place where it
was done were carefully chosen. In ideal circumstances, a seven day
service needs to be provided but this is often impractical. Even
with a five day service, reasonable results have been obtained.[16]
The insemination can be done by nursing or medical staff, but who-
ever it is, they must be in sympathy with the principles of the
therapy, able to achieve a good rapport with the patient and be
able to perform inseminations regularly. Fear and anxiety are well
known as being able to work against fertility in women and thus
the personnel and surroundings must be as relaxed and sympathetic
as possible. The most personalised services can achieve some of the
best results.[2] At the London Hospital, poor pregnancy rates were
obtained when the person doing the inseminations was unsympathetic
and did not communicate with the patients; the rates improved when
a new person took over and the patients recognised the change of
atmosphere.

The timing of AIH is important and in order to try and pinpoint
the best days, the basal body temperature chart(B.B.T.) was usually
used. Others have used the state of the cervical mucus, or the
F.S.H. and L.H. levels. To help to regulate ovulation, we have used
clomiphene citrate which therefore decreased the likelihood of inseminating after ovulation.

Once the day for A.I had been selected, the patient was advised
not to have to travel too far as this in itself will be a disadvantage. Thus distances of more than 100 miles will often be an adverse factor. The husband produced a fresh sample of semen prefer-
ably within an hour of insemination. It was then prepared, if necessary in the way described previously. The insemination was performed in a cystoscopy chair using a 1 or 2 ml. syringe and a no. 12
Intracath. The cervix should not be grasped or manipulated and no
sounding of the cavity done. The vagina and cervix were carefully
cleaned with phosphate buffered solution taking care to wash out
the mucus if there was demonstrable cervical mucus hostility. This
indication will always need at least intracervical insemination
taking care not to inseminate further than 2 cms from the external

cervical os. The procedure should be painless. After injecting the semen, some may run back into the vagina and this is often an advantage. After insemination the woman was asked to rest for 15 minutes or so on her back and told not to douche or wash the vulval region for at least eight hours. The insemination was repeated as least twice in a cycle though there is some evidence to suggest it is worth leaving a day's interval between inseminations. This seems to be a partially psychological phenomenon which may adversely affect either partner. The length of therapy on occasion continues according to the patient's demand long after the doctor's hopes and patience have expired. The age of the women is also a major factor as many women are often over 35 years old at the start of A.I. therapy (Table 2).

RESULTS

In trying to determine the value of AIH, it is usually impossible to give a clear-cut answer in reference to the series that have been reported as there are almost invariably no control groups. However, this is not surprising as the therapy is of a basically practical nature for a group of people who are desperate for help of any sort in achieving a pregnancy. They are thus not suitable as a control group in whom treatment would be positively withheld.

In 1951, Hanson and Rock[8] described their results of the use of newer techniques and in particular with a cervical cap, concluding that it was a worthwhile therapy.

TABLE 2. *Characteristics of 157 couples having AIH at the London Hospital, 1970 to 1976.*

Age of males   : Range 19 to 54 (mean 31.6 years).

Age of females   : Range 18 to 40 (mean 27.0 years).

Length of infertility: Range 1 month to 14 years (mean 6.0 years).

Males

       1° infertility: 136

       2° infertility: 21

Females

       1° infertility: 138

       2° infertility: 19

Mastroianni et al.[10] were amongst the first to make a full appraisal of AIH and its techniques. They only achieved seven pregnancies amongst 113 women and reckoned that intravaginal AIH was the most effective method. Only one pregnancy resulted amongst 29 patients when AIH was performed for poor post-coital tests. Their disillusionment was similarly expressed by Swyer[15] who had only a 17.5% overall success rate but did not give any breakdown as to the number of pregnancies according to indication. Thus, in terms of the use of AIH for cervical hostility or spermatozoa antibodies, one has to look to more recent papers. The best results of anyone are those of Barwin[2] who reported 13 pregnancies in 18 patients(70%) when AIH was done for poor post-coital tests. His overall success rate of 62% was achieved using multiple inseminations, intravenous Premarin and occasionally stored samples from oligozoospermic males.

White and Glass[17] on the basis of post-coital tests done after AIH which showed no improvement consider that intra-uterine inseminations were best for poor post-coital tests. Many of the reported series describe using split ejaculates on the basis of work by Amelar and Hotchkiss.[1] Using this technique, David[3] quotes a 33% overall pregnancy rate though he does not use centrifugation of the spermatozoa unless there is auto-agglutination. We have not used split ejaculates as we have encountered many difficulties on the part of our patients to produce such samples.

In these reported series of AIH, there have been few tests done for circulating spermatozoa antibodies. In the series reported by Usherwood et al.[16] there were four pregnancies in 11 patients. However, in six years experience of AIH involving 157 couples, seven pregnancies were achieved in 22 patients with Kibrick titres of more than 1/32; and of four patients with spermatozoa auto-agglutination, two pregnancies resulted(Table 3). An overall pregnancy rate of 26.7% is the worst result achieved with AIH and this was when it was performed for reasons of severe oligozoospermia(Table 4). However, this is better than is those with oligozoospermia not offered AIH. This is a similar finding to most of the series, especially if there is a poor spermatozoa motility. Speichinger and Mattox[13] only achieved two pregnancies in 24 patients and similarly poor results were obtained by Dixon et al.[4] Retrograde ejaculation on the basis of several case reports[11,5] and the London Hospital results seems to be a good reason for AIH therapy. Steiman and Taymor[14] had equally good results, the best being for poor post-coital tests when a 32% pregnancy rate was achieved.

In terms of complications, there are remarkably few reported in most series though there are occasionally reports of fainting and cramp-like lower abdominal pains. These occur more often in those cases having had intrauterine inseminations.[2] The problem of sepsis is very rare though endometrial biopsies taken after AIH will sometimes reveal inflammatory changes. These tend to occur if

TABLE 3. *Artificial insemination with husband's semen: Indications for therapy amongst 157 couples.*

Indication	Couples	Pregnancies	
Non-consummation	2	1	50 %
Retrograde ejaculation	5	2	40 %
Density $\leqslant$ 20 x10^6 ml before treatment	57	19	33.3%
Low motility < 40% before treatment	35	5	14.3%
Negative P.C.T.	22	7	31.8%
Hormonal/Ovarian	14	2	14.3%
Other	6	0	0 %
Tubal surgery	5	0	0 %
Auto-agglutination of spermatozoa	5	3	60 %
Kibrick $\male$ > 1/32	12	5	41.7%
$\male$ > 1/32	2	1	50 %
$\male$ $\leqslant$ 1/32	16	5	31.3%
$\female$ $\leqslant$ 1/32	15	2	13.3%

TABLE 4. *Spermatozoa density at start of AIH.*

Density x10^6/ml	Couples	Pregnancies
0 - 5	12	3
6 -10	21	4
11 -15	12	4
16 -20	12	5
21- 30	15	5
31 -40	17	5
41 -50	15	4
50	53	12
TOTAL	157	42 (26.6%)

intracervical or intrauterine techniques are used. However, if any
technique is not sufficiently clean, sepsis can result. Intermenstrual
bleeding has also been reported but this is due to faulty technique.
Whilst there can be possible psychological sequelae, it is important
to avoid these by proper selection of couples for the therapy. This
can only be done after close initial interviewing.

There can be no definite time limit as to how long inseminations
should continue as there can be many variable factors. In general,
our experience is that pregnancies are most likely in the first six
cycles and less likely after the first 12 cycles (Figure 1). Thereafter, the patients often become discouraged and disappointed, and
hence stop therapy themselves.

If pregnancy results, there have been varying reports as to the
outcome. Abortion rates of up to 25% have been quoted. This is
only slightly higher than the overall spontaneous natural abortion
rates quoted and may sometimes reflect the widespread use of agents
such as clomiphene citrate for induction of ovulation. In the London
Hospital series, of the 42 pregnancies achieved, 10 aborted spontaneously and seven of these were in women treated with clomiphene.

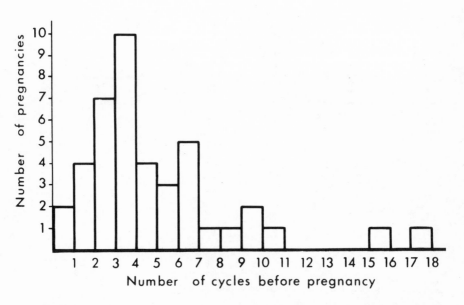

FIGURE 1. Distribution of pregnancies as a function of
the number of treatment cycles.

No doubt AID will be the answer for many couples although in Britain, many of the larger centres offering the service are over-worked. This means that AIH will often be worthwhile and there are still many who would favour the chance of achieving their "own" pregnancy by AIH. For these, the therapy will continue to be used. This is particularly the case when the cause of infertility is thought to be immunological.

ACKNOWLEDGEMENT

I would like to thank Mr. P. Evans, Mr. A. Halim and all the nursing staff for their help and work, and the invaluable advice and encouragement of Professor J.P. Blandy.

REFERENCES

1. Amelar, R.D. and Hotchkiss, R.S. The split ejaculate, its use in the management of male infertility. Fertil. Steril. 16:46-60, 1965.

2. Barwin, B.N. Intra-uterine insemination of husband's semen. J. Reprod. Fertil., 36:101-106, 1974.

3. David, G. Personal communication, 1975.

4. Dixon, R.E., Buttram, V.C. and Schum, C.W. Artificial insemin-ation using homologous semen: A review of 158 cases. Fertil. Steril., 27:647-654, 1976.

5. Fuselier, H.A., Schneider, G.T. and Ochsner, M.G. Successful artificial insemination following retrograde ejaculation. Fertil. Steril., 27:1214-1215, 1976.

6. Halim, A., Antoniou, D., Leedham, P., Blandy, J.P. and Tresidder, G.C. Investigation and treatment of the infertile male. Proceedings of the Royal Society of Medicine, 66: 373-378, 1973.

7. Halim, A., Antoniou, D., Lane, J. and Blandy, J.P. The signi-ficance of antibodies to sperm in infertile men and their wives. British Journal of Urology, 46:65-67, 1974.

8. Hanson, F.M. and Rock, J. Artificial insemination with hus-band's sperm. Fertil. Steril. 2:162-174, 1951.

9. Hendry, W.F., Morgan, H. and Stendrovska, J.   The clinical
    significance of antisperm antibodies in male subfertility.
    British Journal of Urology, 49:757-762, 1977.

10. Mastroianni, L., Laberge, J.L. and Rock, J.   Appraisal of the
    efficacy of artificial insemination with husband's sperm and
    evaluation of insemination techniques.   Fertil. Steril.,
    8:260-266, 1957.

11. Schrum, J.D.   Retrograde ejaculation: A new approach to ther-
    apy.   Fertil. Steril., 27:1216-1218.

12. Shulman, S.   Treatment of immune male infertility with methyl-
    prednisolone.   Lancet, 2:1243, 1976.

13. Speichinger, J.P. and Mattox, J.H.   Homologous artificial in-
    semination and oligospermia.   Fertil. Steril. 27:135-138,
    1976.

14. Steiman, R.P. and Taymor, M.L.   Artificial insemination homo-
    logous and its role in the management of infertility.
    Fertil. Steril. 28:146-150, 1977.

15. Swyer, G.M.   Results of artificial insemination(husband).
    J. Reprod. Fertil., 2:11-16, 1961.

16. Usherwood, M.McD, Halim, A. and Evans, P.R.   Artificial insemin-
    ation(AIH) for sperm antibodies and oligoospermia.   British
    Journal of Urology, 48:499-503, 1976.

17. White, R.M. and Glass, R.H.   Intra-uterine insemination with
    husband's semen. Obstetrics and Gynaecology, 47:119-121,1976.

INTRAUTERINE INSEMINATION AS A TREATMENT

OF IMMUNOLOGICAL INFERTILITY IN THE MALE

K.B. Hansen and T. Hjort

Department of Gynecology and Obstetrics
Kommunehospitalet
Aarhus, Denmark.

INTRODUCTION

Antibodies against spermatozoa membrane antigens can be demonstrated in high titres($\geq$ 64) in serum in three to four percent of men from infertile couples[1,2,3] and in close to 10 percent of the men from couples with otherwise unexplained infertility.[2] The antibodies which can be revealed by the Kibrick gelatine agglutination test, immobilize spermatozoa in the presence of complement. In most men with agglutinating antibodies in serum, the antibodies can also be demonstrated in seminal plasma[2] where they may cause spontaneous agglutination in the ejaculate. Spermatozoa antibodies appear not to affect spermatogenesis, and semen analysis in men with autoantibodies to spermatozoa may reveal completely normal findings with normal sperm counts and a percentage of motile spermatozoa within the normal range. However, Fjällbrant and Obrant[4] found a significant reduction of the motility in men who had autoantibodies.

Spermatozoa from men with autoantibodies to spermatozoa menbrane antigens in seminal plasma reveal reduced penetration into cervical mucus. This can be demonstrated in post-coital tests,[3] in the Kremer cervical mucus penetration test[1,5] and in the sperm cervical mucus contact test.[5] Kremer et al.[5] have described in this latter test the "shaking phenomenon", i.e. the jerking movements of antibody-covered spermatozoa in cervical mucus without any forward progression.

The poor penetration of antibody-affected spermatozoa into cervical mucus forms the rationale for trying intrauterine homologous insemination in women whose husbands have sperm agglutinating antibodies in seminal plasma.[5] We report here preliminary results

from an ongoing study with the aims: (a) To analyse *in vitro* the
mechanisms behind the reduced penetration of antibody-affected
spermatozoa; (b) to investigate the conception rate after intrauterine insemination; and (c) to study whether this treatment may initiate
immune responses to spermatozoa in the females.

MATERIALS

In vitro experiments. Sera from the WHO Reference Bank for
Reproductive Immunology in Aarhus with high titres of spermatozoa
agglutinins were used. The sera were selected to represent different modes of agglutination viz. head-to-head, mixed and tail-to-
tail agglutination.

F(ab')$_2$ fragments of IgG in bank sera were produced by pepsin
digestion as described by Hjort et al.[6] This treatment degrades
the Fc portion of the molecule. Consequently, F(ab')$_2$ fragments
lack the characteristics of IgG which depend on the presence of the
Fc piece, i.e. they do not fix complement and do not attach to Fc
receptors on cell membranes.

Normal cervical mucus was obtained from female donors at mid-
cycle by carefully sucking directly into capillary tubes. Spermatozoa from fresh ejaculates from selected semen donors were used
for the *in vitro* experiments and in the spermatozoa antibody tests
(see below).

Intrauterine inseminations. Five infertile couples have so far
been treated. All five men had tail-to-tail agglutinating autoantibodies in serum and seminal plasma and normal spermatozoa concentration but only one showed normal spermatozoa motility(Table 1).
The women had normal hysterosalpingograms and ovulation. Their cervical mucus revealed normal penetrability when tested by a cervical
mucus penetration test with normal spermatozoa(Table 1).

Sera were collected from the women at the beginning of the insemination and every three months thereafter in order to study any
possible immunological effects of the treatment.

METHODS

Spermatozoa agglutinins were determined in serum and seminal
plasma by means of the gelatine agglutination test(Kibrick test)
and the tray agglutination test(Friberg test) as described by Rose
et al.[7]

TABLE 1. *Results of intrauterine insemination.*

Case	Husband's antibody titre		Husband's spermatozoa		Cervical mucus penetration test (mm/2hrs)		Cycles of treatment
	Serum	Seminal plasma	Motility level*	Motility (%)**	Husband's spz.	Donor's spz.	
1	64	4	2	60	9	65	12
2	256	4	3	65	5	60	8
3	64	16	2	30	1	56	8
4	1024	4	2	35	8	69	6[a]
5	16	16	2	30	6	38	4

*Motility. 1:poor, 2:fair, 3:good, 4:excellent.
**Average of several determinations.
[a] Pregnant.

Indirect immunofluorescent tests with methanol-fixed spermatozoa were performed as described by Hjort and Hansen.[8]

Testing for antibodies to seminal plasma components was performed by double immunodiffusion and by crossed immunoelectrophoresis of normal seminal plasma with the patients serum in the two dimension gel.[9]

The Kremer cervical mucus penetration test was performed as described by Fjällbrant.[1] In the *in vitro* experiments, equal volumes of fresh semen from normal semen donors, adjusted to 40 million spermatozoa per ml, and serum or $F(ab')_2$ fractions were mixed in the reservoir and incubated at 37°C for half an hour before the capillary tube with normal cervical mucus was placed in the reservoir. The maximal penetration of spermatozoa was determined after one hour at 37°C.

When testing the fresh ejaculated spermatozoa from the infertile men with their wives mucus, the incubation time was two hours at room temperature before the maximum penetration was determined.

The intrauterine inseminations were performed under guidance of basal temperature charts and the appearance of preovulatory cervical mucus. A thin plastic catheter was passed through the cervical canal into the uterine cavity followed by injection of 0.1 to 0.2 ml fresh, liquefied semen from a tuberculine syringe. The patient stayed on the couch for 15 minutes for observation of side-effects.

RESULTS AND DISCUSSION OF *IN VITRO* EXPERIMENTS

The results from the cervical mucus penetration tests with normal spermatozoa suspended in normal human serum, agglutinating sera or their corresponding $F(ab')_2$ fragments, can be summarized as follows: Spermatozoa incubated in normal human serum or its $F(ab')_2$ fragments penetrated about 30-50 mm in one hour, and spermatozoa suspended in head-to-head or mixed agglutinating sera or their F $(ab')_2$ fragments revealed practical no penetration into the mucus. The tail-to-tail agglutinating sera reduced the penetration to a few mm, while the corresponding $F(ab')_2$ fragments reduced the penetration to a lesser extent.

The following four explanations for the reduced penetration of antibody-affected spermatozoa may be considered: (1) Crossreaction between antigens in spermatozoa and cervical mucus; (2) binding of the Fc portion of the antibody molecule to cervical mucus; (3) complement dependent immobilization; (4) mechanical effect of the antibodies.

Crossreactions between antigens on spermatozoa and cervical mucus would link the spermatozoa to the mucus. The different agglutination patterns indicate that several antigens exist in the cell membrane of the spermatozoa. Since antibodies to each of the different membrane antigens can reduce penetration, the cervical mucus should consequently contain the very same spectrum of antigen specificities. Further, experiments with egg white as the medium in penetration tests instead of cervical mucus revealed similar results (Hansen and Hjort, to be published), and egg white should therefore also contain the same antigen specificities. Both presuppositions are hard to accept.

The next theory deals with the binding of the Fc piece of the antibody molecule to the cervical mucus glycoproteins.[5] The present experiments lend no support to this assuption as $F(ab')_2$ could reduce the penetration. The third theory which explains the reduced penetration of the antibody-coated spermatozoa by a cytotoxic effect due to complement activity in the mucus is questioned by the fact that $F(ab')_2$ fragments which do not fix complement showed immobilizing effect in the *in vitro* experiments. A complement mediated effect *in vivo* may also be questioned, because a major part of the sperm antibodies in seminal plasma seems to belong to the IgA class, which do not activate complement.[2,10] Consequently, it seems most likely that the reduced penetration is due to a mechanical effect of the antibodies. This might (as mentioned above) cause a decreased spermatozoa motility in the ejaculate and hamper movements in the mucus. Thus, the impaired fertility, or even infertility, of men with autoantibodies seems to be caused by the spontaneous agglutination in the ejaculate and the reduced penetration in cervical mucus, but the spermatozoa might be able to fertilize if they reach the egg. This assuption is supported by reports of conception with men having high concentrations of spermatozoa antibodies.[2,11,12]

INTRAUTERINE INSEMINATION

The evidence that antibody-affected spermatozoa may fertilize if they reach the egg offered an indication for intrauterine insemination in couples with a poor cervical mucus penetration test and autoantibodies in serum and seminal plasma of the male. Preliminary results of this treatment are shown in Table 1. So far, only one woman has conceived (now 6 months pregnant) but treatment of the other women is being continued. No side-effects, i.e. pain during the insemination, signs of infection or allergic reactions have been recorded.

Sera from the women were investigated for antibodies against spermatozoa membrane antigens in the Kibrick test and the Friberg test and for antibodies to sub-surface antigens in the indirect

TABLE 2. *Immunological studies on sera from women treated by intrauterine insemination.*

Immunological test	Sera collected every three months
Gelatine agglutination (Kibrick)	– all sera negative
Tray agglutination (Friberg)	– case No. 3: Weakly positive, unchanged reaction (Titre 4).
Immunofluorescence technique	– case No. 1: Antibody against acrosome, titre 10–20, unchanged.
	– case No. 2: Antibody against acrosome, titre 20, unchanged.
	– case No. 3: Antibody against main tail piece, titre increased from 10 to 20.
Crossed immuno-electrophoresis	– all sera negative.

immunofluorescence test. Finally, crossed electrophoresis was performed in an attempt to detect antibodies against seminal plasma.
Table 2 shows the results. Serum from one patient revealed a weak,
but unchanged reaction in the Friberg Test, and sera from three women reacted in the immunofluorescence test before and during the
treatment without any significant changes.

The results, though scarce, give no indication that intrauterine
insemination induces immune responses to spermatozoa or seminal
plasma.

REFERENCES

1. Fjällbrant, B. Sperm antibodies and sterility in men. Acta
    Obstet. Gynec. Scand., 47, suppl. 4, 1968.

2. Husted, S. and Hjort, T. Sperm antibodies in serum and seminal
    plasma. Int. J. Fertil., 20:97, 1975.

3. Rümke, P. and Hellinga, G. Autoantibodies against spermatozoa
    in sterile men. Amer. J. Clin. Path., 32:357, 1959.

4. Fjällbrant, B. and Obrant, O. Clinical and seminal findings in
    men with sperm antibodies. Acta Obstet. Gynec., Scand., 47:
    451, 1968.

5. Kremer, J. Jager, S. and Kuiken, J. The clinical significance
    of antibodies to spermatozoa. In: Immunological Influence
    on Human Fertility. B. Boettcher Eds., Academic Press, pp. 47,
    1977.

6. H. Hjort, T., Hansen, K.B. and Poulsen, F. The reactivity of
    F(ab')$_2$ fragments of sperm antibodies and their use in the
    investigation of antigen-antibody systems. In: Spermatozoa
    antibodies and infertility, J. Cohen and Hendry W.F., Eds.,
    Blackwell Scientific Publications, p. 101, 1978.

7. Rose, N.R., Hjort, T., Rümke, P., Harper, M.J.K. and Vyazov, O.
    Techniques for detection of iso- and autoantibodies to human
    spermatozoa. Clin. exp. Immunol., 23:175, 1976.

8. Hjort, T. and Hansen, K.B. Immunofluorescent studies on human
    spermatozoa. Clin. exp. Immunol., 8:9, 1971.

9. Weeke, B. Crossed immunoelectrophoresis. Scand. J. Immunol.,
    2, Suppl. 1, 47, 1973.

10. Friberg, J.   Relation between sperm-agglutinating antibodies
     in serum and seminal fluid.   Acta Obstet. Gynec. Scand.,
     Suppl. 36, 1974.

11. Fjällbrant, B.   Fertility in a man auto-immunized to spermato-
     zoa, J. Reprod. Fertil., 14:143, 1967.

12. Rümke, P., van Amstel, N., Messer, E.N. and Bezemer, P.D.   Prog-
     nosis of fertility of men with spermagglutinins in the serum.
     Fertil. and Steril., 25:393, 1974.

FREEZE PRESERVATION OF ISOLATED POPULATIONS

OF HIGHLY MOTILE HUMAN SPERMATOZOA

David F. Katz

Department of Obstetrics and Gynecology
University of California School of Medicine
Davis, California, USA

INTRODUCTION

Contemporary procedures for the freeze preservation of human
and other mammalian spermatozoa involve dilution of the whole semen
with a cryoprotective agent alone, such as glycerol, or a semen ex-
tender(e.g. glycerol-egg yolk-citrate). After suitable equilibration
has occurred, the semen suspension is frozen and stored in liquid
nitrogen. Various quantitative protocols have been applied for the
rates of cooling of the semen suspension before freezing, and the
rates of rewarming during and after thawing. In the human, the great
majority of results have indicated that approximately 30%-70% of
spermatozoa that were motile prior to freezing regained their motility initially after thawing.[1-11] This range of values seems to be
at least as much an indication of the variability of human semen
quality as a result of different freeze-thaw protocols. Indeed,
human semen of very good quality(high percentage motility, vigorous,
progressive sperm swimming) appears to be more resistant to the
stresses of freezing and thawing than human semen of less than optimal quality.[5] This distinction represents a practical limitation
of contemporary human semen freeze preservation: It is difficult to
anticipate *a priori* what the post-thaw motility recovery of a human
sample will be. Consequently, it is of interest to seek improved
methods for freeze preservation of human spermatozoa, methods that
increase the post-thaw recovery of motile, viable spermatozoa, and
in particular, that render less than optimal semen samples suitable
for practical freeze preservation.

A fundamentally different approach is to isolate from the whole
semen a sub-population of highly motile spermatozoa, free from
seminal debris and dead, malformed or otherwise pathological sperm-

atozoa. Such a select subpopulation can then be exposed to a cryo-
protective agent, and frozen via standard procedures. This presentation summarizes a pilot study intended to test the feasibility of
such a new approach.[5]

MATERIALS AND METHODS

Twenty-four semen samples were obtained from thirteen healthy
adult males. The ejaculates were collected by masturbation following a minimum of 48 hours of sexual abstinence. No constraints were
placed on semen quality. After receiving each sample(a maximum of
3 hours after collection), visual determination was made of the volume, count(with a hemocytometer), percentage motility and progressive
motility score. Percentage motility was estimated while regarding
only progressively swimming spermatozoa as motile. Stationary and
agglutinated spermatozoa were not considered progressively motile.
The motility score was a visual assessment of the quality of progressive movement, and was ranked on a scale of 0 to 4 in increments of
0.5(complete absence of progressive motility ranked 0). The same
observer made all visual motility assessments in all experiments in
this study.

A 0.5 ml aliquot of the whole semen specimen was then slowly
diluted 1:1 by volume at room temperature with the egg yolk-glycerol-
glucose citrate cryoprotective medium described by Behrman and
Sawada.[11] Motility was reassessed. This mixture, which served as
an experimental control was then placed in a 2 ml screw-cap plastic
ampule, which was sealed and placed in a Linde model BF-31 freezing
chamber. Cooling was achieved by passing the vapors of liquid nitrogen through the chamber via a temperature feedback-controlled
solenoid valve. The temperature was continuously monitored by the
instrument(Linde model BF-33 controller), using a thermistor placed
in a dummy ampule containing 1 ml of semen extender. The ampules
were cooled at a constant rate that averaged $12.9 \pm 1.5°C$/minute to
a final temperature that varied from -80°C to -100°C. This control
freezing procedure took place an average of 3 hours after semen collection by the donors(range, 1.3 to 4.6 hours). Each sample was
maintained at the final temperature for 15 minutes, after which it
was removed from the freezing chamber and thawed for 40 minutes in
a room-temperature water bath. Immediately after thawing, motility
was reassessed.

Once the above freezing procedure had been initiated for the
control samples, a version of the semen separation technique introduced by Ericsson et al.[12] was applied to the remainder of each whole
semen sample. The sample was diluted 1:1 by volume with sterile
Tyrode's solution(pH 7.4) and then centrifuged at 1300 xg for 15
minutes. After the supernantant was decanted, the spermatozoa were

resuspended in Tyrode's solution at a concentration of 100 million/
ml. Motility was reassessed. Aliquots of this suspension(0.5 ml)
were then overlaid onto each of a replicate series of sperm separation columns, the number of columns being determined by the total
number of spermatozoa in a given sample. The columns were made by
heat sealing Pasteur pipettes at the region of taper. Each column
was filled with solutions of bovine serum albumin(BSA) in Tyrode's
solution, in two different concentrations forming two discrete layers.
The lower layer consisted of 0.5 ml of 17.5% BSA; the upper layer
consisted of 1 ml of 7.5% BSA.

     After 1 hour, the overlaid(top) fraction was pipetted off each
column, pooled, checked for motility, and discarded. After a subsequent 30 minutes, the 7.5% BSA(middle) and 17.5% BSA(bottom) layers
were separately withdrawn, pooled, and evaluated for motility. The
17.5% BSA pool was then diluted 1:1 by volume with Tyrode's solution
and centrifuged at 1300 xg for 10 minutes. All but 0.3 ml of the
supernatant was then quickly decanted, and 0.3 ml of semen extender
was added and gently mixed with the remaining supernatant plus the
pellet of spermatozoa. Visual motility assessment and a hemocytometer count were made of this final preparation. It was then frozen,
stored, thawed and reassessed via the same procedure as for the controls; the average time of freezing after semen collection was 6.2
hours(range, 4.4 to 8.1 hours). The average cooling rate, which
could not be repeated precisely on the freezing instrument, was
15.3 $\pm$ 1.9°C/minute.

RESULTS

Sperm Separation Process

     Sperm motility varied in the different layers of the separation
columns, as summarized in Table 1. Percentage motility and progressive motility score were significantly higher in the 17.5% BSA
fractions than in the 7.5% BSA fractions, top fractions, or parent
semen controls. Motility in the top fractions was markedly inferior
to that in the BSA fractions or semen. The difference in motility
between the 7.5% BSA fractions and parent semen samples was not as
pronounced; while percentage motility in the 24 cases was clearly
higher in the former, a significant difference in motility score
was not detected. The average numbers of motile spermatozoa simultaneously recovered in the 7.5% BSA and in the 17.5% BSA fractions
constituted 25% and 16% respectively, of the numbers of spermatozoa
originally motile in the parent semen samples. The amount of seminal
debris declined dramatically in the successive BSA fractions, appearing to remain primarily in the top fractions. The 17.5% BSA
fractions were virtually devoid of it.

TABLE 1. *Effect of the Separation Technique on Sperm Motility (24 Samples, 13 Donors).*

Sample	% Motility[a]	Progressive motility score[a]
Whole semen	53 ± 14[b]	2.8 ± 0.6[c]
Top fraction	11 ± 8[d]	2.3 ± 0.6[e]
Middle fraction (7.5% BSA)	73 ± 12[f]	3.1 ± 0.5[c]
Bottom fraction ((17.5% BSA)	88 ± 12[g]	3.5 ± 0.5[h]

[a]Means $\pm$ standard deviations. Means bearing different footnote symbols.(b, d, f, g for percentage motility; c, e, h for motility score) differ significantly ($P < 0.05$). (From Glaub, Mills and Katz.[5])

Sperm Freeze Preservation

The spermatozoa recovered from the 17.5% BSA fractions exhibited significantly higher percentage motility and motility score, both prefreeze and post-thaw, than did the spermatozoa in the parent semen controls. The percentage survival of motile spermatozoa was twice as high in these fractions as in the controls. Table 2 presents these results for the 24 semen samples studied. The post-thaw numbers of total motile spermatozoa are extrapolated values for cases wherein the entire ejaculate would either have been frozen as a control or utilized to obtain 17.5% BSA spermatozoa for freezing.

DISCUSSION

The practical objective of the freeze preservation of human spermatozoa is to provide a specimen that can be artificially inseminated at a later time and achieve a normal pregnancy. The association between the "quality" of human semen and its fertility has been appreciated for many years; but interrelationships among different parameters of semen physiology, and distinctions therefrom between fertile and infertile men, are still not well-defined.[13] At present, semen samples exhibiting a high percentage of motile spermatozoa and vigorous, progressive swimming of these motile cells, appear most likely to be fertile.[15-18] Within most semen samples there exist subpopulations of such spermatozoa, which are isolated by techniques such as the one employed in this study. The minimum

TABLE 2. *Motility in the 24 experiments in which the bottom fraction of spermatozoa was frozen.*

Semen donor no.	Prefreeze motility				Post-thaw motility						Total post-thaw motile spermatozoa	
	Control		17.5% BSA		Control		17.5% BSA		% Survival			
	%	Score	%	Score	%	Score	%	Score	Control	17.5 % BSA	Control 17.5 % BSA	
											x 10^6	
1	30	2	95	3.5	15	2	50	3	50	53	11.3	3.2
1	40	3	80	3	20	2.5	60	3	50	75	35.0	12.1
1	60	3	80	3.5	30	2.5	60	3.5	50	75	134.4	23.0
2	40	2.5	90	3.5	5	2	75	3.5	13	83	34.2	44.6
3	45	4	90	4	10	3	50	3	22	56	10.5	7.8
3	75	3.5	90	4	45	3	70	3.5	60	78	63.0	11.8
4	40	3	90	4	5	2	50	2	13	56	5.0	6.6
4	60	3.5	80	3.5	15	2	45	2.5	25	56	5.9	1.8
4	65	3	70	3.5	20	2	40	3	31	57	32.8	4.0
5	60	3.5	90	4	25	2.5	60	3.5	42	67	136.5	20.6
5	60	3.5	65	3	30	2.5	55	3	50	85	140.4	25.2
5	60	3	85	4	20	2	70	4	33	82	78.4	27.4
5	75	3.5	85	4	40	3	60	3.5	53	71	178.4	16.5
6	75	3.5	95	4	10	3	60	3.5	13	63	42.0	25.2
6	75	3.5	80	4	40	2.5	55	3	53	69	30.6	4.8
7	35	2.5	65	3	1	1.5	55	2.5	3	85	2.9	7.4
8	65	3.5	85	3	15	2	45	2.5	23	53	20.0	6.5
8	70	3.5	85	4	30	2.5	60	3.5	43	71	69.9	13.6
9	60	3	70	3	25	2	60	2.5	42	86	30.0	3.2
10	40	3	75	2.5	10	1.5	50	2	25	67	12.6	0.8
10	50	2.5	80	3	15	1.5	40	2	30	50	33.6	2.4
11	65	3.5	85	4	20	2.5	70	3.5	31	82	79.8	13.4
12	60	3	85	4	30	2	70	3.5	50	82	66.3	25.1
13	70	3.5	80	4	10	2	60	3.5	14	75	76.0	57.7
Mean[b]	57[c]	3.1[d]	82[e]	3.6[f]	20[g]	2.3[h]	57[c]	3.0[d]	34[i]	70[j]	55.4	15.2
SD	14	0.4	8	0.5	12	0.5	10	0.6	16	12	49	14

[a]Percentage motile, progressiveness score, percentage survival, and extrapolated total numbers of motile sperm post-thaw. Prefreeze motility values for the control and the bottom fraction were assessed after dilution 1:1 with semen extender.

[b]Means bearing different footnote symbols (c, e, g for percentage motility; d, f, h for progressiveness score; i, j for percentage survival) differ significantly (p 0.05).

(From Glaub, Mills, and Katz[4]).

size of these subpopulations which is adequate for successful artificial insemination is not yet appreciated, and could indeed depend upon the technique of insemination. In any event, it is becoming increasingly evident that sperm numbers of less than 10^7 cells may be adequate for successful insemination. As can be seen from Table 2, such numbers were available post-thaw in this study. Moreover, these subpopulations displayed significantly higher motility quality after thawing than did the parent semen controls. It should be appreciated that the present study involved short-term freezing, and that sperm motility was the sole physiological criterion used to assess the success of the process. Later data does suggest that the differential in motility between isolated and control sperm fractions is maintained after longer-term freezing.   Therefore this new approach appears quite promising in studies of the cryobiology of human spermatozoa, and in their practical application to semen storage and artificial insemination.

REFERENCES

1.   Beck, W.W. and Silverstein, I.   Variable motility recovery of spermatozoa following freeze preservation. Fertil Steril, 26:863, 1975.

2.   Friberg, J. and Gemzell, C.   Insemination of human sperm after freezing in liquid nitrogen vapors with glycerol or glycerol-egg yolk-citrate as protective media. Am. J. Obstet. Gynecol., 116:330, 1973.

3.   Friberg, J. and Gemzell, C.   Sperm-freezing and donor insemination. Int. J. Fertil. 22:149, 1977.

4.   Glaub, J.C., Mills, R.N. and Katz, D.F. Improved motility recovery of human spermatozoa after freeze preservation via a new approach. Fertil. Steril., 27:1283, 1976.

5.   Sawada, Y. and Ackermann, D.R. Use of frozen semen. In: Progress in Infertility, First Edition. Behrmann, S.J. and Kistner, R.W. eds., Boston, Little, Brown and Co, pp. 731, 1969.

6.   Sherman, J.K. Synopsis of the use of frozen human semen since 1964: State of the art of human semen banking. Fertil. Steril., 24:397, 1973.

7.   Silbert, J.A. Large-scale preservation of human semen. Cryobiology, 9:556, 1972.

8.   Smith, K.D. and Steinberger, E. Survival of spermatozoa in a human sperm bank: Effects of a long-term storage in liquid nitrogen. JAMA, 223:774, 1973.

9.   Steinberger, E. and Smith, K.D. Artificial insemination with fresh or frozen semen: A comparative study. JAMA, 223:778, 1978.

10. Tyler, E.T. The clinical use of frozen semen banks. Fertil Steril., 24:413, 1973.

11. Behrman, S.J. and Sawada, Y. Heterologous and homologous inseminations with human semen frozen and stored in a liquid-nitrogen refrigerator. Fertil Steril., 17:457, 1966.

12. Ericsson, R.J., Langevin, C.N. and Nishino, M. Isolation of
     fractions rich in human Y sperm. Nature, 246:421, 1973.

13. MacLeod, J. and Gold, R. The male factor in fertility and in-
     fertility. IV. Semen quality and certain other factors in
     relation to ease of conception. Fertil. Steril., 4:10, 1953.

14. MacLeod, J. and Gold, R.Z. The male factor in fertility and
     infertility. III. An analysis of motile activity in the
     spermatozoa of 1000 fertile men and 1000 men in infertile
     marriages. Fertil. Steril., 2:187, 1951.

15. Hartman, H.G. Correlations among criteria of semen quality.
     Fertil. Steril., 16:632, 1965.

16. Santomauro, A.G., Sciarra, J.J. and Varma, A.O. A clinical
     investigation of the role of the semen analysis and post-
     coital test in the evaluation of male infertility. Fertil.
     Steril., 23:245, 1972.

17. Eliasson. R. Analysis of semen. In: Progress in Infertility,
     Behrmann, S.J. and Kistner, R.W. eds. Boston, Little, Brown and
     Co, pp. 691, 1975.

18. Ericsson, R.J. Isolation and storage of progressively motile
     human sperm. Andrologia, 9:111, 1977.

MOTILITY OF HUMAN SPERMATOZOA AFTER

MIGRATION IN BOVINE SERUM ALBUMIN

Claudette Jeulin

Centre d'Etude et de Conservation
   (CECOS), Kremlin-Bicêtre
Kremlin-Bicêtre, France

Isolation of motile spermatozoa has often been attempted for experimental purposes as well as in an effort to resolve certain problems of male hypofertility. A study by Ericsson et al. in 1973 on migration characteristics of spermatozoa in bovine serum albumin (BSA) solutions showed that it was possible not only to isolate a population which contains a majority of Y bearing spermatozoa but also to significantly increase the proportion of motile forms.[1] These results were contested by Evans et al. and Schilling and Thormaëhlen who found no change in these parameters;[2,3] and Ross et al. were able to determine only an augmentation of motile forms.[4] However, Ericsson's findings have been supported by Broer et al.[5] and David et al.[6,7] who both found a marked isolation of motile forms and Y bearing spermatozoa.

The variability of the above findings are very possibly due to the fact that motility has been subjectively evaluated. The purpose of this study is to objectively analyse spermatozoa motility after migration in BSA as a function of albumin concentration using a Laser Doppler Velocimêter (LDV). This device makes it possible to determine not only the proportion of motile forms but also the instantaneous characteristic velocity and a velocity distribution.

METHODS AND MATERIALS

Semen samples obtained from student volunteers were collected at the laboratory through masturbation. The mean number of spermatozoa was 110×10^6/ml (46 to 199×10^6) of which an average of 65% were motile (50 to 75%).

After liquefaction and less than 1 hour after collection, the semen was diluted volume for volume with Tyrode's solution (pH: 7.5; osmolarity: 285 mOsm./kg; viscosity: 1 centipoise), centrifuged (600 g, 15 min) and then resuspended in the volume of Tyrode's solution necessary to obtain a final concentration of 100 $x10^6$/ml.

Eight ejaculates from three subjects were studied. Glass test tubes were prepared by first adding 1.8 ml of a solution of BSA and Tyrode's solution at BSA concentrations (weight to volume) of either 5, 7.5, 10, 15, 20 or 25%. The pH was adjusted to 7.5 in all cases.

The osmolarity varied from 300 to 320 mOsm/kg and the viscosity from 1 to 2.5 centipoises according to the BSA concentration. Due to its limited volume, one ejaculate could be tested with only three different BSA concentrations. One ml of the spermatozoa suspension (100 $x10^6$ spermatozoa) was carefully placed in the test tube so that an interface was maintained between it and the BSA solution. At this point the tubes were left undisturbed at room temperature for one hour, a migration time chosen based upon preliminary trials which showed sedimentation of non-motile forms in the BSA after 1 1/2 to 2 hours. After migration, the spermatozoa suspension was removed and the BSA solution separated into two equal fractions: F_1 and F_2 according to Figure 1. Only the F_2 fraction was evaluated in this study in order to avoid the artifacts of diffusion and sedimentation which may affect that portion of the BSA adjacent to the spermatozoa suspension.

The following tests were carried out on the F_2 fraction: A sperm count by means of a hemocytometer; determination of the percentage of motile forms by microscopic examination of a 20 μl sample on a glass slide under a cover slip (suspension thickness = 28 μm), ten microscopic fields being observed for each F_2 fraction; and the velocity distribution and characteristic velocity as measured by LDV.[8] LDV analysis has been used by Jouannet et al.[9] to show that spermatozoa in seminal fluid have a unimodal velocity distribution which defines a Poisson curve, the velocities ranging from 0 to 150 μm/sec and corresponding to an exponential light scattering frequency spectrum.

RESULTS

Percentage of Motile Forms (Figure 2)

The eight samples of washed spermatozoa had a mean motility of 50% and a mean semen count of 65 $x10^6$/ml. In order to make the results on the percent of motile forms obtained through the analysis of F_2 more meaningful, the samples were grouped according to 3 ranges of BSA concentration. For the BSA media with concentrations of 5

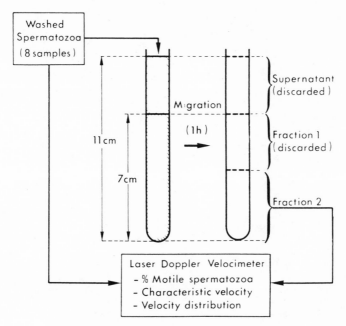

FIGURE 1.   Experimental procedure.

to 7.5%, 10 to 15% and 20 to 25%, the semen count and percentage of motile spermatozoa recovered were respectively 8.5 x10^6 and 26%, 6.5 x10^6 and 20%, and 3 x 10^6 and 9%. For each of these concentration ranges, 90% of those spermatozoa isolated were motile.

Velocity Distribution

In Tyrode's solution, spermatozoa velocities were distributed according to a Poisson curve, as is also observed in seminal fluid. However, the distribution was progressively modified as the BSA concentration increased(Table 1). For example, for one ejaculate tested with a 10% BSA solution(Figure 3), the migrated spermatozoa were still found to have a Poissonian velocity distribution but a cut-off was observed at low velocities, there being no spermatozoa with a velocity below 36 μm/sec. This suggests a filtering effect of the medium. Therefore, at least for this sample, 36 μm/sec could be considered as a velocity "threshold". However, no such threshold was observed in 5 out of 24 tests(Figure 4).

TABLE 1. *Characteristic velocity, velocity distribution and threshold velocity for different spermatozoa populations(semen samples) before and after washing and migration as a function of albumin(BSA) concentration.*

	Number of samples	Mean character- istic velocity (µm/s)	Number with Poissonian distribution	Number present- ing a threshold velocity	Mean threshold velocity (µm/s)
Fresh semen	8	58	8/8	0	-
Washed spermatozoa	8	69	8/8	0	-
BSA: 5 %	6	83	6/6	3/6	34
7.5%	2	85	2/2	2/2	45
10 %	6	81	4/6	4/6	35
15 %	4	-	1/4	4/4	56
20 %	4	-	0/4	4/4	38
25 %	2	-	0/2	2/2	45

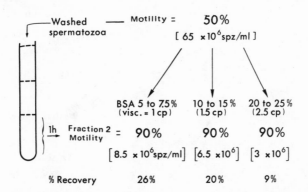

FIGURE 2. The effect of migration in BSA on spermatozoa (SPZ) motility(%) and the sperm count(SPZ/ml).

At BSA concentrations of 15%, 20% and 25%, the velocity distribution no longer conformed to a Poisson curve(Table 1). In fact, the distribution observed was close to that of a cut-off Gauss curve as shown for one sample in Figure 3-C. There appears to have been a population selection in that spermatozoa with high and low velocities were eliminated.

Characteristic Velocity

The mean characteristic velocity after migration in 5, 7.5 and 10% BSA was respectively 83, 85 and 81 μm/s, velocities somewhat higher than those found in Tyrode's solution and seminal fluid which were 69 and 58 μm/s respectively (Table 1). However, it was not possible to determine the Vc for BSA concentrations of 15% or greater due to the modifications which occurred in the velocity distributions (Figure 4). This is illustrated in Figure 3 for one sample after migration in 20% BSA.

DISCUSSION

The results of this study showing an increased concentration of motile spermatozoa after migration in BSA support the findings of certain other investigators.[1,4,5,6] For those studies in which

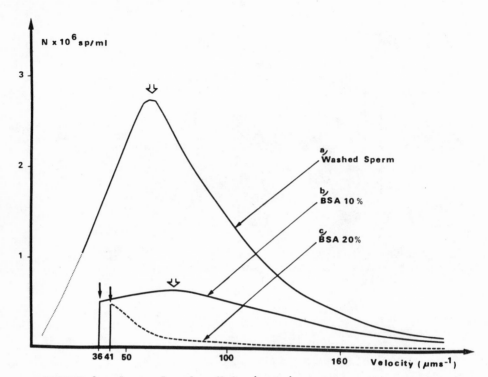

FIGURE 3.   Laser Doppler Velocimetric tests on one semen
sample: Velocity distribution curves for the spermatozoa
after washing(a) and after migration in 10%(b) and 20%(c)
BSA solutions; characteristic velocity(open arrows); and
threshold velocity(solid arrows).

no improvement was noted[2,3] such a result may have been due to the
differences in the experimental conditions such as the time allowed
for migration or the methods used to collect the samples and to measure their characteristics after migration.

The present study has had the advantage of using an objective
measurement technique, Laser Doppler Velocimetry which has made it
possible to carry out a more precise and in depth evaluation of the
effect of BSA on spermatozoa migration. It appears that BSA acts
to impede or retain non-motile forms and forms with low velocities
thus functionning as a "high pass" filter. However, there seems to
be an optimal range of BSA concentration of between 5 and 15% beyond
which a marked loss of spermatozoa with high velocities is observed.

Two hypotheses that can be advanced regarding the modification
of the velocity distribution with high albumin concentrations include the following: A greater medium viscosity slows the more

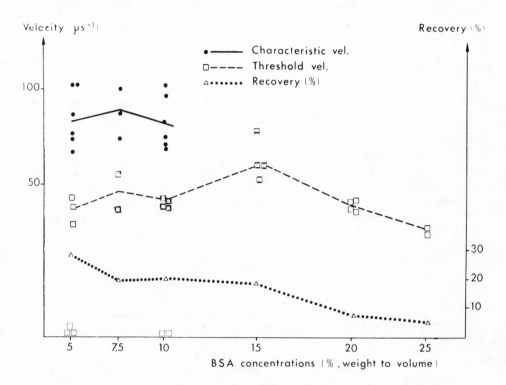

FIGURE 4. Characteristic velocity, threshold velocity and recovery rate after migration as a function of albumin (BSA) concentration.

rapid forms, and albumin depresses spermatozoa activity. In regard
to the former, a survey of the literature revealed only one study
on the effect of medium viscosity: Brokaw[10] has shown that the
effect of 4 to 16 fold increases in viscosity on the beat frequency
of sea urchin spermatozoa reactivated with ATP were nearly undetec-
table at low ATP concentrations whereas at high ATP concentrations,
beat frequency decreased as viscosity increased. Considering the
comparatively negligable changes of medium viscosity in the present
study, it is not likely that it had a significant effect on migration.
Only for those BSA concentrations in which the velocity distribution
curve remains Poissonian(BSA = 5, 7.5 and 10%) has it been possible
to determine a characteristic velocity. The fact that this velocity
is greater for these BSA concentrations than that for either Tyrode's solution or seminal fluid suggests a stimulating effect of the
BSA.

The fertilizing capacity of spermatozoa selected by this technique has been demonstrated clinically. Dmowski et al. have reported 14 pregnancies with 49 couples using artificial insemination with
husband's semen(AIH), 37 of these couples having requested the technique in hope of having male offspring.[15,16] However, Glass et al.
have obtained no pregnancies with 19 couples so treated. We have
yet to demonstrate the efficacy of this technique with our cases
of AIH.

REFERENCES

1. Ericcson, R.J., Langevin, C.N. and Nishino M. Isolation of
       fractions rich in human Y sperm, Nature, Lond., 246:421-424,
       1973.

2. Evans, J.M., Douglas, T.A. and Renton, J.P. An attempt to separ-
       ate fractions rich in human Y sperm. Nature, Lond., 253:
       352-354, 1975.

3. Schilling, E. und Thormäehlen, D. Versuche zur trennung von X
       and Y spermien aufgrund ihrer unterschiedlichen wanderungs-
       gesch win digkeit. Zuch. Thyg., 10:188-190, 1975.

4. Ross, A., Robinson, J.A. and Evans, H. Failure to confirm sep-
       aration of X and Y bearing human sperm using BSA gradients.
       Nature, Lond., 253:354-355, 1975.

5. Broer, K.H., Herrmann, W.P. and Kaiser, R. Semen analysis and
       Y chromatin positive spermatozoa. In: Proceedings of the
       First International Congress of Andrology, FC44, Barcelona,
       1976.

6. David, G., Jeulin, C., Léonard, C., Boyce, A. and Schwartz, D.
    Attempt to increase the percentage motility and the percent-
    age of Y bearing spermatozoa in human sperm. IV ESCO, Madrid,
    1975.

7. David, G., Jeulin, C., Boyce, A. and Schwartz, D. Motility and
    percentage of Y and YY bearing spermatozoa in human semen
    samples after passage through bovine serum albumin. J. Re-
    prod. Fert,, 50:377-379, 1977.

8. Dubois, M., Jouannet, P., Bergé, P., Volochine, B., Serres, C.
    and David, G. Méthode et appareillage de mesure objective
    de la mobilité des spermatozoïdes humains. Ann. Phys. Biol.
    et Med., 9:19-41, 1975.

9. Jouannet, P., Volochine, B., Deguent, P., Serres, C. and David,
    G. Scaterring determination of various characteristic para-
    meters of spermatozoa mobility in a serie of human sperm.
    Andrologia, 9:34-49, 1977.

10. Brokaw, C.J. Effects of viscosity and ATP concentration on the
    movement of reactivated sea urchin sperm flagella. J. Exp.
    Biol., 62:701-719, 1975.

11. Harrison, R.A.P., Dott, H.M. and Foster, G.C. Effect of ionic
    strength, serum albumin and other macromolecule on the main-
    tenance of motility and the surface of mammalian spermatozoa
    in a simple medium. J. Reprod. Fert., 52:65-73, 1978.

12. Eliasson. R., Oxygen consumption of human spermatozoa in seminal
    plasma and a ringer solution. J. Reprod. Fert., 27:385-389,
    1971.

13. Lindholmer, C.H. and Eliasson, R. The effects of albumin, mag-
    nesium and zinc on human sperm survival in different frac-
    tions of split ejaculates. Fert. Steril., 25, 5:424-430,
    1973.

14. Lindholmer, C.H. The importance of seminal plasma for human
    sperm motility. Biol. Reprod., 10:533-542, 1974.

15. Dmowski, W.P., Gaynor, L., Rao, R., Lawrence, M. and Scommegna, A.
    Use of albumin gradients for X and Y sperm separation and
    clinical experience with male sex preselection. Fertil.
    Steril., 31:52-57, 1979.

16. Dmowski, W.P., Gaynor, L., Lawrence, M., Rao, R. and
     Scommegna, A. Artificial insemination homologous with oli-
     gospermic semen separated an albumin columns. Fertil. Ster-
     il., 31:58-62, 1979.

17. Glass, R.H. and Ericsson, R.J. Intrauterine insemination of
     isolated motile sperm. Fertil. Steril., 29:535-538, 1978.

PHARMACODYNAMIC STUDIES ON HUMAN SPERMATOZOA MOTILITY

IN VITRO BY USES OF LASER DOPPLER SPECTROSCOPY

R. Steiner,[*] N. Hofmann,[**] R. Hartmann,[*]
T. Baumeister[*] and R. Kaufmann[*]

[*]Physiology Institute, Dusseldorf University,
Dusseldorf, West Germany

[**]Dermatology clinic, Research Center in Andrology
Dusseldorf, West Germany

With the aid of laser doppler spectroscopy, it has become possible to determine motility parameters of living spermatozoa within a few minutes. This fast and objective method enabled us to perform studies concerning pharmacological effects on sperm motility which are presented in this paper.

Figure 1 is a schematic drawing of the experimental setup. The beam of a CW HeNe laser (1mW) is directed into a special cuvette or capillary which contains the native semen or resuspended spermatozoa. Part of the incident light is scattered by the spermatozoa and if they move, the frequencies shift (Doppler Effect) by a few Hertz. To detect this small frequency shift, the scattered light is mixed with a fixed frequency light coming from stationary scatterers. This allows intensity fluctuations to be easily detected by a photodetector which produces an electrical signal proportional to the intensity of light fluctuations. The frequency spectrum of the statistical fluctuations provides complete information about the motion of the spermatozoa. Signal processing is done either by frequency analysis to obtain the power spectrum or by forming the autocorrelation function (ACF) of the signal in an appropriate autocorrelator.

We used a minicomputer (Plurimat S, Intertechnique), which forms the ACF and extracts the mean spermatozoa velocity parameters using this ACF.

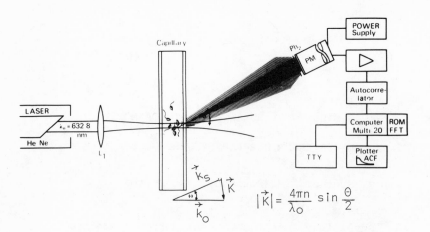

FIGURE 1. Schema of the experimental apparatus.

The computer further controls sample exchange by activating an electrically driven sample stage in which up to ten samples can be mounted. This device enables dose response investigations for test substances or pharmaca over any desired period of time with homogeneous spermatozoa samples using only one experimental setup.

Pharmacological experiments often require the separation of spermatozoa from the seminal liquid in order to avoid undesired effects. For this purpose the spermatozoa are washed twice in an isotonic saline solution following an improved procedure published by Peterson and Freund.[1] They are subsequently resuspended in the same solution and eventually diluted for use in the experiment.

To prevent the growth of bacteria during prolonged experiments, Penicillin G(1M IU/l) and Streptomycin (500mg/l) were added to the suspension medium.

Washing alone induces a decrease in the mean velocity of spermatozoa which drops to about 70% of the initial value. However, the addition of ut to 10mM of glucose can compensate for this depression of motility. Unfortunately, glucose is not equally effective for all samples. The stimulating effect of glucose may be attributed to an increased respiratory rate induced by the washing procedure.[2]

Obviously, sperm motility also depends on the medium. In order to create conditions similar to those in seminal plasma, we introduced human serum albumin (HSA) at different concentrations. The results have been previously reported.[3] Unfortunately, HSA has rather complicated binding properties for many substances and, therefore, might be a handicap in pharmacological studies. As a substitute, a 6% dextran solution has been tried. The effect was negative with the

motility being even more depressed. Therefore, additives which may.
replace HSA are not presently known.

For clinical andrological studies, we investigated substances
such as kallikrein, prostaglandins, caffeine, and others with respect
to their stimulating effects on sperm motility *in vitro*. Figure 2
shows the dose-response curve for kallikrein and the mean sperm velocity. A maximum stimulating effect was observed at 4Kμ/ml. Kallikrein is thought to liberate kinins from inactive kininogen, and
the former is suggested to be responsible for the stimulation of
motility. The full biochemical pathway or mechanism of action of
kallikrein is not yet known. One possible mechanism was suggested
by Palm et al.[4] who proposed that liberated kinins induce prostaglandin synthesis or liberation which in turn acts on the cyclic-
AMP as the second messenger system.

Infertile men turned out to have only 1/3 of the normal prostaglandin concentration in their seminal plasman.[5] However, reinves-
tigations on prostaglandins have demonstrated that this explanation
is too simple. From the prostaglandins investigated so far, only
PGE_2 showed a significant positive effect on sperm motility (figure
3). The maximum effective dose was 0.3μg/ml. The same figure shows
the ineffectiveness of PGE_1. $PGF_1\alpha$, which is not represented in
this figure also had no measurable effect. The stimulation by PGE_2

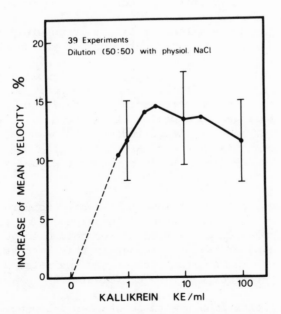

FIGURE 2. Effect of kallikrein on mean spermatozoa velocity.

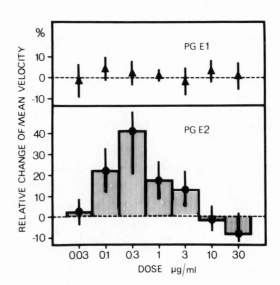

FIGURE 3. Effect of prostaglandins on mean spermatozoa velocity *in vitro.*

could be partially blocked by the addition of salicylic acid which inhibits the prostaglandin producing enzyme (figure 4), whereas the kallikrein induced stimulation was not inhibited by salicylic acid. This suggests different mechanisms for the kallikrein and PGE_2 induced stimulation of spermatozoa motility or possibly the involvement of additional substances or pathways not yet known.

Another substance featuring impressive stimulating effects is caffeine. Figure 5 shows the result of an 8 hour experiment. A rapid increase in mean velocity during the first 30 minutes after application is followed by a period of enhanced velocity which after about 1 1/2 hours, however, drops suddenly below the initial value. The experiment shown in figure 5 has been carried out under the influence of cyclic-AMP (10mM) in both the control and in the test sample.

Nevertheless, subsequent investigations demonstrated that the same kind of effect occurs with caffeine alone. The rapid drop cannot yet be explained. Electron microscopic observations made by Harrison and Sheppard[6] may be relevant in this context. They found severe alterations in the structure of the spermatozoa membrane and in the midpiece after exposure to caffeine.

Amongst the experiments with substances reducing motility, arachidonic acid was most effective. Figure 6 gives a representative

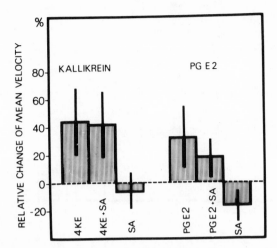

FIGURE 4. Effect of salicylic acid alone and associated with kallikrein and prostaglandins on mean spermatozoa velocity *in vitro*.

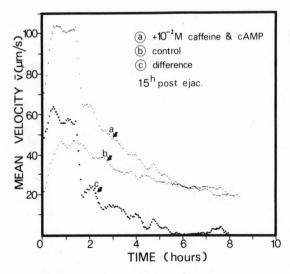

FIGURE 5. Effect of caffeine and cyclic AMP on mean spermatozoa velocity *in vitro*.

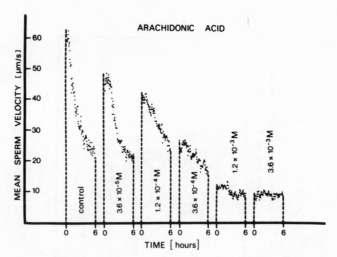

FIGURE 6. Effect of arachidonic acid on mean spermatozoa velocity *in vitro*.

example of such an experiment carried out over a period of 6 hours.

Arachidonic acid (3.6×10^{-5}M) led to a decrease of motility immediately after application. A hundredfold concentration caused all motility to cease. Figure 7 shows the relevant dose-response curves for arachidonic acid, $CuSO_4$, thiourea, and NaF.

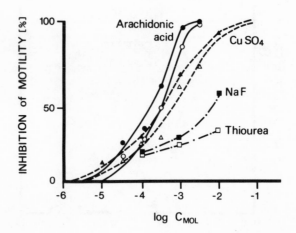

FIGURE 7. Inhibitory effect on spermatozoa motility of increasing concentrations of Arachidonic acid, $CuSO_4$ NaF and Thiourea *in vitro*.

The curves of the first two substances are split because of different initial motility of spermatozoa samples. Samples with high initial motility were found to be more sensitive than samples with low motility. The inhibitory effect of other anorganic componets such as Hg $(NO_3)_2$, $NiCl_2$, $CdSO_4$ not shown here did not significantly affect motility.

REFERENCES

1. Peterson, R.N. and Freund, M.   Reversible Inhibition of the Motility of Human Spermatozoa by Tetraphenylboron. J. Reprod. Fert. 47, 33-38, 1976.

2. Bishop, D.W.   Sperm Motility. Physiological Reviews, 42:1, 1962.

3. Steiner, R., Hofmann, N., Hartmann, R. and Kaufmann, R.   Die Anwendung der Laser Doppler Spektroskopie zur Analyse der Spermatozoen-Motilität in Verschiedenen Medien. Fortschritte der Fertilitätsforschung V, Grosse Verlag, 1977.

4. Palm, S., Schill, W.B., Wallner, O., Prinzen, R. and Fritz, H. Occurence of components of the kallikrein-kinin system in human genital tract secretions and their possible function in stimulation of sperm motility and migration. In : Kinins Pharmacodynamics and Biological Roles, eds : Sicuteri, F., Back, N., Haberland, G.L., Plenum Publishing Corporation, New York, 1976.

5. Bydgeman, M., Fredericsson, B., Svanbork, K. and Samuelsson. 1970. The relation between Fertility and Prostaglandin Content of Seminal Fluid in Man. Fert. Ster., 21, 622-629.

6. Harrison, R.F. and Sheppard, B.L.   Electron Microscopy Studies in Spermatozoa Energized by Caffeine. Vth ESCO, Venice, 1978.

LABORATORY ANALYSIS OF SPLIT EJACULATES

Georges Grignon* and André Clavert**

*Laboratoire de Biologie Médicale, Faculté de Médecine B
Nancy, France.
**Laboratoire d'Embryologie, Faculté de Médecine
Strasbourg, France.

From the works of Mac Leod and Hotchkiss in 1942[1] and Lundquist in 1949,[2] it is generally accepted that during ejaculation in man, the accessory sex glands always secrete in the following order: Cowper's glands, prostate, seminal vesicles. Epididymal fluid which contains the spermatozoa is liberated after release of prostatic fluid and is usually found highly concentrated in the first fraction of split ejaculate. One can therefore obtain a high concentration of male gametes to be used in artificial insemination by collecting this first fraction and thus eliminate problems associated with laboratory manipulation of the entire sample.

The purpose of the present study was to determine the concentration and motility of spermatozoa as a function of the fraction in a split ejaculate and to determine variation in motility with time, also as a function of the fraction.

MATERIALS AND METHODS

Two groups of donors were taken randomly from clinical andrological consultations. Fifty subjects divided their ejaculate into three fractions and fifty others into two. When the volume of ejaculate allowed, we measured volume, concentration of spermatozoa, sperm motility at one and six hours after ejaculation, and fructose content.

RESULTS

Variation in Concentration of Spermatozoa

Ejaculation in Three Fractions. In each of the fractions we measured the percentage of variation in the concentration as a function of the calculated concentration of the total ejaculate. The mean concentration in the first fraction(F1) was 66% higher than that of the total concentration. It was 8% lower in F2 and 36% lower in F3. The highest concentration of spermatozoa is found in F1 in 76% of the subjects, F2 in 12% and F3 in 12%. If we consider only the fraction having the highest concentration, the mean increase is 104%(83.37 percentile).

Ejaculation in two fractions. In 82% of the subjects, F1 had the highest concentration and the mean increase in the fraction having the highest concentration was 107.4%(102.85 percentile).

Factors which Influence the Quality of the Fraction

Total Volume of Ejaculate. A statistical study showed that there exists a correlation between total volume of ejaculate and increase in concentration of spermatozoa within the richest fraction. (coefficient of correlation:+0.378 per 100 subjects, p= 0.01). In other words, the greater the total volume, the greater the concentration within the richest fraction. However, in seven cases the volume was abnormally high(i.e. greater than 6 cc) and the technique was no longer applicable.

Differences in Fructose Content Between F1 and F3. We observed a correlation between the increase in concentration within the highest fraction and the percent of increase of fructose between the F1 and F3 fractions(coefficient of correlation= 0.481 per 43 subjects, p= 0.01). Therefore the greater the separation between seminal vesicle fluid secretion and prostatic secretion, the higher the concentration of spermatozoa in the richer fraction.

Concentration and Number of Spermatozoa in Total Ejaculate. Statistically, in the one hundred cases investigated, we were unable to show a relationship between the total number of spermatozoa and the increase in concentration in the richest fraction. It therefore appears that the quality of the fraction depends not on the number of spermatozoa present but rather on the secretions of the glands of the reproductive tract.

Variations in Spermatozoa Motility in

the Different Fractions of Ejaculate

Motility at one hour. This study was made on the 50 subjects

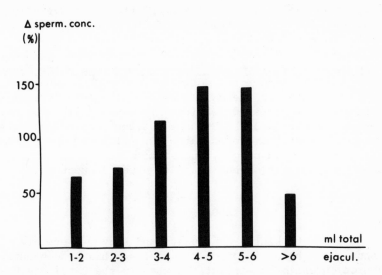

FIGURE 1. Role of the total volume in the efficiency of the split ejaculate technique.

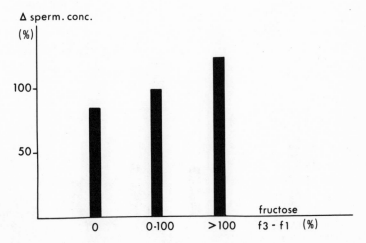

FIGURE 2. Role of the differences in fructose content between F1 and F3 in the increase in concentration of spermatozoa.

whose ejaculate was divided into three fractions. We compared motility in F1 and F3. In F1, a mean of 23.8% of the spermatozoa had good motility(variance= 144.63) while in F3 this mean was only 15.5%(variance= 176.18). Analysis showed that the two means were significantly different(p= 0.05).

Loss in Motility Between One Hour and Six Hours after Ejaculation. We compared loss in total motility in the F1 to the motility of the total ejaculate for the same subject. The mean loss of motility in the ejaculate was 19% while in F1 it was 23%. The number of cases studied was 25 and the Student's t test showed that the two means were significantly different at 0.01. Fluid in the F1 which is primarily prostatic in origin, increases motility of spermatozoa at the moment of ejaculation but their survival is reduced.

DISCUSSION

Mac Leod and Hotchkiss,[1] Lundquist[2] and Harvey[3] were among the first to show that the split ejaculate yields a higher concentration of spermatozoa in one of the fractions than in the total ejaculate.

Our results confirm these observations: In general, the richest fraction has a concentration about 100% higher than the total. There exists a great variation between subjects. In some cases, the increase can be as high as 400%. Regardless of whether the ejaculate was collected in two or three fractions, the mean increase was the same.

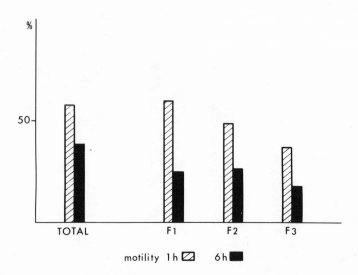

FIGURE 3. Variation in spermatozoa motility in the different fractions of the ejaculate and in the total semen.

In 75 to 80% of the subjects the F1 was the richest in spermatozoa. Prior to artificial insemination it is therefore necessary to test the concentration within the various fractions.

Further analysis allowed us to ascertain that the total volume of ejaculate plays an important role in the efficiency of the split ejaculate technique: The greater the volume of the ejaculate, the greater the increase in the richest fraction. However, in cases where the volume was abnormally high(6 ml) this relationship no longer held(Figure 1).

The concentration effects depend on the separation between secretions of the seminal vesicles and the prostate gland. This observation is supported by the fact that the greater the increase in fructose concentration between F1 and F3, the better the result (Figure 2).

Lindholmer[4] and Lindholmer and Eliason[5] insist that the spermatozoa are more mobile in the first fraction but their survival rate is reduced, probably because the composition of semen in this fraction is different than that of the total.

We have also observed this difference in motility of spermatozoa in the different fractions. We also noted that survival or spermatozoa in the split fraction was reduced compared to that of the total ejaculate(Figure 3).

CONCLUSION

The technique of split ejaculate permits an increase of about 100% in the concentration of spermatozoa. In 76% of the cases studied, the first fraction was the richest, having a greater mobility but a lower survival rate than the total ejaculate. The high variability in our results shows that individual factors intervene in this technique. One of these factors is probably related to the volume of the various secretions.

This technique can be favorably used in artificial insemination either to concentrate spermatozoa in oligospermia or to increase the number of motile spermatozoa in asthenospermia.

REFERENCES

1. Mac Leod, J. and Hotchkiss, R.S. The distribution of spermatozoa and certain chemical constituents in the human ejaculate. J. Urol., 48:225, 1942.

2. Lundquist, F. Aspects of the biochemistry of human semen.

Acta Physiol. Scand., 19, suppl. 66:7, 1949.

3. Harvey, C. The use of proportioned ejaculates in investigation
    the role of accessory secretion in human semen. Stud. Fert.,
    8:3, 1956.

4. Lindholmer, C. Survival of human spermatozoa in different
    fractions of split ejaculates. Fertil, Steril., 24:521,
    1973.

5. Lindholmer, C. and Eliasson, R. The effects of albumine, ma-
    gnesium and zinc on human sperm survival in different
    fraction of split ejaculates. Fertil. Steril., 25:425,
    1974.

USE OF WASHED SPERM FOR REMOVAL

OF SPERM ANTIBODIES

Sidney Shulman

Sperm Antibody Laboratory
New York Medical College
New York, U.S.A.

Certain men and certain women develop sperm antibody activity, and this can be demonstrated in the blood serum; in many cases, this activity can also be shown in the genital secretion. The presence of such antibody is generally associated with a reduction in that person's fertility.[1-5] Hence, it is now considered that, among the various mechanisms that may operate in problems of spontaneous infertility, we can separate a group of patients who are said to have "immune infertility".[3] This antibody activity is usually detected and evaluated by methods of sperm agglutination or immobilization. [6,7] These methods can be adjusted in specificity and sensitivity so that they reflect quite well the clinical relevance of the infertile or the fertile condition.

In our studies of a large population of infertile couples using several agglutination techniques, the frequency of positive results in blood serum samples was found to be 15-18% in the women from such infertile couples, and it was found to be 5-9% in the men from such couples. The exact distributions of the antibody findings depend on the particular technique of agglutination that is used. The same methods gave very low values for the frequency of positive results when they were applied to a fertile population.

In order to treat this kind of infertility problem, several methods have evolved; the methods may differ for the two sexes. In selecting those cases where the male partner has the antibody, an insemination method has been thought to be of special interest. The general plan is to try to remove the antibody from the semen after ejaculation, and then inseminate the female partner with this treated product.[8]

DESCRIPTION OF THE PROCEDURE

Our procedure has actually evolved in two major phases. In our early work, we tried to interrupt the attachment of the antibody molecules to the sperm cells by quickly separating the solid and fluid elements of the semen. In contrast, in our more recent work, we have tried to elute the attached antibody from the sperm cells, assuming then that we were too late to prevent the attachment. We can consider each of these approaches, since both of them may merit further study and evaluation. In either approach, we have termed it the Sperm Washing Insemination Method(S.W.I.M.).

Method 1. The couple must come to the laboratory on the date of ovulation, and the man provides a fresh semen sample. The date is chosen according to the basal body temperature chart for that month and for recent months. We usually try to see the couple twice in each cycle, with the second visit being two days after the first visit; thus we try to bracket the date of ovulation between these two treatment days. On each occasion, the semen sample is diluted immediately (to a four-fold extent) and centrifuged gently. The diluent is 4% human serum albumin; this medium maintains the motility very well throughout the series of manipulations. Other investigators have indicated that this medium is very suitable for preservation of sperm motility.[9] The plasma is discarded, and the pellet is re-suspended in a fresh portion of the diluting medium. The centrifuging("washing") is repeated once or twice more. The final pellet is re-suspended in about 0.50 ml of diluent. This final product, after checking motility and sperm count, is then used for insemination. For this purpose, it is important to stress that the cervical mucus must be considered a deleterious material, that is, a trap for any sperm cells that may still have some antibody on the surface. Hence, the mucus is aspirated as thoroughly as possible; then, the washed sperm is inserted in an intra-uterine fashion. A non-absorbent large tampon is inserted(since this sperm suspension is much less viscous than the normal semen), which the woman can pull out in about 6 hours.

Method 2. As in the description above, the couple is seen on two(or more) occasions in each cycle. The semen is quickly diluted with about 20 ml of the 4% human serum albumin, or the man is asked to ejaculate the semen directly into such a supply of the albumin solution. In order to encourage an elution process, this highly diluted material is allowed to sit for two hours, at 37°C. It is then centrifuged as described above, with a final volume again of about 0.50 ml. The insemination process is exactly the same as in the earlier method.

RESULTS

Although motility is well maintained in these procedures, and the sperm cells look excellent in terms of microscope examination, the success rate for pregnancy has been only about 15% of the cases. The procedure has usually been followed for only 3 or 4 cycles. No evaluation has been made as to the degree of success of removing all of the antibody from the sperm cells.

DISCUSSION

A procedure has been studied that is based on the effort to remove some or all of the sperm antibody in the ejaculate of men who have a sperm antibody activity. Furthermore, there is very little discomfort to the woman in this procedure, presumably because of the removing, by washing, of the prostaglandins.

It is not clear, however, that the antibody has really been removed in all cases, and methods, simple and quick methods, need to be developed for such an evaluation. This could be attempted in either of two ways. One way would be by study of the interaction of the sperm populations with a sample of human or bovine cervical mucus, either as a "penetration" method or a "shaking" method.[10] A second possibility, namely a mixed agglutination of sperm cells and red blood cells, could be attempted for making this evaluation.[11]

The concept of intra-uterine insemination seems to be important in this kind of procedure. This kind of insemination procedure has also been utilized by Kremer for treatment of such cases of male infertility; however, he does not attempt to wash the sperm cells. He uses the better quality portion of a split ejaculate; this is usually the first portion. He does remove all the cervical mucus and then inseminates in intra-uterine fashion. This approach is based on his contention that the cervical mucus acts as a trap for sperm that has antibody attached to it. Thus, one must get past the mucus barrier.

It may be that 3 or 4 cycles is not enough to really judge the efficacy of this method; one should apply at least 6 cycles: Perhaps a larger number than that is needed in a new procedure like this one. It may also be that in some cases the woman still has some cryptic problem that has not been diagnosed, and that this is a contributing factor in the failure of the insemination. Further studies and careful analyses may help with these distinctions.

We may conclude that the early method is probably not suitable in most cases, and that we must make better effort to accomplish an elution of the antibody. Methods must now be perfected for a more complete elution, without any significant damage to the sperm cells.

REFERENCES

1. Shulman, S.   Immunologic barriers to fertility.   Obstet. Gynecol. Survey., 27:553, 1972.

2. Shulman, S.   Sperm antibodies as a cause of problems in infertil-
   ity and in vasectomy.   In: Immunology in Obstetrics and
   Gynaecology, Proceedings of the First International Congress,
   Padua, 1973.   Eds. A centaro and N. Caretti, Excerpta Medica,
   Amsterdam, p. 41, 1974.

3. Shulman, S.   Reproduction and antibody response.   CRC Press,
   Cleveland, 1975.

4. Rümke, P. and Hekman, A.   Auto and iso-immunity to sperm in
   infertility.   In: Clinics in Endocrinology and Metabolism.
   4:473, 1975.

5. Behrman, S.J.   The immune response and infertility.   In: Progress in Infertility, 2nd ed., Eds S.J. Behrman and R.J.
   Kistner, Little Brown, Boston, p. 793, 1975.

6. Rose, N.R., Hjort, T., Rümke, P., Harper, M.J.K. and Vyazov, O.
   Techniques for detection of iso and auto-antibodies to
   human spermatozoa.   Clin. Exp. Immunol., 23:175, 1976.

7. Shulman, S.   Human sperm antibodies and their detection.   In:
   Manual of Clinical Immunology, Eds. N.R. Rose and H. Friedman
   Chap. 95, Waverly Press, Baltimore, p. 710, 1976.

8. Shulman, S. Harlin, B., Davis, P. and Reyniak, J.V.   Immune
   infertility and new approaches to treatment.   Fertil. Steril.,
   29:309, 1978.

9. Lindholmer, C. and Eliasson, R.   The effects of albumin, magne-
   sium and zinc on human sperm survival in different fractions
   of split ejaculates.   Fertil. Steril., 25:424, 1974.

10. Kremer, J. and Jager, S.   The sperm cervical mucus contact
    test: A preliminary report.   Fertil. Steril., 27:335, 1976.

11. Jager, S., Kremer, J. and Van Slochteren-Draaisma, T.   A simple
    method of screening for antisperm antibodies in the human
    male.   Detection of spermatozoa surface IgC with the direct
    mixed antiglobulin reaction carried out on untreated fresh
    semen.   Int. J. Fertil., 23:12, 1978.

FERTILIZATION CAPACITY OF FROZEN

SEMEN IN AUTOPRESERVATION

Françoise Czyglik and Georges David

Centre d'Etude et de Conservation du
Sperme(CECOS), Paris-Bicêtre
Kremlin-Bicêtre, France

INTRODUCTION

The retention of fertilizing capacity is a problem basic to semen cryopreservation, regardless of the purpose for which the technique is employed. At present, there are no data which permit one to accurately define the fertilizing capacity of semen after freezing. Emperically, we retain donor semen for use in artificial insemination which has a high sperm count and above all, a high percentage of motile forms after freezing. In effect, donors are selected based upon semen quality in order to increase the probability of obtaining a pregnancy.

The problem with candidates for autopreservation, that is men about to undergo vasectomy or a treatment which will leave them sterile, is different from that with donor candidates in that there can be no selection. However, for both psychological and practical reasons, autopreservation candidates must not be led to believe that all semen can be preserved.

This study will attempt to assess the practicality of autopreservation on a provisional and approximative basis by extrapolating from the results of artificial insemination with frozen donor semen. Even though no single semen characteristic is of proven reliability as a criterion of fertilizing capacity, certain aspects of spermatozoa motility appear to be most relevant. Our experience with donor semen has indicated that a certain minimum level of spermatozoal motility in a paillette is required for fertilization to occur. Although this lower limit of motility can be considered neither definitive nor universal, it is the most meaningful reference that we have been able to identify.

MATERIALS AND METHODS

From January 1973 to December 1978, 648 requests for autocon-
servation were received by CECOS*, 351(54%) prior to vasectomy and
297(46%) prior to sterilizing treatment. Patients in the latter
group presented with the following disorders: Hematologic(Hodgkins'
disease or leukemia: 140 or 47%); urologic(cancer of the testis:
114 or 38%); nephrologic(renal failure: 20 or 7%); neoplastic(different forms of cancer: 23 or 8%).

Two series of controls were used. One consisted of the ejaculate samples from all 377 fertile men who volunteered as semen donors for AID during the same 5 year period. The other included
ejaculate samples from the first 100 donors whose donated semen had
given a pregnancy in single insemination cycles of an AID program
described elsewhere (p. 211).

Techniques

Semen specimens were collected by masturbation at the laboratory. After liquefaction at 37° for 15 to 20 minutes, a portion was
evaluated for sperm count(n) and percentage of motile forms per ml(m).
When n was inferior to 1 million/ml and/or m was inferior to 10%, the
semen was considered unfreezable since experience has shown that in
such cases recovery is essentially nil.

Semen meeting the criteria of freezability was processed as
follows: The ejaculate was diluted volume to volume with cryoprotector medium, allowed to stand at room temperature for 15 minutes,
distributed into 0.25 ml paillettes or straws(IMV. 61300, L'Aigle,
France) and then frozen and stored using liquid nitrogen. In every
100 ml of medium, there was 20 ml of egg-yolk, 15 ml of glycerol,
1.3 g of glucose, 1.15 g of sodium citrate, 1 g of glycerine, 50 mg
of streptomycine and 100,000 IU of penicillin. The pH was adjusted
to 7.4 with NaOH. Freezing was carried out by placing the paillettes
horizontally 25 cm above the surface of liquide nitrogen(-60°C) for
7 minutes. They were then placed directly into the liquid nitrogen
(-196°C) where they were stored.

On the day of collection and freezing, the semen of one paillette was evaluated for the post-thaw percentage of motile forms
(m_1). From m_1 and the number of spermatozoa per paillette(n_1) where
n_1 equals $\frac{n}{2}$ x 0.25, one obtains the number of motile forms per
paillette$(m_1 n_1)$. The percentage of motile forms recovered(r) was
also calculated from m and m_1.

─────────────

* Centre d'Etude et de Conservation du Sperme, Paris-Bicêtre.

RESULTS

Autocryopreservation was not possible in all cases due either to the failure of ejaculation or an inability to meet freezability criteria as detailed in Table 1. In comparison to donor controls non-productive masturbation was slightly more frequent in vasectomy candidates and much more frequent in nephrologic and urologic disorders. Semen insufficiencies were found often in patients with nephrologic and hematologic disorders, and very often in those with testicular cancer.

For the semen considered as freezable, the recovery of motile forms was by far the lowest for men about to undergo sterilizing treatment(Table 2). The number of motile spermatozoa per paillette ($n_1 m_1$) can be compared in Figure 1: The mean $n_1 m_1$ was similar for donors and vasectomy candidates at 5.7 ± 3.2 and 5.6 ± 3 respectively where as it was only 3.2 ± 3.8 for those to be subjected to a sterilizing treatment. The mean $n_1 m_1$ for donors giving a pregnancy was the highest at 8.1 ± 3.8; their lowest $n_1 m_1$ being 1.9 million. This latter figure has been considered as a paillette motility limit, that is the minimum number of motile forms in a paillette for whicn fertilizing capacity has been proven, and has been used to classify paillettes as sufficient or insufficient(Table 3).

If all the factors identified in this study which militate against fertilizing capacity are grouped for vasectomy candidates and for patients to receive sterilizing treatment(Table 4), the

TABLE 1. *Freezing not practicable.*

	Ejaculate origin					
	Pre-Sterilizing treatment Patients				Pre-Vasectomy	Donors
Cause	Hemat.	Urol.	Nephr.	Others		
	140	114	20	23	351	377
Unsuccessful Masturbation	3 (2.1%)	8 (7%)	4 (20%)	1 (4.3%)	17 (4.8%)	6 (1.6%)
Initial Semen insufficiency[1]	25 (17.9%)	27 (23.7%)	2 (10%)	1 (4.3%)	10 (2.8%)	4 (1.1%)

[1]Sperm count $< 10^6$ and/or $< 10\%$ motility before freezing.

TABLE 2. *Semen characteristics according to origin.*

	Vasectomy candidate	Sterilizing treatment candidates	Donors	100 Fertilizing paillettes[1]
Sperm count $(x10^6)$ ($\pm$ SD)	100,5 (50.5)	83.2 (76.6)	104.2 (54.6)	138.5 (69.7)
Pre-freeze motility(%) ($\pm$ SD)	70.7 (7.6)	61.1 (14.2)	70.7 (9.8)	74.5 (7.5)
Post-thaw motility(%) ($\pm$ SD)	43.9 (13.9)	27.9 (16.9)	45.4 (12.4)	52.2 (8.0)
Post-thaw recovery(%) ($\pm$ SD)	62.1 (17.5)	45.7 (22.7)	64.2 (14.8)	70.1 (10.0)

[1]Measurements for the ejaculates from which paillettes were taken.

TABLE 3. *Cryotolerance as related to indications.*

	Pre-Sterilizing treatment				Vasectomy Candidate	Donors
	Hemat.	Urol.	Nephro.	Other		
Number of Cases	112	79	14	21	324	367
Sufficient cryotolerance	63 (56%)	27 (34%)	10 (71%)	15 (71%)	270 (83%)	321 (87%)
Insufficient cryotolerance	49 (44%)	52 (66%)	4 (29%)	6 (29%)	54 (17%)	46 (13%)

TABLE 4. *Semen freezability in autopreservation candidates.*

	Unsuccessful masturbation	Semen insufficiency[1]	Cryotolerance Insufficient[2]	Cryotolerance Insufficient[3]
Vasectomy candidates (351 cases)	4,5%	3%	14.5%	78%
Sterilizing treatment patients (297 cases)	5.5%	18.5%	37%	38%

[1]A sperm count $<10^6$/ml and/or $<10\%$ motility before freezing.
[2]Motile spermatozoa per paillette($n_1 m_1$) $<1.9 \times 10^6$.
[3]Motile spermatozoa per paillette($n_1 m_1$) $>1.9 \times 10^6$.

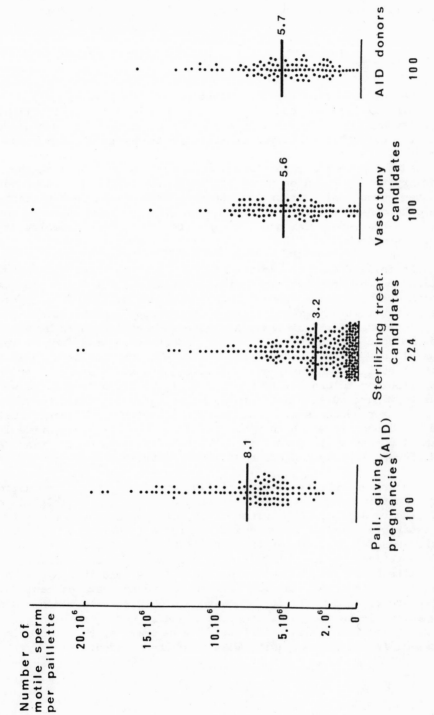

FIGURE 1. Number of motile spermatozoa per paillette (the bar denotes the mean).

difference between them becomes even more pronounced: Overall, 78%
of the former whereas only 38% of the latter present a semen freezability.

DISCUSSION

Vasectomy candidates were found to be very similar to AID donors
regarding failure to produce a semen specimen, inadequate initial
motility and post-thaws recovery of motile forms. This was not the
case for patients to undergo sterilizing treatment who had a greater
number of unsuccessful masturbations and ejaculates with an initially inadequate motility for freezing as well as a lower post-thaw
recovery rate. Based on these criteria, 78% of the vasectomy candidates versus only 38% of the pre-sterilizing treatment patients
could be considered for autocryopreservation in that there is some
evidence that their semen may retain its fertilizing capacity after
frozen storage.

It is difficult to explain the increase in failure of masturbation for the pre-sterilizing treatment group, but their compromised
health status would suggest both physical and psychological causes.
The poorer initial semen quality in this group appears to be related
to the nature of the disease, having been most marked in hematologic
and urologic disorders. Other than hyperthermia, the factors responsible are not yet understood. In this group, the semen's altered
initial quality can as previously demonstrated[1-4] account for the
poor freezing tolerance. Improvements in freezing techniques would
thus be of particular benefit to such patients. It would be useful
to study for each disorder the specific alterations of semen quality
and the manner in which they appear. Such studies may provide information that would permit an earlier decision on semen preservation
and thereby improve the prognosis for preservability.

The semen characteristics of AID donors have been used as controls in this study. One characteristic used as a criteria of fertilizing capacity is the number of motile spermatozoa per paillette
necessary to obtain a pregnancy in a single insemination cycle. This
number was 1.9 million for the first 100 successful donors. However
the tentative status of this figure must be emphasized since its lower limits have not been well explored. It is conceivable that a
paillette with fewer than 1.9 million motile spermatozoa could give
a pregnancy, especially if used with a highly fertile woman. Consequently, it is not possible to refuse a request for semen autopreservation based upon this limit. Nevertheless, the prognosis in
terms of fertilizing capacity must be quite guarded.

REFERENCES

1. Rubin, S.O., Andersson, L. and Bostrom, K. Deep-freeze preserv-
    ation of normal and pathologic human semen. Scand. J. Urol.
    Nephrol., 3:144, 1969.

2. Smith, K.D. and Steinberger, E. Survival of spermatozoa in a
    human sperm bank. Effects of long-term storage in liquid
    nitrogen. J. Amer. Med. Ass., 223:774, 1973.

3. Ulstein, M. Fertility, motility and penetration in cervical
    mucus of freeze-preserved human spermatozoa. Acta Obstet.
    Gynec. Scand., 52:205, 1973.

4. David, G. and Czyglik, F. Tolérance à la congélation du sperme
    humain en fonction de la qualité initiale du sperme.
    J. Gyn. Obst. Biol. Rep., 6:602, 1977.

UROLOGICAL INDICATIONS FOR SPERM PRESERVATION

F. Pontonnier and P. Plante

Urology Service
Hôpital de la Grave
Toulouse, France

INTRODUCTION

In urology, the major indication for semen preservation is
cancer of the testis. Other pathological conditions which may lead
to use of this procedure will also be discussed.

For patients with malignant tumors, semen preservation cannot
be reduced to a simple storage operation; the special psychological
context cannot be disregarded. The perpetuation of life, with the
anguish of death in the background, is strikingly epitomized by this
procedure.

For this problem to be approached correctly, experience is an
undeniable prerequisite, but it is also necessary for the members
of the medical team to act in perfect concert with coordination of
the participants, each being responsible for one phase of the process of semen preservation and delivery.

We have yet to develope a definitive attitude towards guidelines
for collection and distribution for those individuals with malignant
diseases. However, a common way of looking at the question does
exist as a result of frequent joint endeavors and a tacit accord.

In this paper, various treatments used for cancer of the testis
(X-rays, chemotherapy, surgery) will be discussed. We shall also
consider the indications for semen preservation, that is cancer of
the testis and others including mechanical disorders of ejaculation,
organically caused anejaculation, oligospermia and monorchidism.

Effects of Treatments on Spermatogenesis

X-Rays. Their effects were particularly closely studied by
Rowley in 67 volunteers.[5] Between 8 and 600 rads were delivered to
the gonads, most of the subjects undergoing a single radiation session. Their ages varied from 25 to 52. For each, hormonal (testosterone, estrogen, FSH and LH levels) and histological criteria were
analyzed both before and after radiation. This study showed that:
(1) Leydig and Sertoli cells are particularly resistant; and (2) germ
cells are sensitive, the most sensitive being the spermatogonia which
are rapidly affected by more than 8 rads, then the spermatocytes
which are affected at 200 rads and seriously so between 400 and 600
rads and finaly, the spermatides which are affected at higher doses.

Between 50 and 78 rads, oligospermia results, its degree depending on the initial semen quality. Azoospermia does not appear at
these doses. Between 400 and 600 rads, the spermatozoa concentration
falls dramatically over 6 weeks, according to the degree to which
the spermatides are affected. Above 600 rads, Leydig cell modifications and increases in their number are observed. FSH levels depend, as in clinical observations, on the degree of alteration of
the germinal line. The fall of the testosterone level and the rise
of the LH level, seen with high radiation doses, are related to the
Leydig cell involvement.

Evolution of the Germinal Line after Completion of Radiation
Therapy. It is currently recognized in clinical practice that radiation therapy of cancer of the testis does not produce sterility in
men with previously good fertility.[1,2,3] This is the result of the
progress made in the design of radiation sources (photon therapy) and
the skill of radio therapists in cancer treatment centers. The sound
testis usually receives between 40 and 200 rads.

How is the germinal line restored? The more undifferentiated
a cell is, the more it is affected by X-rays. Spermatides, which
are highly differentiated (post-meiotic) cells are 50 times more resistant than spermatogonia. Two points deserve emphasis: (1) Certain spermatogonia, those of type A or Amelar's "young spermatogonia",[1] are more resistant; it is they which are at the origin of
the regeneration since they have not been destroyed; (2) although
the differentiated cells, spermatides and spermatozoids, are more
resistant, they can nevertheless present genetic abnormalities after
being irradiated; it must therefore be recommended that conception
not be envisioned until 18 months after radiation therapy.[2] X-rays
increase the risk of miscarriage, still birth and congenital abnormalities. After being warned of these dangers, couples who do not
desire more children may request vasectomy.

Orecklin's statistics [2] show that out of 77 patients treated
for cancer of the testis(37 by X-rays alone, 21 by lymph mode curettage alone and 19 by both curettage and X rays), 28 desired children: 18 succeeded(65%) and 10 remained sterile. Of the latter, 9
had undergone uni- or bilateral curettage. It should be noted that
among the couples in which the wife became pregnant, there were 6'
spontaneous abortions and one birth of a mongoloïd child.

Histological and biological recovery(spermiogram) are chrono-
logically dissociated. The former occurs much sooner, coinciding
with a gradual decrease in the FSH, the sign of germinal restoration.
According to Rowley,[3] the time required for recovery is: 9 to 18
months for an irradiation of 100 rads; 30 months for an irradiation
of 200 to 300 rads; and 5 years or more for 400 to 600 rads.

Chemical Agents

Chemotherapy is used in urology and elsewhere as an adjuvant
to surgery and X-rays. Its effect on spermatogenesis is less well
known than that of X-rays but it differs from the latter in that it
affects only cells in period of activity through action on RNA and
DNA. Chemotherapy strikes not only cancer cells but healthy ones
as well.

There are several groups of substances: Alkylants, antimetabolites, antibiotics and substances extracted from plants. These
have been classified by Jaffe.[6]

Alkylating agents. The most toxic are Chlorambuci(chloraminophene or Lenkeran) and Cyclophosphamide(Endoxan or Cytoxan). Cumulative doses can produce azoospermia which, according to several
authors, may regress after several years.[7,8]   Among our own patients, we have seen several cases of permanent azoospermia after
treatment of glomerulonephiritis by Chloraminophene. Most alkyla-
tors are teratogenic in animals and most certainly in humans as
well. [9]

Antimetabolites. These are not teratogenic, but may produce
dominant and lethal mutations which are revealed by very early and
hence unrecognized death of the *embryo*. Similarly, recessive mutations, not immediately detectable, may be discovered in the individual several years later or several generations later.

Antibiotics. The most toxic effects are produced by the association actinomycin D - X-rays. Jaffe[6] studied the evolution of
334 children treated for malignant tumors by chemotherapy associated
with surgery or X-rays. The disease had been arrested for at least
5 years. The average age at the time of treatment was 3 and, at
the time of Jaffe's study, 6.   The most common were Wilm's tumors,

neuroblastomas, lymphomas and bone tumors. Of 41 of these patients, who had reached adulthood and had 81 children, those who had been treated for Wilms'tumors(by actinomycine and X-rays) had no children. In the offspring, no increase was observed in perinatal mortality, malformation rate or morbidity. No malignancies were seen in the children born of this series of patients.

Indications for Semen Preservation

There are of two types of indications. First cancer of the the testis and then, all other conditions affecting fertility.

In all these cases, insemination with fresh semen is to be preferred if the volume is sufficient since freezing reduces spermatozoa motility by 30 to 50%. But every specimen reacts differently to temperature change.

Obtaining the ejaculate in cases of retrograde ejaculation and in paraplegia presents special problems. A procedure has recently been developed for the first situation by Delafontaine,[14] who obtained one pregnancy, but with fresh semen. We have obtained a similar result with this procedure. For paraplegics, two methods are used. Cohen[15] prefers rectal electrostimulation whereas Chapelle[16] recommendes, for high paraplegics, intrathecal injection of prostigmine under medical surveillance since a certain risk is involved. Masturbation performed one or two hours after this injection produces ejaculation if T12 and L1 are intact. Because of the dangers of this technique, preservation is advisable if post-thawing motility remains satisfactory(greater than 40%).

A less frequent indication is hypofertility in patients operated on for varicocoele where improvement of motility is observed. Preservation at the peak of improvement can be proposed. We have also preserved semen collected upon spermatocoele puncture performed on a patient who presents deferential agenesia, with spermatozoides present in the epididymial heads. Also less frequently seen are young patients presenting with monorchidisin due to trauma, infection torsion, vascular thrombosis or congenital malformation. We have had occasion to receive requests from this type of patient and we have granted them.

THE EXPERIENCE OF THE SOUTH-PYRENEES CECOS CENTER

WITH PERSONAL REQUESTS FOR PRESERVATION

We have received 13 such requests, 10 due to malignant disease; 7 cases of cancer of the testis, 2 of Hodgkin's disease and one of tumor of the ethmoid; and 3 others including one case each of

spermatocoele, retrograde ejaculation and monorchidism. Preservation
was effected in 8 cases. It was decided against in the 5 remaining
cases with two of these having had previous chemotherapy(1 case of
Hodgkin's disease, 1 of cancer of the testis).

In conclusion, the major indication for semen preservation
occurs in cancer of the testis and other malignant diseases such
as Hodgkin's disease, lymphoma, etc. It can also be useful in congenital or acquired ejaculatory disorders. It can be employed pre-
ventively in monorchidic patients.

Cancer of the testis. [10] Discovery of a testicular tumor more
than any other kind should motivate the general practitioner and
surgeon to consult with a urinary oncology team. The exploration
procedures, from which the treatment plan follows, determine what
will become of the patient. Orchidectomy is performed by way of
an inguinal incision, with initial high ligature of the blood
vessels. Depending on the pathology, hormonal determinations and
lymphographic results, one of several plans may be adopted: Radiotherapy alone, uni- or bilateral lymph mode dissection alone or association of the two; chemotherapy alone or associated with radiotherapy. Bilateral lymph mode curettage is a source of often permanent sterility in a large number of cases.

According to a study performed by Martin [11] (Table 1), germinal
cell tumors represent 93% of all testicular tumors. In a post-
traumatic context, data collected concerned the age of the tumor
patient and the prognosis based upon the histological diagnosis and
the stage. Two tumor types were excluded from this study: Infantile
embryonic carcinoma, occurring between the ages of 3 months and 5
years, and, at the other end of the spectrum, spermatocytic seminoma
affecting men over 50. Semen preservation is to be considered from
adolescence through the forties. We see from the table that its
indications are: Seminoma in its typical form, post-puberty teratoma, embryonic carcinoma of the adult type and complex tumors most
often associating embryonic carcinoma and teratoma.

Procedure Followed for These Patients

If radiotherapy or chemotherapy has already begun, we
prefer to reject preservation since, as we have seen, there is then
a risk of mutation in the more undifferentiated cells of the germinal line which are in a period of cellular activity(meioses).
Spermatozoides descended from these cells and hence possibly damaged
will be produced 2 months after therapy was begun. However, chromosome breakage may also be provoked by X-rays in already mature and
differentiated cells(stocked spermatozoides).

Couples must be warned of the risks of pregnancy in this case.
If a pregnancy occurs, it is advisable to tap the amniotic fluid at

TABLE 1. *Germinal cell tumors (93% of all cases). WHO Classification (Martin*[11]*).*

	Frequency	Major age group	Prognosis		Sensitivity
			2 year survival	15 year survival	
1. Single tumors	3/5				
a. Seminoma (S):					
– typical	35-71%	30-50	92%	75%	X-ray +++
– spermatocytic	rare	50	100%	85%	X-ray +++
b. Embryonic carcinoma (EC):					
– adult type	4-39%	20-30	40%	28%	
– infantile type	60% of tumors of the child.	3 months-3 years	70%	70%	
– polyembryoma	Very rare		40%	0%	
c. Choriocarcinoma (CC	rare	10-30	17%	0%	Chemotherapy
d. Teratoma (T)	40% of tumors of the child	0-30	70%	65%	
e. Tumors on teratomas	Very rare				
2. Complex tumors	2/5 - 14/32%				
EC + T	24%	20-30	50%	40%	
EC + T + S	6.4%	20-30	50%	40%	
EC + S	5%	20-30	40%	28%	
R + S	2%	20-30	72%	64%	
EC + CC + T	1%	20-30	50%	40%	
Other associations	3%				

17 weeks. Malformation can thus be detected and therapeutic abortion considered. In the case of radio or chemotherapy already under way, it is best to ask the couple to put off conception for 18 months.

It is by far Preferable to See the Couple Before Beginning Any Treatment. There are two reasons for this attitude: For one, at this time, there are no risks as regards offspring and, for another, it is of fundamental importance to prepare them psychologically for the future. One is dealing with a young couple, either without children or anxious to have another. Semen preservation has a profound effect on the emotions of the couple, in particular those of the husband who is directly concerned by the disease and for whom it permits the possibility of offspring and biological perpetuation. Semen donation must be integrated into a medical and psychological whole. The surgeon, radiotherapist or chemotherapist can suggest the option of semen preservation but only the physician who collects and analyzes the semen can finally decide for or against. We think it is necessary to warn the couple that the paillettes are destroyed if the husband dies.

Once orchidectomy is performed and the histological diagnosis made, semen collection is indicated for patients with tumors for which the prognosis is good and which are removed at an early stage. It should be carried out 15 to 20 days after the orchidectomy and after 5 days of abstinence. If the sperm count, volume and motility are satisfactory and if the post-thaw test is positive (20 million/cc, 40% motility), we save several ejaculates, obtained at 4 to 5 day intervals. This takes about two weeks, which brings us to about 1 month after the operation. The difficulty in practices lies in having this amount of time at one's disposal; this requires the cooperation of all the members of the medical team. If oligospermia exists at the outset, fractionated collection is used, since in 80% of all cases, the first part is richer than the second.[12]

Semen preservation performed according to these guidelines offers the couple security. It should however, be pointed out that genetic forms of familial cancer exist and are passed from father to son, particularly cancer of the testis.[13]

Other indications

Indications are provided by the presence of an abnormal position of the urethral orifice (hypospadias or surgical sequallae) and sphincter dysfunction due to neuropathy (diabetes), surgical sequellae or destruction of the sympathetic fibers after lombo-abdominal lymph node curettage in cancer of the testis. There are also indications for anejaculation due to paraplegia. These cases involve ballistically inefficient ejaculation (in the case of hypospadia)

or retrograde ejaculation, particularly in the case of resection
or neurological dysfunction of the sphincter.

Here, the advisability of preservation depends upon the individual case. It is worthy of consideration if the husband's work
requires him to be absent during the ovulatory phase. It may also
be of value in that it makes it possible to increase spermatozoid
concentration through the successive collection of several ejaculates. Gain in motility is less certain to be obtained.

REFERENCES

1. Amelar, R.D., Dubin, L. and Hotchkiss, R.S. Restoration of
      fertility following unilateral orchiectomy and radiation
      therapy of testicular tumors. J. Urol., 106:714, 1971.

2. Orecklin, J.R., Faufmann, J.J. and Thompson, R.W. Fertility in
      patients treated for malignant testicular tumor. J. Urol.
      109:293, 1973.

3. Rowley, M.J., Leach, D.R., Warner, G.A. and Heller, C.G. Effect
      of graded doses of ionizing radiation on the human testis.
      Radiat. Res., 59:665, 1974.

4. Frezal, J. and Feingold, J. Genetique In: Frezal, J.,
      Feingold, J. and Tuchmann Duplessis, H. Génétique, Maladies
      du Métabolisme, Embryopathies. Flammarion, Paris, pp. 10-88,
      1971.

5. Baillet, F. and Ciupa, M. Classifications, modes d'action et
      principaux types de chimiothérapie anticancéreuse. VM.,
      18:1607, 1978.

6. Jaffe, N. and Paed, D. Non-oncogenic sequelae of cancer chimo-
      therapy. Radiol., 114:167, 1975.

7. Hinkes, E. and Plotkin, D. Reversible drug-induced sterility
      in a patient with acute leukemia. JAMA., 223:1490, 1973.

8. Sherins, R.J. and Devita, V.T. Effect of drug treatment for
      lymphoma on male reproductive capacity. Studies of men in
      remission after therapy. Ann. Inter. Med., 79:216, 1973.

9. Greenberg, L.H. and Tanaka, K.R. Congenital anomalies probably
      induced by cyclo-phosphamide. JAMA., 188:423, 1964.

10. Delafontaine, D., Taillemite, J.L. and Roux, C.H. La conserva-
      tion de sperme chez les cancéreux jeunes. Contracept. Fert.
      Sexual., 5:131, 1977.

11. Martin, E.D., Rain, B.C., Compain, P. and Imbert, M.C. Anatomie pathologique des tumeurs du testicule. RP., 25:455, 1975.

12. Amelar, R.D. and Hotchkiss, R.S. The split ejaculate. Fertil. Steril., 16:46, 1965.

13. Arcadi, J.A. Testicular neoplasms in father and son. J. Urol. 110:306, 1973.

14. Delafontaine, D., Taillemite, J.L., Colan, J. Cl. and Cornier, E. Ejaculation rétrograde et grossesse. Contracept. Fert. Sexual., 6:345, 1978.

15. Cohen, J. Les stérilités et hypofertilités masculines. Paris, Masson, 1 vol., 244 p., 1977.

16. Chapelle, P.A., Rouffet, M.J. and Pannier, S. Troubles génito-sexuels de l'homme spinal: Eléments de pronostic et déductions thérapeutiques. Contracept. Fert. Sexual., 4:671, 1976.

NEPHROLOGICAL INDICATIONS FOR SEMEN PRESERVATION

Michel Legrain

Service de Nephrologie
Groupe Hospitalier Pitié-Salpêtriere
Paris, France

Many kidney diseases can strike a man at a time which he
desires to be able to procreate. This can lead to sterility in
essentially two ways: The inexorable course of many renal disorders towards kidney failure with associated impotence, and the pre-
scription in certain renal diseases of drugs whose adverse effects
on spermatogenesis are known. Semen preservation represents a means
of alleviating this handicap. It is as yet rarely practiced in so
far as both the general practitioner and the kidney specialist, not
knowing how to judge the risk run by the patient, avoid raising the
question. In this domain, two different situations must be considered, glomerular disease and kidney failure.

Glomerulonephritis

Glomerular disease, often severe, is the most common kidney
disease. It alone accounts for 50% of all patients with terminal
cases of chronic renal failure.

Glomerulonephritis, depending on its clinical and anatomical
features and on the prevailing treatment approach, often consists
of corticosteroid therapy and/or chemotherapy. Among the most
commonly used drugs cited are chloraminophene, azathioprine and
cyclophosphamide.

Corticosteroids, especially when administered in large doses
and for prolonged periods, severely depress spermatogenesis, but
this effect generally seems to be reversible. Consequently, temporary treatment by corticosteroids alone does not carry with it
the risk of permanent sterility.

All forms of chemotherapy used in the treatment of glomerulonephritis,at the doses usually employed, are associated with a high
or very high risk of azoospermia. It is difficult to evaluate from
available data the chances of a recovery resulting in normal spermatozoa, but they seem to be very small.

Under these conditions, we feel that semen preservation should
be envisioned for all male patients with glomerulonephritis or kidney disorders such as those occurring in collagen diseases who are
to be subjected to chemotherapy with or without corticosteroids and
who are likely to desire children.

In the case of a pure nephrotic syndrome in adolescents or
young adults for which intensive but temporary corticosteroid treatment is prescribed, the importance of semen preservation cannot yet
be evaluated. A systematic study of the quality of the semen at a
sufficient distance from this treatment should be undertaken.

Kidney Failure

Statistics show that in the male population aged 15 to 50,
there are 15 new cases per million inhabitants of kidney disease
each year destined to result in terminal kidney failure treatable
only by dialysis or transplantation. These patients are exposed
to a risk of sterility for various reasons.

Impotence frequently occurs and is related to the general non-
specific effects of any severe, prolonged disease as well as by
psychological factors. In certain cases, endocrine and vascular
disorders play an important role. Impotence often persists and sometimes even appears when hemodialysis is instituted. It may disappear, but does not always do so, after a successful kidney transplantation is performed.

Azoospermia may have been induced by chemotherapy used to treat
the kidney disease, usually glomerulonephritis. It may also arise as
a consequence of the corticosteroid treatment and chemotherapy ne-
cessitated by kidney transplantation.

The risk of sterility combined with the duration and quality
of survival which may now be offered to men treated with chronic
terminal kidney failure·has lead us to recommend that semen preservation be routinely proposed to such patients. Taking into account
the possible degeneration in the quality of the semen and the risk
of impotence in advanced chronic kidney failure, we feel semen preservation is indicated when the serum creatinine reaches 30 mg/l.

Observations and Recommendations

The epidemiological data cited above imply that about 20 new kidney patients per million inhabitants each year could benefit from semen preservation. Figures furnished by CECOS-Bicêtre indicate that fewer than 1% of these patients actually use this means of protecting their reproductive potential.

It is up to physicians to inform their patients both of the risks associated with the treatment prescribed and of the possibilities offered by present preservation methods. We are aware of the difficulties which may arise when dealing with young adolescents, an age group for which severe glomerular disease is often a threat. It appears to be important for the patient to be able to collect additional information from persons of his choice, such as another physician, his parents or his wife. It is therefore important that, to the extent possible, the information be furnished early and not be with held until it becomes an emergency issue, that is, a few days before beginning dialysis or even after renal transplantation. In any case, the physician's role is to inform; only the patient can make the decision.

In practice, it is not always possible to obtain a semen specimen. The experience of David and Czyglik indicates that, for reasons which are not always evident but which are likely related to insufficient information, the failure rate in these cases is higher than usual. Semen quality may also be modified, particularly as far as ejaculate volume is concerned. New studies are needed if the origin of these observations is to be understood. However, even if sperm quality is not high, it is better to "over-recommend" semen storage to kidney patients since the ethical and practical condition of subsequent artificial insemination with donor versus husband's semen are very different.

The approach discussed in this paper toward semen preservation is that which is generally taken in the kidney unit of Pitié Salpêtrière. These conclusions were reached in close cooperation with G. David and his coworkers, whom we want to thank for the data which they have provided.

REFERENCE

1. Séminaires d'Uro-Néphrologie de la Pitié-Salpêtrière. Masson, Paris, pp. 84-120, 1979.

DRAFT RECOMMENDATION

ON ARTIFICIAL INSEMINATION OF HUMAN BEINGS

AND EXPLANATORY REPORT

INTRODUCTORY NOTE

1.　The Draft Recommendation and its Draft Explanatory Report were prepared by a Committee of experts of the Council of Europe and adopted by the European Committee on Legal Cooperation(CDCJ).

2.　These texts　are still provisional since they have not yet been examined by the European Committee on Public Health(CDSP) and the Committee of Ministers of the Council of Europe.

A. DRAFT RECOMMENDATION ON ARTIFICIAL

INSEMINATION OF HUMAN BEINGS

The Committee of Ministers,

Considering that the aim of the Council of Europe is to achieve a greater unity between its members in particular through harmonising their legislation on matters of common interest;

Considering that artificial insemination of human beings is increasingly practiced at present in several member States and raises many moral, legal and medical problems;

Considering that the great majority of member States do not possess specific legislation on the matter;

Considering that it would be useful for those States wishing to regulate this matter to do so along uniform lines;

Recommends to the governments of member States which may adopt rules on artificial insemination of human beings or related matters that their law should conform to the rules annexed to this Recommendation.

RULES

ARTICLE 1

These rules apply only to artificial insemination of a woman with the semen of an anonymous donor.

ARTICLE 2

1.   Artificial insemination can be administered only when appropriate conditions exist for ensuring the welfare of the future child.

2.   Artificial insemination shall be administered only on the responsibility of a physician.

ARTICLE 3

1.   No person's semen may be utilised for artificial insemination without his consent.

2.   The consent of the woman and, if she is married, of her husband, is necessary to administer artificial insemination.

3.   The physician responsible for administering artificial insemination shall see that the consent is given in an explicit manner.

ARTICLE 4

A physician or medical establishment receiving semen for artificial insemination must make appropriate medical inquiries and examinations in order to prevent the transmission from the donor of an hereditary condition or contagious disease, or other factor which may present a danger to the health of the woman or the future child. In addition, the physician administering artificial insemination must take all appropriate measures in order to avoid danger to the health of the woman and that of the future child.

ARTICLE 5

The physician and the staff of a medical establishment receiving the donation of semen as well as those administering artificial insemination must keep secret the identity of the donor and, subject to the requirements of law in legal proceedings, the identity of the woman and, if she is married, of her husband, as well as the fact of artificial insemination. The physician shall not administer artificial insemination if the conditions make the preservation of secrecy unlikely.

APPENDIX

ARTICLE 6

1.   No payment shall be made for donation of semen.   However, the loss of earnings as well as travelling and other expenses directly caused by the donation may be refunded to the donor.

2.   A person or a public or private body which offers semen for the purpose of artificial insemination shall not do it for profit.

ARTICLE 7

1.   When artificial insemination has been administered with the consent of the husband the child shall be considered as the legitimate child of the woman and her husband and nobody may contest the legitimacy on the sole ground of artificial insemination.

2.   No relationship of affilation may be established between the donor and the child conceived as a result of artificial insemination. No proceedings for the latter's maintenance may be brought against the donor or by the donor against the child.

B. DRAFT EXPLANATORY REPORT

1. Introduction

1.   Resolution(78) 29 on the harmonization of the legislation of member States relating to removal, grafting and transplantation of human substances, which was adopted by the Committee of Ministers on 11 May 1978, in its paragraph 2 of Article 1 of the annexed rules, excludes from its field of application "the transfer of embryos, the removal and transplantation of testicles and ovaries and the utilisation of ova and sperm".

In fact, due to the particular nature of the problems created by these operations, it was agreed that special rules should be elaborated because of the serious legal and moral consequences particularly those concerning filiation.

2.   This Recommendation deals only with one of the subject not covered by Resolution(78) 29 as it limits itself to the utilisation of semen for artificial insemination. In fact, it was thought that this was the most urgent problem to be studied at present.

3.   Artificial insemination of human beings, is at present practiced in several member States as a remedy for childlessness due to male infertility or any hereditary conditions existing in the couple which would make it undesirable for them to procreate because of the possibility of the conditions being transferred to the child or his descendants. Since the number of childless couples is substantial, recourse to artificial insemination has become more frequent in certain member States in recent years as a result of difficulties in

adoption and of changing social attitudes and technical developments. This practice, although it resolves a family problem, raises also a number of moral, legal and medical issues, which range from the gratuitous character of the semen donation to the legal status of a child conceived as a result of this operation.

4.   Very few member States possess legal provisions on the subject, and those which exist deal only with the problem of affiliation. It is evident that, in the near future, a number of member States, especially those in whose territory artificial insemination is frequently practiced, will introduce specific legislation in this field in order to rectify injustices which may result from the application of the general legislation on affiliation and to curb any abuses of this practice.

As the aim of the Council of Europe is to achieve a greater unity between its members, in particular through harmonizing their legislation on matters of common interest, the Committee of Ministers by this Recommendation recommends the governments of member States, if they introduce legislation on artificial insemination of human beings and related matters, to do so in conformity with the rules annexed to this Recommendation. So as to achieve a harmonized regulation of the problem in Europe.

5.   This Recommendation contains rules which constitute a minimum solution to the problem of artificial insemination. The States may thus adopt additional rules, particularly as to penal sanctions for violations of the rules annexed to the Recommendation.

In this context, the Recommendation does not deal with the problems raised by artificial insemination administered against the system laid down by the rules. This problem is left to national legislation which may adopt specific rules in this field on the condition that the fundamental principles on which the Recommendation is based are respected.

6.   The present Recommendation has been drafted by a joint Committee of Experts under the authority of the European Committee on Legal Co-operation(CDCJ) and of the European Public Health Committee(CDSP) which gave to it as terms of reference, the harmonization of legislations in the field of removal, grafting and transplantation of human substances.

II. Rules

ARTICLE 1

7.   Article 1 defines the field of application of the rules.

They apply only to artificial insemination of a human being with the semen of an anonymous donor.

It follows from this provision that excluded from the field of
application of the rules are artificial insemination with the semen
of the husband, living or deceased, and, in the case of an unmarried
couple, artificial insemination with the semen of the partner.

Artificial insemination of a woman with the semen of her husband or of the partner, when certain medical conditions render natural insemination impossible or difficult, does not raise the same
problems which artificial insemination with the semen of a third
party donor creates and consequently it was not considered useful to
deal with it in this resolution.

ARTICLE 2

8.   Under normal conditions, a married couple or a single woman is
the sole judge as to whether to have a child by natural means or not
to have one. Whatever the health, social and economic situation of
the future mother and father may be, they may have a child if they
so wish and no one outside the couple may interfere with their decision. A married couple or unmarried woman may be advised by a
physician or family counsellor against having a child, but this
advice is by no means binding. Naturally the couple or the unmarried
woman are also solely responsible for the consequences of having the
child.

9.   The situation is somewhat different in the case of artificial
insemination. The physician administering artificial insemination
is also to some extent responsible for the conception of the child.
As a result it is logical that the physician should have the duty to
refuse to carry out such an operation when he considers that the
appropriate conditions do not exist for ensuring the welfare of the
future child. These "appropriate conditions" are, in particular that
the couple or the unmarried woman shall be in good health and sufficiently well-balanced emotionally and psychologically to raise a
child properly.

10. However, it should be noted that paragraph 1 of Article 2 does
not define "appropriate conditions" and does not indicate the person
or the body which is to judge whether they exist. These matters are
therefore left to national legislation.

In particular it is for national legislation, if any, to define
by a general rule, or to give the physician the task of judging case
by case, whether the "appropriate conditions" exist when the insemination is requested by an unmarried woman. This legislation can
also provide for additional rules in order to specify the conditions
of artificial insemination in such a case.

11. Paragraph 2 requires for the benefit of the parties, that artificial insemination must be administered by a physician or under his
control and on his responsibility.

ARTICLE 3

12.   This article concerns the consent which is necessary in order to perform artificial insemination.

Three consent are required: That of the donor, that of the woman and that of her husband if she is married.   This provision stems from the necessity that all those who are concerned in such a delicate and important operation for society, the conception of a human being, are fully aware of the consequences and agree to them.

13.   Paragraph 1 prohibits the utilisation of a man's semen without his consent.   As semen may be received by medical establishments for other reasons than as a donation for artificial insemination, e.g. for medical analysis, this semen should not be utilised for artificial insemination without the consent of that man.

14.   Paragraph 2 requires the consent of the woman as well as her husband, if she is married.   It is evident that the first requirement for artificial insemination is the consent of the woman to whom it will be administered.   In all member States any practice of artificial insemination without the consent of the woman would constitute a criminal offence, no matter whether her husband consented to it or not.

15.   In addition to the woman's consent the article also requires the consent of her husband if she is married.   Therefore, should the husband refuse, the physician or the medical centre must not administer artificial insemination, even if the woman should insist. Although the case where artificial insemination is administered to a woman following the refusal of her husband does not constitute a criminal offence in all member States, it would constitute grounds for divorce and for repudiating the legitimacy of the child in most member States.   In order to avoid such a situation, which would shake or even destroy the family unit, and risk harm to the child's future, this article forbids the practice of artificial insemination without the consent of the husband.

16.   As for the validity and form of the consent required by this article, these matters are left to national legislation.   However, the article requires that such consent must be given in an explicit manner, the intended meaning of "explicit manner" here being some manner of expressing a wish which would not give rise to any doubt or differing interpretation.

The purpose of putting on the physician the obligation of seeing that consent is given in an explicit manner is to draw the attention of practitioners especially to the importance of consent.

ARTICLE 4

17.   This article requires any physician or medical establishment
receiving semen for artificial insemination, to make appropriate medical inquiries and examinations in order to prevent the transmission
from the donor of a hereditary condition or contagious disease or
other factor which may present a danger to the health of the recipient
woman or the future child.

18.   By "hereditary conditions", the article refers primarily to
dominant hereditary conditions but also includes other genetic factors
which may be of equal relevance; by "contagious diseases" it refers to
those which may be transmitted by semen(eg gonorrhoea) and "other
factors" refers to such factors as for example Rhesus factors of the
blood.   But, of course, all these are given merely as examples and if
a physician or medical centre discovers any trace of another hereditary
condition or contagious disease, or other factor which would create a
danger to the health of the mother or future child, artificial insemination with the semen of that donor must not be administered.

   In addition, although the problem is one that can hardly ever arise
in practice, it may be necessary to take precautions not only against
consanguinity of the donor and the recipient but also against producing a
large number of consanguinous children.   To this end physicians should,
so far as possible, avoid using the semen of a particular donor for a
great many artificial inseminations in one centre.

19.   The rules do not contain a provision on the question of whether the
physician should satisfy any wishes of the couple or the unmarried woman
on particular physical characteristics of the donor.   It is left to the
physician, in conformity with paragraph 1 of Article 2, to see whether
in such case the "appropriate conditions" exist to administer artificial
insemination.

20.   The second sentence of the article relates to all other measures and
examinations necessary to perform the operation.   Therefore, if an examination of a woman reveals that artificial insemination would create
undue danger to her health the physician must not administer artificial
insemination.

ARTICLE 5

21.   Secrecy is a matter of the utmost importance in the administration
of artificial insemination in the interest of the donor, of the couple
and of the child.   The article requires that all precautions should be
taken to keep secret the identity of the donor, of the recipient woman
and of her husband, if she is married, as well as the fact that artificial
insemination was used.   Therefore a physician or centre receiving donations of semen or administering artificial insemination is required
to keep secret the names and any other information which could lead to
the identification of the donor, the recipient woman and her husband, and
moreover they must equally keep secret the fact that any particular birth

results from artificial insemination.

22.   The article however allows exceptions to the rules of secrecy
in the case of proceedings before a court, for instance when an action is brought to contest the legitimacy of the child.

In this case the physician is authorised to reveal the existence of the artificial insemination, identity of the woman and her
husband and the existence of their consent.   The identity of the donor must never be revealed; a rule to the contrary might have the
effect discouraging donations of semen.   The secrecy of the identity
of the donor is therefore an absolute rule to which there are no
exceptions.

23.   The article also requires the physician to refuse to administer
artificial insemination when the circumstances in which it is carried
out would put at risk the maintenance of the secret.   For example,
in certain cases family or other links between the donor and the
woman or her husband might emerge, for example, from the sudden and
undesirable discovery that the real father is a close relative or
friend of the family.

ARTICLE 6

24.   Paragraph 1 of this article is on the same lines as Article 9
of the rules annexed to Resolution(78) 29 on harmonization of the
legislation of member States relating to the removal, grafting and
transplantation of human substances, and which is based on the legal
principle existing in most member States which treats human substances as *res extra commercium*.   Semen being a human substance, the donor can receive no material consideration for his donation.   However,
on the same principle as in Article 9 of the annexed rules to the
above-mentioned Resolution, the loss of earnings and travelling and
other expenses incurred as a direct result of the donation may be
refunded to the donor.

25.   Paragraph 2 prohibits the transfer of semen for profit by those
who receive, concerve and treat it.   It is worthwhile, however,
pointing out that only profit is prohibited; the cost of production
may be recovered.

ARTICLE 7

26.   Where a State law has accepted that artificial insemination is
a permissible medical practice, it would be illogical for it to give
anyone the right to dispute the legitimacy of a child conceived by
artificial insemination with the consent of the husband merely on
that account.   This article therefore provides that in such a case
the child shall be considered as the legitimate child of the woman
and her husband and that no-one may dispute the child's legitimacy
on the sole ground of artificial insemination.   This article cov-
ering only the case where birth results from artificial insemination,

is not intended to lead to any other change in the legal provisions
in force in member States which give the husband, or other interested persons, the right to dispute the child's legitimacy on grounds
other than that or artificial insemination.

27. Paragraph 2 of this article prohibits the establishment of a
link of affiliation between the donor and the child on the ground
of artificial insemination. This is quite logical because the donor
does not intend to have a child of his own, but simply to make
artificial insemination possible. If the child, the mother or any
other interested person had the right to bring proceedings to establish his paternity against the donor, despite the promised secrecy,
very few men would feel inclined to donate their semen. As the
establishment of any link of affiliation between the donor and the
child is prohibited, the rules also forbid maintenance proceedings
between the two.

CONTRIBUTORS

Ackman, C.D.F., Department of Urology, McGill University, Montreal
    Canada

Albanese, Ferdinando, Directorate of Legal Affairs, Council of Europe
    Strasbourg, France

Alexandre, Claude, 45 rue de Courcelles, Paris, France

Alnot, M.O., Centre d'Etude et de Conservation du Sperme de Paris-
    Necker, Paris, France

Aron, C., Institut d'Histologie, Faculté de Médecine de Strasbourg
    Strasbourg, France

Baird, O.T., Department of Obstetrics and Gynaecology, University of
    Edinburgh, Edinburgh, Scotland

Barkay, J., Central Emek Hospital, Afula, Israël

Baumeister, T., Physiology Institute, Dusseldorf University,
    Dusseldorf, West Germany

Bissery, Jacqueline, Fondation Vallée, Gentilly, France

Bisson, Jean Pierre, Centre d'Etude et de Conservation du sperme
    Paris-Bicêtre, Kremlin Bicêtre, France

Bolcioni, A.M., Centre d'Etude et de Conservation du Sperme
    Marseille, France

Bremond, A., Clinique Gynécologique, Hôpital Edouard Herriot,
    Lyon, France

Briard, M., Clinique de Génétique Médicale, Hôpital des Enfants
    Malades, Paris, France

Broer, Karl H., Department of Obstetrics and Gynecology, University
    of Cologue, Cologne, West Germany

625

Cabau, Anne, Service of Obstetrics and Gynecology, Hôpital Antoine
     Beclere, Clamart, France

Campana, Aldo, Service of Endocrinology and Gynecology, Ospedale
     Distrettnale di Locarno, Locarno, Switzerland

Chambon, Yves, Centre d'Etude et de Conservation du Sperme (CECOS)
     Rennes, France

Chevret, Marie, Centre d'Etude et de Conservation du Sperme (CECOS)
     Lyon, France

Choux, Michèle, Centre d'Etude et de Conservation du Sperme (CECOS)
     Marseille, France

Clavert, André, Laboratoire d'Embryologie, Faculté de Médecine,
     Strasbourg, France

Conte-Devolx, B., Centre d'Etude et de Conservation du sperme (CECOS)
     Marseille, France

Cottinet, D., Centre d'Etude et de Conservation du sperme (CECOS),
     Hôpital Edouard Herriot, Lyon, France

Cusine Douglas, J., Faculty of Law Old Aberdeen AB 9 2UB, Scotland

Czyba, Jean Claude, Centre d'Etude et de Conservation du Sperme
     (CECOS), Lyon, France

Czyglik, Françoise, Centre d'Etude et de Conservation du Sperme
     (CECOS), Paris-Bicêtre, Kremlin Bicêtre, France

Da Lage, Christian, Centre d'Etude et de Conservation du Sperme
     (CECOS), Paris-Necker, Paris, France

David, Georges, Centre d'Etude et de Conservation du sperme (CECOS),
     Paris-Bicêtre, Kremlin Bicêtre, France

Delezoide, A.L., Centre d'Etude et de Conservation du Sperme (CECOS)
     Paris-Necker, Paris, France

Detlefsen, G. Department of Obstetrics and Gynecology, Frederiksberg
     Hospital, Copenhagen, Denmark

Dervain, I., Service de Gynécologie Obstétrique, Faculté de Médecine,
     Strasbourg, France

Dhont, P., Centre d'Etude et de Conservation du Sperme (CECOS), Paris-
     Necker, Paris, France

Echanojauregui, Abel D., Service of Obstetrics and Gynecology,
    Ciudad Sanitaria "Enrigue Sotomayor" de la Seguridad Social,
    Cruces-Bilbao, Spain.

Ehret, E., Service de Gynécologie Obstétrique, Faculté de Médecine,
    Strasbourg, France

d' Elicio, Giuseppe, Service of Endocrinology and Gynecology
    Ospedale Distrettnale di Locarno, Locarno, Switzerland

Emperaire, Jean-Claude, Centre de Physiopathologie de la Reproduc-
    tion et de la Sexualité Humaine, Hôpital Xavier Arnozan,
    33-Pessac, France

Escalier, Denise, Centre d'Etude et de Conservation du Sperme (CECOS),
    Paris-Bicêtre, Kremlin Bicêtre, France

Frezal, Jean, clinique de Génétique Médicale, Hôpital des Enfants
    Malades, Paris, France

Friberg, Jan, Department of Obstetrics and Gynecology, Downstate
    Medical Center, Brooklyn, New York, U.S.A.

Friedman, Stanley, Department of Obstetrics and Gynecology, UCLA
    School of Medicine, Los Angeles, California, U.S.A.

Gernigon, Claude, Centre d'Etude et de Conservation du Sperme (CECOS)
    Paris-Bicêtre, Kremlin Bicêtre, France

Gigon, Ulrich, Gynecology Clinic, University of Berne, Berne,
    Switzerland

Grignon, Georges, Laboratoire de Biologie Médicale, Faculté de Méde-
    cine B, Nancy, France

Guerin, Jean-François, Centre d'Etude et de Conservation du Sperme
    (CECOS), Lyon, France

Guichaoua, M., Laboratoire d'Histologie, Embryologie, Génétique,
    Faculté de Médecine de la Timone, Marseille, France

Haldemann, R., Gynecology Clinic, University of Berne, Berne,
    Switzerland

Hansen, Brogard K., University Hospital, Aarhus, Denmark

Harrison, Robert F., T.C.D.Department of Obstetrics and Gynecology
    Rotunda Hospital, Dublin, Ireland

Hartmann, R., Physiology Institute, Dusseldorf University, Dusseldorf
    West Germany

Heuche, Vincent, Unité de Recherches Statistiques de l'Institut
    National de la Santé et de la Recherche Médicale, Villejuif,
    France

Hjort, T., Department of Gynecology and Obstetrics, Kommunehospitalet
    Aarhus, Denmark

Hofmann, N., Dermatology Clinic, Research Center in Andrology,
    Dusseldorf, West Germany

Huerre, Patrice, Centre d'Etude et de Conservation du Sperme (CECOS)
    Paris-Bicêtre, Kremlin Bicêtre, France

Iizuka, Rihachi, Department of Obstetrics and Gynecology, Keio
    University School of Medicine, Tokyo, Japan

Jacquard, Albert, Institut National d'Etudes Démographiques, Paris,
    France.

Jeulin, Claudette, Centre d'Etude et de Conservation du sperme (CECOS)
    Paris-Bicêtre, Kremlin Bicêtre, France

Jondet, Michel, Fondation de Recherche en Hormonologie, Paris, France

Jouannet, Pierre, Centre d'Etude et de Conservation du sperme (CECOS)
    Paris-Bicêtre, Kremlin Bicêtre, France

Katz, David F., Department of Obstetrics and Gynecology, University
    of California School of Medicine, Davis, California, U.S.A.

Katzorke, Thomas, Department of Obstetrics and Gynecology, University
    of Essen Medical School, Essen, West Germany

Kaufmann, R., Physiology Institute, Dusseldorf University, Dusseldorf
    West Germany

Kerin, J.F., Department of Obstetrics and Gynaecology, University of
    Edinburgh, Edinburgh, Scotland

Kobayashi, Toshifumi, Department of Obstetrics and Gynecology, Keio
    University School of Medicine, Tokyo, Japan

Kunstmann, Jean Marie, Centre d'Etude et de Conservation du sperme
    (CECOS) Paris-Bicêtre, Kremlin Bicêtre, France

Lansac, Jacques, Centre d'Etude et de Conservation du Sperme (CECOS)
    Tours, France

Laugier, P., Centre d'Etude et de Conservation du sperme (CECOS)
    Marseille, France

Lawson, S., Department of Obstetrics and Gynaecology, University of
    Edinburgh, Edinburgh, Scotland

Lebech, Paul E., Department of Obstetrics and Gynecology
    Frederiksberg Hospital, Copenhagen, Denmark

Lees, MM, Department of Obstetrics and Gynaecology, University of
    Edinburgh, Edinburgh, Scotland

Legrain, Michel, Service de Nephrologie, Groupe Hospitalier Pitié-
    Salpêtrière, Paris, France

Le Lannou, Dominique, Centre d'Etude et de Conservation du sperme
    (CECOS), Rennes, France

Leridon, Henri, Institut National d'Etudes Démographiques, Paris,
    France

Lobel, Bernard, Centre d'Etude et de Conservation du Sperme (CECOS)
    Rennes, France

Macler, J., Service de Gynécologie Obstétrique, Faculté de Médecine
    de Strasbourg Schiltigheim, Strasbourg, France

Maire, F., Hôpital Cantonal de St Gallen, St Gallen, Switzerland

Manuel, Christine, Centre d'Etude et de Conservation du Sperme (CECOS)
    Lyon, France

Marina, Simon, Hospital de la Santa Cruz y San Pablo, Barcelona, Spain

Mattei, A., Centre d'Etude et de Conservation du sperme (CECOS),
    Marseille, France

Mattei, J.F., Centre d'Etude et de Conservation du sperme (CECOS),
    Marseille, France

Mattei, M.G., Centre de Génétique Médicale, C.H.U Timone, Marseille,
    France

Mayaux, Marie-Jeanne, Unité de Recherches Statistiques, Institut natio-
    nal de la Santé et de la Recherche Médicale, Villejuif, France

Mazars,J., Ministère de la Justice, Paris, France

Menezo,Yves, Centre d'Etude et de Conservation du sperme (CECOS)
    Lyon, France

Merckx,Mireille, Fertility Department, Academic Hospital VUB,
    Brussels, Belgium

Millet,Didier, 9 avenue Franco Russe, Paris, France

Mises,Roger, Fondation Vallée, Gentilly, France

Mochimaru,Fumio, Department of Obstetrics and Gynecology, Keio
    University School of Medicine, Tokyo, Japan.

Moreau,N., Laboratoire d'Histologie et d'Embryologie, Lyon, France

Mornaghini,L., Service of Endocrinology and Gynecology, Ospedale
    Distrettnale di Locarno, Locarno, Switzerland

Moser,Hans, Genetic counseling Service, University Department of
    Pediatrics, Berne, Switzerland

Nielsen,N.C., Gynecology Department, Bispebjerg Hospital, Copenhagen,
    Denmark

Nijs,Piet, Institute of Familial and Sexological Sciences,Catholic
    University of Louvain, Louvain, Belgium

Olson, John H., Cryogenic Laboratories, Inc., Roseville, Minnesota,
    U.S.A.

Penochet,Jean Claude, Centre d'Etude et de Conservation du sperme
    (CECOS), Marseille, France

Plante,P., Service d'Urologie, Hôpital de la Grave, Toulouse,
    France

Plas-Roser,S., Institut d'Histologie, Faculté de M&decine de
    Strasbourg, Strasbourg, France

Pontonnier,F., Service d'Urologie, Hôpital de la Grave, Toulouse,
    France

Portuondo, José A., Serivce of Obstetrics and Gynecology, Ciudad
    Sanitaria "Enrique Sotomayor" de la Seguridad Social, Cruces-
    Bilbao, Spain

Poyen,Bernard, Centre d'Etude et de Conservation du sperme (CECOS)
    Marseille, France

Propping,Dirk, Department of Obstetrics and Gynecology, University
    of Essen Medical School, Essen, West Germany

Renaud,R., Service de Gynécologie Obstétrique, Faculté de Médecine,
    de Strasbourg Schiltigheim, Strasbourg, France

Richardson,David.W., MRC Unit of Reproductive Biology, Edinburgh,
    Scotland

Rioux,Jacques E., Department of Obstetrics and Gynecology, Centre
    Hospitalier de l'Université Laval, Quebec, Canada

Rodriguez-Rigau,Luis J.,Department of Reproductive Medicine and
    Biology, University of Texas Medical School at Houston, Houston,
    Texas 77025 U.S.A.

Roulier,R., Centre d'Etude et de Conservation du sperme (CECOS),
    Marseille, France

Roy, David J., Center of Bioethics, Clinical Research Institute of
    Montreal, Montreal, Canada

Sato,Hirohisa , Department of Obstetrics and Gynecology, Keio
    University School of Medicine, Tokyo,Japan

Schoëvaërt,Damien, Centre d'Etude et de Conservation du sperme,
    (CECOS), Paris-Bicêtre, Kremlin-Bicêtre, France

Schoysman,Robert, Fertility Department Academic Hospital VUB,
    Brussels, Belgium

Schoysman-Deboeck,Andrée, Fertility Department Academic Hospital,
    VUB, Brussels, Belgium

Schwartz,Daniel, Unité de Recherches Statistiques,   Institut
    National de la Santé et de la Recherche Médicale, Villejuif,
    France

Segal,Luc, Fertility Department Academic Hospital, VUB, Brussels,
    Belgium

Semenov,Gabrièle, Fondation Vallée, 94-Gentilly, France

Serres,Catherine, Centre d'Etude et de Conservation du sperme
    (CECOS), Paris-Bicêtre, Kremlin-Bicêtre, France

Sheppard,Brian L.,   T.C.D. Department of Obstetrics and Gynaecology
     Rotunda Hospital, Dublin, Ireland

Sherman, Jerome K., Department of Anatomy, University of Arkansas
     for Medical Studies, Little Rock, Arkansas U.S.A.

Shulman,Sidney, Sperm Antibody Laboratory, New York Medical College,
     New York, U.S.A.

Smith,Keith D., Department of Reproductive Medicine and Biology
     University of Texas Medical School at Houston, Houston, Texas
     U.S.A.

Spira, A.,Unité de recherches statistiques ,   Institut National
     de la Santé et de la Recherche Médicale, Villejuif, France

Steeno, O., Institute of Familial and Sexological Sciences,Catholic
     University of Louvain, Louvain, Belgium

Steinberger,Emil, Department of Reproductive Medicine and Biology ,
     University of Texas Medical School at Houston, Houston, Texas,
     U.S.A.

Steiner,R., Physiology Institute, Dusseldorf University, Dusseldorf,
     West Germany

Steppe,A., Institute of Familial and Sexological Sciences, Catholic
     University of Louvain, Louvain, Belgium

Szalmaj,G., Hôpital Universitaire de Basel, Basel, Switzerland

Tauber,Peter F., Department of Obstetrics and Gynecology, University
     of Essen Medical School, Essen, West Germany

Templeton,A.A., Departement of Obstetrics and gynaecology, University
     of Edinburgh, Edinburgh, Scotland

Tignol,J., Service de Psychiatrie, Université de Bordeaux, Bordeaux,
     France

Traina,Giovanni, Contrattista Universitario, Bari, Italy

Traina,Vincenzo, Contrattista Universitario, Bari, Italy

Usherwood,M.McD, Department of Gynaecology, Stoke Mandeville Hospi-
     tal,Aylesbury, Bucks, England

Vekemans,M., Fertility Department, Academic Hospital VUB, Brussels, Belgium

Vendrely,E., Centre d'Etude et de Conservation du sperme (CECOS), Paris-Necker, Paris, France

Verhoeven,Nadine, Fertility Department, Academic Hospital VUB, Brussels, Belgium

Wyss,H., Hôpital Universitaire de Basel, Basel, Switzerland

Young,G.B., Department of Obstetrics and Gynaecology, University of Edinburgh, Edinburgh, Scotland

Zuckerman,H., Central Emek Hospital, Afula,Israël

INDEX

635